Ethnicity and Identity

Herodotus is the epochal authority who inaugurated the European and Western consciousness of collective identity, whether in an awareness of other societies and of the nature of cultural variation itself or in the fashioning of Greek self-awareness – and necessarily that of later civilizations influenced by the ancient Greeks – which was perpetually in dialogue and tension with other ways of living in groups.

In this book, 14 contributors explore ethnicity – the very self-understanding of belonging to a separate body of human beings – and how it evolves and consolidates (or ethnogenesis). This inquiry is focussed through the lens of Herodotus as our earliest master of ethnography, in this instance not only as the stylized portrayal of other societies, but also as an exegesis on how ethnocultural differentiation may affect the lives, and even the very existence, of one's own people.

Ethnicity and Identity in Herodotus is one facet of a project that intends to bring Portuguese and English-speaking scholars of antiquity into closer cooperation. It has united a cross-section of North American classicists with a distinguished cohort of Portuguese and Brazilian experts on Greek literature and history writing in English.

Thomas Figueira is Distinguished Professor of Classics and of Ancient History at Rutgers, The State University of New Jersey, USA.

Carmen Soares is Professor (Professora Catedrática) of Classics of the University of Coimbra, Portugal, and Scientific Coordinator of the Center for Classical and Humanistic Studies of the same university.

Ethnicity and Identity in Herodotus

Edited by
Thomas Figueira
and Carmen Soares

 Routledge
Taylor & Francis Group

LONDON AND NEW YORK

First published 2020 by Routledge

2 Park Square, Milton Park, Abingdon, Oxon OX14 4RN

605 Third Avenue, New York, NY 10017

Routledge is an imprint of the Taylor & Francis Group, an informa business

First issued in paperback 2022

Publisher's Note

The publisher has gone to great lengths to ensure the quality of this reprint but points out that some imperfections in the original copies may be apparent.

British Library Cataloguing-in-Publication Data
A catalogue record for this book is available from the British Library

Library of Congress Cataloging-in-Publication Data
A catalog record for this book has been requested

ISBN: 978-1-138-63111-3 (hbk)
ISBN: 978-1-03-233721-0 (pbk)
DOI: 10.4324/9781315209081

Typeset in Times New Roman
by Apex CoVantage, LLC

Contents

Notes on contributors

Alexandre Agnolon is Associate Professor of Classics at the Federal University of Ouro Preto (Minas Gerais, Brazil). He obtained his PhD in Classics at the University of São Paulo and held a research internship at the University of Oxford. His main areas of interest are Greek and Latin poetry – particularly with regard to the ancient epigram – and Poetics and Rhetoric. He has published *O Catálogo das Mulheres: os epigramas misóginos de Marcial* (2010) and *A Festa de Saturno: o Xênia e o Apoforeta de Marcial* (2017).

Emily Allen-Hornblower is Associate Professor of Classics at Rutgers University. She received her joint PhD in Classics from Harvard and Paris IV-Sorbonne and has published articles on archaic and classical Greek literature (Homer's *Iliad*, Sophocles' *Philoctetes*, Euripides' *Electra*) and Roman historiography (Caesar's *Bellum Gallicum*), as well as on the twentieth-century reception of Greek drama (Gide's *Philoctète*). She is the author of *From Agent to Spectator: Witnessing the Aftermath in Ancient Greek Epic and Tragedy* (2016). In addition to her teaching and scholarship, Allen-Hornblower teaches Classics in medium and maximum-security prisons in New Jersey, as part of NJSTEP (Scholarship and Transformative Education in Prisons).

Steven Brandwood, who did his undergraduate work at Yale, received an MPhil at Rutgers University, where he is a PhD candidate in Classics and is completing a dissertation on cult-song in Hellenistic Athens. He has published articles on Aeschylus and Catullus. His research interests include Greek religion, poetry, and epigraphy, which are reflected in his conference papers. Most recently, he has been Virginia Grace Fellow at the American School of Classical Studies at Athens.

Maria do Céu Fialho is Professor (Professora Catedrática) at the Institute of Classical Studies, University of Coimbra. She obtained her PhD at the University of Coimbra, in the area of ancient Greek tragedy (*Luz e trevas no teatro de Sófocles*). She has written extensively on Greek literature and on poetics and hermeneutics in over 70 publications. She has translated several works into Portuguese, with particular attention given to Sophocles and Plutarch. She also has a deep interest in the reception of classics in Portuguese contemporary literature.

Thomas Figueira is Distinguished Professor of Classics and of Ancient History at Rutgers, The State University of New Jersey. He teaches classical history, Greek and Latin languages and literatures, and classical humanities at all levels including graduate studies. Among his over 140 contributions, articles, and reviews, his publications include *Aegina: Economy and Society* (1981); *Athens and Aigina in the Age of Imperial Colonization* (1991); *Excursions in Epichoric History* (1993); *The Power of Money: Coinage and Politics in the Athenian Empire* (1998); with T.C. Brennan & R.H. Sternberg, *Wisdom from the Ancients: Enduring Business Lessons from Alexander the Great, Julius Caesar, and The Illustrious Leaders of Ancient Greece and Rome* (2001), and he has edited or co-edited *Theognis of Megara: Poetry and the Polis* (1985); *Spartan Society* (2004); *Myth, Text, and History at Sparta* (2016); *Athenian Hegemonic Finances* (2019). For details, see http://classics.rutgers.edu/people/52-people-individual-categories/81-thomas-figueira.

Renaud Gagné is Reader in Ancient Greek Literature and Religion at the University of Cambridge (Faculty of Classics). He is a Fellow of Pembroke College. He has notably published *Ancestral Fault in Ancient Greece* (2013); *Choral Mediations in Greek Tragedy* (2013, with Marianne Hopman); *Sacrifices humains. Perspectives croisées et représentations* (2013, with Pierre Bonnechere); *Regimes of Comparatism: Frameworks of Comparison in History, Religion and Anthropology* (2018, with Simon Goldhill and Geoffrey Lloyd); *Les dieux d'Homère II. Anthropomorphismes* (2019, with Miguel Herrero de Jáuregui).

Brian Hill earned his BA *cum laude* in Classics at Harvard University in 2011, his MPhil in Classics at Trinity College Dublin in 2013, and his doctorate at Rutgers University in 2019. He has presented his work at CAAS, CAMWS, and SCS annual meetings, as well as the Celtic Conference in Classics in Dublin, Ireland and the Symposium Cumanum at the Villa Vergiliana near Naples, Italy. His primary research interests centre on Latin literature, especially late Republican and Augustan poetry and, more broadly, on didactic poetry, the Sophists, and Greek philosophy, ancient athletics, and the dynamics of power in Greece and Rome. His Master's thesis treated failed persuasion and brute force in Ovid's *Metamorphoses*. His dissertation analyzed subtle changes in various recurrent images within Lucretius' *De rerum natura*.

Delfim F. Leão is Professor (Professor Catedrático) at the Institute of Classical Studies and a researcher at the Center for Classical and Humanistic Studies, University of Coimbra. His main areas of interest, in which he has produced many works, are ancient history, law, and political theory of the Greeks, theatrical pragmatics, and the ancient novel. He also has a strong interest in digital humanities. Among his main recent works are D.F. Leão and P.J. Rhodes, *The Laws of Solon. A New Edition, with Introduction, Translation and Commentary* (2015), and a second revised edition in 2016; D.F. Leão and G. Thür (Hrsg.) *Symposion 2015. Vorträge zur griechischen und hellenistischen*

Rechtsgeschichte (2016). Along with Lautaro R. Lanzillotta, he is the editor of the series Brill's Plutarch Studies.

Rosaria Vignolo Munson is the J. Archer and Helen C. Turner Professor of Classics at Swarthmore College. She is the author of *Telling Wonders: Ethnographic and Political Discourse in the Work of Herodotus* (2001)*; Black Doves Speak: Herodotus and the Language of Barbarians* (2005), and several articles on Herodotus and Thucydides. She has edited *Oxford Readings in Classical Studies: Herodotus* (2013). She is co-editing (with Carolyn Dewald) a commentary on Herodotus Book I for the Cambridge Greek and Latin Classics series.

Gregory Nagy is the Francis Jones Professor of Classical Greek Literature and Professor of Comparative Literature, Harvard University, and is the Director of the Center for Hellenic Studies, Washington, DC. In his publications, he has pioneered an approach to Greek literature that integrates diachronic and synchronic perspectives. His books include The Best of the Achaeans: Concepts of the Hero in Archaic Greek Poetry (1979), which won the Goodwin Award of Merit, American Philological Association, in 1982; also Pindar's Homer: The Lyric Possession of an Epic Past (1990), Poetry as Performance: Homer and Beyond (1996), Homeric Questions (1996), Homeric Responses (2003), Homer's Text and Language (2004), Homer the Classic (2008/2009), Homer the Preclassic (2010), The Ancient Greek Hero in 24 Hours (2013). He co-edited with Stephen A. Mitchell the 40th anniversary second edition of Albert Lord's The Singer of Tales (2000), co-authoring with Mitchell the new Introduction. gnagy@fas.harvard.edu.

Nuno Simões Rodrigues is Associate Professor at the University of Lisbon in the Department of History. He holds a PhD in Ancient History, and the main areas of his research have been Cultural History of Ancient Greece, Political History of Rome and Reception Studies (especially Antiquity in Cinema). In recent years, his English-language publications have included *Violence in Ancient and Medieval Worlds* (2018), " '*Like a Ghost of Antigone*': Ganhar a Vida (Get a life), by João Canijo," in C. Moraia, L. Hartwick, and M. de Fátima Silva, *Portrayals of Antigone in Portugal* (2017), and "From Kubrick's Political Icon to Television Sex Symbol," in A. Augoustakis and M. Cyrino, *STARZ Spartacus* (2017). He is currently working on a book on Demeter and Persephone.

Maria de Fátima Silva is Professor (Professora Catedrática) in the Institute of Classical Studies at the University of Coimbra. Her PhD field of research was Ancient Greek Comedy (*Crítica do teatro na comédia antiga*, Coimbra 1987), but she has published widely about Greek literature. She has also published translations, with commentaries, of nine comedies by Aristophanes, Menander's plays and best-preserved fragments, and some of Herodotus' books in collaboration. In recent years she has been particularly interested in reception studies.

Carmen Soares is Professor (Professora Catedrática) of Classics of the University of Coimbra (Faculty of Arts and Humanities) and a member of the Center for Classical and Humanistic Studies of the same university. Teaching activities, research interests and publications include classical literature, ancient Greek history, and food history. She is the author, co-author or co-editor of several books (30), chapters (33), and papers (58), and the translator into Portuguese of Herodotus' *Histories* (Books V and VIII, along with M.F. Silva and J.R. Ferreira), Euripides (*Cyclops*), Plato (*Statesman*), Plutarch (*On Affection for Offspring*) and Archestratus (*Life of Pleasures*). Herodotus' *Histories* has been, since her PhD in Greek Literature (on the topic of death as a narrative way of expressing universal values and ethnic particularisms) one of her main subjects of research. She has published almost 30 titles on Herodotus (in English: *Nomos*, *Anomia* and *Thanatos* in the *Histories* of Herodotus, in *La palabra fundante. The founding word* (2007), "Dress and Undress in Herodotus' *Histories*" (2014). She is Chief Editor of *Humanitas*, the oldest scholarly journal published in Portugal, devoted to Greek, Latin, and Renaissance Classical Studies. For details, see www.cienciavitae.pt/3C1C-F890-F38E.

Rogério Sousa is a Principal Researcher at the Center of History of the Faculty of Humanities of the University of Lisbon. As an Egyptologist, his research interests are focussed on Egyptian funerary material culture and on the Hellenization of the Egyptian tradition. He has published several works on multiculturalism in ancient Alexandria with a particular focus on the Alexandrian cults of Isis and Sarapis. He is currently involved in the study of Egyptian visual culture as used in funerary artifacts dated from the Greco-Roman Period.

Preface

This book grew out of a panel that the editors organized: "Ethnicity and Multi-culturalism in Herodotus: Through Others' Eyes". It was held at the Ninth Celtic Conference in Classics, University College Dublin, June 2016. We would like to thank Anton Powell and Douglas Cairns of the Celtic Conferences and the local hosts, including Dr. Alexander Thein. Our speakers in Dublin included Professor Sarolta Takács, Dean of the Division of Humanities and Social Sciences, City University of New York-Staten Island, who gave the paper "Herodotus' (After) Life in Byzantium". We would like to thank Sari Takács, who was unable to contribute to this volume because of the press of other academic responsibilities, for her participation in our discussions in Dublin.

This project also emerges from our wider commitment to promote intellectual dialogue between Anglophone and Lusophone scholars of the ancient Greek world. Readers will readily see the fruit of this enterprise in the mixture of North American, Brazilian, and Portuguese academics that comprise the roster of our contributors. Hence it also gives us much satisfaction to welcome into this volume two eminent Portuguese scholars of ancient Greece, Delfim Leão of the University of Coimbra and Nuno Simões Rodrigues of the University of Lisbon, whose schedules, ultimately, would not allow them to join us in Dublin, but who, to our great satisfaction, have shared in this volume.

Thomas Figueira would like to express his gratitude to the School of Arts and Sciences of Rutgers, the State University of New Jersey, in New Brunswick for providing him with research funds that helped in the preparation of the manuscript of this volume. Sincere thanks are also owed to Dr. Aaron Beck-Schachter who, as a Valergakis Post-Doctoral Fellow of the Department of Classics, has copy-edited this work. We are also grateful to Carlos Martins de Jesus, a member of the Centre of Classics and Humanistic Studies of the University of Coimbra, for his work on this book's indexes.

Finally, we would like to express our thanks to Michael Greenwood, Elizabeth Risch, and Ella Halstead of Routledge for their patience in bearing with the eventualities that delayed this volume.

Introduction

Thomas Figueira

This introduction will not offer an overview of our subject, ethnicity and ethnology in Herodotus. There have been a number of relatively recent short studies that undertake this mission, including a fine recent example offered by one of the contributors to this volume, Rosaria V. Munson (2014).[1] Rather, it seemed a more sensible enterprise to provide some gauge in broad terms of the state of scholarship on ethnicity, ethnology, and ethnography in general and, specifically on Herodotus, as is portrayed by these various efforts at synthesis. Meanwhile I shall attempt to provide some succinct critical response where appropriate. Since the turn of the millennium, the status of ethnic identity in antiquity has been a very "hot" topic. This reorientation of scholarly interest has in large part been driven by experiential factors arising from our life circumstances in "Western" post-industrial societies. These include the seemingly inexorable rise of identity politics in Western democracies and the counteracting suspicions toward such claims; the activities of emergent ethnic groups and the violence sometimes initiated by them or directed toward them; the perceptions of a "clash" or, more properly "clashes", between civilizations; the general visibility of social gestures meant to combat racism and the corresponding invisibility of neo-racial social coding (often melded with class prejudices and ideological formulas); and a desire to align studies of the ancient world with the preoccupations of other disciplines. This last can be an impulse that is sometimes accompanied by subaltern or sycophantic postures among classicists *vis-à-vis* more ideologized academic disciplines. This emerging focus of research has motivated individual studies,[2] and, perhaps even more notably, a number of collections.[3] And not to be lost from our reckoning, to be sure, is also a series of syntheses on Greek identity.[4]

However, some characteristic tendencies in this scholarship cry out for nuance or conditioning. In my view and as I address in part in my own contribution later in the book (pp. 42–71), critiques may rightfully centre on these issues: first, there has been a recent tendency to locate the stronger distinction between Greeks and non-Greeks (i.e., barbarians) rather later than previously thought, that is, in the early fifth century, and to treat this distinction as an outgrowth of Persian aggression toward homeland Greece and the defeat and deterrence of that threat; second, there has been an inclination to view claims on the basis of ethnic identity as engineered rather than culturally reflexive; and, third, the conviction of certain populations (in particular the Athenians) that their people were autochthonous, i.e., indigenous and derived *ab origine* from their later territory, has also been downdated and sometimes attributed largely to the contrivances of hegemonic policies.

The mechanisms for creation of an ethnic identity were coupled with the evolution of a sociopolitical community in a process that may be called ethnogenesis. It is important to emphasize from the start that the social evolutions at issue here do not merely refer to the development of conceptual systems, that is, a means for archaic or classical Greeks to describe or account for the social and cultural phenomena that they experienced, but ethnogenesis also comprised processes that structured social *praxis* and so actually affected their behaviour, and the organization and conduct of their lives. Recognize at the outset that the ethnogenesis particularly interesting us is the creation of *ethnē* 'communities' as the Greeks understood them (and not for our purposes the phenomenon of panhellenism, the sense of community of the Greeks as a whole). This ethnogenesis reflects an appreciation of shared folkways, of a community of cult and ritual, of a common discourse of storytelling and myth, and a non-problematic or non-marked regime of expressive and receptive language. Ethnogenesis takes on particular relevance in ancient Greek social history as a countervailing factor because the *polis* appears to have had a marked bias toward fission into ever smaller political units, although a balancing impetus could also exist, a force acting toward amalgamation in order to form political alliances, toward the consolidation of regional *ethnē* (such as the Akhaians or Arkadians), and toward the recognition in public of supra-regional *ethnē*, and, finally, toward a panhellenic *koinon*.[5]

Perhaps because of the toxic legacy of nineteenth- and twentieth-century nationalistic ideologies, ethnogenesis in recent classical scholarship has been accorded an aura of artificiality. Thus, there has often been a tendency to interpret such ethnogenesis as a process of self-advertisement or propagandizing and to relegate it to a realm either of elite manipulation or of mere justification for more appetitive communal assertion and aggrandizement. This phenomenon has seemed clearest to scholars among the *ethnē* of the Peloponnesus in the fourth century, where resistance to Spartan hegemony and the sequelae of its weakening took on a strong ethnic coloration. My discussion of the creation of the Messenian identity was an early representative of an investigation of ethnogenesis (Figueira 1999).[6] The proto-Messenians, however, faced substantial and special challenges in ethnogenesis. The Spartans, through repressive and incentive policies, had deculturated non-acquiescent identity features among the Helots so that amid the churning effects of the Laconian socio-economic system déclassé social components were drawn into conformity with Spartan culture, for example in dialect. I was impressed by the signs of organic evolution of ethnic identity in the primarily oral or non-literate, non-elite social order in rural *Lakōnikē*.[7] Any conclusion in favour of an early, organic Messenian ethnogenesis in such a milieu will tend *a fortiori* to convince us that we must take seriously the deeper roots of other Peloponnesian *ethnē*, whose manifestations of identity may only have become more visible in the classical period.[8]

Readers of the *Histories* of Herodotus are well aware that much of his discussion of ethnicity relates to the ethnic identity of individual Greek cities, which may share characteristics of this ethnicity with other cities and wider cultural realms. Everyone recalls how Croesus sought the alliance of the Spartans and Athenians as the paramount *poleis* of the Dorian and Ionian *genē* 'lineages', respectively (Hdt. 1.56.2). In our scholarly context, any exploration of the nature of the *polis* and its ethnology must maintain a sideward glance toward the works of the Copenhagen Polis Centre, and here I also draw on my own review articles.[9] I shall be mindful as we proceed of my *précis* on the basic configuration of the *polis* form,[10] which evolved in reaction to an ambiguity or looseness of criteria applied to identifying city-state societies in Hansen 2000 and 2002. The *polis* was the dominant social and political structure of the Greeks. Its preeminence as the engine for archaic institutional evolution is reflected in the nature of main sites for structural innovation such as Argos, Corinth, and Sparta in the Peloponnese, and in central Greece, Athens, Eretria, and Khalkis. The primacy of the *polis* seems manifest down through the fifth century. Everywhere here, ethnicity in any extra-*polis* manifestation seems decidedly secondary. The most sophisticated structure integrating states was the fifth-century Attic *arkhē*, which appears to assume the *polis* as the 'default' configuration for its members.[11] Moreover, the colonial movement, starting from c. 750 or a little earlier, was primarily an initiative of *poleis*.[12]

Herodotus shows himself to have been acutely sensitive to the ethnic ramifications of Greek colonization, as his catalogue of forces before Salamis is careful to trace such lines of filiation of settlement and potential contemporary affiliation (8.42–48). Here Thucydides followed his lead, using the catalogue of allies at Syracuse to comment on ethnicity and political affiliation (Thuc. 7.57.1–59.1). What we now term colonization was merely the sum of the processes that permitted or actualized a replication of the 'metropolitan' *polis*.[13] Indeed the temptation is strong to understand archaic colonization as an exploitation of the comparative efficiencies of the very order of the *polis* itself in order to tap new pools of resources, to manipulate demographic assets, and to accomplish targeted advancement for specific groups of *politai* and sub-*politai*. As colonization exploited mechanics of common action that the *polis* allowed, it also created kinship between colonizer and the colonists in a common ethnicity. And it is important that this 'replicative' colonial ethnogenesis,[14] which no one would reasonably deny as creating ties of *sungeneia* 'kinship', was both conceptually important and a real factor knitting together *poleis*. Strikingly, however, the terminology of *sungeneia*, specifically as kinship between political units, did not develop until after Herodotus and Thucydides had composed their works.[15] The *oikeiotēs* 'affinity' or *philia* 'friendship' so often later connected with *sungeneia*, had not yet reached the stage of substantial conflation with linkage through ethnicity.[16] And that is a significant finding about the nature of fifth-century ethnicity and its basis in broadly based communal consensus about markers of identity.

Much ethnogenesis in early Greek culture operated within the mechanism of *polis* formation. The conjoined evolution of a *polis* and of its *politai* could, therefore, compete with other types of ethnogenesis, not only in shaping identity, but also in forming institutions. The *polis* was indeed a political order that was fundamentally genetic – of which ethnic fellow feeling is still another manifestation – a community organized into descent units, arrayed upon a genealogical lattice. Such units were also nested within larger units that were treated as collections of lineages of a more distant biological nature (for example, the way in which Attic *genē* are situated among phratries and tribes). When one notes the specification of Athenian tribes as 'Ionian' or Spartan tribes as 'Dorian',[17] one realizes that all Greek biological communalism, whether in small groups or on a culture-wide scale, necessarily subsumes ethnicity. And, since there are variant instantiations of the *polis* form, that is, different constitutional orders that typify individual *poleis*, we are confronted during the classical period with circumstances in which creation of a *polis* assumed a particular normative or even ideological coloration regarding ethnogenesis.[18] Hence Athenian identity is bound up with identification with the Athenian *dēmos*; Lacedaimonian identity with those who had undergone the *agōgē* 'upbringing' with its internalization of the Spartan *diaita* 'lifestyle'. Despite any commonsense criteria that modern scholars might choose to apply, such as common dialect or the absence of cultural markers of alien identity, shared ethnicity for the *polis* could be constrained by political criteria. Athenian slaves who were οἰκογενεῖς 'of origin in the household' were not ethnically Athenian in communal reflection, nor were Helots Lacedaimonian, despite the possession by both those groups of the relevant markers of ethnicity.[19] This suggests again that in archaic and early classical Greece, citizenship initially tended to trump ethnicity as an early organizing principle unless stressing conditions motivated appeals to ethnocultural solidarity.[20]

Herodotus may be regarded as the 'father of ethnological studies' in the Western tradition.[21] The nature of his commentary on this subject dominates the current scholarship. Note how pervasive references to his *Histories* are in some of the recent collections on ancient ethnicity that I noted earlier: in his index Harrison 2002 has 38 call-outs to Herodotus, which cover 86 pages; Malkin (2001) 28 and 71; Zacharia (2008a) 41 and 58; Almagor and Skinner (2013) 45 and 69; and McInerney (2014) has 40 and 53. The single most important text that is cited on Greek views on ethnic identity is the crucial formulation that is offered by Herodotus for the Athenian delegates at Sparta in 479. Their opposition to any thought of Medizing is predicated on a number of factors, first of all and of the greatest significance (μέγιστα) is that they are aware of the ἀγάλματα 'sacred images and οἰκήματα 'structures' that were burnt and destroyed by the Persians. This requires retaliation and not collaboration with the perpetrator. Next they turn to their sense of their Hellenic identity (8.144.2):

αὖτις δὲ τὸ Ἑλληνικόν, ἐὸν ὅμαιμόν τε καὶ ὁμόγλωσσον, καὶ θεῶν ἱδρύματά τε κοινὰ καὶ θυσίαι ἤθεά τε ὁμότροπα, τῶν προδότας γενέσθαι Ἀθηναίους οὐκ ἂν εὖ ἔχοι.

And again there is the *Hellēnikon* 'Greekness', being *homaimon* 'of the same blood' and *homoglōsson* 'of the same language', and common establishments of the gods and homogeneous customs, of which it would not be fitting that the Athenians become traitors.

I shall examine this passage in my chapter for its emphasis on language as a determinant of ethnic identity. Here I merely note its omnipresence in our technical literature on ethnicity among the Greeks. It should not then be surprising that Katerina Zacharia for one even uses her study (2008b) of this passage to begin the series of treatments in her collection (2008a).

Herodotus is so familiar to us as an innovative figure – Cicero's dictum on his status as the "father of History" so well known a catchphrase (*Laws* 1.1.5) – that we still tend to underestimate the brilliance of his achievement. He was not only the first analyst of mere cultural difference, but he also portrayed for his audience the first realizations in our intellectual tradition of the processes of differentiation. However, it is important for us to qualify the nature of his *Histories* on two essential points before proceeding. First, Herodotus' dependence on oral sources and his apparent naivety during his collection of source material over the scale to which his work would aspire meant that an extraordinary stratification and mosaic-effect of Greek observers is manifested throughout his work as transmitted to us. These interactors with the non-Greek world severally grappled with issues of translation (see Brandwood's contribution in this volume), variations of evidentiary standards (e.g., regarding necessity for and nature of autopsy), and distortions of transmission among each other. Herodotus' interlocutors were themselves also fundamentally conditioned by the processes of assimilation, hybridity, and biculturalism that lie at the heart of the *histor*'s own impetus to confront the 'other'. Any imputation to Herodotus – or even to his mainly anonymous interlocutors – of any motivation whatsoever, and especially of animus, is thus greatly complicated.[22] Second, Herodotus and his contemporaries did not have the advantage of their modern scholars in their assurance over canonicity of classical Greek culture. Much that may now strike us as hostilely prejudicial may rather betray defensive posturing in the face of the antiquity, physical scale, and, in the case of the Persians, astounding wealth and power of non-Greek cultures (see Gregory Nagy in this volume [pp. 109–42] on alternative paths of evolution for Hellenicity). As is discernible even in the contemporary world, a degree of ethno-chauvinism can be anticipated from those living in the shadow of populous, wealthy, technologically advanced, and media-dominant societies. Is this not an implicit justification for multiculturalism in modern discourse?

For Herodotus, *nomoi* or *mores* could differ from people to people simply as a manifestation of variation, but at other times perhaps owing to various environmental factors, with substantial effects in the aggregate both for mere subsistence and for affluence (as the Portuguese of the age of discovery recognized, as is shown by Carmen Soares in this volume [pp. 296–325]). In varied settings, humans acted under the influence of *nomoi* directing their existence, as was summed up in his reflection on the adage of Pindar that *nomos* 'law' was *basileus* 'king' (Hdt. 3.38.3–4). This is applied when Dareios, an astonishing and instructive choice for our teacher in the variety of human behaviour, brings the Indian Kalliatai, who ritually eat their dead, into confrontation with the Greeks, who cremate. Yet Herodotus was also a universalist in his own terms, as his reflections on Egyptian religion indicate especially: people tapped the same transcendent order, even if their rituals varied, their awareness of it was imperfect, and their ability to adhere to its dictates may have fallen short or lapsed to a lesser or greater extent. Moreover, Herodotus is not what would now be called an 'essentialist', as he readily conceives that one people may borrow from another – his insistence on the Egyptian origin of Greek cultural motifs has long been emphasized[23] – and, although he lacked a fully explicit concept of hybridity, his willingness to recognize a considerable degree of diffusion or admixture is notable, as is also well illustrated by the Phoenician influence on the Greeks (e.g., Hdt. 5.58–59) and the existence of assorted medial groups. As Alexandre Agnolon's chapter in this volume will show (pp. 159–77), the Scythian Hellenizers dramatize the challenges faced by cultural hybrids (for Skyles, note 4.78–80). There Herodotus' sympathy with the Scythian perspective on Hellenization is conspicuous. Moreover, as I note later, if the Athenians are to be viewed as aboriginally Pelasgians who had traversed a set of self-identifications, originalist biases for Herodotus must be considered to have been significantly muted. And it is important to indicate that, whenever one says "Herodotus" in statements about the content of his accounts of non-Greek societies, they are using a shorthand reference for a unique and perhaps virtually non-duplicable stratigraphy of witnessing on any specific matter.

This Herodotean 'othering' can be viewed as 'mirroring', as Hartog stressed,[24] but we have already recognized that the mirror at issue is not a simple glass for contemplation. Rather, viewing is staged in a hall of mirrors with glasses of various degrees of trueness or distortion. Sometimes the reflections are truly inverted, in which the lives of non-Greeks embody the converse of Greek *nomoi*, although this opposition as in the case of the Egyptians could be to all mankind (Hdt. 2.35.1–4).[25] Such obversions could even continue to the point of perversity, such as general promiscuity,[26] and ritual prostitution,[27] where the negativity of judgment is noteworthy.[28] This phenomenon draws on an archaic propensity for thinking in polarities. Yet, we can also see in mirroring the possibility in which the Greeks can be situated medially between two converses, such as between cultures where clothing is absent or minimal and Asian societies where any nakedness at all is prohibited (cf. Hdt. 1.8.2–4, 11.3–5). Sometimes when this normative deviation has seductive power, our mirror ought to be rendered as a wishing well of fantasy, as in the cases where unproblematic sexual promiscuity is foregrounded (the casual liaisons of the Massagetai or Nasamones: Hdt. 1.216.1; 4.172.2). Herodotus notes this variation of sexual behaviour without titillation or prurient embellishment. It becomes then an open question whether the prominent portrayal of inversions in sexuality do not also serve as a mechanism for coping with the shock elicited by confrontation with the primitive. In some cases, especially regarding Egyptian culture, the image in the Herodotean mirror assumes the authority of a prototype or archetype. Moreover, our Herodotean mirrors possess persistent reflections, so that a succession of interpreters, local guides, non-Greek authorities, Greek *sophoi* 'sages', and *logioi* 'experts', standing in mediation with the 'others', have left their traces in what must be thoroughly composite images.

What is the crucial cultural difference between the Greek world and non-Greek *ethnē* in Herodotus?[29] The Greeks lived in *poleis*, with an articulated political order of *nomoi* about which one could speak rationally in justification or condemnation.[30] It is the very nature of the civic order that determines how 'othering' plays out its course. Each of the significant socio-cultural relations in *polis* society must be articulated in the sense of being fitted together by rules and subjected to processes of operation and integration. The rules governing the status of the countryside versus the town, or those governing how the young relate to their antecedents and how they are reared, or those strictures distributing political power, must be specifiable. Consequently, they must be verbally articulated in order to be evaluated in light of pan-cultural norms of harmony, justice, and beauty. This *habitus* of fitting social relations together and explaining and justifying the elegance of the results puts continual pressure on assaying one's feeling of belonging and alienation. Furthermore, if not as a lived reality, at the very least, communal and personal freedom (*eleutheria*) was an ideal (see Munson's chapter in this volume [pp. 143–58]).[31] In the famous interchange between Damaratos and Dareios (Hdt. 7.101–4), we see that such a style of existence was accompanied by a degree of interiority or of internalization of societal values that seems fundamentally different from the instantiation of the *nomoi* in non-Greek cultures. The lesson of Persian domination of Greek communities is that uttermost essence of otherness lies in its manifestations of arbitrary power, materialism, tyranny, and cruelty.

Thus, the entire history of the 'other' in Western consciousness seems, at the least, foreshadowed, if not exemplified, in the *Histories*. Cultural boundaries are so intensely examined and so minutely explicated in this, the first student of ethnicity and culture, because the earlier, ethnocentric sense of cohesion and foreignness or faith in the possession of divinely sanctioned righteousness wilted before the demands of *polis* life. In the last analysis, the very reason why *historiē* exists at all is that the Greeks of the *poleis* have the capacity to be taught. Hence, the construction of the self for the Greeks, while it drew on Greek images of the 'other', was not exclusively dependent on that 'other' in formulation. It may well be the widespread achievement of the ability to see other cultures from within only became realizable in the early modern period, an age with a very different sense of consciousness and afforded with a much more sophisticated heuristic, not to mention a higher level of resource utilization. However, this concession should not detract from the accomplishments of Herodotus and his contemporaries.

It is unnecessary to summarize our contributions inasmuch as we have provided detailed abstracts for each. Let it suffice here to explain that our work is divided into four parts. Our first, *Part 1: The methodology of ethnic identification in Herodotus*, in which are gathered four chapters, the first of which, by Steven Brandwood, explores the important issue of translation ("Herodotus' Hermēneus and the translation of culture in the *Histories*"). Next I examine "Language as a marker of ethnicity in Herodotus and contemporaries", while Brian Hill focusses on "Protocols of ethnic specification in Herodotus". Emily Allen-Hornblower closes out the first part with "Emotion and ethnicity in Herodotus' *Histories*". Next is *Part 2: Ethnicity among the Greeks* containing another four chapters. Gregory Nagy's study ("Mages and Ionians revisited") concerns a possible alternative evolution of the Greek identity in the event that Xerxes' invasion had been successful. Rosaria V. Munson explores the complexities of freedom in the *Histories* ("Freedom and culture in Herodotus") – these two studies interestingly touch on the so-called *Persian Debate*. Then, in "A goddess for the Greeks. Demeter as identity factor in Herodotus", Nuno Simões Rodrigues explores the goddess Demeter as a factor in Greek identity formation. We have put Alexandre Agnolon's study on the Scythians who had become Hellenized ("Cosmopolitanism and contingency in Herodotus: myth and tragedy in the fourth book of the *Histories*") here because the dramatization of their plight draws on actual tragedy, although this tale of tragic hybridity could well fit into our next part. Our third part, *Part 3: Ethnic identity among the Barbaroi*, concentrates on the two counterposed extremes of the Herodotean world, Egypt and the north, including Scythia. Our Egyptian studies are by Rogério Sousa ("Herodotus' Memphite sources"), who explores the important question of the access of Herodotus both to Egyptian sites of cultural importance and to those knowledgeable about them, and Maria do Céu Fialho, who looks at a tradition about the sojourn of Helen of Sparta in Egypt as example of bicultural amalgamation ("Ethnicity in Herodotus: the story of Helen through the Egyptians' eyes"). As to the northern fringes of the Herodotean world, Renaud Gagné offers "Mirages of ethnicity and the distant north in Book IV of the *Histories*: Hyperboreans, Arimaspians, and Issedones", which understands the account of the *Histories* as operating in juxtaposition and contestation with the *Arimaspea* of Aristeas of Prokonnesos. Nor have we slighted the adversaries of the Greeks in the Persian wars. In "The Greeks as seen from the east: Xerxes' European enemy", Maria de Fátima Silva explores how Herodotus presents Persian views on their own military strengths and those of the Greeks. Our *Part 4: Reflections of Herodotean ethnic historiography* contains two studies. Delfim Leão presents "Barbarians, Greekness, and wisdom: the afterlife of Croesus' debate with Solon", in which he contrasts the treatment of the interaction of Croesus and Solon in Herodotus with the more ethnocentric versions of the episode in later tradition. In our most far-ranging contribution, my fellow editor, Carmen Soares closes out our volume with "Scientific discourse in Herodotus Book II of Histories and its reflection in the age of new world discovery", in which she exposes the influence of the classical historic–scientific matrix (mostly Herodotean and Hippocratic in origin) in the Portuguese narratives on the land and peoples of Brazil.

Notes

1 Another useful overview is Thomas 2001.
2 Among the recent succession of notable monographs has been Hall 1997, 2002; Malkin 1998; Morgan 2003; Skinner 2012; and Vlassopoulos 2013.
3 Nenci 1990; Ulf 1996; Coleman & Walz 1997; Malkin 2001; Harrison 2002; Zacharia 2008a; Dirks & Roymans 2009; Funke & Luraghi 2009; Almagor & Skinner 2013; McInerney 2014.
4 For overviews, note Asheri 1997; Coleman 1997; Nippel 2002; Hall 2002: 9–29; Hall 2007: 49–58; Hornblower 2008.
5 Mitchell 2007 offers discussion with bibliography of panhellenism *vis-à-vis* non-Greek ethnicity.

6 My analysis has been expanded in related studies, one on Helot demography (Figueira 2003), a joint publication applying post-colonial theory to Spartan Helotage (Figueira & Figueira 2009) and another, which is forthcoming, on ethnicity in Thucydides (Figueira forthcoming). Figueira & Figueira did not find that post-colonial theory uncovered much new about Messenian ethnogenesis, but this piece did militate in favour of the relevance of an organic identity evolution there. All these pieces comment on the views of Luraghi (2002a, 2002b, 2002c). Figueira forthcoming addresses Luraghi 2008. See also Figueira 2010.

7 See Figueira forthcoming and Ogden 2004.

8 My views differ from much subsequent work in my insistence that the process of identity formation had started in the early fifth century at the latest, which conditioned the emergence of a Messenian state in the period after Leuktra.

9 Figueira 2006, 2007, 2008b, 2009, 2012.

10 See Figueira 2006: 261–2.

11 See Schuller 1995, while Dreher 1995 finds the same tendency in the fourth-century confederacy (cf. DS 15.28.4) but notes an adjustment to incorporate ethnic *koina* (pp. 179–81). For further discussion, see Figueira 2006: 286–7.

12 Figueira 2015: 321–9.

13 See Figueira 2008a: 427–8, 2015: 319–26, with bibliography. Note also my 'demographic/productive calculus', as explained in Figueira 1991: 161–72.

14 For an overview, see Antonaccio 2001; also de Romilly 1990: 13–55 for the Thucydidean evidence. For its mythological processes, see (e.g.) Malkin 1998: 120–55 on Epeiros.

15 On *sungeneia*, see Crane 1995: 147–61. The work of Curty (1994: 196–7, cf. 1995: 224–41) has been considered useful for the post-classical period, but his *schemata* have been considered too rigid, especially for the classical phenomena. Cf. Hornblower *CT* 2.64–8; Giovannini 1997: 162; Antonaccio 2001: 118–19; Fragoulaki 2013: 43–6.

16 Mere intensity of *oikeiotēs* or *philia* does not prove kinship. Jones (1999: 31) notes the great *philia* and *oikeiotēs* which the Spartans proffered the Athenians after the Athenians had captured the remaining Spartans on Sphakteria (Thuc. 4.19.1), for which see Will 1995: 305–8 and my discussion in Figueira 2019: 189–96; Figueira forthcoming.

17 Note the handy compilation of evidence in Hall 2007: 55.

18 Note Aris. *Pol.* 1276b1–13 for the phrase, πόλις [ἐστι] κοινωνία πολιτῶν πολιτείας '*polis* [is] the commonality of citizens of a political order'. See Murray 1993: 197–8; Hansen 1998: 133–4 for a recent discussion (with Figueira 2006: 281, 2007: 303–4, 2008b: 307–8).

19 These examples seem to demonstrate the criterion of Hansen 2000: 17–18 that city-state identity differs from nation-state identity in its treatment of ethnicity. See the comments of Figueira 2006: 255, 2007: 298 on the importance of the distinction between citizen and inhabitant.

20 In the course of the consolidation of the Athenian state, all Athenians come to have a shared identity as Ἀττικοί (Solon fr. 2.4 W; Alc. fr. 328 LP [Z 105]), but the epithet is poetic and rare. One might anticipate an ethnic Παναθηναῖοι, formed on their festival, the Panathenaia, which would have symbolized their sense of community. It could have been built on parallel with Πανέλληνες (e.g., *Il.* 2.530; Hes. *WD* 528; Arch. fr. 102 [*IEG*]); Παναχαιοί (e.g., *Il.* 2.404; 7.73; *Od.* 24.32; Hellanicus *FGrH* 323a F 21c), or Πανίωνες (Eustath. *Od.* 1.54 (*ad* 1.241). Yet this ethnic is unattested, suggestively, I think, because of an intensity of Athenian focus on their *polis*.

21 Naturally I still share the views on Herodotus as ethnologist that are exemplified briefly (albeit for non-specialists) in Figueira & Figueira 2011. Herodotus' denomination as "tourist", as Redfield 1985 ~ 2002 would have it, belongs to a decontextualized interpretation, blind to issues of technology, social differentiation, and economic structure, a view that is accompanied by condescending and non-empathetical comparisons with modern anthropological research.

22 See, e.g., Isaac 2004: 56–60; Gruen 2011: 21–39.
23 Hdt. 2.49.1–51.1, cf. 2.43.1–44.4. See also 2.81, 123.2–3, 171.3. On the general temporal priority of Egyptian culture, note Hdt. 2.2–4, 109, 177.2.
24 Hartog 1988 ~ 1980. See also Gray 1995.
25 Lloyd 1990: 215–44.
26 Hdt. 1.203.2; 3.101.1; 4.180.5.
27 Hdt. 1.93.3–4, 199.1–5; cf. 2.121ε.1–5, 126.1–2.
28 Kurke 1999: 220–46; Budin 2008: 58–92; Figueira & Figueira 2011: 221–3.
29 These paragraphs draw on Figueira and Figueira 2011: 225–6.
30 See Figueira 2006: 261–2.
31 Cf. Gruen 2011: 22–5.

Bibliography

Almagor, E. & Skinner, J. 2013. *Ancient Ethnography: New Approaches*. London (Bloomsbury Publishing).

Antonaccio, C.M. 2001. "Ethnicity and Colonization." In Malkin 2001, 113–57.

Asheri, D. 1997. "Identità greche, identità greca." In Settis, S., *et al.*, eds., *I Greci: Storia cultura arte società*. Turin (Einaudi), 2.2: 5–26.

Budin, S.L. 2008. *The Myth of Sacred Prostitution in Antiquity*. Cambridge (Cambridge University Press).

Coleman, J.E. 1997. "Ancient Greek Ethnocentrism." In Coleman & Walz 1997, 174–220.

Coleman, J.E. & Walz, C.A., eds. 1997. *Greeks and Barbarians: Essays in the Interaction Between Greeks and Non-Greeks in Antiquity and the Consequences for Eurocentrism.* Occasional Publications of the Department of Near Eastern Studies and the Program of Jewish Studies, Cornell University. Bethesda, MD (CDL Press).

Crane, G. 1995. *The Blinded Eye: Thucydides and the New Written Word*. Lanham, MD (Rowman & Littlefield Publishers).

Curty, O. 1994. "La notion de la parenté entre cites chez Thucydide." *Museum Helveticum* 51: 193–7.

———. 1995. *Les parentés légendaires entre cites grecques*. Geneva (Droz).

Dirks, T. & Roymans, N. 2009. *Ethnic Constructs in Antiquity*. Amsterdam Archaeological Studies 13. Amsterdam (Amsterdam University Press).

Dreher, M. 1995. "Poleis und Nicht-Poleis im Zweiten Athenischen Seebund." In Hansen 1995, 171–200.

Figueira, D.M. & Figueira, T. 2009. "The Colonial 'Subject' and the Ideology of Subjection in Lakōnikē: Tasting Laconian Wine Behind Lacanian Labels." In Hodkinson, S., ed., *Sparta: Comparative Approaches*. Swansea (Classical Press of Wales), 305–30.

———. 2011. "Travels with Herodotus: At Home and Abroad." In Maufort, M., & De Wegter, C., eds., *Old Margins and New Centers: The Legacy of European Literatures in an Age of Globalization: New Comparative Poetics 9*. Brussels (Peter Lang), 215–28.

Figueira, T.J. 1991. *Athens and Aigina in the Age of Imperial Colonization*. Baltimore, MD (Johns Hopkins University Press).

———. 1999. "The Evolution of the Messenian Identity." In Hodkinson, S., & Powell, A., eds., *Sparta: New Perspectives*. London (Duckworth), 211–44.

———. 2003. "Helot Demography and Class Demarcation in Classical Sparta." In Luraghi, N., & Alcock, S., eds., *Helots and Their Masters: The History and Sociology of a System of Exploitation*. Cambridge, MA (Harvard University Press), 193–239.

———. 2006. "The Copenhagen Polis Centre: A Review-Article of Its Publications, Parts 1–2." *Ancient West & East* 5: 252–303.

———. 2007. "The Copenhagen Polis Centre: A Review-Article of Its Publications, Part 3." *Ancient West & East* 6: 294–321.

———. 2008a. "Classical Greek Colonisation." In Tsetskhladze, G.R., ed., *A History of Greek Colonisation and Settlement Overseas*, Leiden (Brill), v. 2, 427–524.

———. 2008b. "The Copenhagen Polis Centre: A Review-Article of Its Publications, Part 4." *Ancient West & East* 7: 304–32.

———. 2009. "The Copenhagen Polis Centre: A Review-Article of Its Publications, Parts 5–6." *Ancient West & East* 8: 262–78.

———. 2010. rev., Luraghi 2008, *Classical Review* 60: 160–3.

———. 2012. "The Copenhagen Polis Centre: A Review-Article of Its Publications – Epilogue." *Ancient West & East* 11: 290–2.

———. 2015. "Modes of Colonization and Elite Integration in Archaic Greece." In Fisher, N.K.E., & van Wees, H., eds., *Aristocracy: Redefining Greek and Roman Elites Ancient Societies*. Swansea (Classical Press of Wales), 313–47.

———. 2019. "The Aristeidian Tribute and the Peace of Nikias." In Figueira, T., & Jensen, S.R., eds., *Athenian Hegemonic Finances: Funding Athenian Domination in the 5th and 4th Centuries B.C.* Swansea (Classical Press of Wales), 167–231.

———. Forthcoming. "Thucydides and Messenian Ethnogenesis." In Debnar, P., & Powell, A., eds., *Sparta in Thucydides*. Swansea (Classical Press of Wales).

Fragoulaki, M. 2013. *Kinship in Thucydides: Intercommunal Ties and Historical Narrative*. Oxford (Oxford University Press).

Funke, P. & Luraghi, N., eds. 2009. *The Politics of Ethnicity and the Crisis of the Peloponnesian League*. Washington, DC (Center for Hellenic Studies).

Giovannini, A. 1997. "Les relations de parenté entre les cités grecques: à propos d'un livre Recent." *Museum Helveticum* 54: 158–62.

Gray, V. 1995. "Herodotus and the Rhetoric of Otherness." *American Journal of Philology* 116: 185–211.

Gruen, E.S. 2011. *Rethinking the Other in Antiquity*. Princeton, NJ (Princeton University Press).

Hall, J.M. 1997. *Ethnic Identity in Greek Antiquity*. Cambridge (Cambridge University Press).

———. 2002. *Hellenicity: Between Ethnicity and Culture*. Chicago, IL (University of Chicago Press).

———. 2007. "Polis, Community, and Ethnic Identity." In Shapiro, H.A., ed., *The Cambridge Companion to Archaic Greece*, Cambridge (Wiley-Blackwell), 40–60.

Hansen, M.H., ed. 1993. *The Ancient Greek City-State*. Symposium on the Occasion of the 250th Anniversary of The Royal Danish Academy of Sciences and Letters July 1–4, 1992. Historisk-filosofiske Meddelelser 67. Copenhagen (The Royal Danish Academy of Sciences and Letters).

———. 1994. *Acts of the Copenhagen Polis Centre 2*. Historisk-filosofiske Meddelelser 72. Copenhagen (The Royal Danish Academy of Sciences and Letters).

———, ed. 1995. *Sources for the Ancient Greek City-State*. Symposium August 24–27.

———. 1998. *Polis and City-State: An Ancient Concept and Its Modern Equivalent*. Symposium, January 9, 1998. Acts of the Copenhagen Polis Centre 5, Historisk-filosofiske Meddelelser 76. Copenhagen (The Royal Danish Academy of Sciences and Letters).

———, ed. 2000. *A Comparative Study of Thirty City State Cultures*. An Investigation Conducted by the Copenhagen Polis Centre, Historisk-filosofiske Skrifter 21. Copenhagen (The Royal Danish Academy of Arts and Letters).

———. 2002. *A Comparative Study of Six City State Cultures*. An Investigation Conducted by the Copenhagen Polis Centre, Historisk-filosofiske Skrifter 27. Copenhagen (The Royal Danish Academy of Arts and Letters).

Harrison, T., ed. 2002. *Greeks and Barbarians*. Edinburgh (Routledge).

Hartog, F. 1988. *The Mirror of Herodotus*. Berkeley, CA (University of California Press) ~ *Le miroir d'Hérodote: Essai sur la représentation de l'autre*. Paris (Gallimard) 1980.

Hornblower, S. 1991–2008. *A Commentary on Thucydides*. Oxford (Oxford University Press) = Hornblower *CT*.

Isaac, B. 2004. *The Invention of Racism in Classical Antiquity*. Princeton, NJ (Princeton University Press).

Jones, C.P. 1999. *Kinship Diplomacy in the Ancient World*. Cambridge, MA (Harvard University Press).

Kurke, L. 1999. *Coins, Bodies, Games, and Gold: The Politics of Meaning in Archaic Greece*. Princeton, NJ (Princeton University Press).

Lloyd, A.B. 1990. "Herodotus on Egyptians and Libyans." In Nenci 1990, 215–44.

Luraghi, N. 2002a. "Helotic Slavery Reconsidered." In Powell, A., & Hodkinson, S., eds., *Sparta: Beyond the Mirage*. Swansea and London (Classical Press of Wales), 227–48.

———. 2002b. "Becoming Messenian." *Journal of Hellenic Studies* 122: 45–69.

———. 2002c. "Helots Called Messenians? A Note on Thuc. 1.101.2." *Classical Quarterly* 52: 588–92.

———. 2008. *The Ancient Messenians: Constructions of Ethnicity and Memory*. Cambridge (Cambridge University Press).

Malkin, I. 1998. *The Returns of Odysseus: Colonization and Ethnicity*. Berkeley, CA (University of California Press).

———, ed. 2001. *Ancient Perceptions of Greek Ethnicity*. Washington, DC (Center for Hellenic Studies).

McInerney, J., ed. 2014. *A Companion to Ethnicity in the Ancient Mediterranean*. Chichester, West Sussex (Wiley-Blackwell).

Mitchell, L. 2007. *Panhellenism and the Barbarian in Archaic and Classical Greece*. Swansea (Classical Press of Wales).

Morgan, C. 2003. *Early Greek States Beyond the Polis*. London (Routledge).

Munson, R.V. 2014. "Herodotus and Ethnicity." In McInerney 2014, 341–55.

Murray, O. 1993. "'Polis' and 'Politeia' in Aristotle." In Hansen 1993, 197–210.

Nenci, G., ed. 1990. *Hérodote et les peuples non grecs: neuf exposés suivis de discussions*. Geneva (Fondation Hardt).

Nippel, W. 2002. "The Construction of the 'Other'." In Harrison 2002, 278–310.

Ogden, D. 2004. *Aristomenes of Messene: Legends of Sparta's Nemesis*. Swansea (Classical Press of Wales).

Redfield, J. 1985. "Herodotus the Tourist." *Classical Philology* 80: 97–118 ~ Harrison 2002, 24–49.

Romilly, J. de. 1990. *La construction de la verité chez Thucydide*. Paris (Julliard).

Schuller, W. 1995. "Poleis im Ersten Attischen Seebund." In Hansen 1995, 165–70.

Skinner, J.E. 2012. *The Invention of Greek Ethnography: From Homer to Herodotus*. Oxford (Oxford University Press).

Thomas, R. 2001. "Ethnicity, Genealogy, Hellenism in Herodotus." In Malkin 2001, 213–33.

Ulf, C., ed. 1996. *Wege zur Genese griechischer Identität: die Bedeutung der früharcaischen Zeit*. Berlin (Akademie Verlag).

Vlassopoulos, K. 2013. *Greeks and Barbarians*. Cambridge (Cambridge University Press).

Will, E. 1995. "SYNGENEIA, OIKEIOTÈS, PHILIA." *Revue Philologique* 69: 299–325.

Zacharia, K., ed. 2008a. *Hellenisms: Culture, Identity, and Ethnicity from Antiquity to Modernity*. Aldershot (Ashgate).

———. 2008b. "Herodotus' Four Markers of Greek Identity." In Zacharia 2008, 21–36.

Part I

The methodology of ethnic identification in Herodotus

1 Herodotus' *Hermēneus* and the translation of culture in the *Histories*

Steven Brandwood

Introduction

Both Plutarch and Aelius Aristides, following traditions unattested in the Herodotean account, relate how Themistocles executed the interpreter accompanying Darius' embassy to Athens in 491 BCE.[1] Plutarch's report in particular emphasizes the ethnolinguistic nature of this interpreter's alleged crimes, namely his use of the Greek language to verbalize the commands of a foreign potentate (Plut. *Them.* 6.3):

> ἐπαινεῖται δ' αὐτοῦ καὶ τὸ περὶ τὸν δίγλωσσον ἔργον ἐν τοῖς πεμφθεῖσιν ὑπὸ βασιλέως ἐπὶ γῆς καὶ ὕδατος αἴτησιν. ἑρμηνέα γὰρ ὄντα συλλαβὼν διὰ ψηφίσματος ἀπέκτεινεν, ὅτι φωνὴν Ἑλληνίδα βαρβάροις προστάγμασιν ἐτόλμησε χρῆσαι.

> His conduct is also praised concerning the translator who was among those sent by the King to demand earth and water. Once he arrested him, he had the man executed by popular decree even though he was an interpreter, because he dared to subject Greek speech to barbarian commands.[2]

Whether Themistocles' actions should surprise us or not, it is noteworthy that this report comes as the first in a list of the great man's praiseworthy achievements, a list that concludes with Themistocles' successful conduct of the Greek war effort.[3] Themistocles would likely not have taken such a measure under normal circumstances – Darius' impending invasion of Attica loomed over the proceedings – but the passage nonetheless provides an interesting glimpse into the possibly charged or precarious position of the interpreter and of bilingualism generally in the sphere of ancient international relations and its historiographic representation.[4]

Themistocles' aversion to interpreters became a part of his legend,[5] but suspicion of bilingualism is a familiar enough trope that was echoed in antiquity after the Persian Wars and even later.[6] Nonetheless, such distrust finds its way into Herodotus' *Histories*, a work centrally concerned with cultural difference, in a notably understated fashion, appearing only in episodes like the death of Skyles, and earning Herodotus' disgust on each occasion.[7] More generally, however, the *Histories* lack the kind of pathological discomfort with interpreters and language difference that Plutarch's Themistocles demonstrates, and the interpreter's death accordingly plays no part in Herodotus' account of the invasion. Language and bilingualism for Herodotus, as Rosaria Munson has comprehensively demonstrated, "represents a particularly unproblematic area of difference", between ethnic groups, and is a difference that can be easily overcome by the use of interpreters.[8]

Such interpreters, however, are conspicuous by their absence from the *Histories*, and appear in name in only six episodes throughout the work, and only once in connection with Herodotus' personal description of his travels.[9] Interpreters do not generally appear in ancient sources as often as they may have been used,[10] but Herodotus' silence concerning the role is still noteworthy. Xenophon, for instance, makes numerous references to his own use of interpreters during his travels with the Ten-Thousand, and demonstrates clear awareness of the many varieties of translation involved in inter-ethnic communication.[11] It is, therefore, possible to read the presence or absence of interpreters within the *Histories* as a matter of "narrative convenience",[12] and it is certainly the case that the overwhelming majority of Herodotean conversations occur without any specified linguistic mediation. The *Histories'* conversational immediacy should not be used to suggest, however, that Herodotus was himself necessarily multilingual and comfortable with either the spoken or written forms of the languages employed by the cultures described in his work.[13] On the contrary, rather than demonstrating any mastery of non-Greek languages, Herodotus in fact occasionally betrays a lack of awareness of the workings of languages like Old Persian, such as in his claim that all Persian names end in the letter *sigma*, or that the names Artaxerxes and Xerxes share a root.[14] Further, Herodotus admits to relying on Greek translations of Persian imperial *stēlai*,[15] and must have employed intermediaries to interpret documents like the Bisitun inscription that were important to his work.[16] It is perhaps reasonable to assume that Herodotus could have attained some degree of practical facility in non-Greek languages over the course of his travels, but, as Lloyd has put it, "this does not mean that [he] would be capable of dealing with Iranian theology or of extracting detailed information on the organization of the army dispatched by Xerxes to bring the Greeks to heel".[17] Herodotus the *histōr* may appear multilingual and conversant with all the languages and cultures that he encounters in the *Histories*,[18] but Herodotus the traveler required linguistic intermediaries, despite their seemingly irregular narrative appearances.

This sustained absence of *hermēnees* throughout the work accordingly leaves the rare moments when they do appear subsequently marked and allows Herodotus to explore the ethnographic and narrative consequences of such figures. Herodotus' treatment of *hermēnees* demonstrates a characteristic of the balance at work in effective cross-cultural communication: language barriers can be easily and straightforwardly overcome by means of an interpreter, but understanding and meaningful communication between ethnic groups can only result from careful cultural explanation and positioning, a kind of ancient "thick description" that the *Histories* and their *histōr* serve to provide.[19] *Hermēnees*, however, appear too seldom in the *Histories* to carry this burden alone or to represent a truly concerted and effective pattern on Herodotus' part. So, their presence must also serve a narrative function. On each of their appearances, therefore, interpreters serve as part of Herodotus' apparatus of inquiry and help to define and focalize the roles of both the *histōr* and his audience, while also marking points in the *Histories'* narrative of cultural translation that require the intervention of the work's arch-translator, Herodotus himself.[20]

The most important appearances of interpreters in the *Histories* occur during the interview between Croesus and Cyrus, the journey of the Ichthyophagoi to Ethiopia, and Herodotus' own interactions with his personal interpreter in Egypt. Before engaging more fully with these episodes, however, it is first necessary to examine Herodotus' more general treatment of *hermēnees* in Egypt, Persia, and Scythia, in order to illuminate some of the patterns that will characterize the figure's employment in the rest of the *Histories*.

Hermēnees in the *logoi*

Egypt

Herodotus mentions his own practical interactions with interpreters on only one occasion,[21] but his discussion of the role of interpreters in Egyptian society, while brief, sheds light on the ethnolinguistic position of these figures and their employers, and on the relationship between interpreters and Herodotus' own patterns of inquiry. The first of these general references appears in Herodotus' description of Psammetikhos I's conquest of Egypt, achieved with the help of Greek and Carian mercenaries, whom he then allowed to settle in the country. Psammetikhos subsequently sent certain Egyptian youths to the Greek encampments to learn the language (Hdt. 2.154.2–3):

καὶ δὴ καὶ παῖδας παρέβαλε αὐτοῖσι Αἰγυπτίους τὴν Ἑλλάδα γλῶσσαν ἐκδιδάσκεσθαι· ἀπὸ δὲ τούτων ἐκμαθόντων τὴν γλῶσσαν οἱ νῦν ἑρμηνέες ἐν Αἰγύπτῳ γεγόνασι.

Moreover, he entrusted Egyptian boys to them to be taught Greek. The interpreters in Egypt today are descended from these boys who had mastered the language.[22]

Herodotus does not openly investigate Psammetikhos' motives for taking such a step, but these interpreters in all likelihood represent part of the pharaoh's attempt to regulate communication with foreign mercenaries.[23] Psammetikhos' preparations chime with his established interests in language acquisition and child-development,[24] and so represent a possible connection between these *hermēnees* and a type of official form of inquiry, a connection that Herodotus compounds in his focus on the relationship between interpreters and *mathēsis*, "learning". *Mathēsis* is a recurring concept in Herodotus' discussion of *hermēnees*,[25] appearing in this instance in the grammatically redundant ἐκμαθόντων τὴν γλῶσσαν, and marks even this bare reference to interpreters as one fundamentally associated with *historiē*.

Herodotus then allows his reader to witness the importance of these *hermēnees* in practice. The Greeks of the *Stratopeda*, "military camps", and the Egyptians, Herodotus relates, engage in bi-directional exchanges mediated by interpreters,[26] such that the Greeks in general gain knowledge of Egypt through them rather than through the Egyptians themselves (Hdt. 2.154.4):

τούτων δὲ οἰκισθέντων ἐν Αἰγύπτῳ οἱ Ἕλληνες οὕτω ἐπιμισγόμενοι τούτοισι τὰ περὶ Αἴγυπτον γινόμενα ἀπὸ Ψαμμητίχου βασιλέος ἀρξάμενοι πάντα καὶ τὰ ὕστερον ἐπιστάμεθα ἀτρεκέως· πρῶτοι γὰρ οὗτοι ἐν Αἰγύπτῳ ἀλλόγλωσσοι κατοικίσθησαν.

Once settled in Egypt, the Greeks intermingled with the Egyptians to such an extent that we now accurately know all Egyptian history, beginning from the reign of King Psammetikhos onward. For these were the first *alloglōssoi* who settled in Egypt.

The kinds of interactions that Herodotus describes here between the Greeks and Egyptians go well beyond the mute cross-cultural exchanges that he details elsewhere in the work.[27] Rather, the Greeks have knowledge of the *history* of the country, τὰ περὶ Αἴγυπτον γινόμενα, and Herodotus is sure to underline the accuracy of this information for his own ethnographic project, stressing that the accounts on which he relies are *atrekēs*.[28] Furthermore, the reference to the Greeks as *alloglōssoi* rather than *xenoi* or *metoikoi*, indicates the importance and persistence of the ethnolinguistic split between the Greeks and the Egyptians in this instance and, notably, from an Egyptian perspective.[29] The Greeks are the outsiders in this encounter, the *alloglōssoi* characterized by their lack of linguistic assimilation, and hence seem to have themselves benefitted from the interpreters they had trained earlier in the same chapter. The lines of inquiry from Egyptian *logioi* to Herodotus hence pass through the *hermēnees* that operated as the *poros* between these Greek and Egyptian communities in the Nile Delta, and Herodotus is clear to emphasize the provenance of the information that he subsequently provides.[30]

Herodotus mentions this class of Egyptian *hermēnees* again in his list of the different castes within Egyptian society, noting that (Hdt. 2.164.1):

ἔστι δὲ Αἰγυπτίων ἑπτὰ γένεα, καὶ τούτων οἱ μὲν ἱρέες, οἱ δὲ μάχιμοι κεκλέαται, οἱ δὲ βουκόλοι, οἱ δὲ συβῶται, οἱ δὲ κάπηλοι, οἱ δὲ ἑρμηνέες, οἱ δὲ κυβερνῆται. γένεα μὲν Αἰγυπτίων τοσαῦτά ἐστι, οὐνόματα δέ σφι κεῖται ἀπὸ τῶν τεχνέων.

There are seven castes among the Egyptians; among these are priests, warriors, cowherds, swineherds, merchants, interpreters, and helmsmen. These are the castes of the Egyptians, and their names derive from their occupations.

In Plato's account of Egyptian social structure, he mentions priests, warriors, hunters, farmers, shepherds, and craftsmen, but no interpreters, and Diodorus, Isocrates, and Strabo, while agreeing on much of the rest, also leave out this group.[31] There is also no mention here of the *cheirōnaktes* and *agoraioi anthrōpoi* that he discusses earlier, perhaps indicating some slippage between different sources in the Egyptian *logos*.[32] Certain scholars have suggested that these interpreters are the descendants of the Egyptian boys taught Greek by the original *alloglōssoi* in the country,[33] while others offer some healthy scepticism, particularly considering the "over-schematization" present.[34]

It does not seem impossible that Herodotus' own *hermēneus* inserted the interpreters into the list of the Egyptian professional *genea* mentioned here, but there is some evidence that interpreters were in fact figures of some importance within the Greek-speaking communities of the Nile Delta during the later fifth century. A Rhodian proxeny decree from 411–407 BCE found at Lindos, *SIG³* 110, honours an unnamed Aiginetan as the Rhodian *proxenos* at Naukratis, and describes him as τ]ὸν ἐγ Ναυκράτ[ιος] ἑρμ[α]νέα.[35] As Figueira points out, the noun *hermaneus* in this inscription represents an official title, one of sufficient prestige to merit reference in a kind of honourific decree that typically avoids discussion of professions.[36] Accordingly, while Herodotus does not mention *hermēnees* each time he employed them, it is not impossible that there is some accuracy to their inclusion in the Egyptian *genea* that Herodotus describes.[37]

This word *genea* itself poses a nearly insoluble problem of translation that emblematizes the nature of the interpreter's role in the *Histories*. The term *genea*, as Lloyd writes, "originally meant 'clan,' a social group of citizens larger than the nuclear family but smaller than a phratry and defined by ties of kinship and religious obligation. It seems extremely improbable that the word bears all these connotations here."[38] For phratry in this instance, we must probably qualify by adducing other similar categories outside Attica.[39] Nevertheless, the interpreter who helped Herodotus to this information could translate the words straightforwardly from Egyptian to Greek, but the cultural components of the terms were perhaps beyond his concern.

Herodotus deals with this dynamic of translation directly in his treatment of the *machimoi*, one of the *genea* mentioned in the catalog of Egyptian castes. The word *machimos* is a very familiar fifth- and fourth-century term, found across genres from Aeschylus to Plato.[40] However, Herodotus' simple translation of the word from Egyptian to Greek is naturally insufficient to transmit the information that he wants, leading to a three-chapter digression in which he specifies the term's exact nature. Rather than simply leave the discussion of the Egyptian *machimoi* as dependent on the easy linguistic equivalence between the Egyptian and Greek words, Herodotus gives information on the *machimoi*'s numbers, hometowns, restrictions, privileges, holdings, and even daily allowances of bread, beef, and wine.[41] These *machimoi* are completely imbricated into their precise cultural context, and the all-too-easy translation of the term between Egyptian and Greek requires the *histōr*'s intervention to specify the cultural difference that the mere linguistic equivalence would otherwise serve to elide. The intervention in this case is of a straightforward nature and involves only the *histōr* and his audience, but the activity of interpreters elsewhere in the *Histories* takes place within the context of narrated conversations and demands more delicate positioning on Herodotus' part.

Persia

Herodotus' *hermēnees* are typically associated with kings, like Psammetikhos I in Egypt, but appear most often in the context of the Persian court, where they seem to function as part of the royal apparatus.[42] Cyrus and Cambyses employ *hermēnees* over the course of military campaigns, but Darius uses interpreters on two occasions while at home in Susa, and so allows for an examination of the peacetime, domestic function of interpreters within the *Histories*.[43] The first of these appearances occurs during the famous interview that Darius sets up between the Greeks and the Indian Kallatiai, which allows Herodotus to affirm the accuracy of Pindar's famous *gnōmē*: *nomos basileus*.[44] Darius acts as the ultimate arbiter of the exchange, but the conversation between the two ethnic groups depends at least in part on the mediation of interpreters (Hdt. 3.38.3–4):

> Δαρεῖος ἐπὶ τῆς ἑωυτοῦ ἀρχῆς καλέσας Ἑλλήνων τοὺς παρεόντας εἴρετο ἐπὶ κόσῳ ἂν χρήματι βουλοίατο τοὺς πατέρας ἀποθνήσκοντας κατασιτέεσθαι· οἱ δὲ ἐπ᾽ οὐδενὶ ἔφασαν ἔρδειν ἂν τοῦτο. Δαρεῖος δὲ μετὰ ταῦτα καλέσας Ἰνδῶν τοὺς καλεομένους Καλλατίας, οἳ τοὺς γονέας κατεσθίουσι, εἴρετο, παρεόντων τῶν Ἑλλήνων καὶ δι᾽ ἑρμηνέος μανθανόντων τὰ λεγόμενα, ἐπὶ τίνι χρήματι δεξαίατ᾽ ἂν τελευτῶντας τοὺς πατέρας κατακαίειν πυρί· οἱ δὲ ἀμβώσαντες μέγα εὐφημέειν μιν ἐκέλευον. οὕτω μέν νυν ταῦτα νενόμισται, καὶ ὀρθῶς μοι δοκέει Πίνδαρος ποιῆσαι, 'νόμον πάντων βασιλέα' φήσας εἶναι.

> Darius summoned certain of the Greeks who were present in his kingdom and asked them at what price they would be willing to eat their fathers' dead bodies. These Greeks declared that they would not do this for any price. Thereupon, Darius summoned certain of the Indians, called the Kalliatai, who do eat their dead parents, and asked, with the Greeks being also present and understanding what was being said by means of an interpreter, at what price they would agree to burn their fathers' dead bodies with fire. The Indians exclaimed loudly and commanded Darius to stay silent about such things. So these matters are governed by tradition, and Pindar seems to me to write correctly when he writes that "custom is King."

Some context is helpful for examining the patterns of translation and interpretation on display in this passage. In the first place, there are four separate parties involved – Darius, the interpreters, the Greeks, and the Kallatiai – and it is not always clear who is addressing whom, how, and in what language. Darius is the host and central figure of the passage, even in terms of geography, a fact that he emphasizes by inviting the farthest-flung subjects of his empire to the interview.[45] The interpreters' role in this passage, however, is somewhat confused. For instance, they only appear when the Greeks are *listening* to the Kallatiai, and not earlier during their conversation with Darius. This could simply mean that, being present in Susa, these Greeks spoke Persian.[46] Such a solution seems attractive, especially considering that a Kallatian–Greek interpreter would be a rarer figure than a Persian–Kallatian one,[47] and it seems unlikely that, in an episode so interested in communication and one in which interpreters are present, a chain of interpreters translating from Kallatian to Persian to Greek would have gone entirely unmentioned.

The interpreters in this episode provide the conduit for linguistic understanding between ethnic groups, but the scene seems almost designed to emphasize their limitations. For instance, it is likely, *pace* Rotolo,[48] that the interpreters are here practising a kind of consecutive translation. Accordingly, no sooner do they begin their work translating Darius' question than Herodotus demonstrates their practical uselessness for real communication between the Greeks, Persians, and Kallatiai. On a functional level, the interpreters become unnecessary as soon as the Kallatiai respond with their sub-linguistic, emotional outburst, οἱ δὲ ἀμβώσαντες μέγα, "they cried out loudly", that would have been intelligible to all observers, regardless of linguistic capacity. Furthermore, the question posed by Darius may be able to be rendered intelligible to each party by means of the interpreter, but strictly on a linguistic level. The Kallatiai and the Greeks do not exchange the vast amounts of explanatory information that would position their funerary practices within their vastly different social structures; hence the shock and anger of the Kallatiai at the very thought of Darius' question.

The episode concludes for its characters with an injunction to silence, *euphēmeein*,[49] rather than explanation, and it is only Herodotus' Pindaric framing that can demonstrate that "custom is king" to his Greek audience. Conceivably, Darius' inquiry was more self-enhancing than intended to educate his subjects – Darius seems primarily motivated here to demonstrate the breadth of his domain, both geographically and ethically, and, hence, the need for universal monarchy – and it is only in Herodotus' narration of the episode that it takes on any educative character.[50] Accordingly, the one-way direction of the *hermēnees'* activity in this scene displays a kind of structure. The *Histories* are themselves written for the Greeks, and the interpretations offered are given in their own cultural and linguistic medium. The interpreters in this scene serve as the conduit to the Greeks of a certain kind of ethnographic information, involved with the kind of explanations that the *histōr* provides throughout the work. Consequently, as part of the apparatus of inquiry, the interpreters are oriented *towards the Greeks*, in this case indicating the truth of Pindar's *nomos basileus* and that Herodotus' interventions are essential for any understandings of such *nomoi*.

These *hermēnees* continue in their role as the indicators of inquiry in the other episode involving Darius at his court: his interactions with the Samian exile Syloson. The presence of interpreters in this episode helps to emphasize their role in the act of royal and historical inquiry, but their inconsistent deployment here may demonstrate their essential marginality within the *Histories'* narrative. Herodotus provides numerous levels of discourse in this passage, which allows him to dwell on the interpreters' narrative functions (Hdt. 3.140.1–3):

ἀναβὰς δὲ ἐς τὰ Σοῦσα ἵζετο ἐς τὰ πρόθυρα τῶν βασιλέος οἰκίων καὶ ἔφη Δαρείου εὐεργέτης εἶναι. ἀγγέλλει ταῦτα ἀκούσας ὁ πυλουρὸς τῷ βασιλέϊ· ὁ δὲ θωμάσας λέγει πρὸς αὐτόν· 'καὶ τίς ἐστι Ἑλλήνων εὐεργέτης τῷ ἐγὼ

προαιδέομαι, νεωστὶ μὲν τὴν ἀρχὴν ἔχων, ἀναβέβηκε δ' ἤ τις ἢ οὐδείς κω
παρ' ἡμέας αὐτῶν, ἔχω δὲ χρέος ὡς εἰπεῖν οὐδὲν ἀνδρὸς Ἕλληνος; ὅμως δὲ
αὐτὸν παράγαγε ἔσω, ἵνα εἰδέω τί θέλων λέγει ταῦτα.' παρῆγε ὁ πυλουρὸς
τὸν Συλοσῶντα, στάντα δὲ ἐς μέσον εἰρώτων οἱ ἑρμηνέες τίς τε εἴη καὶ τί
ποιήσας εὐεργέτης φησὶ εἶναι βασιλέος. εἶπε ὦν ὁ Συλοσῶν πάντα τὰ περὶ
τὴν χλανίδα γενόμενα καὶ ὡς αὐτὸς εἴη κεῖνος ὁ δούς.

After he went up to Susa, Syloson sat before the doors of the King's palace and claimed that he was a benefactor of Darius. The gatekeeper, once
he heard this, reported to the King, but he was amazed and replied to the
gatekeeper, "But who is this Greek benefactor to whom I am in debt? I have
only recently gained my kingdom, and almost nobody has even approached
us from among the Greeks. Furthermore, I have no use for any Greek, so to
speak. Nonetheless, bring him in, so that I might learn to what end he is saying such things." The gatekeeper brought Syloson in, and, as he stood in the
middle of them, the interpreters asked him who he was and what he had done
to claim to be the King's benefactor. Syloson related all that had happened
concerning the cloak, and that he had been the one who had given it.

Syloson's involvement with Darius comes in two stages and provides a useful
look at the nature of inter-ethnic communication. In the first instance, Syloson
gave Darius his cloak as a gift while the two were in Egypt. In this exchange,
there is no mention of the language used between the Greek and the Persian soldiers, each speaking a language other than the local Egyptian, and it does not
seems unlikely that the conversation took place by means of gesture, Quintilian's
omnium hominum communis sermo.[51] Franke has suggested that Syloson may
have been proficient in either Egyptian or Persian,[52] but this is unnecessary considering the passage's focus on communication and would render otiose any practical need for a *hermēneus* in the royal audience scene. Regardless of language
used or mediation available, this initial interaction nonetheless achieved success:
the giving and receiving of a gift.[53] Such straightforward communication between
the two ends there, however, encapsulated in linguistic lack of understanding.

For instance, Syloson gains entrance to the royal audience chamber in Susa
by claiming to be the king's "benefactor", *euergetēs*, an impossibility as far as
Darius is concerned because of the relative novelty of his reign. Herodotus is
elsewhere interested in the concept of a Persian *euergetēs*, and glosses the word
in Persian as *orosangēs* during his description of the Battle of Salamis.[54] These
orosangai, however, were not the equivalent of the Greek conception of an ordinary *euergetēs*, but rather were much grander figures – given their own thrones
and audience chambers, meals with the king, and sizable gifts of land.[55] Again,
there is a functional linguistic equivalence between *euergetēs* and *orosangēs*, but
the cultural gulf separating the two terms is enough to provide a communicative
misfire between Syloson and the court, perhaps resulting in his royal audience.

It is notable that no *hermēneus* is mentioned in Syloson's interaction with the
gatekeeper, even though this conversation is the starting-point of the scene's
communication problems. Gehman suggests that an official figure like the king's

gatekeeper would be obliged to understand a number of languages, if not speak them fluently,[56] an attractive solution and one that prepares the communicative misfire that takes place in the king's presence. It is equally possible, however, that a third party, familiar to either the gatekeeper or to Syloson himself, could have acted as interpreter in this more informal interview, but not in the throne-room, where a higher level of privilege of access would be required. Interpreters become involved in the scene mainly as part of the apparatus of the court, but also as the arbiters of royal inquiry and markers of a heightened level of interlocution. They, rather than Darius himself, ask Syloson, "who he was and what he had done to claim to be the King's benefactor", possibly adding a narrative touch to aggrandize the king's throne-room presence.[57] By involving the *hermēnees*, however, Herodotus, also invites some scrutiny on the language at issue in the passage, particularly in regard to the operative word *euergetēs*, and so underscores the importance of his own work's mediation of cultural difference.

Scythia

Herodotus' discussion of interpreters is typically associated with royal courts, but also occurs as an indicator of inquiry in his discussion of the far north of Scythia. In discussing the Argippaioi, Herodotus describes the network of translators that is required to speak with them, through whom knowledge is effectively gained:

> καὶ γὰρ Σκυθέων τινὲς ἀπικνέονται ἐς αὐτούς, τῶν οὐ χαλεπόν ἐστι πυθέσθαι, καὶ Ἑλλήνων τῶν ἐκ Βορυσθένεός τε ἐμπορίου καὶ τῶν ἄλλων Ποντικῶν ἐμπορίων. Σκυθέων δὲ οἳ ἂν ἔλθωσι ἐς αὐτοὺς δι' ἑπτὰ ἑρμηνέων καὶ δι' ἑπτὰ γλωσσέων διαπρήσσονται.

> Some of the Scythians come to them, from whom it is not difficult to gather information, and from some of the Greeks as well who come from the *emporion* [marketplace] of Borysthenes and the other Black Sea *emporia*. The Scythians who do go there do business by means of seven interpreters in seven languages.

The marker, οὐ χαλεπόν ἐστι πυθέσθαι, characterizes this description as a discussion of the process of inquiry, and the presence of the *hermēnees* serves to compound this description. The chain of interpreters that Herodotus says are necessary to communicate with the Argippaioi, however, would render communication functionally impossible. And the special number seven only adds to the folkloric quality to communication with the Argippaioi,[58] while the numerical repetition of *hepta* chimes with traditional language found in both Herodotus and elsewhere.[59] Importantly, however, despite the ease with which Herodotus claims to be able to converse with these people, the information he offers is almost entirely visual – the construction of their houses, the length of their noses and chins, and the fruit that they eat, *aschy*, an untranslated word that could be learned without recourse to interpreters.[60] In the Scythian *logos*, therefore, the translators again serve as indicators of inquiry and the markers of Herodotean *historiē*.

Cases of special interest

Aside from the smaller-scale scenes mentioned earlier, the most important scenes in the *Histories* for analyzing the role of interpreters are the interview between Croesus and Cyrus, the Ichthyophagoi's journey to Ethiopia, and Herodotus' own interactions with his personal translator in Egypt.[61] Up to this point, Herodotus' engagement with *hermēnees* has demonstrated the importance of the practitioner's skill as a marker of inquiry and narrative intervention, and these three episodes will serve to continue their characterization as markers of and surrogates for Herodotean inquiry. The interview between Croesus and Cyrus is an important one for the work in general,[62] but particularly so for the character of the work's *hermēnees*, as it clearly demonstrates their role in the *Histories'* cultural translation as markers of the *histōr*'s intervention.

Croesus and Cyrus (Hdt. 1.86–7)

The first of these scenes, describing Croesus' fall and his aborted execution on the pyre, has much to do with communication between people who cannot communicate, or at any rate cannot communicate well.[63] From the beginning of the episode, Herodotus thematizes difficult communication, beginning with his description of Croesus' mute son, and the equally inscrutable oracle about him from Delphi.[64] The passage's first instance of language difference, however, occurs with this son's first utterance of his life, when he shouts to the Persian soldier chasing his father, ὤνθρωπε, μὴ κτεῖνε Κροῖσον, "Don't kill Croesus, man!",[65] and successfully halts the attacker, despite the lack of a common language. There is clearly no interpreter in this scene, but the desired statement, nonetheless, has immediate effect, perhaps demonstrating the easy difference between languages that Munson has described, particularly in such emotionally charged circumstances.[66] It is likely, however, that the language barrier was broken simply by the name *Croesus* that served almost as an extra-linguistic tag for the man to whom it was applied,[67] and that the name itself may have provided the linguistic passage between the two in its function as an emblem.[68] The son cries out the name in an attempt to stop his father's death, and the attacker hears the name and instantly recognizes his quarry's value. The two seem to have communicated effectively without an interpreter, but it is only through their briefly aligned immediate frames of reference.

The following scenes, despite their grisly character, are, nonetheless, ones of real inquiry. Cyrus must have had speedier means of execution than a dramatic immolation, but he chooses to proceed in the way he does for the sake of investigation. As Herodotus relates, he proceeded the way he did because (Hdt.1.86.2):

ἐν νόῳ ἔχων εἴτε δὴ ἀκροθίνια ταῦτα καταγιεῖν θεῶν ὅτεῳ δή, εἴτε καὶ εὐχὴν ἐπιτελέσαι θέλων, εἴτε καὶ πυθόμενος τὸν Κροῖσον εἶναι θεοσεβέα τοῦδε εἵνεκεν ἀνεβίβασε ἐπὶ τὴν πυρήν, βουλόμενος εἰδέναι εἴ τίς μιν δαιμόνων ῥύσεται τοῦ μὴ ζώοντα κατακαυθῆναι.

He intended either to offer them as the first-fruits to one of the gods, or indeed because he wanted to fulfill a vow, or, since he heard that Croesus was a pious man, and on account of this forced him to mount the pyre, wishing to learn whether or not some divinity would save him from being burned alive.

As Segal has pointed out,[69] Cyrus' inquisitive thought process is on full display in this scene, a point that Herodotus is clear to repeat three times in the same tricolonic sentence: ἐν νόῳ ἔχων, πυθόμενος, and βουλόμενος εἰδέναι. Herodotus' narrative here reflects his own pattern of inquiry into Cyrus' reasoning, creating the beginning of the *mise-en-abîme* effect that characterizes the passage: Herodotus enquires into Cyrus' patterns of inquiry in order to demonstrate a feature of inquiry itself,[70] and to distinguish his own *historiē* from the cruel manipulations of a despot like Cyrus or Psammetikhos.[71] It is at this point that Croesus voices his emblematic utterance, "Solon", to the bafflement of Cyrus and his *hermēnees* (Hdt. 1.86.3–4):

τῷ δὲ Κροίσῳ ἑστεῶτι ἐπὶ τῆς πυρῆς ἐσελθεῖν, καίπερ ἐν κακῷ ἐόντι τοσούτῳ, τὸ τοῦ Σόλωνος, ὥς οἱ εἴη σὺν θεῷ εἰρημένον, τὸ ʽμηδένα εἶναι τῶν ζωόντων ὄλβιον᾽. ὡς δὲ ἄρα μιν προσστῆναι τοῦτο, ἀνενεικάμενόν τε καὶ ἀναστενάξαντα ἐκ πολλῆς ἡσυχίης ἐς τρὶς ὀνομάσαι ʽΣόλων᾽. καὶ τὸν Κῦρον ἀκούσαντα κελεῦσαι τοὺς ἑρμηνέας ἐπειρέσθαι τὸν Κροῖσον τίνα τοῦτον ἐπικαλέοιτο, καὶ τοὺς προσελθόντας ἐπειρωτᾶν. Κροῖσον δὲ τέως μὲν σιγὴν ἔχειν εἰρωτώμενον, μετὰ δέ, ὡς ἠναγκάζετο, εἰπεῖν· ʽτὸν ἂν ἐγὼ πᾶσι τυράννοισι προετίμησα μεγάλων χρημάτων ἐς λόγους ἐλθεῖν.᾽

Even though he was in such disaster as he stood upon the pyre, it occurred to Croesus that Solon's remark, "no man among the living is happy," had been spoken with divine direction. And when this idea came to him, after much silence, he sighed, groaned, and called out the name "Solon" three times. Cyrus heard him and commanded his interpreters to ask Croesus whom he was calling upon. They approached him and asked. Croesus, however, kept silent during their questioning and only spoke after being compelled: "I would have preferred even to great wealth that this man converse with every ruler!"

Just as in the earlier interaction between Croesus' son and the Persian soldier, the name "Solon" has a certain emblematic character to it, expressing in extraordinarily condensed fashion the entire history between these two men, and the folly of Croesus' inability to understand him. It is a term that requires no interpreter as far as its linguistic identity is concerned, but requires the *Histories* at large, chapters 1.30–33 in particular, and Herodotus himself to explicate.

The interpreters present for the interview, in their first appearance in the work, nonetheless, find Croesus' utterances impossible to transmit, despite their linguistic capabilities. As Hollman puts it, *hermēnees* "are translators, but they are far from hermeneuts".[72] Croesus' language remains *asēma* and demands greater intervention than linguistic equivalency can provide, so Herodotus allows Croesus to act as his surrogate in this passage (Hdt. 1.86.5–6):

ὡς δέ σφι ἄσημα ἔφραζε, πάλιν ἐπειρώτων τὰ λεγόμενα. λιπαρεόντων δὲ αὐτῶν καὶ ὄχλον παρεχόντων, ἔλεγε δὴ ὡς ἦλθε ἀρχὴν ὁ Σόλων ἐὼν Ἀθηναῖος, καὶ θεησάμενος πάντα τὸν ἑωυτοῦ ὄλβον ἀποφλαυρίσειε οἷα δὴ εἴπας, ὥς τε αὐτῷ πάντα ἀποβεβήκοι τῇ περ ἐκεῖνος εἶπε, οὐδέν τι μᾶλλον ἐς ἑωυτὸν λέγων ἢ οὐκ ἐς ἅπαν τὸ ἀνθρώπινον καὶ μάλιστα τοὺς παρὰ σφίσι αὐτοῖσι ὀλβίους δοκέοντας εἶναι. τὸν μὲν Κροῖσον ταῦτα ἀπηγέεσθαι, τῆς δὲ πυρῆς ἤδη ἀμμένης καίεσθαι τὰ περιέσχατα. καὶ τὸν Κῦρον ἀκούσαντα τῶν ἑρμηνέων τὰ Κροῖσος εἶπε, μεταγνόντα τε καὶ ἐννώσαντα ὅτι καὶ αὐτὸς ἄνθρωπος ἐὼν ἄλλον ἄνθρωπον, γενόμενον ἑωυτοῦ εὐδαιμονίῃ οὐκ ἐλάσσω, ζώοντα πυρὶ διδοίη.

They asked him again what he had said, since he was saying things that were unintelligible to them. And since they were begging him and forming a crowd, he said that Solon was an Athenian who had come to his kingdom, and upon seeing all of his wealth, made little of it and said as much; now everything had turned out for him exactly as Solon had said, speaking not so much to him as to all of humanity, and especially to those who imagine that they are fortunate. As Croesus related these things, the fire was kindled and the edges of the pyre began to burn. Cyrus heard what Croesus said by means of his interpreters, and changed his mind, recognizing that he himself was a human and was preparing to commit to the fire another human, who had been no less than himself in happiness.

Initially, Croesus does not comply with their questions, and only enigmatically provides further information on Solon under compulsion: "I would have preferred even to great wealth that this man converse with every ruler!" Even in this oracular type of definition,[73] which remains *asēma* to the onlookers, the communication breakdown is stark. Croesus *did* meet Solon and *did* converse with him, without any lost fortune at the time, and still did not come to any understanding with him, primarily through their different definitions of the linguistically shared term *olbios*.[74] Thus, even when language difference is entirely erased, the intervention of the *histōr* is still required between speakers and still determines the effectiveness of the communication.

As the interview continues, Solon becomes less obscure, explaining to the assembled *okhlos* a succinct summary of Herodotus 1.30–33: Solon was an Athenian who came to Sardis, made light of what he saw, and told Croesus to look to the *telos*, which he failed to do at his own peril. The Herodotean translation that Croesus provides extends ἐς ἅπαν τὸ ἀνθρώπινον, an appropriate marker for the universality of the *histōr*'s intervention. Accordingly, as Demont and others have remarked,[75] Croesus for this *logos* takes on the role of the *histōr* and Cyrus the reader or audience of the *Histories* in this passage, hearing and changing his mind, *metagnonta*, and recognizing, *ennōsanta*, his common humanity with his captive.[76]

The reader and the king may share perspective here, but it is the *interpreters* that provide the connection, a fact that Herodotus is at pains to make. He is very clear, for instance, to demonstrate that the interpreters are the arbiters of this conversation, occupying the middle zone, physically and linguistically, between the two interlocutors. Contrary to the earlier depiction of interpreting given at Hdt. 3.38, Herodotus provides a completely textbook description of consecutive translation in this passage: Cyrus instructs his *hermēnees* to question Croesus, κελεῦσαι τοὺς ἑρμηνέας ἐπειρέσθαι τὸν Κροῖσον τίνα τοῦτον ἐπικαλέοιτο; the interpreters repeatedly question him, persisting even through misunderstanding, λιπαρεόντων δὲ αὐτῶν καὶ ὄχλον παρεχόντων; the *hermēnees* refer the information to Cyrus, καὶ τὸν Κῦρον ἀκούσαντα τῶν ἑρμηνέων τὰ Κροῖσος εἶπε; and he changes his mind, μεταγνόντα τε καὶ ἐννώσαντα. Herodotus thematizes the translation of cultural information in this passage, in which the interpreters play the most straightforward and least problematic of roles.

Cyrus and the reader can come to their *anthrōpinon* realization, but only the interpreters make this possible. Interpreters transmit information easily from one linguistic code to another,[77] but are nonetheless placed under significant limitations that demand context and explanation. In this episode, however, the interpreters are a featured part of Herodotus' inter-ethnic communicative network, serving as the medium for both linguistic and cultural explanation that can lead to recognition and understanding. Importantly, once Croesus has communicated effectively with Cyrus and Herodotus has underlined the importance of narrative mediation, the interpreters vanish from the scene, and do not recur in any of Croesus' further conversations with Persian kings.[78]

There are numerous other lines of communication present in this passage – Croesus to the *okhlos*, Croesus to the Gods, the Gods to the *okhlos*, etc. – but a further question remains to be asked about the nature of the interpreters depicted in this scene: from which language are they translating for Cyrus?[79] There is no indication one way or another whether we are to imagine Croesus speaking in Lydian to the interpreters and to the gods, and his pronunciation of the name "Solon" would probably remain similar regardless of which language he employed.[80] Imagining that the conversation took place by means of Persian to Lydian interpreters, and was subsequently translated into Greek for Herodotus' source and subsequent relation of the tale, places an even squarer focus on the necessity of the *histōr*'s role in these proceedings. Without Herodotus, the Persian to Lydian to Greek translations could be effectively accomplished as far as linguistic equivalency is concerned, but the long exchange from Solon to Croesus to Cyrus to the *logioi* to Herodotus would have become so muddied as to render the discussion permanently *asēma*.

The Ichthyophagoi

The Croesus episode provides the clearest treatment of *hermēnees* in the *Histories*, if we limit ourselves to where they are referenced by their proper name. But there are instances throughout the work when translators are used or represented without the use of the term. The most extended treatment of non-*hermēneus* interpreters comes in the discussion of the Ichthyophagoi and their journey to Ethiopia as Cambyses' spies. The Ichthyophagoi, as their name implies, are something of a hybrid, in-between group of individuals, placed somewhere between the meat-eating Ethiopians and the grain-eating Persians on a kind of Herodotean anthropological continuum.[81] They are, however, fundamentally figures of inquiry, and differ from their fellow *hermēnees* in being both the inquirers *and* interpreters of the information sought. By virtue of their linguistic ability, Cambyses sends these men as spies, a fact that Herodotus repeats seven times over the course of the episode.[82] Their role in investigating Ethiopian *nomoi* causes them in a certain way to stand as surrogates for the *histōr* himself, pursuing inquiry, but for an end notably inferior to true *historiē*.[83]

The Ichthyophagoi's linguistic ability does not eliminate the need for the *histōr*, however, as the introductory chapter to the episode demonstrates. Herodotus opens the journey to Ethiopia with a short digression on the legendary "table of the sun" that is constantly covered with boiled meats, although he reveals that this is the work of officials rather than any miraculous occurrence. The very existence of the table in the *Histories*, however, speaks to a problem constant throughout the *Histories* of the translation of metaphor. As How and Wells note, the "Table of the Sun" is possibly a myth misunderstood in translation, connected to the "Meadow of Offerings" familiar from the Egyptian Underworld.[84] This metaphorical "table" then becomes concretized into a real structure in need of explanation, which the *histōr* is keen to provide. The Ichthyophagoi, therefore, set out on a journey of translation and investigation into a subject of inquiry that is *itself* a possible mistranslation, requiring Herodotus' great efforts to remedy and placing a certain focus within the episode on the nature of translation and inquiry.

As in the interview between Cyrus and Croesus, communication and language are once again of central importance in the meeting between the Ichthyophagoi and the king of the Egyptians, particularly in the realm of truth-value. An interpreter can easily transmit a lie to another party, and may gain the goal of the original speaker, but real communication will have failed.[85] The king of the Ethiopians recognizes this and quickly remarks that (Hdt. 3.21.2):

οὔτε ὁ Περσέων βασιλεὺς δῶρα ὑμέας ἔπεμψε φέροντας προτιμῶν πολλοῦ ἐμοὶ ξεῖνος γενέσθαι, οὔτε ὑμεῖς λέγετε ἀληθέα (ἥκετε γὰρ κατόπται τῆς ἐμῆς ἀρχῆς) οὔτε ἐκεῖνος ἀνήρ ἐστι δίκαιος.

The king of the Persians has not sent you bearing gifts because he greatly values that he become my guest-friend, nor do you yourselves speak the truth – you have come as spies into my kingdom – nor is that man just.

The lies that the Ichthyophagoi tell are perhaps the clearest indicator of the ease of linguistic transfer, but its essential meaninglessness for communication and, in this case, to inquiry itself.

The King's response also includes the gift to Cambyses of an unbendable bow. This bow has obvious folkloric parallels,[86] but also serves a number of communicative purposes. For instance, the Egyptian hieroglyphic symbol for Ethiopia was a bow,[87] possibly causing the object to stand for the country in the eyes of its interpreter, Cambyses, while its unbendable nature would have served as its own objective form of meaning. By bypassing the use of language altogether, the King of the Ethiopians has achieved greater power of communication than the interpreters deputized to gather information.

In the second part of their conversation with the King, the Ichthyophagoi further demonstrate the limitations of strict linguistic translation for effective communication. The king again focusses on the truth-value of the statements made to him, declaring the myrrh and the scarlet robes to be *dolera*, "treacherous",[88] even though he can see and hold their material reality in his hands. Importantly, however, he is unable or unwilling to understand the Ichthyophagoi's explanations of the jewelry that they give as gifts (Hdt. 3.22.2–3):

δεύτερα δὲ τὸν χρυσὸν εἰρώτα, τὸν στρεπτὸν τὸν περιαυχένιον καὶ τὰ ψέλια· ἐξηγεομένων δὲ τῶν Ἰχθυοφάγων τὸν κόσμον αὐτοῦ γελάσας ὁ βασιλεὺς καὶ νομίσας εἶναί σφεα πέδας εἶπε ὡς παρ᾽ ἑωυτοῖσί εἰσι ῥωμαλεώτεραι τουτέων πέδαι.

Next, he asked about the braided golden bracelets and necklace, and after the Ichthyophagoi explained the jewelry, the King laughed and, imagining that they were chains, said that there were stronger chains than these in his kingdom.

Even when the ornaments have been explained, they remain no clearer to the king, and are even the subject for joking, although it does seem that the king was being facetious. This line of reverse inquiry continues as the interview progresses, with the two groups engaging in numerous communicative misfires. Among these are the Ethiopian opinion of bread as *kopros* and the relative unimportance of gold in Ethiopia, a fact that Herodotus is able to explain easily, based on its relative plenty in the country.[89]

In the case of the ages of men, however, it is possible that a real misfire has taken place, that neither the Ethiopians, Ichthyophagoi, nor Herodotus notice. The Ethiopians eat only meat and drink only milk, and live to 120, while Persians live to 80 and eat bread.[90] As How and Wells point out, it is possible that this represents a different reckoning of how to count years, or at any rate, how to determine "a long time",[91] a circumstance common enough in our own day.[92] There is no need to accept Speke's ratio of five months to the year observed along certain stretches of the Nile, but it is entirely possible that the translation of "year" from one language to another involved different units of time. One does not have to reduce the Ethiopian lifespan from 120 to 50 to recognize this possibility.

The Ichthyophagoi are both the interpreters and the inquirers after information, but their audience is Cambyses, whose outraged reaction leads to the invasion and the inquiry's failure in the discomfiture. This again serves to highlight the narrative role played by interpreters in the *Histories*: the Ichthyophagoi are surrogates for Herodotean inquiry only in so far as they seek information. They are *katoptai* and so inevitably deceitful and distinct from *histōres*, and their information consequently cannot be interpreted effectively. By bookending Cambyses' malign motivation and his obviously erroneous reaction to the information around the story, Herodotus further thematizes the importance of his own brand of *historiē*, one that can comprehend the bad inquiries of other seekers and use the information to explicate more fully the cultural material between different ethnic groups.

Herodotus' translator in Egypt

There are times, however, when the basic limitations of the interpreter preclude effective communication, and no place is this more apparent than in Herodotus' own interactions with his personal translator while travelling through Egypt. In his only reference to his personal *hermēneus*, Herodotus relates how his guide translated an inscription on the great pyramid of Cheops for him (Hdt. 2.125.6–7):

> σεσήμανται δὲ διὰ γραμμάτων αἰγυπτίων ἐν τῇ πυραμίδι ὅσα ἔς τε συρμαίην καὶ κρόμμυα καὶ σκόροδα ἀναισιμώθη τοῖσι ἐργαζομένοισι· καὶ ὡς ἐμὲ εὖ μεμνῆσθαι τὰ ὁ ἑρμηνεύς μοι ἐπιλεγόμενος τὰ γράμματα ἔφη, ἑξακόσια καὶ χίλια τάλαντα ἀργυρίου τετελέσθαι. εἰ δ᾽ ἔστι οὕτως ἔχοντα ταῦτα, κόσα οἰκὸς ἄλλα δεδαπανῆσθαί ἐστι ἔς τε σίδηρον τῷ ἐργάζοντο καὶ σιτία καὶ ἐσθῆτα τοῖσι ἐργαζομένοισι, ὁκότε χρόνον μὲν οἰκοδόμεον τὰ ἔργα τὸν εἰρημένον, ἄλλον δέ, ὡς ἐγὼ δοκέω, ἐν τῷ τοὺς λίθους ἔταμνον καὶ ἦγον καὶ τὸ ὑπὸ γῆν ὄρυγμα ἐργάζοντο, οὐκ ὀλίγον χρόνον;
>
> It is written on the pyramid in Egyptian lettering how much was spent on radishes, onions, and garlic for those who constructed it; and, as I remember well, the interpreter, when he explained these things to me, said that sixteen hundred talents of silver had been spent. If so much was spent on these things, how much is it likely was spent on the iron with which they worked, and on the food and clothing for the workers, when the stated amount of time went into the building was no small amount, especially, as it seems to me, that time during which they cut and dragged the stone and dug out the ditches in the earth?

There were writings on the surfaces of the pyramids, but these were more along the line of travellers' graffiti and would not have included official records of construction logistics.[93] Moreover, as Lloyd notes, neither Greece nor Egypt were money economies in the era of the pyramids' construction, and the items listed – radishes, onions, and garlic – would represent a bizarrely limited account of the materials needed for construction, such as grain, beer, fish, and linen, not to mention building materials (even accepting that Old Kingdom accounts would have been conceptualized along the lines of classical Greek inscribed building accounts).[94] The translator certainly gave Herodotus information, but seems to have misled him, perhaps hoping to disguise his own hieroglyphic illiteracy.[95]

Before treating the actual text of the inscription itself, it is important to look carefully at the process of mistranslation that Herodotus' *hermēneus* demonstrates.

Most importantly, he translates for Herodotus without a present interlocutor. If Herodotus were speaking to, say, a priest, the *hermēneus* would almost certainly have gone unmentioned, as he does over the course of the rest of the work, and the words would have been straightforwardly attributed to Herodotus' speaking interlocutor, regardless of the language constructs required to share information. In this opportunity to appear in the story, however, the interpreter performs the Herodotean task of cultural translation, putting the incomprehensible scratching on the pyramid or stele into a language that Herodotus can understand: that of monetary summary. 1,600 talents of silver were an amount selected to impress a listener who knew the contemporary value of a talent and, in this sense, was successful – the Athenian treasury held 6,000 at the start of the Peloponnesian War.[96] In a way similar to Herodotus' own pattern of cultural translation, the translator took his limited information and put it into a medium that was understandable for his listener.[97] Accordingly, the translator appears explicitly only when he surpasses the role of a mere translator.

It is immaterial to an extent what this, quite possibly incidental, inscription under discussion really said, but it seems likely that it was a royal decree, the onion being the hieroglyphic symbol for *nesut*, meaning "king", and the papyrus and lotus, possibly mistaken for radishes and garlic, were part of the king's title as "lord of upper and lower Egypt".[98] Translator's errors like these are fatal to Herodotus' plan of explaining other cultures, and his mention of his interpreter in this instance may in fact offer a way for Herodotus to distance himself from the information. Herodotus' own memory is sound, ὡς ἐμὲ εὖ μεμνῆσθαι,[99] and so preserves the integrity of his project of *historiē* while attributing any error to his source.

Whether or not there is a mistranslation in this instance, the possibility of a flawed translation or interpretation looms large over Herodotus' study, and this may contribute to the portrayal of *hermēnees* throughout the *Histories*. Herodotus' interaction with his interpreter is the only appearance of the figure outside of an embedded story, and so the only instance of a real translator at work.

Conclusion

In a later work of ethnographic interest, Strabo provides a famous anecdote of Alexander's journey through India and his lieutenant Onesikritos' encounter with the most famous Indian sophists. Although Onesikritos is eager to discourse with these philosophers, the wisest of them, Mandanis, refuses, remarking that (Str. 15.1.64 C715–6):

αὐτῷ δὲ συγγνώμη εἴη, εἰ δι' ἑρμηνέων τριῶν διαλεγόμενος πλὴν φωνῆς μηδὲν συνιέντων πλέον ἢ οἱ πολλοί, μηδὲν ἰσχύσει τῆς ὠφελείας ἐπίδειξιν ποιήσασθαι· ὅμοιον γὰρ ὡς ἂν εἰ διὰ βορβόρου καθαρὸν ἀξιοῖ τις ὕδωρ ῥεῖν.

There should be some understanding if, discoursing by means of three interpreters who, aside from the language, understand no more than anyone else, a man will not be able to demonstrate the value of his argument. For it would be similar if someone thought it reasonable that water could flow pure through mud.

Mandanis' objections to this conversation are not necessarily an objection to translation generally, but to the use of multiple interpreters who do not understand the philosophy under discussion. The language can be transmitted, but the meaning and complexity cannot without the aid of learned intervention. A similar dynamic characterizes the use of interpreters in Herodotus' *Histories*, and, significantly, it is Herodotus himself who provides that intervention. The languages of the barbarians can be understood as language easily enough, but their context and content only achieve their moral effect through Herodotus' careful action as a *hermēneus* on the readers' behalf. The remaining interpreters, whether Persian, Egyptian, Scythian, Lydian, or Greek, are no more than characters in the narrative and so subject to the scrutiny of Herodotean inquiry. This is their function: to mark points in the narrative of cultural translation that require the intervention of the work's arch-translator, Herodotus himself.

Notes

1 Plut. *Them*. 6.3; Aristid. *Or*. 46.184. This account does not appear in the Herodotean depictions of the various Persian embassies to Athens, for which see Hdt. 6.48; 7.133. There seems to be some confusion or condensation of traditions surrounding this execution in the later sources. Paus. 3.12.7, for instance, ascribes the act to Miltiades, and Aristides does not mention Themistocles in his other treatment of the episode, for which see Aristid. *Or*. 13. 122. Frost (1980: 95–6) provides a clear treatment of the complexities of the tradition and concludes that, in spite of Herodotus' remarks on the lack of any Persian embassy, Plutarch may have moved the episode to the debate before Salamis in 481. The ultimate source may lie in patriotic oratory or Atthidography or even some combination thereof.
2 Text from Plutarch is drawn from Ziegler 1969 and all translations are my own.
3 The execution of the *hermēneus* is followed in Plutarch's account by Themistocles' outlawing of Arthmios of Zelea (Plut. *Them*. 6.4) and his conclusion of domestic wars to focus attention against Persia (Plut. *Them*. 6.5).
4 Plutarch's use of the substantive adjective δίγλωσσον may itself represent this lack of trust. The simplest meaning of the word is 'bilingual', and it is used accordingly by Thucydides (Thuc. 4.109.4; 8.85.2), but Hesychius attests to associations of duplicity in his gloss, διχόμυθον, 'double-speaking' (Hesych. s.v. δίγλωσσον, Δ 1483 Latte). This fear of duplicity or treachery is notably absent from Herodotus' treatment of *hermēnees* within the *Histories*, and even the Ichthyophagoi (Hdt. 3.17–23), although described as "spies" on seven occasions (see n. 82), are portrayed as effectively faithful transmitters of linguistic and ethnographic information, despite Cambyses' malign intentions in sending them.
5 See Plut. *Them*. 29.3; Thuc. 1.138.1–2 for Themistocles' rejection of interpreters during his audiences with Artaxerxes. No value judgments on such learning are offered by Plutarch or Thucydides, but Cornelius Nepos' account grandiosely makes Themistocles a more-fluent Persian speaker than those speaking it as a native tongue (Nep. *Them*. 10.1). See Frost (1980: 218–19) for discussion of Themistocles' linguistic abilities, and Harrison (1998: 6) for discussion of the differing Roman and Greek approach to bilingualism that Nepos' admiration represents.

6 Suspicion of interpreters is richly attested in the ancient sources. Aristophanes, for instance, writing at roughly the same time as Herodotus, dramatizes in his *Acharnians* the distrust felt even for the Athenian interpreters of the "eye of the king", Pseudartabas (Ar. *Ach.* 98–122). In a later era, Cassius Dio relates that Caracalla would have his interpreters executed after their translation of politically sensitive material (DC 79.6). More modern examples are also forthcoming, ranging from the famously ambiguous figures Squanto and La Malinche from the colonial period in North America and Mesoamerica to current anxieties over the status of interpreters taking part in the War on Terror, for which see, e.g., Foust 2009.

7 For bilingualism and its accompanying dangers, see Hdt. 4.76–80 for discussion of Anakharsis and Skyles, and Hdt. 6.138.2–4 for treatment of the Athenian children on Lemnos. Kyaxares' inadvertent cannibalism can be added to this list, although the Greek language is not involved (Hdt. 1.73). See Harrison (1998: 6–7) for discussion of the function of these passages within the *Histories*.

8 Munson 2005: 78. See Munson (2005: 70–83) for discussion of the status of the *hermēneus* in the *Histories*.

9 The term ἑρμήνευς appears in the *Histories* twice in the interview between Cyrus and Croesus (186.4 and 1.86.6); once in the description of the Egyptian pyramids (2.125.6); once in the description of Psammetikhos' caste of interpreters (2.154.2); once in the description of the classes of Egyptian society (2.164.1); once in Darius' famous interview with the Greeks and the Kallatiai (3.38.4); once in the interview between Darius and Syloson (3.140.3); and once in the description of communication chains in the north of Scythia (4.24.1). This catalogue does not include the innumerable instances in which the presence or absence of interpreters is simply elided.

10 Gehman (1914: 64) notes concerning this dynamic that, "affairs of everyday knowledge are those least often mentioned in books". One may consider an analogous situation involving slaves as omnipresent agents of action, yet only infrequently mentioned in historical accounts. Herodotus, for instance, mentions δοῦλοι on only 40 occasions in the *Histories*, and θέραποντες and θεράπαιναι 16 times combined. Herodotus provides an illuminating example of the possibly troubling prominence of slaves and hierarchical inferiors in imperial activity in his account of the exposure and rescue of Cyrus in Book I (Hdt. 1.108–13). For example, Astyages orders Harpagos directly, λάβε τὸν Μανδάνη ἔτεκε παῖδα, φέρων δὲ ἐς σεωυτοῦ ἀπόκτεινον· μετὰ δὲ θάψον τρόπῳ ὅτεῳ αὐτὸς βούλεαι, "take the child which Mandane bore, and, once you have taken it to your home, kill it. Then bury it in whatever way you wish" (1.108.3). Rather than committing the act himself, however, Harpagos then entrusts the child to the herdsman Mitradates and even ensures the completion of the action by means of further subordinates, πέμψας δὲ ὁ Ἄρπαγος τῶν ἑωυτοῦ δορυφόρων τοὺς πιστοτάτους εἶδέ τε διὰ τούτων καὶ ἔθαψε τοῦ βουκόλου τὸ παιδίον, "Harpagos then sent the most trustworthy of his bodyguards and, through them, both saw and buried the cowherd's child" (1.113.3). It is at least partly Herodotus' intent in this episode to emphasize Harpagos' error, but he, nonetheless, provides an illuminating account of the involvement of slaves or inferiors, as far as the official, imperial account would be concerned, in the conduct of any action.

11 Xenophon gives numerous and varied reports of his interactions with interpreters during his travels through the Persian Empire. For Persian–Greek interpreters, see Xen. *An.* 2.3.18; 2.5.35; 4.5.10; 4.5.34. For Cyrus' royal interpreter, Pigres, see Xen. *An.* 1.2.17; 1.8.12. For non-Persian languages of the Persian empire, see Xen. *An.* 4.2.18 (Kardouchian); 4.4.5 (Armenian); 5.4.5 (Mossynoikian). For Thracian, see Xen. *An.* 7.2.19; 7.6.9; 7.6.43. In one instance, Xen. *An.* 4.8.4, Xenophon uses a slave originating from the local area but raised in Athens to communicate with the Makronians. See (Gehman 1914: 33–46) for a discussion of these passages.

12 Harrison 1998: 14.

13 Mandell 1990 maintains that, because of the lack of textual appearance of interpreters during Herodotus' ethnographic *logoi*, it is reasonable to assume that he spoke at least Aramaic. Both Miller (1997: 105) and Munson (2005: 29 n. 51) reject this claim as unconvincing *argumentum ex silentio*.

14 For the discussion of Persian names, see Hdt. 1.139 and Chamberlain (1999: 289), who points out that only Persian names with stems ending in – *i* or – *u* would terminate in a sigma, while names like *Khshayârshâ*, 'Xerxes', that have stems terminating in – *a* or other letters do not. It is further clear, as Chamberlain (1999: 268) points out, that Herodotus is not familiar with the nature of Artaxerxes' Persian name at Hdt. 6.98. The prefix *Arta-* can mean 'great', but the names derive from different words meaning 'king', *Khshayârshâ* in Xerxes' case and *Kshatra* in the case of Artaxerxes. See Miller (1997: 105–6) for discussion of Herodotus' errors in Old Persian.

15 Hdt. 4.87. See West (1985: 281–2) for discussion of this *stēlē*.

16 Lewis (1997: 346–7) notes that Herodotus' error of including *Aspathines* rather than *Ardumaniš* among his catalogue of the Seven conspirators at Hdt. 3.70 and his lack of awareness of the political context of Darius' ascent shows that he did not personally read the text of the Bisitun inscription, but rather relied on a reasonably reliable informant, as compared with Ktesias, who gets only one name of the Seven entirely correct, despite his access to official Persian records. Lewis (1977: 12–14) notes the presence of official clerks in the Persian Empire who wrote in Greek and were referred to as *Yaūna*, i.e. 'the Ionian', in surviving fragments of clay tablets, and he suggests that such figures could have served as intermediaries for Herodotus' inquiries into Persian documents, such as his catalogue of the Persian army at Hdt. 7.61–98.

17 Lloyd *ap.* Briant 1990: 109.

18 Munson 2005: 29.

19 For the original anthropological discussion of "thick description", derived from Gilbert Ryle, see Geertz (1973: 3–30, and esp. 5–10). Although anachronistic as applied to the *Histories* as a whole, the concept provides a useful framework for Herodotus' treatment of the language and the explanation of culture within the work.

20 Hollman (2011: 3.2.1) notes in regard to the interview between Cyrus and Croesus that *hermēnees* appear, "only in situations where the narrative is concerned to draw attention to the distance in language and culture that separates two or more parties".

21 Hdt. 2.125.2. The presence of interpreters is largely elided over the course of the *Histories*' ethnographic excurses.

22 Text from Herodotus is drawn from Hude 1955.

23 See Figueira (1993: 320) for discussion of these mercenaries.

24 Hdt. 2.2.2–5. See Gera (2003: 66–111) for detailed discussion of Psammetikhos' experiment and its subsequent reception.

25 Note that μανθάνω and related markers of inquiry and learning appear repeatedly in connection with interpreters: Hdt. 3.38.5, παρεόντων τῶν Ἑλλήνων καὶ δι᾽ ἑρμηνέος μανθανόντων τὰ λεγόμενα; Hdt. 3.21.2, ὁ δὲ Αἰθίοψ μαθὼν ὅτι κατόπται ἥκοιεν, λέγει πρὸς αὐτοὺς τοιάδε; Hdt. 1.86.6, ἐνθαῦτα λέγεται ὑπὸ Λυδῶν Κροῖσον μαθόντα τὴν Κύρου μετάγνωσιν; Hdt. 1.87.2, οὕτω δὴ μαθόντα τὸν Κῦρον ὡς εἴη ὁ Κροῖσος καὶ θεοφιλὴς καὶ ἀνὴρ ἀγαθός. The verb πυνθάνομαι also helps to characterize the scenes in which *hermēnees* appear: e.g., Hdt. 1.24.1 καὶ γὰρ Σκυθέων τινὲς ἀπικνέονται ἐς αὐτούς, τῶν οὐ χαλεπόν ἐστι πυθέσθαι.

26 The precise location of the *Stratopeda* is contested and does not allow for archaeological investigations that could confirm the kind of segregation between Greek and Egyptian that this passage can be made to imply. For the possible locations and dating for the *Stratopeda*, see Lloyd 1975a: 137. A similar kind of social arrangement appears to have occurred at Naukratis, where, despite the long coexistence of Greek and Egyptian populations, for example, intermarriage and integration was rare enough that the settlement functioned like any typical Greek *polis*, and one that, at times, such as under the reign of Amasis, as Hdt. 2.179 makes clear, was strictly demarcated from

Egyptian territory. See Roebuck 1950: 242–3; Armayor 1978: 66; Bresson 1980: 296 for a discussion of the Greek character of Naukratis. Möller (2000: 184–91) does not contradict the Greek cultural character of the city, but interrogates Herodotus' use of the word *polis* to describe it at Hdt. 2.178, concluding that the settlement could not be considered a *polis* in the Greek constitutional sense until the fourth century BCE when the city begins to produce its own coinage and the *ethnikon* Ναυκρατίτης gains some currency, for which see Bresson 1980: 316.

27 See Hdt. 4.96 for the mute, economic exchanges between the Carthaginians and Libyans, and Hdt. 4.110 for the more complicated patterns of language-free courtship between the Scythians and Amazons.

28 Words formed from the root ἀτρεκ- appear 54 times within the *Histories*, and Lateiner (1989: 63) notes that such words are typically used, in contrast to this instance, to exhibit "the limits of [Herodotus'] certainty". Crane (1996: 50–65) provides the fullest available analysis of the term, its use by earlier authors such as Homer, and its place in Herodotus' historiographic programme. See Greenwood & Cartledge (2002: 362–3) for a discussion of Herodotean *atrekeia* and the word's consequences for Herodotus' characterization of *historiē*.

29 Herodotus' language in this instance is reminiscent of the famous Abu-Simbel Inscription of 591 BCE inscribed on the leg of a colossus of Rameses II, *SEG* 16: 863.4 = *ML* 7a.4, ἀλογλόσος δ' ἦχε Ποτασιμτο, Αἰγυπτίος δὲ Ἄμασις·, "Potasimto led those of foreign speech, and Amasis led the Egyptians." See also *IG* XII. 3. 328. 20 for the application of ἀλλόγλωσσος to non-Greek individuals, in this case to dead bodies ransomed by the Therans in the third century BCE. See Gera (2003: 77) for discussion of the Egyptian perspective of this passage.

30 See Lloyd (1975a: 116–20) for discussion of Herodotus' local Greek sources of information on Egypt and Egyptian history.

31 Pl. *Tim.* 24a-b; DS 1.73–4; Isoc. *Bus.* 15–18; Str. 17.1.3 C787.

32 Hdt. 2.141.4, See Lloyd 2007: 363–4 for discussion of this omission.

33 How & Wells 1967: 244; Bresson 1980: 306.

34 Figueira 1993: 320; Lloyd 2007: 364. For the overzealous Greek systemization of Egyptian society and the possible influence of Hippodamos of Miletus, a fellow colonist to Thourioi, on Herodotus, see Lloyd 1975b: 182–8.

35 *SIG³* 110.4–5. For discussion of this inscription, see Figueira 1993: 318–22. Bresson (1980: 300–7); and Vlassopoulos (2013a: 98–9) argue for the emendation Αἰγύπτιον, rather than Αἰγινάταν favoured by the original editors and by Figueira.

36 Figueira 1993: 321.

37 Vlassopoulos (2013a: 98) notes the importance of occupational markers in Egyptian society, but adduces Hdt 2.154 as evidence of this. As far as material evidence is concerned, Vlassopoulos relies on *IG* II² 7967, an Attic funerary monument (for which see also Bresson 1991: 39–42) that commemorates a certain Hermaios, Αἰγύπτιος ἐχ Θηβῶν [γ]ναφαλλουφάντης, "an Egyptian wool-merchant from Thebes". If Bresson and Vlassopoulos are correct in their argument that occupations, however humble, could appear in decrees and commemorations, it is not impossible that the Rhodian *proxenos* of *SIG³* 110 was both commemorating his official designation and adopting a local Egyptian practice.

38 Lloyd 1975b: 184.

39 Consider, for instance, the *phylai* and *obai* at Sparta, among the numerous other forms of social structure evident in the Greek world contemporary with Herodotus. See Jones 1987: *passim* and 118–23 for Spartan social organization.

40 The earliest appearances of *machimos* occur in Aeschylean choral odes: Aes. *Supp.* 811; *Ag.* 123. The word is otherwise common and occurs, for instance, nine times in Thucydides, 15 times in Herodotus, four times in Aristophanes, seven times in Plato, and twice in both Isocrates and Xenophon.

41 Hdt. 2.164–8.

42   For the presence of interpreters in the Persian court, see Munson 2005: 28, 73; Rotolo 1972: 401. Kings are central to the majority of episodes in the *Histories* that make explicit mention of the figure of the ἑρμήνευς. The Egyptian king Psammetikhos is responsible for the caste of interpreters at Hdt. 2.154.2 and possibly remains involved in the subsequent discussion of interpreters' role in Egyptian social structure at Hdt. 2.164.1, for discussion of which, see Lloyd 2007: 346. The Persian king Cyrus appears in his interaction with Croesus (Hdt. 186.4 and 1.86.6), and Darius is twice associated with the figure of the ἑρμήνευς, in his famous interview with the Greeks and the Kallatiai (3.38.4), and once in his exchange with Syloson (3.140.3). Although the word is not used in connection with the Ichthyophagoi (Hdt. 3.18–25), the bilingual *katoptai* are the agents of the Persian king Cambyses. The other two appearances of the word, concerning the Egyptian pyramids (Hdt. 2.125.2), and the chain of Scythian interpreters (Hdt. 4.24.1), do not explicitly involve kings. See Munson 1991 and Christ 1994 for the relationship between Herodotean kings and the *Histories*' patterns of *historiē*.

43   Cyrus and Cambyses both employ interpreters, in the Croesus and Ichthyophagoi passages respectively (Hdt. 1.86; 3.17–25, see the following paragraphs), but Darius employs them on two separate occasions (Hdt. 3.38; 3.140), and both times while in residence at Susa. As Vlassopoulos (2013b: 67) notes, Darius enjoys a similar reputation in his appearance in the Septuagint *I Esdras* 3–4, in which his court is again the venue for inquiry, in this case allowing the Jewish bodyguard Zerubbabel to argue for the supremacy of truth. This argument encourages Darius to permit the Jews to return to Jerusalem and rebuild the temple, a story that perhaps echoes the Herodotean Darius' treatment of Syloson and his return to Samos (Hdt. 3.140–4) and highlights the perhaps arbitrary character of Persian administration.

44   Pin. fr. 169a S/M: νόμος ὁ πάντων βασιλεύς/ θνατῶν τε καὶ ἀθανάτων/ ἄγει δικαιῶν τὸ βιαιότατον/ ὑπερτάτα χειρί, "Custom is the king of all, mortal and immortal, and leads them, making even the most violent just with its superior strength." Plato preserves the fragment in Kallikles' speech at *Gorg.* 484a-c, for which see Dodds 1990: 270–2. For Herodotus' employment of the poem, see Gigante 1993: 72–122, esp. 112–13; see Ostwald 1965 for the tradition surrounding the Pindaric fragment.

45   Asheri 2007: 436 notes the "barbaro-centric" nature of the passage's staging.

46   Gould (1989: 24) argues that the Greeks present at Susa would not have been able to communicate without an interpreter, while Munson (2005: 29) discusses the "obstinate monolingualism of the ancient Greeks in general". On the other hand, Harrison (1998: 11) argues for a greater awareness of Persian or Aramaic by Greeks than is attested in the ancient sources, while Mandell (1990) argues that Herodotus himself, like certain Greek travellers in the Persian empire, knew Aramaic at least. This last claim has been dismissed by Miller (1997: 105) as having "not even likelihood to recommend it".

47   Harrison (1998: 13) suggests that the exchange could be mediated by means of a single Greek–Kallatian interpreter, but also notes the rarity of such an individual.

48   Rotolo (1972: 402) suggests that the interpreters in this scene provide an early example of simultaneous translation, a technique formally developed in the 1940s for use initially at the Nuremberg Trials. For the development of the technique, see Gaiba 1998.

49   Gigante (1993: 111) notes that this is the only use of the verb or of the noun *euphēmia* in Herodotus. The translation of the Kallatiai's command for silence into such a loaded religious concept for the Greeks may itself represent the *histōr's* engagement in the passage. For definition and discussion of *euphēmia*, see Montiglio 2000, esp. 16–18.

50   See Christ (1994: 199–200) for the superiority of Herodotean *historiē* to that practised by the kings in his narrative.

51   See Quint. *Inst.* 11.3.8. Luc. *Salt.* 64 and Ath. 1.20c-d also provide information on ancient ideas on the expressiveness of gesture and movement, as in some cases superior to language. Herodotus provides two instances of such communication within the *Histories*: the trade conducted between the Carthaginians and Iberians (Hdt. 4.196); and the "courtship" of the Scythians and Amazons (Hdt. 4.110).

52 Franke 1992: 87.
53 Following Gould 1991; van der Veen (1995) reads this exchange as the key kind of communication in this passage and in Herodotus as a whole.
54 See Hdt. 8.85.3. There appears to have been some contemporary interest in the Persian word and associated concept, as it appears twice in the fragments of Sophocles, frs. 183 and 634, in the *Marriage of Helen* and *Troilus*, respectively. The position ὀροσάγγης appears to be an official one in Herodotus' description, as Phylakos is "recorded" as a benefactor of the king, ἀνεγράφη, possibly in the royal archives or on a *stēlē*, as Macan (1908: 492) has argued. There could in fact be some linguistic slippage in this case as well, as Photius glosses the word as σωματοφύλακες βασιλέως, indicating perhaps some relationship with Phylakos' given name (Phot. s.v. ὀροσάγγαι ο, 349.11 Theodoridis).
55 On benefactors' thrones, see DS 17.14.2; for meals with the king, see Darius' treatment of Demokedes at Hdt. 3.132.1; the episode at Phylakos at Hdt. 8.85.3 and of Xenagoras at Hdt. 9.107.3 indicate the gift of land for official benefaction as well. See Asheri (2007: 518) for discussion of the term and its possibly etymology.
56 Gehman 1914: 35, "no doubt a man in his position was required to know several languages". See Munson (2005: 73, n. 28) for discussion of the roles of the official figures surrounding the Persian king in Herodotus.
57 Rotolo 1972: 401.
58 Fehling (1989: 225–6) offers numerous parallels for the "fabulous and novelistic" use of the number seven in Herodotus, such as the seven oracles that Croesus consults (Hdt. 1.46.2), and the seven Persian ships at Marathon (Hdt. 6.115). Geus (2014: 149–50) follows such analysis to demonstrate the subjective and "typical" character of the units that Herodotus employs, especially concerning distance, of which the seven interpreters are an indirect type of indication. Corcella (2007: 599) argues against Fehling and points out that it is possible to accord these seven linguistic changes with the different peoples that Herodotus mentions from 4.21 onwards, provided that the Budini and Geloni speak different languages. See Mosley (1971: 2); Harrison (1998: 13); Gera (2003: 195) for discussion of the practical functioning of such a chain of interpreters, and Braund (2007: 61–77) for discussion of the realities of river-based trade networks in the Scythian hinterland that this passage describes. Fehling's folkloric understanding of the seven interpreters in this passage picks up on the vast distances, both geographic and linguistic, that Herodotus invokes in this description of the furthest-flung reaches of the Scythian plain. See also Gagné, pp. 241–2 in this volume.
59 Elsewhere in Herodotus, the number seven is repeated in close contact several times: Hdt. 3.129.3, Ἐπ' ἑπτὰ μὲν δὴ ἡμέρας καὶ ἑπτὰ νύκτας ὑπὸ τοῦ παρεόντος κακοῦ ὁ Δαρεῖος ἀγρυπνίῃσι εἴχετο; Hdt. 7.56.1, Διέβη δὲ ὁ στρατὸς αὐτοῦ ἐν ἑπτὰ ἡμέρῃσι καὶ [ἐν] ἑπτὰ εὐφρόνῃσι. Compare with Eur. *Supp.* 963, ἑπτὰ ματέρες ἑπτὰ κούρους ἐγεινάμεθ'; Soph. *Ant.* 141, ἑπτὰ λοχαγοὶ γὰρ ἐφ' ἑπτὰ πύλαις.
60 Hdt. 4.23.
61 See respectively, Hdt. 1.86–7; 3.17–25; and 2.125.2.
62 See Sebeok & Brady 1979: 19 for a discussion of the programmatic nature of the episode.
63 Sebeok & Brady (1979: 16) argues that Croesus represents, "an embodied symbol for all human beings, bombarded with information which all of us must decode and interpret if we are to survive".
64 Hdt. 1.85.1–2.
65 Hdt. 1.85.4.
66 Munson 2005: 28.
67 See Chamberlain 1999 for discussion of Herodotus' patterns of onomastic translation. Munson (2005: 35) notes Herodotus' "special sense of the occasional, mysterious transparency of foreign languages", particularly in regard to names such as Battos (Hdt. 4.155.2–4).

68 On the emblematic nature of names, Hartog (1988: 242) notes in his discussion of Democr. fr. 142 DK, that the names of the gods should be *agalmata phōnēenta*, and so possibly emblematic of themselves, although the fragment is rather difficult to interpret. A similar debate about the emblematic nature of names occurs in Pl. *Cratyl.* 422d-432e, with possible Democritean influence, for which see Baxter 1992: 156–60.

69 Segal 1998: 286.

70 See Demont 2009 for discussion of this effect, esp. p. 197.

71 Note Hdt. 2.2–3.

72 Hollman 2011: 3.2.1.

73 Sebeok & Brady (1979: 18) argue that Croesus becomes a Sibylline character after his realization.

74 Munson (2005: 71–2) observes that the communication-breakdown in this instance centres on personal definitions of the word *olbios*.

75 For a discussion of this dynamic, see Sebeok & Brady 1979: 20; Munson 2005: 75; Demont 2009: 197.

76 Segal (1998: 285–8) focusses on Cyrus' learning-process over the course of the episode.

77 Hollman 2011: 3.2.1.

78 Franke 1992: 87. For Croesus' later career as an adviser to the Persian kings, see Hdt. 1.155–6; 3.34–6;

79 This question raises a number of additional questions. Herodotus claims to use a Lydian source for his telling of the encounter between Croesus and Cyrus (Hdt. 1.87.1): ἐνθαῦτα λέγεται ὑπὸ Λυδῶν, "thereupon it is said by the Lydians". This could imply that Herodotus' account is itself a translation, or a telling of a translation, from a Lydian original, although Croesus speaks Greek during his interview with Solon (Hdt. 1.29–33) and in his intermediated interactions with the Delphic Oracle (Hdt. 1.47.3; 1.55.2; 1.85.2). Cyrus could have been speaking any of the three languages present in the Bisitun Inscription – Old Persian, Neo-Babylonian, Elamite – or Imperial Aramaic, which seems perhaps the most likely candidate as the *lingua franca* of the Achaemenid Empire, for which see Miller 1997: 131; Mandell 1990: 105.

80 The name does not appear in Old Persian inscriptions, but Herodotus' Greek transliterations of Persian names represent significant similarity with the Persian originals. Consider, for instance, the following names on the Bisitun Inscription: *Dâryavuš* for Δαρεῖος, *Pârsa* for Πέρσαι, and *Kûruš* for Κῦρος. On the other hand, Ξέρξης is rendered in Old Persian as *Khshayârshâ*, and pronounced in Biblical Hebrew as *Ăhašwērôš*, from which derives the name Ahasuerus of the King James Bible *Book of Esther*. Contemporary Farsi writes the name سولون, and pronounces it "Sōlōn".

81 Longo (1987: 13) makes this point and provides a thorough account of the appearances of the Ichthyophagoi in other sources such as Nearchos and Agatharkhides of Knidos.

82 Note κατόπτας (Hdt. 3.17.2); κατοψομένους (3.17.2); κατασκόπους (3.19.1); κατόπται (twice), 3.21.2; κατάσκοποι, 3.23.3; κατάσκοποι, 3.25.1.

83 See Christ (1994: 180–2) for a discussion of the consequences of such spying on Herodotean *historiē*.

84 How & Wells 1967: 261. There is also the suggestion of a Greek frame of reference for such an understanding of the myth, considering the feasts of the Ethiopians in Homer, e.g., Hom. *Od.* 1.20–6.

85 Such a situation of "insincerity" would fulfill what J.L. Austin termed an "abuse" of the illocutionary act, corresponding to Γ1 of his "felicity conditions", for which see Austin 1962: 12–38, esp. 15–20.

86 Hartog (1988: 43–4) discusses the recurrence of the bow motif in Ktesias' account of communication between Darius and the Scythians, with the bow acting as universal symbol of the strength and interchangeability of those living at the "margins of the world". The figure of the unbendable bow is familiar from Hom. *Od.* 21, but there are further resonances with the Sanskrit epic *Mahabharata*, which features Karna's unbendable bow Vijaya, for which see, e.g., *Mahabharata* 8.72.

87 How & Wells 1967: 262.
88 Hdt. 3.22.1.
89 Hdt. 3.23.4.
90 Hdt. 3.22.4–23.1.
91 How & Wells (1967: 262) relates the findings of the nineteenth century explorer John Hanning Speke, who observed that certain tribes along the Upper Nile counted only five months to the year. Speke was not an anthropologist, but his report does not fundamentally conflict with the observations of E.E. Evans-Pritchard on the conception of time among the Nuer, who inhabit the Upper Nile valley in what is now South Sudan. Evans-Pritchard (1939: 190) notes that a 'year' (*ruon*) in Nuer usage, is the period split between the wet season (*tot*) and the dry season (*mei*), each of which can also be independently considered a 'year' (*ruon*), although this is uncommon. Importantly, as Evans-Pritchard (1939: 198) notes, "The words *tot* and *mei* stand for the cluster of social activities, especially economic activities, of the wet and dry seasons. They are not pure units of time-reckoning, but are expressions which signify social activity." Accordingly, numerical mechanisms for calculating duration of time or even personal age were lacking during the period of Evans-Pritchard's study of the Nuer, for which see Evans-Pritchard 1939: 209–16. For a more contemporary discussion of Evans-Pritchard's methods and findings concerning time-reckoning among the Nuer, see Gell 1992: 15–22.
92 In South Korea, for instance, a child born on July 1 is immediately considered to be one year old, and becomes two years old on New Year's Day, when it would turn six months old in the United States. In modern Ethiopia, the new year starts in September and is always between seven and eight years behind the Gregorian calendar.
93 See Lloyd (2007: 332) for a discussion of the original graffiti with bibliography.
94 See Lloyd 1975a: 70–1, 2007: 332 for the nature of the anachronisms present in this passage.
95 West (1985: 295) writes that such illiteracy would be common, as "knowledge of cuneiform and hieroglyphic scripts was practically restricted to small professional groups, and a Greek curious to know the meaning of a Persian or Egyptian inscription was more than likely to fall victim to guesswork by natives anxious not to seem disobliging".
96 Gould 1989: 24–5.
97 It is important that Herodotus does not refer to his guide as an *exēgētēs*, a *cicerone*-type figure familiar from Pausanias who was responsible for explicating points of interest to sightseers. For discussion of the role of these *exēgētai*, see Jones 2001.
98 How & Wells 1967: 229.
99 Hdt. 2.125.6.

Bibliography

Armayor, O.K. 1978. "Did Herodotus Ever Go to Egypt?" *Journal of the American Research Center in Egypt* 15: 59–73.

Asheri, D. 2007. "Book III." In Murray, O., & Moreno, A., eds., *A Commentary on Herodotus: Books I-IV*. Oxford (Oxford University Press), 379–527.

Austin, J.L. 1962. *How to Do Things with Words*. Cambridge, MA (Harvard University Press).

Baxter, T.M.S. 1992. *The Cratylus: Plato's Critique of Naming*. Leiden (Brill).

Braund, D. 2007. "Greater Olbia: Ethnic, Religious, Economic, and Political Interactions in the Region of Olbia c. 600–100 BC." In Braund, D., & Kryzhitskiy, S.D., eds., *Classical Olbia and the Scythian World*. Oxford (Oxford University Press), 37–77.

Bresson, A. 1980. "Rhodes, L'Hellénion et Le Statut de Naucratis (VIe-IVe Siècle a.C.)." *Dialogues d'histoire ancienne* 6: 291–349.

————. 1991. "Le Fils de Pythéas, Égyptien de Naukratis." In Fick, N., & Carrière, J.-C., eds., *Mélanges Étienne Bernard*. Besançon (Université de Franche-Comté), 37–42.

Briant, P. 1990. "Hérodote et la Société Perse." In Nenci, G., & Reverdin, O., eds., *Fondation Hardt Entretiens XXXV: Hérodote et les Peuples Non Grecs*. Geneva (Fondation Hardt), 69–113.

Chamberlain, D. 1999. "On Atomics, Onomastics, and Metarhythmic Translations in Herodotus." *Arethusa* 32: 263–312.

Christ, M.R. 1994. "Herodotean Kings and Historical Inquiry." *Classical Antiquity* 13: 167–202.

Corcella, A., Murray, O. & Moreno, A., eds. 2007. "Book IV." In Murray, O., & Moreno, A., eds., *A Commentary on Herodotus: Books I-IV*. Oxford (Oxford University Press), 543–721.

Crane, G. 1996. *The Blinded Eye: Thucydides and the New Written Word*. Lanham, MD (Rowman & Littlefield Publishers).

Demont, P. 2009. "Figures of Inquiry in Herodotus' Inquiries." *Mnemosyne* 62: 179–205.

Dodds, E.R. 1990. *Plato: Gorgias*. Oxford (Oxford University Press).

Evans-Pritchard, E.E. 1939. "Nuer Time-Reckoning." *Africa: Journal of the International African Institute* 12: 189–216.

Fehling, D. 1989. *Herodotus and His Sources*. Translated by J.G. Howie. Leeds (Cairns).

Figueira, T.J. 1993. "Four Notes on the Aiginetans in Exile." In Figueira, T.J., ed., *Excursions in Epichoric History: Aiginetan Essays*. Lanham, MD (Rowman & Littlefield Publishers), 294–324.

Foust, J. 2009. "Maladies of Interpreters." *The New York Times*, September 21.

Franke, P.R. 1992. "Dolmetschen in Hellenistische Zeit." In Müller, C.W., Zier, K., & Werner, K., eds., *Zum Umgang Fremden Sprachen in Der Griechischen-Römischen Antike*. Stuttgart (Franz Steiner), 85–96.

Frost, F.J. 1980. *Plutarch's Themistocles: A Historical Commentary*. Princeton, NJ (Princeton University Press).

Gaiba, F. 1998. *The Origins of Simultaneous Interpretation: The Nuremberg Trial*. Ottawa (University of Ottawa Press).

Geertz, C. 1973. *The Interpretation of Cultures*. New York, NY (Basic Books).

Gehman, H.S. 1914. "The Interpreters of Foreign Languages Among the Ancients." Dissertation, University of Pennsylvania, PA.

Gell, A. 1992. *The Anthropology of Time: Cultural Constructions of Temporal Maps and Images*. Oxford (Berg).

Gera, D.L. 2003. *Ancient Greek Ideas About Language, Speech, and Civilization*. Oxford (Oxford University Press).

Geus, K. 2014. "A 'Day's Journey' in Herodotus' 'Histories'." In Geus, K., & Thiering, M., eds., *Features of Common Sense Geography: Implicit Knowledge and Structures in Ancient Geographical Texts*. Münster (LIT Verlag), 147–56.

Gigante, M. 1993. *Nomos Basileus*. Naples (Bibliopolis).

Gould, J. 1989. *Herodotus*. New York, NY (St. Martin's Press).

————. 1991. *Give and Take in Herodotus*. A Lecture Delivered at New College, Oxford on May 23, 1989. J.L. Myre's Memorial Lectures 15. Oxford (Leopard's Head Press).

Greenwood, E. & Cartledge, P. 2002. "Herodotus as a Critic: Truth, Fiction, Polarity." In Bakker, E., De Jong, I.J.F., & van Wees, H., eds., *Brill's Companion to Herodotus*. Leiden (Brill), 351–72.

Harrison, T. 1998. "Herodotus' Conception of Foreign Languages." *Histos* 2: 1–45.

Hartog, F. 1988. *The Mirror of Herodotus: The Representation of the Other in the Writing of History*. Translated by Janet Lloyd. Berkeley, CA (University of California Press).

Hollman, A. 2011. *The Master of Signs: Signs and the Interpretation of Signs in Herodotus' Histories*. Hellenic Studies 48. Washington, DC (Center for Hellenic Studies).

How, W.W. & Wells, J. 1967. *A Commentary on Herodotus*. Oxford (Oxford University Press).

Hude, C. 1955. *Herodoti Historiae*. Oxford (Oxford University Press).

Jones, C.P. 2001. "Pausanias and His Guides." In Cherry, J.F., Alcock, S., & Elsner, J., eds., *Pausanias: Travel and Memory in Roman Greece*. Oxford (Oxford University Press), 33–9.

Jones, N.F. 1987. *Public Organization in Ancient Greece: A Documentary Study*. Philadelphia, PA (American Philosophical Society).

Lateiner, D. 1989. *The Historical Method of Herodotus*. Toronto (University of Toronto Press).

Lewis, D.M. 1977. *Sparta and Persia*. Leiden (Brill).

———. 1997. "Persians in Herodotus." In Lewis, D.M., ed., *Selected Papers in Greek and Near-Eastern History*. Cambridge (Cambridge University Press), 345–61.

Lloyd, A.B. 1975a. *Herodotus Book II: Commentary 99–182*. Leiden (Brill).

———. 1975b. *Herodotus Book II: Introduction*. Leiden (Brill).

———. 2007. "Book II." In Murray, O., & Moreno, A., eds., *A Commentary on Herodotus: Books I-IV*. Oxford (Oxford University Press), 219–378.

Longo, O. 1987. "I Mangiatori Di Pesci: Regime alimentare e quadro culturale." *Materiali e discussioni per l'analisi dei testi classici* 18: 9–55.

Macan, R.W. 1908. *Herodotus: The Seventh, Eight, and Ninth Books*. London (Macmillan).

Mandell, S. 1990. "The Language, Eastern Sources, and Literary Posture of Herodotus." *The Ancient World* 21: 103–8.

Meiggs, R. & Lewis, D.M. 1989. *A Selection of Greek Historical Inscriptions*. Oxford (Oxford University Press).

Miller, M.C. 1997. *Athens and Persia in the Fifth Century B.C.: A Study in Cultural Receptivity*. Cambridge (Cambridge University Press).

Möller, A. 2000. *Naukratis: Trade in Archaic Greece*. Oxford (Oxford University Press).

Montiglio, S. 2000. *Silence in the Land of Logos*. Princeton, NJ (Princeton University Press).

Mosley, D. 1971. "Greeks, Barbarians, Language, and Contact." *Ancient Society* 2: 1–6.

Munson, R.V. 1991. "The Madness of Cambyses." *Arethusa* 24: 43–65.

———. 2005. *Black Doves Speak: Herodotus and the Language of Barbarians*. Hellenic Studies 9. Washington, DC (Center for Hellenic Studies).

Ostwald, M. 1965. "Pindar, Nomos, and Heracles." *Harvard Studies in Classical Philology* 69: 109–38.

Roebuck, C. 1950. "The Grain Trade Between Greece and Egypt." *Classical Philology* 45: 236–47.

Rotolo, V. 1972. "La Communicazione Linguistica Fra Alloglotti nell'Antichità Classica." *Studi Classici in Onore Di Quintino Cataudella* 395–414.

Sebeok, T.A. & Brady, E. 1979. "The Two Sons of Croesus: A Myth About Communication in Herodotus." *Quaderni urbinati di cultura classica* New Series, 1: 7–22.

Segal, C. 1998. "Croesus on the Pyre: Herodotus and Bacchylides." In Segal, C., ed., *Aglaia: The Poetry of Alcman, Sappho, Pindar, Bacchylides, and Corinna*. Lanham, MD (Rowman & Littlefield Publishers), 281–93.

van der Veen, J.E. 1995. "A Minute's Mirth: Syloson and His Cloak in Herodotus." *Mnemosyne*[4] 48: 129–45.

Vlassopoulos, K. 2013a. *Greeks and Barbarians*. Cambridge (Cambridge University Press).

———. 2013b. "The Stories of the Others: Storytelling and Intercultural Communication in the Herodotean Mediterranean." In Almagor, E., & Skinner, J., eds., *Ancient Ethnography: New Approaches*. London (Bloomsbury Publishing), 49–75.

West, S. 1985. "Herodotus' Epigraphical Interests." *Classical Quarterly* 35: 278–305.

Ziegler, K. 1969. *Plutarchi Vitae Parallelae*, Fourth Edition, Vol. 1. Leipzig (Teubner).

2 Language as a marker of ethnicity in Herodotus and contemporaries

Thomas Figueira

Introduction

To understand Greek views on ethnicity in the fifth century, we must turn to Herodotus, who provides us a touchstone expression of identity at a most historically fraught moment, not only of his *Histories*, but also of the entire history of the Greek *polis*.[1] This interchange takes place at the critical meeting at which the Athenians attempt to induce the Spartans in 479 to take energetic action north of the Isthmus of Corinth against Mardonios, commander of the Persian forces left behind by Xerxes. The Attic delegates reaffirm their intention not to Medize, expressing their mindfulness of the sacred places and objects destroyed by the Persians. I reproduce their further specification, one based on their sense of their Hellenic identity (Hdt. 8.144.2).[2]

> αὖθις δὲ τὸ Ἑλληνικόν, ἐὸν ὅμαιμόν τε καὶ ὁμόγλωσσον, καὶ θεῶν ἱδρύματά τε κοινὰ καὶ θυσίαι ἤθεά τε ὁμότροπα, τῶν προδότας γενέσθαι Ἀθηναίους οὐκ ἂν εὖ ἔχοι.
>
> And again there is the *Hellēnikon* 'Greekness', being both *homaimon* 'of the same blood' and *homoglōsson* 'of the same language', and common establishments of the gods and customs *homotropa* 'of the same orientation', of which it would not be fitting that the Athenians become traitors.

Here is a template of affinity applicable whether on the grand scale of the Hellenes and other peoples or applied in ethnic differentiation among the Greeks themselves. We find here as well a phenomenon that characterizes early Greek ethnology. What we would term the genetic, actual biological connection is usually juxtaposed with cultural affinity, which will be important in our examination. From this passage and in general in early Greek sociolinguistics, one can state the principle that the categories of language or dialect and of people, nation, or ethnic group were treated equivalently.[3] Hence, in Herodotus, language or dialect is juxtaposed with biological connection, here expressed by ὁμαίμων 'same-blooded'.[4] Moreover – let me note as corroboration – universal homophony necessarily belongs to the realm of animal fable,[5] probably because that genre has already confounded the most fundamental of all distinctions of heredity, namely the difference between humans and beasts.

Hence, we must confront the shortcomings of some recent scholarship on ethnicity, especially that either written or influenced by Jonathan Hall. The recognition of the close relationship of language and ethnic identity that is yielded by our
testimonia is not to be vitiated by observing – as Hall has done repeatedly[6] – that
ethnic identity was culturally constructed. That is because everything people do
must be socially or culturally constructed in the absence in our species of instinc-
tual hardwiring on a neurological level.[7] Accordingly, processes of cultural construction had to proceed within the parameters of perceived cultural *realia*, such
as linguistic similarity and differentiation or shared and variant folkways, among
which homologies in cultic or other ritual behaviour loomed large. Moreover, the
existence of isoglosses does not militate against my thesis, because a linguistic
boundary that seems blurred to us is, nonetheless, a boundary that may well have
been intuitively experienced as significant by classical Greeks. Nor does the failure of ancient dialectal classifications to align exactly with our own categories
erase the fact that making such categories was as meaningful for the ancients as
it is for us.[8] One might just as well upbraid the Greeks for primitive zoological
taxonomy, although the exercise would never convince us that they could not
distinguish a wolf from a lion.

Although it is possible to muster a good deal of special pleading against con-
ceding that language meaningfully determines ethnic identity,[9] the cost in analytic
force is thus considerable. Therefore, Hall ought not to be followed in downplay-
ing the role of language in Herodotus 8.144.2 by asserting that the historian has
put the criteria of ethnicity in reverse order, so that the concept expressed by
the word ὁμόγλωσσος becomes of least importance. It is certainly no accident
that Herodotus' Mardonios starts his characterization of the cultural unity of the
Greeks (7.9β.2) by using the very same term in what is likely historiographical
projection. Indeed, similarity of language or dialect was the most effective factor
in determining ethnicity and, thus, unsurprisingly, least tractable to gross manipulation or mere willful ascription. And we shall see shortly that such, ultimately
rather theoretical, objections to this conclusion can hardly overcome the examples
that one can collect. The other factors mentioned by the Athenians at Sparta will
only come into my presentation for the light they help shed on the function of
language in establishing ethnicity and, therefore, must be relegated to a secondary
level. Characteristic tribal orders and other *polis* subdivisions can be noted as ethnic markers only with reservations. Unlike dialects, they are seldom adduced as
foolproof indicators of ethnicity. Even in rather more encompassing ethnic classifications, such as the Ionians and eventually even the three-fold Dorians, the
effects of consolidation of disparate groups and other modes of political restruc-
turing are often manifest in *polis* tribal or component structures. Each *polis* was
itself a genetic entity of expressive *sungeneia* whose binding force in the archaic
and classical periods tended to trump other ethnic bounds (see the *Introduction*
and Figueira forthcoming).

Relationships of kinship based on shared myth are both omnipresent and
were readily susceptible to reshaping by parties with an agenda in ethnogenesis. Rather than acting as demonstrators of their standing alongside dialect and

ἤθεα as determinants of *sungeneia*, their ubiquity indicates the intensity of the impulse to deny or, better, to transcend φωνή and social practice. The depth of these fissures occasioned much ingenuity to surmount by the process of 'discovering' *sungeneia*. Let it suffice to note a strikingly early diplomatic effort. The attempt to connect the dominant Thracian *ethnos* called the Odrysians and their dynasty founder Teres with the mythological Thracian Tereus, an ally by marriage of the early Attic king Pandion, had to be forcefully corrected by Thucydides.[10] His effort was, however, to little avail. This contrived connection was reused by a later Odrysian king Seuthes in dealings with Xenophon. Interethnic affinities proposed by non-Greek and Hellenized communities became a mainstay of post-classical Greco-Roman diplomacy, but the stakes were then often much lower and such contrivance had become a politeness of diplomacy.[11]

That descent established ethnic identity is doubtless true, as the Athenian remarks in Herodotus imply.[12] However, unfortunately for historical analysis, it is also tautological: the quality of being 'same blooded' (ὁμαίμων) can confirm 'common birth' (συγγένεια). It did not assist ethnogenesis in the Greek conceptual order; rather, it was itself ethnogenesis as social process or result of process. Were the status of shared blood or birth among Greek groups or between Greeks and their neighbours as self-evident as the differentiation of a group of Hellenes that might adjoin a population of Ethiopians, for example, other markers of affinity would be much less salient. And even then, that would only be valid until the two groups intermingled. Genetic gradations among Greeks, and often with their neighbours as well, however, were too subtle and contentious to be sustained on the basis of obvious or tacit unanimities on *sungeneia* (in terms recognizable to us as hereditary); thus, other markers dominate the historical dynamic in Hellenic foreign affairs. The frailty of positive *sungeneia* is well illustrated by Plato's Socrates in the *Theaetetus*. He mocks a *gennaios* 'person of good lineage' for his painfully limited range of affinity when this elite person boasts of just seven notable antecessors.[13] There are a number of ways in which classical Greeks implied that the lines of actual descent forming the major Greek dialectal subdivisions were not strictly biological (in our terms) but rather symbolic/cultural (even fictive) aggregates. I limit myself here to noting the function of the concept ἀρχηγέτης 'founding hero' in legitimizing *polis* structures, because *arkhēgetai* so clearly transcended actual biological connection with their successors.[14]

Literary generic boundaries help underline my point. It is characteristic of tragic drama that it tends to treat recapitulation of genealogy through distant affiliation based on heroic connection in myth as truly authentic.[15] That is, however, merely a function of its location *in illo tempore*, the other time of heroic action. Such claims do appear in actual foreign affairs; an example is the Theban effort circa 506 to acquire military help from the Aiginetans against the Athenians. This was predicated on the relationship of their eponyms, the nymphs Thebe and Aigina as sisters, both daughters of the river god Asopos.[16] As the context in Herodotus makes clear for the Theban appeal, such an attempt required a considerable leap in reasoning, making for a strained construal of the motivating oracle. For us, it must surely smack of an elite initiative for manipulation of popular opinion. Such claims formed a diction of interconnectedness, but they seem to have lacked the visceral impact of personal identification.

For Herodotus, the highest level of ethnographic category that is expressed in political terms among the Greeks is the alliance of the Hellenes which we conventionally call the Hellenic League, that is, the Greeks swearing to defend against Xerxes' invasion and recognizing Spartan hegemony. Even this unity, however, is necessarily an amalgamation of lower-hierarchy ethnicities, as Herodotus underlines in his roster of the Greek allies at Salamis. This list is a paradigmatic classification marked by ethnicizing description. The first six Peloponnesian states that Herodotus notes are of the Dorian, and so necessarily for him, the 'Macedonian', *ethnos*,[17] with the exception of the Hermioneans, who are Dryopians.[18] Next an elaborate derivation is offered for the Athenians, in which Herodotus both restates his earlier contention that they were originally Pelasgians who were Hellenized and specifies a series of their successive identities.[19] He culminates with the observation that "when Ion, the son of Xouthos, became their leader in war, they were called Ionians after him". Herodotus notes next that Megarians, Ambrakiots, and Leukadians "are Dorian in *ethnos* from Corinth", while the Aiginetans are Dorians from Epidauros.[20] Right afterward come the Khalkidians and Eretrians: they are Ionians.[21] From the Cyclades, the speakers of Ionic Greek are more closely associated with the Athenians: Keians, Ionian in *ethnos* from Athens, and the Naxians, Ionians from Athens.[22] However, the Styrians of Euboia and the Kythnians are Dryopians;[23] the Krotoniates are Achaeans;[24] the Melians are in *genos* 'extraction' from Lakedaimon;[25] and, finally, the Siphnians and Seripheans are (once again) Ionians from Athens.[26] For Herodotus to understand the aggregate of the Greeks required a specification of disparate origins, and this variety is fundamentally linguistic in nature. In the meaningful case of the Athenians, an evolution was presented that worked through a series of varying denominations and identities that Herodotus carefully notes (cf. Hdt. 2.51.2). Yet the end result is grounded in linguistic reality: the Pelasgians of Attica learned to speak Greek of a dialect that the Athenians shared with the other Ionians.

We see also in Herodotus' catalogue of the Greek forces facing Xerxes how overarching emphases existed in the array of *poleis*, deriving from dialect, and came to establish the vectors of late archaic ethnogenesis. The two most significant higher-level distinctions are Dorian and Ionian, and, even in the catalogue at Salamis, their mention tends necessarily to evoke the cities of Sparta and Athens. Much earlier in his work, Herodotus had already foregrounded this theme. In treating Kroisos' plans for seeking allies circa 546, Herodotus had highlighted the preeminence of Sparta and Athens in terms of ethnicity. These were the δυνατωτάτους 'most powerful' and προέχοντας 'prominent' over, respectively, the Dorian and the Ionian *genē* 'lineages'.[27] That both Athens and Sparta could proffer wider political claims on the basis of this dominance and influence over one of the primary ethnolinguistic subdivisions of the Greeks depends in turn on a panhellenic sensibility, i.e., understanding that all Greeks are themselves members of a community established by shared language, gods, cults, and poetry.[28] As we shall see, a bipolar Greek world, riven by power blocs that were led by Athens and Sparta, implies a binary linguistic and ethnic configuration for Greece.

We saw at the outset how in Herodotus τὸ Ἑλληνικόν is elevated by the Athenians at Sparta to a determining role in formulating policy. While Herodotus recognizes the Athenians as preeminent among the Ionians, he also insists that they and the other Ionians were not Greek in origin, but Pelasgians (Hdt. 1.56–8). This is indeed the same position that he was to take in his later enumeration of the Greek allies of the Hellenic League at Salamis. Stress falls in Herodotus on the mutability of the Athenians, and especially on how their Ionian identity was the result of an evolution through varying cultural stages. Concomitantly, he has offered a correction to what one might now be tempted to call 'essentialism' in his general treatment of the Ionian *ethnos*.[29] He undermines the Attic origin of the Ionians along two axes: he notes in detail the non-Ionian elements – Euboian Abantes, Orkhomenian Minyans, Kadmeioi, Dryopes, Phokians, Molossians, Arkadian Pelasgians, and Dorian Epidaurians – who participated in the settling of Ionia, and he recognizes that even the settlers from Athens would have taken Karian wives.[30] Following the example of Herodotus, later Greek historians accepted that accounting for such heterogeneity in Greek colonies should play a part in their brief as historians.[31] In framing what would now be called a cultural-historical definition, Herodotus is willing to term Ionian all 'from Athens', which is not meant in some genetic sense, and all who celebrate the festival of the Apatouria.[32] Subsequent commentary paralleled the Herodotean treatment: Thucydides observes a marker of affinity in the festival of Dionysos in Limnai celebrated during Anthesterion by the Athenians and οἱ ἀπ' Ἀθηναίων Ἴωνες 'the Ionians [derived] from Athenians' (Thuc. 2.15.4).

Herodotus' willingness to see ethnic identity as an acculturation is concordant with his emphasis on the initial identity of the Athenians as Pelasgians, despite any note of disparagement that might be detected in that non-Greek origin. His Pelasgian theory is balanced by his appreciation of the Athenian capacity for plasticity in identity.[33] Herodotus seems to have grappled – perhaps achieving only partial success in our eyes – with three fundamentally hard to reconcile 'facts': Athenian autochthony; the Pelasgian character of pre-Hellenic Greece; and Attica as the origin point of eastward colonization. Thus, accounting for ethnogenesis was central to the Herodotean understanding of historical cultural change.

Language and ethnic identity

Now let us leave Herodotus momentarily and turn to some other cases where ethnic identity is clearly predicated upon linguistic circumstances. Here the boundaries between dialects were significant cultural demarcations, as many passages reveal. Especially striking are cases that seem to record spontaneous reactions, reflect conventional behaviour, or present gnomic pronouncements.

1   For example, it was a *topos* that dialectal differences in public assemblies served to establish ethnic identity.

   (a) Xenophon reports that a disputant among the Ten-Thousand was credited as Greek for his use of the Boiotian *phōnē* 'dialect', until his ears, pierced like a Lydian, were noted (Xen. *An.* 3.1.26–32 [**spontaneous**]).

(b) Socrates in Plato's *Apology*, because of his inexperience in court, asks for indulgence of the very same sort the jurors might show a ξένος 'alien' with different φωνή 'speech' and τρόπος 'manner' in which that person was raised (Plato *Apol.* 17D-18A [**conventional**]). This ξένος could be either a Greek speaking a different dialect or even a Hellenized person.

(c) In his speech *For the People of Megalopolis*, Demosthenes upbraids some previous fellow Athenians speaking in the assembly for their promotion of Spartan and Arkadian interests (Dem. 16.1–2 [**spontaneous**]). It is only his knowledge of their identity and their speaking the Attic dialect (τὸ τῇ φωνῇ λέγειν Ἀττικῶς) that disallows identifying them as Arkadians and Lakonians and permits recognition of them as Athenians.

2   Judgment on dialect's role in detection of ethnic boundaries is well informed by Old Comedy,[34] where, unlike prose genres and tragedy, variation of speech characterizes members of other cultures and ethnicities, and linguistic divergence is put to good comic effect. Undoubtedly, barbarous substandard Greek could be raw material for amusement, as illustrated by the *loci classici* of the Scythian archer/policeman in the *Thesmophoriazusae* (1001–7, 1082–97)[35] and the Triballian god in the *Birds* (1565–1693: [both **conventional**]).[36] One vector of abuse of the demagogues is their tainted foreign background, which can have an ethnolinguistic basis [**conventional**].[37] Aristophanes has notable sections of accurately rendered Laconian Doric, Megarian Doric, and Boiotian.[38] Whether dialect variation is meant as comic *per se* is disputed, and our judgment is dependent on its interactions with other comic effects, which the difference in dialect appears to enhance.[39] It is simply incorrect, however, to maintain (after Hall) that a Megarian seemed different to an Athenian merely by an ascription of ethnicity based on cultural prejudice and not on the basis of his actual linguistic divergence. There were probably other examples in Old Comedy of the dramatization of identity specification through dialect that have been lost. Hermippus, an older contemporary of Aristophanes, could adapt this type of characterization by describing someone with the *dialektos* and face of a lamb but the insides of a snake (**gnomic**, fr. 3, *PCG* 5.564–5).[40] By contrast, as an aspect of genre, differences of dialect and degrees of mastery of Greek seem to be excluded in tragedy. In Aeschylus' *Choephoroi* 560–4, Orestes states the intention that he and Pylades will disguise themselves as foreigners by imitating the Phokian dialect, but there is no representation in the play of any deviation from Aeschylean Attic.[41] The Phrygian in Euripides' *Orestes* (1369–1502) may be a parodic figure marked by ethnocentric coloration and over-wrought expressively, with questionable stylistic choices, but his Greek appears unobjectionable and Attic.[42]

3   The boundaries of Attic Greek, a mainland dialectal enclave of Attic-Ionic amid other dialects, are strikingly prominent.

(a) In an early and dramatic manifestation of linguistic ethnic identity, Solon described the deracination suffered by Athenians beset by the agrarian crisis not only by portraying them as wandering refugees but also as "persons no longer putting forth the Attic tongue".[43] Such a *démarche* was for them a personal and for him a communal disaster. I have sought to explain this assertion by the hypothesis of an assimilation of Dorian accents for those dislodged from Attica who had become acculturated on nearby Aigina (and perhaps at Megara).[44] By comparison, there is an apposite passage in Demosthenes reporting the plight of a person whose family was deprived of Athenian citizenship because his father spoke with a foreign accent acquired when he was a prisoner during the Dekeleian War (Dem. 57.18–19). He may well have assimilated a Doric accent, having been sold into slavery on Leukas, probably by one of Athens' Peloponnesian adversaries.[45]

(b) Solon's comment alone would tend to indicate deep consciousness of a significant linguistic and cultural boundary between the 'oldest land of Ionia' (fr. 4a W [**conventional**]) and its Saronic Gulf neighbours. Moreover, even if one discounts the factuality of the erection of boundary *stelae* that demarcated zones of dialect and ethnicity,[46] the common assertion by Attic local historians that such markers did indeed exist shows the powerful hold that this line of separation exerted over historical consciousness.[47] Along the Megarian-Corinthian border, after the Ionians were expelled from the Peloponnesus, *stelae* were supposedly placed cooperatively by Ionians and Peloponnesians. On each, the Corinthian face stated τάδ᾽ οὐχὶ Πελοπόννησος ἀλλ᾽ Ἰωνία 'this is not the Peloponnesus, but Ionia' and the Megarian face stated τάδ᾽ ἐστὶ Πελοπόννησος οὐκ Ἰωνία 'this is the Peloponnesus, not Ionia'. This demarcation was eventually altered by the Dorians, who attacked Attica and were outmaneuvered by Athenian king Kodros.[48] Then the Peloponnesians Dorianized the Megarid and destroyed the *stelae*. This story, however fanciful, apparently became a mainstay of Athenian collective memory. Herodotus reveals its place in the traditional enumeration of Dorian invasions of Attica (5.76). Thucydides referenced a poetic/oracular tradition speaking of a "plague" or a "famine" that would accompany a future Δωριακὸς πόλεμος (**gnomic**), which is surely reflected in the tradition of an earlier such invasion (2.54.1–3). The story of an early Peloponnesian invasion beautifully represented the early defensive tenor of Ionian ethnicity at Athens in its central Greek setting. In its present form, the story of the *stelae* and their destruction perhaps derived from a phase of ethnicization of Attic foreign affairs after the initial break with Sparta in 510, after which Megara stood at the outer edge of the Peloponnesian League.[49] Euphemos, the Athenian envoy to the conference of the Sikeliots at Kamerina in winter 415/14, counters the Dorian chauvinistic claims of the Syracusan ambassador, Hermokrates,[50] by depicting Attica as a salient beset by more numerous Dorian enemies (Thuc. 6.82–7). Congruently, Euphemos recognizes an important attestation in Hermokrates' speech: τὸ ... μέγιστον μαρτύριον 'the greatest testimony' is that οἱ Ἴωνες αἰεί ποτε πολέμιοι τοῖς Δωριεῦσιν εἰσίν 'the Ionians are always enemies to the Dorians' (**gnomic**, 6.82.2). Outnumbered by Dorian Peloponnesians, the Athenians in his view acquired ships and sought the military strength to protect themselves (Thuc. 6.82.3). In this mythology and the politics derived from it, dialect establishes ethnic and political identity.

(c) Consequently, claims touching on issues of identity and ownership in the Ionian–Dorian border region had to work around ethnolinguistic issues. Salamis was disputed between Megara and Athens.[51] Hence Solon is reported to have claimed in an arbitration conducted before Spartan judges that sundry Delphic responses had described Salamis as Ionian (Plut. *Solon* 10.4). However, there had likely been demographic instability on the island, where Athenian and Megarian occupations succeeded each other, perhaps at times even coexisting. In a situation where identification of dialect could not be probative, Athenian local history recounted how folkways proved a claim over the ethnic identity of the inhabitants of Salamis. Solon supposedly proved to the arbitrators the authenticity of Attic claims by observing that the style of burial of the early inhabitants of the island conformed to Athenian, not Megarian usage, a contention the Megarians seem to have contested.[52]

(d) The Athenians felt less threatened along their northern flank with the Boiotians. During the late archaic period that was so critical for the crystallization of politicized mythography, Athens had had so much of an advantage over the Thebans that the ethnolinguistic boundary there was less relevant for the purposes of power politics. Moreover, the late archaic expansion of Athens northwestward had encompassed ethnically diverse communities, either incorporated like Oropos or sympathetic like Plataia. However, the basis of the political boundary in differences in dialect was always apparent, as demonstrated by several pieces of evidence. In the fourth century, Epaminondas supposedly contested ownership of a border site called *Sidē* by noting its toponym only made sense as 'pomegranate' in Boiotian and not Attic.[53] In the *Seven against Thebes*, Aeschylus calls the Argive army attacking Thebes a ἑτερόφωνος στρατός 'army of different speech', which is a *non sequitur* in its mythological context, before respectively the Dorian conquests and the arrival of the Boiotians.[54] But such an ethnological distinction sounded natural to Attic ears in this context. I would conclude that the controversies over the nature of the boundaries of Attica indicate how linguistic contentions can try to trump territoriality.

We may now return to Herodotus for further evidence on cultural assimilation, alienation, or reassimilation. It is worthwhile to note that Thucydides can be brought in repeatedly here in order to adduce similar patterns of thought.[55] On ethnogenesis, Thucydides was clearly a Herodotean: for him language established ethnicity, and cultural metamorphoses generally had a linguistic dimension.

Where the Athenian master-historian differed from the Halikarnassean was not in their shared recognition of the ubiquity of ethnic fellow sentiment and arguments based on ethnicity in political affairs. Rather, it lay in Thucydides' insistence on the insincerity, even the insubstantiality, of ties between *poleis* based on ethnicity under the influence of opportunism founded on *Realpolitik*. His catalogue of the allies on either side before the climactic battle at Syracuse is thus a masterly dramatization of the interplay of calculated communal self-advantage with ethnic feeling (Thuc. 7.57.1–59.1). Yet it is also noteworthy even here that Thucydides did concede that ethnic ties between mother-city and colony – albeit often betrayed – had a more substantial role in international politics.

In Herodotus, assimilation through linguistic adaptation is exemplified by the adoption of the Doric dialect and Argive culture by the Kynourioi (8.73.3). Similarly, Thucydides presents Nikias in his speech of exhortation to his troops at Syracuse as alluding to the pride possessed by Athenian metics for their knowledge of the Attic dialect (here φωνή) and their assimilation of Attic *tropoi* 'customs' (7.63.3). I have already noted how celebration of the festival of the Apatouria is central in Herodotus to an individual being identified culturally as an Ionian.[56] From Thucydides, we can add the rural Dionysia for the Ionians and the Karneia for the Dorians.[57] Another instance of the ways in which social customs or folkways became loaded ethnically is the way in which Herodotus presents the Athenian abandonment of Doric dress for Ionic dress for their women after an early war with the Aiginetans.[58] The change became necessary when Athenian women misused their dress pins to murder the sole survivor of a defeat on Aigina. They could not be trusted to dress with long pins, while the Aiginetans and their Argive allies lengthened their women's pins in commemoration of their victory over the Athenians. Indeed, Dorian girls' dress was itself a cultural marker with important moral connotations and signified for Ionians shamelessness and sexual advertisement.[59] The verb δωριάζω 'behave Dorian' meant 'dress in a sexually provocative fashion' for Anacreon (Anacr. fr. 54 [*PMG* 399]). Yet it could also mean 'speak Doric Greek' (Anacreont. 11.6; Philostr. *VS* 1.529). Hence it was equivalent to the more common verb δωρίζω in denoting speech in the Doric dialect.[60] Here note how speech in these examples is the apex differentiator to whose conceptualization other cultural markers conform.

In the *Arkhaiologia*, Thucydides consistently portrays the means by which ethnic identity is acquired as centred upon assimilation of the Greek language. According to him, the development of the Greek identity occurred in a context typified by expulsions of populations who were being plotted against continually by ἀλλόφυλοι 'people of different origins'.[61] The name Hellene itself spread from Phthiotis among varied *ethnē*, among whom the Pelasgians predominated, imposing itself as the Greek communities came to understand each other.[62] Elsewhere in Thucydides, we can see this process operating in the historical period. The Amphilokhian Argives are Hellenized to their present speech by contact with the Ambrakiots.[63] He also appreciated cultural hybridity: the Akte peninsula of the Khalkidike is inhabited by "mixed *ethnē* of *diglōssoi* [bilingual] barbarians", with a Khalkidian element, but a larger Pelasgian component and the presence of various Thracian groups.[64] For Thucydides, being Greek for the people of the Akte might involve only a small Greek ancestral cohort and a larger non-Greek one, and revealed a retention of non-Greek languages, while still encompassing life in a *polis*. The Athenians at Sparta in Herodotus, as I noted earlier, predicated their Hellenic character on ἤθεα or 'customary practices', notably because they are ὁμότροπα 'of the same orientation' (8.144.2). The same thinking is highlighted in Thucydides. At Himera νόμιμα Χαλκιδικά 'Khalkidian social practices' prevailed in a settlement of mixed Ionic and Doric *phōnē*, while Gela was founded with νόμιμα Δωρικά, where νόμιμα probably encompassed the Doric dialect.[65] It is uncertain whether Thucydides meant that Himeran *phōnē* remained mixed or that the use of Doric receded there as the *nomima Khalkidika* prevailed (the literary dialect of Stesichorus is of course not probative).[66] Moreover, Thucydides emphasizes on two occasions that the great damage suffered by the Spartans after the Athenian occupation of Pylos depended on the status of Messenian raiders as speakers of the Lakonian variant of the Doric dialect: they were *homophōnoi*.[67] Homophony as the most probative differentiator also signified the possession of a common cultural apparatus, and it deserves emphasis here as appearing in a context where shared self-identification was in default.

Thucydides saw ethnic identity as a dynamic process: he is unsurprisingly the first Greek author to use the verb ἑλληνίζω 'to become Greek', as we have seen regarding Amphilokhian Argos. His addition of the qualifying phrase τὴν νῦν γλῶσσαν 'in their present speech/dialect' not only expresses his understanding that achieving a new collective identity resided primarily in acquisition of a new language/dialect, but also reveals a corollary, namely that linguistic attainment did not necessarily subsume everything that becoming Hellenic required. I adduce particularly the fourth-century attestations, where Xenophon, Plato, and Aristotle attest to the meaning 'to speak Greek' for ἑλληνίζειν.[68] Aeschines brings in the nuance that Thucydides was after: τὰ δ' ἀπὸ τῆς μητρὸς Σκύθης βάρβαρος ἑλληνίζων τῇ φωνῇ· ὅθεν καὶ τὴν πονηρίαν οὐκ ἐπιχώριός ἐστι "regarding his maternal lineage, [Demosthenes] is a Scythian barbarian although being Greek in *phōnē*, hence he is not a native even in his criminality" (3.172). Although later sources do still use the verb predominantly in its more strictly linguistic connotation,[69] the wider sense of acculturation into Greek values is also attested a few times.[70] This could be depreciating when speaking of a not fully acculturated, fluent speaker of Greek, but could also mark a high degree of Hellenization. I juxtapose Clearchus of Soli (fr. 6 W) who reports Aristotle's judgment after his encounter with the Jewish sage Hyperokhides: Ἑλληνικὸς ἦν οὐ τῇ διαλέκτῳ μόνον, ἀλλὰ καὶ τῇ ψυχῇ "he was Greek not only in *dialektos* [speech], but also in his soul" (*apud* Joseph. *Contra Apionem* 1.180–1). However, to become Greek usually meant to learn Greek, and being identified as Greek depended on speaking Greek properly.

Such judgments about dialect and ethnicity reflect contemporary public life. Thucydides quotes Perikles as explaining Athenian military advantages over the Peloponnesians not only by noting their adversaries' lack of a single deliberative apparatus and their need to achieve consensus among allies who were *isopsēphoi* 'of equal votes', but by also citing their diverse intentions, which in turn were based on their not being 'of the same ethnicity'.[71] That looks like a riposte aimed at Dorian ethnic chauvinism, equating the Peloponnesians with Dorians, among, most prominently, the Spartans and Corinthians.[72] Contemporary discourse indicates clearly how this primary ethnic and dialectal fault line between the Athenians and Spartans played out in its political ramifications. It is then noteworthy that verbs like ἀττικίζω (with ἀττικιστὶ) and λακωνίζω and their related nouns (ἀττικισμός and λακωνισμός or λακωνιστής) mean, without further verbal nuance, both 'to speak in the Attic or Spartan dialect'[73] and 'act in the interests either of the Athenians or of the Spartans' (and, by implication, not in those of one's own people). Our historiographical evidence for this phenomenon comes from Thucydides and Xenophon, and our literary evidence derives from comedy.[74] It may well be significant that our first attestations of *Attikismos* are accusations of disloyalty among other Boiotians that Thucydides attributes to the Thebans, where there is a clear implication of their dishonest pleading.[75] While the Thebans were naturally sensitive to speaking a different dialect from the Athenians, it should not, however, be surprising that they also operated under acute feelings of grievance over the loyalty or unfaithfulness to their ethnicity on the part of other Boiotians.[76] Despite Thucydides' efforts to condition ideological ethnicization, the Peloponnesian War exacerbated ethnic subdivisions, leading to some striking categorical formulations.[77]

It was doubtless in reflection of classical political sociology that, in the third century, Heraclides Criticus explicitly connects the differentiation of Greek dialects with ethnic identities inherited from the lineage of Hellen.[78] Collocations of the term διάλεκτος with terminology based on ἔθνος often appear in the grammarians thereafter.[79] As Cassio has explained, it becomes customary in later Greek phonetics and musicology to associate Greek dialects with normative and cultural meanings that tracked the common prejudices about the characteristics of Greek *ethnē*, and especially those of the two higher-order ethnicities, the Dorians and Ionians.[80] The significant discussion of the *harmoniai* or modes in Plato's *Republic*, where we find them associated with various moral dispositions, constitutes an intellectualization of systems of belief in which we find musical modes and dialects correlated with value systems.[81]

The ethnicity of Greeks and barbarians

If speaking Greek and what Greek one spoke established ethnic identity, then speaking a non-Greek language as one's mother tongue and lacking Greek fluency excluded a person from acceptance as a member either of the Hellenic *ethnos* in general or of a Greek *ethnos* in particular. To be sure, it has been a cliché of recent scholarship that would assign the barbarian counter-image to the fifth-century aftermath of the Persian invasion.[82] There had earlier been significant countervailing scholarship,[83] but the hypothesis of the late emergence of the Greek/barbarian dichotomy has already been subjected over the last several decades to such spirited and convincing riposte that those scholars objecting are almost too many even for a mere listing.[84] In what follows we will be interested in exploring the matter as regards the issue of language as a criterion for ethnic identity. Another variant of the same line of interpretation sees a fundamental difference in the evolution of Greek self-awareness as a single people by asserting that ethnogenesis was aggregative pre-480, i.e., based on growing perceptions of communality, and oppositional thereafter, i.e., driven by differentiation from non-Greek 'others'.[85] While this discussion does not offer me the scope for a thorough rebuttal,[86] I would emphasize that these two processes of conceptualization operated synergistically, although their specific dynamic doubtless differed in varying social and cultural settings (as I shall note several times in what follows).

We are fortunate in exploring this dichotomy that Strabo chose to give two overviews of the tradition. In his Book VIII (8.6.6 C370), he provides a noteworthy discussion of the early use of the terms *panhellenes* and *barbaroi*, partly to correct Thucydides (1.3.3–4), who had asserted Homer did not speak of *barbaroi*. Thus, he collected an important body of evidence about this central cultural fissure, because he not only cites the *Iliad* (2.684, 867 [*barbarophōnoi* Karians]) and the *Odyssey* (1.344, 15.80), but quotes Hesiod (fr. 130 MW) and Archilochus (fr. 102W) for the appellation *panhellēnes*, and finally the Hellenistic savant Apollodorus (*FHG* 1.458, fr. 172) for the early geographical limitation of the Hellenes. Moreover, Strabo returned to the subject in Book XIV (14.2.28 C661–3), where the particular context is a discussion of the Karians, starting with the *barbarophōnoi* of *Il.* 2.867 and Thucydides' aforesaid comments. Apollodorus is noted once again for the idea of a particular Homeric/Ionian contempt for the Karians.[87] However, Strabo also notes that 'barbarian speech' was initially attached to all with impaired patterns of pronunciation, and he envisages the application of *barbaroi* as a term of ethnic differentiation from the Greeks as a secondary and misguided generalization about a supposedly thick or harsh enunciation of speakers of non-Greek languages. It is quite clear from his framework of citation that Strabo imagined that this classification of non-Greeks as *barbaroi* was quite early and pejorative; it is unlikely that his citations were anything other than selective or that he exhausted relevant material to be found in earlier authors.

The Greek world functioned as a cultural unit in manner different both from the traditional peasant agriculture-based Near Eastern societies and from the tribal nations of Europe. Through colonization Greek *poleis* spread widely along the coastlands of the Mediterranean and Black Sea basins. The surface area or boundary of interaction between Greeks and non-Greeks was thus vastly greater than the border regions (often sparsely populated) of other earlier, albeit sometimes quite large, non-Greek linguistic, ethnic, and cultural units. Significant economic and military interaction with non-Greeks characterized the littoral disposition of many Greek colonies. This ensured the rate of personal contacts by ordinary Greeks with non-Greeks had to differ quantitatively, and hence qualitatively, from other Mediterranean and Near Eastern societies. Not only were there inevitably indigenous groups operating culturally at various levels of Hellenization, but some Greeks themselves had practical rationales for achieving a degree of fluency in languages other than Greek (even when factors of ideology and chauvinism militated against this development or against its advertisement). The ubiquity and growing intensity of the institution of chattel slavery was another factor in Hellenization, because predominantly non-Greek slaves were imported (in large numbers) who then became Hellenized through interaction with their social context and for the sake of economic purposes. Repatriation from Greek cultural milieus appears rare, so that the number of Greeks grew beyond rates of natural increase and necessarily contained partially Hellenized individuals.

Strabo goes on to note in 14.2.28 C663 that the Karians were *barbarophōnoi* because they were in the process of becoming Hellenized. On the basis of later usage, I would observe that the combination of *barbaros* with a *phōn-* word-element would conventionally be specifying or concessive in sense – on the model of phrases like "Hellenized in *phōnē*" – suggesting Karian assimilation of Greek culture while retaining the primary use of their native tongue; this emphasis on acculturation seems to fit a catalogue citing the *fortes* of Trojan allies. In any case, the majority of the later speakers of imperfect Greek in the archaic and classical periods were doubtless those Hellenizing, but other social markers must often have stigmatized or marginalized them. Therefore, the verb τὸ βαρβαρίζειν tended to be applied to those speaking Greek badly and not in its obvious application to persons speaking languages other than Greek. Strabo notes this situation, adding in the rarer terms τὸ βαρβαροφωνεῖν, βαρβαροφώνοι, and καρίζειν. Strikingly, Herodotus uses βαρβαροφώνοι as 'speaking a language other than Greek' in citing two oracles of Bakis, supposedly associated with the fighting of 480–79 (8.20.2, 9.43.2), but he is the exception.[88] Regarding βαρβαρίζειν, it is used to describe gibberish or inarticulate cries like those of birds,[89] and speaking poor Greek,[90] alongside the surface meaning of speaking a language other than Greek.[91]

Therefore, it was fundamental for understanding ethnic identity for Herodotus and his contemporaries to realize that they were constantly aware of the contrast between Greek and non-Greek, which had been well established by 550 at the latest.[92] The successful defence against the invaders of 480 did indeed shape appraisals of non-Greeks, both negatively and positively, but perceptions of a profound cultural divide had long been ethnicized. The *barbaroi* as a collective, which, while including different peoples, is to be envisioned as an opposite or mirror-image to the Greeks, and often implicitly as their inferiors, can be found in a determinative number of early attestations and in later passages that have a fair claim to derive from early material in substance or theme. Thus, the divide is a foundation of Greek ethnic identity, and it is primarily linguistic. Some of these examples could in principle (one supposes) be dismissed as rather late, if they did not have the appearance of commonplaces. Let me present some instances in a sort of general chronological order.

1   Any consideration of Homeric epic must start from a recognition of the strong universalizing and humanistic tenor of the representation of individual and communal existence in the *Iliad* and *Odyssey*. Nor for our purposes does the argument turn perforce on detecting ethno-chauvinistic attitudes in what would necessarily have to include hundreds of contributors to oral

poetic traditions. Rather our question more narrowly concerns whether ethnic variety was determined primarily by language for the audience of epic and whether the distinction of non-Greek from Greek was already taking on its polar disposition and a tone of derogation of the non-Greek. We have already noted the *barbarophōnoi* (*Il.* 2.867), to whom the *agriophōnoi* 'wild [or savage]-voiced' Sintians might be added (*Od.* 8.294). Greek homogeneity of speech is contrasted with meaningless variety among non-Greeks, as notably in *Iliad* 2.802–6, where Hector alludes to the linguistic variation of the Trojan allies, or in the pejorative descriptions of the multilingual, bestial clamour of the Trojan forces (3.1–7; 4.433–8).[93] And, if the distinction between *barbaroi* and Greeks necessarily embodies the concept of ethnic superiority based in part on language, that is the way in which the ancient commentators imply that *Iliad* 2.802–6 was to be read.[94] Sourvinou-Inwood sensibly notes that the catalogue of Trojan allies not need be ethnocentric in terms of the classical period, but reflects the Greek/barbarian polarity in its Dark Age context.[95] Mackie has argued skillfully that such distinctions are carried into *Iliadic* dichotomous treatment of Greek and 'Trojan' political comportment.[96] In *Il.* 3.1–7, the pejorative character of the comparison of the Trojan vociferations with the cries of birds has often been denied. The later *topos*, however, that 'barbarian' speech resembles birds' voices is so well established that the generalizing ethno-chauvinism of the *Iliadic* lines must be conceded.[97] Against this background the epithet of *panakhaioi* for the assembled Greeks appears to be stylizing archaism for *panhellēnes*[98] – though *panhellēnes* slips into *Il.* 2.530 – especially because the latter is attested in hexametric poetry (Hes. *WD* 527–8; fr. 130 MW). Thus Archilochus' "the misery of the *panhellēnes* rushing together in Thasos" (fr. 102 W) is a pointedly ironic evocation of Greek commonality.

2   Diodorus Siculus preserves an archaic oracle stating that Battos will face the resistance of *barbaroi* when he embarks on the colonization of Kyrene.[99] This quite possibly reflects a naïve comment by Delphic cult personnel regarding a peripheral target for settlement whose inhabitants were largely unknown.

3   According to Hermippos, Thales (or perhaps Solon) thanked the gods in a μακαρισμός for his possession of certain innate qualities, among which he celebrated birth as a human and not an animal, as a male, not a woman, and as a Greek, not a *barbaros*.[100]

4   Anacreon fr. 313b (Page *Supp.*) contains the admonition μή πως βάρβαρα βάξηις "lest you speak barbarous [things]". It has been combined by editors with fr. 423 (*PMG*), which is discussed later.

5   Heraclitus expounds on the fallacious interpretation of sensory data by attributing such deficiencies to those having "barbarian souls".[101] The analogy naturally suggests a longstanding derogatory attitude towards the cultural attainments of non-Greeks well before its utterance.

6   A number of early references to the Hellenes occur in official contexts, where the clear counterpoint is provided by non-Greeks who are conceptualized as single entity. The Olympic games were reserved for Greek contestants

exclusively, with *barbaroi* being excluded, as the dispute over the eligibility of Alexander I of Macedonia (c. 496) indicates (Hdt. 5.22.1–2; cf. 2.160.3).[102] As early as the turn of the fifth century, the judges at the games were called *Hellanodikai*.[103] While the institution of the great games was aggregative in its consolidation of various groups of Greeks, it was also oppositional because an exclusion of non-Greeks was integral to this process of integration.

7   Similarly, although eligibility for initiation at Eleusis was open to all *poleis* and *ethnē*, to all classes, and to slaves as well as freemen, the initiate could not be a *barbaros* and had to possess sufficient active and receptive knowledge of Greek.[104] At the latest this criterion was probably imposed during the Peisistratid reorganization of the cult. This is another example of aggregative ethnogenesis that also embodies an oppositional distinction.

8   Another similar indication involves the authorization of Naukratis by the Pharaoh Amasis as the sole Greek *emporion* in Egypt. The main common Greek sanctuary in the town, which exercised control over the market, was the Hellanion (Hdt. 2.178.1–3).[105] The cities controlling this sanctuary appointed the *prostatai* 'supervisors' of the *emporion* at Naukratis, constituting thereby the managers of the sole licit vehicle for Greek commerce with Egypt. These arrangements were a skillful measure taken to limit the preponderance and mutual rivalries of the three most powerful commercial states active at Naukratis: Miletos, Samos, and Aigina. The understanding of the cult of the Hellanion and of the management of the market as enterprises of the Greeks in common illustrates the aggregative process whereby Greeks reciprocally recognized their common identity. Yet we must also note a simultaneous process of differentiation, where Greeks were not only distinguished obviously from the native Egyptians (who remained under close pharaonic supervision), but also from other transactors, like the Phoenicians (who were probably excluded). Herodotus' identification of Amasos as *philellēn* (2.178.1, the only such designation in his work) completes our conceptual map of the ethnology of the foundation of Naukratis by providing an ethnic differentiator for its patron.

9   According to Plato's Protagoras, even so respected a figure as the Mytilenean statesman Pittakos, usually one of the Seven Sages, could be criticized because, as a Lesbian, he had been reared in a supposedly barbaric dialect (Λέσβιος ὢν καὶ ἐν φωνῇ βαρβάρῳ τεθραμμένος), that is, Greek typified by some assimilation of non-Greek vocabulary.[106] Protagoras is thinking of Simonides' correction of a famous maxim of Pittakos (fr. 37, *PMG* 542).

10   Hecataeus characterized the inhabitants of the Peloponnesus before the Greeks as *barbaroi*, next going on to differentiate the specific pre-Hellenic populations of particular Greek regions.[107]

11   In practical terms, when people of unknown identity are confronted in dramatic situations where fighting is possible, hearing spoken Greek is crucial. Our evidence is classical, but the motif has every indication of being a *topos*. In Sophocles' play, Philoktetes is only assured of his visitors' identity by hearing them address him in Greek (*Phil.* 219–38). The author of the *Rhesus*,

a play handed down in the corpus of Euripides, reverses this conceit: a Trojan shepherd ceases his fear only after realizing an unknown force is *not* speaking Greek ([Eur.] *Rh.* 284–95).

There is another angle of approach to understanding the psychological and normative valence of the demarcation between the Greeks and *barbaroi*. This examination is hinted at by Strabo, who would later sum up the tradition by connecting the verb σολοικίζειν 'to solecize' with βαρβαρίζειν 'to speak like a barbarian'. Exploring imperfect linguistic assimilation yields material that not only supports the conclusion that this distinction was strongly dichotomized, indeed even polarized, but substantiates the idea that the *barbaroi* were early judged to be morally, politically, and culturally inferior. I am referring to the evidence that the ethnolinguistic demarcation between Greek and non-Greek was fraught with profound angst on an individual scale. There exists a wealth of early evidence regarding the anxiety over self-betrayal as a non-Greek through imperfect mastery of linguistic norms.

The phenomenon is nowhere more evident than in the concept of σολοικισμός 'solecism' (i.e., linguistic error).[108] Our first attestations of the concept derive from the sixth century. Hipponax was aiming for comic effect when he observes that the σόλοικοι 'solecists' are caught, sold, and set to work as Phrygians milling barley at Miletos.[109] Yet this jest does indeed attest to the debased servile and non-Greek essence of those labeled 'solecists'. Anacreon prayed to Zeus that he might put solecistic speech to sleep (fr. 76, *PMG* 423). We have already noted that his stated rationale for this entreaty may well have been in order to preclude barbarous speech. And these are merely the bare remains of a rich diction on the phenomenon. Herodotus himself attests to the prevalence of sensitivity in cultural affiliation when he imagines solecism by the Sauromatians *vis-à-vis* Scythians because of imperfect transmission of the Scythian language through the Amazons (4.117). In a telling example from later oratory, Apollodorus would rail against Phormio, while projecting onto the jurors the intuition that, because he solecizes, they must have already concluded that he is a *barbaros* and therefore contemptible (Apollodoros: [Dem.] 45.30). The term ἀσόλοικος is derived from the same root element, but merely means 'refined' or 'unspoiled'.[110] That connotation stands as a remarkable testimony to Greek anxiety over tainting or adulteration from foreign influences, since lack of such contamination becomes equivalent to excellence by itself.[111]

Furthermore, the prevailing ancient theory of the origin of this diction is revelatory in several ways. During his post-legislative travels, the Attic statesman Solon supposedly travelled to Cilicia. There he founded a city called Soloi that included a few Athenian colonists.[112] According to Diogenes Laertius and assorted lexical notices, these settlers, having become deculturated, were said to solecize. I am not interested here in authenticity of a story that reeks of later fabrication on the basis of the similarity of the name Soloi to Solon. The detail that even Athenian settlers could become de-Hellenized renders acute the threat of dissimilation, which any Greek ought to fear through intensive contact with non-Greek settings. Moreover, this etiology reminds us of anti-Athenian polemics. To Athenian democrats the presence of slaves and freedmen, metics, and allied and foreign visitors was a testimony to the wealth, power, and vitality of the *paideusis* of Hellas. In the hostile, Laconizing perspective of the *Constitution of the Athenians*, preserved for us among the works of Xenophon, these contacts result in contamination. The author notes that "hearing every φωνή, the Athenians have chosen an element from one, another element from another. And the Greeks use rather their own φωνή, lifestyle, and dress, while Athenians use mixed φωνή, lifestyle, and dress from all the Greeks and barbarians".[113] The introduction of the barbarians here, and the deliberate contrast with the Greeks, establish an undertone of depreciation of the Athenians.

The fate of Soloi also exhibits the larger scale existential risk that an entire community might be brought down through a loss of proficiency in Greek and the extinction of other qualities of panhellenic culture. This communal barbarization is sometimes expressed by the verb ἐκβαρβαρόω and is caused by a loss of fluency in Greek.[114] Athenaeus cites Aristoxenos for a poignant deployment of this concept regarding the people of Poseidonia in Italy (fr. 124W [Athen. 14.632A]). Starting out Greek, they had been barbarized to become Etruscans (or is that Latins/Romans?), with their speech and social practices transformed. However, they still celebrated one Greek festival at which they recalled the ancient words and νόμιμα amid tears and lamentations. The attrition of Greek culture in southern Italy was eventually a commonplace: Strabo considered that all the *poleis* were barbarized except for Taras, Neapolis, and Rhegion (Strabo 6.1.2 C253). There are other examples of the dread over past incidents of barbarization and anxiety over its future occurrence. Isocrates in his *Evagoras* notes that Cypriot Salamis, although founded by Teucer, had been corrupted by a Phoenician interloper who had barbarized the city and subjugated Cyprus to the Persians for the sake of personal power (9.20). The author of the eighth Platonic epistle attributes the appointment of Dionysios the Elder to mastery over Syracuse as motivated by the danger that Sicily would be completely barbarized by the Carthaginians ([Plato] *Ep.* 8.353A-B). There is a common trope in local historiography wherein native peoples encountered by Greek colonists are interpreted as deculturated Greeks from Heroic-Age colonization. One wonders whether this degeneration could provide exculpation (even if subconsciously) for colonial aggression.

Summation

Let me recapitulate my main points. Ethnogenesis among the archaic and classical Greeks was not a superficial process, or one dominated by propaganda, by arbitrary assertions, or even by mere prescription. It rested on observations of genuine cultural phenomena and involved elements of personal identity. Although there was a role to be played by ἤθεα, among which folkways and shared ritual activities were noteworthy, the single most important factor establishing proximity or distance in kinship was shared dialect and other common elements of speech, such as onomastics. Loss of one's original φωνή was a personal catastrophe. Hence, the distinction between Greeks and non-Greeks was linguistic in ordinary consciousness on the level of initial interaction. Even before 500, well before Xerxes' expedition was repulsed, Greek and *barbaros* were polarized, dichotomous categories, with cultural superiority accorded to the Hellene. To be exposed as anything other than an authentic Greek was considered a grave subversion of identity. Thus, solecism spotlighted a steep and slippery slope of potential deculturation. Loss or deterioration of fluency in Greek could represent communal barbarization, a cultural disaster and fearsome lesson. Herodotus' sensitivity to issues of ethnic identity and his pattern of continual reversion to matters involving distinctions between the European Greeks and Asiatic *ethnē*, dominated by the Persians, is not merely a byproduct of the initial fear and subsequent relief associated with Xerxes' invasion. Rather, the invasion itself highlighted the significance of cultural differentiation as a powerful influence in human relations. This variation possessed a predominantly linguistic quality.

Having started with Herodotus, it is fitting to end with Thucydides, whose *Histories* demonstrate the omnipresence of ethnicized thinking, while Thucydides himself reveals ironically the lack of sincerity of appeals to ethnicity by his contemporaries. In Book VII, in 413, the nighttime assault on the heights of Epipolai at Syracuse stood as a stratagem to put right the Athenian attempt to capture that city (Thuc. 7.44.5–8.). When a possibility of the attack's success still existed, the singing of the paean by Doric-speaking Athenian allies, explicitly the Argives and Corcyreans, engendered panic and was the largest factor in the Attic defeat.[115] Note first the almost incalculably vast impact for the eventual fate of Athens and Greek democracy had there been a favourable outcome to this battle. The error in understanding linguistic differentiation here adds an undertone of irony to the treatment of ethnicity elsewhere in Thucydides. The psychological effect of the negative reception of the paean, whether sung by Dorian friends or enemies, was wholly dependent on the rooted prejudice that a Doric-speaker equalled an enemy of Athens. On the basis of our investigation, such prejudice, however ruinous, must be envisaged as deeply seated in the classical psyche.

Notes

1 This study is the first of a triptych on Hellenic ethnogenesis and typology that will eventually include Figueira (forthcoming) and an exploration in draft on ethnicity after the Peloponnesian war which will be partially presented in a conference on Xenophon in 2020.

2 See (in general) Zacharia 2008; Munson 2005: 15–18, 2014: 344–7; also Hall 1989b: 172–81; Jones 1996: 315, n. 4. Cf. Hall 2002: 189–94. This crucial interchange must have been authorized in advance by the *stratēgoi* and *boulē* at a minimum; its successful outcome would have rendered it still quite memorable when Herodotus was conducting his inquiries. The suggestion that it was a free composition of the historian is quite cavalier.

3 For language as equivalent to ethnic identity: in brief, e.g., Willi 2002: 135: "both language and dialect were clearly felt to be indicators of national and tribal identity"; Colvin 2014: 96: "the Greeks, like most peoples ancient and modern, associated language (dialect) with ethnic group". For background, see also, e.g., Consani 1991: 15–27 and pp. 47–53 this volume.

4 The only other appearance of the term in Herodotus is strikingly in another appeal to the Spartans that is made by Aristagoras of Miletos before Kleomenes on behalf of the subjugated Ionians (5.49.3). This may suggest that the stress on the characteristic of "same-bloodedness" may be designed to overcome Spartan or Dorian prejudices about the Hellenicity of east Greeks.

5 Animal fable: Aesop *Fab.* 302.1; *Vita Aesopi* (G) 97, 99, 133 (for which see Petrocelli 2001: 69–70).

6 Hall 1996, 1997: 44–7, 177–81, 2001: 169–70 (where Herodotus supposedly gives his criteria in reverse order); 2002: 111–17, 175, 2007: 56–9; Hall *et al.* 1998: 267–8). Cf. Harrison 1998: 1–2; Konstan 1997: 99–100, 106–7; Anson 2009: esp. 6–7.

7 Hall emphasizes ethnic construction as discursive, though I fail to understand how that 'quality' would render ethnicity unconditioned by cultural realities like dialect. And our views about the contingent nature of ethnocultural construction do not neatly overlap with those of the archaic/classical Greeks. See Hall 1995a: 9–10, 15–16; Hall *et al.* 1998: 267; cf. S. Jones in Hall *et al.* 1998: 271–3.

8 See Willi 2002: 136–7, n. 29. See also Konstan 1997: 106; Anson 2009: 7–11 for dialect recognition in literary sources, and Haarmann 2014, who treats the determinative role of language in ethnic identification as uncontroversial.

9 See Hall 1996.

10 Teres & Tereus: Thuc. 2.29.3 with scholia; Xen. *An.* 7.2.31 with Jones 1999: 29–30.

11 Post-classical *sungeneia*: note the monographs of Curty (1995: esp. 254–63). See Will 1995 and Jones (1999: esp. 132–6) for important correctives of Curty 1995. See also, Giovannini 1997; Patterson 2010: 109–23.

12 Hall 2002: 189–90, 1997: 44–5. Cf. Antonaccio 2001: 115–16; Morgan 2009: 18–20.

13 Plato *Theaet.* 174E–175B. Cf. Aris. *Rhet.* 1360b26–30.

14 *Arkhēgetai* as colony patrons/protectors: Pin. *Ol.* 7.78–80; *Pyth.* 5.60; fr. 140a.58; Thuc. 6.3.1. Erikhthonios: Strabo 13.1.48 C604. Attic eponymous heroes: Dem. 43.66, citing an oracle; Arist. fr. 135, *PCG* 3.2.93; Phot. s.v. ἀρχηγέται α 2926; Hesych. s.v. α 7583. Heroes at Plataia: Plut. *Arist.* 11.3–4. Herakles at Sparta: Xen. *HG* 6.3.6. Cf. Hdt. 9.86.

15 Tragic genealogies: e.g., Aes. *Supp.* 274–335; Eur. *Phoen.* 202–60; frs. 696; 727b from the *Telephos*. Cf. Hall 1989b: 172–6, also 35–7. On Attic comedy, cf. p. 48.

16 Hdt. 5.79–81. See Figueira 1993: 54, 135–6, cf. 209; Figueira 2012.

17 Hdt. 8.43: οὗτοι πλὴν Ἑρμιονέων Δωρικόν τε καὶ Μακεδνὸν ἔθνος . . . οἱ δὲ Ἑρμιονέες εἰσὶ Δρύοπες . . .

18 For the Dryopes, see Wallace & Figueira 2019: 80, 95–6 (with bibliography).

19 Hdt. 8.44.2: Ἀθηναῖοι δὲ ἐπὶ μὲν Πελασγῶν ἐχόντων τὴν νῦν Ἑλλάδα καλεομένην ἦσαν Πελασγοί, ὀνομαζόμενοι Κραναοί, ἐπὶ δὲ Κέκροπος βασιλέος ἐπεκλήθησαν Κεκροπίδαι, ἐκδεξαμένου δὲ Ἐρεχθέος τὴν ἀρχὴν Ἀθηναῖοι μετωνομάσθησαν, Ἴωνος δὲ τοῦ Ξούθου στρατάρχεω γενομένου Ἀθηναίοισι ἐκλήθησαν ἀπὸ τούτου Ἴωνες. See Hdt. 1.56–58; cf. 6.137–40.

20 Megarians, Ambrakiots, and Leukadians: ἔθνος ἐόντες οὗτοι Δωρικὸν ἀπὸ Κορίνθου (Hdt. 8.45.1). Aiginetans: Αἰγινῆται δέ εἰσι Δωριέες ἀπὸ Ἐπιδαύρου (Hdt. 8.46.1).

21 Khalkidians and Eretrians: οὗτοι δὲ Ἴωνές εἰσι; Keians: ἔθνος ἐὸν Ἰωνικὸν ἀπὸ Ἀθηνέων (Hdt. 8.46.2).

22 Naxians: Ἴωνες ἀπὸ Ἀθηνέων (Hdt. 8.46.3).

23 Styreans and Kythnians: Δρύοπες (Hdt. 8.46.4).

24 Krotoniates: Ἀχαιοί (Hdt. 8.47).

25 Melians: γένος ἐόντες ἀπὸ Λακεδαίμονος (Hdt. 8.48).

26 Siphnians and Seripheans: Ἴωνες ἐόντες ἀπ' Ἀθηνέων (Hdt. 8.48).

27 Hdt. 1.56.2: ἱστορέων δὲ εὕρισκε Λακεδαιμονίους τε καὶ Ἀθηναίους προέχοντας, τοὺς μὲν τοῦ Δωρικοῦ γένεος, τοὺς δὲ τοῦ Ἰωνικοῦ. ταῦτα γὰρ ἦν τὰ προκεκριμένα, ἐόντα τὸ ἀρχαῖον τὸ μὲν Πελασγικόν, τὸ δὲ Ἑλληνικὸν ἔθνος. On *genos* and *ethnos* in Herodotus here: Jones 1996: 317–18 and Hill p. 74 in this volume.

28 In the present state of the evidence, it is unclear to what extent the binary Ionians/
    Dorians – Athens/Sparta was influenced by the poetic turn illustrated by Ibycus fr.
    282A.23–35, where an honorand is *kallistos* 'fairest' among the Ionians and at
    Lakedaimon.

29 Though claims both to solidarity on the basis of ethnicity and to superior embodiment
    of general cultural ideals by ethnic groups were common from the late fifth century,
    both Herodotus and Thucydides were sceptical (see pp. 51–3). Will (1956: esp. 61–3)
    offered a classical discussion of the 'divide' between Ionians and Dorians.

30 Hdt. 1.146.1–2: τούτων δὴ εἵνεκα καὶ οἱ Ἴωνες δυώδεκα πόλις ἐποιήσαντο, ἐπεὶ ὥς
    γέ τι μᾶλλον οὗτοι Ἴωνές εἰσι τῶν ἄλλων Ἰώνων ἢ κάλλιόν τι γεγόνασι, μωρίη πολλὴ
    λέγειν, τῶν Ἄβαντες μὲν ἐξ Εὐβοίης εἰσὶ οὐκ ἐλαχίστη μοῖρα, τοῖσι Ἰωνίης μέτα οὐδὲ
    τοῦ οὐνόματος οὐδέν, Μινύαι δὲ Ὀρχομένιοί σφι ἀναμεμίχαται καὶ Καδμεῖοι καὶ
    Δρύοπες καὶ Φωκέες ἀποδάσμιοι καὶ Μολοσσοὶ καὶ Ἀρκάδες Πελασγοὶ καὶ Δωριέες
    Ἐπιδαύριοι, ἄλλα τε ἔθνεα πολλὰ ἀναμεμίχαται. Hdt. 1.146.3: οἱ δὲ αὐτῶν ἀπὸ τοῦ
    πρυτανηίου τοῦ Ἀθηναίων ὁρμηθέντες καὶ νομίζοντες γενναιότατοι εἶναι Ἰώνων, οὗτοι
    δὲ οὐ γυναῖκας ἠγάγοντο ἐς τὴν ἀποικίην ἀλλὰ Καείρας ἔσχον, τῶν ἐφόνευσαν τοὺς
    γονέας.

31 Note (e.g.) Hellanicus *FGrH* 4 F 101 for the Kadmeioi at Priene (cf. Paus. 7.2.10); see
    also Strabo 14.1.3 C632–3. Paus. 7.2.1–4, adds to the complexity by trying to account
    for cases where, just as the Ionian colonization of Kodros, expeditions comprised eth-
    nically differentiated leaders and followers (ἐκ δὲ τῆς Ἑλλάδος τρίτος δὴ οὗτος στόλος
    ὑπὸ βασιλεῦσιν ἀλλοίοις ὄχλοις τε ἀλλοίοις ἐστάλησαν).

32 Hdt. 1.147.3: εἰσὶ δὲ πάντες Ἴωνες, ὅσοι ἀπ' Ἀθηνέων γεγόνασι καὶ Ἀπατούρια ἄγουσι
    ὁρτήν. ἄγουσι δὲ πάντες πλὴν Ἐφεσίων καὶ Κολοφωνίων· οὗτοι γὰρ μοῦνοι Ἰώνων
    οὐκ ἄγουσι Ἀπατούρια, καὶ οὗτοι κατὰ φόνου τινὸς σκῆψιν.

33 See Sourvinou-Inwood 2003: 140–2; for the Pelasgians, see Sourvinou-Inwood 2003:
    esp. 136–40.

34 See Colvin 1999: 119–31, 297–308 (with reservations). Cf. Hall 1996: 88–9.

35 See Long 1986: 130–56; Hall 1989a: esp. 40–1; Prato 2001: 311–13. Willi (2003:
    198–231) astutely analyzes the Scythian's Greek as an example of "foreigner talk" (see
    also Willi 2002: 142–9). Cf. Sier 1992: esp. 67–9; Colvin 2000: 287–8.

36 Dunbar 1995: 715–16, 724–5, 727–8, 735–6.

37 See Hyperbolos in Plato Com. frs. 182–3, *PCG* 7.505–7; and Kleophon in Arist. *Ranae*
    679–83, with scholia; Plato fr. 61, *PCG* 7.0458. Cf. Colvin 2000: 288–91.

38 Arist. *Ach.* 729–835 (Megarian Doric), 860–954 (Boiotian); *Lys.* 81–244, 980–1013,
    1076–1189, 1242–1321 (all Spartan Doric). Other poets: Epilycus fr.4, *PCG* 5.171–2
    (Laconian); Eubulus fr. 11, *PCG* 5.191 (Boiotian).

39 To hold that "there is little evidence that the Greeks looked down on other dialects of
    Greek" (Colvin 2014: 89) is a bit misleading. Even Colvin has to concede that Strat-
    tis fr. 49 (*PCG* 7.646–7, from his *Phoinissai*) presents an Athenian who is mocking
    semantic deviations in the Theban dialect. Our body of evidence is largely Athenian.
    There is little doubt that the Athenians claimed cultural superiority over other Greek
    ethnic groups in large part distinguished by dialectal differences. Many rationales are
    activated for this superiority, with which any claims specifically on behalf of Attic
    Greek had to compete, but it is clear from Nikias' final speech at Syracuse that Attic
    phōnē could provide one such contention (Thuc. 7.63.3). It may ultimately be unclear
    to what extent dialect speech could sustain humor by itself, as in New York vaudeville.
    And the tone of such scenes varied from the bitter ridicule of the Megarian in the
    Acharnians to the emollient treatment of the Spartans in the *Lysistrata*. Willi (2002:
    132–41) has offered a provocative hypothesis that the acceptance of Laconian Dorian
    (offensive as mere *rhēsis*) in the *Lysistrata* depends on its presentation as sung poetry.
    I note that this theory starts from the premise that spoken Laconian aroused "a highly
    negative psychological response in the average Athenian" (p. 139). This is just the

setting one might predict for such ridicule. Note also Brixhe (1988: 137): "la xénopho-
bie ordinaire, qui s'exercait non pas seulement à l'égard du non-Grec, mais aussi du
Grec non attique".

40 Sometimes dialectal variation might yield mere invective, as in Strattis fr. 49 (a contemporary of Aristophanes), who has a character denigrate the Thebans when he attributes their semantic variants to their ignorance or stupidity.

41 Aes. *Cho.* 560–4: ξένῳ γὰρ εἰκώς, παντελῆ σαγὴν ἔχων, ἥξω σὺν ἀνδρὶ τῷδ᾽ ἐφ᾽
ἑρκείους πύλας Πυλάδη, ξένος τε καὶ δορύξενος δόμων. ἄμφω δὲ φωνὴν ἥσομεν
Παρνησίδα, γλώσσης αὐτὴν Φωκίδος μιμουμένω.

42 Note Willink 1986: 305; West 1987: 276–7.

43 Solon fr. 36.10W: γλῶσσαν οὐκέτ᾽ Ἀττικὴν ἱέντας. See Noussia-Fantuzzi 2010: 471–
2. Cf. Solon fr. 4aW: γινώσκω, καί μοι φρενὸς ἔνδοθεν ἄλγεα κεῖται, | πρεσβυτάτην
ἐσορῶν γαῖαν ['Ι]αονίης | κλινομένην.

44 Figueira 1993: 82–3. Cf. Mülke 2002: 379–80, for a destination in Ionia.

45 In Dem. 57.18–19, the term for this alienation of speech patterns is ξενίζειν, used three
times, which probably derives from the more common meaning 'surprise by a strange
sight' (*LSJ s.v.* ξενίζω, II). See n. 77.

46 Androtion *FGrH* 324 F61a-b; Philochorus *FGrH* 328 F107; Strabo 3.5.5 C171; 9.1.6–7
C392–3. See Harding 1994: 189–91. Plut. *Thes.* 25.3 attributes the stele to Theseus.

47 Strabo 9.1.6–7 C392–3. Dorian war of aggrandizement: Andron *FGrH* 10 F 14; cf.
Hellanicus *FGrH* 4 F 75, 78.

48 Hellanicus *FGrH* 323a F 23; cf., e.g., Pherecydes *FGrH* 3 F 154; Hdt. 5.76; Lyc.
Leoc. 84–7; Strabo 9.1.7 C392–3; Justin 2.6.16–21; Vell. Pat. 1.2.1–2; Phot. s.v.
εὐγενέστερος Κόδρου (Demon *FGrH* 327 F 22?). This foray caused the Dorianization
of the Megarid, formerly part of Attica (cf. also Plato *Critias* 110D–E).

49 Cf. Figueira 1985: 298–300.

50 Thuc. 6.76–80. Observe especially how he presents to the Dorian Kamarineans both
that the Attic allies are habitual slaves to be contrasted to Δωριῆς ἐλεύθεροι ἀπ᾽
αὐτονόμου τῆς Πελοποννήσου 'free Dorians from the autonomous Peloponnesus'
(6.77.1) and both that the Athenians as τοὺς μὲν φύσει πολεμίους 'enemies by nature'
and that and the Syracusans as τοὺς δὲ ἔτι μᾶλλον φύσει ξυγγενεῖς 'even more so kins-
men by nature' (6.79.2). See also Figueira forthcoming.

51 Figueira 1985: 280–8, 291–2, 300–3; see also Legon 1981: 122–31, 136–40 and now
Robu 2014: 76–81. That the insertion of Solon into an arbitration, which may be late
sixth century, might be apocryphal does not alter the nature of what constituted tokens
of ethnicity.

52 Plut. *Solon* 10.3; Ael. *VH* 7.19, cf. 5.14; DL 1.48. The Megarian local historian Hereas
denied that the Megarians buried differently from the Athenians (*FGrH* 486 F 4). In
Strabo we see a similar rationale: Athena's priestess eats only foreign cheese, including
Salaminian (9.1.11 C395).

53 Agatharchides *FGrH* 86 F 8 (Athen. 14.550F-651A). See F. Geyer, s.v. 'Sidai', *RE*
2.2.2207–8; s.v. 'Side (8)' cols. 2209–10. For the site as Pyle (Derbenosialesi/Dherve-
nosialesi), see Wallace 1979: 90–1; Buck 1979: 17.

54 Aes. *Septem* 170 for the *heterophōnos stratos* 'army of different speech', where the
effect may be deliberately marked (cf. *Trag. Adesp.* fr. 645 K/S). Consider E. Hall
1989b: 177–9: "Aeschylus wanted to suggest the deep psychological fear which alien
speech can arouse, even if only an alternative dialect of the same language."

55 See Figueira forthcoming.

56 Hdt. 1.147.2. Note also Herodotus' discussion of Ionian *glōssai* 'dialects' (1.142.3),
which are said to be *paragōgai* 'divergences' (J.E. Powell) or 'alterations', possibly
even in the sense of 'perversions' (Asheri *Hdt. I–IV* 173). Have they diverged from or
perverted Attic Greek?

57 Dionysia: Thuc. 2.15.4; Karneia: Thuc. 5.54.2; cf. Paus. 3.13.3–4.

58 Hdt.5.87.1–88.3; Duris *FGrH* 76 F24. Cf. Figueira 1993: 41–4.

59 Doric dress: Ibycus fr. 58 (*PMG* 339); Soph. fr. 872 Radt; for which cf. Plut. *Comp. Lyc. et Num.* 3.3–4 (also citing Eur. *Andr.* 597–8); Eur. *Andr.* 594–601, *Hec.* 933–4; ΣEur. *Hec.* 934M, with Duris *FGrH* 76 F2; Call. fr. 620a Pf; Anacr. fr. 54 (*PMG* 399).

60 See, e.g., Theoc. *Id.* 15.89–93 (also featuring the possible *hapax* Πελοποννασιστί for speaking in a Peloponnesian fashion); Strabo 8.1.2 C333; Plut. *Philop.* 2.2; *Mor.* 421B.

61 See Thuc. 1.2.1–6 on the ecological interpretation of the early lack of settled conditions in Hellas, exempting Attica because of its infertility. Note 1.2.4: διὰ γὰρ ἀρετὴν γῆς αἵ τε δυνάμεις τισὶ μείζους ἐγγιγνόμεναι στάσεις ἐνεποίουν ἐξ ὧν ἐφθείροντο, καὶ ἅμα ὑπὸ ἀλλοφύλων μᾶλλον ἐπεβουλεύοντο.

62 Thuc. 1.3.1–4, noting 1.3.4: οἱ δ᾽ οὖν ὡς ἕκαστοι Ἕλληνες κατὰ πόλεις τε ὅσοι ἀλλήλων ξυνίεσαν.

63 Amphilokhian Argos: Thuc. 2.68.5: καὶ ἡλληνίσθησαν τὴν νῦν γλῶσσαν. Cf. *HCT* 2.201–2; Hornblower *CT* 1.352.

64 Thuc. 4.109.4: ξυμμείκτοις ἔθνεσι βαρβάρων διγλώσσων, καί τι καὶ Χαλκιδικὸν ἐνι βραχύ, τὸ δὲ πλεῖστον Πελασγικόν, τῶν καὶ Λῆμνόν ποτε καὶ Ἀθήνας Τυρσηνῶν οἰκησάντων, καὶ Βισαλτικὸν καὶ Κρηστωνικὸν καὶ Ἠδῶνες . . . Cf. Hdt. 7.22.2: ὁ γὰρ Ἄθως ἐστὶ ὄρος μέγα τε καὶ ὀνομαστόν, ἐς θάλασσαν κατῆκον, οἰκημένον ὑπὸ ἀνθρώπων . . ., where Macan (1.1.34) believed that ἀνθρώπων had to be modified by βαρβάρων or διγλώσσων . . . The former is more likely, turning the passage into grounds for correction by Thucydides. Cf. Hornblower *CT* 2.347–8; *HCT* 3.588–9.

65 Gela: Thuc. 6.4.3. Himera: Thuc. 6.5.1.

66 Cf. Hornblower *CT* 3.291, 297–8; also *HCT* 4.217–8.

67 Thuc. 4.3.4: καὶ τοὺς Μεσσηνίους οἰκείους ὄντας αὐτῷ τὸ ἀρχαῖον καὶ ὁμοφώνους τοῖς Λακεδαιμονίοις πλεῖστ᾽ ἂν βλάπτειν ἐξ αὐτοῦ ὁρμωμένους; 4.41.2: οἱ ἐκ τῆς Ναυπάκτου Μεσσήνιοι ὡς ἐς πατρίδα ταύτην . . . πέμψαντες σφῶν αὐτῶν τοὺς ἐπιτηδειοτάτους ἐλήζοντό τε τὴν Λακωνικὴν καὶ πλεῖστα ἔβλαπτον ὁμόφωνοι ὄντες. See Figueira 1999: 213; Petrocelli 2001: 88–90; Figueira & Figueira 2009: 312–14. For two Thucydidean examples of false identification through misinterpreting dialect, see 3.112.4; 7.44.6.

68 Xen. *An.* 7.3.25; Plato *Protag.* 327E; *Meno* 82B; *Charm.* 159A; *Alcib.* I 111A, C. The same pattern prevails for our few Hellenistic attestations: Poseidippos Comicus fr. 30, *PCG* 7.576–7: Posidonius *FGrH* 87 F28(4) (Strabo 2.3.4 C98); note Agatharcides *De Mari Erythraeo* 5 (*GGM* 1.112–13), where the Persian Boxos ἑλλήνισαι γλῶσσαν καὶ γνώμην 'hellenized his speech and mindset'. For Aristotle, the connotation of speaking Greek correctly or idiomatically is present: *Rhet.* 1407a20, 1413b6; *SE* 182a14, 34.

69 Nic. Dam. *FGrH* 90 F 100 (Strabo 15.1.73 C719); Strabo 14.2.28 C662–3*ter*; Plut. *Mor.* 1116E; Clem. Alex. *Strom.* 2.1.3; Aristid. 23.281; 44.571J; Paus. 9.23.6; App. *Sam.* 7.4; Dio Cassius (e.g., especially for translation of Latin official terminology into Greek) 45.12.3; 53.14.6, 16.8; cf. 74.8.2; Luc. *Deor. Conc.* 9 (τῇ φωνῇ), *Philops.* 16, 34; Heliod. *Aeth.* 2.12.4, 21.4, 30.4; 7.14.2; 9.25.3; 10.9.6, 31.1, 39.1; Philostr. *VA* 5.35; Dio Chrys. *Or.* 4.55; 15.15; 36.9, 19. The usage of the grammarians also conforms to this pattern: Aristonicus *De sign. Od.* 3.402, *De signis Il.* 1.68; Apoll. Dys. *De adverbiis GGM* 2.1.162; Hdn. Περὶ σολοικισμοῦ καὶ βαρβαρισμοῦ 311; Anon. *De Barbar. et soloec.* 178, 181, 290. Connotation of pure Greek: DH *Dem.* 5; *Pomp.* 2.5; Athen. *Deipn.* 3.121f, 6.231b; Philostr. *VS* 2.623 Sext. Emp. *Math.* 1.175, 176. 184, 185, 186, 188*bis*; 191, 193; 235, 246, 247*bis*: 2.56, 57. Medical writers use this diction to specify correct terminology: Galen *De meth. med.* 10.71 (contrasted with σολοικίζειν); *De comp. med.* 12.961; *Inst. Log.* 4.6; *In Hipp. lib. iii epid. Comm.* 17a.625; *In Hipp. prog. comm.* 18b.307–8; Rufus *De corp. hum. appell.* 133.

70 Diog. Laert. 1.102 (of Anacharsis); Plut. *Mor.* 328D; Aristid. 32.403; Philostr. *VS* 1.489 (quoting Favorinus). The verb ἀφελληνίζω means to 'Hellenize/civilize thoroughly': Philo *Legatio* 147; Dio Chrys. 37.26; Pollux 5.154.

71 Thuc. 1.141.6: ὁμόφυλοι.

72 See Figueira forthcoming and consult Thuc. 1.124.1; 5.9.1; 6.77.1, 80.1, 3; 7.5.4; 8.25.5.

73 Attic dialect (I limit myself to select classical attestations): Eupolis fr. 99.23–5, *PCG* 5.345 (*Dēmoi*), cf. fr. 268.39, *PCG* 5.455 (*Taxiarkhoi*), fr. 390, *PCG* 4.413 (?); Plato Com. fr. 183, *PCG* 7.505–7. ἀττικιστὶ: Antiphanes fr. 97, *PCG* 2.162 (*Euthydikos*); Alexis fr. 200, *PCG* 2.134 (*Proskedannumenos*). Spartan dialect: λακεδαιμονιάζω: Arist. fr. 97 (*Babylonioi*), *PCG* 3.2.76, which Stephanus Byzantius (*Ethn.* 408) equates with λακωνίζω and λακωνιστής; cf. Plut. *Mor.* 150B: λακωνίζω (of Kheilon).

74 *Attikismos*: Thuc. 3.62.2, 64.5 (of the Plataians); 4.133.1 (Thespians); Xen. *HG* 1.6.13; 6.3.14; Isoc. *De pace* (8) 108*bis*. For Laconism: λακεδαιμονιάζω: Arist. fr. 97, *PCG* 3.2.76 (cf. *Vespae* 1169 for διασαλακώισον); Xen. *HG* 1.1.32; 4.4.2, 4.4.15, 4.8.28; 6.3.14; 7.1.46; 7.4.35; Isoc. *Paneg.* (4) 110; *De pace* (8) 108; *Panath.* (12) 155; *Plat.* (14) 30; *Antid.* (15) 318. Cf. Theopompus *FGrH* 115 T2 (the historian's father); DL 2.15 (of Xenophon); Plut. *Kimon* 15.3 (Kimon); *Per.* 10.2–3 (Kimon); 29.2 (Lakedaimonios, son of Kimon); Paus. 3.10.1; 4.35.2; Philostr. *VS* 1.16 (Kritias).

75 Macleod (1983: 116) rightly recognizes ἀττικίζειν and ἀττικισμος as neologisms in the mouths of the Thebans – I would suggest of the period of the Thirty Years Peace. Hornblower (*CT* 2.411) cites Hellanicus *FGrH* 4 F 81 (Steph. Byz. *Ethn.* 678) for the verb ὀρχομενίζω 'to have sympathy with Orkhomenos' to suggest that "such coinages were common". I would note, however, the common Boiotian context for the first appearance of Atticism and for 'Orkhomenism' (itself an isolated formation), with the occasion for F 81 being almost certainly the ultimately disastrous expedition of Tolmides to Boiotia in 446 (e.g., Thuc. 1.113.1–4).

76 We have already seen that βοιοτιάζω can mean speak in the Boiotian dialect (Xen. *An.* 3.1.26–32; also *Com. Adesp.* fr. 875K, *PCG* 8.253; Arr. *An.* 6.13.5; Dio Chrys. *Or.* 43.5). Unsurprisingly, it came in the fourth century to mean 'to follow a pro-Theban policy line', for which see Xen. *HG* 5.4.34; Aesch. 2.106, 3.139; Plut. *Nic.* 10.7; *Pel.* 14.1; *Mor.* 575D.

77 Figueira forthcoming. Note how Plato in the *Cratylus* could apply diction using *xenik-* 'alien' (cf. n. 45) to describe vocabulary differentiations between dialects (401b–c, 407b, 412b, 417c, 419c, 426c*bis*, with Anson 2009: 11 with n. 21). According to Aelian (*VH* 4.15), probably based ultimately on Atthidography, Alkibiades achieved a virtual *trifecta* of perverse sentiment: he was not only *philolakōn*, but at other times he played the Boiotian (βοιατιάζω) or the Thessalian (Θετταλίζω). The latter verb usually means 'speak in the Thessalian dialect' (Steph. Byz. *Ethn.* 311; Parth. *Am.* 24.2; Dio Chrys. *Or.* 11.23b).

78 Heraclides Criticus: frs. 3.2, 3.2*bis* (also *FHG* 2.263–4, under Dicaearchus fr. 61; cf. *GGM* 1.LI-LIII), for which see Pfister 1951: 90.24–92.3, 224–8. See Morpurgo-Davies 2002 (1987): 161–2, with n. 17. Here the point is not the precision which Greeks brought to linguistic classification, but its use by them to determine ethnic identity. Cf. Hall 1996: 87–9.

79 Morpurgo-Davies 2002: 162–3 with n. 18: e.g., Diogenes Babylonius fr. 20 (*SVF* 3.213) *apud* DL 7.56; Clem. *Strom.* 1.21.142; cf. Strabo 8.1.2 C333–4. See also Hainsworth 1967: 64–8.

80 Cassio 1984: 116–31.

81 *Rep.* 398E-399C: ἀλλὰ κατάλειπε ἐκείνην τὴν ἁρμονίαν [the Doric], ἣ ἔν τε πολεμικῇ πράξει ὄντος ἀνδρείου καὶ ἐν πάσῃ βιαίῳ ἐργασίᾳ πρεπόντως ἂν μιμήσαιτο φθόγγους τε καὶ προσῳδίας, καὶ ἀποτυχόντος ἢ εἰς τραύματα ἢ εἰς θανάτους ἰόντος ἢ εἴς τινα ἄλλην συμφορὰν πεσόντος, ἐν πᾶσι τούτοις παρατεταγμένως καὶ καρτερούντως ἀμυνομένου τὴν τύχην (but note that the Ionian mode is not disparaged); cf. Aris. *Pol.* 1342a28-b34 (the last material in the treatise!); Heraclides Ponticus fr 163W.

82 Cf., e.g., Hall 1989b: 3–13, 54–5 (p. 54: "the all-embracing genus of anti-Greeks later to be termed 'the barbarians' does not appear until the fifth century"); Malkin 1998: 18, 27; Hall 2002: 172–89.

83 E.g., Weiler 1968 (however hesitant to generalize); Lévy 1984 (fundamental); see also Asheri 1997: 14–19.
84 See (selectively) Harrison 1998: 1–3, 40–1; Tuplin 1999: 48–57; Zacharia 2008: 25–9; Coleman 1997: 175–8, 186–9 (although with my reservations); Petrocelli 2001: 69–74; Sourvinou-Inwood 2005 (esp. 29–34; cf. 26–8, for general misgivings). See also Georges 1994: 1–46, 244–6; Thomas 2000: 75–100; Nippel 2002 (1996): 279–93; Mitchell 2007: 54–75; Skinner 2012: 239–50.
85 Hall 1996: 91–2, 1997: 47–8; Hall in Hall *et al.* 1998: 280–1 (with some retreat in light of criticism); Malkin 1998: 18, 59–60 (offering some reservations).
86 Note Konstan 1997: esp. 107–9; I. Morris in Hall *et al.* 1998: 270; S. Morris in Hall *et al.* 1998: 274–5; Mitchell 2007: 39–54.
87 Apollod. (*FHG* 1.460) fr. 177.
88 Strabo is himself responsible for a notable proportion of the usage of the words of the βαρβαροφων- family, with the rest deriving from grammarians and lexicographers (e.g., Pollux 2.111). Cf. Rochette 1997/98. As to καρίζειν, despite Strabo, it is (in extant texts) prominently attested in the sense 'to speak Carian' only in the ethnocentric and negative proverb Πρὸς Κᾶρα καρίζεις (Diogen. 7.65, *CPG* 1.297; Macar. 7.36, *CPG* 2.205).
89 Aes. fr. 450 Radt (cf. *Ag.* 1050); Hdt. 2.57.2. See n. 97.
90 Plato *Alc.* 120B, cf. Plato *Lys.* 223A-B; Arist. *SE* 165b20–1; Polyb. 39.1.7; Plut. *Mor.* 59F, 375F; Dio Chyrs. *Or.* 36.26.
91 Athen. 14.652d. Note Xen. *HG* 5.2.35, where the verb describes the supposed Medism of Ismenias; cf. Max. Tyr. *Dialexeis* 33.2. The concept can be extended to connote a non-Greek lifestyle, as in Ach. Tat. 3.9.2.
92 Kim (2013: 28–30) opts for a somewhat later sixth century date (noting Anacreon and Heraclitus), but suggests that Persian ethnological thinking provided a model for Greek ethnic classification (pp. 31–7).
93 Cf. Gera 2003: 1–3.
94 Eustath. *Il.* 1.548.1–11; 783.2–19. See Petrocelli 2001: 70–1.
95 Sourvinou-Inwood 2005: 38–47.
96 Mackie 1996: 15–41.
97 Cf. Aes. *Ag.* 1050–2; fr. 450 Radt; Hdt. 2.57.2; Soph. *Ant.* 1000–2; Ion fr. 33 Snell; Arist. *Ran.* 679–82, cf. *Av.* 199–200, 1680–1. See Harrison 1998: 18; Tuplin 1999: 50; Gera 2003: 191–4; also Dunbar 1995: 736–7.
98 *Il.* 2.404; 7.73, 159, 327, 385; 9.301; 10.1; 19.193; 23.236, all of which except 9.301 involve the formula. . . ἀριστῆας Παναχαιῶν. See also *Od.* 1.239; 14.369; 24.32 for the hexameter: τῷ κέν οἱ τύμβον μὲν ἐποίησαν Παναχαιοί. See Sourvinou-Inwood 2005: 36–7.
99 DS 8.29: an oracle in nine hexameters; cf. Hdt. 4.155.3 (variant of the first two lines). Although Parke & Wormell (1956: 1.75–6, 2.18, 31–2) would treat the longer version as a subsequent elaboration, their rationale regarding the evolution of the monarchy at Cyrene is not particularly probative, and even this down-dating preserves the oracle as late archaic. Cf. Fontenrose 1978: 174–5, 283–4.
100 Hermippos *FGrH* 1026 F 13 (DL 1.33 = 11 A 1 D/K). Cf. J. Bollansée in *FGrH* IVA.3.186–9; also Wehrli 1974: 51–2. Cf. *Apoph. Sept. Sap.* 5.9.
101 Heraclitus (22) B107 D/K. Robinson (1987: 150–1) stresses that failure to understand the appropriate language is central to the analogy. See also Marcovich 1967: 45–8, 1978: 31–3; Conche 1987: 266–8.
102 See Hornblower 2013: 116–18; in general, Anson 2009: 20–2.
103 Pin. *Ol.* 3.10–15 with scholia, including Hellanicus *FGrH* 4 F 113; *LSAG* "Elis" #15 (p. 220); Aris. fr. 499.1–2 Gigon; cf. Paus. 5.9.4–5 (note the manuscript variant in Hdt. 5.22.2). Compare the epigram celebrating the Pythian victory of Ekhembrotos, in his words singing *melea* and *elegoi* for the Hellenes, traditionally dated to 582 (Paus. 10.7.5–6: West, *PEG* 2.62). See also Sourvinou-Inwood 2005: 46–9.

104 Isoc. 4.157. Origen (*Contra Celsum* 3.59–60) cites Celsus' statement that among other criteria an initiate must be φωνὴν συνετός 'cognizant in [Greek] speech' (cf. Willi 2002: 136), while Libanius notes the admonishment against anyone Ἑλλήνων φωνῆς ἀξύνετος (*Dec.* 13.1.52). Note also Theon Smyrn. *De util. math.* p. 14.23–4 Hiller.

105 See Figueira 1981: 252–64, 2006: 293; also Sourvinou-Inwood 2005: 52–7.

106 Plato *Protag.* 341C; note Sim. frs. 541–2. Cf. Plato *Lys.* 223A–B for barbarized Greek. Note Werner 1991.

107 Hecataeus *FGrH* 1 F 119 (Strabo 7.7.1 C321B). Although the specific context is lost for Corinna fr. 655, fr. 4.4 (*PMG*), the reference to *barbaroi* presumably involves a retelling of Boiotian myth.

108 E.g., Aris. *SE* 165b20–1; DL 1.51; Plut. *Mor.* 59F; *Etym. Gud.* s.v. σολοικισμός, σ 507.26–32.

109 Hipp. fr. 27 W; cf. fr. 92 for a woman λυδίζουσα for speaking Greek contaminated by Lydian in an obscene context.

110 The usage of ἀσόλοικος: Eubulos fr. 6, *PCG* 5.191–2, in emendation [from the *Amaltheia*]; Zeno fr. 81, *SVF* 1.23 (DL 7.18); Plut. *Cleom.* 13.4. Cf. Soph. fr. 629 Radt.

111 Even during the High Empire in a Roman imperial world of ethnic mixture, embedded cultural assumptions rendered labelling as a 'solecist' humiliating. This terminology was particularly favoured by Lucian, whose works well illustrate later usage, where this diction could still embody anxiety over authentic identity, while presenting juxtapositions with barbaric Greek. Lucian even wrote a playful exploration of the subject called the *The False Sophist or Solecist*. For Lucian's usage (note * for items with *barbar-* allusion), see for imperfect diction: *Dem.* 40; *Vit. Auct.* 23; *Merc. Cond.* 35; *Rh. Pr.* 17*, 23*; not socialized behaviour: *Nigr.* 31; mistakes in performance: *Salt.* 27, 80; *Soloec. passim* (5*).

112 DL 1.51; also *Anec. Gr. Bach.* 1.367.31–2; ΣPlato *Rep.* 599e; cf. Hecataeus *FGrH* 1 F 268; *Suda* s.v. Σόλων, Ἐξηκεστίδου, σ 779 Adler.

113 [Xen.] *Ath. Pol.* 2.8: ἔπειτα φωνὴν πᾶσαν ἀκούοντες ἐξελέξαντο τοῦτο μὲν ἐκ τῆς, τοῦτο δὲ ἐκ τῆς· καὶ οἱ μὲν Ἕλληνες ἰδίᾳ μᾶλλον καὶ φωνῇ καὶ διαίτῃ καὶ σχήματι χρῶνται, Ἀθηναῖοι δὲ κεκραμένῃ ἐξ ἁπάντων τῶν Ἑλλήνων καὶ βαρβάρων.

114 See Bowersock 1992: esp. 256–7.

115 See *HCT* 4.423–4; Hornblower *CT* 3.629–30; Petrocelli 2001: 85–8, 90–4.

Bibliography

Anson, E.M. 2009. "Greek Ethnicity and the Greek Language." *Glotta* 85: 5–30.

Antonaccio, C.M. 2001. "Ethnicity and Colonization." In Malkin 2001, 113–57.

Asheri, D. 1997. "Identità greche, identità greca." In Settis 1997, 2.2: 5–26.

Bowersock, G. 1992. "Les Grecs 'barbarisés." *Ktema* 17: 250–7.

Brixhe, C. 1988. "La langue de l'étranger non-Grec chez Aristophane." In Lonis, R., ed., *L'Étranger dans le monde grec*. Nancy (Presses Universitaires de Nancy), 113–38.

Buck, R.J. 1979. *A History of Boeotia*. Edmonton (University of Alberta Press).

Cassio, A.C. 1984. "Il 'carattere' dei dialetti greci e l'opposizione Dori – Ioni: testimonianze antichi e teorie di età romantica (su Arist. Quint. 2. 13, Iambl. *v. Pyth* 241 sgg., sch. in Dion. Thr. p. 117, 18 sgg. Hilgard." *Annali dell'Università degli Studi di Napoli "L'Orientale" (filol.).* 6: 113–36.

Coleman, J.E. 1997. "Ancient Greek Ethnocentrism." In Coleman, J.E., & Walz, C.A., eds., *Greeks and Barbarians: Essays on the Interaction Between Greeks and Non-Greeks in Antiquity and the Consequences for Eurocentrism*. Bethesda, MD (Occasional Publications of the Department of Near Eastern Studies and the Program of Jewish Studies, Cornell University), 175–220.

Colvin, S. 1999. *Dialect in Aristophanes and the Politics of Language in Ancient Greek Literature*. Oxford (Clarendon Press).

———. 2000. "The Language of Non-Athenians in Old Comedy." In Harvey, D., & Wilkins, J., eds., *The Rivals of Aristophanes: Studies in Athenian Old Comedy*. Swansea (Classical Press of Wales), 285–98.

———. 2014. *A Brief History of Ancient Greek*. Chichester (Wiley-Blackwell).

Conche, M. 1987. *Héraclite Fragments 2*. Paris (Presses Universitaires de France).

Consani, C. 1991. *ΔΙΑΛΕΚΤΟΣ: Contributo alla storia del concetto di 'dialetto'*. Pisa (Giardini).

Curty, O. 1995. *Les parentés légendaires entre cités grecques*. Geneva (Droz).

Dunbar, N. 1995. *Aristophanes Birds*. Oxford (Clarendon Press).

Figueira, D.M. & Figueira, T.J. 2009. "The Colonial 'Subject' and the Ideology of Subjection in Lakōnikē: Tasting Laconian Wine Behind Lacanian Labels." In Hodkinson, S., ed., *Sparta: Comparative Approaches*. Swansea (Classical Press of Wales), 305–30.

Figueira, T.J. 1981. *Aegina*. New York, NY (Times Books).

———. 1985. "Archaic Megara, 800–500 B.C." In Figueira, T.J., & Nagy, G., eds., *Theognis of Megara: Poetry and the Polis*. Baltimore, MD (Johns Hopkins University Press), 261–303.

———. 1993. *Excursions in Epichoric History: Aiginetan Essays*. Lanham, MD (Rowman & Littlefield Publishers).

———. 1999. "The Evolution of the Messenian Identity." In Hodkinson, S., & Powell, A., eds., *Sparta: New Perspectives*. London (Duckworth), 211–44.

———. 2006. "The Copenhagen Polis Centre: A Review-Article of Its Publications, Parts 1–2." *Ancient West & East* 5: 252–303.

———. 2012. "The Aiakidai, the Herald-less War, and Salamis." In Bers, V., Elmer, D., Frame, D., & Muellner, L., eds., *Donum natalicium digitaliter confectum Gregorio Nagy septuagenario a discipulis collegis familiaribus oblatum*. Washington, DC (Center for Hellenic Studies). http://chs.harvard.edu/wa/pageR?tn=ArticleWrapper&bdc=12&mn=4610

———. Forthcoming. "Ethnogenesis and Hegemony in Classical Power Politics." In Debnar, P., & Powell, A., eds., *Sparta in Thucydides*. Swansea (Classical Press of Wales).

Fontenrose, J. 1978. *The Delphic Oracle: Its Responses and Operations*. Berkeley & Los Angeles, CA (University of California Press).

Georges, P. 1994. *Barbarian Asia and the Greek Experience: From the Archaic Period to the Age of Xenophon*. Baltimore, MD (Johns Hopkins University Press).

Gera, D.L. 2003. *Ancient Greek Ideas on Speech, Language, and Civilization*. Oxford (Oxford University Press).

Giovannini, A. 1997. "Les relations de parenté entre les cités grecques: a propos d'un livre récent." *Museum Helveticum* 54: 158–62.

Haarmann, H. 2014. "Ethnicity and Language in the Ancient Mediterranean." In McInerney 2014, 17–33.

Hainsworth, J.P. 1967. "Greek Views of Greek Dialectology." *Transactions of the Philological Society*: 62–76.

Hall, E.M. 1989a. "The Archer Scene in Aristophanes' Thesmophoriazusae." *Philologus* 133: 38–54.

———. 1989b. *Inventing the Barbarian: Greek Self-Definition Through Tragedy*. Oxford (Oxford University Press).

Hall, J.M. 1995. "Approaches to Ethnicity in the Early Iron Age of Greece." In Spencer, N., ed., *Time, Tradition and Society in Greek Archaeology: Bridging the 'Great Divide'*. London (Routledge), 6–17.

————. 1996. "The Role of Language in Greek Ethnicities." *Cambridge Philological Society* 41: 83–100.

————. 1997. *Ethnic Identity in Greek Antiquity*. Cambridge (Cambridge University Press).

————. 2001. "Contested Ethnicities: Perceptions of Macedonia Within Evolving Definitions of Greek Identity." In Malkin 2001, 159–86.

————. 2002. *Hellenicity: Between Ethnicity and Culture*. Chicago, IL (University of Chicago Press).

————. 2007. "Polis, Community, and Ethnic Identity." In Shapiro, H.A., ed., *The Cambridge Companion to Archaic Greece*. Cambridge (Cambridge University Press), 40–60.

Hall, J.M., Morris, I., Jones, S., Morris, S. & Renfrew, C. 1998. "Review Feature: Ethnic Identity in Greek Antiquity." *Cambridge Archaeological Journal* 8: 265–83.

Harding, P. 1994. *Androtion and the Atthis: The Fragments Translated with Introduction and Commentary*. Oxford (Oxford University Press).

Harrison, T. 1998. "Herodotus' Conception of Foreign Languages." *Histos* 2: 1–45.

————, ed. 2002. *Greeks and Barbarians*. Edinburgh (Routledge).

HCT = Gomme, A.R.W., Andrewes, A. & Dover, K.J. 1945–1981. *A Historical Commentary on Thucydides*, 5 vols. Oxford (Oxford University Press).

Hdt. *I–IV* = Asheri, D., Lloyd, A. & Corcella, A. 2007. *A Commentary on Herodotus Books I–IV*. Edited by O. Murray & A. Moreno. Oxford (Oxford University Press).

Hornblower *CT* = Hornblower, S. 1991–2008. *A Commentary on Thucydides*, 3 vols. Oxford (Oxford University Press).

————. 2013. *Herodotus: Histories: Book V*. Cambridge (Cambridge University Press).

Jones, C.P. 1996. "ἔθνος and γένος in Herodotus." *Classical Quarterly* 46: 315–20.

————. 1999. *Kinship Diplomacy in the Ancient World*. Cambridge, MA (Harvard University Press).

Kim, H.J. 2013. "The Invention of the 'Barbarian' in Late Sixth-Century BC Ionia." In Almagor, E., & Skinner, J., eds., *Ancient Ethnography: New Approaches*. London (Bloomsbury Publishing), 25–48.

Konstan, D. 1997. "Defining Ancient Greek Ethnicity." *Diaspora: A Journal of Transnational Studies* 6: 97–110 [reviewing Hall 1997].

Legon, R.P. 1981. *Megara: The Political History of a Greek City-State to 336 B.C.* Ithaca, NY (Cornell University Press).

Lévy, E. 1984. "Naissance du concept de barbare." *Ktema* 9: 5–14.

Long, T. 1986. *Barbarians in Greek Comedy*. Carbondale, IL (Southern Illinois University Press).

Mackie, H. 1996. *Talking Trojan: Speech and Community in the Iliad*. Lanham, MD (Rowman & Littlefield Publishers).

Macleod, C.W. 1983. "Thucydides' Plataean Debate." In *Collected Essays*. Oxford (Oxford University Press).

Malkin, I. 1998. *The Returns of Odysseus: Colonization and Ethnicity*. Berkeley and Los Angeles, CA (University of California Press).

————, ed. 2001. *Ancient Perceptions of Greek Ethnicity*. Washington, DC (Center for Hellenic Studies).

Marcovich, M. 1967. *Heraclitus: Greek Text with a Short Commentary*. Merida, Venezuela (Los Andes University Press).

————. 1978. *Eraclito. Frammenti*. Florence (La Nuova Italia).

McInerney, J., ed. 2014. *A Companion to Ethnicity in the Ancient Mediterranean*. Chichester (Wiley-Blackwell).

Mitchell, L. 2007. *Panhellenism and the Barbarian in Archaic and Classical Greece*. Swansea (Classical Press of Wales).

Morgan, C. 2009. "Ethnic Expression on the Early Iron Age and Early Archaic Greek Mainland: Where Should We Be Looking?" In Derks, T., & Roymans, N., eds., *Ethnic Constructs in Antiquity: The Role of Power and Tradition.* Amsterdam (Amsterdam University Press), 11–36.

Morpurgo-Davies, A. 2002. "The Greek Notion of Dialect." In Harrison 2002, 153–71, ~ *Verbum*, 1987, 7–27.

Mülke, C. 2002. *Solons politische Elegien und Iamben (Fr. 1–13; 32–37 West): Einleitung, Text, Übersetzung, Kommentar.* Munich & Leipzig (K.G. Saur).

Munson, R.V. 2005. *Black Doves Speak: Herodotus and the Language of Barbarians.* Hellenic Studies 9. Washington, DC (Center for Hellenic Studies).

———. 2014. "Herodotus and Ethnicity." In McInerney 2014, 341–55.

Nippel, W. 2002. "The Construction of the 'Other.'" In Harrison 2002, 278–310 ~ Settis 1997, 1.165–96.

Noussia-Fantuzzi, M. 2010. *Solon the Athenian, the Poetic Fragments.* Leiden (Brill).

Parke, H.W. & Wormell, D.E.W. 1956. *The Delphic Oracle*, 2 vols. Oxford (Basil Blackwell).

Patterson, L.E. 2010. *Kinship Myth in Ancient Greece.* Austin, TX (University of Texas Press).

Petrocelli, C. 2001. "Le parole e le armi: omofonia/omoglossia in guerra." *Quaderni di Storia* 54: 69–97.

Pfister, F. 1951. *Die Reisebilder des Herakleides, Sitzungberichte der Akademie der Wissenschaften.* Wien (Phil.-Hist.), 227.

Prato, C. 2001. *Aristophane: Le donne alle Tesmoforie.* Milan (A. Mondadori).

Robinson, T.M. 1987. *Heraclitus: Fragments: A Text and Translation with a Commentary.* Toronto (University of Toronto Press).

Robu, A. 2014. *Mégare et les établissements mégariens de Sicile, de la Propontide et du Pont- Euxin: Histoire et institutions.* Bern (Peter Lang).

Rochette, B. 1997–1998. "La langue des Cariens à propos de B 867." *Glotta* 74: 227–36.

Settis, S., ed. 1997. *I Greci: Storia cultura arte società: 1: Noi e I Greci; 2: Una storia greca: II. Definizione.* Turin (Giulio Einaudi).

Sier, K. 1992. "Die Rolle des Skythen in den 'Thesmophoriazusen' des Aristophanes." In Müller, C.W., Sier, K., & Werner, J., eds., *Zum Umgang mit fremden Sprachen in der Griechisch-Römischen Welt.* Stuttgart (Franz Steiner), 63–83.

Skinner, J.E. 2012. *The Invention of Greek Ethnography: From Homer to Herodotus.* Oxford (Oxford University Press).

Sourvinou-Inwood, C. 2003. "Herodotos (and Others) on Pelasgians: Some Perceptions of Ethnicity." In Derow, P., & Parker, R., eds., *Herodotus and His World: Essays from a Conference in Memory of George Forrest.* Oxford (Oxford University Press), 103–44.

———. 2005. "Ethnicity and the Definition of Greekness." *Hylas, the Nymphs, Dionysos and Others*, Acta Instituti Atheniensis Regnae Sueciae[8] 19. Stockholm (Paul Åströms Förlag), 24–63.

Thomas, R. 2000. *Herodotus in Context: Ethnography, Science and the Art of Persuasion.* Cambridge (Cambridge University Press).

Tuplin, C. 1999. "Greek Racism? Observations on the Character and Limits of Greek Ethnic Prejudice." In Tsetskhladze, G.R., ed., *Ancient Greeks West and East.* Leiden (Brill), 47–75.

Wallace, M.B. & Figueira, T.J. 2019. "Karystos in Euboia and Attic Hegemony." In Figueira, T., & Jensen, S.R., eds., *Athenian Hegemonic Finances: Funding Athenian Domination in the 5th and 4th Centuries B.C.* Swansea (Classical Press of Wales), 79–108.

Wallace, P.W. 1979. *Strabo's Description of Boiotia: A Commentary*. Heidelberg (Carl Winter).

Wehrli, F. 1974. *Die Schule des Aristoteles: Suppl. Bd. 1: Hermippos der Kallimacheer.* Basel (Schwabe).

Weiler, I. 1968. "Greek and Non-Greek in the Archaic Period." *Greek, Roman and Byzantine Studies* 9: 21–9.

Werner, J. 1991. "Das Lesbische als barbarische Sprache?" *Philologus* 135: 55–62.

West, M.L. 1987. *Orestes: Euripides*. Warminster (Aris & Phillips).

Will, E. 1956. *Doriens et Ioniens: Essai sur la valeur du critère ethnique appliqué à l'étude de l'histoire et de la civilisation grecques*. Paris (Les Belles Lettres).

———. 1995. "SYNGENEIA, OIKEIOTÈS, PHILIA." *Revue de Philologie* 69: 299–325.

Willi, A. 2002. "Languages on Stage: Aristophanic Language, Cultural History, and Athenian Identity." In Willi, A., ed., *The Language of Greek Comedy*. Oxford (Oxford University Press), 111–49.

———. 2003. *The Languages of Aristophanes: Aspects of Linguistic Variation in Classical Attic Greek*. Oxford (Oxford University Press).

Willink, C.W. 1986. *Orestes*. Oxford (Clarendon Press).

Zacharia, K. 2008. "Herodotus' Four Markers of Greek Identity." In Zacharia, K., ed., *Hellenisms: Culture, Identity, and Ethnicity from Antiquity to Modernity*. Aldershot (Ashgate).

3 Protocols of ethnic specification in Herodotus

Brian Hill

Herodotus often employs a particular and idiosyncratic vocabulary in his ethnographic inquiries in the *Histories*. In this chapter, my focus will be Herodotean ethnic vocabulary, specifically the terms ἔθνος and γένος, and therein we shall explore the different ways in which Herodotus employs this terminology. These words have already been discussed by Weil 1960[1] and Jones 1996,[2] but our understanding of Herodotus' particular and idiosyncratic deployment of these terms requires in my view still further refinement. The words ἔθνος and γένος form a crucial element of Herodotean vocabulary about identity in so far as they appear to take on a rather specialized meaning in Herodotus *vis-à-vis* the words' more general definitions as 'people' and 'stock', respectively, in other Greek authors.[3] In order to cast the specifically Herodotean usages of these words into sharper relief, we will examine here those instances in the *Histories* when ἔθνος and γένος appear in close connection and textual proximity to one another. As such, this chapter undertakes to analyze the specifically Herodotean flavour of the ethnic terminology used in differentiating the meanings of ἔθνος and γένος in the *Histories*, supporting many of the claims proposed by Jones 1996 while also nuancing and extending his arguments.

An appropriate beginning for our discussion of Herodotus' vocabulary of ethnic specification will be to examine the first instances in the *Histories* where each of these terms occurs. Herodotus first makes mention of the word ἔθνος quite early, when he describes the Persians' perception of their domain at 1.4.4:

> τὴν γὰρ Ἀσίην καὶ τὰ ἐνοικέοντα ἔθνεα βάρβαρα οἰκηιεῦνται οἱ Πέρσαι, τὴν δὲ Εὐρώπην καὶ τὸ Ἑλληνικὸν ἥγηνται κεχωρίσθαι.
>
> The Persians claim Asia and the foreign peoples dwelling there as their own; Europe and that which is Greek they consider to be separate from them.[4]

A few important points are raised in this brief but illustrative statement. First, Herodotus thrusts the reader out of the past and into the present when discussing ἔθνεα in this passage. The Persians' attitude toward the ἔθνεα of Asia stretches into the present day, as Herodotus indicates with his use of the present-tense verb οἰκηιεῦνται. The present tense stands out after the preceding narrative of past wrongdoing and blame-counting between the Greek and Persian sides. The main verbs of the independent clauses that precede this section likewise emphasize the historian's present. The reader naturally assumes a present-tense verb such as ἐστί *vel sim.* in the *sphragis* that forms the first sentence of the work, and in addition the discourse remains rooted in the present even as Herodotus guides his reader through the events and accusations of the past: the learned among the Persians today (νυν) assert (φασὶ) that the culpability lies with the Phoenicians at 1.1.1. Likewise, Herodotus proceeds to relate the Persians' account in indirect discourse until he returns to finite verbs at 1.2.1 and restores his reader to the present tense: the Persians say (λέγουσι) that the account under narration constituted the first wrongdoing between the two sides, and they aver (φασὶ) that some Greeks kid-napped Europa, daughter of the king; even the optative εἴησαν (1.2.1) keeps the finite verbs of the account fixed within the present. Again at 1.3.1 Herodotus rein-forces the present-day nature of relating of these tales by noting that the Persians say (λέγουσι) what will follow. And, finally, at 1.4.4 we once more emerge from indirect discourse regarding past events and return to Herodotus' own day for the main verb, when the Persians claim for their own the peoples living in Asia at that time (οἰκηιεῦνται). For all the relating of past events being conducted here, nev-ertheless these verbal cues continue to remind Herodotus' contemporaries of the implication that these accounts are not only all being relayed in the present day, but their implications also play out in the present. The Persians in question are very much the Persians of the present moment, not those of the distant past. This temporal component is important to emphasize even in this early employment of the word ἔθνος.

McInerney (1999) has suggested that the term ἔθνος may allow for a purposeful vagueness in its application, at least in certain authors. In Thucydides, for instance, McInerney notes that the word was employed to refer to 'more than just marginal, frontier tribes'. As contact between Greeks and non-Greeks increased, *ethnos* served as a conveniently loose label equivalent to the vague English term 'people' (1999: 23). While such nonspecific usage may well hold true for the application of the word ἔθνος in Greek writers more generally, I suggest that Herodotus in particular maintains a specialized meaning of the word that is activated by the very temporal markers outlined by Jones 1996. However, in contrast to Jones, I would assert that ἔθνος stands as a specific temporal subset of γένος: Herodotus uses the term ἔθνος when referring to a group in a particular time period or generation and employs γένος when considering the ways in which a people's lineage stretches through time. Again, however, just as we must be cautious before taking the famous for-mulation of τὸ Ἑλληνικὸν at 8.144.2 as a final and singularly authoritative articula-tion of what our author must unequivocally understand Greek identity to constitute, likewise we must remain cognizant of the particular context in which Herodotus situates this vocabulary.[5] In this famous passage, for example, it is important to con-sider that these words are put in the mouths of Athenians who aim to demonstrate to Alexander and the Spartan envoys not only the tight bond that they, the Atheni-ans, share with other Hellenes, but also the Athenians' singular position as histori-cal leaders of the Greeks and thereby their distinct status even within that broader grouping of notional continuity or identity. Consequently, and unsurprisingly, this passage must not be interpreted as a statement of fact from our author, but rather it ought to be understood as being refracted through several narratological lenses. It is the Athenians who constitute the party issuing this determinative proclamation, and so Herodotus may indeed be attaching a certain amount of commentary to the designs of his own Athenian contemporaries on leadership in a way that colours his articulation of what these Athenian representatives define as τὸ Ἑλληνικὸν before Alexander and the Spartans.

To return to *Histories* 1.4, let us also be attentive to the fact that here we are similarly taking the perspective of another party, here the Persians, and must consider the effect on the narrative by the imposition on it of such framing. According to Herodotus, the Persians indeed claim Asia's ἔθνεα for their own, and here Herodotus employs the noun ἔθνος in a specific way, whatever the surrounding modifiers may owe to the perspective of the Persians. I follow Jones' assessment that "Herodotus uses ethnos in a very restricted way, and practically every case can be translated 'people' or 'nation'" (1996: 316). I am also quite in agreement with Jones that ἔθνος constitutes a more narrowly defined entity than that which is indicated by γένος; however, I disagree regarding the nature of the relationship between the specificity inherent in Herodotus' use of ἔθνος and the broader, intergenerational signification of γένος. Jones sees no taxonomic relation between the two terms. I maintain, however, that Herodotus regularly presents these words in just such a dynamic within the *Histories*. In addition to the roles Herodotus' vocabulary plays with respect to intension or focalization, these terms also signify different temporal preoccupations. To propose a crude analogy – and one that draws on an evidently obsolescent technology – we might imagine a series of cylindrical towers of CDs. Each CD tower stands for a particular γένος stretching vertically through multiple generations. A horizontal disc or discs within that vertical stack, and others at the same height in any adjacent CD stacks, represents a given ἔθνος at a certain point in time within the histories of those bloodlines. That is to say, I would classify ἔθνος as a synchronic excerpt of a diachronic γένος or γένεα. For Herodotus, ἔθνος can signify a people within a bounded span of time; γένος imports notions of ancestry into the narrative. Jones 1996 prefers to understand the meanings of these words in terms of intension rather than taxonomy. Intension certainly plays a crucial role, but a mutual taxonomy asserts itself as well: for Herodotus, an ἔθνος can be made up of various γένεα (e.g., the topmost CD on any of six adjacent CD towers), and a γένος can contain any number of temporally-specified ἔθνεα within it (a single vertical tower comprised of many stacked CDs). Let us turn to examples of this complex and idiosyncratic usage in Herodotus for further investigation.

The first occurrence of the word γένος in the *Histories*, not long after Herodotus' first use of ἔθνος in the work, sheds light on this distinction. At 1.6.1, Herodotus offers his description of Croesus, the first man, as far as can be reckoned, to have subjugated Greeks:

Κροῖσος ἦν Λυδὸς μὲν **γένος**, παῖς δὲ Ἀλυάττεω, τύραννος δὲ **ἐθνέων** τῶν ἐντὸς Ἅλυος ποταμοῦ, ὃς ῥέων ἀπὸ μεσαμβρίης μεταξὺ Συρίων τε καὶ

Παφλαγόνων ἐξιεῖ πρὸς βορέην ἄνεμον ἐς τὸν Εὔξεινον καλεόμενον πόντον. οὗτος ὁ Κροῖσος βαρβάρων πρῶτος τῶν ἡμεῖς ἴδμεν τοὺς μὲν κατεστρέψατο Ἑλλήνων ἐς φόρου ἀπαγωγήν, τοὺς δὲ φίλους προσεποιήσατο.

Croesus was Lydian by birth, son of Alyattes, sovereign over those peoples within the river Halys, which, flowing from the south between the Syrians and the Paphlagonians, goes out toward the northern wind into the sea called the Euxine. This Croesus was the first of the foreigners of whom we know who subdued some of the Greeks into payment of tribute and added others of them as allies.

We will examine this passage more fully in what follows, but at this initial juncture it is important to note that Herodotus' use of γένος in this account illustrates the typical association of this word with lineage or historical background. Croesus was Lydian "by birth," where γένος indicates his "descent-group".[6] And while Herodotus employs γένος in service of a variety of different functions in the *Histories* (including the accusative of respect, as here), the abundance of applications of this word with regard to lineage owes much to its root relation to γίγνομαι.[7] In many ways this first occurrence of γένος lays the foundation for the use of this word in Herodotus: this term signals a consideration of lineage and an intergenerational backdrop, in contradistinction to the narrower frame suggested by ἔθνος.

In order to gain a clearer understanding of the semantic differences between ἔθνος and γένος in their idiosyncratic usage in Herodotus, let us turn our attention to those passages in which these words occur in close proximity to one another in order to cast their separate meanings into sharper relief.[8] At 1.56–9 we can begin to see these subtle differences at work. This passage details Croesus' investigation into the might of the Greeks at the time when he was looking to join into an alliance with whichever Greek people proved to be the most attractive ally. As Jones 1996: 317 points out, the word γένος occurs only at the outset of Croesus' inquiry; afterward in this discussion the operative word becomes ἔθνος. What might this lexical shift suggest? The initial employment of the word γένος clearly makes reference to the Spartans' and Athenians' heritage or bloodline:

ἱστορέων δὲ εὕρισκε Λακεδαιμονίους καὶ Ἀθηναίους προέχοντας τοὺς μὲν τοῦ Δωρικοῦ **γένεος** τοὺς δὲ τοῦ Ἰωνικοῦ.

By inquiry he discovered that the Lacedaemonians and the Athenians were foremost, the one being of Doric stock, the other of Ionic.

This emphasis on lineage, however, gives way to considerations of a people of a particular epoch, as reflected in the narrative and in the historian's switch from γένος to ἔθνος. Herodotus adds immediately thereafter:

ταῦτα γὰρ ἦν τὰ προκεκριμένα, ἐόντα τὸ ἀρχαῖον τὸ μὲν Πελασγικὸν τὸ δὲ Ἑλληνικὸν**ἔθνος**.

For these were the distinguished entities, being, in antiquity, the one a Pelasgian and the other a Hellenic people.

The phrase τὸ ἀρχαῖον situates these peoples in the distant past, tying them to a particular historical moment.[9] The period in question is not otherwise qualified, and yet the mere act of associating the peoples in question with a given moment in time, albeit apparently nonspecific it may seem, assigns those peoples to a notional chapter in history. Accordingly, Herodotus' use of the term ἔθνος instead of the word γένος, which he employed directly beforehand, suggests more than idle *variatio* on the part of the historian and it reflects, rather, the subtle shades of meaning appropriate to each of these terms. Similarly, the subsequent instances of ethnic specification in this passage refer to "peoples (Pelasgians, Hellenes, Spartans, Athenians) as language-groups, as ones that 'split off' or 'joined' others".[10] The line is now broken; Herodotus shows us not a continuum of one γένος through time but of several disparate ἔθνεα that branched off at one stage and which thus constitute a discrete break in the chain, notionally delimited by a particular historical moment. The focus on language and on offshoots from a main line demonstrates these subtle shifts in the vocabulary of ethnic specification.

A similar differentiation motivates the historian's alternation from one term to the other at 1.101, where Herodotus describes first a people of a particular period and then a series of peoples identified by their heritage:

Δηιόκης μέν νυν τὸ Μηδικὸν **ἔθνος** συνέστρεψε μοῦνον καὶ τούτου ἦρξε· ἔστι δὲ Μήδων τοσάδε **γένεα**, Βοῦσαι Παρητακηνοὶ Στρούχατες Ἀριζαντοὶ Βούδιοι Μάγοι. **γένεα** μὲν δὴ Μήδων ἐστὶ τοσάδε.

Deiokes then gathered together the Median people alone and ruled over it; the tribes of the Medes are as many as the following: Busai, Paretakeni, Stroukhates, Arizantoi, Budioi, Magoi. So many are the tribes of the Medes.

Herodotus' preoccupation with identifying each of the six tribes in the latter portion of this statement aligns with the notion that the lineage of these tribes extends through time; as Jones points out, these are clearly "hereditary" groups (Jones 1996: 318), and thus they are properly understood as γένεα. In the earlier part of the passage, by contrast, Herodotus uses the term ἔθνος because there the historian is describing the population of a particular moment in time, namely that of Deiokes' day, as indicated by the adverb νυν. So far, then, the aforementioned schema appears straightforward and consistent in its application. How do we explain its function in more complicated deployments?

An illustrative example occurs at 7.185.2, where Herodotus lists the sources of the hundreds of thousands of soldiers in Xerxes' army provided from populations of Europe. Interestingly, the historian names the various peoples who provided troops, and his use of the noun ἔθνεα (τούτων τῶν ἐθνέων, #of these peoples") suits this reference to the peoples of a particular period, namely the buildup to Thermopylai. However, within his litany of demonyms constituting Xerxes' massive force (Παίονες καὶ Ἐορδοὶ καὶ Βοττιαῖοι, "Paeonians and Eordoi and Bottiaioi", among several others), Herodotus diverges from simple adjectival classification when he describes the Khalkidians with the phrase τὸ Χαλκιδικὸν γένος, "the Khalkidian race". This pivot again raises the question of signification, and the historian seems to be emphasizing the historical lineage of this people when he uses this phraseology.[11] Further, I would suggest that Herodotus not only reminds the reader of this people's descent but likewise points to the Khalkidians' longstanding tradition as a people of militaristic stock, highlighting their history through this pointed word choice. Indeed, as Hammond 1995 points out, "'the Chalcidian race' was called on for infantry only. It was therefore a military power", and this characterization may likewise draw on their contentious history with the colonists who "expelled or subjugated those of the Chalcidian race who were in occupation of the best harbour sites on the Chalcidic peninsula. Thereafter there must have been conflicts between them."[12] That is, the Khalkidians could hardly be called a naval people given their history, and Herodotus' use of γένος recalls their longstanding reputation as infantry forces.

Similar concerns motivate Herodotus' phraseology at 8.43–8 during his catalogue of the Greek naval forces readied at Salamis. I include the relevant selections here:

(8.43)   Σικυώνιοι δὲ πεντεκαίδεκα παρείχοντο νέας, Ἐπιδαύριοι δὲ δέκα, Τροιζήνιοι δὲ πέντε, Ἑρμιονέες δὲ τρεῖς, ἐόντες οὗτοι πλὴν Ἑρμιονέων Δωρικόν τε καὶ Μακεδνὸν **ἔθνος**, ἐξ Ἐρινεοῦ τε καὶ Πίνδου καὶ τῆς Δρυοπίδος ὕστατα ὁρμηθέντες. . .

(8.45)   . . . Ἀμπρακιῶται δὲ ἑπτὰ νέας ἔχοντες ἐπεβοήθησαν, Λευκάδιοι δὲ τρεῖς, **ἔθνος** ἐόντες οὗτοι Δωρικὸν ἀπὸ Κορίνθου. . .

(8.46)   μετὰ δὲ Κήιοι τὰς αὐτὰς παρεχόμενοι, **ἔθνος** ἐὸν Ἰωνικὸν ἀπὸ Ἀθηνέων. . .

(8.47)   Κροτωνιῆται δὲ **γένος** εἰσὶ Ἀχαιοί. . .

(8.48)   Μήλιοι μὲν **γένος** ἐόντες ἀπὸ Λακεδαίμονος δύο παρείχοντο. . .

(8.43)   The Sikyonians provided fifteen ships, the Epidaurians ten, the Troizenians five, and the Hermionians three, being, apart from the Hermionians, a Dorian and Macedonian people, driven most recently from Erineus and Pindos and the land of Dryopis. . .

(8.45)   . . . the Ambrakiots assisted by bringing seven ships, and the Leukadians three, being a Doric people from Corinth. . .

(8.46)   After that were the Keans, providing the same number of ships, being an Ionic people from Athens. . .

(8.47)   The Krotoniates are Achaean by lineage. . .

(8.48)   . . . the Melians, being from Lakedaimon by lineage, provided two. . .

Here the terms recur in close proximity, shedding further light on their subtle differences in Herodotus. The final two excerpts employ γένος in the familiar construction of the accusative of respect ("in lineage", "with respect to lineage"), and consequently their meaning is easily grasped. Yet, as Jones 1996: 319 notes in regard to the preceding expressions that employ ἔθνος, "it is harder to explain the two phrases in which ἔθνος is accompanied by a prepositional phrase". Namely, Herodotus uses the word ἔθνος to describe the Sikyonians, Epidaurians, and Troizenians as a collectively Dorian and Macedonian people; he dubs the Leukadians a Doric ἔθνος; and the Keans he calls an Attic ἔθνος. We might otherwise be tempted to treat the word ἔθνος as being interchangeable with γένος in these sentences, particularly if we consider the ethnic ties which likely helped to motivate these groups to participate to the Greek effort. While that is no doubt the case, the temporal valence of Herodotus' usage of ἔθνος serves to focus the reader on the population providing ships at Salamis at this particular historical juncture; hence his use of ἔθνος rather than γένος. By contrast, the historian employs γένος in those statements that are meant to recall the long heritage of the people in question, just as he does in the case of the Krotoniates (8.47). What, precisely, was the Krotoniates' claim to fame? At 3.131.2, Herodotus describes Croton's reputation as doctors owing to the work of Demokedes (καὶ ἀπὸ τούτου τοῦ ἀνδρὸς οὐκ ἥκιστα Κροτωνιῆται ἰητροὶ εὐδοκίμησαν, "and it was not least from this man that the Crotoniates were renowned as healers"). The Krotoniates' good name (εὐδοκίμησαν) precedes them.[13] The historian's praise for the people of Croton is made quite clear when he points out their willingness to stand with the Greeks at Salamis despite the distance from Italy: τῶν δὲ ἐκτὸς τούτων οἰκημένων Κροτωνιῆται μοῦνοι ἦσαν οἳ ἐβοήθησαν τῇ Ἑλλάδι κινδυνευούσῃ μιῇ νηί, τῆς ἦρχε ἀνὴρ τρὶς πυθιονίκης Φάυλλος ("of those dwelling beyond these people, the Krotoniates were the only ones who gave aid to Hellas in her venture by providing one ship, headed by Phaullos, a man with three victories at the Pythian Games"). By recalling their heritage with the word γένος Herodotus offers more full-throated praise for the Krotoniates.

Likewise, Herodotus' reference to the Melians' Lacedaemonian lineage emphasizes their historical reputation. This passage includes the only express mention of the Melians in the *Histories*; however, references to the Lacedaemonians and their famously warlike attitude are of course peppered throughout the work. A preoccupation with descent is not out of place in a Spartan setting. Earlier,[14] Herodotus traces Leonidas' descendance from Heracles by naming every individual forefather in the intervening generations.[15] The combination of Lacedaimonian military prowess, regularly alluded to in the *Histories*, coupled with Herodotus' concern for tracing heritage with particular care in a Spartan setting, neatly illustrates the historian's care in demonstrating a longstanding Lacedaimonian military pedigree. Using the word γένος allows Herodotus to subtly and succinctly import the Melians' storied legacy into this catalogue of Greek forces at Salamis.

Other collocations of ἔθνος and γένος prove similarly illustrative. We may here return to 1.6.1, that passage briefly adduced earlier as the first appearance of γένος in the *Histories*. The word γένος in this passage is followed in close order by ἔθνος. Applying the distinction between these two words allows us to understand the subtleties of this word choice. At this point in the *Histories*, at the very outset of the enterprise, Herodotus has just been musing on the fickle nature of human prosperity. In effect, the historian tells us that he will offer a simultaneously synchronic and diachronic account, remarking that once-great communities have since fallen to ruin, and, likewise, previously minor entities have subsequently risen to prominence (1.5.3–4). This gnomic statement even correlates well with Herodotus' vocabulary: the historian remains sensitive both to snapshots of a given people at a given time (i.e., how an ἔθνος behaves in a particular historical moment) and to the broader historical trajectory of a people (i.e., the manifestations of a γένος over long stretches of time).

Following upon this gnomic rumination, then, the excerpt at 1.6.1 is informed by this appreciation of diachrony and synchrony, and Herodotus layers his vocabulary into this same overarching schema. Croesus is described as being Lydian in γένος, and thus we focus on his lineage. And while the word γένος suggests a reach back into Croesus' familial past, the ἔθνεα over which Croesus exercises control offer a snapshot of the peoples he rules at the moment of the story's first unfolding, the peoples over which Croesus ruled at that particular time. In this account, Herodotus gently guides us from familial past to immediate paternal background, and then to contemporaneous rule, all with the subtle tone changes of specific vocabulary such as ἔθνος and γένος to mark the transitions. Even the particles μὲν and δὲ sustain a narrative thrust which likewise juxtaposes different aspects of Croesus' identification. These particles possess an adversative touch contrasting his past with his present, his familial history with his status as ruler within the scope of the narrative.[16] This early pairing of ἔθνος and γένος thus bridges past and present to activate different elements of Croesus' story in an immediately appreciable fashion even on a lexical level.

Consider, too, 1.143.2, amid Herodotus' description of the Greeks of Asia Minor. I would suggest that a mutually taxonomic understanding of the terms ἔθνος and γένος asserts itself here as well, whereby the ἔθνεα of a particular time period stand as the specific strata of various γένεα, and any particular level of a γένος can be called an ἔθνος. Again, it is on this point that I differ emphatically from the classification proposed by Jones 1996, since Jones prefers to avoid assigning any taxonomic relationship to the two terms. Now, at the same time, intension is surely at play in such a usage as well; that is, characterizing the Hellenic race as a γένος is acceptable here precisely because Herodotus focusses on the features of this group's genetic continuity, the features that are thought to be tied to a specific bloodline. Then, once Herodotus establishes this legacy-minded characterization and suggests the Hellenes' identity has something to do with familial ties, at that point the historian deploys the word τότε to indicate that the Ionic people was "at that time" by far the weakest of the various ἔθνεα then populating the area. The important distinction to draw is that γένος evokes the extended pillar of previous Hellenic heredity up to that point in time, a designation that is then brought to bear among the contemporary ἔθνεα described in the narrative. A Herodotean ἔθνος thus again relies on temporal placement within the longer line of history behind a given γένος.

Accordingly, Herodotus also nods toward chronological concerns at 3.67–8. The peoples of Asia are properly referred to as ἔθνεα when they are envisioned as the populations governed briefly by Smerdis the *magos*. Indeed, the temporal markers of this scene serve to foreground the concern with a particular historical moment. The peoples in question are the subject states of Smerdis for a period specified as seven months (μῆνας ἑπτὰ) and the edicts of that era are expressly tied to their historical context as well (διαπέμψας γὰρ ὁ Μάγος ἐς πᾶν ἔθνος τῶν ἦρχε προεῖπε ἀτελείην εἶναι στρατηίης καὶ φόρου ἐπ᾽ ἔτεα τρία. "For the *Magos*, sending word to every people of those over whom he ruled, declared that there was an exemption from military service and tribute for three years" [3.67]). By contrast, γένος, which occurs not long after ἔθνος in this passage, is employed as a dative of respect here, performing in shorthand its familiar function as intergenerational designation. Indeed, the very placement of the word is important in this sentence, as γένος occurs immediately after Herodotus introduces Otanes by his patronymic. As such, the historian evokes the concept of Otanes' bloodline even at the level of phraseology when identifying Otanes in the narrative.

The protocols that we have witnessed are fully on display at 4.46, where Herodotus refers to the Scythians first as an ἔθνος and then as a γένος. Again, it is possible to show how this lexical shift suggests more than mere *variatio*. At first the historian describes the populations on the Black Sea, and this account clearly includes the Black Sea denizens of Herodotus' day, as the tenses of the verbs make clear. As such, the temporally-specific designation of ἔθνος is appropriate in the first part of this passage:

Ὁ δὲ Πόντος ὁ Εὔξεινος, ἐπ᾽ ὃν ἐστρατεύετο ὁ Δαρεῖος, χωρέων πασέων παρέχεται ἔξω τοῦ Σκυθικοῦ **ἔθνεα** ἀμαθέστατα. οὔτε γὰρ **ἔθνος** τῶν ἐντὸς τοῦ Πόντου οὐδὲν ἔχομεν προβαλέσθαι σοφίης πέρι οὔτε ἄνδρα λόγιον οἴδαμεν γενόμενον, πάρεξ τοῦ Σκυθικοῦ **ἔθνεος** καὶ Ἀναχάρσιος.

Of all places, the sea called Euxine, against which region Darius campaigned, offers, outside of the Scythian body, the most unlearned peoples. For neither can we propose a people, of those in the Black Sea region, that comes close to wisdom, nor do we know of any intelligent man produced there, aside from the Scythian people and Anacharsis.

Herodotus is describing the inhabitants of the Black Sea region who are his contemporaries, as we plainly observe in παρέχεται, ἔχομεν, and the present-tense force of the formally perfect οἴδαμεν. The word ἔθνος, then, again denoting a particular period of time, suits the context. However, the very next sentence sees the historian take a new direction:

τῷ δὲ Σκυθικῷ **γένεϊ** ἓν μὲν τὸ μέγιστον τῶν ἀνθρωπηίων πρηγμάτων σοφώτατα πάντων ἐξεύρηται τῶν ἡμεῖς ἴδμεν, τὰ μέντοι ἄλλα οὐκ ἄγαμαι.

Now, among the Scythian race the single greatest of all mortal affairs of which we know has been most wisely discovered, though I do not admire them with regard to other matters.

Herodotus has switched from the noun ἔθνος to the noun γένος; why? I propose that the historian's use of γένος here emphasizes the intergenerational nature of the "discovery" that Herodotus credits to the Scythians. Their means of protection against potential attackers strikes Herodotus as ingenious, and their reputation for this technique is clearly a time-honoured technique honed over generations, and no invention of any single creator of Herodotus' day. The historian's praise for the Scythians' defensive discovery reaches backward into time immemorial, and, as such, his phraseology reflects his emphasis on their heritage. The nomadic lifestyle of the Scythians stretches across time in a continuous and far-reaching manner, such that Herodotus can comfortably employ the term γένος here in reference to a longstanding cultural practice that reaches from the past to the present. In this light, then, we can appreciate that Herodotus uses the term ἔθνος to describe his contemporary Scythians, whereas the Scythian γένος constitutes the historical populace across time.

As we have noticed in the foregoing discussion, then, Herodotus employs the terms ἔθνος and γένος in a particular and idiosyncratic fashion, and the two, while related, are not wholly synonymous. The historian employs ἔθνος when highlighting a populace of a particular time period, whereas γένος in the *Histories* emphasizes legacy and bloodline across generations. In addition, *pace* Jones 1996, I find that Herodotus' use of ἔθνος indeed functions not only for intension but also taxonomically, suggesting a substratum of a broader γένος or γένεα. What, then, does this specification offer us in reading the *Histories*? Are we merely constructing a distinction without a difference? I would suggest that our attempt to disentangle the strands of ἔθνος and γένος in the complex web of Herodotus' *Histories* allows us to see the historian's language of ethnic specification with a degree of focus and clarity. Ultimately Herodotus remains true to his promise as laid out at the opening of the work: in carefully distinguishing between synchronic ἔθνεα and diachronic γένεα, Herodotus succeeds in offering us an account that demonstrates not only the scatter-plot points of a specific people's affairs, but also gives us a sense of the larger historical arc that they trace. By applying this lens to the *Histories*, we can appreciate more fully the nuanced precision with which Herodotus presents his many and varied ethnographic inquiries.

Notes

1 Weil 1960: 385: "Hérodote définit mal l'‘ethnos'. C'est pour lui tantôt une subdivision du ‘génos', tantôt au contraire un ensemble de ‘génè.'"
2 Jones 1996: 315: Herodotus' "distinction between the two words is not taxonomic, but instead is to be explained by linguistic ‘intension': that is, his choice of one or the other is determined not only by the object referred to or ‘referent' (‘extension') but by the way he wishes to present them (‘intension')."
3 In Thucydides, for instance, Morris 1891 actually finds the terms ἔθνος and γένος to be interchangeable at 1.24.2, 4.61.14, 7.27.2, and 7.29.23. See also Fragoulaki 2013 for a more detailed look at specific Thucydidean ethnic terminology, including ἔθνος and γένος. Cf. also Johansen 1998: 199 on the terms' distinctions in Plato. For a discussion of the hierarchical (or non-hierarchical) use of ἔθνος in Paul, see Wan 2000 as well as Buell & Johnson Hodge 2004.
4 All translations my own.
5 See Konstan 2001 and Munson 2014 for a detailed discussion of this passage. Also Figueira pp. 43–6.
6 Jones 1996: 317.
7 See Blanc & de Lamberterie 2015: 128–30 for recent remarks on the etymological connection between these words.
8 A number of these passages have been discussed in Jones 1996, but I shall also add illustrative examples omitted in that study.

9 As Rijksbaron 2006 and de la Villa 2013 demonstrate, temporal adverbs paired with the definite article (*vis-à-vis* temporal adverbs without the article) suggest that the time period in question is specifically delimited.

10 Jones 1996: 318.

11 Thus Jones 1996: 318–19: "There must be a reason why Herodotus designates the Chalcidians settled in Thrace, whom elsewhere he calls Χαλκιδέες (8.127), as 'the Chalcidic tribe' in this list of ἔθνεα. What distinguishes them from the others is that they are colonists who take their name from a parent-group, the Chalcidians of Euboea."

12 Hammond 1995: 309.

13 On Herodotus' praise for (and 'amusement' by) Demokedes' machinations, see Lateiner 1990: 232. For a discussion of Herodotus' admiration of physicians and his use of medical sources in the *Histories*, see, e.g., Dawson & Harvey 1986 and Raaflaub 2002: 161–4.

14 Hdt. 7.204: Τούτοισι ἦσαν μέν νυν καὶ ἄλλοι στρατηγοὶ κατὰ πόλιας ἑκάστων, ὁ δὲ θωμαζόμενος μάλιστα καὶ παντὸς τοῦ στρατεύματος ἡγεόμενος Λακεδαιμόνιος ἦν Λεωνίδης ὁ Ἀναξανδρίδεω τοῦ Λέοντος τοῦ Εὐρυκρατίδεω τοῦ Ἀναξάνδρου τοῦ Εὐρυκράτεος τοῦ Πολυδώρου τοῦ Ἀλκαμένεος τοῦ Τηλέκλου τοῦ Ἀρχέλεω τοῦ Ἡγησίλεω τοῦ Δορύσσου τοῦ Λεωβώτεω τοῦ Ἐχεστράτου τοῦ Ἤγιος τοῦ Εὐρυσθένεος τοῦ Ἀριστοδήμου τοῦ Ἀριστομάχου τοῦ Κλεοδαίου τοῦ Ὕλλου τοῦ Ἡρακλέος, κτησάμενος τὴν βασιληίην ἐν Σπάρτῃ ἐξ ἀπροσδοκήτου. "At that time they all had different generals in each of their cities, but the most admired and the one leading the entire army was Leonidas the Lacedaimonian, descendant of Anaxandrides, Leon, Eurykratides, Anaxandros, Eurykrates, Polydoros, Alkamenes, Teleclos, Arkhelaos, Hegesilaos, Doryssos, Leobates, Ekhestratos, Agis, Eurysthenes, Aristodemos, Aristomachos, Kleodaios, Hyllos, and Herakles; he held the kingship in Sparta without having sought it out."

15 Cf. Hdt. 8.131.2 on the lineage of the Spartan king/admiral Leotykhidas for a comparably lengthy aside, again regarding specifically Lacedaimonian genealogy.

16 Cf. Bentein 2016: 39 on the subtle contrasts of intension which Herodotus can signal with verbal forms, as well as with μέν . . . δέ constructions.

Bibliography

Bentein, K. 2016. "Aspectual Choice and the Presentation of Narrative: An Application to Herodotus' *Histories*." *Glotta* 92: 24–55.

Blanc, A. & de Lamberterie, C. 2015. "Chronique d'étymologie grecque N° 15 (*CEG* 2016)." *Revue de Philologie* 89.2: 117–72.

Buell, D.K. & Johnson Hodge, C. 2004. "The Politics of Interpretation: The Rhetoric of Race and Ethnicity in Paul." *Journal of Biblical Literature* 123.2: 235–51.

Dawson, W.R. 1986. "Herodotus as a Medical Writer." With Notes by F.D. Harvey. *Bulletin of the Institute of Classical Studies* 33: 87–96.

de la Villa, J. 2013. "Πάλαι/τὸ πάλαι, πρίν/τὸ πρίν, παραχρῆμα/τὸ παραχρῆμα." *Glossa* 89: 222–41.

Fragoulaki, M. 2013. *Kinship in Thucydides: Intercommunal Ties and Historical Narrative*. Oxford (Oxford University Press).

Hammond, N.G.L. 1995. "The Chalcidians and 'Apollonia of the Thraceward Ionians.'" *Annual of the British School at Athens* 90: 307–15.

Johansen, T.K. 1998. "Truth, Lies and History in Plato's 'Timaeus-Critias'." *Histos* 2: 192–215.

Jones, C.P. 1996. "ἔθνος and γένος in Herodotus." *Classical Quarterly* 46.2: 315–20.

Konstan, D. 2001. "'To Hellēnikon ethnos': Ethnicity and the Construction of Ancient Greek Identity." In Malkin, I., ed., *Ancient Perceptions of Greek Ethnicity*. Cambridge, MA (Harvard University Press), 29–50.

Lateiner, D. 1990. "Deceptions and Delusions in Herodotus." *Classical Antiquity* 9.2: 230–46.

McInerney, J. 1999. *The Folds of Parnassos: Land and Ethnicity in Ancient Phokis*. Austin, TX (University of Texas Press).

Morris, C.D. 1891. *Commentary on Thucydides Book 1*. Boston, MA (Ginn & Company).

Munson, R.V. 2014. "Herodotus and Ethnicity." In McInerney, J., ed., *A Companion to Ethnicity in the Ancient Mediterranean*. Malden, MA & Oxford (Wiley-Blackwell), 341–55.

Raaflaub, K.A. 2002. "Philosophy, Science, Politics: Herodotus and the Intellectual Trends of His Time." In Bakker, E.J., de Jong, I.J.F., & van Wees, H., eds., *Brill's Companion to Herodotus*. Leiden (Brill), 149–86.

Rijksbaron, A. 2006. "The Meaning and Word Class of πρότερον and τὸ πρότερον." In Crespo, E., de la Villa, J., & Revuelta, A.R., eds., *Word Classes and Related Topics in Ancient Greek*. Leuven (Peeters), 441–54.

Wan, S. 2000. "Collection for the Saints as an Anti-Colonial Act: Implications of Paul's Ethnic Reconstruction." In Horsley, R.A., ed., *Paul and Politics: Ekklesia, Israel, Imperium, Interpretation; Essays in Honor of Krister Stendahl*. Harrisburg, PN (Trinity Press International), 191–215.

Weil, R. 1960. *Aristote et l'Histoire. Études et Commentaires* 36. Paris (Klincksieck).

4   Emotion and ethnicity in Herodotus' *Histories*

Emily Allen-Hornblower

In Book III of his *Histories*, Herodotus presents us with a story that is intended to support his conviction that the Persian king Cambyses was raving mad. Clearly, he contends, the king was insane since he actually went into sanctuaries and desecrated them, ridiculing corpses and statues alike, and thus mocking both tradition and religion. No one but a madman goes against his own customs, which one inevitably considers to be the best in the world. Herodotus then famously provides the example of a conference that took place during Darius' reign, in which the Persian king is said to have brought together Greeks and Indians to inquire about their respective sources of disgust, fear, or horror.[1] The Persian first asks the Greeks how much money it would take for them to eat their fathers' corpses (no amount in the world would be enough). The Indian tribe (the Kallatiai), on the other hand, reply that they always *do* eat their parents and would not cremate them for all the riches in the world: in fact, they cry out in horror at the mere idea. This is the famous passage where Herodotus uses an Iranocentric perspective on two peoples living beyond the eastern and western borders of the Persian empire to declare that "*nomos* is king": they are both barbarians, and yet both highly civilized; they are also fundamentally different in culture.[2] This passage provides a good entryway to what I propose to examine in this chapter; it shows how much Herodotus (and, in this case, his internal observer, Darius) embraces the belief that emotional responses to certain stimuli, as well as the contexts and ways in which these emotions manifest themselves, are (to some extent at least) culturally relative and can be revealing, on a fundamental level, of the values and beliefs of a given individual, people, culture, or ethnic group.[3] Munson convincingly has shown in her work on the language of barbarians that there are different cultural or linguistic codes used in this dialogue, including a communicative code (how things are said, with expressions and gestures), and a code of customs.[4] I suggest that there is much to glean from instances in which cultural codes translate into displays of emotion, and that Herodotus' repeated stress on emotional displays (and others' perception of them) shows the extent to which he believed (or at any rate held his fellow Greeks to believe) these to be revealing of certain broader character traits and values defining the individual or group under scrutiny.[5]

The emotions in the classical world, as well as their place in the ancient works of ancient historians and historiography (be it the emotions of their characters, or those that they seek to elicit from their readers) have received a good amount of scholarly attention, including recently.[6] I propose to approach the question of the depiction of the emotions within Herodotus' *Histories* from a novel angle. In what follows, I offer an (inevitably brief and cursory) examination of a number of select scenes in which Herodotus depicts a few prominent characters' emotional responses (individual or collective) to a given situation or event. Specifically, I propose to look at those instances in which he depicts certain characters' judgments of and (often emotional) reactions to other characters' displays of emotion. The scenes of particular interest to the present inquiry are those in which representatives of one culture are shown in the process of observing another, and of evaluating, echoing, rejecting, or downright misunderstanding their (often, but not always, foreign or 'other') counterparts' emotional displays.

I wish to examine, then, not just Herodotean depictions of a given character, group, or people's emotions, but specifically how these emotions are evaluated by others observing them. In some cases, the character observing another's emotional display is of the same ethnicity as the one whose emotions are being watched and evaluated; of particular interest to me in what follows, however, are those cases in which they are not. At times, the observer is intradiegetic (that is, an internal observer from within the Herodotean narrative proper); sometimes, the observer is, more or less implicitly, Herodotus of Halikarnassos, *qua* Greek, observing, describing, and implicitly or explicitly judging and reacting to the characters whose emotional displays he has chosen to relay.

The question of the historicity and veracity of any of these emotional responses arises, as it does with any specific speech or isolated narrative detail that Herodotus mentions in his *Histories*.[7] I am not concerned in the present analysis with whether or not such and such a laugh or other sign of mirth, anger, fear, grief, or pity ever actually took place, nor am I seeking to determine whether such and such a figure ever actually had the opportunity to watch such another's reaction and evaluate it, and whether they ever did show or voice a response of their own.[8] The question I am focussing on, rather, is that of the broader narrative function these emotional displays – and others' reactions to them – fulfill within the greater arc of Herodotus' storytelling, by paying due attention to which emotional outbursts Herodotus attributes to whom; what reactions (he says) these responses prompt from others watching; and, as the case may be, how Herodotus himself views them.[9]

My principal interest here lies in the use of emotions as a narrative device, and especially as a tool for characterization. Herodotus resorts to the mention and description of the emotions not just to lend greater vividness or verisimilitude to his portrayals, but also to characterize a given figure or group in a particular manner.[10] I want to examine in particular one specific way in which Herodotus as narrator avails himself of the connection (whether implied or explicit) between emotion and *ethos* when he depicts his characters in the *Histories*, and the connections between *pathos, ethos,* and *ethnos* in particular. Emotions – how and when they are felt, and especially how they are processed – reflect a particular set of values and priorities (and this whether they are spontaneously and genuinely felt, or deliberately displayed or concealed).[11] They thus serve as a useful tool for characterizing certain individuals and the larger groups they represent.

The moment in which an emotion is displayed by a given figure is not just an opportunity to provide information that is ultimately central to the characterization of that figure; it is also an opportunity to characterize *others*, based on their reactions to the emotion of the character in question: whether they in turn show an emotional response, or voice or suggest what their judgment of that emotion is. Sometimes they misinterpret the emotion they see others display or misunderstand what motivates it; sometimes they simply react to it in a manner that is telling and worth examining in and of itself. In short, emotional displays are not just an opportunity for the historian to characterize those who feel the emotions, but also those who are watching and evaluating those responses in turn.

Comparative approaches and situations in which a representative or representatives of one group observe and assess another's emotions and actions provide fertile ground for voicing judgment (implicit or explicit) of a given individual, and of the political regime (say) or ruling style that this individual epitomizes. One particular group I consider here are those in positions of authority or, in shorthand, 'leaders'. In displaying the emotions of a given leader, Herodotus exposes their character and motivations, as well as the nature of their relationship to their subjects and other leaders. The characterization of individuals of a certain class or social and political category is an important part of the Herodotean means of portraying the socio-cultural and political systems to which these individuals belong or which, in the case of leaders, they represent.

The emotional reactions of leading figures are predicated on their conception of their own place and role within the society where they wield such power, and their conception of their own status and rights in relation to others, and to power and the law.[12] Thus, how a given character experiences and processes emotions that then translate into actions is a reflection of how they conceive of their power (or how Herodotus imagines them to), and directly influences how they wield it – very simply put, justly or not. In focussing on the emotional process and the actions taken in consequence of a given leading figure's emotion(s), Herodotus addresses his broader concern with what makes a given political regime functional, durable, and commendable – a question he explores largely by showing what does not.

That the emotions felt, decisions made, and actions taken by certain political leaders in the *Histories* reflect the internal dynamics and workings of a particular political system is made apparent and clearly stated in the constitutional debate of Book III in which Herodotus casts a Persian, Otanes, in the role of speaker for democracy.[13] In his speech, Otanes connects in no uncertain terms the political regime of monarchy with a specific emotion, *hubris*, which serves as a driving motivation for a despotic monarch's every decision and action (Hdt. 3.80.3):

κῶς δ᾽ ἂν εἴη χρῆμα κατηρτημένον μουναρχίη, τῇ ἔξεστι ἀνευθύνῳ ποιέειν τὰ βούλεται; καὶ γὰρ ἂν τὸν ἄριστον ἀνδρῶν πάντων στάντα ἐς ταύτην ἐκτὸς τῶν ἐωθότων νοημάτων στήσειε. ἐγγίνεται μὲν γάρ οἱ ὕβρις ὑπὸ τῶν παρεόντων ἀγαθῶν, φθόνος δὲ ἀρχῆθεν ἐμφύεται ἀνθρώπῳ.

How can monarchy be an orderly affair, when a monarch has the license to do whatever he wants, without being accountable to anyone? Make a man a monarch, and even if he is the most moral person in the world, he will leave his customary ways of thinking. All the advantages of his position breed arrogant abusiveness in him and envy is ingrained in human nature anyway.

Herodotus goes on to use Otanes as a mouthpiece for specifying monarchical traits that his subsequent stories illustrate repeatedly. A monarch is erratic and fickle, ἀναρμοστότατον δὲ πάντων; his emotions always end in anger, one way or the other.[14] This erratic fickleness, along with anger prompted inconsistently by opposite stimuli, is precisely what characterizes one of the worst if not the worst abuser of his monarchical powers in all of the *Histories*: the Persian Cambyses, as we will see in several examples that follow.

Fear

Hubris is a character trait often typical of a narrow group (usually) in authority. What of the emotions that are manifested in all humans? Take fear – an interesting emotion to consider in Herodotus, particularly in terms of how it is assumed by one group to be present or absent in another, sometimes wrongly and tellingly so. The assumption by one people or individual that another from a foreign or otherwise ethnically different group is experiencing or displaying a certain emotion is influenced by their own mindset. To that extent, a given people's reading of another's emotions tells us as much or perhaps more about the observer than it does about the observed. Fear is not prompted by the same stimuli in the same people for the same reasons nor in the same circumstances, and its presence or absence, as well as the wrongful assumption by one group of its presence or absence in another, is a useful tool that Herodotus uses to indicate certain character or cultural traits, not only (if at all) in those being watched, but rather in those making such assumptions. Let us turn to one particularly illustrative example: that of the outstanding courage of the Greeks in the face of hordes of invading non-Greeks.

In Book VII, the Persian king Xerxes is preparing to march against Greece, and sends for Demaratos, the deposed Spartan king, who now serves as his adviser. It is his hope that, because Demaratos is Greek, he might enlighten a Persian such as himself regarding the reactions and decisions of the Greeks as a group. The great King's question to the Spartan is simple: Will the Greeks stand against him? Will they resist?[15] After being reassured that Xerxes wants to hear the truth, and not just a comforting reply, Demaratos declares that the Greeks will face the Persians because of courage (*aretē*), intelligence (*sophia*), and the force of law (*nomos iskhuros*), driven by the desire to keep poverty and despotism at bay.[16] He restricts his assessment to those he knows best, and states with certainty that the Lacedaimonians will *not* give in before the threat of slavery, no matter how outnumbered they are. Xerxes laughs in disbelief.[17] This is noteworthy, because confrontation of the two camps depicted here has not actually been played out – it is merely an imagined scenario, and a fine example of how much Herodotus uses portrayals of Greek and barbarian imaginings, preconceptions, and misconceptions about their own people and others as a means of characterisation, all of which are at play here.[18]

The basis for Xerxes' disbelief is his misunderstanding of the sources and mechanics of fear in Lakedaimon. Demaratos pinpoints the misguided nature of that disbelief in his explanation. The fear Xerxes assumes must drive the Lacedaimonians' decisions is based on a Persian vision of what drives an army to fight, and is, hence, erroneous. The Persian ruler imagines the Greeks must feel great fear because they are so outnumbered; this assumption betrays a fundamental misunderstanding of his opponents' willingness to fight to the death, as well as an incapacity to fathom the Greeks' determination – one so fierce it can eliminate or overcome fearsome odds. The only fear that he imagines could motivate the Greeks to face their opponent at a ratio of a thousand to one would be "if they had a single leader in the Persian mold, for then fear of him might make them excel themselves . . . urged on by the whip".[19] In fact, Demaratos retorts, the Lacedaimonians are best at fighting in groups precisely because they are free: the only master they fear is the law.[20] Again Xerxes laughs. His ignorance and misunderstanding of the Greeks' respect for law and the communal good serve as a foil to the Greeks' exceptional behaviour, one that is due to the collaborative nature of their political and social organization. Emotional misevaluation serves as a benchmark for underscoring political disparities between Persia and Greece. The Persian ruler's incapacity to conceive of any other motivation for battle to the death in the face of unlikely odds than fear of a despotic master underscores the shortcomings of the regime that this ruler epitomizes. We will see this characteristic further illustrated on the Persian side in a later example, involving a weeping Persian noble.

When Demaratos affirms that the Lacedaimonians will not back down regardless of the number of Persians facing them, the narrative implicitly characterizes the Lakonians as honourable because of their lack of fear (or, perhaps, their ability to act in spite of that fear) and pays tribute to their courage and dedication. When that affirmation is met with Xerxes' disbelief, the degree to which their behaviour is commendable is put into further relief. By the same token, the Persian leader's inability even to conceive of the other-directed, communal, and fundamentally egalitarian frame of mind that underlies such lack of fear highlights the emotional and social disparities between these different groups and the political regimes that shape such wildly different emotional responses.[21]

The Athenians also receive due honour in the Herodotean narrative earlier in the *Histories*, by way of the Persians' misunderstanding of the Athenians' motivations. In Book Six, Herodotus positions his reader as an observer on the enemy's side by having his reader watch along with the Persians as the Athenians charge their invaders at a run, though they have the support of neither cavalry nor archers. The Persians are baffled (Hdt. 6.112.2):

οἱ δὲ Πέρσαι ὁρέοντες δρόμῳ ἐπιόντας παρεσκευάζοντο ὡς δεξόμενοι, μανίην τε τοῖσι Ἀθηναίοισι ἐπέφερον καὶ πάγχυ ὀλεθρίην, ὁρέοντες αὐτοὺς

ὀλίγους καὶ τούτους δρόμῳ ἐπειγομένους, οὔτε ἵππου ὑπαρχούσης σφι οὔτε
τοξευμάτων.

When the Persians saw the Athenians running towards them, they got
ready to receive them, but thought the Athenians must be mad – mad enough
to bring about their utter destruction – because they could see how few of
them there were.

Because they do not perceive any trace of fear in the Athenians charging towards
them, the Persians can only assume that they are mad. The glaring and surprising
absence of fear thus indirectly and conspicuously underscores the Athenians' courage,
but in a subtler and more convincing manner than if Herodotus were to mention it
explicitly. In case the point about their courage had not been grasped (courage being
not the absence of fear, but courageous action taken despite it), we then shift to the
Athenian perspective: the Athenian men are "the first Greeks known to charge enemy
forces at a run, and the first to endure the sight of Persian dress and the men wearing it.
Up until then even the word 'Persian' had been a source of fear in Greece."[22] The glo-
rification of the Athenians in relation to the other Greeks is more implicit than explicit,
yet it is powerful. This is the beginning of the iconic battle of Marathon.

An analogous scenario plays out in Book VIII, where the narrative provides
a naval equivalent to the land army's bravery. When Xerxes' troops and their
commanders see the modest number of ships coming at them, they assume that
the Greeks have gone mad, and victory awaits. First, Herodotus emphasizes the
Greeks' courage and intelligence in the face of unlikely odds by stressing the
Persians' unsuspecting hope, one that he concedes is "not unreasonable," before
underlining how that hope turns out to be premature delight (Hdt. 8.10.1):

ὁρῶντες δὲ σφέας οἵ τε ἄλλοι στρατιῶται οἱ Ξέρξεω καὶ οἱ στρατηγοὶ
ἐπιπλέοντας νηυσὶ ὀλίγῃσι, πάγχυ σφι μανίην ἐπενείκαντες ἀνῆγον καὶ αὐτοὶ
τὰς νέας, ἐλπίσαντες σφέας εὐπετέως αἱρήσειν, οἰκότα κάρτα ἐλπίσαντες.

When Xerxes' troops and their commanders saw the small number of
Greek ships bearing down on them, they were certain that the Greeks must
have gone mad. They too put out to sea, expecting an easy victory, not an
unreasonable hope.

This is not presumptuous confidence; it is, as the narrator himself concedes, not
an unreasonable hope.[23] The narrative then further highlights the Greeks' superior
courage and underlines the forthcoming effectiveness of their strategy by introducing an additional sub-category of observers to the battle, through whose eyes
he briefly makes his reader watch and anticipate with anxiety what seems to be a
likely outcome for the Greeks (Hdt. 8.10.2):

ὅσοι μέν νυν τῶν Ἰώνων ἦσαν εὔνοοι τοῖσι Ἕλλησι, ἀέκοντές τε ἐστρατεύοντο
συμφορήν τε ἐποιεῦντο μεγάλην ὁρῶντες περιεχομένους αὐτοὺς καὶ
ἐπιστάμενοι ὡς οὐδεὶς αὐτῶν ἀπονοστήσει· οὕτω ἀσθενέα σφι ἐφαίνετο εἶναι
τὰ τῶν Ἑλλήνων πρήγματα.

However, some of the Ionians of the Persian fleet, who were pro-Greek and had joined the expedition against their will, were very concerned at the sight of the Greeks being surrounded. They were sure that, given the apparent weakness of the Greek forces, none of them would return home.

The Ionian subjects' loss of hope when assessing the situation, along with their fear for their fellow Greeks' prospects, is an important means of stressing the courage, solidarity, resilience, and superior strategy of their free Greek counterparts.

Contrast Xerxes' fear and dismay after the battle of Salamis: "realizing the extent of the disaster, Xerxes became afraid and resolves on flight".[24] To hide his fear, he makes further military preparations, in order to give the impression that he is preparing another sea battle. Mardonios, the Achaemenid nobleman and chief lieutenant of Xerxes (who, according to Herodotus) had been the chief proponent of the campaign, advises the Persian king to either attack the Peloponnesus immediately, or head home and leave him behind with 300,000 men to "make him the master of Greece". Xerxes proceeds to consult with Artemisia, the ruler of Persian Halikarnassos specifically, because she had advised him to avoid the battle of Salamis, and he now realizes she was right.[25] He claims, in his own words, to wish to follow her opinion because her advice had been best. But Herodotus then steps in and suggests another motive for Xerxes' desire to follow Artemisia's advice: he sees the king's hasty agreement to withdraw to his homeland and leave Mardonios and key troops behind to enslave Greece as motivated by fear: "I think he was so frightened that he would not have stayed even if every man and every woman had told him to."[26] Thus, Herodotus the Greek provides a contrast between the Persian king's self-representation and face-saving tactic before his advisers, and his own, harsher assessment of the Persian ruler. The latter, he suggests, was not motivated by reason; he was simply terrified (καταρρωδήκεε) of the Greeks.

Mardonios in Book IX fulfills a similar function. According to the Persian general himself, there was a Greek among the Greeks named Pausanias, the regent uncle of the son of Leonidas, commanding the Greek forces, who was afraid of the Persians. The Athenians, meanwhile, were ready to face the Persians head-on, and to leave the Spartans to face the medizing Boiotians and Thessalians. Herodotus underscores the disparity in courage between Athenians and Spartans by using Mardonios as an internal observer and commentator (from the Persian side), who finds great satisfaction in mocking the Spartans' decision to manoeuvre away from the Persians, while the Athenians remain to face them. This manoeuvre, Mardonios (in this case, rightly) assumes to stem from Spartan fear. He sends a herald to proclaim to them the following (Hdt. 9.48.1–2):

'ὦ Λακεδαιμόνιοι, ὑμεῖς δὴ λέγεσθε εἶναι ἄνδρες ἄριστοι ὑπὸ τῶν τῇδε ἀνθρώπων, ἐκπαγλεομένων ὡς οὔτε φεύγετε ἐκ πολέμου οὔτε τάξιν ἐκλείπετε, μένοντές τε ἢ ἀπόλλυτε τοὺς ἐναντίους ἢ αὐτοὶ ἀπόλλυσθε. τῶν δ' ἄρ' ἦν οὐδὲν ἀληθές· πρὶν γὰρ ἢ συμμῖξαι ἡμέας ἐς χειρῶν τε νόμον ἀπικέσθαι, καὶ δὴ φεύγοντας καὶ στάσιν ἐκλείποντας ὑμέας εἴδομεν, ἐν Ἀθηναίοισί τε τὴν πρόπειραν ποιευμένους αὐτούς τε ἀντία δούλων τῶν ἡμετέρων τασσομένους.

Men of Lakedaimon, you are held by everyone in this part of the world to be the bravest of men. They boast that you never retreat and never break ranks but keep to your post until you either kill your opponents or are killed yourselves. But this is all a pack of lies, apparently. Before the battle has even started, before we have got to close quarters, you've already pulled back and left your post – we saw you do it! You're putting the Athenians out in front, while you yourselves take up a position facing mere slaves of ours.

This is not an actual interchange, but a purely rhetorical, non-dialectical bit of direct speech, with which Herodotus expands upon the emotional disparity between the Lacedaimonians' fear and the Athenians' courage. He further harps on these in what follows, focussing on an equally telling geographical disparity between the two groups: while both Athenians and Spartans are on the move toward a new site from which they might be in a better position to face the Persians, Herodotus notes that "as instructed, the Athenians took the alternative route from that taken by the Lacedaimonians: whereas the Lacedaimonians kept to the hillocks and the spurs of Cithaeron because they were afraid of the Persian cavalry, the Athenians made their way down to the plain".[27]

Anger

Anger is another emotion whose display appears to exhibit a marked historiographical valence. While Herodotus mentions fear mainly in reference to collective military entities, anger is (mostly) displayed by individuals, particularly those in a position of power.[28] The actions these individuals take as a result of their anger are revealing both of their character and nature, and an illustration of the shortcomings of the political regime that, he suggests, both enables and allows their anger to take the forms that it does. Aristotle, and his view of anger in particular, are useful to bring into consideration as we proceed to consider Herodotus' (often) implicit didacticism and moral judgments regarding the sources, forms, and results of the anger of those in power in the *Histories*.[29] It is likely that many Athenians, in the fourth century and possibly before, shared a vernacular version of Aristotle's view: that anger should not necessarily be avoided altogether (revenge certainly is not frowned upon), but rather that a person of the right character (*ethos*) should seek to feel anger toward the right people, for the right reasons, in the right manner (i.e., to the proper degree), at the right moment, and for the right length of time.[30] Sometimes, if the offense is egregious, anger that is *not* moderate may even be required. This opinion provides a useful framework to bear in mind as we consider how Herodotus presents various characters in a position of power; the ways in which he foregrounds how and why they feel anger and the actions they take as a result; and how he implicitly suggests, from the reactions of those around them to that anger, whether their anger is warranted or not, just or not, commensurate or not, apposite or not, timely or not, and so on. There is no time here to consider many of the instances we find in the *Histories*. I shall limit myself to representative examples, which shed light on each other by the contrasting exemplars they put forward, both positive and negative.

One case of anger control (or lack thereof) provides a rich case study for evaluating the function of socialized anger in Herodotus, particularly when it comes to a ruling figure in power.[31] In Book I, while Croesus of Lydia is Cyrus's prisoner, the Lydian Tabalos leads an uprising against the Persian administration in Sardis, and lays siege to the city. The Persian king turns to his captive Croesus, the former king who has become his adviser. He is tempted, he tells the latter, to reduce the Lydians to slavery for all the trouble and work they are causing. He is, in fact, somewhat indignant to find them rebelling, considering that, though he has taken their king (Croesus), he left them their city. This is an interesting scenario: a Persian ruler is asking a Lydian (former) ruler how he should treat the latter's people. Croesus is afraid, Herodotus tells us, that Cyrus might drive his people out of Sardis, and responds accordingly with a word of caution, encouraging moderation (1.155.3–4):

ὦ βασιλεῦ, τὰ μὲν οἰκότα εἴρηκας, σὺ μέντοι μὴ πάντα θυμῷ χρέο, μηδὲ πόλιν ἀρχαίην ἐξαναστήσῃς ἀναμάρτητον ἐοῦσαν καὶ τῶν πρότερον καὶ τῶν νῦν ἐστεώτων. . . . Λυδοῖσι δὲ συγγνώμην ἔχων τάδε αὐτοῖσι ἐπίταξον, ὡς μήτε ἀποστέωσι μήτε δεινοί τοι ἔωσι· ἄπειπε μέν σφι πέμψας ὅπλα ἀρήια μὴ ἐκτῆσθαι, κέλευε δὲ σφέας κιθῶνάς τε ὑποδύνειν τοῖσι εἵμασι καὶ κοθόρνους ὑποδέεσθαι, πρόειπε δ' αὐτοῖσι κιθαρίζειν τε καὶ ψάλλειν.

My Lord, what you've said is perfectly reasonable, but you shouldn't be motivated completely by anger. Don't turn an ancient city into ruin when it wasn't to blame for the earlier situation and isn't now either. I was responsible for the first incident and on my head fell the consequences. . . . You can be lenient toward the Lydians and still issue them a directive to ensure that they never rebel and are no threat to you. Send a message that they are forbidden to own weapons of war, that they are to wear tunics under their clothes and coats and slippers on their feet, that they are to take up the cithara and the harp.

Cyrus likes the idea. He calms down and tells Croesus that he will do as he suggested. The Lydians, we are told, completely altered their lifestyle as a result.[32]

This vivid narrative, with conversations reported in direct speech, is one of several in which Herodotus presents us with representatives of different peoples and ethnicities exchanging thoughts, ideas, judgments, and advice on a given situation that they are both in the process of assessing. What is interesting to note for our present purposes is the central place of the emotions in defining and assessing the characters of the leaders involved. It is not often that two individuals – especially two leaders, or a leader and an adviser, see eye to eye in Herodotean discourse – including one who is the other's former enemy and current captive. That Cyrus is able to follow the advice "not to yield to anger" (μὴ πάντα θυμῷ χρέο) is very much to his credit as a ruler and military commander, and this seems to be the main point of the story. While Croesus may have a protective agenda for his people when he urges Cyrus to put aside his anger, Cyrus' ability to follow his advice marks him as a superior leader who is able to heed others' opinions for the benefit of the community, rather than putting his impulsive reactions, individual self and pride first. The Persian leader does *not* allow anger to overcome him, and thus provides a foil for the others who do.

The captive Croesus becomes an adviser to the Achaemenid Cambyses as well, albeit with quite different results. At 3.36.1–3, Herodotus reports a conversation that Cambyses allegedly had with the former Lydian king Croesus – one in which the latter is (ironically, considering what we have been told about Croesus while he was still ruling) recommending that the former show more restraint and self-control. The context is worth mentioning: Cambyses has just killed his own wine-bearer, the son of his most trusted adviser, Prexaspes (to whom I shall return in a moment). Immediately after, he also had twelve of the highest-ranking Persians, persons deemed guilty of "a paltry misdemeanor", buried alive up to their necks in the ground. When Croesus recommends more restraint and self-control, Cambyses reacts by exhibiting just the opposite: in extreme and uncontrolled anger, he tries to kill Croesus on the spot by grabbing the very same bow and arrows with which he just recently killed Prexaspes' son.[33] Croesus leaps out of the room just in time. When Cambyses orders his attendants to find and kill the Lydian king, they know Cambyses' fickleness well enough to realize that he may subsequently come to have a change of heart and resent them for carrying out an order he may come to regret (and rather soon), because he likes Croesus. Accordingly, they spare the former Lydian king. Predictably, Cambyses soon comes to miss the very same Croesus whom he ordered his men to execute. When he discovers that Croesus is in fact still alive, he claims to share in his attendants' happiness – and it is clear that he does. Yet he nonetheless puts to death (3.36.6) those who kept Croesus alive for not following orders – that is, those who are the very source of his happiness and relief. Fickleness here is tied to lack of moderation, including when it comes to anger: when the very same figure comes to see their past actions (and the decisions that stemmed from their brash and immoderate emotions) with regret, the misguided nature of their emotions and actions are brought to the fore. In this instance, the fickleness of Cambyses's shifting emotions, moods, and decisions is compounded by his nonsensical punishment of those who tried to save him from himself, as it were. His poor leadership is further emphasized by the fact that his subjects are more reasonable than he is. Though they anticipate the inconsistency of his moods and attempt to preempt his unjust responses, they still meet their doom. This is a notable lesson on the behavioural perversions of unchecked authority – and its cost to those subjected to it.

In this example, in which the good adviser Croesus nearly meets his end for speaking truth to power, we are reminded of the horrifying episode that immediately precedes it and contributes to prompt the foregoing encounter, an example that well illustrates the nature of the relationship between Cambyses and his subjects: one characterized by a sadistic lack of any moderation.[34] When Cambyses' favourite adviser Prexaspes provides the monarch with a truthful answer to the question of what the Persians think of him: namely, that he drinks too much (3.34.2), he responds by shooting an arrow through Prexaspes' son's heart right then and there, to "prove his sanity" (thereby, of course, demonstrating the absence of any such thing).[35] This incident touches on the Herodotean appraisal of such acute emotional reactivity among ruling figures: one proves one's *sōphrosunē* by being *sōphrōn*, while any impulsive act demonstrates its absence. At the centre of this episode is not so much the perversion of Cambyses and his personality disorder, but the pitfalls inherent in a political and social context in which such unbridled emotional impulsivity meets with no checks or balances whatsoever: namely, absolute autocracy.

Herodotus also portrays the manifestations and consequences of fear and anger within the Greek camps themselves. The narration of episodes that feature these emotions in context – how and when they are felt and acted upon, and how they are perceived by others – is a tool he uses to distinguish Greeks from Persians, but also to differentiate between the members of different Greek *poleis*, especially when it comes to how and when they choose to face the Persian invader. The modalities of that anger and its results, however, are very different from what we have seen among the Persians.

The Spartan Amompharetos is a commander in charge of the Pitanate battalion who refuses – in spite of Pausanias' commands – to retreat further from the Persian cavalry's advance, stating that, "he would never bring shame to Sparta by retreating from 'strangers'". His refusal to obey orders makes Pausanias and his fellow officer Euryanax (son of Dorieus) furious (9.53.2). Yet despite experiencing extreme fear (of the massive Persian cavalry contingent) and great anger (that one of their men should thus disagree and refuse to carry out orders and plans as they have been laid out), they do not punish but rather seek to persuade their fellow Greek.

Clearly, leading figures handle and act upon their anger very differently within the Greek camp. Moreover, their anger itself is based on tellingly different motives from those that provoke the anger of, say, Cambyses: Pausanias and Euryanax are furious that Amompharetos disagrees and disobeys, but what really drives them to try and change Amompharetos' mind by way of discussion and persuasion (*parēgoreuon*) is that "they found even more disturbing the prospect of abandoning the Pitanate battalion, which they would have to do, if Amompharetos remained stubborn, because they would be abandoning Amompharetos and his men to their deaths" (9.53.3). And so they remain where they are, angry at Amompharetos because they are concerned for his (and others') survival. In their anger, they try to persuade Amompharetos to change his mind. Meanwhile, Amompharetos voices his strong dissent by picking up a rock with both hands and putting it down before Pausanias's feet: this is his 'vote' against retreating from strangers.[36] Here too, there is a noteworthy gap between the way in which the Greeks handle disagreements among themselves – including regarding matters of great military importance, involving life-and-death decisions – and the way Herodotus shows Persians handling such disagreements, especially when these disagreements involve those in command being disobeyed by those receiving commands. Important conceptions of the appropriate *modus operandi* that should govern interrelationships between fellow citizens among Greeks transpire in these depictions of Greek responses to situations of extreme fear (caused by the enemy) and anger (stemming from dissent among fellow citizens). The entire scene between

Pausanias, Euryanax, and Amompharetos takes place in the presence of an Athenian messenger, who has come to see what it is the Spartans are actually going to do in the end (since the Athenians, as Herodotus tells us, expect the Spartans to say one thing, but then do another).[37] He watches and listens while the Lacedaimonians disagree, then returns to the Athenian lines to report this internal quarrel, as well as Pausanias' wish that they retreat away from the Persians, as the Lacedaimonians intend to do. In the outcome of this episode, the reader is reminded of the contrast Herodotus established between the Athenians' comportment at Plataia (discussed previously in this chapter) and that of the Lacedaimonians when, as anticipated by the Athenians, Amompharetos subsequently changes his mind. His leaders call his bluff and give orders that all others retreat – thereby abandoning him and his troops until they, too, follow suit. In their fear of the Persian cavalry, the Lacedaimonians keep to the hills, while the Athenians march in the plains.[38]

Pity . . . and grief

I turn now to a few select examples of pity, an emotion that is based on the ability to see oneself in others, and hence perhaps the most democratic in its principles.[39] Whether or not a given individual, and especially a leader, is inclined to feel, show, or act on pity (or not) provides fruitful ground for pointing up differences between various leadership styles, and the political systems that the leaders epitomize.

Let us look at a particularly interesting example of a Herodotean autocrat shown in the process of testing, reacting, and responding to the emotions of one of his foreign captives: the Persian Cambyses' infamous psychological experiment, in which he deliberately torments the deposed Egyptian pharaoh Psammenitos after the siege of Memphis.[40] The experiment involves "putting to the test the Egyptian king's courage" and his ability *not* to display emotion in the face of painful evidence paraded before him of the desperate situation in which he, his family, and his people now find themselves.[41] The Herodotean narrative here presents us with a rather complex scenario involving the orchestration by one ruler of an emotional experiment, for the purposes of indulging in the voyeuristic evaluation of an enemy ruler's responses to it.[42] The Persian is shown in the process of both staging and testing a conquered foreigner's emotional response to his downfall, for the sake of his own curiosity and enjoyment.

To conduct the experiment, Cambyses has the ex-king's daughter dressed as a slave and sent out to fetch water along with the other daughters of the leading men of Egypt, also dressed as slaves. The ex-pharaoh and his fellow Egyptians are thus forced to take in the spectacle of their loss of power and downfall: to watch how low they have fallen as a people and look on as their enslaved daughters are paraded before their eyes, crying out and bursting into tears. All of the men echo their daughters, responding with cries and tears of their own.[43] But not Psammenitos: "he understood what was happening", and merely bows his head to the ground.[44] Next, Cambyses has Psammenitos' son paraded before his father, along with 2,000 other young Egyptian men, with ropes around their necks and bits in their mouths, all being taken to their deaths. All of the other Egyptians weep and wail, but not Psammenitos; once more, he merely bows his head. After the two processions and the orchestrated portion of the emotional testing are over, he catches sight of an elderly man who used to be his friend, who happens to be walking by.[45] When he sees this friend reduced to begging from the army, Herodotus says, he breaks down: letting out a loud groan, he calls out his friend's name and strikes his head in distress.[46]

One important piece to our understanding this episode may lie in Herodotus' mention that Psammenitos "sees and then understands" (*proidōn kai mathōn*).[47] He sees what is happening; but what is it that Psammenitos "understands" when he sees the procession of enslaved women that includes his daughter? What he understands is, perhaps, the test to which Cambyses is subjecting him (διεπειρᾶτο αὐτοῦ τῆς ψυχῆς, 3.14.1). He senses that this is all a purposely choreographed spectacle of pain, meant to provide gratification to its stage director (Cambyses) – a textbook example of *Schadenfreude* (taking pleasure in observing the [displays of emotional] pain of others) with an additional, spectatorial twist: the victor puts the conquered and their demise right before the leader of the fallen, in order to sit back and monitor how the latter simultaneously experiences and witnesses his own downfall and that of his people. In other words, Psammenitos realizes that Cambyses is treating himself, not just to the spectacle of the Egyptians' downfall, but also to that of their leader (himself) in the process of being made to watch and react to it. If this interpretation is correct, then we might understand what follows as resulting from Psammenitos' realization that there is a double level of scrutiny at hand, and that his decision stems from the desire not to gratify Cambyses with the spectacle of his pain. By withholding tears, he wields what little power he has left – that of depriving Cambyses of the sight of him weeping. In the earlier moments, he knows he is on display, and chooses gestures (the bowing of his head) that show grief but maintain his dignity in the face of an experiment designed to inflict extreme humiliation on him. He is asked to provide a reason for his tears, and he does (more on this later); but perhaps the real reason he gives in to tears when he sees his friend reduced to beggary is because the elderly man and friend over whom he weeps is *not a* part of Cambyses' test of his courage (he just 'happened' to be walking by, 3.14.7); hence, this is a spectacle to which he can respond spontaneously, because avoiding humiliation is not a concern.

There are additional layers of complexity to this intentional set-up, for there are two different stages in the observation and evaluation of Psammenitos' emotional display, involving two different sets of emissaries. In the first stage (involving parading war captives before their leader), Psammenitos' emotions are being deliberately provoked and tested, and their expression and manifestations examined. When the Persian ruler hears from the emissaries that Psammenitos did not protest nor cry on seeing his daughter humiliated and his son marched to his death but *did cry* when he saw his old friend begging the army, the former Egyptian king's reactions leave him puzzled. Why is it that he did not break down in the face of the two indignities involving his daughter (*kekakōmenēn*) and son, but did show grief, "a mark of respect" (*etimēsas*), for the beggar?[48] Cambyses continues

his fascinated, sadistic inquiry by sending more emissaries to inquire about the
motives for the deposed pharaoh's emotional responses. To this, the former pharaoh responds with a gnomic statement: the distance between self and other allows
for an other-directed, compassionate response for his friend; his own despair, on
the other hand, was beyond tears.[49] Aristotle later makes reference to this very
passage in order to illustrate the distinction that he draws between those scenarios
that move to pity and those that are too close to home to allow for pity (Ar. *Rh.*
2.8.12 1386a):

ἐλεοῦσι δὲ τούς τε γνωρίμους, ἂν μὴ σφόδρα ἐγγὺς ὦσιν οἰκειότητι· περὶ
δὲ τούτους ὥσπερ περὶ αὐτοὺς μέλλοντας ἔχουσιν· διὸ καὶ ὁ Ἀμάσιος ἐπὶ
μὲν τῷ υἱεῖ ἀγομένῳ ἐπὶ τὸ ἀποθανεῖν οὐκ ἐδάκρυσεν, ὡς φασίν, ἐπὶ δὲ τῷ
φίλῳ προσαιτοῦντι· τοῦτο μὲν γὰρ ἐλεεινόν, ἐκεῖνο δὲ δεινόν· τὸ γὰρ δεινὸν
ἕτερον τοῦ ἐλεεινοῦ καὶ ἐκκρουστικὸν τοῦ ἐλέου καὶ πολλάκις τῷ ἐναντίῳ
χρήσιμον·

The persons men pity are those whom they know, provided they are not
too closely connected with them, for if they are, they feel the same as if they
themselves were likely to suffer. This is why Amasis [*sic*] is said not to have
wept when his son was led to execution but did weep at the sight of a friend
reduced to beggary, for the latter excited pity, the former terror. The terrible
is different from the pitiable, for it drives out pity, and often serves to produce
the opposite feeling.[50]

We need not necessarily take at face value the explanation Psammenitos gives to
Cambyses' messengers for his lack of tears in the first instance. If he had sent to
the monarch a reply that had, for instance, stated that he had concealed his grief
because of his unwillingness to gratify Cambyses with the spectacle of pain and
humiliation he was hoping for, such an admission would surely have been deemed
a form of direct resistance and met with further abuse, as (presumably) would any
admission that the reason he gave in to a full display of sorrow when he saw his
friend reduced to beggary was because (if we are correct) he was, at that point,
outside of the framework of the experiment devised by Cambyses, and hence outside of the perverse emotional test contrived by the latter. Perhaps Herodotus is
suggesting that the power dynamics are not as they appear here. Cambyses seeks
to demonstrate his power by conquering and humiliating his conquest; he attempts
to gain control over his enemies' former leader's emotional responses to defeat,
in order to revel in the contrived experiment. However, if there is some cunning
dissimulation in the Egyptian monarch's way of portraying and explaining his
own emotional displays to the one scrutinizing them, then by maintaining some
degree of control over when and how he displays his pity and grief, and especially
when and how he represents these to those watching him, then he retains what little power and freedom he has in relation to the gratuitously abusive and hybristic
Cambyses.

The other level of emotional evaluation and differentiation in this episode
comes at the end of the story, when Herodotus turns his attention back to the

curious observer Cambyses and his royal entourage. This entourage includes another deposed ruler, the Lydian Croesus, and other Persian grandees present at the time – a most unlikely detail, and likely a very deliberate, additional narrative device used by Herodotus to distinguish between the various members of this internal audience according to their emotional responses and respective cultural identities. On hearing the emissaries report Psammenitos' explanation for the tears he withheld (as opposed to the tears he shed), Croesus himself cries, as do the high-ranking Persians (3.14.11), while Cambyses does not. Interestingly, it is not the account of Psammenitos' grief itself, but the deposed Egyptian pharaoh's *explanation* for his different emotional reactions, that moves (most of) his Persian and Lydian 'audience' to tears.

Cambyses does not weep; but he is, we are told, overcome with an uncharacteristic, belated, "certain amount of pity" for Psammenitos.[51] Such pity, following as it does the intricate conception and implementation of a blatantly sadistic psychological test, provides another instantiation of autocratic fickleness, and underscores Cambyses' sociopathic nature. While the presence of "some pity" may seem to show his humane side, it actually underscores the misguided nature of the monarch's entire initiative to begin with. Even *he* comes to realize that he was ill-advised in his cruelty and extreme punishment; witness the fact that he ultimately tries to rescind the order he gave, and to have Psammenitos' son rescued from death. Cambyses' emotional turnaround comes too late: by the time the relevant parties have been informed that his order was rescinded, Psammenitos' son has already been put to death.

Fickleness in feelings of pity is an important and recurring motif that highlights authoritarian leaders' abuse of power and lack of self-control, in which they are exposed as being emotionally at odds with their own, earlier emotive selves. The result, in this case, is irreparable regret (for those belatedly pitying), and death (for those belatedly pitied). Meanwhile, Psammenitos has retained his dignity, and even earned the respect ("he had spoken well") and pity of his tormentor.

In another interesting example, Herodotus uses the emotion of grief – the grief experienced by a subject rather than a leader, this time – as a means of portraying the nature of the relationship between subject and master or king, within the framework of the Persian monarchy. This example, another of the many Herodotean *logoi* to explore emotional resonance that seems too good to be true, has all the trappings of a literary *paradeigma*, and yet Herodotus is intent on highlighting its veracity: he claims it is one of only two instances in which someone sheds tears before an eyewitness who reported the instance right back to him.[52] This example is especially worthy of examination because it involves an internal observer: specifically, a Greek, who watches a Persian weep and inquires as to what causes his tears. The context is as follows. Thersandros of Orkhomenos is a distinguished Boiotian who finds himself at a banquet in which fifty Persians and fifty Thebans (ostensibly) of the highest rank all convene, Mardonios himself included.[53] Every Persian shares a couch with a Theban. During the drinking that follows the meal, the Persian with whom he has been dining tells Thersandros his pessimistic view of the current military situation. To plan for his own safety, he says, as he begins to weep, the Theban should be aware of the fact that most of the Persians present along with most of those in the army encamped nearby will soon be dead. Thersandros responds to this statement (and its speaker's tears) with wonder: wonder at the fact that his Persian friend is not voicing this view to his military and political superiors, including Mardonios and other higher-ranking Persians. His question is fundamentally Greek in its assumption that opinions and influence could travel up and down the hierarchical ladder of command – something we saw happen on the Greek side, in the case of Amompharetos symbolically 'voting' and remonstrating against his superiors' decision to retreat from immediate confrontation with the Persians, and that we continue to see in Pausanias' and Euryanax's efforts to sway him through discussion rather than coercion, in spite of their combined fear and anger.[54] The Persian's reply to the Theban is an opportunity to remind Thersandros (and us readers) of the nature of the relationship between the Persians and their leaders: one that precludes any such form of exchange between those of different ranks: "no one is willing to believe even those who tell the truth".[55] Although many Persians are well aware of the likelihood of a fatal outcome for most of them, if not all, "<they> follow <their> leaders because <they> have no choice".[56] The Persian ends by voicing the great pain (ἐχθίστη δὲ ὀδύνη) that is inherent in this strange combination of complete lucidity regarding what awaits, and the utter powerlessness to do anything about it: "there's no more terrible pain a man can endure than to see clearly and be able to do nothing".[57] The dysfunctional nature of Persian political power and organization is epitomized in this emotional scene: both in the Persian's grief, and in his Greek counterpart's bafflement that such a display of grief should be followed by complete inaction, owing to the Persian's sense of utter powerlessness. This powerlessness and the harm that come with it, it is clear, stem from his and others' lack of participation in any military or political decision-making.

Emotional displays also take on a significant role in the Herodotean narrative when intimate, interpersonal dynamics are written on a communal scale. While Herodotus' portrayals of the Persians play up the disparities between Persian subjects' emotions and those of their leaders, among the Greeks, by contrast, his narrative explores shared emotions as a signal and a factor of communal solidarity, demonstrating and facilitating the pursuit of common interests and goals within a given community (or, as the case may be, a surprising and potentially corrosive lack thereof). On the level of an entire community, sharing in the emotions of others – and prominently displaying the fact that one does – can serve as a telltale, public sign and statement that one group feels a sense of community and identity with another (or not). Displays of grief become veritable diplomatic demonstrations of solidarity, while their absence can be the manifestation of a diplomatic incident.

When the city of Miletos is sacked by the Persians, most of the male population is killed; the women and children are reduced to slavery; their main shrine (Didyma) is plundered and burnt; and any survivors are rounded up and taken back to King Darius in Susa.[58] As Miletos endures this horrible fate, the Sybarites commit an emotional *faux pas* that also constitutes a political and diplomatic incident: they fail to show any signs of compassion or shared grief at the news of the Milesians' downfall. This lack of grief (or at least of a display of one) is all the more shocking, Herodotus tells us, as the Milesians themselves – the entire population – had in the past shaved their heads to signal *their* deep grief when Sybaris was destroyed by the Krotoniates, "because there are no known states which have closer ties than Miletus and Sybaris".[59] In not publicly displaying any sign of shared pain, the Sybarites betray that tie, and "a debt fails to be repaid".[60] The Sybarites' (political, diplomatic, and presumably military) shortcomings are highlighted not just by the absence noted by the Milesians of any prominent display of grief that would constitute a sign of solidarity on their part, but more so still by the fact that there is another ethnic group that *does* express its sorrow at the fall of Miletos: the Athenians. "*Even* the Athenians behaved better than the Sybarites . . . and . . . burst into tears <at Phrynikhos' production of his tragedy about *The Fall of Miletos*>", fining him 1,000 drachmas for showing them a disaster that was "so close to home", even banning (as the story goes) any future productions of the play.[61] The Sybarites' lack of emotional display serves, in fact, as a foil for underscoring the Athenians' greater solidarity with their 'fellow Greeks' in the face of the Persian invader.

The display of emotions (in this case grief) – or a lack thereof – on a collective level is an important sign and signal of a given group's conception of the nature of their relationship with another population or ethnic group facing misfortune. Whether these emotions are sincerely felt or not is, of course, not a question we can answer. What we can say is that the prominent display of emotions is presented here as a form of public statement, intended to be perceived and recognized by others as such. It is implicit that certain military and other forms of mutual duties and obligations follow such "feelings" of solidarity. This is, in sum, the emotional expression of political and military alliances and one that plays up the superior solidarity of the Athenians with other, allied Greek communities.

Conclusion

The historicity of any and all of these accounts, and of the emotion-filled moments at their core, is at best questionable – though they certainly make for excellent story-telling.[62] Yet the 'truth' of Herodotean anecdotes and *logoi* is too complex to pinpoint by simply drawing a boundary between what demonstrably or plausibly may have happened, and what is a Herodotean invention or borrowing from tradition.[63] Whether, when, and how such and such an instance of fear, pity, anger, or cruel *Schadenfreude* occurred, and how it was perceived, viewed, and perhaps misinterpreted by others – such questions must inevitably remain largely unanswered and often unanswerable.[64] Be that as it may, what remains undeniably worth examining is how Herodotus resorts to these anecdotal (and perhaps entirely imaginary or borrowed) accounts of emotional displays and (mis)interpretations as a means of characterizing and contrasting various individuals and peoples, and the political regimes or *poleis* to which these individuals (rulers and subjects) belong. These intricate, close-up accounts of the (perceived) internal workings and motives of others bring out the connection between the social, military and political actions taken by individuals, communities, and those in a position to lead them, on the one hand, and the way in which these individuals, communities, and leaders experience, process, and act on their emotions, on the other. How individuals, and people, and cultures process emotions, in turn, shapes how they understand others – sometimes correctly, often not – in a manner that is revealing of their own values and preconceptions. Emotional responses across the board (and how they are viewed by others) – be they those responses that others seek to elicit and watch, those that are observed and misunderstood, those that are consciously hidden or displayed, or those that are (perhaps) spontaneously given in to – all are a subtle means the historian repeatedly uses to characterize and differentiate between distinct political and social dynamics, between Greeks and foreigners, and even, as we have seen, among the Greek *poleis* themselves.

Notes

1 Hdt 3.38.3–4. See, e.g., the commentary of Asheri *et al.* on this much-discussed passage.
2 All translations are Waterfield & Dewald (1998). On this passage and the question of cultural relativism in Herodotus, see Munson in this volume (pp. 250–3); regarding the "*nomos* is king" statement in particular, see Demont 2013.
3 Regarding the experiential nature of every culture's emotional categories, and the extent to which emotional concepts vary from one individual and *a fortiori* from one linguistic community to another, see the important distinctions pointed up by Cairns 2016. On Greek portrayals and conceptions of 'barbarians', see for instance the work of Hall 1989, and the recent work of Gruen 2011; on Herodotus and Persia, see Flower 2006; regarding Herodotus and foreign lands more broadly, Hartog 1980 remains a reference; see also Burkert 1990, and Rood 2007. Concerning the rhetoric of otherness in Herodotus, see Gray 1995. See also Figueira's chapter in this volume, particularly concerning the question of Greek conceptions of ethnicity (see pp. 43–53), and Munson 2014.
4 Munson 2005: 76–7.
5 On emotional responses as a means of characterization in other genres, see Allen-Hornblower 2016.
6 On the emotions in the classical world, see e.g., Cairns & Nelis 2017, with ample bibliography, including reference to Cairns' significant, prior work on the emotions. See also Oxford's Emotions of the Past series, including the volume on disgust edited by Lateiner & Spatharas (2017); and the recent edited volume on hope (Kazantzidis & Spatharas 2018). Lateiner's work on laughter, tears, and the emotions in Herodotus also provides excellent discussion of several passages examined here (see Lateiner 1977, 2009). The question of whether and which emotional responses are visceral and universal, and which might be said to be culturally relative, is a disputed matter; see e.g., Allen-Hornblower 2017, Cairns 2016, and the introduction by Lateiner & Spatharas (2017). For a fresh and insightful study of collective (choral) emotions, see Visvardi 2015.
7 On the matter of veracity and historicity in Herodotus, particularly when it comes to myths and narratological patterns, see e.g., Lateiner 1989 and the excellent introduction to Baragwanath & de Bakker 2012; see also Thomas 2000, 2018. Regarding traditional elements within Herodotus and their sources, see Giangiulio 2005.
8 Lateiner 1977 deals with the question of the 'truth' in Herodotean stories involving laughter and tears.

9 The implicit judgments within the *Histories* can be a rich source of information concerning Herodotean (and broader) Greek conceptions of what is and is not an appropriate emotional response, and what is or is not an appropriate action taken as a result of that response.

10 Regarding characterization in Herodotus, see de Bakker 2017.

11 Lateiner & Spatharas 2017's introduction offers an excellent discussion of disgust as a good example of a visceral, bodily emotional response – and of the importance of noting that the visceral and psychophysical nature of the emotion nonetheless does not necessarily mean that all individuals or cultures experience disgust in response to the same stimuli, nor in the same way. On the related question of the emotions, the body, and the information to be gleaned from the metaphors that convey them, see Cairns 2016.

12 Regarding how this applies in the case of *hybris* in particular, see Fisher 1992.

13 Hdt. 3.80.3–6. Cf. Nagy pp. 130–6 and Munson pp. 151–3 in this volume. Regarding the constitutional debate, see e.g., Rhodes 2018, as well as Lateiner 2013.

14 Hdt. 3.80.5. Bratt 1985 provides a thorough overview of common character traits among Eastern leaders in Herodotus. On *hybris* in general, see Fisher 1992. On viewing, spectatorship, and monarchs in Herodotus, see Boedeker 2018.

15 Hdt. 7.101.2.

16 Hdt. 7.102.1–2.

17 On laughter as a narrative tool and marker of imminent demise in Herodotus, see Lateiner 1977 and Flory 1978.

18 It may well be that members of Demaratos' entourage returned to Sparta after the expedition. Others have pointed to the Athenian Dikaios, an explicit informant of Herodotus, as a possible source for this episode.

19 Hdt. 7.103.1.

20 Hdt. 7.104.4: ἔπεστι γὰρ σφι δεσπότης νόμος. There is fear implicit in *turannos* – cf. Solon fr. 36 W. Munson (in this volume) discusses the different forms and conceptions of freedom in this passage (pp. 151–3) and others.

21 On Herodotus and democracy, see Rhodes 2018.

22 Hdt. 6.112.3: πρῶτοι δὲ ἀνέσχοντο ἐσθῆτά τε Μηδικὴν ὀρέοντες καὶ τοὺς ἄνδρας ταύτην ἐσθημένους· τέως δὲ ἦν τοῖσι Ἕλλησι καὶ τὸ οὔνομα τὸ Μήδων φόβος ἀκοῦσαι.

23 Regarding hope in ancient literature, history, and art, see the recent volume edited by Kazantzidis & Spatharas (2018).

24 Hdt. 8.97.1: Ξέρξης δὲ ὡς ἔμαθε τὸ γεγονὸς πάθος, δείσας.

25 Concerning women in Herodotus, Dewald 1981 remains a reference. On Artemisia in particular, see e.g., Munson 1988.

26 Hdt. 8.103.1: οὐδὲ γὰρ εἰ πάντες καὶ πᾶσαι συνεβούλευον αὐτῷ μένειν, ἔμενε ἂν δοκέειν ἐμοί· οὕτω καταρρωδήκεε.

27 Hdt. 9.56.2: Ἀθηναῖοι δὲ ταχθέντες ἤισαν τὰ ἔμπαλιν ἢ Λακεδαιμόνιοι· οἱ μὲν γὰρ τῶν τε ὄχθων ἀντείχοντο καὶ τῆς ὑπωρέης τοῦ Κιθαιρῶνος φοβεόμενοι τὴν ἵππον, Ἀθηναῖοι δὲ κάτω τραφθέντες ἐς τὸ πεδίον.

28 See Bratt 1985 for an exhaustive overview of all relevant passages.

29 Ar. *Rh.* 2.2. Regarding ancient anger in general, see Braund & Most 2003, including Konstan's chapter on Aristotle and anger (ch. 4); see also Konstan 2006 (ch. 2). On the moral didacticism within historiographic writings from Herodotus on, see e.g., Pelling 2006 (with useful bibliography), and Hau 2016. Fisher 2002 points up the underlying complexities of seemingly simple morality in Herodotean storytelling.

30 Ar. *NE* 4.5.1125b27–1126b10. Harris 2001 argues for this shared vernacular position.

31 On restraining anger as a commendable form of self-control in the classical world, see Harris 2001 (see ch. 10 in particular, regarding angry rulers).

32 On the complex significance of this passage, see Asheri 2007, *ad loc.*

33 Hdt. 3.35.5.

34 Hdt. 3.34.1–35.5.

35 Hdt. 3.35.2.

36 On the humor of this passage, and distinctions in wit and humor between various *poleis* and ethnicities within Herodotus, see Dewald 2006.

37 Hdt. 9.54.1.

38 Hdt. 9.56.2.

39 On pity, power, and politics, see Sternberg 2005. On the place, role, and importance of pity in the context of the *polis* as exemplified in tragedy, see for instance Allen-Hornblower 2013, 2017. Visvardi 2015 deals with pity as well as other emotions in political context. On pity in ancient Greece more broadly, see Konstan 2001, 2006 (ch. 10).

40 Hdt. 3.14.1–15.1.

41 Hdt. 3.14.1.

42 On the metahistorical dimensions of Herodotus' representation of inquiring kings, see Christ 1994.

43 Hdt. 3.14.3.

44 I shall return in a moment to how we might interpret what it is Herodotus means by Psammenitos "understanding".

45 At Hdt. 3.14.7 (παρελθόντων δὲ καὶ τούτων), the coincidental nature of their encounter is underlined by Herodotus as a way of marking this event as distinctly outside of the carefully orchestrated processions that preceded.

46 Hdt. 3.14.7. On tears in Hellenic historiography, see Lateiner 2009 (see 110ff. regarding the tears of Herodotean autocrats in particular).

47 Hdt. 3.14.6.

48 Hdt. 3.14.9.

49 Psammenitos' reply is gnomic, and the entire scene follows the tears–question–*gnōmē* scheme pinpointed by Flory 1978.

50 Ar. *Rh.* 2.8.12–14 1386a (trans. J.H. Freese). The importance of a certain degree of emotional distance in pity in Aristotle's definition is underscored by Konstan 2001, 2006 (ch. 10). For further discussion of pity and emotional detachment in Aristotle, see Visvardi 2012.

51 Hdt. 3.14.11: αὐτῷ τε Καμβύσῃ ἐσελθεῖν οἶκτόν τινά.

52 On the paradigmatic nature of these tearful manifestations, see Lateiner 2009.

53 Hdt. 9.16.1–5.

54 See pp. 94–5.

55 Hdt. 9.16.4: οὐδὲ γὰρ πιστὰ λέγουσι ἐθέλει πείθεσθαι οὐδείς.

56 Hdt. 9.16.5.

57 Hdt. 9.16.5: ἐχθίστη δὲ ὀδύνη ἐστὶ τῶν ἐν ἀνθρώποισι αὕτη, πολλὰ φρονέοντα μηδενὸς κρατέειν. On conscious human powerlessness in Greek tragedy, see Allen-Hornblower 2016; this is a typically tragic motif (one thinks of Sophocles in particular).

58 Hdt. 6.18.1–20.1

59 Hdt 6.21.1.

60 Hdt. 6.21.1: οὐκ ἀπέδοσαν τὴν ὁμοίην Συβαρῖται.

61 Hdt. 6.21.2: καὶ δὴ καὶ ποιήσαντι Φρυνίχῳ δρᾶμα Μιλήτου ἅλωσιν καὶ διδάξαντι ἐς δάκρυά τε ἔπεσε τὸ θέητρον, καὶ ἐζημίωσάν μιν ὡς ἀναμνήσαντα οἰκήια κακὰ χιλίῃσι δραχμῇσι, καὶ ἐπέταξαν μηδένα χρᾶσθαι τούτῳ τῷ δράματι.

62 Regarding Herodotean story-telling, see Bowie 2018.

63 For more on the question of the historicity of emotional displays, see for instance the conclusion to Lateiner 1977. On the question of truth in Herodotus, see Baragwanath & de Bakker 2012.

64 See Lateiner 2009.

Bibliography

Alaux, J., ed. 2013. *Hérodote: formes de pensée, figures du récit*. Rennes (Presses Universitaires de Rennes).

Allen-Hornblower, E. 2013. "Sounds and Suffering in Sophocles' 'Philoctetes' and Gide's 'Philoctète'." *Studi Italiani di Filologia Classica* 11: 5–41.

————. 2016. *From Agent to Spectator: Witnessing the Aftermath in Ancient Greek Epic and Tragedy*. Berlin & Boston, MA (De Gruyter).

————. 2017. "Moral Disgust in Sophocles' 'Philoctetes'." In Lateiner & Spatharas 2017, 69–87.

Asheri, D., Lloyd, A. & Corcella, A. 2007. *A Commentary on Herodotus Books I–IV*. Edited by O. Murray & A. Moreno. Oxford (Oxford University Press).

Baragwanath, E. & de Bakker, M., eds. 2012. *Myth, Truth, and Narrative in Herodotus*. Oxford (Oxford University Press).

Boedeker, D. 2018. "Tyrants' Spectacles in Herodotus." In English & Fratantuono 2018, 13–25.

Bowie, A. 2018. "Herodotus the Story-teller." In Bowie 2018, 25–36.

Bowie, E., ed. 2018. *Herodotus: Narrator, Scientist, Historian*. Berlin (De Gruyter).

Bratt, K.D. 1985. *Herodotus' Oriental Monarchs and Their Counsellors: A Study in Typical Narration*. Thesis, PhD, Princeton University, NJ.

Braund, S. & Most, G., eds. 2003. *Ancient Anger: Perspectives from Homer to Galen*. Cambridge (Cambridge University Press).

Burkert, W., ed. 1990. *Hérodote et les peuples non-grecs*. Genève (Fondation Hardt).

Cairns, D. 2016. "Mind, Body, and Metaphor in Ancient Greek Concepts of Emotion." *L'Atelier du Centre de Recherches Historiques* (Online) 16.

Cairns, D. & Nelis, D., eds. 2017. *Emotions in the Classical World: Methods, Approaches, and Directions*. Stuttgart (Franz Steiner Verlag).

Christ, M. 1994. "Herodotean Kings and Historical Inquiry." *Classical Antiquity* 13: 167–202.

De Bakker, M. 2017. "Herodotus." In De Bakker, De Temmerman, & Van Emde Boas 2017, 135–52.

De Bakker, M., De Temmerman, K. & Van Emde Boas, E., eds. 2017. *Characterization in Ancient Greek Literature: Studies in Ancient Greek Narrative*, Vol. 4. Leiden (Brill).

Demont, P. 2013. "Le Nomos-Roi: Hérodote, III, 38." In Alaux 2013, 37–45.

Dewald, C. 1981. "Women and Culture in Herodotus' Histories." In Foley, H., ed., *Reflections of Women in Antiquity*. London (Routledge), 93–127.

————. 2006. "Humour and Danger in Herodotus." In Dewald & Marincola 2006, 145–64.

Dewald, C. & Marincola, J., eds. 2006. *The Cambridge Companion to Herodotus*. Cambridge (Cambridge University Press).

English, M. & Fratantuono, L., eds. 2018. *Pushing the Boundaries of Historia*. London (Routledge).

Fisher, N. 1992. *Hybris: A Study in the Values of Honour and Shame in Ancient Greece*. Liverpool (Liverpool University Press).

————. 2002. "Popular Morality in Herodotus." In Bakker, E., De Jong, I.J.F., & van Wees, H., eds., *Brill's Companion to Herodotus*. Leiden (Brill), 199–224.

Flory, S. 1978. "Laughter, Tears and Wisdom in Herodotus." *American Journal of Philology* 99: 145–53.

Flower, M. 2006. "Herodotus and Persia." In Dewald & Marincola 2006, 274–89.

Giangiulio, M., ed. 2005. *Erodoto e il 'modello erodoteo': formazione e trasmissione delle tradizioni storiche in Grecia*. Trento (Labirinti).

Gray, V. 1995. "Herodotus and the Rhetoric of Otherness." *American Journal of Philology* 116: 185–211.

Gruen, E. 2011. *Rethinking the Other in Antiquity*. Princeton, NJ (Princeton University Press).

Hall, E.M. 1989. *Inventing the Barbarian: Greek Self-Definition Through Tragedy*. Oxford (Oxford University Press).

Harris, W. 2001. *Restraining Rage: The Ideology of Anger Control in Classical Antiquity.* Cambridge, MA (Harvard University Press).

Harrison, T. & Irwin, E., eds. 2018. *Interpreting Herodotus.* Oxford (Oxford University Press).

Hartog, F. 1980. *Le Miroir d'Hérodote: Essai sur la représentation de l'Autre.* Paris (Gallimard).

Hau, L. 2016. *Moral History from Herodotus to Diodorus Siculus.* Edinburgh (Edinburgh University Press).

Kazantzidis, G. & Spatharas, D., eds. 2018. *Hope in Ancient Literature, History, and Art: Ancient Emotions I.* Berlin (De Gruyter).

Konstan, D. 2001. *Pity Transformed.* London (Bloomsbury Publishing).

———. 2003. "Aristotle on Anger and the Emotions: The Strategies of Status." In Braund & Most 2003, 99–120.

———. 2006. *The Emotions of the Ancient Greeks: Studies in Aristotle and Classical Literature.* Toronto (University of Toronto Press).

Lateiner, D. 1977. "No Laughing Matter: A Literary Tactic in Herodotus." *Transactions of the American Philological Association* 107: 173–82.

———. 1989. *The Historical Method of Herodotus.* Toronto (University of Toronto Press).

———. 2009. "Tears and Crying in Hellenic Historiography: Dacryology from Herodotus to Polybius." In Fögen, T., ed., *Tears in the Graeco-Roman World.* Berlin (De Gruyter), 105–34.

———. 2013. "Herodotean Historiographical Patterning: The Constitutional Debate." In Munson, R.V., ed., *Herodotus: Vol. I.* Oxford (Oxford University Press), 194–211.

———. 2017. "The Emotion of Disgust, Provoked and Expressed in Earlier Greek Literature." In Cairns & Nelis 2017, 31–52.

Lateiner, D. & Spatharas, D., eds. 2017. *The Ancient Emotion of Disgust (Emotions of the Past).* New York, NY (Oxford University Press).

McInerney, J., ed. 2014. *A Companion to Ethnicity in the Ancient Mediterranean.* Chichester, West Sussex (Wiley-Blackwell).

Munson, R.V. 1988. "Artemisia in Herodotus." *Classical Antiquity* 7: 91–106.

———. 2005. *Black Doves Speak: Herodotus and the Language of Barbarians.* Hellenic Studies 9. Washington, DC (Center for Hellenic Studies).

———. 2014. "Herodotus and Ethnicity." In McInerney 2014, 341–55.

Pelling, C. 2006. "Educating Croesus: Talking and Learning in Herodotus' Lydian 'Logos.'" *Classical Antiquity* 25: 141–77.

Rhodes, P.J. 2018. "Herodotus on Democracy." In Harrison & Irwin 2018, 265–77.

Rood, T. 2007. "Herodotus in Foreign Lands." In Dewald & Marincola 2018, 290–305.

Sternberg, R. 2005. *Pity and Power in Ancient Athens.* New York, NY (Cambridge University Press).

Thomas, R. 2000. *Herodotus in Context: Ethnography, Science, and the Art of Persuasion.* Cambridge (Cambridge University Press).

———. 2018. "Truth and Authority in Herodotus' Narrative: False Stories and True Stories." In Bowie 2018, 265–84.

Visvardi, E. 2012. "Minimizing the Distance? On Pity and Emotional Detachment." www.chs-fellows.org/2012/12/04/minimizing-the-distance-on-pity-and-emotional-detachment-2/

———. 2015. *Emotion in Action: Thucydides and the Tragic Chorus.* Leiden (Brill).

Waterfield, R. & Dewald, C. 1998. *Herodotus: The Histories.* New York, NY (Oxford University Press).

Part II
Ethnicity among the Greeks

5   Mages and Ionians revisited

Gregory Nagy

In *Classical Inquiries: Studies on the Ancient World from CHS* I published an online essay entitled "Mages and Ionians".[1] This piece drew on the same research that I presented in part for the panel "Ethnicity and Multiculturalism in Herodotus: Through Others' Eyes", at the Ninth Celtic Conference in Classics, University College Dublin, June 2016.[2]

Now I am publishing here a set of retrospective comments on that essay in further exploration of Greek ethnic identity. These comments are intended as responses to my friend, Thomas Figueira, who had read my original text and had shared with me his thoughts about my arguments. He had tried to read my essay as a social historian. That was back in mid-July 2017, less than one month after my original essay had been published online. Ever since then, I have been trying to find the best way of responding to these annotations by Figueira, which had opened up for me so many new possibilities for further thinking. In the end, for better or for worse, I have come up with the comments that I present here, which I intend as a dialogic response to Tom's original annotations. Where they exist a lightly edited version of my original text ("Mages and Ionians" as written in mid-July 2017) will be followed by a comment of mine. We are preserving the original paragraph numbers (as given in my original text) to help in cross-reference and inserting an original set of page numbers.[3] For the sake of clarity, where necessary I shall annotate with my initials, GN, and the relevant annotations by Thomas Figueira, as written shortly thereafter in mid-July 2017, will be preceded by his initials, TJF.[4] More recent thoughts and supplementations or revisions from the two of us are also incorporated.

§0. {|₉₇} There is a problem with the meaning of the word 'mage', *mágos* (μάγος) in Greek, which was borrowed into Greek from a language known to linguists as Old Persian. In the Bisitun Inscription, which celebrates the accession of Darius the First in 522 BCE and his subsequent successes as the new king of the Persian Empire, the corresponding Old Persian word is *maguš*, referring to a man named Gaumāta whom Darius accused of usurping the Persian kingship (column 1 lines 35–43, etc.). In the *History* of Herodotus (3.61–79), there is a convergent narrative about a *mágos* who usurped the kingship, though his name is given there as Smerdis.[5] In any case, here is the problem: aside from the idea that, once upon a time, a *maguš/mágos* usurped the kingship of the Persian Empire, the contexts of *mágos* in Greek sources do not match neatly the contexts of Old Persian *maguš* and of its cognates as found in other Iranian languages. Aiming at a solution to this problem, I argue that the Greek and the Iranian contexts of the word can best be understood by taking a closer look at historical evidence for interactions between Greeks and Persians in the sixth, fifth, and fourth centuries BCE.[6] On the basis of such evidence, I also argue that the original mediators for the word *mágos* and for the ideas underlying this word were the *Ionians*.[7]

TJF, in his introduction to his relevant annotations, comments on my overall essay:

> This is most original and provocative, and stakes out much new ground, especially for those uninitiated into Nagyian thought. At more than one point, the stages of your argument clicked into conviction for me. I do feel some of the further steps of the argument pressed too far, lacked sufficient substantiation, or needed tweaking. Please take my suggestions as constructive criticism and use your own best judgment. I would not want to lose the freshness of your piece.

GN comments, responding here to TJF by making three points, listed in the order of ABC:

> A. I treasure the praise and I happily accept the criticism. In further annotations by TJF, which will appear here, he gives some telling examples of situations where I may well have taken my arguments too far. 'A bridge too far. . .'
>
>   B. I feel both honoured and intimidated by the term 'Nagyian thought'. One of these days, I should try and figure out, in some definitive way, if there really is anything distinctive about my thinking. For now, let me just take a preliminary step in that direction . . . What perhaps sets me apart, at least to some extent, is the effort I make in analyzing the linguistic aspect of any problem where the original wording needs to be analyzed in its historical contexts. I should stress that such analysis needs the application of both synchronic and diachronic perspectives. I think I say it best in Nagy 2011a, as listed in the Bibliography. In this context, I need to comment on a missed opportunity, dating back to an early phase of my publications. In *Best of the Achaeans*, Nagy 1969, I had decided to avoid using the terms *synchronic* and *diachronic*. As time went by, I came to regret that avoidance, and, twenty years later, I tried to make up for the missed opportunity. This was in the new Introduction to the second edition of that book, Nagy 1999, where I explain how my overall thinking is shaped by combining synchronic and diachronic perspectives.
>
>   C. I should put on record that the criticisms of my work by TJF have always been for me a model of collegial debate. TJF: In other words, any sharpness here is meant as fun between friends. As to the epithet 'Nagyian', I offer this gloss: "showing an intention to read all texts as imbricated in their sociocultural matrix, during which analysis every insight is relentlessly

and wholeheartedly pursued, without respect to prevailing consensus, until its interpretative potency is exhausted".

A problem with the word *mágos*

§1. On the surface, in popular cultures that flourish in what is vaguely understood to be the 'West', the word *mágos*, which I translated as 'mage' in the title of this {|₉₈} presentation, does not seem to be all that problematic. We know that this word is somehow related to the word *magic*. So, a 'mage' must be some kind of a practitioner of *magic*, no? The meaning seems esoteric or even exotic, but understandable. So, what is the problem here?

> GN on §1–15: There is not much that I can add at present to what I originally said in §§1–15 about the mágoi or 'mages' in the Persian Empire – except perhaps to cite an article by Kai Trampedach (2017) about the role of these *mágoi* in the overall narrative of Herodotus. As Trampedach argues in terms of this narrative, the *mágoi* who advise Persian royalty – especially in the case of Xerxes – are programmed, as it were, to fail. That is to say, the narrative makes them suffer the same patterns of mistakes that are suffered by their royal advisees. Herodotus delineates these mistakes as offenses against the cosmic order that takes shape in his narrative.

§2. The problem has to do with origins. If we look up the word in any encyclopedia, the basic fact emerges: this word *mágos* originates from Iranian civilization. But the meaning of such a word in its Iranian contexts does not square with our superficial 'Western' understanding of the word. I say Iranian *contexts*, not *context*, since the historical background of the word *mágos* in Iranian civilization is multiple – and complicated. By contrast with the modern 'Western' understanding, which is superficially simple, there is no unified 'Eastern' meaning of the word. The Iranian contexts of *mágos* are quite diversified: the word seems to mean different things at different times and in different places within the vastly diverse world of Iranian civilization.[8] There are clearly multiple understandings, and a unified explanation has up to now eluded any consensus – even among experts in Iranian civilization.[9]

Another problem with the word **mágos**

§3. Now we come to a second problem. Adding to the complications that I have already sketched is the fact that the word *mágos* crosses into the 'Western' world by way of the ancient Greeks, and that *their* uses of the word, like the 'Eastern' uses, are problematic in their own right. In this case, the problem is not a divergence of meanings, but an evolving convergence, eventually centering on the idea, already noted, that a *mágos* (μάγος) is some kind of a practitioner of *magic*. It is Greek civilization, which we consider to be the fountainhead of Western civilization, that has given to the modern world the seemingly unified meaning of this word – by contrast with Iranian civilization, representing the 'mysterious' East, where the real meaning is multiple and complicated.

§4. But there is more than one way of thinking about Greek civilization. Here the problem is hidden, because Greek civilization as articulated by the Greek language seems to be on the surface so unified, so monolithic. After all, there is and always has {|₉₉} been only one Greek language, and it has survived to this day as one single Greek language. There is evidence to show that this language has lasted continuously for over 3,000 years of world history. By contrast, when we consider this same period of three or so millennia, we find evidence for many different Iranian languages. If we track Iranian languages as they existed during this stretch of time, we find many different languages conveying many different cultures that were or are in many ways discontinuous from each other. The only Iranian continuum that is comparable to the Greek language is represented by the languages known to linguists as Old Persian, Middle Persian, and New Persian.

§5. There is no time for me to go into details here about Iranian discontinuities, and I content myself with just one obvious example that goes back to the earliest recoverable times: when we consider the sacred texts of what is generally known as the *Avesta*, it is obvious that the language of these texts cannot simply be traced forward in time to match what is generally described as Old Persian, which was the official Iranian language of the Achaemenid dynasty.

§6. To resume my main argument . . . By comparison, as I said a moment ago, with the Iranian languages, the Greek language tends to be viewed as some kind of a miraculously ongoing continuum – as an exceptionally unified vehicle of Greek civilization. It can even be said, and I did say it already, that the Greek language is something of a monolith. Granted, there were always Greek dialects, but such subgroupings clearly belonged to a single language that we now recognize as one single Greek language. So, if the teleology of the Iranian word *mágos* as used in Greek points to an eventual meaning that we may tentatively define as a practitioner of *magic*, then such an outcome may seem to be good enough for us. But it is not at all good enough.

§7. The appearances of a monolithic Greek language can be deceptive, and this deceptiveness can become an overall problem for me as I look further into the meaning of the Greek word *mágos* as borrowed from the Old Persian word *maguš*. This overall problem can be broken down into two specific problems with reference to the Greek word *mágos*:

1   It is only in relatively later Greek texts, stemming from the Hellenistic and later eras – so, in texts dated after the death of Alexander in 323 BCE – that we find unambiguous attestations of the word *mágos* in the sense of *magician* or *practitioner of magic*.

2   In earlier Greek texts, the word *mágos* is used in a different and more complicated sense. And this different sense, as we will see, operates not in the Greek language considered as a whole but only in one dialect of the Greek language. That dialect, as we will also see, is Ionic, as spoken by Ionians. And here we will be looking at a situation where the history of the Greek language

cannot be viewed monolithically: one dialect will reflect a world view that is significantly different from the world view reflected by the other dialects. And the different sense of the {|₁₀₀} word *mágos* as used in the Ionic dialect can be viewed as a most telling sign of such differences in world views.

§8. We are about to explore, then, a glaring example of discontinuities as well as continuities in the Greek language, which turns out to be not as monolithic as it might appear to be at first sight. The example focusses on the positive as well as the negative uses of the word *mágos* in Greek.

Some positive and negative views of the word mágos

§9. I start with negative uses. In later Greek texts, a notorious example of the word *mágos* in a negative sense is the narrative about one Simon the Mage in *Acts of the Apostles* 8:9–24. This *mágos* named Simon is viewed as a magician who threatens to invalidate the authority of the apostle Peter himself in a set of confrontations. Even more vivid confrontations between Simon the Mage and Peter can be found in the Apocrypha, as in *Acts of Peter* 32, where we see Simon in the act of captivating his onlookers by performing for them magic tricks like levitating high in the air, in imitation of Christ ascending to heaven. Seeing Simon levitate, Peter feels threatened, and he reacts by praying that Simon should crash. Peter's prayers are answered. Unlike Christ, Simon now comes crashing down to earth, humiliated and disempowered.

§10. In such narratives about Simon the Mage, we can see that *mágoi* have the potential to authorize themselves as authorities in their own right, and this potential is seen as esoteric and even exotic. Viewed negatively, such a potential for esoterism and exoticism can be demonized as *magic*.

§11. Viewed positively, however, the esoterism and exoticism of *mágoi* can be exalted as the power of authority, which can validate authority itself. Such a positive view is evident in the Gospel according to Matthew 2:1–12, where the wise men who visit the infant Jesus are *mágoi* from the exotic 'East' whose role is to recognize and thus to validate the kingly authority of the divine child.[10]

TF: This is understandable if we accept the conjecture that they represented emissaries from communities of Iranian Jews (cf. Albright & Mann 1971: 12–16). I add that the *Contra Celsum* (1.28, 32, 38) of Origen refers to a Jewish tradition, transmitted by Celsus, that Jesus himself became a *mágos* by virtue of his sojourn in Egypt (Jesus as 'magician' being a common adversarial charge). Could it have been the birth of a potential *mágos* with an ability to authorize kingship that frightened Herod about this Jesus?

§12. From such relatively later Greek contexts, then, we can see that *mágoi* have the potential to validate as well as to invalidate authority, and that only their potential to invalidate could be viewed negatively as *magic*. By contrast, if this same potential of the *mágoi* is viewed positively, then it becomes an exalted and even sacred power.

§13. That said, what can we say about the relatively earlier Greek contexts of the same word *mágos*? Here we will need to be all the more careful in avoiding the assumption that this word consistently conveys the idea of *magic*, which as we have seen is only a negative view of the word as used in its later Greek contexts. The positive view, as we have also seen, is that the potential of the *mágos* to validate authority must be a sacred power. Further, as we will soon see from the evidence of earlier {|₁₀₁} Greek contexts, such a positive view must have allowed for the power of the *mágos* to invalidate an authority that is supposedly bad, not only the power to validate an authority that is supposedly good.

§14. When the authority is supposed to be good, it is visualized as a form of kingship that is sacralized by a divinity who protects kingship. In the case of the Bisitun Inscription, for example, the god Ahuramazdā protects the kingship of Darius. In this case, however, as we read in the text of the Bisitun Inscription, the rebellious *maguš* is supposedly bad, not good, and only the king Darius is good. Correspondingly, in the matching Greek text of Herodotus, the *mágos* there too is supposedly bad, not good. In this case, then, it is presumed that a good king has invalidated a bad *mágos*. In an alternative unfolding of events, however, it could have been a good *mágos* who invalidated a bad king. Either way, the point remains this: in the relatively early Greek context where Herodotus narrates events that match what is narrated in the Old Persian text of the Bisitun Inscription, the bad *mágos* is viewed not as a magician. Rather, in terms of the negative view as shaped in the Greek text of Herodotus, the supposedly bad *mágos* is a false king, a usurper. And, similarly in the Old Persian text of the Bisitun Inscription, the negative view of the supposedly bad *maguš* presents him not as some magician but as a false king, a usurper.

§15. Still, lexicographers tend to interpret *mágos* as conveying the idea of a magician even when the word is found in earlier Greek contexts. My favourite example comes from Sophocles, *Oedipus Tyrannus* 387, where we see one of the earlier Greek attestations of the word: here the king Oedipus refers to the seer Teiresias insultingly as a *mágos*. It is commonly thought that the king in this context is accusing the seer of acting like some kind of a magician. But is Teiresias here really a practitioner of magic, as we think of magicians? Or is he more of a usurper? Here I return once again to the Old Persian word *maguš*, as attested in the Bisitun Inscription: there, as we saw from the beginning, the word refers to a man who was accused by the king Darius of usurping the kingship of the Persian Empire (column 1 lines 35–43, etc.). In that context, the *maguš* is viewed as an evil usurper, not as an evil magician, and his success in usurping the kingship is not linked with magic. A similar formulation applies to the *mágos* in the *History* of Herodotus (3.61–79): here too the role of this *mágos* is evidently the same, a usurper. And a similar formulation applies even to Teiresias in the *Oedipus Tyrannus* of Sophocles: when the king Oedipus calls Teiresias a *mágos* at verse 387, he is in effect accusing the seer of threatening the king's kingship. And what exactly is so threatening about the role of Teiresias as a would-be *mágos*? My answer is this: the knowledgeability of Teiresias about the cosmos – both physical and political – is viewed here as a potential threat, not only as a potential aid, to king-ship. And, as we will now see, such knowledgeability is exactly what can seem to be so threatening about the role of the *mágoi* in the overall context of the Persian Empire. {|₁₀₂}

TJF: Here is a line of accusation along which Oedipus also abuses him. GN com-ments: I agree. Also, as I go on to argue in GN §16, Oedipus himself suspects Teiresias of being a usurper. GN comments further on his §15: The knowl-edgeability of Teiresias about the cosmos – both physical and political – is viewed here at *Oedipus Tyrannus* 387 as a potential threat, not only as a potential aid, to kingship. TJF: Is it not significant that this expertise also has received Apolline endorsement (*OT* 377)?

GN: I agree.

Ionian views of the word mágos

§16. So far, we have found nothing inherently magical about *mágoi* in early Greek sources as represented by Herodotus. But there is, as we will now see, something inherently priestly about them. Such a view of the *mágoi*, as priests of some kind, was transmitted into the Greek language by way of one dialect in particular, and that dialect was Ionic as spoken by Ionians. As I have already indicated, I will be arguing that speakers of the Ionic dialect were transmitters of a world view that was different from other world views as reflected by speakers of other Greek dialects, and that this difference in world views is exemplified by the use of the word *mágos* by Ionians during a specific period of their history. In what follows, I will concentrate on the historical context of that period as I proceed to analyze the special use of the word *mágos* by Ionians.

TJF: The assumption, in the writings of Herodotus, of the seamlessness of transla-tion may reflect a peculiarly Ionian attitude toward distinction by language. For more discussion, see Brandwood pp. 31–2 this volume.

GN: I agree. As we will see further on, Herodotus views the *mágoi* as a priestly class, and his narratives about these *mágoi* consistently reflect this basic understanding of his.

§17. In the course of my analysis, I will re-examine the relevant evidence of two major Greek sources: one is the *History* of Herodotus, composed in the Ionic dialect, and the other is the Derveni Papyrus. More needs to be said about the sec-ond source. Though the writing-down of the text that we read in the Derveni Papy-rus is generally dated to the fourth century BCE, the author of the text itself can be dated further back, to the fifth century BCE, and so he may be roughly contem-poraneous with Herodotus himself.[11] Moreover, just as the text of Herodotus was composed in Ionic, that is, in the dialect of the Ionians, so too the language used by the author of the Derveni Papyrus is heavily influenced by the Ionic dialect.[12]

§18. Both of these fifth-century Greek sources provide essential pieces of information about the role of *mágoi* in the era of the Achaemenid dynasty, which ruled the Persian Empire from around 550 to 330 BCE.

§19. According to Herodotus (1.101), the *Mágoi* (Μάγοι) were one of six social subdivisions (*éthnea*) of the Iranian people known as the Medes (Μῆδοι). Even in the Bisitun Inscription, the Babylonian portion of the trilingual text refers to the *maguš* there as a 'Mede' (line 15: *ma-da-a-a . . . ma-gu-šu, /madaya magušu/*). Accordingly, we may at first sight think of the *mágoi* as a priestly class within the overall framework of the Persian Empire. A closer look, however, suggests that the *mágoi* were already a priestly class in the empire of the Medes, which preceded the more multi-ethnic Persian Empire, and that the status of *mágoi* as imperial priests in this later empire was no longer so strictly linked to their original status as an ethnic grouping that was also sacerdotal within the empire of the Medes themselves.[13] {|₁₀₃}

TJF: Is the narrative in Herodotus implying that the *mágoi* had lost their status as a clerical caste in the Achaemenid empire, but simply maintained that status among the still influential Medes?

GN: I agree that the *mágoi* cannot really qualify any more as a clerical caste in the Achaemenid empire, but I think they still functioned as imperial priests, as we will see in what follows.

TJF: I think that the reciprocal legitimatization of Achaemenid kings and of the individual *mágoi* serving them is a telling point here. In general, I note that Bickerman & Tadmor 1985 is a notable counterpoint to GN on the identity of Gaumāta the usurper and the nature of the *mágoi*.

§20. I concentrate here on what we read in Herodotus (1.132.2–3) about the role of the *mágos* (μάγος . . . μάγου) in authorizing *thusíai* (θυσίας) 'sacrifices' by way of *epaeídein* (ἐπαείδει) 'singing incantations', where the *epōidḗ* (ἐπαοιδήν) 'incantation' is described as a *theogoníē* (θεογονίην) 'theogony'.

§21. Keeping in mind such a role for the *mágoi* as sacrificer, I now highlight what we read in column VI (after Ferrari) of the Derveni Papyrus. Here it is said that the *mágoi* (μάγων at line 2, μά[γο]ι at line 5, μάγοις at line 9) are models for the performance of rituals by initiands (lines 8–9), where the word I am translating as 'initiands' is *mústai* (μύσται at line 9). Here is the way I translate the relevant wording (at lines 8–9): 'the *mústai* perform-preliminaries-of-sacrifice [*prothúein*] to the Eumenides in the same way as the *mágoi* perform-preliminaries-of-sacrifice' (μύσται | Εὐμενίσι προθύουσι κ[ατὰ τὰ] αὐτὰ μάγοις). Within this overall context, we find three most relevant words that seem to be connected with the activities of the *mágoi*:

1   *eukhḗ* 'prayer' ([εὐ]χαί at line 1, to be compared with εὐχῆς at column I line 6)[14]
2   *thusiā* 'sacrifice' (θυσ[ί]αι correlated with ([εὐ]χαί, at line 1; also θυσ[ία]ν π[οιοῦσ]ι[ν] . . . | οἱ μά[γο]ι at lines 4–5)
3   *epōidḗ* 'incantation' (ἐπ[ωιδὴ δ]ὲ μάγων at line 2).

§22. The first and the third of these words are in regrettably fragmentary condition, but a majority of editors agree on the restorations that I have given here. All three of these words are most relevant to what I cited just a moment ago from Herodotus (1.132.2–3), who speaks about the role of the *mágos* (. . . μάγο ς . . . μάγου . . .) in authorizing *thusíai* (θυσίας) 'sacrifices' by way of *epaeídein* (ἐπαείδει) 'singing incantations', where the *epōidḗ* (ἐπαοιδήν) 'incantation' is described as a *theogoníē* (θεογονίην) 'theogony'.[15] Here we see the idea of singing about the cosmos – even *singing the cosmos* – linked with the idea of *authorizing a sacrifice*. From a comparative point of view, as we know from surveying a wide variety of cross-cultural evidence, *the performance of a theogony* can function as *an authorization of kingship*. We read similar ideas about the correlation of cosmos and kingship in the work of Xenophon known as the *Education of Cyrus* (8.1.23) with specific reference to the ritual activities of the *mágoi*: two relevant words used there are *humneîn* (ὑμνεῖν) 'performing hymns' and *thúein* (θύειν) 'sacrificing'. Here too, *mágoi* are viewed as coefficient with the king of the Persian Empire in sustaining cosmic order by way of sacrifice and incantation.

TJF: We may compare what happens in the Hesiodic *Theogony*, where the narrative about the genesis of divinities is followed by catalogues (*Eoiai*) of female heroes who were impregnated by male divinities and gave birth to founders of royal lineages (albeit of reduced Dark Age kingships). This is authorization that is based on theogony.

§23. Even more relevant is what we read in Herodotus (7.191.2) about *mágoi* who are described as 'sacrificing' (*éntoma poieûntes*) and 'singing incantations' (*kataeídontes* {|₁₀₄} *boêisi*) in response to a violent wind that had at that time seriously damaged the fleet of the Persian Empire by destroying many of its ships anchored in the shallows at Cape Sepias. The context here makes it clear that the *mágoi* were performing these rituals in order to salvage the royal project of Xerxes, successor to Darius as king of the Persian Empire, who was attempting to conquer the Greeks inhabiting the mainland situated on the European side of the Aegean Sea. In the same narrative of Herodotus (7.191.2), these *mágoi* are described as also sacrificing (*thúontes*) to the goddess Thetis, mother of Achilles, and to her sister goddesses, the Nereids. Herodotus says more (again, 7.191.2): the *mágoi* sacrificed (*éthuon*) to Thetis because of what they had heard 'from the Ionians' (*parà tôn Iṓnōn*). What they heard, as Herodotus recounts (again, 7.191.2), is a sacred narrative about Cape Sepias, the place situated on the European coast where the fleet of the Persian Empire was damaged by the violent wind: it was at this same place, the Ionians told the *mágoi*, that Achilles was conceived when his immortal mother Thetis was impregnated by his mortal father Peleus.

§24. Given the fact that the native Greek narratives attributed cosmic powers to the goddess Thetis, I argue that we see here another example of a link between the idea that the *mágoi* have the power to *sing the cosmos* and the idea of their *authorizing a sacrifice* by way of their *incantations*.

§25. But who were these Ionians who had narrated for the *mágoi* the sacred narrative that led to the *magian* sacrifice to divine forces worshipped by the Greeks? It is clear from what we read in Herodotus (7.191–2) that these Ionians were Asiatic Greeks fighting on the side of the Persians and against the Greeks of Europe who were defending their homeland from the invasion initiated by Xerxes. These Ionians were serving in the invading navy of the multi-ethnic Persian Empire.

§26. By studying the political and cultural identity of these Greeks who called themselves Ionians, I argue, we can develop a holistic explanation for the meaning of the word *mágos* in Greek. And that is because these Greeks, as Ionians, were the primary transmitters of Persian civilization beyond the Persian-speaking world.

TJF: on GN's wording "the primary transmitters": The definite article here disquiets me. What about Iranian estate-holders in the satrapies (such as those in Anatolia or Syria, for example, as interacting with Xenophon in Asia Minor (e.g., *Anabasis* 5.3.4–7) or the Jews returning to Jerusalem? See respectively Briant 2002: 75–6, 596–9; Shaked 1984.

GN: Point well taken.

Ionians and the Persian Empire

§27. The point that I just made about Ionians as the primary transmitters of Persian civilization beyond the Persians is, I think the most consequential aspect of my overall argument. When I say *Persian civilization* in this context, I use the term in an inclusive rather than exclusive sense. Such a civilization was not at all exclusively Persian in its ethnicity, since the Persian Empire promoted a multi-ethnic world {|₁₀₅} view that prided itself on its Greek-speaking constituency as a singularly prestigious aspect of its overall civilization.[16]

§28. I am arguing that the civilization of the Ionians was a jewel in the crown for the Persian Empire – at least, from an Ionian perspective. And such an argument requires a rethinking of four subjects, three of which are ideas and one of which is a historical fact:

1   the idea of 'Ionians' as defined by the so-called Ionian Dodecapolis, a confederation of 12 states, which took shape in the late eighth and early seventh centuries BCE;
2   the idea of a Debate of the Constitutions, as dramatized by Herodotus (3.80–4), which supposedly took place among Persian elite conspirators in 522 BCE;
3   the historical fact of an Ionian revolt against the Persian Empire in 499–494 BCE;
4   the idea of 'Ionians' as viewed after the sea battle at Salamis in 480 BCE.

§29. I have listed these four subjects in chronological order here, but the order of my analysis will be 1–4–3–2.

The idea of 'Ionians' and the Ionian Dodecapolis

§30. The name of the region *Ionia* (*Iōníē*), and the name of the people, *Ionians* (*Íōnes*), are hardly even recognized in the popular cultures of the 'West'. Nor are they all that well understood by experts in the history of Greek civilization. The name *Ionian* is ordinarily used today with reference to populations that spoke *Ionic*, which was a dialect of the unified language that was Greek. This *Ionic* dialect, as linguists can tell us, was closely related to another dialect, *Attic*, spoken in *Attica*, which was the name given to a region dominated by the city-state of Athens in the classical period of the fifth century BCE and beyond. Linguists think of Attic as a dialect spoken in one part of a larger dialect-area that they describe as *Attic-Ionic*, while Ionic is understood to be the dialect spoken in the other part. But how to define that other part? Whereas Attica, the original area where Attic was spoken, can be defined easily, since it is situated on the mainland of what we know as Europe, it is much more difficult to define the areas where Ionic was spoken.

TJF: It is perhaps worth noting that this undeniable linguistic classification may be obscuring ideological and cultural differences between the Athenians and Ionians. (Particularly evident are the differences in economic practices, such as the degree of involvement in long-distance commerce.) The process of equation drew force from the fifth- and fourth-century championing of the Ionians by the Athenians against the Persians. Anti-Medism was accompanied by mythological and cultic syntheses of Athenian and Ionian tradition, which provoked some passionate resistance. I would differ from you in emphasizing that the less Athenocentric myths about the foundation (*ktisis*) of Ionian cities might have been promoted by some archaic (and even classical) Ionians. See Sakellariou 1958: 39–243, esp. with summary table on 239–41, 254–302; more recently, Vanschoonwinkel 1991: 367–421. I think particularly of the variants about the settlement of Samos that highlight the Argolid instead of Attica (Paus.7.4.2–4; Menodotos *FGrH* 541 F1; cf. *EM* s.v. Ἀστυπάλαια). See also Figueira pp. 45–6.

§31. The fact that I need to say plural *areas* and not singular *area* is already an indication of the difficulties that await us. Contributing to these difficulties is the fact that the Ionians who were most active and influential in defining Ionian identity were exclusivist in using the name *Ionian*. As we are about to see, these exclusivist Ionians were the proud inhabitants of a region they called *Ionia*, situated in what we know as Asia Minor, on the east side of the Aegean Sea. They mythologized themselves as {|₁₀₆} descendants of adventurers who had followed kingly leaders stemming from Athens, capital city of Attica in Europe, in crossing over from the west side of the Aegean Sea and establishing on the east side 12 states at sites located along the central coastline of mainland Asia Minor and on two important offshore islands.

§32. These 12 states were consolidated into a confederation known as the Ionian Dodecapolis. Herodotus (1.142.3) lists all 12 states: of these 12, the ten Asiatic mainland city-states were Miletos, Myous, Priene, Ephesos, Kolophon, Lebedos, Teos, Klazomenai, Phokaia, and Erythrai, while the two Asiatic island-states were Samos and Chios.

§33. The self-mythologizing of Ionian states as offshoots of settlements originating from Athens can be seen as the most prominent feature of a much broader set of myths that can be categorized under the heading *Ionian Migration*, where the Greek word that I translate as 'migration' is *apoikiā* (as used in Strabo 13.1.3 C582 and elsewhere).[17] Although the mythmaking of the Ionian Dodecapolis must have screened out or at least minimized alternative myths that would have aetiologized the founding of other Ionian states that were not members of the 12-state confederation, we have evidence for the survival of such alternative myths, as we see for example from a passing remark made by Pausanias (7.3.3) concerning an Ionian migration from Athens to Naxos – which was one of the most important islands in a chain of islands known as the Cyclades. Evidently, the Ionian populations of the Cyclades were excluded from the confederation of the Ionian Dodecapolis. Another example of exclusion is Euboia, a large and most important Ionian island situated offshore to the northeast of Attica.

TJF: about the self-mythologizing of Ionian states as offshoots of settlements originating from Athens: This formulation can work in terms of the final reckoning, which was shaped by classical political realities.

GN: Very attractive, the hermeneutics of the term 'final reckoning'!

TJF: After the Athenian victory at Eurymedon (c. 468) affiliation in some form with Athens was established as the only viable alternative to Persian domination. Any 'final reckoning' reflects this situation that is contemporary with crystallization of the myths on which GN is focussing.

§34. Even if we define the Ionians narrowly, restricting the field of vision to the Asiatic Greeks of the Ionian Dodecapolis, I maintain that their importance was still paramount in the history of Greek civilization. But the problem is, the achievements of these Ionians, especially in science and in philosophy, are today generally seen as merely an aspect of Greek civilization viewed as a unified whole. It is almost as if the localization of such achievements by Ionians inhabiting the Asiatic region called Ionia were simply a historical accident. Or, to put it another way, it is as if the Asiatic Greeks of the Ionian Dodecapolis were no different from European Greeks.

TJF: Instead of saying *European Greeks*, I would suggest the *Attic, Euboian, and Cycladic Ionians*.

GN: I agree that the wording of TJF is more accurate, as we reconstruct backward in time. But I would still say, as we reconstruct forward in time toward what we may call the 'final reckoning', that the term 'European' works in the long run.

TJF: I concede GN's point, but I would continue to assert that the conjectural 'difference' with 'European Greeks' was most dramatic in comparison with the Attic and Euboian Ionians.

§35. But the fact is, the Asiatic Greeks of the Ionian Dodecapolis had their own distinct Greek identity – or, as I would prefer to say, their own self-defined ethnic identity. For these Ionians of the Ionian Dodecapolis, this ethnic identity was formalized by way of celebrating a seasonally recurring festival named the *Paniōnia*, the venue for which was a place named the *Paniōnion*. As Douglas Frame has shown in an important book about the myth of Nestor, king of Pylos (Frame 2009), the apogee {|₁₀₇} of this Ionian confederation – and of the festival of the Paniōnia as celebrated at the Paniōnion – can be dated to the late eighth and early seventh centuries BCE, and there survives a specific reference already in Homeric poetry to the festival that formalized the identity of the celebrants (*Iliad* 20.403–5).

§36. As Frame (2009: ch. 10) has also shown, the original leader of this 12-state confederation was the city-state of Miletos, and the rulers of this state claimed that they were descended from Neleus father of Periklymenos, who was a brother of Nestor, and that Periklymenos was an ancestor of Kodros, a king of Athens, who in turn was the father of a second Neleus. The Athenian Neleus founded not only Miletos but also, ultimately, the entire confederation of the Ionian Dodecapolis – according to the mythology propagated by Miletos about the Ionian migration, as we read in a fifth-century source, Hellanicus (*FGrH* 323a F 11; see also a later source, the Parian Marble *FGrH* 239F A27; see also *Suda* under the entry Πανύασις, where the early-fifth-century poet Panyasis is cited as another source).

§37. Alternatively, however, as we read in another fifth-century source, Pherecydes (*FGrH* 3 F 155, via Strabo 14.1.3 C632–3), the leader of the Ionian migration from Athens to Ionia (ἄρξαι δέ φησιν ῎Ανδροκλον τῆς τῶν ᾿Ιώνων ἀποικίας) was another son of Kodros the king, Androklos of Athens, who was known as the 'legitimate' son of Kodros (υἱὸν γνήσιον Κόδρου τοῦ ᾿Αθηνῶν βασιλέως) and who was the founder of the city-state of Ephesos (γενέσθαι δὲ τοῦτον ᾿Εφέσου κτίστην), establishing in that city a *basíleion* 'royal centre' for all the Ionians (διόπερ τὸ βασίλειον τῶν ᾿Ιώνων ἐκεῖ συστῆναί φασι) – which is why, says this source, the descendants of Androklos in Ephesos retained the title of *basileîs* 'kings' (καὶ ἔτι νῦν οἱ ἐκ τοῦ γένους ὀνομάζονται βασιλεῖς). So, the city-state of Ephesos, which as we have already seen is listed by Herodotus as a member of the Ionian Dodecapolis, was a rival of Miletos in claiming to be the city-state that dominated the new homeland of the Ionians in Asia Minor.

TJF: If you are correct, the advancement of Ephesos must have been managed by the satrapal regime in Sardis. Ephesos may have been a late joiner of the Delian League, as the landfall there of Themistokles, in flight from the Athenians and Spartans, seems to suggest (Thucydides 1.137.2-3; cf. Nepos *Themistocles* 8.7). Ephesos appears otherwise so much less significant than Miletos – until the eclipse of Miletos under the Athenians during 465–45. Even then the two cities seem to be on a similar economic level from the later 440s (Ephesos assessed at 6 talents; Miletos at 5).

GN: On the management of Ephesos by the satrapal regime in Sardis, I have something to say in what follows, at GN §40.

TJF: On reconsideration, I would also note that Pherecydes appears to have been close to Kimon (note F 2) so that the prominence of Androklos at Ephesos was probably acceptable in Kimonian circles at Athens in the early years of the Delian League.

§38. What we see here are two mutually contradictory versions of an overall myth about the Ionian migration. According to one version, the state of Miletos was clearly in the forefront of a grand movement of Ionians travelling from Athens to their new home in Asiatic Ionia, while in the other version it was the state of Ephesos that took the lead – and became the dominant city in Ionia.

§39. An explanation is needed for the emergence of Ephesos, at the expense of Miletos, as the dominant city of the Ionian Dodecapolis. As I will argue, this dominance took shape in an era that postdated by around two centuries the apogee of the Ionian Dodecapolis, which, as I already said, can be dated to the late eighth and early seventh centuries BCE. During those two centuries, as I will also argue, it was still Miletos and not Ephesos that maintained a position of dominance over the Ionian Dodecapolis.

§40. The question for now is this: how did Ephesos emerge as a serious rival to Miletos? The answer, as we will see, has to do with the fact that the entire region of {|₁₀₈} Ionia was for a long time under the domination of the Persian Empire, which was exerting its control over the cities of Ionia through the primary agency of the satrap of Lydia, stationed in the inland city of Sardis, the capital of what had once been the Lydian kingdom. For further background, here are two basic historical facts about the era of Persian domination over Ionia:

1   The Persian domination of Ionia got underway in 546 BCE, when the Persian Empire overwhelmed the Lydian kingdom, which had dominated mainland Ionia beforehand.
2   During the era when the Ionian Dodecapolis was dominated by the Persian Empire, it was secondarily dominated by the city-state of Miletos – and Miletos must have maintained this secondary domination of Ionia till the end – about which I will have more to say in §41.

TJF: I am sympathetic to your hypothesis and seeing Miletos as the dominant city in mainland Ionia seems unproblematic (I have written a bit about Milesian colonization); it was advantaged by its mastery of techniques for long-distance trade (including emplacement of *emporia*, especially in Egypt and the Black Sea). It is the period before 700 (or a little later) that gives me some pause. I would be encouraged if the traditions about the ramifications of the Lelantine War could be brought in (via Eretria) – and if some archaeology from Miletos were cited as well.

GN: TJF here is far too modest in the way he cites his own research on the history of Miletos as the mother city or metropolis of numerous daughter cities. For an introduction, I recommend a reading of TJF's relevant comments in the book *Theognis of Megara* (1985: 289–90, 294–6), edited by TJF and GN, as listed in the Bibliography. About the Lelantine War, I offer some relevant observations in *Classical Inquiry* 2018.06.01, "Lelantine War, Eretria and Chalkis, and the Contest of Homer and Hesiod."

TJF: On Milesian trade and colonization, consult now Figueira 2015: 329–30.

§41. The end for Miletos came with the Ionian revolt, which lasted from 499 to 494 BCE. This revolt was started by Miletos and ended with the sack of this city by the Persian Empire in 494 BCE. This disaster, as narrated by Herodotus (6.18), was commemorated in a tragedy produced soon thereafter in Athens, composed and directed by the dramatist Phrynichus (6.21.2).

§42. I will postpone till later my analysis of the Ionian revolt, except to say this much already now: before the end came, Miletos could still claim to be the primary originator of the Ionian migration. Most relevant is what we read in Herodotus: when Aristagoras of Miletos went to Athens for the purpose of persuading the Athenians to come to the aid of the Ionian Revolt (5.97.1), he referred to the myth of the Ionian migration: or, to put it in terms of the rhetoric paraphrased by Herodotus, Aristagoras reminded the Athenians of the claim that the people of Miletos were *ápoikoi* 'colonists' originating from the city of Athens (5.97.2) – in other words, that Athens was the originator of the *apoikiā* or 'migration' of Ionians to the East.

The idea of 'Ionians' as viewed after the sea battle at Salamis

§43. The ethnic self-definition of the Asiatic Greeks who called themselves *Ionians* (*Íōnes*) must be contrasted with a rival ethnic self-definition of European Greeks who called themselves *Hellenes* (*Héllēnes*). To drive this point home, I start by asking a hypothetical question. This question centres on a major event in world history, namely, a sea battle that took place at the island of Salamis in 480 BCE, where the naval forces of Athens, combined with smaller naval forces sent by the island state of Aegina and by other allied states, decisively defeated the combined naval forces of the Persian Empire. The question is, what would have happened if the Persian Empire had won this naval battle, and if Athens and its allies had lost? Well, in terms of my line of argument, the Persian Empire would have conquered European Greece, and there would have been, after that, no more Hellenes in Europe. There would continue to be Greek-speaking populations there, yes, and they would even be much the same populations as before, but they would not be calling themselves Hellenes anymore. {|₁₀₉} Instead of Hellenes, there would now be Ionians in Europe – that is, in the region of Athens known as Attica and in such outlying islands as nearby Euboia – just as there were Ionians already in Asia Minor. To put it more broadly, Greekness would have been reconfigured in terms of the self-representation of the Eastern Greeks, with the obliteration of Greekness as configured by the Western Greeks of Europe who had up to now called themselves Hellenes.[18]

TJF: Certainly the fact that the European enemy alliance called itself the Hellenes (e.g., Herodotus 7.145.1) would have weighed in the kind of shift in nomenclature that you posit. Also, ought you not make the point right here that the Persians and other Near East peoples were already calling our Greeks 'Ionians'?

GN: See now n. 18.

§44. This formulation is relevant not only to the European Greeks who were Ionians but also to other European Greeks who were Aeolians and Dorians. If the forces of the Persian Empire had been victorious in the sea battle at Salamis, then there would have been a more general realignment affecting

1   the Ionians of Europe, like the populations inhabiting Attica and the offshore island of Euboia
2   the Aeolians of Europe, like the populations inhabiting Boiotia and Thessaly
3   the Dorians of Europe, like the populations inhabiting most of the land masses situated to the north as also to the south of the Corinthian Gulf.

TJF: on GN's category 1: I have come around to the position that late ninth- and eighth-century central Greece was a sort of *ēpeiros* or *peraiā* of the island of Euboia in structural and cultural terms (Figueira 2015: 325).
GN: I find this formulation of TJF most intuitive. Perhaps a similar formulation could be made with regard to the northern coast of Asia Minor at a comparably earlier period: in this case, that area could be seen as a sort of *ēpeiros* 'mainland' or *peraiā* 'mainland-that-faces-the island' of Lesbos.
TJF: Certainly the major eastern Aegean islands (Chios, Samos, and on Lesbos Mytilene; and, outside Ionia, Lindos on Rhodes) all secured extensive sub-hegemonies on their *peraiai* in the first period of the Delian League. In general, see Jensen 2010. GN's conclusions accommodate nicely the likely balance of power between insular and mainland Ionia. Outside of Miletos, after the Persian conquest, the rest of the mainland lost wealth and power relative to the Chians, Samians, and Lesbians. This power/wealth balance is illustrated by the rebel Ionian naval contingents at Lade in 494 (Herodotus 6.7–8). As GN notes, Miletos suffered grievously in the defeat of the revolt (492), while Chios also suffered heavy losses at Lade. The early Delian League period saw a resurgence, largely expressed through the sub-hegemonies in neighbouring islands and *peraiai*, in which Miletos shared for a time until succumbing to internal and hegemonic stresses in mid-century (note Rhodes-Osborne *GHI* 1, #123).

§45. These populations of European Greeks, who had all been calling themselves Hellenes at this moment in history when the sea battle took place, would thereafter have been realigned respectively with the following populations of Asiatic Greeks:

1   the Ionians in the central coastlands of Asia Minor as also in the outlying islands of Chios and Samos
2   the Aeolians in the northern coastlands of Asia Minor as also in the outlying islands of Lesbos and Tenedos

3   the Dorians in the southern coastlands of Asia Minor as also in the outlying
islands of Rhodes and beyond.

TJF: on GN's categories 2 and 3: With regard to 2 . . . And we recognize that the
eastern Aeolians were already aligned with the eastern Ionians in politics and
institutions. With regard to 3 . . . Moreover, Herodotus of Halicarnassus – a
city that belonged to the Dorian Hexapolis – writes in Ionic. Herodotus was
closely connected with Samos and is saturated with Ionian thought.

§46. But none of this happened. In the end, after the defeat of the Persian Empire's
naval forces in the battle of Salamis and, later, after the defeat of its land forces at
Plataia, the Greekness of the Hellenes in the West prevailed over the Greekness of
the Ionians and the Aeolians and the Dorians in the East. And, hurrah, the democracy that had been the new way of life for Greeks of the West as represented primarily by Athens could now prevail over the tyranny that was the old way of life for the
subjugated Greeks of the East as represented primarily by the Ionians.

§47. What I have just formulated is a common contemporary understanding
of what happened after the sea battle at Salamis in 480 BCE – followed by the
land battle at Plataia in 479 BCE. But this formulation is oversimplified. In the
case of Ionia, for example, we are about to see that the cities of that region were
at this same moment in history governed by regimes that were considered to be
democracies, and $\{|_{110}\}$ such democratic regimes had been installed at the initia-
tive of the Persian Empire. As I am about to argue, the victory of the European
Greeks at Salamis and at Plataea in 480 BCE and 479 BCE may have been seen
as a victory for democracy as we know it, yes, but the fact remains that an alternative victory for the Persian Empire could have been likewise ideologized as a
victory for democracy – at least, for those Greeks who were Ionians. And such
an ideology would have been promoted by the Persian Empire itself. In terms
of the multi-ethnic ideologies of this empire, I argue, such a victory would have
been equated with a victory not for Persians but rather for Ionians – that is, for the
Asiatic Greeks who populated Ionia. At this point in history, as we are about to
see, these Ionians could have promoted an alternative version of democracy that
supposedly rivaled the democracy as configured in European Athens.

TJF: especially with regard to GN's wording "the dominion over Ionia and over
other Greek-speaking regions in the East was lost by the Persian Empire and
was won by Athens, which thereafter evolved into what we know retrospectively as the Athenian Empire": A crude and old-fashioned view. For one
thing, this ignores the phenomenon of sub-hegemony where the major east
Greek allies of the Athenians acquired sizable spheres of influence during the
Attic hegemony (for which see earlier mention). Was the Athenian domination as intrusive as the Persian? Judgment varies (I am skeptical). It was most
assuredly not so fiscally. And there was much less room for arbitrary authority. The Athenians almost always acted (in the absence of outright revolt)
through adjudication.

GN: Here is one of those areas in my overall argumentation where my friend thinks I have gone too far. 'A bridge too far. . .'. I am guessing that, if I had not used the term 'Athenian Empire', I would not have seemed quite so far at variance with TJF's own assessment of what happened after the Persian Empire lost control over the Greek-speaking populations in the East. I could say in my defence that the rationale for my speaking in terms of an 'Athenian Empire' was not ideological but historical. Or, to put it more accurately, I was trying to take a historical approach in analyzing the conflicting ideologies, current in the ancient world, concerning a basic question: what does it mean for one city-state to have *arkhē* or 'rule' over other city-states? I offer relevant analysis of such conflicting ideologies in *Homer the Classic* (Nagy 2009|2008 4§§174–175, §§177–180), as cited at the end of my original discussion in GN §48.

TJF: Note in support of GN's position how Herodotus is quite emphatic on the energy with which the majority of the Ionians fought against the Greek alliance at Salamis (8.85.1–3).

§48. Before I can proceed with my argument, I need to highlight a basic fact of history. As a consequence of the sea battle of Salamis in 480 BCE, where the navies of the Persian Empire were on the losing side while the navy of Athens was on the winning side, the dominion over Ionia and over other Greek-speaking regions in the East was lost by the Persian Empire and was won by Athens, which thereafter evolved into what we know retrospectively as the Athenian Empire. To say it more bluntly, Athenians became the super-Greeks of the East. In the Greek-speaking world of the East, the Athenians could now dominate the Ionians in the form of the Delian League, but eventually they dominated also the Aeolians to the north of the Ionians and the Dorians to the south. And the domination extended even further, to the regions of the Hellespont and the Propontis and beyond. An architectural landmark of this new dominion of Athens over the Asiatic Greeks was the Odeum of Pericles, built to replicate the Grand Tent of Xerxes, which had been confiscated by the Athenians after their victory in the naval battle at Salamis. Plutarch (*Pericles* 13.9–11) gives a most vivid description of this new imperial building, adjacent to the Theatre of Dionysus: here was a People's Palace for all Asiatic Greeks to admire as an orientalizing *stupor mundi*, situated in the heart of a European city that could now also play the role of an Asiatic metropolis.[19]

TJF with regard GN's statement about Athenian domination of Aeolians and Dorians in the East: The major Aeolian states and most of the Doric Hexapolis (except for Halicarnassus) belonged to the alliance from the outset.

GN: Point well taken.

TJF: In support of GN's characterization of the Delian League as Ionian, I think that the following is helpful for context. Most of the allies in the early league were smaller *phoros*-paying *poleis*, a large number of which were under their larger neighbours' hegemony. Only c. 24 allies contributed ships and men, actively participating in planning operations. Fourteen of these were Ionian in dialect, including the large islands of Chios, Samos, Thasos, Naxos, and Paros. Aeolic speakers were mainly the alliance of Lesbian cities, perhaps with their Thracian colony Ainos, and at some rather early stage Kyme in mainland Aeolis. The only Dorians were the Rhodians in their three cities and the Poteidaians. If one uses *phoros*-assessment and ship-contingents as a gauge of wealth and indirectly of population size, the early Delian League was at least 70% Ionian, with the rest mostly Aeolic Lesbians (>18%).

§49. The new domination of Eastern Greeks by Athens was viewed by most Greeks as tyranny – a new form of tyranny that superseded the old domination of these same regions by the Persian Empire. Yes, Athens could still be considered a democracy on the inside, but it had now become a tyranny on the outside (Pericles is quoted as saying this much by Thucydides 2.63.1–2).[20] Ionia could now be controlled from Athens in Europe, not from Sardis in Asia Minor. And a parallel formula of control could now be extended to the Aeolians and to the Dorians situated respectively to the north and to the south of the Ionians in Asia. {|₁₁₁}

TJF: with reference to GN's use of the term 'tyranny' here: The idea of Athens as a *turannos polis* was formulated in highly propagandistic terms, especially by the Peloponnesians. In general, this idea did push some elite contemporaries' buttons quite effectively. Recall, however, that the Athenians were themselves quite effective at recovering allies after Laconizing interludes. As to being true, that is another question. Reading the account of Syloson's accession to the Samian tyranny in Herodotus (especially at 3.139–41, 146.1–149) helps to understand the significant difference separating Athenian hegemony from Persian authority, with its caprice and solipsism.

TJF: with reference to the thinking of Pericles as reported by Thucydides 2.63.1–2: For Pericles, it was like a tyranny in a certain way (being difficult to give up), but it was Kleon who then went the next step to equate with tyranny (Thucydides 3.37.2), and even he was acting under extreme pressure, given the danger posed by the revolt of Mytilene.

GN: Again, I will say in my defence that my aim was merely to report on ancient ideologies, not to highlight my own value judgments. More in *Homer the Classic* (Nagy 2009|2008 4§24). as cited in GN §49. TJF: Our disagreement is perhaps owed to seeing the same phenomenon from different angles. As noted earlier, the *turannos polis* interpretation of the Attic hegemony cannot be corroborated by the evidence, yet its hold on Greek elite opinion is well attested (as GN observes), particularly by Thucydides. Ionian elites longed for *eleutheria* in isolation, both accompanied by preservation of their political and social privileges and benefitted in perpetuity by the material gains afforded by political status. That this aspiration sought restoration of something never existent (especially as uncontested) evokes for me GN's appeal to 'ideologies'. As Athenians or Persians appeared the chief hindrances or facilitators of such Ionian elite wish-fulfillment, they varied as objects of admiration and fealty or antipathy and resistance.

§50. By contrast, if the forces of the Persian Empire had won at Salamis, the new super-Greeks would have been not the Athenians as controllers of Ionians and beyond but the Ionians as controllers of Aeolians to the north and of Dorians to the south in Asia Minor. And, in fact, the prototype for such a smaller-scale empire was already visible in the context of what historians today call the Ionian revolt. As I will now argue, such a smaller-scale empire could be described as an Ionian Empire in the making. But such an empire was only *in the making*, since the Ionian revolt ultimately failed.

Ionian revolt

§51. Most relevant to the historical contingencies during the fifth and fourth centuries of Ionian identity was the Ionian revolt, which lasted from 499 to 494 BCE. This revolt of Ionians from the Persian Empire – along with its grim aftermath – is documented primarily and in fact almost exclusively by Herodotus (5.23.1– 6.42.2), whose narrative highlights the many successes and failures experienced by both sides in the conflict, which in any case culminated in the decisive victory of the Persian Empire.

§52. In undertaking my analysis of the historical background, I will focus on four Ionian states as the primary settings for various events that I will be foregrounding:

1   the city-state of Miletos, situated on the mainland in Asia Minor
2   the city-state of Ephesos, situated on the mainland in Asia Minor
3   the outlying island-state of Samos
4   the city-state of Athens, situated on the mainland on the other side of the Aegean Sea, in Europe.

§53. And I will focus on four relevant historical facts:

1   The city-states of Miletos and Ephesos, as well as the island-state of Samos, were all members of the Ionian Dodecapolis.
2   The city-state of Miletos claimed Athens as its mother-city or *mētropolis*. Such a claim was actualized, as we have seen, in the Milesian version of myths about an Ionian migration.
3   The Ionian revolt, led by the state of Miletos, failed partly because the state of Samos defected at a critical moment in a decisive sea battle at Lade in the year 494 BCE. As for Ephesos, which like Samos was becoming a most serious rival of Miletos in claiming leadership of the Ionian Dodecapolis, the forces of this city were not even present at the sea battle of Lade. Our primary source for such telling details is Herodotus (6.14.2–3).
4   The failure of the Ionian revolt led to the capture of Miletus and to its obliteration as a viable state in 494 BCE, followed by other harsh forms of retribution inflicted on other Ionian states by the victorious forces of the Persian Empire in 494–493 BCE. Again, our prime source is Herodotus (6.18 and

31–2). At this point, as I infer {|₁₁₂} from the account of Herodotus (6.33), much of the punitive naval action against the Asiatic Greeks seems to be blamed on the Phoenicians.

§54. Finally, I will focus on four most relevant *dramatis personae* in the story as narrated by Herodotus:

1   *Histiaios*. He was tyrant of Miletus and the foremost ally of Darius, king of the Persian Empire, in an imperial expedition against the nomadic Scythians in 513 BCE. Our primary source here is Herodotus (4.137–8). In this context, it is made clear that the Ionian city-states, including Miletus, were at that time ruled by tyrants who had been installed by the Persian Empire, and the relevant word used here by Herodotus is *turanneúein* 'rule as a tyrant' (4.137.2). As tyrant of Miletos, Histiaios assumed the role of chief spokesman for the Ionians, and Herodotus quotes him as saying that all the tyrants of the Ionians owe their political power to Darius, without whose domination the Ionians would rather "have democracies" than "have tyrannies" – and the relevant words used here are *dēmokrateîsthai* and *turanneúesthai* (again, 4.137.2). Although Histiaios collaborated with Darius, he had so much personal power in Ionia that he was eventually relocated to the Persian capital (Herodotus mentions only the administrative capital at Susa, not the other capital at Persepolis), supposedly as the honoured guest of Darius (Herodotus 5.25 and 30).

2   *Aristagoras*. He became the next tyrant of Miletos. At the time of his rule, Miletus maintained its status as the most eminent and successful state among all the states in Ionia. Again, our primary source is Herodotus, who describes Miletos as "the pride [*proskhēma*] of Ionia" (5.28: τῆς Ἰωνίης . . . πρόσχημα). In this context, as Herodotus reports further (5.38.1), Aristagoras became the main instigator of the Ionian revolt, and he arranged for the tyrants of the various Ionian cities, as formerly installed by the Persian Empire, to be removed. I interpret these actions as indications of an overriding motive: *Aristagoras and his co-conspirators were attempting to form an Ionian Arkhē*, dominated by Miletos, and this empire would be independent or quasi-independent from the Persian Empire.[21] To support my argument that the motive of Aristagoras was to form some kind of a breakaway empire, I cite the reportage of {|₁₁₃} Herodotus (5.109.3) concerning the expression used by the delegates of the Ionians in referring to their constituency at this time: *tò koinòn tôn Iốnōn* 'the commune of the Ionians'. This same term *koinón* 'commune', as I have argued in another project, was used decades later by the Athenians in referring to their own empire (as we see for example by way of Thucydides 2.60.4, 2.61.4).[22] I will have more to say presently about the eventual Athenian Empire, but for now I must continue to concentrate on the would-be Ionian Empire. Although the motive of Aristagoras in instigating the Ionian revolt was imperialistic, as I argue, he claimed that his motive was democratic: as Herodotus puts it, Aristagoras renounced his own *turannis* 'tyranny'

in Miletos and proclaimed as its replacement the principle of *isonomiē* 'equitable participation' for the city (5.37.2). Here I must return to a passage of Herodotus that I have already cited earlier (3.80–4), about the Debate of the Constitutions, the dramatic date for which is 522 BCE. In the context of this Debate as dramatized by Herodotus, the same word *isonomiē* is used to express the idea of democracy, advocated by one of the three debating Persian nobles, Otanes, as the best form of government for the Persian Empire (3.80, 3.83). At a later point in the narrative, Herodotus will cross-refer to this passage, and, in the context of his cross-reference, the word he uses for the idea of democracy is now *dēmokratiē* (6.43.3), which is clearly meant here as a synonym of *isonomiē*. I should add that Herodotus uses the same word *dēmokratiē* (6.131.1) in referring to the establishment of democracy in Athens by Cleisthenes in 508–507 BCE. I should also add here a detail that I have already noted: Herodotus uses the word *dēmokrateîsthai* 'have democracy' (4.137.2) in referring to the negative attitude of Histiaios, tyrant of Miletos, toward the very idea of democracy. I will soon consider further the context of the reference made by Herodotus to *dēmokratiē* in his cross-reference to the Debate of the Constitutions (6.43) but for now I will stick to the present context of his reference to the *isonomiē* (5.37.2) declared by Aristagoras for the state of Miletos in 499 BCE. It is relevant to such a context that the city-state of Athens is linked with this declaration of Aristagoras. Recruited as supporters of the Ionian revolt were two Ionian city-states on the European side of the Aegean Sea. According to Herodotus (5.77 and 5.99) one of these states was Eretria, an Ionian city situated on the island of Euboia and an old ally of Miletos; and the other state was, not coincidentally, Athens, the notional mother city of Miletos. The government of Athens at this time had been a *dēmokratiē* ever since this form of government was established there by Cleisthenes in 508–507 BCE, and this democratic identity would have been compatible with the ideology newly declared by Aristagoras for Miletos and, by extension, for all the states of Ionia. After the Ionians were joined by the Athenians and the Eretrians, they undertook an ultimately unsuccessful attack on Sardis in the year 498 BCE. After this serious provocation against the Persian Empire, {|₁₁₄} there was no turning back for the Ionians participating in the revolt, as Herodotus darkly observes (5.103). And these Ionians now included not only the states of the Ionian Dodecapolis but also the states of Athens and Eretria. But now let me finish with Aristagoras: during the final phases of the Ionian revolt, which was already collapsing, Aristagoras had to leave Miletos and was killed in the course of a military side-adventure in Thrace (5.126).

TJF: commenting on the interpretation of the rationale for the actions taken by Aristagoras and Histiaios: Quite a bold hypothesis, given that the background to the revolt was an expedition to subjugate Naxos *for* Persia. What such an 'empire' would have looked like has to be shaped by the sphere of influence acquired by Polykrates of Samos in the 530s and 520s (Herodotus 3.122.2; cf. 3.39.4; also Thucydides 1.13.6). If one accepts that the limitations accepted by Polykrates would have to have been observed by Aristagoras and Histiaios (perhaps for a new satrapy governed at Miletos by Histiaios), then you may indeed have gauged their rationale.

GN: commenting on a rewritten §54: On the events reported by Herodotus (5.30–8) concerning the failed military expedition of Aristagoras to capture the Ionian island of Naxos, I confine myself here to noting two arguments I plan to develop in a separate project. One, with reference to the 200 triremes that were authorized by Darius himself for Aristagoras to use in his expedition (5.30–33), I will argue that this contribution undertaken by the Persian Empire was more directly a contribution fulfilled by the cities of the Asiatic Greek world, which were ruled at the time by tyrants appointed by the empire – just as Miletos was ruled by such an appointee in the person of Aristagoras himself. Two, I will argue that the narrative of Herodotus about the double-crossing of these Greek tyrants by Aristagoras (5.36–8) leaves room for interpretations that differ from the one that the narrator himself prefers, which is, that Aristagoras feared retribution from Darius for the failure of the expedition. In terms of my own interpretation, Aristagoras seized an opportunity to capitalize on this failure by attempting to turn it into a successful revolt against his Persian sponsors. In any case, as Herodotus notes (5.35–6), Aristagoras may well have been secretly aided and abetted by his predecessor Histiaios.

TJF: It is worth exploring to what extent the ambitions toward (regional) hegemony of Aristagoras (and possibly Histiaios) need have differed under Persian domination or free of that control. Notable also is that our appraisal of Herodotus' account of the death of Aristagoras may be affected by a probable lacuna at the end of Book VI (6.126).

3   *Artaphernes.* He was a brother of Darius and ruled Ionia by virtue of his royal appointment as satrap of Lydia, with headquarters in the inland city of Sardis.[23] As we read in Herodotus (5.70–4), Artaphernes was involved in a political crisis that took place in the city of Athens after 510 BCE, which was the year when Hippias, of the lineage of the Peisistratidai, was overthrown and exiled as tyrant there: at around 507 BCE, in the context of an ongoing effort by proponents of democracy as led by Cleisthenes to seek external allies in their political struggle against proponents of oligarchy as led by Isagoras, ambassadors were sent from Athens to Artaphernes, satrap at Sardis, and they agreed to offer tokens of earth and fire, thus signaling submission to the Persian Empire (5.74).[24] Around eight years later, as we read in Herodotus (5.96), Artaphernes sent a threatening message to the Athenians, ordering them to undo their prevailing democratic regime and to restore to power the lineage of the Peisistratidai, who remained exiled from Athens. It was at this same point, says Herodotus (5.97.1), that Aristagoras of Miletos happened to arrive in Athens for the purpose of asking the Athenians to come to the aid of the Ionian revolt. As I have already noted, one of the arguments presented by Aristagoras to persuade the Athenians to join the Ionians in their revolt was

his reference to the myth of the Ionian migration (5.97.2). After noting this new involvement of Artaphernes in the politics of the Athenians, Herodotus has no more to say about this Persian until his narrative reaches the final phases of the Ionian revolt. It was near the time of the bitter end, as we follow the narrative of Herodotus (6.30), that this same Artaphernes got involved in the capture of Histiaios, whom he promptly executed. Herodotus (6.32) goes on to narrate the horrific obliteration of Miletos in 494 BCE together with the ghastly retributions suffered by other Ionian states in the grim aftermath, and he concludes this part of the narrative by gravely observing that the Ionians, now that their revolt was utterly defeated, became once again what they had been before, that is, slaves of the Persians. In the course of narrating this bitter end, Herodotus keeps Artaphernes out of his narrative. But then, Herodotus (6.42) starts to narrate what seems to be a {|₁₁₅} new beginning of sorts, and, at this point, Artaphernes is reintroduced into the narrative: the satrap now convenes representatives of the remaining Ionian states and proceeds to set up new treaties with them – arrangements that are described in most positive terms by Herodotus. There is another reference to these new arrangements by Diodorus of Sicily (20.25), and we learn from this later source that a chief negotiator for the Ionians in their dealings with Artaphernes was Hecataeus of Miletos. As I argue in another project, Herodotus thought of this Hecataeus as one of the *lógioi* 'word-masters' of the Persians; in other words, the Persian 'party line' about the wars between Hellenes and Persians was represented not by Persians but by Ionians like Hecataeus who spoke as collaborationists promoting the agenda of the Persian Empire.[25] As we know from Herodotus (5.36.2–4), Hecataeus had been an outspoken opponent of the Ionian Revolt.

TJF: commenting with regard to the reportage of Herodotus (6.42) about the initiatives taken by Artaphernes, satrap of Sardis, in setting up treaties for the Ionian cities after the failure of the Ionian Revolt. TJF points out that these treaties would have bound these cities to each other.

GN: I agree, but I think that such treaties could also have originally bound these Ionian cities in a special way to the Persian Empire itself.

TJF: While I suspect that any genuine democratic, populist, concessionary aspects of Artaphernes' intervention were modest, GN is undoubtedly correct in seeing the underlying *tradition* as laudatory, apologetic, and programmatic. Cf. Scott 2005: 191–3, 544–8.

4   *Mardonios.* A son-in-law of Darius, he was put in charge as the leader of a military expedition sent to Europe in 493 BCE for the purpose of punishing Athens and Eretria, which had been the two Ionian city-states in Europe that had supported the revolt of the Asiatic Ionians. That is what Herodotus (6.43) reports, adding that the real motive was to extend the power of the Persian Empire to the European side of the Aegean Sea. At this point, the narrative of Herodotus (again, at 6.43) reveals a most interesting detail about the actions of Mardonios

as the generalissimo of the military forces that had been sent off to subdue the European Greeks: advancing from the south of Asia Minor toward the north, where he would make his eventual crossing into Europe at the Hellespont, Mardonios separated from his infantry and sailed with his navy along the entire coastland of Ionia, travelling from south to north, and what he proceeded to do upon arrival at each Ionian city was to dismiss each *túrannos* 'tyrant' that had been appointed by the Persian Empire, establishing *dēmokratíai* 'democracies' in their place (δημοκρατίας κατίστα). We see a double-headed strategy here: while Artaphernes as satrap at Sardis was establishing new treaties between the Persian Empire and the states of Ionia, Mardonios as generalissimo of the empire's armed forces was ensuring a democratic base for all these Asiatic Ionians. At this point, Herodotus (again, at 6.43) makes a most ostentatious remark: the Greeks of his own generation, he says, hearing more than half a century later what he has just said about things done by a general of the Persian Empire (in 493 BCE), would find it unbelievable that Mardonios could have done such things in Ionia, namely, that "he was establishing democracies in the cities" (δημοκρατίας κατίστα ἐς τὰς πόλιας) – just as it may seem unbelievable for these Greeks who are living in the time of Herodotus to hear that there had once taken place, at an even earlier time (522 {|₁₁₆} BCE), the so-called Debate of the Constitutions, on which occasion some of the Persian elites actually argued that they needed to establish a democracy for themselves (ὡς χρεὸν εἴη δημοκρατέεσθαι Πέρσας). In this context, then, Herodotus is ostentatiously cross-referring to an earlier moment in his *History* where he narrates this Debate of the Constitutions (3.80–4) – and where he says that one of the three debating Persian nobles, Otanes, actually advocated democracy and not monarchy or oligarchy as the best form of government for the Persian Empire. But Herodotus insists (again, at 6.43) that Mardonios did in fact establish democracies throughout Ionia before he proceeded with his navy to the Hellespont, where he would be joined by his infantry. I will not proceed to review what Herodotus narrates (again, at 6.43) about the misfortunes that awaited Mardonios and his combined armed forces after they all crossed the Hellespont – except to note that they got bogged down in the region of Mount Athos, and that Mardonios was then relieved of his command as generalissimo (6.94.2). Thus, the subsequent combination of (A) success for the Persian forces at Eretria and (B) failure for them at Marathon in 490 BCE must be attributed to military leaders other than Mardonios. We will have to wait 13 years for Mardonios to re-emerge as a *dramatis persona*, when he becomes once again the generalissimo of the Persian Empire in the expedition of 480–79 against the Hellenes of Europe, culminating in the defeats at Salamis and Plataea.

Debate of the constitutions

§55. The so-called Debate of the Constitutions, dramatized by Herodotus (3.80–4) as happening in 522 BCE, is often dismissed as pure invention: many have gone on record to claim that Persian elites at this point in history could not have been thinking of three forms of government as conventionally described in ancient Greek traditions: monarchy, oligarchy, democracy.[26] In my own work on the Debate passage, by contrast, I have argued against such claims of invention, emphasizing (1) the accuracy of Herodotus in his use of wording to describe the three forms of government and (2) the applicability of this wording to forms of government as they actually existed in the Greek-speaking world at this time.[27] My argument is, these three forms of government – or at least the idea of these forms – already existed in the Greek-speaking world that belonged to the Persian Empire at this time, 522 BCE. My argument goes further: the Persian elites as pictured by Herodotus in the Debate of the Constitutions would have been debating in real life not the ideal form of government for the Persians as Persians but for the Asiatic Greeks who inhabited the westernmost part of their empire, especially for the Ionians, who were considered to be the dominant {|₁₁₇} culture of the Asiatic Greek-speaking world by contrast with the Aeolians to the north and the Dorians to the south.

TJF: I have always thought that Herodotus' trust in the historicity of the Debate derived from the circulation of an earlier Ionian written version of the 'event'. If it could be considered 'Persian' in so far as it was Ionian constitutional thinking that was attributed to the Persians (perhaps those sympathetic with Greek values) for application to Ionia, I would find this theory most congenial. Whether such a forerunner was necessarily fixed in 522 would be uncertain, but GN is hitting the right note with his suggestion that follows that the Debate in its present form can only be properly viewed retrospectively from a later, fifth-century vantage point. That even the adding the names of Darius and his fellow conspirators to the story could be subsequent may not be problematical. The most famous transition in the period of Persian domination might have drawn to itself this tradition, embodying so powerful an ideological debate. On the Debate, see also Munson pp. 151–3.

§56. And here I return to what Herodotus says (6.43) about the actions of Mardonios in 493 BCE: as we have already seen, Mardonios established democracies in the cities of Ionia, deposing the Ionian tyrants who had been installed by the Persian Empire to rule these cities. I argue that the Debate of the Constitutions, as narrated in the *History* of Herodotus (3.80–4), makes sense only retrospectively. In other words, the things that were supposedly being said in 522 BCE, which was the dramatic date of the Debate, could only be understood in terms of the things that were being done by Mardonios in 493 BCE. In the Debate dramatized by Herodotus, as we have already seen, the word *isonomiē* is used to express the idea of democracy, advocated by Otanes, one of the debating nobles, as the best form of government for the Persian Empire (3.80, 3.83). Later, when Herodotus cross-refers to this passage in the context of narrating the establishment of democracies by Mardonios, he uses the word *dēmokratiē* (6.43), which as we have already seen is clearly meant there as a synonym of *isonomiē*. And, as we have also seen already, Herodotus uses the same word *dēmokratiē* (6.131.1) in referring to the establishment of democracy in Athens by Cleisthenes in 508–507 BCE. Conversely, Herodotus uses the word *isonomiē* (5.37.2) in referring to the democracy proclaimed in Miletos by Aristagoras in 499 BCE. And there were even earlier prototypes of such democracy, at least conceptually. Herodotus (3.142.3) mentions a striking example: he says that *isonomiē* was proclaimed in Samos by Maiandrios, the new tyrant of that island state, successor to Polycrates, who died not long after 522 BCE. In this case, however, Herodotus goes on to narrate how the proclamation failed (3.142.4–143.2). Failure or no failure, however, democracy was an option to be reckoned with in the Greek-speaking regions of the Persian Empire.

§57. But now I move fast-forward in time from 493 to 480 BCE. The cities of the Ionians who were fighting on the side of the Persian Empire had presumably still retained democratic forms of government as established by Mardonios 13 years earlier.[28]

§58. In any case, the question remains: what would have happened if Mardonios had been victorious in the grand expedition that culminated in the naval battle at Salamis? Well, if we follow the reportage of Herodotus (7.6.1), Mardonios would have become the satrap of the entire Greek-speaking world of Europe.[29] But there is more {|₁₁₈} to it. I think that the Ionians who were his collaborators would have played a major role in the political reorganization of the European Hellenes. Besides Asiatic Ionia, there could now be a European Ionia as well, with the annexation of Attica together with such outlying islands as Euboia, and the capital city of such a reconfigured Greater Ionia could have remained Athens, which was after all the original mother city or metropolis of the mythical Ionian migration. And this venerable metropolis could even have remained a democracy of sorts – at least in name.[30]

TJF: I must remark (fondly, as always) that there is a tendency here for a major step forward in analysis to get lost as an intermediate step toward a conclusion that is somewhat over-reaching. The significant insight of GN for me is that those who were tarred with the brush of Medism and opposition to democracy during the Athenian hegemony may well have objected by offering a plausible defence through the following sequence: (1) the argument of Otanes in favor of *isonomiē* in the Debate of the Constitutions; (2) the initiatives of Mardonios in suppressing Ionian tyrants; and (3), I add, an offer, made by Mardonios, of autonomy to Athens – as reported by Herodotus (8.140.2). (And what about Gobryes, then, the father of Mardonios? Was he one of the two Persians nobles [Herodotus 3.83.1] who sided with Otanes for *isonomiē* against Darius and monarchy?) Thus, the Persian Debate could be seen as a living issue in the period of the Athenian *arkhē* 'rule'. As to an overreaching dimension, I think that, external to the apologetics of former Medizers, one has to concede the regular status of 'tyrant'-led subject *poleis* (including the Ionians), beyond Strattis of Chios (GN n. 28) and the returning Peisistratids and Aleuadai (n. 30): Plutarch *Mor.* 859C notes tyrants expelled from Miletos, Phokis, Thasos, and Thessaly (a *dunasteia*); the *Suda* (s.v. Ἡρόδοτος, η 536; Πανύασις, π 248 Adler) notes a tyrant at Halikarnassos.

TJF: commenting further on the possibility I raise, that Athens could have remained a capital city, as it were, even within the Persian Empire: Given that the Athenians were offered autonomy by Mardonios (8.140.2), the city-state of Athens could have become, as Miletos once was, an island of autonomy inside a Persian satrapy. Alternatively, the capital of such a satrapy could have been relocated to a city on the island of Euboia – perhaps to Karystos – or to the island of Naxos. In the case of Naxos, Delos would have been closely attached. Both Karystos and Naxos resisted the early Delian League (Thucydides 1.98.3–4).

TJF: concluding: Even in situations where they professed to abolish tyranny, I doubt that the Persians were intending to replace or exclude one-man rule. Rather, they were simply setting up a system where one leader, appointed by them, would consult with other organs of government and the wider community. Such an arrangement might not be much different from how the 'king' of a Phoenician city operated under Persian control (Bondi 1995: 293–5).

One last time, back to the *mágoi*

§59. It can be debated whether the Ionians would really have become new continuators of democracy if Mardonios as generalissimo of Xerxes had defeated the Athenians. Speaking for myself, I am not certain. But I would be more certain of something else: if the Persian Empire had won at Salamis, the Ionians would have become far more important politically as well as culturally. And, leaving aside such hypothetical questions, I am even more certain about a simple fact that has emerged all too clearly in the course of this presentation: the Ionians were and always had been very important for the Persian Empire. Here we come back one last time to the *mágoi*.

§60. Because these *mágoi*, like the Ionians, were very important for the Empire, it stands to reason that the Ionians understood well the *mágoi* just as the *mágoi* understood the Ionians. I close this presentation with two examples that illustrate the point I just made.

§61. The first example centres on a most famous Ionian intellectual, Heraclitus, the dating of whose lifespan stretches from the middle of the sixth century BCE down to a few years beyond the year of the naval battle at Salamis, 480 BCE. This Ionian was a native of one of the greatest cities of the Ionian Dodecapolis, Ephesos, which had stayed under the domination of the Persian Empire during practically the entire extent {|₁₁₉} of his lifetime, except perhaps for a few years after the events of 480 BCE. In Heraclitus Fragment 14 (= B 14 DK), as mediated by Clement of Alexandria (*Protrepticus* 2.22.2–3), Heraclitus is said to be "speaking as a seer" (*manteúein*) to various kinds of occultists, described by Clement as *nuktipóloi* 'those who go roaming at night'/*mágoi* 'mages'/*bákkhoi* 'devotees of Dionysus'/*lênai* 'she-devotees of Dionysus'/*mústai* 'initiands', and he warns them about various possible punishments, including fire, in a negative kind of afterlife – supposedly because they conducted rituals of initiation "in a way that is not sacred [*an-hierōstí*]" (Τίσι δὴ μαντεύεται Ἡράκλειτος ὁ Ἐφέσιος; "Νυκτιπόλοις, μάγοις, βάκχοις, λήναις, μύσταις", τούτοις ἀπειλεῖ τὰ μετὰ θάνατον, τούτοις μαντεύεται τὸ πῦρ· "τὰ γὰρ νομιζόμενα κατὰ ἀνθρώπους μυστήρια ἀνιερωστὶ μυοῦνται"). The wording of Clement strikes me as a composite of many different contexts where Heraclitus was referring to many different kinds of initiations and initiands.[31] Most relevant to this fragment of Heraclitus is column VI of the Derveni Papyrus: here, as we have already seen, the author mentions *mágoi* (lines 2, 5, 9) as models for *mústai* 'initiands' (line 9). Also relevant, with respect to two other fragments of Heraclitus (22 B 3 and B 94 DK), is column IV of the Derveni Papyrus: there, as Franco Ferrari argues, the author of the Papyrus refers to Heraclitus (Ἡράκλειτος, line 5) in the context of this savant's thinking about ritual practices, and among those practices are rituals of sacrifice as practiced by the Persians, as we can see from the restored wording [Π]έρσαι θύρυ[σι] "the Persians sacrifice [*thuein*]" (line 11).[32] The Persians who are sacrificing in this context, I think, are the *mágoi*.[33]

§62. My second example centres on the Ionians who advise the *mágoi* to sacrifice and sing incantations in order to appease the wind of the Hellespont and the mother of Achilles, as we read in the narrative that I cited earlier on from Herodotus (7.191.2). To me, that narrative says it all – in its very own microcosm.

Notes

1 https://classical-inquiries.chs.harvard.edu/magoi-and-ionians. For ease of reference, the enumeration of the notes of the original version are included here in square brackets [/].

2 The original text was also the basis for a lecture I presented in Budapest, Hungary (June 6, 2017), on the occasion of my induction as a corresponding member of the Hungarian Academy of Sciences (Magyar Tudományos Akadémia). The lecture, which I had composed in Hungarian, was an abridged version of what I present here in English.

3 These page numbers ({|[no.]}) derive from the version reprinted in C. Mora, C. Zizza *Antichi Persiani. Storia e rappresentazione*, Biblioteca di Athenaeum 60. Bari (2018) 97–121.

4 We have edited for style and in reflection of the process of maturation for this contribution.

5 [1] For more on Smerdis/Gaumāta, I strongly recommend the work of Shayegan 2012; I follow up on his interpretations in Nagy 2016.

6 [2] On such Greek/Persian interactions, I refer in general to the pioneering work of Benveniste 1929; also Benveniste 1938. A most incisive set of observations on Greek / Persian interactions can be found in the work of Panaino 2009, especially at p. 25 with reference to the word *mageíā* in the Platonic *Alcibiades* I (22a), which is defined there as *theōn therapeíā* 'caring for the gods' (ἔστι δὲ τοῦτο θεῶν θεραπεία). In Nagy 2013 6§54, I survey Greek examples of *therapeúein* in the specialized sense of 'ritually care for, take care of' with reference to whatever is considered to be sacred.

7 [3] In general, what I will argue is inspired by the remarks of Tsantsanoglou 2014: 16, who emphasizes the importance of an Ionian reception for the *mágoi*.

8 [4] A particularly significant attestation of Iranian *magu-* is Pahlavi *mowbad*, reconstructed as **magu-pat-* and meaning something like 'master of the *magu*-s': see

Panaino 2009: 24. On the authority of the generic *mōbad* in classical Persian poetics, as represented in the *Shāhnāma* of Ferdowsi, I follow the interpretation of Davidson 2013: 43.

9   [5] For background on the concept of *mágos* in Iranian contexts, along with ample bibliography, I recommend the admirable analysis of Panaino 2011, where he also considers the role of Zoroaster/Zarathuštra (especially pp. 344–7). Likewise relevant is what Panaino 2009 has to say (especially at p. 25) with reference to the use of the word *mageíā* in the Platonic *Alcibiades* I (22a), since the author there connects this Greek word with 'Zōroastēr son of Ōromazos' (μαγείαν τε διδάσκει τὴν Ζωροάστρου τοῦ Ὠρομάζου – ἔστι δὲ τοῦτο θεῶν θεραπεία). As for the presentation I offer here, what I will be arguing with reference to the *mágoi* is relevant to what I have to say about Zoroaster/Zarathuštra in Nagy 2017.04.19 §§15–17.

10 [6] Panaino 2015, with further analysis. More in Panaino 2011: 361–3.

11 [7] On the Derveni Papyrus in general, I always learn something new whenever I read Betegh 2004. Especially useful for me in the present context is his interpretation of Diogenes Laertius 1.7, who refers to the practices of *mágoi* in interpreting *eidōla* 'images' – in the sense of *insubstantial images of the dead*.

12 [8] On this point, see Ferrari 2014: 57.

13 [9] Most informative here is the analysis of Panaino 2011: 347–61.

14 [10] This word *eukhḗ* 'prayer' is relevant to what I have to say about Zoroaster/ Zarathuštra in Nagy 2017.04.19 §§15–17. A work on Zoroaster that I find singularly useful is the article of Skjærvø 2015.

15 [11] I interpret *theogoníē* 'theogony' as a kind of *eukhḗ* 'prayer': here I invoke the context of the word *eukhḗ* as used in the Derveni Papyrus. See §21.

16 [12] An authority on the subject of the multi-ethnic nature of the Persian Empire is Briant 1996, 2002.

17 [13] In Nagy 2011b, I survey the myths about an Ionian migration and compare them with the rival myths about the Aeolian migration.

18 [14] On this point, I offer further argumentation in Nagy 2014. Also, as Rahim Shayegan points out to me, the so-called 'Daiva Inscription' of Xerxes, found at Persepolis (XPh 23–5), already refers to the Asiatic Greeks and the European Greeks together as 'the Ionians who live by the sea and who live across the sea': *yaunā taya drayahiyā dā|rayatiy utā tayaiy paradraya dārayat|iy.*

19 [15] Nagy 2009|2008 4§§174–175, §§177–180.

20 [16] Nagy 2009|2008 4§24.

21 [17] Now see our discussion on p. 131.

22 [18] Nagy 2009|2008 4 §25.

23 [19] Artaphernes was involved in the events reported by Herodotus (5.30–8) concerning the failed military expedition of Aristagoras to capture the Ionian island of Naxos. In my earlier footnote about this expedition, I already noted that Herodotus speaks of 200 triremes that were authorized by Darius himself for Aristagoras to use in his expedition (5.30–3); in that same context, I must now add, Herodotus also speaks of the role of Artaphernes himself in persuading Darius to make such an authorization.

24 [20] I do not have enough space here to delve into the complexities of this political crisis in Athens.

25 [21] Nagy 2014. I would now add this observation: the use of the word *Héllēnes* by Hecataeus (FGH 1 F 1) in referring to Greeks as makers of multiple and laughably unreliable *lógoi* 'words' was meant to be a negative reference to the mythmaking of European Greeks in his era, to be contrasted with the supposedly reliable mythmaking of Asiatic Greeks.

26 [22] Sissa 2012 resists such negative claims (with bibliography at p. 230, n. 7). For further analysis (with further bibliography), see Panaino 2001.

27 [23] Nagy 1990: 181–92, 265–6.

28 [24] One exception at this time, and there may have been more, was the island-state of Chios: within the time-frame of the year 479 BCE, Herodotus (8.132.2) mentions in passing that a tyrant by the name of Strattis was in charge there at that point in time. Elsewhere, Herodotus (4.137.2) mentions that Strattis was in charge of Chios already during the events narrated for 513 BCE. In this case, then, the tyrant may have been deposed in 499 BCE and then may have made a comeback, as it were, even after the democratic deals made by Mardonios with the cities of Ionia in 493 BCE.

29 [25] As Rahim Shayegan points out to me, there existed an Old Persian word for such a 'super-satrap', to be reconstructed as *kārana-*, which is attested in Greek as *karanos* (κάρανος). For example, Cyrus the Younger was such a *karanos* (κάρανος), as we read in Xenophon *Hellenica* 1.4.3–4. He was appointed the ruler of three satrapies in Asia Minor: Lydia, Greater Phrygia, and Cappadocia. See Shayegan 2017.

30 [26] I can see a possible objection to my raising this possibility. In Herodotus 7.6.1–5, where Mardonios is portrayed as agitating at the court of Xerxes for war against the European Greeks, and where his motive is said to be his ambition to rule over all the Greeks (7.6.1), it is also said that the Athenian family of the Peisistratidai and the Thessalian family of the Aleuadai were also present at the court of Xerxes – and were also agitating for war. Text and comments in Nagy 2010|2009: 348–9 (see also Haubold 2007: 52–4). Still, we cannot assume that Mardonios and the other agitators were all on the same political side. Even if the Peisistratidai, as former 'tyrants' of Athens, would not have been advocating a democracy for Athens, the same kind of advocacy cannot be assumed for Mardonios, who must have had his own political agenda. As for what happened 13 years earlier at Marathon, when the Persian Empire was ready to reinstate the Peisistratidai as tyrants of Athens by restoring Hippias to power, I need to recall the fact that Mardonios had already been relieved of his command of the forces on the Persian side, as we see from the reportage of Herodotus (6.94.2). If Mardonios had still been in command in 490 BCE, I think that Hippias would not have been given another chance to attempt a political comeback in Athens.

31 [27] I think that Plato in *Theaetetus* 179e is making references to comparable contexts of initiation as interpreted by latter-day followers of Heraclitus in Ephesos (Nagy 2009|2008 2§137 and 3§96).

32 [28] Ferrari 2014: 63–5. I am grateful to Ioanna Papadopoulou for reminding me of this restoration.

33 [29] Such an argument is actually made by Ferrari 2011, who also cites further sources, with bibliography (especially valuable are his observations at p. 71, with reference to the important work of Horky 2009 and others).

Bibliography

Albright, W.F. & Mann, C.S. 1971. *Matthew: Introduction, Translation, and Notes*. Garden City, NY (Doubleday).

Asheri, D. 1983. *Fra Ellenismo e Iranismo*. Bologna (Pátron).

Benveniste, E. 1929. *The Persian Religion According to the Chief Greek Texts*. Paris (Paul Geuthner).

———. 1938. *Les Mages dans l'ancien Iran*. Paris (Librairie Orientaliste: Paul Geuthner).

Bernabé, A. 2014. "On the Rites Described and Commented Upon in the Derveni Papyrus, Columns I – VI." In Papadopoulou, I., & Muellner, eds., *Poetry as Initiation: The Center for Hellenic Studies Symposium on the Derveni Papyrus*. Hellenic Studies 63. Cambridge, MA, & Washington, DC (Center for Hellenic Studies), 19–52.

Betegh, G. 2004. *The Derveni Papyrus: Cosmology, Theology and Interpretation*. Cambridge (Cambridge University Press).

Bickerman, E.J. & Tadmor, H. 1985. "Darius I, Pseudo-Smerdis, and the Magi." In Bickerman, E.J., Gabba, E., & Smith, M., eds., *Religions and Politics in the Hellenistic and Roman Periods*. Como (New Press), 230–61.

Bondi, S.F. 1995. "Les institutions, l'organisation politique et administrative." In Krings, V., ed., *La civilisation phénicienne et punique: Manuel de recherche: Handbuch der Orientalistik 40*. Leiden (Brill), 290–302.

Briant, P. 1996. *Histoire de l'Empire Perse: De Cyrus à Alexandre*. Paris (Fayard).

———. 2002. *From Cyrus to Alexander: A History of the Persian Empire*. Translated by P.T. Daniels. Winona Lake, IN (Eisenbrauns).

Davidson, O.M. 2013. *Poet and Hero in the Persian Book of Kings*. Cambridge, MA (Harvard University Press).

Ferrari, F. 2011. "Rites Without Ordeals: Magi and Mystae in the Derveni Papyrus." *Zeitschrift für Papyrologie und Epigraphik* 79: 71–83.

———. 2014. "Democritus, Heraclitus, and the Dead Souls: Reconstructing Columns I–VI of the Derveni Papyrus." In Papadopoulou, I., & Muellner, L., eds., *Poetry as Initiation: The Center for Hellenic Studies Symposium on the Derveni Papyrus*. Hellenic Studies 63. Cambridge, MA, & Washington, DC (Center for Hellenic Studies), 53–66.

Figueira, T.J. 1985. "Archaic Megara, 800–500 B.C." In Figueira, T.J., & Nagy, G., eds., *Theognis of Megara: Poetry and the Polis*. Baltimore, MD (Johns Hopkins University Press), 261–303.

———. 2015. "Modes of Colonization and Elite Integration in Archaic Greece." In Fisher, N., & van Wees, H., eds., *"Aristocracy" in Antiquity: Redefining Greek and Roman Elites*. Swansea (Classical Press of Wales), 311–45.

Frame, D. 2009. *Hippota Nestor*. Hellenic Studies 34. Cambridge, MA, & Washington, DC (Center for Hellenic Studies).

Haubold, J. 2007. "Xerxes's Homer." In Bridges, E., Hall, E., & Rhodes, P.J., eds., *Cultural Responses to the Persian Wars: Antiquity to the Third Millennium*. Oxford (Oxford University Press), 47–63.

Horky, P.S. 2009. "Persian Cosmos and Greek Philosophy: Plato's Associates and the Zoroastrian magoi." *Oxford Studies in Ancient Philosophy* 37: 47–103.

Jensen, S.R. 2010. *Rethinking Athenian Imperialism: Sub-Hegemony in the Delian League*. Dissertation, Rutgers University, NJ.

Nagy, G. 1969. *The Best of the Achaeans: Concepts of the Hero in Archaic Greek Poetry²*. Baltimore, MD (Johns Hopkins University Press).

———. 1990. *Pindar's Homer: The Lyric Possession of an Epic Past*. Baltimore, MD (Johns Hopkins University Press). http://nrs.harvard.edu/urn-3:hul.ebook:CHS_Nagy.Pindars_Homer.1990.

———. 1999. *The Best of the Achaeans: Concepts of the Hero in Archaic Greek Poetry²*. Baltimore, MD (Johns Hopkins University Press).

———. 2009|2008. *Homer the Classic*. Printed|Online version. Hellenic Studies 34. Cambridge, MA, & Washington, DC (Center for Hellenic Studies). http://nrs.harvard.edu/urn-3:hul.ebook:CHS_Nagy.Homer_the_Classic.2008.

———. 2010|2009. *Homer the Preclassic*. Printed|Online version. Berkeley & Los Angeles, CA (University of California Press).

———. 2011a. "Diachrony and the Case of Aesop." *Classics@. Issue 9: Defense Mechanisms in Interdisciplinary Approaches to Classical Studies and Beyond*. http://nrs.harvard.edu/urn-3:hlnc.essay:Nagy.Diachrony_and_the_Case_of_Aesop.2011.

———. 2011b. "The Aeolic Component of Homeric Diction." In Jamison, S.W., Melchert, H.C., & Vine, B., eds., *Proceedings of the 22nd Annual UCLA Indo-European Conference*, 133–79. Bremen. In Nagy 2012, v 1.

————. 2013. *The Ancient Greek Hero in 24 Hours*. Cambridge, MA (Harvard University Press). http://nrs.harvard.edu/urn3:hul.ebook:CHS_NagyG.The_Ancient_Greek_Hero_in_24_Hours.2013.

————. 2014. "Herodotus and the 'Logioi' of the Persians." In Korangy, A., & Sheffield, D.J., eds., *No Tapping Around Philology: A Festschrift in Honor of Wheeler McIntosh Thackston Jr.'s 70th Birthday*. Wiesbaden (Harrassowitz). http://nrs.harvard.edu/urn-3:hlnc.essay:Nagy.Herodotus_and_the_Logioi_of_the_Persians.2014.

————. 2016. "The Idea of an Archetype in Texts Stemming from the Empire Founded by Cyrus the Great." In Bintliff, J., & Rutter, K., eds., *The Archaeology of Greece and Rome: Studies in Honour of Anthony Snodgrass*. Edinburgh (Edinburgh University Press), 337–57. http://nrs.harvard.edu/urn-3:hlnc.essay:Nagy.The_idea_of_an_archetype.2016.

————. 2017. "Thinking Iranian, Rethinking Greek." *Classical Inquiries*. http://classical-inquiries.chs.harvard.edu/thinking-iranian-rethinking-greek/.

————. 2018. "Lelantine War, Eretria and Chalkis, and the Contest of Homer and Hesiod." *Classical Inquiries*. https://classical-inquiries.chs.harvard.edu/lelantine-war-eretria-and-chalkis-and-the-contest-of-homer-and-hesiod/.

Panaino, A. 2001. "Greci e Iranici: confronto e conflitti." In Settis, S., ed., *I Greci: Storia, Cultura, Arte, Società: Vol. 3: I Greci oltre la Grecia*. Torino (Einaudi), 79–136.

————. 2009. "Aspetti della complessità degli influssi interculturali tra Grecia ed Iran." In Riedweg, C., ed., *Grecia Maggiore: Intrecci culturali con l'Asia nel periodo arcaico/Graecia Maior: Kulturaustausch mit Asien in der archaischen Periode: Atti del simposio in occasione del 75° anniversario di Walter Burkert/Akten des Symposions aus Anlass des 75: Geburtstages von Walter Burkert*. Basel (Bibliotheca Helvetica Romana 30: Schwabe), 19–53.

————. 2011. "Erodoto, i Magi e la Storia Religiosa Iranica." In Rollinger, R., Truschnegg, B., & Reinhold Bichler, R., eds., *Herodot und das persische Weltreich*. Wiesbaden (Harrassowitz), 343–70.

————. 2015. "Jesus' Trimorphisms and Tetramorphisms in the Meeting with the Magi." In Szántó, I., ed., *From Aṣl to Zā'id: Essays in Honour of Éva M. Jeremiás*. Piliscsaba (Klaus Schwarz), 167–209.

Papadopoulou, I. & Muellner, L., eds. 2014. *Poetry as Initiation: The Center for Hellenic Studies Symposium on the Derveni Papyrus*. Hellenic Studies 63. Cambridge, MA, & Washington, DC (Center for Hellenic Studies). http://nrs.harvard.edu/urn-3:hul.ebook:CHS_PapadopoulouI_MuellnerL_eds.Poetry_as_Initiation.2014.

Sakellariou, M.B. 1958. *La migration grecque en Ionie*. Athens (Collection de l'Institut français d'Athènes).

Scott, L. 2005. *Historical Commentary on Herodotus Book 6*. Leiden (Brill).

Shaked, S. 1984. "Iranian Influence in Judaism: First Century B.C.E. to Second Century C.E." In Davies, W.D., & Finkelstein, L., eds., *The Cambridge History of Judaism: Vol. 1: Introduction; The Persian Period*. Cambridge (Cambridge University Press), 308–25.

Shayegan, M.R. 2012. *Aspects of History and Epic in Ancient Iran: From Gaumāta to Wahnām*. Hellenic Studies 52. Cambridge, MA, & Washington, DC (Center for Hellenic Studies).

————. 2017. "Persianism: Or Achaemenid Reminiscences in the Iranian and Iranicate World(s) of Antiquity." In Strootman, R., & Versluys, M.J., eds., *Persianism in Antiquity*. Stuttgart (Franz Steiner), 401–55.

Sissa, G. 2012. "Democracy: A Persian Invention?" *Mètis: Anthropologie des mondes grecs anciens* 10: 227–61.

Skjærvø, P.O. 2015. "The 'Gāthās' as Myth and Ritual." In Strausberg, M., & Vevaina, Y.S.-D., with the assistance of A. Tessmann, eds., *The Wiley Blackwell Companion to Zoroastrianism*. Chichester (Wiley-Blackwell), 59–67.

Trampedach, K. 2017. "Die Priester der Despoten: Herodots Persische *Magoi*." In Klinkott, H., & Kramer, N., eds., *Zwischen Assur und Athen: Altorientalisches in den Historien Herodots*. Stuttgart (Franz Steiner), 197–218.

Tsantsanoglou, K. 2014. "Some Desiderata in the Study of the Derveni Papyrus." In Papadopoulou, I., & Muellner, L., eds., *Poetry as Initiation: The Center for Hellenic Studies Symposium on the Derveni Papyrus*. Hellenic Studies 63. Cambridge, MA, & Washington, DC (Center for Hellenic Studies), 1–18.

Vanschoonwinkel, J. 1991. *L'Égée et la Méditerranée orientale à la fin du IIe millénaire: temoignages archéologiques et sources écrites*. Louvain-la-neuve (Publications d'histoire de l'art et d'archéologie de l'Université catholique de Louvain).

**Freedom and culture
in Herodotus**

Rosaria Vignolo Munson

Among the many reasons, right or wrong, that were given for past American
military interventions abroad, one was ideological and not entirely insincere: the
belief that everyone yearns to be free, so that people over there would welcome
being liberated from an oppressive form of government and joining the consor-
tium of liberal democracies.[1] This way of thinking resonated with many Americans because it seemed ethnocentric on our part – as it still does – to theorize
that certain societies are incapable of conceptualizing freedom. Many years later,
some political commentators have expressed more cynical views.[2]

The citizens of the fifth-century European Greek *poleis* lived in a world in
which autocracy and domination were almost everywhere else the norm. Aware
of their exceptionalism, they tended to consider freedom as their exclusive ethnic
trait thanks to some vague combination of nature, environment, and tradition.[3]
Herodotus, however – an Asiatic Greek, who was born a subject of the Persian
Empire, became a subject of the Athenian Empire, and ended up as a free citizen
in Thourioi (an Athenian colony) – displays towards non-Greeks unique expertise and 'charity'.[4] His attitude on the differences between Greeks and *barbaroi*,
including in the sphere of ideas about freedom, is complicated by his overarching
view of culture (expressed in *nomos*), which he considers to be the most crucial
area of ethnic differentiation – more important, that is, than other characteristics,
such as ancestry, race, language, religion, or territory.[5]

With a famous phrase, borrowed from Pindar, Herodotus concludes his commentary on the crazy deeds of the Persian king Cambyses by declaring that "custom is king of all" (νόμον πάντων βασιλέα, 3.38.4). Here Herodotus reflects on
the wide variety of customs among peoples in the world so that, for example,
in the Greek funeral one cremates the dead, while the funeral of an Indian tribe
called the Kallatiai includes the ritual of eating the flesh of their deceased parents. Herodotus implies that the two types of ceremony are equivalent – they both
amount to a funeral – yet they are both so engrained in their respective cultures
and so different from each other that the Kallatiai are just as horrified at the Greek
custom as the Greeks are disgusted when asked if they would consider cannibaliz-
ing their dead the way the Kallatiai do: neither of the two peoples would consider
doing anything but what they do. This shows how each society is attached to its
own customs so that, if all the customs of the world were on display as in a bazaar

in view of a possible exchange, people would look at them all, but ultimately would end up choosing to keep their own (3.38.1):

> Εἰ γάρ τις προθείη πᾶσι ἀνθρώποισι ἐκλέξασθαι κελεύων νόμους τοὺς καλλίστους ἐκ τῶν πάντων νόμων, διασκεψάμενοι ἂν ἑλοίατο ἕκαστοι τοὺς ἑωυτῶν.

For if someone were to display their customs to all the people in the world, asking them to select the most beautiful among them, they each would consider them carefully and then choose their own.[6]

The problem with cultural relativism

Herodotus is a cultural relativist, but of a special type. For him 'different strokes for different folks' means, on the one hand, that we are not entitled to consider our own customs as the exclusive expression of an absolute moral correctness; but, on the other hand, unlike some sophistic thinkers of his time, he establishes that we are not entitled, either, to devalue customs as unimportant conventions, whether our own or those of others. In particular, with regard to foreign practices, the only sane response is to treat them with the utmost respect, even in cases when we may not particularly like them and would never consider adopting them.

This position makes Herodotus a very satisfying author for modern readers to work with, and he becomes even dearer to us – I propose – when we realize the cognitive dissonance it entails. Cultural relativism is hard to defend in certain cases, and we are just as embattled and occasionally inconsistent as Herodotus was.

First of all, the area of *nomos* (no matter what society we are talking about) is ordered hierarchically. Certain customs, such as sacred rituals, were considered (and, still now, tend to be considered) as more compelling than others. The derision toward Egyptian religion shown by Cambyses – who tortures the corpse of an Egyptian king, stabs the Apis bull, or desecrates Egyptian graves, mocks cult statues, and barges into Egyptian temples (3.16, 29, 37) – is an unforgivable offence. At the opposite end of the spectrum, some customs that have to do with material culture (like diet and clothing), unless they are motivated by religion, often simply depend on ecological factors; even if they reveal something about a people's tastes and values, one can safely joke about them. By the rules implicitly stipulated by the *Histories*, for example, it is perfectly fine for the king of the Ethiopians, who only eat meat, to ridicule the Persians (3.22.4) because they eat bread (he calls them eaters of dung).[7] Not all customs need to be taken seriously in the same way.

Secondly, custom is conservative, but not immune to alteration, on account of external influences or other historical factors. Herodotus records numerous cases of practices dropped or adopted.[8] Thirdly – and this is the most important point – not every custom, religious or not, is tolerable from the point of view of a broader human community. It is not just a matter of *not liking* certain forms of behaviour – as when Herodotus cringes at the fact that almost all foreign peoples do not have a taboo against sexual intercourse in sanctuaries (2.64). Culturally subjective cringing is inconsequential, but Herodotus actually crosses into moral condemnation, for example, when he describes the Babylonian prostitution ritual in honour of Aphrodite-Mylitta as "most shameful" because it compels women to sleep with a stranger for a coin and subjects them to all sort of discomforts and humiliation (1.199).[9]

Herodotus' relativism, which prescribes the utmost respect for the customs of other people, finds its limits when confronted with practices that are oppressive to members of the society to which the custom belongs. Although it occurs rarely, there is here, for him, such a thing as a bad custom. For the relevance of this problem to our times I only need to mention, for example, contemporary discussions on female genital cutting – whether it represents mutilation or just a scratch, whether it is cruel or acceptable because embraced by those involved, whether it should be declared a human rights abuse or whether we should altogether stay out of it.[10]

Political customs and the meaning of freedom

But what about political customs? Like all other customs, these vary from culture to culture. In Herodotus they are largely secular, though sometimes supported by religious structures or claims.[11] They are often handed down by tradition, but they may also be deliberately chosen at a determinate historical moment.[12] They are in fact more subject to change than many other customs, but profoundly serious. Inhabitants of the so-called Western world nowadays disapprove of autocracy. To what extent does Herodotus think that some political systems are morally wrong, in an absolute sense?

These questions lead us to an overarching theme in the *Histories*, also expressed by other sources at least starting from the first quarter of the fifth century BCE, namely that a society that practices or at least values political freedom is morally better than one that does not.[13] The concept of 'freedom' is most frequently expressed with the noun ἐλευθερίη and related words. What is striking about the Greek freedom discourse (as opposed to our own) is its constant use of the opposite set of words that in a literal sense denote legal slavery (δουλοσύνη, δουληίη δοῦλος, δουλόω),[14] but are even more frequently applied in a metaphorical sense to a number of political restrictions considered to make the status of a free citizen even just one step closer to the condition of a literal slave.[15] In Herodotus these terms are not neutral; they carry great emotional impact and a measure of moral condemnation, directed in part against the enslaver, but more notably against the ones enslaved (a case of blaming the victim, if you will), unless they perceive that constraint and want to be free.

Political freedom as 'national' independence among the Greeks

It is perhaps obvious to say that political freedom has two main aspects in Herodotus, external and internal. On the one hand, words of the ἐλευθερίη family are used in reference to the independence of any state from external domination by a different ethnic group or state. At a minimum, what counts for national non-freedom in the fifth century is obligation to pay tribute to an external power or having no say in one's own foreign policy.[16] So, for example, Herodotus reports that "all the Greeks were free" before Croesus exacted tribute (φόρος) from the Greek cities of Asia (1.6.2–3). He is of course interpreting history retrospectively. At the time when Herodotus was writing, at any rate, and since the Persian invasions of Greece, the concept of *eleutheria* as state independence had become urgent in Greek thought and a major theme in Greek authors.[17] In Herodotus there are numerous ἐλευθ- passages (I have counted 28) that talk about the Greeks reacquiring, valuing, or defending their freedom from Eastern powers.[18] Different Greek speakers proclaim that they will fight against the Persians on behalf of freedom, or encourage others to do so – Aristagoras at Sparta and Athens, Dionysios of Phokaia at Lade, Miltiades at Marathon, Spartans and Athenians in Syracuse, to name just a few.[19] There are Greeks who do not display sufficient energy in defending the cause or are not part of the group of Greeks who "want to be free", to use Herodotus' phrase (7.178.2). These are treated with contempt.[20]

Political freedom as 'national'" independence among non-Greeks

Some of the passages cited earlier seem to echo the widespread Greek view that love of freedom is a defining Greek *nomos* and an essential part of Greek ethnic identity. On the eve of his expedition, Xerxes expresses the hope that the Greeks, once they realize the extent of his power, will be persuaded to give up their "distinctive freedom" (ἰδίην ἐλευθερίην, 7.147.1).[21] But how distinctive is it, or in what sense? According to Herodotus, national freedom is highly valued also among non-Greeks. The Egyptian conqueror Sesostris sets up celebratory honourific inscriptions for the peoples of Asia who fought bravely against him "for their freedom", but he erects *stelai* representing female genitals for those who did not (2.102–4–5). The Scythians exhort the Ionian Greeks to free themselves from Persian domination (4.137.1); when their suggestion is rejected, they say that the Ionians are excellent slaves devoted to their master but worthless as free men (4.142.2). The Persian sage Artabanos advises Xerxes that if the Ionians do not assist their fellow Greeks of the mainland in their fight for freedom, they will prove to be the "most unjust of men", so why would Xerxes want them as allies anyway (7.51.2). In fact, in the *Histories* the non-Greeks who are most vocal on the subject of national freedom are the Persians – that is to say, the power that is intent on enslaving everyone else and that played a major role in the development of the Greek concept of *eleutheria*. This suggests a zero-sum notion of national freedom. Cyrus delivers the Persians from Median rule ("Obey me and you will be free!" he says), while at the same time subjecting the Medes to the Persians. Throughout the *Histories* several Persian speakers recall that foundational event and celebrate their own freedom as a nation as well as their power over others.[22]

Greek political freedom

What is so special, then, about the Greek notion of *eleutheria* in contrast to everyone else's? It is simply that it combines the idea of the independence of a state from other states with that of the constitutional freedom of the citizens within the state. The most frequent antonym to the internal type of freedom is 'tyranny', meaning subjection to autocratic rule.[23] Scholars, especially Raaflaub, have convincingly argued that this second meaning of *eleutheria* is older than the idea of state independence. It goes back to the sixth century and has its root in the constitutional development of the Greek *poleis*, many of which experienced a period of autocratic rule not connected to a previous tradition of hereditary kingship.[24]

The opposition between freedom and tyranny becomes almost obsessive in the sections of the *Histories* where Herodotus deals with internal Greek politics and sixth-century Greek dictatorial regimes.[25] In any given city people who support or enable tyrannies are the object of blame. They are those who "do not want to be free", like the Samians, when they oppose the reforms of Maiandros (οὐ γὰρ δή, ὡς οἴκασι, ἐβούλοντο εἶναι ἐλεύθεροι, 3.143.2), or those who "find tyranny more welcome than freedom", like the supporters of Peisistratus in Athens (ἄλλοι . . . τοῖσι ἡ τυραννὶς πρὸ ἐλευθερίης ἦν ἀσπαστότερον, 1.62.1). By contrast, the liberation of Athens from the Peisistratids, while having nothing to do with an external threat to the city's autonomy at the time, represents for Herodotus a major turning point on the road to greatness, eventually enhancing Athens' ability to defend Greek national freedom in the Persian Wars.[26] Herodotus describes how this type of freedom manifested itself in Athens (5.78):

Ἀθηναῖοι μέν νυν ηὔξηντο. Δηλοῖ δὲ οὐ κατ' ἓν μοῦνον ἀλλὰ πανταχῆ ἡ ἰσηγορίη ὡς ἐστὶ χρῆμα σπουδαῖον, εἰ καὶ Ἀθηναῖοι τυραννευόμενοι μὲν οὐδαμῶν τῶν σφέας περιοικεόντων ἦσαν τὰ πολέμια ἀμείνονες, ἀπαλλαχθέντες δὲ τυράννων μακρῷ πρῶτοι ἐγένοντο. Δηλοῖ ὦν ταῦτα ὅτι κατεχόμενοι μὲν ἐθελοκάκεον ὡς δεσπότῃ ἐργαζόμενοι, ἐλευθερωθέντων δὲ αὐτὸς ἕκαστος ἑωυτῷ προεθυμέετο κατεργάζεσθαι.

So, the Athenians then became more powerful. It is clear not only from one case but in general that equal-speech is a sensible system, if also the Athenians when they were being ruled by a tyrant were no better than their neighbours in war, but once they got rid of the tyrants became by far the best. This then makes clear that when they were subjected they behaved sluggishly thinking that they were working for a *master*, but *once they became free*, each person was eager to work for himself.

The aspect of internal freedom Herodotus here chooses to emphasize has to do with speech: ἰσηγορίη, which means the right of any citizen to address the sovereign assembly on public matters.[27] It overlaps with our own notion of 'freedom of speech' in the sense that deliberation includes clashes of opinions and criticism of officials and policies.[28] Other times in Herodotus, *eleuther-* words occur in connection with free speech: the Corinthian Sokles, for example, "speaks freely" against tyranny in the Peloponnesian assembly (5.93.2). Artabanos expresses his opinion "freely" to Xerxes when he attempts to persuade him not to march against Greece (7.46.1), although that does not go well.[29] But the main point of Athenian *isegorie* is that by means of speech the individual citizen, regardless of his status, has the opportunity to influence policy decisions such as waging war; the practical result, according to Herodotus, is that he is also motivated to participate more enthusiastically in their execution, which in turn increases the potential for success of the city as a whole.[30]

Complementary to this description of the advantages of freedom for Athens is one that discusses freedom among the Spartans while underlining again, although in a different way, how a state that is governed constitutionally is also better equipped to handle its own defence. On the eve of the battle of Thermopylae, Xerxes argues to the Spartan king Demaratos that the Greeks, since they are free, cannot possibly be successful against his much larger army (7.103.3–4):

Κῶς ἂν δυναίατο χίλιοι ἢ καὶ μύριοι ἢ καὶ πεντακισμύριοι, ἐόντες γε <u>ἐλεύθεροι</u> πάντες ὁμοίως καὶ <u>μὴ ὑπ' ἑνὸς ἀρχόμενοι</u>; . . .

<u>Ὑπὸ μὲν γὰρ ἑνὸς ἀρχόμενοι</u> κατὰ τρόπον τὸν <u>ἡμέτερον</u> γενοίατ' ἂν δειμαίνοντες τοῦτον καὶ παρὰ τὴν ἑωυτῶν φύσιν ἀμείνονες, καὶ ἴοιεν ἀναγκαζόμενοι μάστιγι ἐς πλέονας ἐλάσσονες ἐόντες· <u>ἀνειμένοι δὲ ἐς τὸ ἐλεύθερον</u> οὐκ ἂν ποιοῖεν τούτων οὐδέτερα.

How would 1,000 or 10,000 or 50,000 men, at least when they are all equally <u>free</u> and <u>not ruled by one man</u>, be able to confront such a great army as mine? . . .

For if they were <u>ruled by one man</u>, *as is our way,* through fear of him they would display valour even beyond their nature and would go compelled by the whip against a greater number of enemies despite being outnumbered; but being <u>released to freedom</u>, they would not do either.

While Xerxes speaks about freedom as being a way of life for all the Greeks, Demaratos focusses more specifically on his own city (7.104.4–5):

Λακεδαιμόνιοι κατὰ μὲν ἕνα μαχόμενοι οὐδαμῶν εἰσι κακίονες ἀνδρῶν, ἁλέες δὲ ἄριστοι ἀνδρῶν ἁπάντων. <u>Ἐλεύθεροι</u> γὰρ ἐόντες <u>οὐ πάντα ἐλεύθεροί εἰσι</u>· ἔπεστι γάρ σφι <u>δεσπότης νόμος</u>, τὸν ὑποδειμαίνουσι πολλῷ ἔτι μᾶλλον ἢ οἱ σοὶ σέ· ποιεῦσι γῶν τὰ ἂν ἐκεῖνος ἀνώγῃ· ἀνώγει δὲ τὠυτὸ αἰεί, οὐκ ἐῶν φεύγειν οὐδὲν πλῆθος ἀνθρώπων ἐκ μάχης, ἀλλὰ μένοντας ἐν τῇ τάξι ἐπικρατέειν ἢ ἀπόλλυσθαι.

In single combat the Lacedaemonians are certainly inferior to no one, but all together they are the best in the world, because, although they are <u>free</u>, they are <u>not free</u> in all respects. They have <u>law/custom as their master</u>, whom they fear much more than your subjects fear you, so that they do what it commands them. And it always commands the same thing: not to flee in battle regardless of the number of enemies but stand firm at their post and either conquer or die.

As we see, the Athenians' conception of their position as citizens as formulated at 5.78 is more individualistic than that of the Spartans, who rather emphasize their collective allegiance and their collective goal. In Athens effective action is preceded by speech, for the Spartans the only speech is the command of the law. This shows that internal freedom can take different constitutional and cultural forms; it is always, however, freedom from autocratic rule, whether by a tyrant in the technical sense, like Peisistratos and other sixth-century Greek tyrants, or by a hereditary king like Xerxes.[31] To both types of monarch the passages apply the word δεσπότης (master), thereby including internal subjection in the semantic field of 'enslavement', which is the common metaphor for subjection to an outside power.

Dual freedom as a distinctive characteristic of Greeks

What makes the Greeks special, then, is that for them freedom from out-of-state domination and internal freedom are strictly intertwined. This fusion makes sense since, when fighting the Persian aggression, the Greeks were actually defending both at once. The Ionian revolt from Persia gained momentum as a freedom war against Persian-sponsored tyrants.[32] At Marathon the Athenian general Miltiades tells the *polemarkhos* Kallimakhos that by confronting the Persians in battle he will ensure his city's freedom and gain as much glory for himself as the tyrannicides Harmodios and Aristogeiton (6.109.3). The appearance of the Athenian former tyrant Hippias with the Persian force at Marathon must have made clear that Persian domination of Greece would entail the return of the tyrannical regime in Athens.[33] This double threat, both external and internal, created a global concept of freedom similar to the one encoded, for example, in our phrase 'free world', old-fashioned and much maligned but still currently used in an oppositional sense. What today is the free world? Whom does this expression exclude? It clearly excludes nations governed by autocratic regimes as well as those who hold other nations in subjection (or attempt to do so), and nations that are dominated by foreign rule.

Non-Greeks in Herodotus are largely oblivious to the idea of internal enslavement. The Egyptians, once liberated (ἐλευθερωθέντες) from Ethiopian rule, nevertheless "could at no time live without a king" (οὐδένα γὰρ χρόνον οἷοί τε ἦσαν ἄνευ βασιλέος διαιτᾶσθαι, 2.147.2). The satrap Hydarnes tells the Spartan heralds Sperkheios and Boulis that his own prosperous circumstances are proof of how advantageous it is to become friends with the Great King, so that they should try it too. They answer that this sort of advice can only come from one who has never experienced freedom (7.135.3):

> Ὕδαρνες . . . τὸ μὲν γὰρ <u>δοῦλος</u> εἶναι ἐξεπίστεαι, <u>ἐλευθερίης</u> δὲ οὔκω ἐπειρήθης, οὔτ' εἰ ἔστι γλυκὺ οὔτ' εἰ μή. Εἰ γὰρ αὐτῆς πειρήσαιο, οὐκ ἂν δόρασι συμβουλεύοις ἡμῖν περὶ αὐτῆς μάχεσθαι, ἀλλὰ καὶ πελέκεσι.
>
> Hydarnes . . . you know what it is to be a <u>slave</u>, but you have never experienced <u>freedom</u>, whether it tastes sweet or not. If you had, you would advise us to fight for it not only with spears, but also with axes.

Obviously Sperkheios and Boulis are here talking first and foremost about fighting on behalf of their city's freedom, anticipating the narrative of the heroic Spartan resistance at Thermopylae. At the same time, the enslaved status they here attribute to Hydarnes can only be of the other kind. He is not a "slave" as a national Persian – ethnic Persians are very proud of their national freedom – but (from the Greek point of view) he is a slave as a subject of the Great King.[34]

The Greek double notion of freedom emerges from Herodotus' interpretation of the early vicissitudes of a foreign nation like the Medes, who used to be subject to the Assyrians (1.95.2–96.1):

> Ἀσσυρίων ἀρχόντων τῆς ἄνω Ἀσίης ἐπ' ἔτεα εἴκοσι καὶ πεντακόσια, πρῶτοι ἀπ' αὐτῶν Μῆδοι ἤρξαντο ἀπίστασθαι· καί κως οὗτοι <u>περὶ τῆς ἐλευθερίης</u> μαχεσάμενοι τοῖσι Ἀσσυρίοισι ἐγένοντο ἄνδρες ἀγαθοὶ καὶ <u>ἀπωσάμενοι τὴν δουλοσύνην ἐλευθερώθησαν</u>. Μετὰ δὲ τούτους καὶ τὰ ἄλλα ἔθνεα ἐποίεε τὠυτὸ τοῖσι Μήδοισι. Ἐόντων δὲ <u>αὐτονόμων</u> πάντων ἀνὰ τὴν ἤπειρον, ὧδε <u>αὖτις ἐς τυραννίδα περιῆλθον</u>.

> The Assyrians ruled upper Asia for 520 years, and the Medes were the first to revolt from them. And somehow, fighting for <u>freedom</u> against the Assyrians, they displayed valour, and <u>casting off slavery they became free</u>. After them, also the other ethnic groups did the same thing as the Medes. When they all on the continent were <u>autonomous, they reverted again to tyrannical government</u>, and they did so in the following way.

Desire for freedom, which is shared by many ethnic groups, motivates the Medes to fight well, enabling them to become independent from foreign domination. This independence is here called αὐτονομίη, a term used only one other time in Herodotus,[35] but significant in this context because it includes the concept of law/ custom (*nomos*) with which we have begun our discussion and which we have seen in the Spartan passage already quoted (7.104.4). By throwing off Assyrian rule, the Medes are left free to govern themselves according to their own and not someone else's *nomoi*. The sentence introduces the narrative of what they chose to do with that opportunity. After their liberation they suffer from a period of ἀνομίη, that is to say, of lawlessness, presumably because of a void of institutions suitable for safeguarding societal stability and justice. In the hopes of establishing εὐνομίη (1.97.3: "law-abidingness", in the apt translation of Cartledge 2016: 44), they elect a monarch. To Herodotus and his audience, this measure marks a return ("they reverted *again*", αὖτις . . . περιῆλθον) to a state of non-freedom, albeit internal, denoted as 'tyranny'.[36]

The ordinary Mede Deioces, once the people have put him in power, founds a dynastic kingship, which is inherited by Cyrus who is royal only from his Median mother's side. In the tradition followed by Herodotus, therefore, only now does monarchy become an established Persian *nomos*, and that happens at the same time as Cyrus liberates the Persians from Median subjection. A Persian speaker (the future king Darius) says as much at a special moment in Herodotus' narrative, when the abusive king Cambyses and his Median usurper are both dead and there is no king. The Persians here find themselves in a situation somewhat similar to that of the Medes after their liberation from the Assyrians, in that they too have the opportunity to determine what will constitute their *nomos* from now on.[37] Persian notables meet to consider the issue arguing what form of government might suit them best for the future.

One of the most interesting, if neglected, aspects of this much-studied scene, the so-called 'Constitutional Debate, is that it once again brings together ἐλευθερίη and νόμος and attempts to define them dialectically. Here the Persians reproduce for real the thought-experiment Herodotus envisions at 3.38.1 [p. 144]): they look at different customs and then, just as Herodotus predicts there, they end up keeping their own. Darius concludes that this is the right thing for the Persians to do, while also connecting monarchy with Persian freedom (3.82.5):

Κόθεν ἡμῖν ἡ ἐλευθερίη ἐγένετο καὶ τέο δόντος; Κότερα παρὰ τοῦ δήμου ἢ ὀλιγαρχίης ἢ μουνάρχου; Ἔχω τοίνυν γνώμην ἡμέας ἐλευθερωθέντας διὰ ἕνα ἄνδρα τὸ τοιοῦτο περιστέλλειν, χωρίς τε τούτου πατρίους νόμους μὴ λύειν ἔχοντας εὖ.

Where did our freedom come from, and who gave it to us? The people, an oligarchy, or a monarch? Well, then, I am of the opinion that we, who *were freed thanks to one man*, should preserve this system, and, aside from this, we should not disassemble ancestral customs (πατρίους νόμους), since they serve us well.

For Darius, freedom is the national Persian independence that Cyrus acquired in fighting the Medes; renouncing monarchy, moreover, would be tantamount to overturning Persian *nomoi* established since the time of the same Cyrus. But there are dissenting voices. The system founded by Deioces the Mede may have solved the problem of rampant *anomiē* but has also sown the seeds of the ruler's disregard of *nomos*. The two Persians who speak before Darius in the Constitutional Debate are both in favour of replacing monarchy with a collective government, be it a democracy or an oligarchy. To the first of them Herodotus attributes an indictment of monarchy more violent than any judgment we find anywhere else in the *Histories* (3.80.3–6, excerpts):

Κῶς δ' ἂν εἴη χρῆμα κατηρτημένον μουναρχίη, τῇ ἔξεστι ἀνευθύνῳ ποιέειν τὰ βούλεται; . . . τὰ μὲν γὰρ ὕβρι κεκορημένος ἔρδει πολλὰ καὶ ἀτάσθαλα, τὰ δὲ φθόνῳ. Καίτοι ἄνδρα γε τύραννον ἄφθονον ἔδει εἶναι, ἔχοντά πάντα τὰ ἀγαθά . . . Τὰ δὲ δὴ μέγιστα ἔρχομαι ἐρέων· νόμαιά τε κινέει πάτρια καὶ βιᾶται γυναῖκας κτείνει τε ἀκρίτους. Πλῆθος δὲ ἄρχον πρῶτα μὲν οὔνομα πάντων κάλλιστον ἔχει, ἰσονομίην.

How could monarchy be an appropriate asset, when it makes it possible for a man to do what he wants without being held accountable? . . . Glutted with affluence he does many reckless things out of arrogance, and some out of envy. And yet a tyrant should be immune from envy since he has all advantages. . . . And here is the most important thing I am going to say: he overturns ancestral customs, does violence to women, and puts people to death without due process. When a multitude rules, on the other hand, this has the most beautiful name, equality of law.

Otanes preemptively contradicts Darius on several counts. He establishes that monarchy is synonymous with tyranny and, therefore, by definition the opposite of freedom (meaning free government), thereby disregarding in advance the notion that, as Darius will say, monarchy has been the cause of Persian freedom (meaning national independence).[38] Otanes' antonym for monarchy/tyranny is here not *eleutheriē*, but ἰσονομίη, which we can vaguely translate as 'equality of law', just as we have translated ἰσηγορίη at 5.78 as 'equality of speech'.[39] *Isonomia* is a somewhat fluid term, which began to be used by opponents of Greek tyrannical rule earlier than *eleutheria* and could be applied to a variety of constitutional systems in different city-states.[40] Eventually it became a catchword for the Kleisthenic democracy, some of whose features are (anachronistically) included in Otanes' description of his favourite form of government.[41] Here, however, we should not be excessively narrow in the denotation of the term at the cost of forgetting the resonances of its basic components: the aspect of freedom that *isonomia* underlines is first and foremost the status of what Otanes calls νόμαια, customary norms, as a *collective* and shared possession. These are the *nomoi* such as Herodotus describes in his Persian ethnography in Book I, where he portrays an assertive and self-confident community, with the king a secondary figure only mentioned twice and subject to the same *nomoi* as other Persians (1.137.1):

αἰνέω δὲ καὶ τόνδε, τὸ μὴ μιῆς αἰτίης εἵνεκα μήτε αὐτὸν τὸν βασιλέα μηδένα φονεύειν, μήτε τινὰ τῶν ἄλλων Περσέων μηδένα τῶν ἑωυτοῦ οἰκετέων ἐπὶ μιῇ αἰτίῃ ἀνήκεστον πάθος ἔρδειν.

I [Herodotus] praise also the following law, namely that neither the king himself may put anyone to death for a single offence, nor may any other Persian inflict capital punishment on any of his slaves for a single offence.

In Herodotus' historical narrative, as a matter, of fact, this and many other laws and customs are violated by the Persian kings many times.[42] In the view of both Herodotus and his character Otanes, *isonomiē* is incompatible with absolute monarchy, which often deviates from the collective *nomoi*. Herodotus' narrative even goes one step further making clear that monarchy follows norms of its own.[43] As far as the Persians are concerned, one of these royal Achaemenid norms is *arkhē*, perpetual and limitless rule over others, a *nomos* that Xerxes will claim to have inherited from his predecessors and that he is bound to follow by invading Greece.[44]

Needless to say, Otanes loses the debate, but on the topic of freedom and *nomoi* he has the last word. Once his colleagues reject his proposal of an isonomic form of government, he chooses to opt out of the regime altogether (3.83.2):

Ἐγὼ μέν νυν ὑμῖν οὐκ ἐναγωνιεῦμαι. Οὔτε γὰρ ἄρχειν οὔτε ἄρχεσθαι ἐθέλω· ἐπὶ τούτῳ δὲ ὑπεξίσταμαι τῆς ἀρχῆς, ἐπ' ᾧ τε ὑπ' οὐδενὸς ὑμέων ἄρξομαι, οὔτε αὐτὸς ἐγὼ οὔτε οἱ ἀπ' ἐμέο αἰεὶ γινόμενοι.

I am not going to compete with you [for the kingship]. I do not wish either to rule or be ruled. And I renounce ruling on this condition: that neither I nor my descendants will be ruled by any of you.

And this is the narrator's comment (3.83.3):

Καὶ νῦν αὕτη ἡ οἰκίη διατελέει μούνη <u>ἐλευθέρη</u> ἐοῦσα Περσέων καὶ <u>ἄρχεται</u>
<u>τοσαῦτα ὅσα αὐτὴ θέλει, νόμους οὐκ ὑπερβαίνουσα τοὺς Περσέων</u>.

And so even now the family of Otanes is the only one among the Persians
that continues to be <u>free</u>, and <u>is ruled only as much as it wishes, without trans-
gressing the laws of the Persians</u>.

Here ἐλευθέρη responds to Darius' use of ἐλευθερίη (to denote national freedom):
it means not being subject to autocratic rule, which goes hand in hand with following collective *nomoi*. Otanes in effect comes close to the Spartan principle
(7.104.4–5, quoted on p. 148) of rejecting a personal master in favour of law as
the only master. He also anticipates the allegiance to *isonomia* that is typical of the
Athenians after their liberation from tyranny.

Conclusion

The dialogic density of this last passage is almost overwhelming, but I would like
to conclude by taking away three interrelated points.

First, the "custom/law king of all" statement with which we have begun our discussion (3.38.4) emphasizes the validity of different *nomoi* for different peoples
and establishes that the only correct response to the *nomoi* of others is respect.
The Constitutional Debate contributes to reconciling this relativistic position with
Herodotus' opinion, expressed elsewhere, that oppressive *nomoi* are not morally acceptable because they violate absolute principles. For Herodotus freedom,
internal and external, is just such a non-renounceable principle and autocratic rule
is essentially illegitimate.

Second, modern scholars agree that the Constitutional Debate is both anachronistic and an extreme case of cultural translation – that is to say, it is an expression
of Greek political thought, in particular sophistic theorizing, fictitiously transferred to a foreign setting.[45] But Herodotus insists that, believe it or not, it really
happened in the way he is reporting it.[46] I have argued elsewhere that this scene,
as part of Herodotus' overall representation of Persian society, is likely based
on his interactions with real Persians interpreting themselves and their past in
that cultural middle-ground that was fifth-century Asia Minor.[47] In that case, the
anachronism of the Debate may be theirs rather than owed to Herodotus, and the
cultural translation may also be partly theirs. I would like to believe, for example,
that the narrator who defines the family of Otanes as uniquely "free" (3.83.4)
is not just Herodotus, but a Persian of a certain kind, somewhat critical of the
Achaemenid regime, an admirer or *soi-disant* descendant of Otanes,[48] perhaps
Herodotus' drinking friend in Samos or elsewhere, and his source for this episode.

Historical imagination aside, my last point is that Otanes introduces into the
Debate words and ideas that have to do with 'ruling'. The liberty Herodotus attributes singularly to him and his family as the next best thing to "a collectivity that
rules" (πλῆθος . . . ἄρχον, 3.80), entails *not to rule* as well as not being ruled. On

the other hand, the Persian liberty mentioned by Darius is often envisioned as freedom (indeed, necessity) to rule others.[49] Otanes himself, this almost Socratic figure in the Debate who rejects both ruling and being ruled, adapts to the system: he will soon appear in the subsequent narrative using brutal force to re-establish Persian rule in Samos (3.141–49).[50]

At the time when Herodotus was writing, however, the terminology of ruling (*arkhē*, *arkhein*, etc.), including the construed inevitable alternative between ruling or being ruled, would have evoked not so much Persian domination anymore, but the Athenian empire. We have been aware at least since Fornara's study in 1971 that Herodotus' representation of Persian expansionism is in large part informed by Greek political circumstances of his day. And since the "ruling multitude" (πλῆθος . . . ἄρχον) of isonomic Athens now ruled over other fellow-Greeks, the 'enslaved' ones (to use once again common discourse) were envisioned as being subject both to a local tyrant (the whole city of Athens or the *dēmos* as tyrant), and to an external power comparable to Persia.[51] The Greeks' awareness of their historical failure to actualize full freedom among themselves both intensified and challenged the notion of a special Greek freedom. Herodotus responds by looking abroad. When he finds the most complete articulation of the idea of *eleutheriē* among a tiny minority in the most autocratic nation he knows, what he sees in microcosm is the same fragmentation, contradiction, and paradox that problematize freedom as an essential component of Greek self-definition.

Notes

1 See, e.g., President George W. Bush, on the occasion of his visit with the troops at Fort Irwin, California, April 4, 2007 during the Iraq War that begun in 2003: "I believe liberty is universal. I don't believe it is just for the United States of America alone. I believe there is an Almighty, and I believe the Almighty's gift to people worldwide is the desire to be free. And I think, if given a chance, people will seize that moment."

2 P. Noonan 2014. "What Americans Think About Iraq." *Wall Street Journal*, June 20: "[T]he old American emotionalism, the assumption that the people of Iraq want what we want, freedom and democracy, is over. Ten years ago if you announced you had reservations about what the people of Iraq really want, and maybe it isn't freedom and democracy first, such reservations were called ethnocentric, belittling, bigoted. That's over, too. We are hard-eyed now." Freedom is however a value at least nominally embraced by most developed countries and enshrined in the Universal Declaration of Human Rights.

3 Aes. *Pers.* 181–99 (but see Gruen 2011: 19–21), 242; Hippocr. *Aer.* 16.30. For Aristotle (*Pol.* 7.6.1, 1327b), freedom is part of the Greek φύσις. For a history of the notion of freedom and its origins in the West, see Patterson 1991.

4 For ethnological 'charity', see Asad 1986.

5 Munson 2014.

6 All translations from the Greek are my own.

7 He also makes fun of the Persian king's gift of a gold twisted necklace and bracelets (3.22.2), but these are connected with the idea of enslavement, like the golden shackles Darius gives Demokedes of Croton (3.130.4).

8 See, e.g., 1.135; 1.155–56; 1; 1.96.5; 5.87.

9 See also Herodotus' less explicit disapproval of the pragmatic cannibalism of the Padaian Indians, who hurry the death of sick people so that they can use their flesh as food

(3.99), in contrast to the consensual ritual sacrificing/eating of the dead practised by Massagetai (1.216.2) and Kallatiai (3.38.4).

10 See the discussion in Pam Bellock and Jon Cochrane. 2016. "UNICEF Report Finds Female Genital Cutting to Be Common in Indonesia." *The New York Times*, February 4.

11 Hdt. 4.68–69, 71–72 (Scythian kingship); 5.66.2 (Kleisthenic democracy); 8.137–38 (Macedonian kingship).

12 See, e.g., the Spartan change from a bad government to a good constitution (1.65.2–66.1).

13 Raaflaub 2004: 58–117.

14 As in Hdt. 2.135.1.

15 Evidence points to the early 470s as the time when slavery words start being used metaphorically in reference to political non-freedom. Raaflaub 2004: 59–63.

16 For Athenian tribute as a mark of slavery, see n. 51. Freedom is explicitly opposed to slavery (*doulosunē* and related words) e.g. at Hdt. 1.95.2 (Medes), 1.126.2 (Persians), 1.170.2 (Ionians), 1.210.2 (Persians).

17 Pohlenz 1966: 10–17; Raaflaub 2004: 58–89.

18 Hdt. 1.6.3, 170.2; 4.133.2, 136.4, 137.1, 139.2, 142; 5.49.2, 109.2, 116; 6.11.2 bis; 109.3; 10.6; 7.51.2, 139.5, 157.2, 178.2; 8.77.2, 132.1, 140α4, 142.3, 143.1; 9.41.3, 45.2, 60.1, 98.3.

19 Hdt. 5.92.2, 6.11.2bis, 6.109.3, 7.157.2; see also 1.170.2 (Bias of Priene to the Ionians); 4.137.1 (Miltiades to the Greek tyrants in Scythia); 5.109.2 (tyrants of Cyprus to the Ionians; 8.132.1 (Ionian messengers implore the Lacedaemonians to free Ionia); 8.142.3 (the Spartans say that it would be intolerable for the Athenians to be responsible for the enslavement of Greece, when they have always been liberators of many). See also 8.140α4 and 8.143.1 (Alexander of Macedon to the Athenians and Athenian response); 9.45.2 and 3 (Alexander at Plataia says the he does not wish that Greece be enslaved rather than free and that the Athenians should remember him and his efforts towards their liberation); 9.60.1 (Pausanias to the Athenians); 9.98.3 (Leutykhides to the Ionians). Divine encouragement occurs at 7.168.2 (Delphians to "the Greeks who wanted to be free") and 8.77.2 (oracle).

20 See, e.g., the Ionians, who clamour that they prefer enslavement (δουληίην, 6.12.3) to Persia rather than freedom achieved through harsh military discipline (6.11.1–2).

21 For Herodotus' use of ἴδιος in reference to distinguishing ethnic features, see, e.g., 4.18.3, 23, 106.2. Cf. Munson 2001: 80–1, 2005: 23–4.

22 Hdt. 1.126.6 (Cyrus to the Persians); 127.1 (Persian response); 210.2 (Hystaspes to Cyrus); 3.82.5*bis* (Darius to the Persian nobles); 7.2.3 (Xerxes in Persian council). Cf. 3.65.3, (Cambyses urges the Persians to recover their freedom from the Median usurper Smerdis). For freedom entailing necessity to rule, see pp. 153–5.

23 Normally exercised by one man (a *mounarkhos*), but sometimes even by a small despotic group, like the Bakkhiad μούναρχοι in Corinth (5.92α), or the 12 kings of Egypt (2.147). The appearance in Greek antiquity of the modern notion of individual freedom from constitutionally enacted laws that are perceived as intrusive can be detected in the complaints of the oligarchs who feel constrained by the democratic system (see, e.g., [Xen.] *Ath. Pol.*); these complaints are expressed in terms of *douleia* e.g. in Plato, *Gorgias* 484a. In *Republic* 563d the excessively free citizens of the democratic state resent being enslaved by the laws.

24 Raaflaub 2004: 53–89.

25 On Greek tyrants in Herodotus, see Dewald 2003.

26 Hdt. 5.55, 5.62.1, 5.62.2, 5.64.2 5.65.5, 5.78, 5.91.1, 6.122.1–2, 6.123.2; cf. 5.63.1, 5.91.2.

27 Griffith 1966.

28 As does the related notion of *parrhēsia* ("saying anything/everything"), a term that does not occur in Herodotus; see Saxonhouse 2006: esp. 94.

29 See also 1.116.1, Astyages finds the answer of young Cyrus "rather free". See Hohti 1974.
30 Confirmed by the calculations of the Spartans at 5.91.1. This is not to say that a sovereign assembly cannot make the wrong decision when it comes to voting in favour of aggressive wars; see 5.97.2. As I mention elsewhere (pp. 146, 153–4), freedom in practice combines the impulse or necessity to dominate others.
31 In replacing any human *despotēs* with *nomos* as an even more forceful *despotēs*, Demaratos speaks in terms that Xerxes would be able to understand. See however Millender, who argues for a less charitable interpretation on Herodotus' part of the Spartan devotion to freedom on the basis of this passage and the generally ambivalent representation of the Spartans throughout the *Histories* (Millender 2002a), and particularly in light of Herodotus' awareness of the despotic aspects of the Spartan dual kingship (2002b). *Contra*, e.g., Munson 1993.
32 See 6.5.1: the Milesians are not eager to accept another *turannos*, having tasted *eleutheria*.
33 Hdt. 6.102. Raaflaub 2004: 100.
34 See, e.g., 8.102–3. Herodotus' Persian speakers, by contrast, call "slaves" only non-Persian subjects (7.8β2, 7.9.2, 7.11.4, 7.39.1, 8.100.2, 9.48.2).
35 In Xerxes' offer of autonomy (8.140α2) and freedom (8.140α4) reported by Mardonios to the Athenians. Elsewhere *autonomia* and related words occur in literary sources and documents largely in reference to fifth-century Greek inter-state relations; cf. Ostwald 1982: esp. 9–14; Figueira 1990.
36 It is possible that the subject of this last sentence is all the Asiatic people who had been subject to the Assyrians (rather than only the Medes), and that "tyrannical government" refers to their eventual common external subjection to the Persians down the line. But this is not the most immediate and instinctive interpretation.
37 Walter in Meier, Patzek, & Walter: 2004.
38 On the paradox of " 'freedom' as an argument for tyranny" in Darius' speech, see Pelling 2002: 145.
39 On Herodotus' concern for equality, expressed by *iso*-words, see Saxonhouse 1996: 31–57.
40 See Raaflaub 2004: 95: "[I]t is crucial that *isonomia* always characterizes a political system that stands in sharp contrast to tyranny or other forms of despotic rule, including narrow oligarchy, and that the notion of equality inherent in the term is not necessarily that of democracy." Herodotus also uses the term in reference with Maiandros' attempt to re-establish freedom on Samos (3.124.3–4), and Aristagoras' abdication of his tyranny in Miletus (5.37.2). In contrast to tyranny, Herodotus also once uses ἰσοκρατίη ("equal power"), which according to Sokles is most consistently upheld by the Spartans (5.92α).
41 For a history and definition of the term, see especially Ostwald 1969: 96–136.
42 Lateiner 1989: 154–5.
43 In Eur. *Suppl.* 431–32 the tyrant is represented as the singlehanded owner of *nomos*. In Thuc. 3.62.2–3 the Thebans claim that the narrow oligarchy that ruled their city at the time of the Persian Wars was contrary to *nomos* and closest to a tyranny. Herodotus' acknowledgement that Peisistratos did not upset existing public offices (τιμάς) or changes regulations (θέσμια) does not use the term νόμος (1.59.6).
44 Hdt. 7.8α. A micro-illustration of this law occurs when Xerxes' general and cousin Mardonios attacks at Plataea in spite of unfavourable omens, because activism is the Persian *nomos* (9.41.4); he is a true loyalist, so that for him the royal and the national *nomos* are one and the same.
45 E.g., Brannan 1969; Lasserre 1976; Evans 1981; Pelling 2002; Gruen 2011: 23–5; Roy 2012; Provencal 2015: 66–71.
46 Hdt. 3.80.1; cf. 6.43.3; Thomas 2000: 114–17.

47 Munson 2009. See also Nagy pp. 133–6 in this volume.
48 Briant (2002: 132–5) shows that claims to descend from one or the other of the Seven were not infrequent: according to Diodorus (31.19.1–4) the kings of Cappadocia traced their ancestry to both Cyrus and Otanes (Anaphas); Polybius (5.43) records that Mithridates of Pontus "boasted of descent from one of the Persian Seven who killed the Magus".
49 See Hdt. 7.11.3; 9.121.3.
50 Pelling 2002: 139–41.
51 See Raaflaub 1979; Henderson 2003. According to Thucydides (1.98.3), the first Greek city the to be 'enslaved' by the Athenians was Naxos, which apparently tried to get out of paying tribute to the Delian League; cf. pp. 232–3. For the alternative between ruling and being ruled in Athenian discourse, see Thuc. 2.61.1, 63.2–3.

Bibliography

Asad, T. 1986. "The Concept of Cultural Translation in British Social Anthropology." In Clifford, J., & Marcus, G.E., eds., *Writing Culture: The Poetics and Politics of Ethnography*. Berkeley, CA (University of California Press), 141–64.

Brannan, P.T. 1969. "Herodotus and History: The Constitutional Debate Preceding Darius' Accession." *Traditio* 19: 427–38.

Briant, P. 2002. *From Cyrus to Alexander: A History of the Persian Empire*. Translated by P.T. Daniels. Winona Lake, IN (Eisenbrauns).

Cartledge, P. 2016. *Democracy: A Life*. Oxford (Oxford University Press).

Dewald, C. 2003. "Form and Content: The Question of Tyranny in Herodotus." In Morgan, K.A., ed., *Popular Tyranny: Sovereignty and Its Discontents in Ancient Greece*. Austin, TX (University of Texas Press), 25–58.

Evans, J.A.S. 1981. "Notes on the Debate of the Persians Grandees in Herodotus 3.80-82." *Quaderni urbinati di cultura classica* n.s. 7: 79–84.

Figueira, T. 1990. "AUTONOMOI KATA TAS SPONDAS (Thuc.1.67.2)." *Bulletin of the Institute of Classical Studies* 37: 63–88.

Griffith, G.T. 1966. "'Isegoria' in the Assembly at Athens." In Badian, E., ed., *Ancient Society and Institutions: Studies Presented to Victor Ehrenberg on His Seventy-Fourth Birthday*. Oxford (Blackwell & Mott), 115–38.

Gruen, E.S. 2011. *Rethinking the Other in Antiquity*. Princeton, NJ (Princeton University Press).

Henderson, J. 2003. "Demos, Demagogue, Tyrant in Attic Comedy." In Morgan, K.A., ed., *Popular Tyranny: Sovereignty and Its Discontents in Ancient Greece*. Austin, TX (University of Texas Press), 155–79.

Hohti, P. 1974. "Freedom of Speech in Speech Sections in the 'Histories' of Herodotus." *Arctos* 8: 19–27.

Lasserre, F. 1976. "Hérodote et Protagoras: le débat sur les constitutions." *Museum Helveticum* 33: 65–84.

Lateiner, D. 1989. *The Historical Method of Herodotus*. Toronto (Toronto University Press).

Meier, M., Patzek, B., Walter, U., & Wieshöfer, J. 2004. *Deiokes, König der Meder: Eine Herodot-Episode in ihren Kontexten*. Wiesbaden (Franz Steiner Verlag).

Millender, E. 2002a. "Herodotus and Spartan Despotism." In Powell, A., & Hodkinson, S., eds., *Sparta: Beyond the Mirage*. Swansea & London (The Classical Press of Wales), 1–61.

————. 2002b. "Νόμος Δεσπότης: Spartan Obedience and Athenian Lawfulness in Fifth-Century Greek Thought." In Robinson, E., & Gorman, V., eds., *Oikistes: Studies in Constitutions, Colonies, and Military Power in the Ancient World Offered in Honor of A.J. Graham.* Leiden (Brill), 33–59.

Munson, R.V. 1993. "Three Aspects of Spartan Kingship in Herodotus." In Rosen, R.M., & Farrell, J., eds., *Nomodeiktes: Greek Studies in Honor of Martin Ostwald.* Ann Arbor, MI (University of Michigan Press), 39–54.

————. 2001. *Telling Wonders: Ethnographic and Political Discourse in the Work of Herodotus.* Ann Arbor, MI (University of Michigan Press).

————. 2005. *Black Doves Speak: Herodotus and the Language of Barbarians.* Hellenic Studies 9. Washington, DC (Center for Hellenic Studies).

————. 2009. "Who Are Herodotus' Persians?" *Classical World* 102: 457–70. Reprinted in Munson, R.V., ed., 2013. *Oxford Readings in Classical Studies: Herodotus.* Oxford (Oxford University Press), II, 321–35.

————. 2014. "Herodotus and Ethnicity." In McInerney, J., ed., *A Companion to Ethnicity in the Ancient Mediterranean.* Boston, MA (Wiley-Blackwell), 341–55.

Ostwald, M. 1969. *Nomos and the Beginnings of the Athenian Democracy.* Oxford (Clarendon Press).

————. 1982. *Autonomia: Its Genesis and Early History.* American Classical Studies II. Chico, CA (Scholars Press).

Patterson, O. 1991. *Freedom: Vol. I: Freedom in the Making of Western Culture.* New York, NY (I.B. Tauris).

Pelling, C. 2002. "Speech and Action: Herodotus' Debate on the Constitutions." *Proceedings of the Cambridge Philological Society* 48: 123–5.

Pohlenz, M. 1955. *Griechische Freiheit: Wesen und Werden eines Lebensideals.* Heidelberg (Quelle und Meyer). English trans. Pohlenz. 1966.

————. 1966. *Freedom in Greek Life and Thought: The History of an Ideal.* Translated by C. Lofmark. Dordrecht (D. Reidel).

Provencal, V. 2015. *Sophist Kings: Persians as Other in Herodotus.* London (Bloomsbury Academic).

Raaflaub, K. 1979. "Polis Tyrannos: Zur Entstehung einer politischen Metapher." In Bowerstock, G., Burkert, W., & Putnam, M.C.J., eds., *Arktouros: Festschrift B.M.W. Knox.* Berlin (De Gruyter), 137–52.

————. 2004. *The Discovery of Freedom in Ancient Greece.* Translated by R. Franciscono. Chicago, IL (University of Chicago Press).

Roy, S. 2012. "The Constitutional Debate: Herodotus' Exploration of Good Government." *Histos* 6: 298–320.

Saxonhouse, A.W. 1996. *Athenian Democracy: Modern Mythmakers and Ancient Theorists.* Notre Dame (Notre Dame University Press).

————. 2006. *Free Speech and Democracy in Ancient Athens.* Cambridge (Cambridge University Press).

Thomas, R. 2000. *Herodotus in Context: Ethnography, Science, and the Act of Persuasion.* Cambridge (Cambridge University Press).

7 Cosmopolitanism and contingency in Herodotus

Myth and tragedy in the Book IV of the *Histories*

Alexandre Agnolon

Introduction

Herodotus was considered *pater Historiae* 'father of History' by Cicero in *De legibus*. The Latin author, however, assigned to him – as well as to Theopompus – an excessive fondness for *fabulae*, which sometimes converted the historian's prose into something quite like the compositions of the poets,[1] in whose endeavour, as we know, delight plays a fundamental role.[2] This intimate connection, often organic, between λόγος and μῦθος in Herodotus' *Histories* was not only noted by the ancients,[3] but was also, and above all, an issue of dispute in ancient historiography.[4] This connection was often manifested by the comparative effort proper to an ἀγών 'contest' between one author and another, in particular regarding an enumeration of virtues taken as symmetrically opposed. I am thinking of Quintilian, who contrasts the pleasure gained from reading the poetic prose of Herodotus – almost Homeric – to the concision and vigour of Thucydides.[5] Or we might note the almost direct criticism of Thucydides himself, who, for example, at the beginning of his work, censures a certain model of historical composition whose exemplar is Herodotus, an author who, with a greater intention of pleasing the ears of his audience, forges narratives difficult to substantiate, since they cannot be verified; in time, these narratives "prevailed into the territory of the fable" (ἐπὶ τὸ μυθῶδες ἐκνενικηκότα).[6]

Among modern authorities, the controversy does not seem to be too different. Murray, in his synthesis of ancient Greek literature, immediately at the beginning of his essay on Herodotus' prose, calls him a "storyteller"; he then remarks that it is not a question of saying that Herodotus was an "improviser", but rather a prose analogue of the bard, a narrator of the achievements of real men and a describer of foreign places.[7] This aspect of Herodotus' prose contributes to the amplification of his narrative in time and space. In defiance of the chronological sequence of events, the narrative is always interrupted, and the author adds extensive comments and other minor narratives.[8] Murray's observation obviously alludes to Thucydides and Cicero – perhaps also to Quintilian. These authors considered it to be the task of the historian to reveal factual truth, from which emanated the intelligibility and possible knowledge that could be deduced from the past.[9]

Here Murray follows, at least in part, earlier scholars of nineteenth-century historicism. Leopold von Ranke and his followers understood history as political history, military history, state history, and the history of great men, an indelible product of a truth obtained through historical research in sources – that is, mainly textual, with an emphasis on proof. They followed methods and specific precepts that were consistent with the practices of a particular discipline, a form of scientific history.[10] The emphasis of these historians on the document and on the archive motivated, therefore, society (subjects upon which Herodotus focussed) be put aside, or considered a product of simple dilettantism.[11]

This sort of 'scientificity effect', mainly because of the historicists of the preceding century, relegated Herodotus, despite his importance in antiquity, to the place of coadjuvant.[12] In a way, as a consequence of following these traditions, since they were unreliable from the prevailing view of proper methodology, the historian suffered from a reputation for unreliability.[13] Despite this reputation, in the beginnings of the modern age as a consequence of the 'age of discovery' and the contact with native peoples, several scholars satiated the curiosity of the European public with respect to the wonders of the New World, emulating, therefore, the narrative schemes of Herodotus. The Greek historian was a fundamental model for the 'ethnographers' of the sixteenth and seventeenth centuries.[14]

At the beginning of the twentieth century, there was a real change of perspective regarding Herodotus. Two causes, in my view, were responsible for this: on the one hand, the appearance of works such as those of Jacoby and Pohlenz[15] supported by a wide range of archaeological sources; on the other hand, in parallel with the revaluation of Herodotus' work, the various debates in academic circles that problematized the methodological models (and claims) of traditional modern historiography, particularly the critiques in the manner of the *nouvelle histoire*, which incorporated contributions from sociology and anthropology.[16]

Regardless of the significance attributed to Herodotus, regardless of the diatribes or the quarrels that, as we have seen, had already put the authority of the historian in question, it is necessary to consider his enterprise as one of the summations of a broad and longlasting movement dating from at least the eighth century BC that worked on behalf of the expansion of the cultural and territorial horizons of Greek civilization. The expansion of trade and colonies along both shores of the Mediterranean Sea was marked by the resumption of contacts with the Orient, interrupted for centuries by the fall of Mycenaean civilization.[17] Now, from the shores of Ionia, the Greeks consolidated their ties with Lydia within the interior of Anatolia. Trade relations and cultural integration intensified ever more: the Greeks, already in the middle of the seventh century, had extended the tentacles of their colonization and commerce to Africa and the Iberian Peninsula in the west and to the Black Sea in the east, surpassing, by the connections that they established, the interaction within the eastern basin of the Mediterranean.[18]

This enlargement or expansion of these frontiers, which in origin is more or less contemporaneous with the advent of the πόλις (according to Vernant, a social structure "whose originality will be fully felt by the Greeks")[19] corresponds, intellectually, to the development of speculative thinking in Greece. This development included the emergence of philosophy, which ensured the central theoretical instrument for the description of the world. The philosophical conceptions of Thales of Miletus and Anaximander's cosmology,[20] for example, which were largely a product of close cultural intercourse with Babylonian astronomers – Thales of Miletus was said to have predicted a solar eclipse in 585 BC[21] – rejected mythic structures of thought in favour of a rational system of organization of experience. In the field of history, the work of Herodotus was situated in this same rational movement of the understanding of human reality and represented more than the mere narrative of the war waged against the Persian aggrandizement, or a union of more or less unified oral histories.

Through the detailed description of foreign peoples, the historian endeavoured, by means of research and 'inquiry' (ἱστορίη), to give intelligibility to the representation of the 'other'. He endeavoured to make the Greek public 'see' (through θεωρίη) the distant territories he describes, the cultural attitudes of the foreigner and, ultimately, the Greeks themselves, in a specular reflective fashion and within a profoundly dialectical dimension. In other words, the enlargement of the Greek view on the 'other' in Herodotus' work immediately implies the detailed composition of an enlarged κόσμος, marked by the vision of the historian's privileged position as an experienced observer, which is the consequence of the experience he had gained in his travels and his relations with contemporary philosophical culture.[22] Even if Herodotus conceived his world as influenced markedly by the boundary between Europe and Asia, this did not prevent him from being "sensitive to ethnic-cultural diversity".[23]

The purpose of this chapter is thus to focus on the episodes of Anacharsis and Skyles, which are part of the Book IV of the *Histories* (4.76.1–80.5), in order to demonstrate how Herodotus, assuming the role of a 'cultural translator', puts under the Greek gaze practices and customs of the Scythian people. The historian makes a pervasive use of symbolic structures known to the Greeks, particularly originating from tragedy and myth. These structures must be understood in Herodotus as devices of representation of the other. In other words, we intend to show that the extended κόσμος of Herodotus to which we have already referred, and which is an indication as well of the profound complexity of the contemporary cultural exchanges that crossed the Mediterranean from the West to the East, is correlated with an effort to represent the 'other' by means of what was familiar to the Greeks. That is to say, the intention to bring the strange customs of the barbarians closer to the Greeks implies the effort to accommodate them in Greek structures of thought. We find him envisioning simultaneously presence and absence of difference, proximity and distance, and establishment and erasure of boundaries between Greeks and barbarians.

The tragic episodes of Anacharsis and Skyles

The conventions of tragedy,[24] broadly employed in Herodotus' narratives dedicated to Anacharsis and Skyles, as we shall see, constituted not only a sort of 'rhetorical–mythical–poetic' apparatus that framed Greek culture, but above all were indicative of the tensions and ambiguities inherent in the city itself; as such they were the result of its social, cultural, and historical dynamics, acutely perceived at the heart of Greek sensibility in the classical period. For that reason, these conventions not only corresponded to the dramatic purposes of their narrative,[25] but were also convenient for the representation of otherness as well (not however necessarily exploiting the conventions of drama that indicated a tragic vision of the world). This alterity could only be fully forged by a process of close identification with the other, generating the terror and piety typical of the drama. Furthermore, it was capable of making the barbarian a little Greek;[26] to know the other and to perceive alterity was only possible for the historian if Greeks and barbarians, temporarily and virtually, inhabited a grey common area, a point of intersection between cultures.

It is not by chance that both narratives – which serve in Herodotean *historiē* to exemplify the irreducible character of the Scythian people, its aversion towards the adoption of foreign customs, especially those of the Greeks – have as their scene Milesian colonies.[27] Situated on the edge of the Greek-speaking world, Kyzikos and Olbia were localities, now attested by surviving archaeological findings, which were in close contact with the northern and eastern peoples in a kind of 'free zone' of commerce. Moreover, because they existed within a region of persistent contact between Greeks and barbarians, Kyzikos and Olbia were cities of intense cultural exchanges. This interaction depended, as we have seen, on a process that presupposed concomitant mutual cultural exchanges and the marking of differences, imposing sometimes the visibility of the frontier and sometimes obscuring it. Although the superiority of the Greeks is well marked in Herodotus, this 'panhellenic sensibility' is not fixed, but always changing and highly aware that it is the product of cultural interactions; the 'frontier' is, therefore, a territory of formation of identities and the identity is, paradoxically, 'acculturation' itself.[28]

The narratives about Anacharsis and Skyles are more or less homologous.[29] Broadly speaking, both were aristocrats belonging directly to the Scythian royalty. The first, as Herodotus testified, is the brother of King Saulios;[30] the second becomes king of the Scythians, loses his throne, and then falls into disgrace. He is succeeded by his half-brother, Oktamasades.[31] Later, because both practised Greek cults, thus denying, according to the reasoning of the Scythians, their culture and religion, they are killed by their respective brothers: Anacharsis is struck by Saulios; Skyles is beheaded by Oktamasades.[32] The misfortunes of both, murdered by relatives, resemble, although with some differences, some of the extrajudicial practices of Scythia (referenced by Herodotus), those allowing the assassination of relatives in cases of discord. There is also a macabre fact: in the presence of important guests, the skulls of those assassinated, in the manner of enemy spoils, were brought forth by the host as a sign of distinction; at the same time, the host would also expound the motive for the quarrel that had led to the assassination, although it was among members of the same family.[33]

The story of Anacharsis, more briefly, begins with his return to Scythia (4.76.1–6). After many years of travelling, having known many lands (γῆν πολλὴν θεωρήσας) and, in these far-off places, being accepted by all as a man of great wisdom (ἀποδεξάμενος κατ ‛αὐτὴν σοφίην πολλὴν),[34] he was about to return to his kinfolk. Soon after crossing the Hellespont, Anacharsis reached the Milesian colony of Kyzikos, just as its citizens were celebrating, with great fanfare, the festival dedicated to the Great Mother, Cybele (an Asia Minor deity of a vegetal character and, therefore, associated with nature, who will among the Greeks be identified with Demeter).[35] It was then that Anacharsis, in the midst of the feast in Cyzicus, promised to the Great Mother, that, if he returned home safely, he would offer sacrifices in her name, analogous to those given to her by the inhabitants of that city, as well as observe the ritual of a "waking night vigil" (παννυχίς). In Scythia, precisely in the region called Hylaie, Anacharsis initiated the rituals he had promised, celebrating them with tympanums and images of the goddess and of Attis (her consort) attached to his body. The narrative now reaches its climax. A compatriot, on seeing him celebrating the honours of the goddess, informed the king Saulios what was happening. The king went immediately to Hileia. After he saw with his own eyes the celebrations that were being offer to the Great Mother, he killed Anacharsis with an arrow. Finally, Herodotus reports that no one among the Scythians claimed to know even who Anacharsis was because he went to Greece and adopted foreign customs.

The story of Skyles takes place, according to Herodotus, many years later (4.76.1, 78–80). The historian, almost fulfilling the protocols of what later will inform the genre of epideictic rhetoric, begins the narrative with the birth and origin of his character: Skyles was the elder son of Ariapeithes, king of the Scythians, with a woman from Istria. She was, therefore, Greek.[36] For this reason, she taught her child the Greek language and culture (τὸν ἡ μήτηρ αὐτὴ γλῶσσάν τε Ἑλλάδα καὶ γράμματα ἐδίδαξε). Soon after the death of Ariapeithes – murdered by the king of the Agathyrsi, Spargapithes – Skyles became king of Scythia, taking for himself, his father's wife, Opoie.

Although he was king and exercised, therefore, power over his people, Skyles had no inclination for Scythian habits. He identified himself much more with Greek customs, through which he had been educated by his mother from childhood. Thus, every time Skyles went to the city of the Borysthenites (that is, Olbia, another Milesian colony), after leaving his forces outside the walls, he entered the city, abandoned his clothes, and dressed in Greek dress. Within the limits of the city, he lived as a Greek, adopting their gods, and practising Greek religion according to the usage and rules professed by them. Skyles spent months in Olbia and then left the city with his army, again wearing Scythian dress. According to Herodotus, it was the custom of the king to behave thus, so much so that he had built a very large and sumptuous mansion in Olbia, with sphinxes and griffins carved in white marble. He also married a Greek woman, whom he settled in that same house. On one occasion, because "it was necessary that things go badly" (δὲ ἔδεέ οἱ κακῶς γενέσθαι), when Skyles determined that he should initiate himself in the Dionysian rites, there was a great prodigy: his mansion was grievously struck by lightning and burned completely. Nevertheless, Skyles maintained his determination to be initiated into the cult of Dionysos.

Meanwhile, one of the Borysthenites – most likely a disaffected one – scoffingly informed the Scythians about the intentions of their king to be initiated into

Dionysos' Bacchic rites. With the help of this man, the Scythians reached one of the towers of the wall where, with their own eyes, they were able to see Skyles, in an altered state of consciousness, parading in the company of the *thiasos*, taken by the Bacchic trance. As soon as he returned, the Scythians at Oktamasades' urging were revolted by what they had witnessed. Expecting the worst, Skyles ran away and found refuge with Sitalkes, king of the Odrysian Thracians. Oktamasades now held the power that formerly belonged to his brother. Determined to initiate a campaign against the Thracians to capture his brother, he left for Thrace with his troops; but on the Istros, when they were about to fight, Sitalkes proposed an agreement. There was to be an exchange of prisoners: since the pair were relatives – Oktamasades was the son of a sister of Sitalkes – the Thracian king saw no need of a clash between their armies, which would not only cause great slaughter, but above all could put them both in danger. Sitalkes, therefore, asked that in exchange for Skyles the Scythians give him a brother of his, who was under the protection of Oktamasades. The offer was accepted promptly. As soon as he was delivered to his brother, Skyles was beheaded under the orders of Oktamasades, as punishment for his rejection of the Scythian way of life and acceptance of the Greek gods.

Tragedy and narrative

The references to the lineage of the characters, in Herodotus' narrative, work in close correlation with the trajectories of their lives. Anacharsis, as we noted, was Saulios' brother; Skyles was a king, although, from one perspective, a bastard (he was one of the many sons of King Ariapeithes). Even so, both experienced similar destinies: they were killed because they violated cultural and religious interdictions. Indeed, the affinity between high birth and themes of a tragic nature was so familiar to the Greek audience of the period that they were able to identify these characteristics with the misfortunes of the famous aristocratic houses of the legendary past that were staged in the theatre. Aristotle, dealing precisely with the designs for the character of the heroes of tragedy, declares that, although he was not distinguished by virtue or justice, the hero necessarily must be one of those men belonging to illustrious γένη and enjoying a great reputation.[37]

For the philosopher, the hero's misfortune should not depend on his supposed bad character, but on a 'mistake' (ἁμαρτία). Thus, because it belongs to the same semantic field of ἄτη, the 'error-perdition', the ἁμαρτία presupposes in turn the idea of transgression. It includes an idea of trepassing limits of a religious order, whose punishment, although juridical in principle, still holds very clearly in the memory of the Greeks of the multifarious societies contemporary to Herodotus. These punishments are remnants of sacrificial rites and expiation, which bring the outcome of the narratives in question even closer to a depiction of the destiny of the great heroes of legend. However, this approximation is capable of generating a certain unexpected effect, namely, it establishes an analogy between the contemporary practices of the Scythian people – especially with regard to their warrior and religious morality – and the legendary past of Greece sung by the poets, an aspect of fundamental identity for the Greeks in the fifth century BC.

If it is true that the Greeks are distinguished from the Scythians, a datum that is often reiterated in the historian's prose,[38] it is no less true that the tragic sense with which these episodes are permeated can lead the reader on the opposite path, which is to bring the Greeks and barbarians closer together. This tragic affect shuffles the cultural limits among them; the reader is, in this sense, placed in the position of Anacharsis and Skyles, who transgressed the limits of one culture to move toward another. This is not only because of the affections that inspire terror and piety, which are fundamental to the alterity forged by the historian, but mainly because the fate of Anacharsis and Skyles display the same fluctuating character and the same ambivalence of the words present in the tragic poets.

These poets have programmatically explored the ambiguous nature of utterance, reflecting both the religious universe and the urban and secular ambience. This reflection converts speech into a quasi-amalgam (in itself difficult to categorize) whose new nature expresses the game of tensions and ambiguities to which the tragic hero is exposed. In a world full of contingencies, the consequences of heroic action depend simultaneously on human will and on the imperatives of destiny; thus, the punishment of tragic heroes is both legal and religious; it is at same time a sanction and an expiation. The narrative of Herodotus, like the rewriting of traditional myth in the tragedians, enhances the ambiguity of the sign itself and formulates propositions in which the true and the false are almost equivalent in the eyes of the other. Just as the Scythian people do not perceive the differences between celebrating the mysteries of Dionysos and a surrender to μανία – for the Scythians, the terms are equivalent, as they are ignorant of Greek religious culture[39] – so also in the *Philoctetes*, Sophocles makes the 'salvation' and the 'false' interchangeable terms: the ambiguity of words here is the fruit of the syntactic ambiguity innate in the Greek phrase: is it the false that contains salvation or is it salvation that contains the false? (τὸ σωθῆναί γε τὸ ψεῦδος φέρει).[40]

This near lack of distinction between what establishes the space of religious traditions and that of proper legal or social traditions coincides very much with Vernant's conception of the practice of the tragedians of the fifth century BC, who, using the legal categories of the time, played "deliberately with their uncertainties, their fluctuations, their lack of finishing: imprecision of terms, changes of meaning, inconsistencies and oppositions that reveal disagreements within the juridical thought itself, also translate their conflicts with a religious tradition".[41] This blurring, the forgetting of the frontier, as proposed by F. Hartog,[42] must be understood in truth as a τόπος of tragedy, and is part of Herodotus' rhetorical-poetic apparatus, which incorporates in his narrative particular characteristics not only originating from the mythical repertoire common to the Greek-speaking world, but above all from tragedy as a genre practised by Aeschylus and Sophocles.[43] Surpassing limits, through ignorance or forgetfulness, is related to ὕβρις, an essential component of the tragic hero's character.

Moreover, the theme of a transgression of certain limits that are imposed by men or by the gods themselves – a transgression, by the way, motivated by ὕβρις – is a tragic theme *par excellence*. Indeed, as far as the characters in particular are concerned, it is important to note, as Hartog has already pointed out, that the actions of Anacharsis and Skyles are deeply conditioned by their respective characters. That is, the transgression of cultural boundaries – or, as the French historian proposes, the 'forgetting' of these frontiers – is a common ingredient in both characters. Dangerous contact between the two cultures is associated not only with an excess, which motivates the breaking of the limits imposed on these subjects, but especially with the privileged position enjoyed by both. Here, it is not a question of social position, but of the position of the gaze, of seeing more, and of seeing beyond one's own limits: Anacharsis has a keen eye; as Herodotus himself observes, the man saw many peoples and places and gave repeated proofs of wisdom. Skyles, because he was δίγλωσσος, 'bilingual', half-Scythian and half-Greek, was also in a privileged position; as a speaker of both languages he knew both cultures profoundly.[44] Moreover, Skyles' preference for his Greek identity implies the knowledge of the Greek language.

The relationship in Anacharsis's story between travel and knowledge (σοφία) is equivalent, in Skyles' story, to the ability to be bilingual. Knowledge is an ambiguous aspect of the constitution of the character of both figures, since it is simultaneously virtue and vice. On the one hand, knowledge is positive, since it inscribes the characters in a privileged position in relation to the cultural dynamic with the Greeks; indeed there is no Scythian at all who knows the 'other' more than these two. On the other hand, this knowledge is the evil from which both suffer. Both are displaced characters, true strangers in the land itself, and neither of them is seen as fully Scythian, although the case of Skyles is more evident, since he does not identify with the Scythian habits of life. The theme of knowledge and the transgression of borders, deeply interconnected in the history of Anacharsis and Skyles, has special relations with themes that are related to the tragic genre and the myths of 'resistance'.

Transgression, punishment, and tragedy

Transgression, especially religious – the reason why Anacharsis and Skyles die – is an important theme of Attic tragedy, which establishes points of contact between the narratives of Herodotus and tragedy. In Sophocles' *Philoctetes*, for example (a play already mentioned earlier) the character who gives his name to the play, despite his heroic values, is punished by the gods, since on his way towards Troy he penetrates sacred space reserved for the goddess of Kryse[45] (the Greeks went there to offer sacrifices). Upon invading the enclosure, the hero is bitten by a serpent guarding the temple. The wound, although not fatal, does not heal, and becomes purulent and foul-smelling.

Because of his terrible cries of pain, Odysseus and Atreus' sons decided to leave the hero on the island of Lemnos.[46] Exile, abandonment, and a savage existence, far removed from all civilization, having as sole companions the purulent wound and the bow of Heracles, all this constitute the punishment for the audacity of the hero, who had transgressed the space reserved for the deity.[47] In fact, in the play, the theme of transgression occupies a place of fundamental centrality, since it goes beyond the strictly religious dimension, and leads to the centre of the stage important ethical dilemmas for the classical political society. It is in this sense that perhaps we should understand both the agile and forceful dialogue at the beginning of the drama between Neoptolemus and Odysseus,[48] which advocates the use of all possible means to achieve the conjoined ends – deception and deceit.

This theme is also not strange to Sophocles' *Oedipus Rex*, perhaps not only the most famous tragedy, at least for us moderns, but, according to Aristotle, also the best, owing to the complexity of its plot: the Stagirite, in several passages of the *Poetics*, more than once praises the structuring of the work. For him, this tragedy is the best since the poet engineers the convergence of *pari passu*, *peripeteia* and recognition (ἀναγνώρισις). Sophocles, however, makes a number of changes regarding the presentation of the traditional myth, in the first place, because the tragedy begins in the time after Laius' death and the incest has already been consummated.

The tragedian shows, in spite of the plague that is destroying the city, the figure of Oedipus, who appears immediately in the prologue, almost *in medias res*, in all his glory as an absolute tyrant. Secondly, Sophocles' focus is not on the traditional motifs involving taboo offences, such as the murder of relatives and incest, but on the investigation of Laius' murder and, afterwards, the question of the true identity of Oedipus. In the midst of all this is the conflict, always tense and ambiguous, between the mysterious forces of fate and human will, driven to the centre of the scene, thus relegating to the background the theme of the family curse, which is more important for the delineation of the myth in other ancient sources, as, for example, the *Odyssey*, in whose verses the encounter between Odysseus and Jocasta in Hades is narrated. In this passage of the epic, Homer alludes to the curse that falls on Oedipus and his family that is determined by the avenging Erinyes. Besides this, there are also references to the suicide of Jocasta, the incest, and the misfortunes of Oedipus.[49]

The changes made by Sophocles to the myth of Oedipus directly affect the poet's treatment of transgression. The family curse, incest, and parricide are obviously transgressive themes, but they lose visceral strength in Sophocles' drama. Although we may suppose that the Greek spectator of the Classical period, familiar with the Oedipus legend, was able to associate these elements with the hero, a figure who was able to transgress certain limits in a manner (from the legal and religious point of view) forbidden to men in general. Because of this it seems evident that Oedipus will inexorably suffer sanctions. The poet's emphasis on Oedipus' ceaseless seeking to make his authority legitimate is quite remarkable throughout the drama. His government, however, has no legal basis. Oedipus is, for all intents and purposes, a stranger who, by his own merit, since he defeated the Sphinx, fills the void of power left by the former king. Oedipus is a usurper who takes over the throne of Thebes and Laius' wife. This situation is associated with his effort to legitimize his reign, since it is through Jocasta that the hero ties his offspring to the Kadmos' bloodline.

The fragility of the bases upon which the power of Oedipus is supported is most strikingly revealed in his dialogue with Teiresias, when, for the first time in the drama, his guilt is revealed.[50] Faced with the evasive answers of the priest of

Apollo and, finally, with the accusation that imputes guilt to him, Oedipus immediately condemns Teiresias and his brother-in-law, Kreon, on the charge of conspiring to enact a *coup d'état*. This dimension of the tragedy, which becomes a kind of 'tragedy of power', is present only in the Sophoclean version of the myth, and is expressed by the presence of the oracle, alluded to in the play, consulted by the hero himself. He knows that he will be directly responsible for the death of his father, and that he will marry his mother. It is the oracular speech that motivates, in the poet's drama, the hero's flight to Thebes, the enscenement of the tragedy, because it is in the city of Kadmos that the prediction is fulfilled in an overwhelming way.

The power exercised by Oedipus (after the victory over the Sphinx, absolute power, by the way) and the oracle mentioned earlier are responsible for generating a rather important paradoxical effect for the tensions uncovered by the play. If it is true that the simple fact of the limitless power of which Oedipus is the master and the faith that the population has in the capacities of its tyrant – as the priest's initial speech suggests in the prologue[51] – paradoxically anticipates the sudden collapse of the hero, it is no less true that the actions of Oedipus, understood as a consequence of his visit to the Delphic sanctuary, are carried out with the simple aim of escaping his terrible destiny. However, paradoxically, the more he seeks to escape destiny, the more he goes forward to encounter it.

To flee from destiny and to play with absolute, almost divine power – let us remember that the priest, in his initial speech, even compares it to that of the gods[52] – is to surpass, to transgress limits that are beyond what is given to mortals: the hero is shrewd and extremely overconfident in his own abilities. Therefore, his principal virtues, amid the paradoxes of Sophocles' tragedy, become a φάρμακον: indeed, Oedipus uses his abilities in order to save himself and the city. However, his virtues are excessive and will lead him to ruin, since through his intelligence and cunning the hero seeks in every possible way to avoid the inevitable. The will of Oedipus enters upon a direct collision course with the divine designs. Thus, having the tragedy as support, recurrent themes of the Greek mythic universe, such as the idea of knowledge, intelligence, performance of power, and transgression are potentialized, powerfully embedding themselves in the Hellenic mind. The hero who transgresses these boundaries will inexorably suffer sanctions.

Thus, regardless of the veracity of Herodotus' narrative, it is necessary to note that the historian's account is constructed according to narrative topical strategies peculiar to the myths already known to the Greeks, but above all according to strategies, which must be understood as commonplaces, repeatedly present in contemporary tragedy. These strategies can be seen in the examples taken from *Philoctetes* and *Oedipus* in which transgression, associated with ὕβρις, plays a fundamental role in the fate of the titular characters. They can also be seen in the fate of Anacharsis and Skyles: both the Scythians aristocrats are, like the tragic heroes, transgressors and therefore must be punished. Their 'identity crime', because it transgresses the Scythian customs, is equivalent to the sin of Philoctetes penetrating the temple at Kryse and the crimes of the arrogant Oedipus. In addition, the tragic tonalities of both narratives can be noted in the deities themselves whom they worship: in Cybele's myth the subject of transgression, figured in Attis, occupies a central place; Dionysius is simply the god of tragedy and his cult is the performance situation of the genre itself.

This schematic logic of plotting (it can be expressed as a triad: transgression, inexorability, and sanction) has profound connections not only with tragedy but also with the mythic universe. These connections are clearly present in the exemplary narratives dedicated to Anacharsis and Skyles in the Book IV of Herodotus' *Histories*. In fact, we have seen that both men, members of the Scythian royalty, transgress cultural boundaries, and are punished with death. The punishment they suffer is abrupt, as can be seen in Herodotus' account, but it is also inexorable as in a tragedy. The marks of this tragic inexorability, a product of divine and human tensions and a result of the gods' will and of the error and fault of the heroes themselves, are far more remarkable in Skyles' story; it is present not only in the elements that compose his narrative (we must remember the destruction of his house in Olbia, a fundamental oracular component) but also in the elements connected to the discourse: the historian at the beginning refers to the misfortune: δὲ ἔδεέ οἱ κακῶς γενέσθαι.

The 'mythic–tragic' structure in the stories of Anacharsis and Skyles, at least in the way Herodotus presents them to us, also establishes interesting relations with the so-called 'resistance myths' especially as regards the inversion of each's constituent ingredients. Such 'resistance myths', as they are known, are associated with the legendary cycle of several deities, and were based on the binomial 'refusal-punishment'. Basically, a mortal refused a deity or the deity's cult, and he or she was, therefore, terribly punished by the god. There are several examples of this kind of myth in antiquity, but the most important are the history of Lykourgos, the myths related to the daughters of Minyas, the myth of Attis, and the histories of Hippolytos and Pentheus.[53]

All these stories, except that of Hippolytus and Attis, centre on Dionysos, a figure who is not only the god of drama, connected with poetry in general and with close ties to tragedy, but who is also precisely the god who presides, as we have seen, over the rites in which Skyles participates at the end of Herodotus' narrative of his downfall. Note also that the mythology of Attis relates him to Cybele, the great mother, the goddess whom Anacharsis is worshipping when he was surprised by his countrymen. The Scythian aristocrat incidentally, according to the Herodotean narrative, had celebrated her cult with images of Attis applied to his body. It is not surprising, therefore, if we think here of the tragic destiny of Anacharsis, that Cybele would be connected with another story of unrestrained suffering where the punishment is reserved for those who resisted the designs of the goddess.[54] Anacharsis, however, does not contradict the dictates of the goddess, but contradicts, from the Scythian point of view, his ancestral customs. Thus, the images he has attached to the body symbolize not only his devotion to the goddess, but also anticipate prophetically his terrible fate.

Of all the ancient surviving sources, *The Bacchae* by Euripides (405 BC) is the most elaborate portrayal not only of ancient Dionysism,[55] at least as it was in the mid-fifth and early fourth centuries BC, but especially of the patterning of 'resistance myths'. The tragedy focusses on the story of Pentheus, king of Thebes, and the elite matrons of the city, including Agave, the mother of the young ruler, who, by rejecting the cult of Dionysos, is punished by the god. The women, taken by the frenzy that inspired the god, abandon their Theban homes and leave, with the *thiasos*, towards the fields beyond the city walls. In order to bring back the bacchants, Pentheus, after an unsuccessful attempt to imprison the deity – who takes the form of a Lydian foreigner – departs for Mt. Cithaeron because he wants to find the women and ostensibly restore the ancestral order. Pentheus is a 'curious' man and, therefore, wants to observe them. However, Pentheus, when he contemplates the women, penetrates a space that is forbidden to him. Transgression, as determined by the logic of the theme, results in the punishment of the transgressor.

It is there that, instigated by Dionysos, he dresses in a woman's clothes to approach the *thiasos*. Pentheus falls into the trap of the god, since the implacable influence that Dionysos exerts on the women causes the illusion that Pentheus is a lion: immediately attacked by the crazed *thiasos*, the bacchanals kill him by σπαραγμός, that is to say, Pentheus is torn in pieces by women led by his own mother. Agave, believing herself to be have slain a lion, returns to Thebes displaying the head of the beast as a trophy. It is only later that she realizes that she was carrying the head of her own son. The punishment takes effect, and Thebes definitely embraces the Dionysian cult.

At first, it may seem improbable that there is any similarity between Herodotus' narratives devoted to the misadventures of Anacharsis and Skyles, and the resistance myths just mentioned, especially the one related to Pentheus, except when we consider the fact that, in these stories, there is a presence of deities deeply identified with states of frenzy as well as with catastrophic outcomes. In fact, as Munson observes in the case of Skyles, there is non-resistance because the Scythian king embraces the Greek god and his cult.[56] It is possible even to see the contrary, that is, the presence of characteristics absolutely opposite to a 'resistance myth'. In the tragedy of Euripides, Dionysos is represented as barbarian – remember here the chorus formed by the Lydian devotees and Dionysos himself, characterized as a beautiful alien stranger – whereas, in Herodotus, Dionysus appears as an index of Greek identity, providing the reason for the deaths of Anacharsis and Skyles. Thus, because only with bloodshed would it become possible to restore balance in the κόσμος, the narratives would most closely resemble myths of sovereignty, as narrated, for example, in Hesiodic poetry.[57] What, then, is the relation of those stories told by Herodotus and such 'resistance myths'?

The historian generates an interesting effect by reversing the roles of Greeks and barbarians. Assuming a position different from that which is most common in the *Histories*, that is, a position that generally presupposes the Greeks as observers, Herodotus subjects the Greeks to the intrusive sight of barbarians who now serve as the watchers or observers. This inversion is made notable not only by the fact that Anacharsis, in his many journeys through the Greek-speaking world, made commentaries on the various cities and customs, but also by the fact that Skyles, who is in a sense a *mestizo*, also contemplates, with Scythian eyes, the

Greek cultural universe. He contemplates both realms, in fact, from a privileged position, since he is able to see with detachment: the stories take place in the confines of the world, where barbarians and Greeks mingle.[58]

Moreover, it is the Scythians themselves (represented by the brothers of Anacharsis and Skyles) who, observing the two men as they celebrate Greek ritual and cultural practices, decide to execute them, and thus preserve the purity of the customs of their people. In this sense, it is possible to understand these narratives, by virtue of the change in perspective through which they look, as a kind of rewriting of resistance myths. In fact, by giving themselves to the cult of deities that represent the Greek identity, Anacharsis and Skyles abrogate their autochthonous customs and gods and are, therefore, punished by death, which, as we have seen, has close links with the Scythians' own legal-religious practices, and thus maintains, as in Euripides' *Bacchae*, the 'refusal-punishment' scheme represented by the 'resistance myths' to which we have already referred.

Conclusion

Throughout this chapter, I have tried to demonstrate that the narratives about Anacharsis and Skyles presented in the Book IV of the *Histories* were not simply exemplary stories that dramatized the irreducible character of the Scythian people. To be sure, they were so proud of their customs and traditions that they punished transgressors with death. Yet we need to transcend this valid observation that these *logoi* were important exemplary narratives because they are useful in outlining, from a structural point of view of Book IV, the character of the people that will confront Darius' armies during his Scythian expedition. Indeed, as we have seen, they are more than that. In a certain way, by attempting to 'translate' barbarian customs into the Greek spiritual universe by assigning intelligibility to them, Herodotus accommodates the foreign practices in the schemes of a mythological conceptual tradition that was familiar to the Greeks, where the rewriting depended greatly on tragedy, functioning as a kind of vector for these legendary stories. In addition, it is necessary to observe that the crimes for which Anacharsis and Skyles are punished are related to Greek notions of identity, marked mainly by language, religion, and customs.[59] For the Scythians, both characters renounce their language, religion, and customs by indulging in Greek ritual practices. In this sense, we also perceive, in these same narratives, the presence of various schemes and conventions typical of the genre, fundamental to give meaning to the experience, while encapsulating it in Greek modes of thought. Moreover, it is interesting to note that, in a way, the typical logic of 'resistance myths' – understood as denying the worship of some deity, followed then by the punishment of the transgressor – assumes a deeply ironic sense in the narrative and at the same time puts in perspective Herodotus' relativistic representation of the two Scythians. On the one hand, the resistance/negation does not occur by the denial of Greek deities (as in Pentheus' case in the *Bacchae*, for example), but, on the contrary, it occurs precisely by the adhesion to the Greek gods. On the other hand, when the characters indulge in the worship of Dionysos and the Great Mother, they simultaneously deny the rites of their native gods. This kind of relativism, therefore, condensed in the form of tragic discourse, brings Herodotus' gaze closer to the typical relativism of the sophists.

Notes

1 Cf. Boedeker 2002: 97: "Readers of Herodotus both ancient and moderns have found the imprint of Homeric epic on all levels of his text, from the occasional use of special poetic words, to literary tropes such as set speeches and dialogues, to overall range and purpose. Herodotus occasionally refers to epic characters and deeds; moreover, story patterns familiar from myths emerge from time to time in the *Histories*."

2 Cf. Cic. *Leg.* 1.1.5: *QVINTVS: Intellego te, frater, alias in historia leges obseruandas putare, alias in poemate. MARCVS: Quippe cum in illa ad ueritatem, Quinte, referantur, in hoc ad delectationem pleraque; quamquam et apud Herodotum patrem Historiae et apud Theopompum sunt innumerabiles fabulae.*

3 For Aristotle (*Gen. An.* 775b6), Herodotus was a μυθολόγος. See also Aul. Gell. 3.10.11. Regarding the relations between Herodotus and myths, see Luc. *Philops.* 2.

4 On the numerous old debates about the work of Herodotus, see Momigliano 1958: 1–13. The 'fabulous' character often associated with Herodotus' prose is related to the diuturnal use by the historian of oral tradition. On the enormous number of oral sources used by Herodotus, see Lateiner 1991: 56. On Herodotus in the ancient theoretical discourse, see Pernot 1995: 125–36.

5 Cf. Quint. *Inst.* 10.1.73–4. Other authorities (Dion. Hal *Thuc.* 23; [Longinus] *Subl.*13.3; Strab. 1.3.18 C59; and Luc. *Hist. Conscr.* 14) compare Herodotus' prose with the Homer's poetry. On Herodotus' relations with the epic and the legendary tradition, see Boedeker 2002: 97–118.

6 Thuc. 1.21.1.

7 See Murray 1912: 132.

8 Cf. Munson (2001: 21): "On the whole, the narrative proceeds chronologically, but the discourse interrupts the story sequence by constantly introducing explanations and expansions of this or that story element. In most cases, these formally subordinated narratives recount events belonging to a specific previous or later story time (flashbacks or follow-ups) or are descriptions in the present tense."

9 For example, see Cic. *De orat.* 2.36: [. . .] *historia vero testis temporum, lux veritatis, vita memoriae, magistra vitae, nuntia vetustatis, qua voce alia nisi oratoris immortalitati commendatur.*

10 On the systematization of the so-called 'historical method', see Langlois & Seignobos 1897.

11 See Burke 1990: 18–19. From this new academic discipline focussed on the history of political events, all history that was not political was often excluded. See Gilbert 1965: 315–87. There were, however, a few voices that sounded far differently from that of Ranke throughout the nineteenth century. Michelet, Burckhardt, Fustel de Coulanges, and even Marx in a sense are prominent examples.

12 On the origins of this devaluing of Herodotus, see Morelo 2014: 171–84.

13 Immerwahr 1966: 2.

14 About the Herodotus' rehabilitation as an historiographical model during this period, see Soares in this volume (p. 299).

15 See Jacoby 1913; Pohlenz 1937. See also Pereira 1994: 17.

16 See Trabulsi 1985: 51.

17 Concerning Mycenaean palatial culture, social structures, and our sources in Linear B, see, e.g., Ventris & Chadwick 1956; Bennett 1956: 103–33; and finally the classic work of Finley 1957: 133–59.

18 On the enlargement of Greek areas in the Mediterranean Sea and contact with the East, see Bérard 1957; Dunbabin 1957; Roebuck 1959.

19 See Vernant 1962: 53; also Ehrenberg 1937: 147–59, 1950: 519–48.

20 On the cosmology of Anaximander, see Kahn 1960.

21 Hdt. 1.73–4.

22 On Herodotus and his travels, see Redfield 1985: 97–118. Travel in Herodotus' *Histories* is strictly connected with storytelling and knowledge. See Griffiths 2007: 130–45; Friedman 2007: 165–78; Rood 2007: 290–306. Several authors have already demonstrated the alignment of Herodotus with the philosophical thought of the fifth century BC. See, for example, in this volume Soares p. 298 and Thomas 2006; Raaflaub 2000.

23 Soares 2001: 51.

24 In ancient sources, an explicit association between Herodotus and tragic poetry is rare (see, for example, Plut. *Mor.* 347a). Several modern authors have already observed many properly tragic aspects linked to the Herodotus' *Histories*, such as Fohl 1913. For the positions of modern critique that have dealt with the reverberations of tragedy in Herodotus, see Said 2002: 117–47; Griffin 2007: 46–59.

25 See Evans 1991: 5.

26 Immerwahr (1966: 69) classified the episodes of Anacharsis and Skyles as 'dramatic *logoi*'. See also Soares 2001: 73.

27 See Hdt. 4.76.1. Vinogradov (1981: 35–6) points out that the deaths of these Scythian aristocrats, separated by about 150 years, may reveal a change in relations between the Greek colonies and Scythians over time. In parallel with the narrowing of contact with the Greeks, it is possible that Scythian elites had gradually become more attached to their autochthonous values. See Soares 2001: 73.

28 Cf. Figueira in this volume (p. 46): "panhellenic sensibility, i.e., understanding that all Greeks are themselves members of a community established by shared language, gods, cults, and poetry"; "Herodotus' willingness to see ethnic identity as an acculturation is concordant with his emphasis on the initial identity of the Athenians as Pelasgians, despite any note of disparagement that might be detected in that non-Greek origin".

29 On the extensive discussion about Anacharsis, see Kindstrand 1981. On the role of deities in the fate of Anacharsis and Skyles, see Hall 1989: 153–4. See also Hartog 1988: 62–84; Munson 2001: 30–50; Soares 2014: 222–34.

30 Hdt. 4.76.6. The historian attributes the information about the Anacharsis' genealogy to Timnes, ambassador of Ariapeithes, the Scythian king.

31 Hdt. 4.78.2; 80.1.

32 In Herodotus' view, the violation of νόμοι represents immediate danger to an individual's character in the *Historiae*. See Lateiner 1989: 1404. See also Soares 2014: 223: "Those who exceed the limits of what is considered reasonable commit the sin of hybris, and therefore, like tragic heroes, deserve to fall, according to the principle of retribution. This principle dictates that the offender incurs the ultimate punishment of death for his criminal behaviour."

33 Hdt. 4.65.2. The skulls were also used as cups. The practice, common among the barbarians, is confirmed by archaeological findings and also by various textual sources, among them Pl. *Euthyd.* 299e; Strab. 7.3.7 C300 and Pompon. 2.13.

34 In Herodotus, there is a profound relationship between travel, wisdom, and experience, as Boedeker (2002: 99) observes, "Herodotus in some ways resembles the curious and well-traveled Odysseus." See also Hartog 1988 and Nagy 1990.

35 According to ancient sources, there was in Kyzikos a temple dedicated to Cybele erected by the Argonauts. Cf. Strabo 12.8.11 C575.

36 Istria, now Dobrudja, was a Milesian colony situated at the mouth of the Danube river.

37 Aris. *Poet.* 1453a. The relation between serious themes and the fate of the aristocrats adds an inherent *decorum* to tragedy, even before Aristotle. In the *Frogs* of Aristophanes, Aeschylus accuses Euripides of inserting into drama elements that are foreign to it, thus injuring the *decorum* of the genre, which always values the grave (note, for example, vv. 1058–62). Horace, in the *Ars Poetica*, considers high-class characters as subjects of high genres, such as epic and the tragedy (*Ars. P.* vv 73–4, 80–1); Ovid does the same in his elegy *Amores* 3.1. See also Auerbach (2001: 29), in

opposition. For the author, Antiquity was unable to thematize the everyday in a serious, but nevertheless comical way, in a low style. That means that the serious, and the
tragic, therefore, always belonged alongside serious themes, dramatized only a certain
type of character, one who is superior to us in actions, as we do not belong to the social
status that they occupy.

38 Hdt. 4.31.1–2. Herodotus at all times demarcates the frontiers of 'Greek' in relation to
what is barbarous: the Scythians, unlike the Greeks, do not understand the difference
between celebrating the bacchanals and surrendering to the god, in his μανία. See Hartog 1988: 122.

39 Hdt. 4.79.4: Ἐπείτε δὲ ἐτελέσθη τῷ Βακχείῳ ὁ Σκύλης, διεπρήστευσε τῶν τις
Βορυσθενεϊτέων πρὸς τοὺς Σκύθας λέγων· Ἡμῖν γὰρ καταγελᾶτε, ὦ Σκύθαι, ὅτι
βακχεύομεν καὶ ἡμέας ὁ θεὸς λαμβάνει· νῦν οὗτος ὁ δαίμων καὶ τὸν ὑμέτερον βασιλέα
λελάβηκε. See Hartog 1988: 83.

40 Soph. *Phil.* 109.

41 Vernant & Vidal-Naquet 1998: 3.

42 Hartog 1988: 101.

43 Said (2002: 137): "Herodotus knew and used Aeschylus' *Persians*, as is demonstrated
by a series of verbal echoes particularly in reported or direct speeches."

44 Cf. Figueira p. 44 in this volume: "similarity of language or dialect was the most effective fator in determining ethnicity". See also Brandwood p. 15 in this volume.

45 There was in Kryse a temple dedicated to Athena. Kryse was also the epithet of the
goddess.

46 Cf. Soph. *Phil.* 6–10; 264.

47 Cf. Soph. *Phil.* 264–75. The disgrace of Philoctetes is also referred to in Hom. *Il* 2.
716–25. Between the verses 192 and 200, Neoptolemus, certainly moved by Philoctetes, attributes the hero's misfortune to the divine will. Note, then, the game of
ambiguities of the poem, which, as pendular, sometimes assigns the guilt to the gods,
sometimes to the transgression of the hero.

48 Cf. Soph. *Phil.* 52–122.

49 Cf. Hom. *Od.* 11.271–80.

50 Cf. Soph. *OT* 300–462.

51 Cf. Soph. *OT* 14–57.

52 Cf. Soph. *OT* 31.

53 Cf. Trabulsi 2004: 173–90. See also Massenzio 1970. This author inserts these 'resistance' myths in the broad set of myths of acceptance or hospitality, that is, he inserts
them as their exact opposite.

54 On Attis and Cybele, see Paus. 7.19 and Strab. 12.5.3 C567.

55 On Euripides, Dionysus, and 'resistance myths', see Guthrie 1950; Dodds 1960; Murray 1965; Winnington-Ingram 1997; Thumiger 2007; Segal 1997; Sousa 2010: 79;
Trabulsi 2004; Riu 1999. For 'resistance myth' in *Histories*, see, e.g. Hdt. 9.34.

56 Cf. Munson 2001: 120.

57 On myths of sovereignty, see, e.g. Hes. *Theog.* On the idea that the sovereign, in mythic
thought, exercises his government beyond the civic sphere, see Vernant 1962: 119.

58 In the prologue (Eur. *Bacch.* 17–19), the incarnated Dionysus mentions the places of
the world to which he has travelled, his dominions. Referring to Asia, the god alludes
to the walled great cities in the territories, full of Greeks and barbarians all together.

59 See Zacharia 2008; Anson 2009.

Bibliography

Anson, E.M. 2009. "Greek Ethnicity and the Greek Language." *Glotta* 85: 5–30.

Auerbach, E. 2001. *Mimesis*. São Paulo (Perspectiva).

Barth, F. 1969. *Ethnic Groups and Boundaries: The Social Organization of Culture Difference*. Oslo (Universitetsforlaget).

Bennett, E.L. 1956. "The Landholders of Pylos." *American Journal of Archaeology* 60: 103–33.

Bérard, J. 1957. *La colonisation grecque de l'Italie Mériodionale et de la Sicile dans l'Antiquité*. Paris (Presses Universitaires de France).

Boedeker, D. 2002. "Epic Heritage and Mythical Patterns in Herodotus." In Bakker, E.J., de Jong, I.J.F., & van Wees, H., eds., *Brill's Companion to Herodotus*. London, Boston, & Köln (Brill), 97–116.

Burke, P. 1990. *The French Historical Revolution: The Annales School 1929–1989*. Stanford, CA (Stanford University Press).

Dodds, E.R. 1960. *Euripides. Bacchae*². Oxford (Clarendon Press).

Dunbabin, T.J. 1957. *The Greeks and Their Eastern Neighbours: Studies in the Relations Between Greece and the Countries of the Near East in the Eight and Seventh Centuries*. London (Society for the Promotion of Hellenic Studies).

Ehrenberg, V. 1937. "When Did the Polis Rise?" *Journal of Hellenic Studies* 57: 147–59.

———. 1950. "Origins of Democracy." *Historia* 1: 519–48.

Evans, J.A.S. 1991. *Herodotus, Explorer of the Past: Three Essays*. Princeton, NJ (Princeton University Press).

Finley, M.I. 1957. "Homer and Mycenae: Property and Tenure." *History* 6: 133–59.

Fohl, H. 1913. *Tragische Kunst bei Herodot*. Dissertation, Rostock. Borna-Leipzig (Buchdruckerei Robert Noske).

Friedman, R. 2007. "Location and Dislocation in Herodotus." In Dewald, C., & Marincola, J., eds., *The Cambridge Companion to Herodotus*. Cambridge (Cambridge University Press), 165–78.

Gilbert, F. 1965. "Three 20th-Century Historians." In Higham, J., Krieger, L., & Gilbert, F., eds., *History*. Englewood Cliffs, NJ (Prentice-Hall), 315–87.

Griffin, J. 2007. "Herodotus and Tragedy." In Dewald, C., & Marincola, J., eds., *The Cambridge Companion to Herodotus*. Cambridge (Cambridge University Press), 46–59.

Griffiths, A. 2007. "Stories and Storytelling in the Histories." In Dewald, C., & Marincola, J., eds., *The Cambridge Companion to Herodotus*. Cambridge (Cambridge University Press), 130–45.

Guthrie, W.H.C. 1950. *The Greeks and Their Gods*. Boston, MA (Beacon Press).

Hall, E. 1989. *Inventing the Barbarian: Greek Self-Definition Through Tragedy*. Oxford (Oxford University Press).

Hartog, F. 1988. *The Mirror of Herodotus: The Representation of the Other in the Writing of History*. Berkeley, CA (University of California Press).

Immerwahr, H.R. 1966. *Form and Thought in Herodotus*. Cleveland, OH (American Philological Association).

Jacoby, F. 1913. "Herodotos." In Kroll, W., ed., *Paulys Real-Encyclopädie der classischen Altertumswissenschaft*, Supplement-Band II. Stuttgart (J.B. Metzler), cols. 205–520.

Kahn, C.H. 1960. *Anaximander and the Origins of Greek Cosmology*. New York, NY (Columbia University Press).

Kindstrand, J.F. 1981. *Anacharsis: The Legend and the Apophthegmata*. Upsala (Almquist & Wiksell).

Langlois, C.V. & Seignobos, C. 1897. *Introduction aux Études Historiques*. Paris (Hachette).

Lateiner, D. 1989. *The Historical Method of Herodotus*. Toronto (University of Toronto Press).

Massenzio, M. 1970. *Cultura e crisi permanente: la "xenia" dionisíaca*. Roma (Edizioni dell'Ateneo).

Momigliano, A. 1958. "The Place of Herodotus in History of Historiography." *History* 43: 1–13.

Morelo, S. 2014. "Metodologia e Perspectivas de Relativização da Verdade nas Histórias de Heródoto." *Revista Mundo Antigo* 171–84.

Munson, R.V. 2001. *Telling Wonders: Ethnographic and Political Discourse in the Work of Herodotus*. Ann Arbor, MI (University of Michigan Press).

Murray, G. 1912. *A History of Ancient Greek Literature*. London (William Heinemann).

———. 1965. *Euripides and His Age*. Oxford (Oxford University Press).

Nagy, G. 1990. *Pindar's Homer: The Lyric Possession of an Epic Past*. Baltimore, MD, & London (Johns Hopkins University Press).

Pereira, M.H. da R. 1994. "Introdução Geral." In Heródoto, ed., *Histórias*. Lisboa (Edições 70), 1.

Pernot, L. 1995. "Le plus panégyrique des historiens." *Ktema* 20: 125–36.

Pohlenz, M. 1937. *Herodot, erste Geschichtsschreiber des Abendlandes*. Leipzig (Wissenschaftliche Buchgesellschaft).

Raaflaub, K.A. 2000. "Philosophy, Science, Politics: Herodotus and the Intellectual Trends of His Time." In Bakker, E.J., Jong, I.J.F. de, & Wees, H. van, eds., *Brill's Companion to Herodotus*. Leiden (Brill), 149–86.

Redfield, J. 1985. "Herodotus the Tourist." *Classical Philology* 80: 97–118.

Riu, X. 1999. *Dionysism and Comedy*. Lanham, MD (Rowman & Littlefield Publishers).

Roebuck, C. 1959. *Ionian Trade and Colonization*. New York, NY (The Archaeological Institute of America).

Rood, T. 2007. "Herodotus and Foreign Lands." In Dewald, C., & Marincola, J., eds., *The Cambridge Companion to Herodotus*. Cambridge (Cambridge University Press), 290–305.

Saïd, S. 2002. "Herodotus and Tragedy." In Bakker, E., de Jong, I.J.F., & van Wees, H., eds., *Brill's Companion to Herodotus*. Leiden (Brill), 117–47.

Segal, C.P. 1997. *Dionysiac Poetics and Euripides' Bacchae*. Princeton, NJ (Princeton University Press).

Soares, C. 2001. "Tolerância e Xenofobia ou a Consciência de um Universo Multicultural nas 'Histórias' de Heródoto." *Humanitas* 53: 49–80.

———. 2014. "Dress and Undress in Herodotus' 'Histories'." *Phoenix* 68: 222–34.

Sousa, E. 2010. *As Bacantes de Eurípides*. São Paulo (Hedra).

Thomas, R. 2006. "The Intellectual Milieu of Herodotus." In Dewald, C., & Marincola, J., eds., *The Cambridge Companion to Herodotus*. Cambridge (Cambridge University Press), 60–75.

Thumiger, C. 2007. *Hidden Paths: Self and Characterization in Greek Tragedy: Euripides' Bacchae*. London (Institute of Classical Studies).

Trabulsi, J.A.D. 1985. "O Imperialismo Ateniense, Tucídides e a Historiografia Contemporânea." *Ensaios de Literatura e Filologia* 5: 51–73.

———. 2004. *Dionisismo, Poder e Sociedade na Grécia até o Fim da Época Clássica*. Belo Horizonte (Editora da Universidade Federal de Minas Gerais).

Ventris, M. & Chadwick, J. 1956. *Documents in Mycenaean Greek*. Cambridge (Cambridge University Press).

Vernant, J.P. 1962. *Les origines de la pensée grecque*. Paris (Presses Universitaires de France).

Vernant, J.P. & Vidal-Naquet, P. 1998. *Mito e Tragédia na Grécia Antiga*. São Paulo (Perspectiva).

Vinogradov, J.G. 1981. "L'anello del re Skyles: Storia politica e dinastica degli Sciti nella prima metà del V secolo a.C." *Epigraphica* 43: 9–37.

Winnington-Ingram, R.P. 1997. *Euripides and Dionysus, an Interpretation of the Bacchae.* Bristol (Bristol University Press).

Zacharia, K. 2008. "Herodotus' Four Markers of Greek Identity." In Zacharia, K., ed., *Hellenisms: Culture, Identity, and Ethnicity from Antiquity to Modernity.* Aldershot (Ashgate).

8 A goddess for the Greeks

Demeter as identity factor in Herodotus

Nuno Simões Rodrigues

Introduction – Herodotus and the role of the Gods

Although the formulations by which Herodotus refers to the gods of the Greeks do not coincide with what we read in Homeric poems – the *Histories* contribute little material about what we might call Olympian mythology – divine entities are present in the historian's narrative. Most often, we find circumstantial and casual references, which serve for instance to contextualize divine entities in their identifications and religious functions (ritual and cultural), while generally juxtaposing them with 'theological' discourses and formulations that are then attributed to other peoples. In this sense, Book II of the *Histories* might be considered characteristic, if not paradigmatic. Yet at other times, gods appear with specific functions that, even if not exactly mythological, seem to contribute toward the construction of the Herodotean text and the 'ideology' that the historian seems to adopt and intends to present.

Thus, in the end of his report on the Battle of Salamis, in Book VIII of the *Histories*, Herodotus credits Themistocles with the following statement (Hdt. 8.109.2–3):

> ἡμεῖς δέ, εὕρημα γὰρ εὑρήκαμεν ἡμέας τε αὐτοὺς καὶ τὴν Ἑλλάδα, νέφος τοσοῦτο ἀνθρώπων ἀνωσάμενοι, μὴ διώκωμεν ἄνδρας φεύγοντας. ' τάδε γὰρ οὐκ ἡμεῖς κατεργασάμεθα, ἀλλὰ θεοί τε καὶ ἥρωες, οἳ ἐφθόνησαν ἄνδρα ἕνα τῆς τε Ἀσίης καὶ τῆς Εὐρώπης βασιλεῦσαι ἐόντα ἀνόσιόν τε καὶ ἀτάσθαλον: ὃς τά τε ἱρὰ καὶ τὰ ἴδια ἐν ὁμοίῳ ἐποιέετο, ἐμπιπράς τε καὶ καταβάλλων τῶν θεῶν τὰ ἀγάλματα: ὃς καὶ τὴν θάλασσαν ἀπεμαστίγωσε πέδας τε κατῆκε.

> Now, we Athenians and the whole of Greece have already benefited from our luck in repelling such an immense swarm of men; they have already taken to their heels, so why should we go after them? In any case, it was not we who accomplished this, but the gods and heroes, who did not want to see a single man ruling both Asia and Europe – and a man who commits terrible atrocities too.[1]

This passage does not necessarily present Herodotus' opinion on religion and its manifestations,[2] but rather offers a practical example of the methodology for the presentation of *ta legomena*, that is, it offers "what [supposedly or by means of an account] has been said". I say this without prejudice concerning the possibility that some of such presented information seems little, or not at all, likely to belong to Herodotus himself. Nonetheless, acting like an investigator (*histōr*) and as a conduit for transmitting information, Herodotus has credited Themistocles with an idea, which would surely have been shared by many Greeks of his time: that the gods were responsible for the Persians' expulsion from the Hellenic territory south and west of the Hellespont. This is a conception shared, for example, by Aeschylus. In the *Persians*, the messenger reporting the battle of Salamis to the Persian queen says, "No, it was some divine power that tipped the scale of fortune with unequal weight and thus destroyed our host. The gods preserve the city of the goddess Pallas" (*Pers.* 345–7, transl. H. Weir Smyth).[3]

Two perspectives on Demeter in Herodotus: from the goddess and her *timē* to the intervener deity

Prominent among the gods who appear in relevant roles in the Herodotean narra-tive on the invasion of Xerxes is Demeter, a deity associated with the earth, agri-culture, and, particularly, cereal production (as in fact Herodotus himself explains in a metonymic manner at various points in the *Histories* 1.193.2–3; 4.198.2; 7.141.4). These are surely, however, not the historian's most significant refer-ences to the goddess. In point of fact, in Book VIII, another passage, charged with oracular and metaphysical overtones, effectively establishes a relation between Demeter and the Greeks' victory at Salamis. The Herodotean narrative revolves around two Greek renegades who had joined the Persian forces. Shortly before the confrontation at Salamis, when Xerxes had pillaged Attica, this pair faced a situ-ation in the Thriasian Plain (near Eleusis in Attica) that they deemed strange. The renegades were Dikaios, an Athenian exile, and Demaratos, a former Spartan king from the house of the Eurypontids, who had defected to the Persian side and had thereby achieved high political status. According to the account, whose source Herodotus identifies as Dikaios, the two men witnessed in Eleusis such a dust cloud as might have been caused by a throng of 30,000 people. A sound emanated from the crowd that seemed like the hymn of the initiates, normally chanted to Iakkhos at the occasion of the Eleusinian mysteries celebrated in honour of Dem-eter and her daughter Persephone (Hdt. 8.65.1).[4]

The Eleusinian aspect of Herodotus' report is immediately apparent. Neverthe-less, the Greek historian wishes to assign Demaratos an inconceivable ignorance as to what was going on at Eleusis, so that Dikaios has the expository opportunity not only to explain the episode, but also to add his opinion – which, in itself con-stitutes a prophetic reading of the manifestation concerning the imminent con-frontation in Salamis. So, Dikaios asserts that the "divine chant", associated with the festival, annually celebrated in honour of the Mother and Daughter, and during which any Athenian or other Greek could be initiated, originated from Eleusis and had come in aid of the "Athenians and their allies" (Hdt. 8.65.2).

The reference to Mother and Daughter (*Mētēr kai Korē*) was easily understood by Herodotus' audience as an allusion to Demeter and Persephone (the Eleusinian deities). In fact, the place of the supposed event, Eleusis, leaves no doubt about that interpretation. However, as indicated earlier, this incident is not the first time that the historian has cause to mention Demeter. Apart from the metonymic references just noted, in Book II we find the first specific allusions to the goddess. As also happens with other deities, within the ambit of the Egyptian *logos* Herodotus presents an Egyptian origin of Demeter that, far from being an original in the overall framework of his writings, is one more confirmation of his idea that the Greeks would have inherited almost all divine *onomata* 'names' from the Egyptians (2.50).[5] This derivation conforms to the organizing principle evident in the *Histories*, that the systematic belief in the gods is a common macro-structure for all peoples.[6] Thus, when Herodotus presents the religious festivals of the people of the Nile, he mentions several Egyptian gods, listing them, however, not only with the name of the Greek deity he deems to be the same, but also with a different Egyptian name, because, as Scullion notes: "Herodotus is manifestly aware that nations identify the same gods by different vocables."[7] Also for this reason the historian claims that "Isis in the Greek language is Demeter" (2.59.2) or even that "Demeter is Isis" (Δήμητηρ δὲ Ἶσις: 2.156.5). It is in that sense that, when reporting episodes of Egyptian mythology, Herodotus uses the names Isis and Demeter interchangeably. Rhampsinitos, for example, when descending into the Netherworld, played dice with Demeter, here used naturally as an equivalent of Isis (2.122). This is curious because, in the Greek tradition, it must be Persephone, the daughter, and not Demeter, the mother, who would be playing dice in the hellish underworld with whomsoever. Identifying Demeter, the goddess of crops, as the one present and not her daughter, endorses the intentionality of comparing deities in a mutual interpretive system.[8] Along the same analytic line, Demeter's sanctuary and the ritual associated with it, mentioned in the same chapter, operate as a narrative hook to allow Herodotus to expand on conceptions of soul and death among the Egyptians. In this way he can offer *interpretationes graecae* of Isiac rituals, for which Demeter (and also Dionysos, here understood as the Greek counterpart of Osiris) is mostly an aid in decoding (2.123).

The etiology that the historian later provides for the Thesmophoria is not exactly of the same type as the instances mentioned earlier (2.171). In this passage, which is concerned with the rituals surrounding Osiris, Herodotus refers to practices that he calls *musteria* and that he deems to be the origin of the Athenian festival known as the Thesmophoria. For that reason, the historian restrains himself from providing further details, because he considers that, just as with the parallel Greek ceremonies and rituals, the several procedures associated with the ritual at issue, being mysteries, should remain as such while avoiding disclosure or exposure. Herodotus here reveals his scruples and respect for the sacred, which does not mean, however, that he necessarily shared the beliefs associated with the ritual.[9] Along the same lines, since he held that part of the Greeks' rituals and beliefs were rooted in Egypt, the historian suggests that it must have been the Danaids who took these *teletai* to Hellas (Hdt. 2.171). Therefore, it is not merely a Greek reading of Egyptian religious phenomena at issue, but an Egyptian etiology for the Greek ritual.

In another passage in Book V, Herodotus presents a complementary version of the origin of Demeter's mysteries, where the goddess is classified under the epithet of *Akhaia* ('the painful'), as she was known in the Peloponnese (see Arist. *Ach.* 709; Plut. *Is. et Os.* 69 [*Mor.* 378E]). Here we read that the Gephyraeans, the clan to which the tyrannicides Harmodios and Aristogeiton belonged, were of Phoenician origin, that their ancestors taught the alphabet to the Greeks, and that their descendants built temples with restricted access at Athens for the cult of Demeter and for the respective celebration of the mysteries (Hdt. 5.58, 61). With these references, Herodotus signals his conviction that these rituals were of oriental origin, although this is a controversial issue among historians still to this day.[10] Nevertheless, it should be recognized that the Herodotean understanding of Demeter as an important transcultural deity influenced his receptivity toward a report such as that provided by Dikaios.

In these passages, Herodotus also marks a process of differentiation of motifs in the references he makes to Demeter. In some parts of his work he refers to the goddess of crops (as well as other Greek deities) as only a Hellenic expression of what was ultimately an Egyptian religious category (that is, the name, the origin, or the essential mythological contexts of the goddess). In other settings, the historian introduces Demeter into the narrative not because of the inherent mythical-religious nature of the deity, but essentially on account of political circumstances, in which the role of the goddess or her domain of action or influence are pertinent to the context of the narrative process to which he is dedicated at the moment in question. It is precisely in this second subject or category that Demeter becomes more interesting to our investigation, because she assumes a unique cultural and primarily socio-political importance that can be summarized in a single inquiry: 'What was the importance of Demeter and her cult to Herodotus and for the Greeks of his time?'

An example of this second perspective on the goddess of cereals and crops is in Book VI. In the context of a digression on the Spartan royal families, Herodotus reports that one of the Eurypontids, Demaratos – precisely the same man who would become one of the protagonists of the aforementioned episode on the Thriasian Plain (Hdt. 8.65) – was accused of illegitimacy by the other Spartan king, the Agiad Kleomenes. This was so that Demaratos would be considered ineligible for the kingship, and thus be removed from power (Hdt. 6.64–69). Herodotus claims that the hostility between the pair dated back to the invasion of Attica by the Spartans; Demaratos had abandoned the campaign at Eleusis, owing to a disagreement over policy, and this had ended the invasion (Hdt. 5.74-76). Following this difference between the two kings, according to Herodotus, the Spartans would establish a rule never to authorize the simultaneous departure of the two kings for war. The hostility between both would intensify when Kleomenes decided to intervene against the Aiginetans because they had become supporters of the Persians (Hdt. 6.64). Thereupon, the Kleomenes decided to conspire against Demaratos, convincing another member of the Eurypontid family, Leotykhidas, to support him in his disputing his opponent's legitimacy, achieving this by means of offering him the possibility of occupying the position of the eventually deposed Demaratos in the dyarchy (Hdt. 6.65). Within a context of intensified political hostility, Leotykhidas accepted the offer and accused Demaratus of being the illegitimate son of the previous king. Aiming to know the truth about Demaratos' origin, the Spartans decided to consult the Delphic oracle, but Kleomenes bribed the Pythia to declare publicly the illegitimacy of the Demaratos' succession to the throne (Hdt. 6.65–66).

Following this conspiracy, Demaratos was deposed, eventually abandoned Sparta, and joined the Persians and King Darius by whom he was particularly welcomed (Hdt. 6.67–70). Leotykhidas took Demaratos' place on the Spartan throne and, together with Kleomenes, in 491 BC, intervened on Aigina to punish the Aiginetans for having supported the Persians (Hdt. 6.73). At this time, the two Spartan kings took ten prominent Aiginetans hostages, handing them over to the Athenians. Meanwhile, the conspiracy against Demaratos had been discovered, and Kleomenes fled from Sparta to Arkadia, where he conceived a plan to seek revenge from the Spartans. Fearing the consequences, they decided to accept Kleomenes home again. The king, however, went insane and ended up committing suicide (Hdt. 6.75).[11]

Herodotus presents three then current opinions among the Hellenes about the causes for Kleomenes' fate. For many Greeks, the king's madness and suicide arose from the fact that he had bribed the Pythia when Demaratos had been deposed. For the Argives, however, the cause of the Spartan king's fate was Kleomenes' ambush and murder of the Argive soldiers who had sought refuge as supplicants in a sacred wood, thus disrespecting that those harbouring there had been placed under a deity's protection, as well as his polluting the sanctity of the location itself, which he subsequently ordered to be set on fire (cf. Hdt. 6.76–84).[12] Still for the Athenians, Kleomenes' madness and cruel death derived from the invasion of Eleusis and the defiling of the sanctuary of the two goddesses (Hdt. 6.75; cf. 5.74–76).

Herodotus does not choose any explanation immediately, presenting all three to his audience. However, common in all of them is the quality of *hybris*, of excessive behaviour toward the established order, in this case a religious dispensation, which is defied and transgressed, leading to the destruction of the transgressor. However, it is not accidental that the historian presents still a fourth reason for the Spartan king's madness, far more pragmatic and physiological, and less mystical (thus relevant for Herodotus' perception of religious influences) than the preceding ones: Kleomenes became insane not through a divine force, but because, by influence of the Scythians, he had become addicted to drinking pure wine (not diluted in water, as it was customary for the Greeks to drink). Therefore, for the Spartans Kleomenes would have become an alcoholic, leading him to mental imbalance and eventual suicide (Hdt. 6.84). Still, the historian makes sure to point out the case of Demaratos and how his treatment explains Kleomenes' punishment (Hdt. 6.84.3). In any event, it seems relevant to us that the Athenians preferred the idea that Kleomenes' transgression was related to Eleusis and the profanation of the sanctuary of Demeter and Persephone.

In the same Book VI, another passage refers to a similar situation in formal terms. As in the previous case, it is not related to Demeter's mythology, but to the relevance of her cult. Herodotus tells us that, after Kleomenes' death, the Aiginetans tried to achieve the release of the hostages, who had been delivered to the Athenians, by demanding Leotykhidas' cooperation (Hdt. 6.85). The Athenians, however, were reluctant to deliver up the hostages. The Aiginetans reacted by capturing an Athenian ship near Cape Sounion with some important persons on board, trying to acquire assets for an exchange of captives. The Athenians, nonetheless, responded by cooperating with a revolt led by Nikodromos, an elite Aiginetan dissatisfied with the island's oligarchy. Yet, the uprising of Nikodromos and his allies was suppressed by the Aiginetan regime. The Aiginetans took the rebels out of the city for the purpose of killing them. This event tarnished the Aiginetans with a sacrilege that, according to Herodotus, would lead to their expulsion from their Aigina by the Athenians in 431 BC (Hdt. 6.91):

> What happened was that they were in the process of taking seven hundred prisoners out of the town for execution when one of them broke free of his chains and took refuge at the porch of the temple of Demeter the Lawgiver, where he seized the door handles and hung on to them. They could not get him to let go by pulling him away from the door, so they chopped off his hands and took him away for execution like that – while his hands remained gripping the handles.

As in the previous case, the excessive act (*hybris*) is here defined also by disrespect to what was deemed sacred, namely the idea that an individual could place himself under the protection of a sanctuary, choosing to hand his life own over to it and to its guardian deity, and that act would be respected by his fellow citizens.[13] The Aiginetans had not respected the idea of sanctuary, and were thus punished.[14] It is also significant that Herodotus mentions the term *thesmophoros* as epithet of Demeter on Aigina. This name emphasizes the goddess' attribute as 'legislator' or 'law, norm, or custom enforcer', focussing on the social ordinances of an agrarian society.

Herodotus also refers to Demeter Thesmophoros in the context of his narrative on Miltiades – one of the Athenian generals in the Battle of Marathon in 490 BC. The historian tells that, because of this military success, Miltiades gained special prominence in Athens. Taking advantage of that situation, he decided to conduct an expedition against the Parians and, to this end, requested human and material commitments from his Athenian compatriots without, however, revealing to them the whole project, only brandishing the possibility of returning from the enterprise enriched with gold. Herodotus mentions that Miltiades was actually moved by a desire to feed his resentment and satisfy personal revenge. When the Athenians reached Paros, however, the Parians decided to resist, and were besieged. It is in this context that, according to Herodotus (basing himself on Parian sources), a war prisoner named Timo appears, who was also the priestess for Demeter and Persephone, mentioned in the text as "chthonic goddesses" (*khthoniōn theōn*: Hdt.

6.134.1). Timo's advice to Miltiades was that if his intention was to take Paros, then he should act as she told him.

Following the meeting, Miltiades went to the hill located in front of the city and tried to enter the sanctuary of Demeter Thesmophoros. As he could not open the temple's doors, Miltiades decided to jump over the wall and enter the temple's *megaron* 'chamber', possibly steal some sacred object. However, as he approached the doors, Miltiades was struck by a negative feeling that made him return along the path by which he had come. Then, when leaping over the wall again, Miltiades injured his hip, according to some, or his knee, according to others. At any rate, unsuccessful, Miltiades withdrew back to Athens where the Athenians accused him of *apatē* 'deception'. In the end, the general ended up dying of gangrene, stemming from the injury sustained when leaving the temple of Demeter.

In turn, the Parians decided to punish the priestess of the two goddesses, for allegedly having aided Miltiades to conquer Paros and revealing the "sacred mysteries prohibited to men" (Hdt. 6.135.2). After having consulted the Delphic oracle, however, the Pythia stated that Timo was innocent, because what appeared before Miltiades would have been a spectre of the priestess and not herself. However, the general was fated to end poorly, and the apparition bearing Timo's image would only have been the triggering element of that process, leading him to a predefined end (Hdt. 6.134–6).

The proffered explanation for the appearance of Timo's 'clone' (or *eidōlon*) reminds us, naturally, of the discussion not only by Herodotus himself, in a long section in Book II, commenting on the journey of Helen to Egypt (2.112–20) where she was separated from Paris,[15] but also by the lyric poet Stesichorus who had Helen replaced in the company of Paris by an *eidōlon* (frs. 15–16, *PMG* 192–3). Effectively, as D. Leão notes following other researchers, the possibility must be taken into account that the oracle mentioned by Herodotus was spurious and simply created, possibly even by the Parians, perhaps on the basis of the traditions around figures such as Aeneas and Helen. Yet, as the same scholar appropriately notes, for Herodotus, Miltiades' marked fate also functions to lessen the impact caused by an inglorious end for one who had been and should have continued to be one of Athens' heroes in the fight against the Persians.[16] Besides, lest we forget, there is the Herodotean practice of invoking divine intervention in order to absolve an individual from responsibility.[17]

The references to Demeter in Book VI are, thus, essentially circumstantial, even if not necessarily without a wider sense in the work's general scope. In these sections, the goddess is revealed under several aspects, but mostly as avenger and patron of multiple spaces disseminated throughout Hellas, from Athens and Eleusis to Aigina, continuing to Paros. Another aspect of these references is their occasional tendency to allude to the issue of gender segregation in the scope of Demeter's cult.[18]

The panhellenic identity-function of Demeter in Herodotus

Another noteworthy reference to Demeter within this essentially political circumstantial framework, is the one in Book IX, which was mentioned at the beginning of this study (Hdt. 9.65) and with which we must relate three other references made in *Histories*. Effectively, it seems to us that it is within this context that we may defend the idea that Herodotus, on his own initiative or motivated by the political circumstances experienced during his inquiries, has either reflected a tradition on Demeter or transformed her into an emblem of identity intended to serve the idea of panhellenism.[19]

As we have noted, the section that contains the Thriasian 'miracle' appears within the narration of the events involving the Battle of Salamis of· 480 BC (Hdt. 9.65). Along with the battles of Marathon (490 BC), Plataia (479 BC), and Mykale (479 BC), this confrontation has been recognized since antiquity as one of the key moments in Hellas' struggle with the Persian enemy.[20] Boedeker even claims that these were events that shaped the identity of the Hellenes.[21] In this sense, we may call the battles Greece's foundational struggles. Recently, Whitmarsh has described them as part of a collective Greek mythology, especially one that is filtered by an Athenian perspective.[22] Therefore, we deem it relevant that in the Herodotean treatment of three of these battles, there are repeatedly references to Demeter and her respective cults.

In effect, what we read in Book VIII corresponds to a type of miracle, translating an idea of divine intervention, on the one hand apparently strange to Herodotus' religious thought, given that in *Histories* we never find gods intervening in a Homeric manner, but on the other hand, perfectly consistent with what we read in other parts of the *Histories*. Besides, it is possible to uncover within the text, what we may call an ideological agenda that, as we will try to demonstrate, seems to feature the idea of panhellenism and of a "pan-Hellas" defeating Persian barbarity.

Let us resume our discussion at the moment in which two Greek renegades (an Athenian and a Spartan) see on Eleusis' horizon what appears to be a group of 30,000 people shouting Iakkhos' invocation (Hdt. 8.65). This episode, which Boedeker calls the "phantom Eleusinian procession",[23] evidently referred to the ceremony consisting of the procession that was made in autumn, along the known Via Sacra or Sacred Way, and in which the so-called 'holy things' associated with Demeter and Persephone were transported (cf. Ar. *Ran.* 398–413). The manner in which the episode – later referenced by Plutarch in *Themistocles* (*Them.* 15) in a clear reference to Herodotus – is narrated suggests a marked symbolic-metaphorical charge that must not be ignored.

First, the idea that this procession would comprise 30,000 participants certainly alludes to the *mustai* and *epoptai* that annually formed the march, which marked the beginning of the celebrations associated with the mysteries of Eleusis.[24] As has been noted, 30,000 is a figure that may be related to the total number of Athenian citizens at the time of Herodotus. Understood in this way, the reference to that amount of individuals surely indicates that the Athenians joined the festivities in honour of the two goddesses *en masse*, such was its importance to the city of Athens (see Plut. *Alcib.* 34), even if that may not seem materially possible.[25] Then, note the fact that that the two Greek renegades are actually experiencing this divine intervention. The Spartan Demaratos exhibits an inconceivable ignorance of the phenomenon, and this provides Herodotus an opportunity to allow it to be explained by Dikaios as a prophecy. At last, Herodotus stresses precisely this prophetic quality that the Athenian provided in his explanation: if the praise chant of Iakkhos reached the Peloponnese, then the Persian king and his army would be in danger; if, on the contrary, it reached the ships based on Salamis, then the Persian fleet would be threatened (Hdt. 9.65.3-6). As we know historically, this second possibility was the one realized, as revealed in the Greek victory.

It is relevant that the figures of Demeter and Persephone are associated with the victory at Salamis, where, unlike Plataia, there was no sanctuary dedicated to the goddesses. Thus, the anecdote about the alleged Thriasian miracle, in effect, makes the association. This relevance in the realm of cult is implicit in Herodotus' explanation of the number of individuals participating, corresponding to the celebrants (and the total number of Athenians) who in the vision participate in the procession.

Concomitantly, we must observe that Eleusis is normally associated with Attica, which grants an even more expressive symbolic load to the episode. All the details, including the explanation placed in the mouth of Dikaios the Athenian,[26] converge so that Athens become the *polis* primarily associated with the episode: the staging at Eleusis, the connection to Athens through the Via Sacra and the Eleusinian procession, the number of individuals coinciding with that of the Athenian civic body, and the prophetic explanation by Dikaios. As noted by How and Wells, not all Athenian citizens were initiated or initiates in the mysteries.[27] Therefore the reference can only be a sort of metonymy, almost in rhetorical exaggeration by Herodotus, where men and women or Athenians and foreign celebrants are rendered equivalent to male citizens. His purpose might be to show that the city as a whole could manifest itself at the moment of the ceremony. Thus, ultimately, the celebration of Eleusis' mysteries is conflated with Athens and, accordingly, it is Athens that becomes the prophetic entity earning victory at Salamis.

It is clear that the Greeks' victory at Salamis was the result of cooperation among a number of Hellenic cities. But Herodotus' report stresses the capital importance of Athens in this process, in a framework in which both goddesses of panhellenic significance would gain special relevance by operating in their primary Eleusinian sphere. Thus, the impact of an ideology of panhellenism, headed by Athens, appears particularly strong in Herodotus' text.

Finally, the relevance of the episode is also reflected by its arising from supernatural prompting, springing out of divine origin. It emerges from within Eleusis itself and, as such, is probably rooted in the influence of the local goddesses. Boedeker goes further, recognizing in the report in 8.84–85, where the *phasma* 'apparition' of a woman incited the Greeks to fight at Salamis, an epiphany by Demeter (and not Athena as some have thought).[28]

In fact, this idea seems to be reinforced by other instances of the cult of Demeter in Herodotus' text. When he describes the geography of the Thermopylai, the historian clearly mentions that in the environs of that place (probably in Anthele) there was a temple dedicated to Demeter Amphictyonis (Hdt. 7.200.2).[29] Despite the defeat of the Spartan Leonidas and his companions in the pass along the

Malian Gulf in the spring of 480 BC, Thermopylai had become a great moment and mark of the heroic resistance of Hellas to the Persian advance. Thus, it does seem significant in our analysis that the historian explicitly mentions the proximity of Demeter's temple in the immediate region. The fact that Demeter is qualified in this passage as *amphiktyonis*, that is, protector of the Delphic confederacy of *poleis*, further draws our perspective to the horizon of panhellenism.

Herodotus also alludes to the worship of Demeter during the narration of the Battle of Plataia, located north of the Thriasian plain of Eleusis, on the border with Boiotia. There, in 479 BC with the support of a disciplined hoplite phalanx, the Spartan Pausanias and the Athenian Aristides defeated the Persians. Herodotus mentions that the most intense part of the confrontation between Hellenes and Persians happened precisely near the goddess' temple (Hdt. 9.62.2).[30] The battle ended with a Greek victory that, the historian emphasizes, also avenged the death of Leonidas at Thermopylai (Hdt. 9.64.1; 78). In this sense, Plataia functions as the conclusion or final stage of the battle at Thermopylai. In this framework, the references to Hera (Hdt. 9.61.3) and Demeter have particular relevance, because they appear almost subliminally as divine interventions during the course of the events. And while, in the case of Hera, Herodotus even claims that it was following prayers of Pausanias to the goddess that the results of the fight started to be favourable to the Greeks (Hdt. 9.62.1), in the case of Demeter the historian is even more assertive and suggestive: despite the fight having taken place near the goddess' sanctuary, "not a single Persian, as it turned out, either entered the precinct or died in there" (Hdt. 9.65; the same sanctuary is mentioned later in the context of the same battle: Hdt. 9.69.1). Immediately afterward, Herodotus felt the need to justify this statement in claiming: "I think the goddess herself kept them away because they had burnt her temple in Eleusis" (Hdt. 9.65).[31]

This reflection by Herodotus is significant for two reasons. The first is related to the ambivalent attitude, almost opportunistic, that the historian has adopted toward the divine, which has already been stressed by several students of Herodotus, out of whom we note Harrison.[32] The second rationale draws force from my analysis earlier: Herodotus chose to exhibit Demeter as an especially protective goddess of the Hellenes in their fight against the Iranian forces. Also, Plataia meant a significant win for Hellas; therefore, by granting the goddess of agriculture the relevance we read in the text, Herodotus is, once again by association, accrediting her with a protagonist's role in the maintenance of independence and freedom for the Greeks.[33] This leading role for Demeter is reinforced when Herodotus proposes a reason for the goddess' 'behaviour' on this occasion by raising the possibility of retaliation for the Persians having set fire to Demeter's sanctuary at Eleusis. In truth, this is the historian's first and only reference to this fire. Yet it is quite possible it occurred during the looting of Attica by Xerxes in 480 BC, just as, according to Herodotus, Thespiai and Plataia were set afire, and Athens itself was destroyed (Hdt. 8.50).

Nevertheless, it should seem important to us that the author of *Histories* expresses a cause and effect relation between the supposed fires and the supernatural lack of Persian casualties in Demeter's sanctuary in Plataia. The phenomenon is understood as the rejection by the goddess of actions or factors, such as death and the dead bodies of the Persian enemies, which could pollute her territory. In fact, this association follows an idea present in other passages in the historian's work: acts of sacrilege are always punished by deities as an expression of cosmic justice.[34]

The third reference to Demeter during the hostilities between Greeks and Persians is one that assured the definitive expulsion of the Persians from the Hellenic territory and involves the confrontation at Mykale. At this point, it must be mentioned that, according to the tradition, the battle took place on the Ionian coast, near Samos and Miletos, precisely on the same day of the clash at Plataia. It is possible, however, that the coincidence of the date is nothing more than historiographical rhetoric, taken up subsequently by learned or popular tradition, that intended to dramatize the importance of these events in the fight against the enemies of Greece. Yet it is also significant how Herodotus builds his narrative around these events and their synchronicity. In fact, apparently, the historian interprets the coincidence of the events as a sign of providential intervention in human affairs.[35]

After the Persians' retreat to the Ionian coast, Leotykhidas takes the command of the Greek fleet which, making landfall at Mykale, attack the enemy destroying their ships. Herodotus tells the episode with some detail: once in Ionia, the Persians pass through the sanctuary that the historian identifies as being of the 'Mistresses' or 'Ladies' (τὸ τῶν Ποτνιέων ἱρὸν).[36] The reader is directed afterwards to the temple of Demeter Eleusinia which, according to the historian, would have been instituted by Philistos on the occasion of the foundation of Miletos (Hdt. 9.97). Near the temple of Demeter Eleusinia, the Persians then built a palisade of rock and wood, waiting for the Hellenes to strike (Hdt. 9.102.1). A force of mostly Athenians and Spartans had disembarked at Mykale and were preparing to attack the Persians, when they got news that, at Plataia, the Greeks had been victorious over Mardonios (Hdt. 9.100). At this point, Herodotus' reflection is particularly relevant to our inquiry (Hdt. 9.100.2):

> There is plenty of convincing evidence that the divine plays a part in human affairs. Consider how, on this occasion, with the Persian defeat at Plataia and their imminent defeat at Mykale happening on the same day, a rumour of Plataia reached the Greeks at Mykale, boosting their morale and making them even more willing to face danger.

Following this note, Herodotus reinforces the judgment that divine providence is present in history, without this concept absolutely coinciding with the figuration of the Homeric gods. The historian then points out two other coincidences between the battles that occurred at Plataia and Mykale: both of them had taken place on sacred spaces dedicated to Demeter (Hdt. 9.101.1) and both of them resulted in victories for the Hellenes (Hdt. 9.106). The relation between the two factors is, naturally, created from the Herodotean report. In fact, the goddess' protection had already been implied chapters before, when, apropos of the imminence of

Mardonios' attack, the historian reports that the Spartans – who according to the text wished the best for Hellas (Hdt. 9.19.1) – and Athenians united and organized themselves to face the Persian threat. When passing through Eleusis, the confederate armies would have made sacrifices, supposedly to Demeter and Persephone, having obtained favourable omens for the common enterprise (Hdt. 9.19.2).

Conclusion

Following Boedeker, we must conclude that the great battles in which the Greeks defeated the Persians – Salamis, Plataia, and Mykale – are described by Herodotus in clear association with Eleusis and Demeter.[37] To those conflicts we add Thermopylai, which, despite not being a canonical victory, is the founding battle of 'Greek liberty' and a central step in the process of resistance to the eastern invader. In this sense, the Thermopylai is a kind of foundational defeat that, nonetheless, in Herodotus is also related to Demeter. This seems to us another important issue since the heroes of the Thermopylai are essentially Spartans, who have thus become closer to the agriculture goddess, particularly in her Eleusinian expression, which was essentially Attic.[38]

So, it seems to us likely that, regardless of Herodotus' belief or disbelief in deities such as Demeter, there is in the historian's text an intentionality that coincides with his historiographical material and with the value judgments expressed by the *personae* of the *Histories*. That intentionality was based on the idea that the agriculture goddess was a deity of panhellenic character who become fundamental for the victory of the Greeks over the Persians. It is not unlikely that this proposition was grounded in a trans-Herodotean tradition that made Demeter, and Eleusinian Demeter in particular, the protective goddess of the Hellenes in the Greek–Persian clash. This perspective would be parallel to the Delphic tradition, which alternatively presented Apollo (a deity with particular manifestations in the Spartan context[39]) as the protective god of the Greeks in the confrontation against the Persians, an interpretation that is also present in the historian's work (Hdt. 8.121–122; 9.81.1).[40] Moreover, it also seems to us unquestionable that Herodotus utilizes disparate traditions that existed in service of an ideology that sought to uncover the identity of the Greeks through mytho-religious elements that linked them. Eleusis' Demeter provided one of them. Just as Delphi, Eleusis was an appropriate space for the disclosure of panhellenic attitudes.[41]

Then what explains this dependence on Demeter, who is not even a martial goddess?[42] Why not reinforce what militant capacity was acknowledged in Apollo? Possibly because Apollo was too Spartan[43] and would not be Athenian enough, and Herodotus on Demeter seems to operate mainly so that the focus could be placed on Athens. This being so, then why not Athena, who besides all else was a war goddess? Certainly, this was because Athena was too Athenian,[44] with a risk of, for that reason, not being accepted in a panhellenic perspective by the remaining *poleis*, especially in the Peloponnese, as a supra-*polis* deity for the Hellenes and thus serving as a factor for establishing the Hellenic identity. On the other hand, Demeter, particularly Demeter Eleusinia, albeit still associated to Attica, would be ideal to perform this function in a more consensual manner; that is, an Athenian emphasis without an Athens too exposed or obvious; almost subliminal. Effectively, Demeter seems to take a more or less tacit, more or less explicit, pan-hellenic character as an ethnic identifier. Hence also derives Herodotus' interest in explaining the involvement by both Athenians and Spartans in the aforementioned sections, and in mentioning the goddess' sanctuaries, scattered throughout the Greek world, regardless of the epithet associated with her locally.

We must not forget that Eleusis and the cult of Demeter had assumed the role both of a legitimizer of territorial control and of a signifier of Greekness, as is shown by the number of cults and sanctuaries dedicated to the goddess spread throughout Hellas (even if the epithet 'Eleusinia' was not always used to characterize the goddess locally).[45] In fact, the common practice often was that a deity assumed for itself characteristics, and, therefore, epithets, that translated or imitated the historic or physical, political, or social idiosyncrasies of each location. This fact favoured, naturally, a general acceptance of Demeter as a goddess of identity for the Greeks, surely far more than Athena, a goddess especially associated with Athens in the fifth century and, therefore, a possible generator of conflicts of interest among the other *poleis*.[46]

Furthermore, the efforts from Athens aiming to boost the political character of Eleusis would have also favoured this process. Eleusis' association with Athens was old. As we have already noted, the location of the sanctuary must have been integrated with the Athenian *polis* relatively soon, dating back, at least to the eighth century BC or even to a previous period (some suggest the thirteenth century BC or the Mycenaean period[47]). However, the augmentation and development of the mystery rituals must be deeply associated with the Athenian domination.[48] Note that, according to *Athenaion Politeia*, the organization of the Eleusinian festivals depended on Athens' archon *basileus* ([Aris.] *Ath. Pol.* 57.1). In addition, the procession throughout the more than 30 kilometres of the Via Sacra was intended to mark that integration of the Eleusinian cult in Athens, or even, as noted by some commentators, to compensate for a potential flaw in the definitive transfer of the cult to Athens, which discrepancy may have also be reflected in the subdivision of the ritual into the Minor Mysteries, celebrated in Athens, and the Greater Mysteries, celebrated at Eleusis, on different occasions within the year.[49] If the transfer process, however, was imperfect ritually, the continual reinforcement of the association between Eleusis and Athens did not fail.[50]

Boedeker reminds us that, in 430 BC, at the same time that the Athenians invited those who were not contributing first fruits to Eleusis to do so, Athens decreed that all its allies were to annually send Demeter Eleusinia their first fruits (*IG* I[3] 78.24–26).[51] Simultaneously, in Athenian art, there appear representations of Triptolemos as an emissary sent by the goddess through the world to spread agriculture and her cult.[52] This can be understood as a mechanism for the Greeks to assume the tight bond to their land, like the Athenians did with their own. Worshipping Demeter naturalized them as aboriginals. Behind these measures, there could only be a political agenda of panhellenic character that promoted the goddess of agriculture, that must be linked to what we have analyzed for Herodotus.

Shortly afterwards, Isocrates would state that the Mysteries and the growing of cereals were two gifts from Demeter that humankind received through Athens.[53] And Nilsson has already claimed that the Thesmophoria, connected with Demeter Thesmophoros, was the mostly widely disseminated festival and cult throughout the Greek world.[54]

In any case, we are more particularly interested in highlighting the intrinsically Athenian character of Demeter Eleusinia, totally perceivable in the fifth century BC and precisely derived from those circumstances that we have seen illustrated in our references in Herodotus. By valuing Demeter in this context, it contributed toward the promotion of a panhellenism built on an idea of Athenocentrism, and that must be related to the association and admiration, however more or less objective we deem it, that the historian apparently had for this city.[55] Note, for example, how Herodotus accredits the Athenians with a defence of panhellenism amid assurance of their opposition to Persian autocracy (Hdt. 8.144.2):

> Then again, there is the fact that we are all Greeks – one race speaking one language, with temples to the gods and religious rites in common, and with a common way of life. It would not be good for Athens to betray all this shared heritage.[56]

As noted by Whitmarsh, there were formal mechanisms which enabled the establishment of a consolidated panhellenic perspective, such as the Olympic Games, the Delphic Oracle, and the common cultural investment in Homer's and Hesiod's poetry.[57] It seems to us that Eleusis and the cult to Demeter celebrated there may have fulfilled similar conditions for Greek integration, and, based on what we have analyzed in the *Histories*, Herodotus had contributed towards the promotion of yet another 'anti-imperialist' conceptualization that was grounded in Greek ethnic identity.[58]

There is another aspect of Demeter that seems essential for understanding this issue. In Greek religious thought Demeter can be a chthonic goddess, Herodotus himself noting her as such (Hdt. 6.134). And this goddess of land and agriculture also takes the function of a deity that delineates borders, a characteristic in fact visible in Herodotean *logoi* (e.g., Hdt. 9.65). That role can be conflated with the idea of autochthony, so dear to the Greeks, especially the Athenians, mostly from the sixth century BC onwards.[59] As shown by Valdés Guía, it is more often Gaia who is the goddess who helps to establish the function of autochthony in Athenian thought.[60] Nevertheless, there is in Herodotus' references a series of elements which allow us to think of Demeter as a goddess focussed on defending territory, both in Attica in particular and Greece in general, in a fashion evoking autochthony or quasi-autochthony. Thus, by not allowing any dead Persian to stain her holy precinct in Plataia, Demeter symbolically expels the enemy from the Greek land, actualizing her peasant, rural, agrarian connections as a defender of her land (while encompassing common Greek territory). And if she is not exactly the chief goddess of autochthony, she is unquestionably a divinity who through her tutelage over agriculture binds the Greeks as an *ethnos* to their soil and so grants them an invincible claim against Xerxes to their territories, as confirmed by Herodotus' text.[61] By protecting her space, the goddess protects the whole of Hellas.[62] She assists in fusing an idea of territory with ethnic identity, which in the case of the Greeks begins with language, but will eventually encompass other domains including religion in its cultural, ritual, and mythological aspects.

Herodotus himself acknowledges the central role of Athens and of the Athenians in the fight against the Persians (Hdt. 7.139).[63] But the fact that the historian acknowledges that importance does not ensure that contemporaries from the other Greek cities had also acknowledged it; therefore, the presentation of an ethnolinguistic-cultural identity and an integrative element such as the cult and symbolism of Demeter gains special sense and justification. As Harrison has noted, it does not seem that Demeter in Herodotus is particularly associated with revenge, while having a function in panhellenic identity and unity (as proposed by Boedeker).[64] Having Demeter in a central role in this process seems key also to Athens' being recognized as a leader in the fight against the Persians and as a mentor of Greek freedom, but not necessarily as their oppressor. Thus, themes associated with Demeter proved a significant element for Herodotus' historiographical project, which is also qualified by several remarkable political elements.[65]

The interpretation of religion by Herodotus may be considered essentially prov-identialist and universalist, but sometimes even rationalist. By considering divine action as a logical regulation of the world and human actions,[66] the historian does not hesitate in using Demeter as a specific expression of the divine at work among Greeks. In a way, this position is linked with what Scullion called an "ambivalent attitude to custom and convention" and reflects the historian's recourse to the so-called uncertainty principle concerning religion.[67] The intervention of the divine does not work in the mode of myth-history, even if Immerwahr has defended the idea that the events portrayed in Book IX suggest that the historian "himself thought of the local gods as participating in the battle",[68] but through evoking ritualistic factors at the service of a pro-Athenian ideology, though one not yet necessarily 'imperialist'. Gods participate in the battle not in a Homeric manner with the physical presence of deities – Herodotus resists associating the divine with forms of corporeality, as noted by Scullion[69] – but in a more intelligible and providential form of divine action affecting human history.

Notes

1 All translations are adapted from Waterfield 2008. This research was developed under the project UID/ELT/00196/2013 of the Centre for Classical and Humanistic Studies, funded by the Portuguese FCT – Foundation for Science and Technology.
2 E.g., Shimron 1989: 37–9; Soares 2002: 31.
3 Soares 2002: 71, n. 124.
4 The same framework is suggested in tragic and comic theatre: see, e.g., Eur. *Ion* 1079–86; Arist. *Ran.* 316, 398–413.
5 On the meaning of the passage, see Scullion 2006: 198.
6 Whitmarsh 2016: 26.
7 See Scullion (2006: 197–8) who deems Herodotus a proponent of cultural dissemination.
8 In another passage of the same book (Hdt. 2.156.5–6), Herodotus refers to a lost tragedy by Aeschylus in which the Greek playwright presents Artemis as daughter

of Demeter. The historian reasons that the poet would have done this because he was inspired by Egyptian tradition that considered (according to Herodotus) Apollo and Artemis as offspring of Dionysos and Isis. As Isis is identified as Demeter, Artemis, consequently, must be her daughter.

9   On Herodotus' relation with the religious and sacred in general, see Scullion 2006: 192–208; Harrison 2002; Mikalson 2012: 187–98.

10 On this issue, see, e.g., Sourvinou-Inwood 1997: 132–64; Dietrich 1982: 445–71.

11 On the character and death of Kleomenes, see Soares 2003: 448–61.

12 On the offence about supplication in Herodotus, see Mikalson 2003: 73–4; on how the historian approaches the topic of sanctuaries, see Mikalson 2012: 187–98.

13 Mikalson 2003: 73–4.

14 On disrespect for the sacred space in Herodotus, see, e.g., Hdt. 8.129. The subject is particularly well discussed in Harrison 2002: 96–7, 169–73.

15 See in this volume pp. 258–68. Also Euripides in 412 BC in the *Helen*, follows and develops that tradition, which built a justification for the less laudable actions of the Greek heroine, by stating that what had been conveyed to Troy would have been an image or *eidōlon* of the Spartan queen and not Helen herself, who had been retained in the country of the Nile (Eur. *Hel.* 30–5, 580–90; cf. Pl. *Rep.* 9.586B-C). We must not rule out the hypothesis of an intertextual process between Herodotus and Euripides' works. If the poet wrote the tragedy after the historian composed his work, the influence on the latter must be considered. Equally, the tragedy *Philoctetes* by Sophocles, presented in 409 BC, seems to contain elements from Miltiades' story, namely the gangrenous leg, despite the fact that the *Iliad* 2.716–720 already mentions the injury of Philoktetes. Perhaps we must consider, however, the possibility of the treatment in Herodotus having received earlier influences. Nor should we forget both that the subject of a malicious *eidōlon* already appeared in the *Iliad* when Apollo forges a double for Aeneas to confuse the enemy and thus save the hero (*Il.* 5.449–51), and that Helen's *eidōlon* dated back to Stesichorus at least (regarding which see, e.g., Oliveira 2015: 20–1; Pulquério 1973/1974: 265–73). Moreover, inside the universe of the *Histories*, we have another protagonist dying of gangrene, the madman Cambyses (following a wound in the corresponding place where he had wounded the sacred bull of the Egyptians, the god Apis: Hdt. 3.64–6). Consequently, both Herodotus and Euripides may have drawn on common thematic matrixes, regarding this subject. Regardless of whether the Parians were Herodotus' likely sources or not, there is an underlying literary *topos* that Herodotus reproduces (Hdt. 6.134). I thank our colleague C.L. Soares for commentary regarding this note.

16 Leão & Ferreira 2000: 47.

17 Harrison 2002: 228.

18 See Larson 2007: 70–2.

19 During the Persian Wars, a panhellenic sentiment and an ethnic consciousness increased among the Greeks, as we can read in Simonides, Pindar, and Aeschylus, but also in Sophocles, Euripides, Aristophanes, and Thucydides. See Ferreira 1992: 299–460; Ferreira 2005: 15–42.

20 Boedeker 2007: 67.

21 Boedeker 2007: 65; Ferreira 2013: 275–313.

22 Whitmarsh 2016: 72.

23 Boedeker 2007: 69.

24 On this ceremony, see Burkert 1983: 278–9; Bremmer 2014: 5–16.

25 Soares 2002: 71, n. 127; also How & Wells 1928: 256–7.

26 On Herodotus as narrator and how, in that quality, he approaches religion, see Scullion 2006: 197–8; Harrison 2002: 180–1.

27 How & Wells 1928: 256–7.

28 Boedeker 2007: 69.

29 Scott 2015: 111–13, 204, 222.

30 On archaeological traces of a sanctuary possibly dedicated to Demeter near Plataia, see Boedeker 2007: 67–8 and bibliography quoted there.

31 This reference contrasts with Hdt. 9.27.3, where it is mentioned that the Argive dead who had fallen in the expedition of the Seven against Thebes were buried in the sanctuary of Eleusis by the Athenians. Albeit Argives, these dead were nevertheless Hellenes (just as their Theban adversaries). In this context, it is relevant to mention, as D. Boedeker does (2007: 68), that in his *Aristeides*, Plutarch follows this tradition, alluding to Demeter Eleusinia as the deity in whose soil, according to the Delphic oracle, the Battle of Plataia must be fought (Plu. *Arist.* 11.3–7; cf. Paus. 9.4.3). In the section in question, apart from Demeter and Kore, other deities are mentioned, to whom the Greeks must pray for help for the victory over the Persians: Zeus, Hera, Pan, and the Sphragitides nymphs, apart from a series of venerable heroes. But it is regarding Demeter and her daughter, namely through the reference to the Eleusinian sanctuary, that Plutarch is emphatic. In this same chapter of the biography of Aristides (also one of the Attic generals at Marathon), Plutarch notes the Athenian hoplites, whom he led at Plataia, as well as the Spartans and remaining Hellenes, commanded by Pausanias, the overall commander.

32 Harrison 2002.

33 On the issue of freedom, see Moles 2002: 33–52.

34 Scullion 2006: 194; Whitmarsh 2016: 80–1; Harrison 2002: 102–7.

35 Niskanen 2004: 99.

36 Hdt. 9.97. Some editions of Herodotus (e.g., Marincola 2003: 593) identify the *Potniai* as the Eumenides; others, however (e.g., Strassler 2007: 712, n. 9.97.1a), identify them as Demeter and Persephone (see Soph. *OC* 1050, Arist. *Thesm.* 1149, and Paus. 9.8.1). It is likely that the 'Ladies' were in fact the Eleusinian goddesses, even if the following explicit reference to Demeter Eleusinia renders the meaning somewhat redundant.

37 Boedeker 2007.

38 Boedeker 2007: 67–9. Based on the work by Polemon, Boedeker claims that, apart from the referenced battles, Marathon (490) was also, in the Greek tradition, associated with Demeter and her daughter Persephone (Boedeker 2007: 72–4). Although this reference does not appear in Herodotus, there are reasons to think that the Greek tradition made that association.

39 Graf 2009: 116–20; Pettersson 1992.

40 See Boedeker 2007: 73–4; Mikalson 2012: 189–91, who refer to three panhellenic gods: Olympian Zeus, Isthmian Poseidon, and Delphian Apollo. In a certain manner, Plut. *Arist.* 11.3–7, by signalling that the Delphic oracle determined that the confrontation of Plataia would occur in realm of Demeter Eleusinia, implies a fusion of both traditions.

41 An idea already proposed by Boedeker 2007: 66.

42 Effectively, Nilsson already noted (1961: 24) that Demeter is a deity to whom the Homeric warriors paid little attention. She is mostly a peasants' goddess.

43 Pettersson 1992.

44 On this aspect of Athena, see Deacy 2008: 74–91. One must recall however that, when Herodotus was writing his *logoi*, controversial cults of Athena Polias were being established by Athenian partisans among the allied cities. On this subject, see Deacy 2008: 99, 124.

45 Boedeker 2007: 66–8, 75–6; Clinton 1994: 161–72; Graf 1985: 273–8. Pausanias still accounts for that in the second century, as shown by the following examples: Attica: Paus. 1.1.4; 2.4; 13.7; 14.1; 22.3; 37.3–4; Corinth: 2.4.7; 11.3; 21.5; 34.8; 36.4; Lakonia: 3.20.5; 21.8; Messenia: 4.17.1; 31.9; Elis: 5.5.6; 6.21.1; Achaea: 7.21.4; 25.5; Arkadia: 8.8.1; 9.2; 25.2–4; 29.5; 35.7; 44.5; 53.7; 54.5; Boiotia: 9.24.2; Phokis: 10.33.6; 35.5.

46 The subject is suggested by Boedeker 2007: 76.

47 Padgug 1972: 148–50; Walton 1952: 108–9. Some, like Parke 1977: 57, consider that the incorporation took place c. 600 BC.

48 Padgug 1972: 135–50; Sourvinou-Inwood 1997: 132–64; Walton 1952: 112.

49 On this issue, see Padgug 1972: 145–6 and the bibliography discussed and quoted there; cf. Walton 1952: 110.
50 Sourvinou-Inwood 1997: 132–64.
51 Boedeker 2007: 75.
52 Through Triptolemos the goddess benefits the whole world and invites everyone to come to Eleusis and be initiated in order to obtain happiness in this life and the after-life. See Johnston 2013; Boedeker 2007: 75; Clinton 1992: 100–3; Raubitschek 1991: 229–38; Walton 1952: 106, 112.
53 Isoc. 4.28–31.
54 Nilsson 1957: 313; Nilsson 1961: 24.
55 Moles 2002: 49–52. This author pertinently notes that Herodotus admires Athens as defender of Greek liberty and condemns it as promoter of 'imperialism'. In fact, Herodotus prefers a genuine panhellenism to this other option.
56 Identical arguments appear in 1.6.3; 7.138.1; 8.3.1.
57 Whitmarsh 2016: 19–20.
58 On account of these arguments, we stressed earlier the fact that the Athenians consider Kleomenes' transgression toward Demeter as an assault on Athens. See Hdt. 6.84.
59 On this issue, see, e.g., Valdés Guía 2008.
60 Valdés Guía 2008: 47–88.
61 See Mikalson 2003: 126–7; Boedeker 2007: 78; see still Cole 1994: 199–216; Nilsson 1961: 24.
62 In this connection, note the relation and parallelism that Loraux established between the character of Persephone, daughter of Demeter in Athenian tradition, and Creusa, a mythological figure embodying paradigmatically the issue of Athenian autochthony. See Loraux 1990: 196–251 (esp. 245–7); see also Loraux 1996; Leão 2011: 105–22; Leão 2010: 445–64. We thank our colleague L.N. Ferreira for this helpful suggestion.
63 Moles 2002: 33–52.
64 Harrison 2002: 181; Boedeker 1988: 46.
65 Because of the clear mythological affinities between Demeter and Isis, namely the quest for a lost daughter/husband, perhaps it must not be overlooked that Demeter is identified with Isis, one of the more important deities of the Egyptian pantheon.
66 See Whitmarsh 2016: 80–1; Scullion 2006: 195; Harrison 2002: 177–81.
67 Scullion 2006: 192, 202; Harrison 2002: 191.
68 Immerwahr 1986: 295.
69 Scullion 2006: 202.

Bibliography

Boedeker, D. 1988. "Protesilaos and the End of Herodotus' 'Histories'." *Classical Antiquity* 7: 30–48.

———. 2007. "The View from Eleusis: Demeter in the Persian Wars." In Bridges, E., Hall, E., & Rhodes, P.J., eds., *Cultural Responses to the Persian Wars: Antiquity to the Third Millennium*. Oxford (Oxford University Press), 65–85.

Bremmer, J. 2014. *Initiation into the Mysteries of the Ancient World*. Berlin (De Gruyter).

Burkert, W. 1983. *Homo Necans: The Anthropology of Ancient Sacrificial Ritual and Myth*. Berkeley, CA (University of California Press).

Clinton, K. 1992. *Myth and Cult. The Iconography of the Eleusinian Mysteries*. Stockholm (Paul Åströms förlag).

———. 1994. "The Eleusinian Mysteries and Panhellenism in Democratic Athens." In Coulson, W.D.E., *et al.*, eds., *The Archaeology of Athens and Attica Under the Democracy*. Oxford (Oxford University Press), 161–72.

Cole, S.G. 1994. "Demeter in the Ancient Greek City and Its Countryside." In Alcock, S.E., & Osborne, R., eds., *Placing the Gods: Sanctuaries and Sacred Space in Ancient Greece*. Oxford (Clarendon Press), 199–216.

Deacy, S. 2008. *Athena*. London (Routledge).

Dietrich, B. 1982. "The Religious Prehistory of Demeter's Eleusinian Mysteries." In Bianchi, U., & Vermaseren, M.J., eds., *La soteriologia dei culti orientali nel'impero Romano*. Leiden (Brill), 445–71.

Ferreira, J.R. 1992. *Hélade e Helenos: Génese e Evolução de um Conceito*. Coimbra (Instituto Nacional de Investigação Científica, Centro de Estudos Clássicos e Humanísticos da Universidade de Coimbra).

————. 2005. "Hélade, Pan-Helenismo e Identidade Helénica." In Fialho, M.C., Sousa e Silva, M.F., Rocha Pereira, M.H. da, coords., eds., *Génese e Consolidação da Ideia de Europa: Vol. I: De Homero ao Fim da Época Clássica*. Coimbra (Imprensa da Universidade), 15–42.

Ferreira, L.N. 2013. *Mobilidade poética na Grécia Antiga: Uma leitura da obra de Simónides*. Coimbra (Imprensa da Universidade de Coimbra).

Graf, F. 1985. *Nordionische Kulte: Religionsgeschichdiche und epigraphische Untersuchungen zu den Kulte von Chios, Erythrai, Klazomenai und Phokaia*. Zürich (Schweizerisches Institut in Rom).

————. 2009. *Apollo*. London (Routledge).

Harrison, T. 2002. *Divinity and History: The Religion of Herodotus*. Oxford (Oxford University Press).

How, W.W. & Wells, J. 1928. *A Commentary on Herodotus With Introduction and Appendixes II*. Oxford (Clarendon Press).

Immerwahr, H.R. 1986. *Form and Thought in Herodotus*. Atlanta, GA (Scholars Press).

Johnston, S.I. 2013. "Demeter, Myths, and the Polyvalence of Festivals." *History of Religions* 52: 370–401.

Larson, J. 2007. *Ancient Greek Cults: A Guide*. London (Routledge).

Leão, D.F. 2010. "Cidadania, autoctonia e posse de terra na Atenas Democrática." *Cadmo* 20: 445–64.

————. 2011. "Autoctonia, filiação legítima e cidadania no 'Íon' de Eurípides." *Humanitas* 63: 105–22.

Leão, D.F. & Ferreira, J.R. 2000. "Introdução." In *Heródoto: Histórias, Livro 6°*. Lisboa (Edições 70).

Loraux, N. 1990. *Les enfants d'Athéna: Idées athéniennes sur la citoyenneté et la division des sexes*. Paris (Éditions du Seuil).

————. 1996. *Né de la terre: mythe et politique à Athènes*. Paris (Éditions du Seuil).

Marincola, J.M. 2003. "Introduction." In *Herodotus: The Histories*. Translated by A. Sélincourt. London (Penguin).

Mikalson, J.D. 2003. *Herodotus and Religion in the Persian Wars*. Chapel Hill, NC (North Carolina University Press).

————. 2012. "Religion in Herodotus." In Bakker, E.J., De Jong, I.J.F., & van Wees, H., eds., *Brill's Companion to Herodotus*. Leiden (Brill), 187–98.

Moles, J. 2002. "Herodotus and Athens." In Bakker, E.J., De Jong, I.J.F., & van Wees, H., eds., *Brill's Companion to Herodotus*. Leiden (Brill), 33–52.

Nilsson, M.P. 1957. *Griechische Feste von religiöser Bedeutung mit Ausschluss der attischen*. Darmstadt (Wissenschaftliche Buchgesellschaft).

————. 1961. *Greek Folk Religion*. Philadelphia, PA (University of Pennsylvania Press).

Niskanen, P. 2004. *The Human and the Divine in History: Herodotus and the Book of Daniel.* London (T & T Clark International).

Oliveira, A.C.J.N. 2015. "Estudo introdutório." In *Eurípides: Helena.* Coimbra & São Paulo (Imprensa da Universidade de Coimbra/Annablume), 11–105.

Padgug, R.A. 1972. "Eleusis and the Union of Attika." *Greek, Roman and Byzantine Studies* 13: 135–50.

Parke, H.W. 1977. *The Festivals of the Athenians.* London (Thames & Hudson).

Pettersson, M. 1992. *Cults of Apollo at Sparta: The Hyakinthia, the Gymnopaidiai and the Karneia.* Stockholm (Paul Åströms Förlag).

Pulquério, M.O. 1973/1974. "O problema das duas palinódias de Estesícoro." *Humanitas* 25–26: 265–73.

Raubitschek, A.E. 1991. "The Mission of Triptolemos." In Obbink, D., & Waerdt, P.A.V., eds., *The School of Hellas: Essays on Greek History, Archaeology and Literature.* Oxford (Oxford University Press), 229–38.

Scott, M. 2015. *Delfos. Historia del Centro del Mundo Antiguo.* Barcelona (Editorial Planeta).

Scullion, S. 2006. "Herodotus and Greek Religion." In Dewald, C., & Marincola, J., eds., *The Cambridge Companion to Herodotus.* Cambridge (Cambridge University Press), 192–208.

Shimron, B. 1989. *Politics and Belief in Herodotus.* Stuttgart (Steiner)

Soares, C. & Ferreira, J.R. 2002. *Heródoto: Histórias, Livro 8°.* Lisboa (Edições 70).

Soares, C. 2003. *A morte em Heródoto: Valores universais e particularismos étnicos.* Lisboa (Fundação Calouste Gulbenkian).

Sourvinou-Inwood, C. 1997. "Reconstructing Change: Ideology and the Eleusinian Mysteries." In Golden, M., & Toohey, P., eds., *Inventing Ancient Culture: Historicism, Periodization, and the Ancient World.* London (Routledge), 132–64.

Strassler, R.B., ed. 2007. *The Landmark Herodotus: The Histories.* New York, NY (Anchor Books).

Valdés Guía, M. 2008. *El nacimiento de la autoctonía ateniense: cultos, mitos cívicos y sociedad de la Atenas del s. VI a.C.* Madrid (Universidad Complutense de Madrid).

Walton, F.R. 1952. "Athens, Eleusis, and the Homeric Hymn to Demeter." *Harvard Theological Review* 45: 105–14.

Waterfield, R., ed. 2008. *Herodotus: The Histories.* Oxford (Oxford University Press).

Whitmarsh, T. 2016. *Battling the Gods: Atheism in the Ancient World.* London (Faber & Faber).

Part III

Ethnic identity among the Barbaroi

9   Herodotus' Memphite sources

Rogério Sousa

Introduction

Herodotus' accounts on Egypt provided medieval and modern scholars with a het-
erogeneous picture of the Nile valley and pharaonic civilization. Although Herodotus certainly aims at celebrating the 'remembrance of actions of men' (from
the proem) the way he looks at this foreign land and people lies well beyond the
historical scope of his work *in stricto senso* and is greatly shaped by scientific reasoning. The history of Egypt is introduced through geographical and 'ethnographical' observation, and is interspersed with zoological and botanical comments,
providing a vivid background on the life in the Nile valley. Herodotus' inquiry is
deeply influenced by scientific, philosophical, and rhetorical developments.

This integrative view of the land and its people has deeply shaped the Western
vision of Egypt. Nearly 2,300 years after Herodotus' journey, when Bonaparte
led his expedition to Egypt, a similar way of looking at this land reemerged. The
Description de l'Égypte unveils before our eyes the geography, botany, zoology,
ethnography, and archaeology of the land of the pharaohs,[1] providing the first
integrated scientific publication of an entire ecosystem. Curiously enough, the
first scientific expedition to Egypt would provide a wealth of illustrations of landscapes, animals and plants, cities and monuments revealing to Western eyes the
same mental images narrated by Herodotus more than 2,000 years ago.

Only in the aftermath of Napoleon's campaign, with Champollion's decipher-
ment of hieroglyphic writing, could Egyptian sources start to be studied directly
by contemporary scholars, revealing for the first time the enormous inconsistencies of the picture provided by Herodotus on the history of Egypt. In this respect,
it is notable that the surviving fragments of the work of Manetho, who lived under
the rule of Ptolemy II (246–221 BC), are far more consistent with the Egyptian
sources. Indeed, his division into 30 dynasties is still in use by Egyptologists
and provides the backbone of pharaonic historiography.[2] This fact alone reveals a
paradox. The Hellenized Egyptian priest Manetho wrote the *History of Egypt* in
Greek, and he was certainly knowledgeable in the writings of Herodotus. However, in terms of the historical account, he greatly surpassed his master both in the
consistency of his methodology and in the reliability of his sources.

The Greek sources of Herodotus

Manetho was knowledgeable in hieroglyphic texts, and, unlike Herodotus, he had the advantage of undertaking a direct inquiry of the Egyptian written sources. He did have access to the Royal Lists and to other records concerning the main achievements of each reign.[3] Moreover, as Herodotus noticed, the Egyptians had developed highly sophisticated methods for the reckoning of time (Hdt. 2.4).[4] Chronology and kingship had always been a matter of the highest importance in Egyptian royal ideology and the precision of pharaonic records largely explains the outstanding results achieved by Manetho. Not surprisingly, using the historio-graphical method borrowed from Herodotus, Manetho synthesized the Egyptian sources in a way never achieved before.

Herodotus used three methods in his historical approach: observation (autopsy), surmise on the basis of considered opinion, and inquiry.[5] Although he relied on oral accounts (2.99.1), he clearly enjoyed access to Greek written sources as well. He used direct observation to describe the monumental sites,[6] the land,[7] and the life on the river banks.[8] In general terms, the corpus of his observations provides a reliable account of life in the Nile valley. Moreover, Herodotus also undertakes a personal inquiry (2.99.1). It is clear that his privileged sources were the Greeks settled in Egypt, but these were only useful for the recent past (2.154.4):[9]

> From the date of the original settlement of these persons in Egypt (Carian and Ionian mercenaries), we Greeks, through our intercourse with them, have acquired an accurate knowledge of the several events in Egyptian history, from the reign of Psammetikhos onwards.[10]

Herodotus also mentions Egyptian sources, and he is keen in showing that he consulted with the priests from the most important temples of Egypt (in Thebes, Memphis, and Heliopolis), which in Book II are quoted on several occasions (2.2.5, 3.1, 10.1, 13.1, 19.1; 28; 54–5, 73.1, 99–143). However, the ultimate soundness of the information provided by these sources is highly questionable, to say the least.

In fact, in terms of the historical account itself two major sequences are clearly distinguishable in terms of historical accuracy and merit. The first account going back to the origins of Egypt continues down to the Kushite dominion (2.99–142), while the second part deals with the Dodecarchy (Libyan Period) and the Late Period down to Amasis (2.147–82).[11] Herodotus' recent history of Egypt stands out as one of the most important historical sources for the period,[12] but the histori-cal account provided for the more distant past of Egypt is imprecise and filled with distorted and confused statements. This situation has been interpreted as resulting from an insufficient knowledge of the Egyptian sources themselves concerning their own traditions:

> The general opinion of older scholars that they were low-grade members of the hierarchy has little to be said for it. It is far from improbable that

Herodotus had access to high-ranking priests, and the distorted and confused
information which he obtained from them, particularly on history, is by no
means inconsistent with that view. Egyptian priests were certainly not as well
informed as we are inclined to think.[13]

However, this view of the Egyptian priesthood is not consistent with the breadth
and scope of the works achieved by Manetho, nor with the prevailing dynamism
and vitality of Demotic culture.[14] Behind the sharp contrast between the two historical accounts provided by Herodotus we may certainly find a far more complex
situation.

The precision of the account on the recent history of Egypt is largely related
to the close association of the Greek settlers with the pharaonic establishment during the Late Period. In fact, Greek merchants and soldiers are detected in Egypt
long before the sixth century BC.[15] Greek mercenaries are identifiable in the early
years of the reign of Psammetikhos I and played an important political role in
winning Egyptian independence from Assyrian domination and in the re-estab-
lishment of a unified government in the country by 656 BC.[16] Greek and Carian
mercenaries, as well as Jews and Phoenicians, guaranteed its security from external attack and provided a counterweight within the country to the power of the
makhimoi, the native Egyptian warrior class, who were in fact Libyans in origin,
and posed a significant threat to royal authority.[17]

These foreign troops were settled in permanent camps on the northeastern frontier, providing a barrier against Asian invaders.[18] Herodotus himself informs us that
stratopeda ('camps') were established between Bubastis and the sea on the Pelusiac
branch of the Nile. He claims that these camps were occupied without a break for
over a century. The preference shown to these foreign troops was far from welcome
to the *makhimoi* and tensions between the native Egyptian warrior class and the
Greek mercenaries eventually occurred.[19] According to Herodotus, during the reign
of Psammetikhos I a large contingent of *makhimoi* mutinied and withdrew from
Egypt to a site that may well have lain somewhere in the vicinity of the Blue Nile
and Gezira area near Omdurman (2.30). By the time of Apries (589–570 BC), the
situation eventually reached a disastrous level when the king was swept from the
throne by a backlash from the *makhimoi* against the privileged position of Greeks
and Carians in the military establishment.[20] This revolt cost Apries the crown and
ultimately his life (2.161.3–4, 163, 169). His successor, Ahmose I, Amasis to the
Greeks (570–526 BC), prudently withdrew the Greek mercenaries from their camps
on the northeastern frontier and stationed them in the city of Memphis, with this
redeployment creating in that city the half-castes called Karomemphitai and Hel-
lenomemphitai, resulting from Greek and Egyptian marriages (2.154.3).[21]

Greek merchants were also encouraged to settle in Egypt early in the reign of
Psammetikhos I (664–610 BC). By the end of the seventh century the Milesians
had established a major commercial centre at Naucratis.[22] This well-documented
trading centre was established on the Canopic branch of the Nile not far from the
capital of the Twenty-Sixth Dynasty, Sais, and possessed excellent communica-
tions for internal and external trade. Excavation there has revealed a series of

sacred enclosures dedicated to Greek cults, a scarab factory producing material for export, and a Late Period platform that may have been military in purpose but could equally well have had civilian, administrative functions.[23]

Closely related to the political strategy of the Saite kings, these Greek communities certainly provided Herodotus with sound historical sources for this period, most of them available in written record.[24]

Herodotus' tour of Egypt

The economic growth fostered by the Saite kings would not have been possible without an easy circulation of goods and people. This concern was extended far beyond the borders of Egypt. Herodotus mentions that Nekau (Nekho) constructed a fleet of war galleys with rams, some of which were used in the Mediterranean and others in the Red Sea. Indeed, it may be that the abortive Red Sea canal was intended, in part, to facilitate the transfer of naval forces from the Red Sea to the Mediterranean as circumstances required.[25]

Under the Persian occupation this policy was kept and when Herodotus visited Egypt, under Artaxerxes I (465–424 BC),[26] he found excellent conditions for travelling. Moreover, Greek merchants and mercenaries settled in the country certainly provided Herodotus with an important network of contacts that would make his journey easier.

Herodotus explicitly mentions several localities from the Delta down to the First Cataract and, at first sight, we are tempted to accept that Herodotus sojourned all over the country and visited all the main sites. We may easily assume that he went to every place that he mentions, but the actual extent of his visits is highly debatable to say the least.

In fact, when examined in detail, his observations reveal a sharp contrast between the vivid description of certain places and the lacunose, not to say evasive, references to others. Generally speaking, his observations about Egyptian territory are correct from the geographical standpoint. He points to the geographical particularities of the Nile Delta – to which he refers correctly as an alluvial land (2.5) – and those of the territory of the Nile Valley up to the First Cataract (2.9). He also makes accurate descriptions of the temples he visited. Regarding the description of the monuments, in particular, it is clear that Herodotus enjoys providing as much detail as possible. The Temple of Bastet at Boubastis – referred to by him as the Temple of Artemis – is perhaps the best example in this respect, as it provoked in Herodotus a strong aesthetic admiration. Not only did Herodotus consider it the most beautiful of the temples that he had seen but its description is actually quite helpful in terms of reconstruction of an archaeological site of which little has survived (2.137.5). Despite the thorough description of the site, it is clear that his account focusses on the exterior impressions of the sacred island, and no important feature of the inner precinct is mentioned, suggesting that Herodotus could do no more than see it from outside.

However, an insider view is provided of the temple precinct at Sais, where Herodotus was able to enter the sacred precinct. There he saw the royal tombs of the Saite kings (2.169)[27] and wooden colossal statues that he interpreted as depicting the servants of Mykerinos' daughter. Most importantly, he was able to see the venerated image of the cow, which he was told was the coffin of Mykerinos' daughter (2.130).

According to his own account, Herodotus was initiated into the Osirian mysteries in the Temple of Sais (2.170–1). Those rituals were performed in the sacred precinct of the Goddess Neith, today almost completely lost. Herodotus provides an important description of the site (170–1):

> Here too, in this same precinct [of Athena at Sais], is the burial-place of one whom I think it not right to mention in such a connection. It stands behind the temple, against the backwall, which it entirely covers. There are also some large stone obelisks in the enclosure, and there is a lake near them, adorned with an edging of stone. In form it is circular, and in size/ . . . On this lake it is said that the Egyptians present by night his sufferings whose name I refrain from mentioning, and this representation they call their Mysteries. I know well the whole course of the proceedings in these ceremonies, but they shall not pass my lips.

Herodotus accurately describes a ritual tomb of Osiris, and this account is consistent with the widespread use of Osirian temples in almost every sacred precinct during the Late Period. These crypts were usually shaped as a sacred hill and built next to a sacred lake.[28] However, Herodotus seems to think that the structure which existed at Sais was the actual tomb of Osiris, apparently unaware that many other such 'Osirian tombs' existed in Egyptian territory.[29]

Another Egyptian monument that Herodotus classifies as a wonder "greater than the Pyramids" is the Labyrinth (2.148.3), the funerary complex of the Pharaoh Moeris (Amenemhat III) in the Fayum oasis. His descriptions are again extremely valuable not only to reconstruct the original splendor of the site, but also for understanding that such an immense structure was still easily accessible for tourists more than a thousand years after its construction (2.148–9). Also fascinating is the description of the two enthroned *colossi* of Moeris facing the lake, which Herodotus classifies as a wonder greater than the Labyrinth itself. He states that nearly in the centre of the lake stood two high platforms, each crowned with a colossal quartzite statue of the king sitting upon a throne. Today the statues are lost but the platforms where they stood have been located, giving credit to the description of Herodotus (2.149.2):

> It is manifestly an artificial excavation, for nearly in the center there stand two pyramids, rising to the height of fifty fathoms above the surface of the water, and extending as far beneath, crowned each of them with a colossal statue sitting upon a throne. Thus, these pyramids are one hundred fathoms high, which is exactly a furlong [*stadion*] of six hundred feet: the fathom being six feet in length, or four cubits, which is the same thing, since a cubit measures six, and a foot four palms.

It is worth noting that the Labyrinth itself was described by six classical writers, including Manetho (*BNJ* 609 F 3b), Diodorus Siculus (1.61), Strabo (17.1.3, 37, 42 C787, 811, 813), Pliny (*NH* 36.13), and Pomponius Mela (1.9.56) revealing that the Fayum area was not only easily accessible, but was in fact a favourite destination for visitors touring Egypt, possibly as important as the Giza pyramid field, of which Herodotus also has much to say (2.8.3, 10.1; 12.1, 15.2; 125.6; 127.1). The Great Pyramid itself is described as "built entirely of polished stone, fitted together with the utmost care", which in fact corresponds to the archaeological evidence. In Giza, Herodotus reveals a great deal of interest in the gigantic causeway that linked the pyramid on the plateau downward to the valley temple. This once impressive structure was still standing at that time (2.124):

> It took ten years' oppression of the people to make the causeway for the conveyance of the stones, a work not much inferior, in my judgment, to the pyramid itself. This causeway is five furlongs in length, ten fathoms wide, and in height, at the highest part, eight fathoms. It is built of polished stone and is covered with carvings of animals.

Such description is fully consistent with the archaeological evidence too.[30] A sacred crypt is reported to have been built in Giza, which Kheops intended as vaults for his own use; these last were built on a sort of island, surrounded by water introduced from the Nile by a canal (2.124).

This description clearly reminds us of the *Osireion* of the Temple of Seti I in Abydos, also designed as an underground crypt. During the Nile flood, it was partially filled with phreatic water recreating the primordial hill in its midst. Although not thoroughly published, evidence of such a structure was found near the causeway of Kafre at Giza, comprising three successive shafts and two chambers, the lower one carved 25 metres underground.[31] The central sarcophagus was surrounded by infiltrating water, reminiscent of the Osireion of Seti I.[32] This symbolic tomb of Osiris could not have been built before the Late Period.

The vivid accounts that Herodotus gives of these monuments are highly contrasting with his parsimonious words regarding well-known monuments of Thebes, such as the Temple of Amun-Re in Karnak, the avenue of sphinxes, the Temple of Luxor, or the *Colossi* of Memnon that stood on the Theban West Bank. In fact, the only reference to the Temple of Karnak is misleading, making reference to the "inner sanctuary, which is a spacious chamber with a multitude of colossal statues in wood" (2.143). According to Herodotus, these statues depicted the complete genealogy of the priests of Amun. Although statues of high dignitaries were common in temple precincts,[33] they were not exactly colossal. Moreover, while genealogy played an important role in priestly communities from the Third Intermediate Period onwards,[34] there is no archaeological record of such galleries, except for the kings themselves. In fact, in the precinct of Karnak, the Chamber of the Ancestors – now kept in the Louvre Museum – lists the lineage of 61 pharaohs from Djoser (2667–2648 BC) to the Eighteenth Dynasty (1550–1295 BC).[35] During the Third Intermediate Period (1069–664 BC), this part of the temple – the

Festival Hall of Thutmose III – was used for the initiation of the priests and it is a possibility that statues of the royal ancestors were displayed there too.[36] It is thus likely that somehow the information regarding this Chamber of the Ancestors was 'lost in translation', and Herodotus perceived it as representing the lineage of high priests of Thebes. This mistake also shows that he overlooked here one of the most important historical records regarding the history of Egypt. In contrast, references to the High Priestesses, the famous god's wives of Amun – some of them daughters of the Saite pharaohs – are not mentioned at all.[37]

Given the erroneous or parsimonious commentaries on the Theban temples and sites, it is rather likely that Herodotus was not received with open arms by the Theban priests. Despite that, Herodotus locates in Thebes some of the sources referring to the origins of the oracles of Zeus at Siwa and Dodona, as well as the genealogy of Hecataeus (2.3.1, 55, 143). These statements seem decorative, or rather like narrational embroidery, and in fact they could well have been obtained somewhere else as they do not seem to have any relevant relationship with the core of the Theban theological tradition. The cold reception from the Theban priests is better understood in light of the traumatic events suffered under the invasion of Assurbanipal, who plundered the Temple of Amun-Re and took the sacred images as booty to Assyria.[38] This inconceivable profanation of one of the most revered holy places of the ancient world was decisive in triggering a cultural response to trauma in the form of xenophobia, which remained particularly intense under Persian occupation. Demotic literature shows abundant signs of this reaction in the form of oracles, such as the *Oracle of the Lamb* or the *Potter's Oracle*, where foreign occupation is clearly seen as resulting from a weak adherence to divine laws. After the traumatic experience of witnessing the profanation and estrangement of their divine images, which have always been the core of the Egyptian experience of sanctity, temples intensified religious taboos to avoid contamination and pollution.

A similar situation seems to have occurred in Heliopolis, by far the largest religious centre in Egypt. Again, Herodotus quotes Heliopolitan priests on the antiquity of Egypt (2.3.1) but no description is provided of the sacred city itself, which must have been truly impressive.[39] As in Thebes, important pieces of information seem to arise from his supposed Heliopolitan sources, but intermediation may be suspected. The openness towards an interaction with the Greek element will only take form under Ptolemaic rule, with Ptolemaic rulers restoring to Egypt the stolen images of the gods and thereby establishing their reign as the promised age of salvation.[40]

The doubts concerning the real extent of Herodotus' contacts with Egyptian priests increase when we examine the 'explanations' offered by the author regarding the meaning of the sites he visited. Here, Herodotus describes the sacred cow in the Temple of Sais (Hdt. 2.130–2):

[It lies in] a chamber richly adorned. Every day there are burnt before it aromatics of every kind; and all night long a lamp is kept burning in the apartment. . . . As for the cow, the greater portion of it is hidden by a scarlet coverture; the head and neck, however, which are visible, are coated very thickly with gold, and between the horns there is a representation in gold of the orb of the sun. The figure is not erect, but lying down, with the limbs under the body; the dimensions being fully those of a large animal of the kind. Every year it is taken from the apartment where it is kept and exposed to the light of day.

While the description of the sacred image fully corresponds to the depiction of the goddess Mehet Ueret, the embodiment of Neith as the Great Flood, the primordial Ocean, Herodotus then explains that the statue is used as a coffin for the corpse of the daughter of Mykerinos who committed suicide (Hdt. 2.132). Herodotus then adds: "They say that the daughter of Mykerinos requested her father in her dying moments to allow her once a year to see the sun." This piece of information is extremely important since ritual images of deities were effectively brought to the daylight during the Festival of the New Year. These rituals became especially important from the Late Period onwards. In this episode, Herodotus faithfully describes the iconography of the sacred image of Neith, as well as the ritual of the New Year but fails completely in his exploration of their meaning. Accounts like these clearly show that the Herodotus' indigenous sources are able to lead him to certain places but were badly informed on essential matters.

From the Egyptological standpoint, how can we interpret Herodotus' erroneous information? Should we see it as resulting from the low levels of cultural literacy among the Egyptian priests as is usually advanced? Could the priests of the Late Period be so badly informed about their own traditions? Every piece of evidence that we possess attests that the Egyptian priesthood was extremely knowledgeable and – perhaps more than ever before – they were extremely cultivated in their own traditions.

In this scenario it is much more likely that, despite Herodotus claims, he probably failed to gain contact with Egyptian priests. In the same way that we cannot simply assume that he visited every place he mentions,[41] we should also consider that Egyptian priests might not have always been as open to Herodotus as he wants his readers to believe.

On most of the relevant occasions, he used interpreters who – as Herodotus himself explains – descended from Egyptian children raised by the Greek mercenaries.[42] Most of Herodotus' accounts regarding the distant past of Egypt had been probably reported by these Egyptian interpreters, who certainly felt compelled to form a corpus of curiosities and stories to entertain and impress Greek visitors.[43]

It is no matter of chance that many of the Greek anecdotic tales, passed down about the pharaohs of old, revolve around prostitutes or cheating wives. With no funds to finish his pyramid Kheops could find no better source of income than making his daughter a prostitute (2.126.1). Moreover, as legend had it and Herodotus retold it, one of the small pyramids in Giza was a product of the enterprise of one of the same Khufu's daughters. In addition to payment, the princess had also asked each of her clients for a block of stone, which she used to build her own pyramid (2.126.1).[44] The same expedient was used by Rhampsinitos (Ramses II), who sent his daughter to the brothel to find out the thief of his treasure (2.121.1). The blinded Pharaoh Pheron could hardly find "a woman who had been faithful to her husband" in order to recover his sight (2.111). Besides these risqué legendary accounts, Herodotus is particularly keen in providing stories of the most celebrated Greek courtesans based in Egypt (Hdt. 2.135):

> Naucratis seems somehow to be the place where such women are most attractive. First there was this Rhodopis of whom we have been speaking, so celebrated a person that her name came to be familiar to all the Greeks; and, afterwards, there was another, called Archidike, notorious throughout Greece, though not so much talked of as her predecessor.

These are, in fact, the kind of stories that would be expected to be told in the renowned brothels of Naukratis. His interpreters and guides, serving the Greeks mercenaries and merchants living in Egypt for several generations, certainly provided him with most of these entertaining stories, and it is possible that they become part of oral tradition in the Greek communities. These stories reveal 'othering' in which Greek intermediaries projected onto the Egyptians sexual practices that transgressed their own norms.

Aware of this fact, when describing the third pyramid at Giza, Herodotus is clear about the stories made up by the Greeks on the history of Egypt (Hdt. 2.134):

> Some of the Greeks call it the work of Rhodopis the courtesan, but they report falsely. It seems to me that these persons cannot have any real knowledge who Rhodopis was; otherwise they would scarcely have ascribed to her a work on which uncounted treasures, so to speak, must have been expended. Rhodopis also lived during the reign of Amasis, not of Mykerinos, and was thus very many years later than the time of the kings who built the pyramids.

In another occasion he says (Hdt. 2.3): "The Greeks, among other foolish tales, relate that Psammetikhos had the children brought up by women whose tongues he had previously cut out." One senses that Herodotus might have appreciated this difficulty as a serious obstacle to overcome, but it is certain that he failed in getting more reliable authorities. Egyptian xenophobia in the fifth century BCE would explain this difficulty.[45] This attitude towards foreigners had nothing to do with racism or nationalism *per se*; rather, it reflected their concern that foreigners might act in a blasphemous way toward the gods, who, offended, might then turn away from Egypt,[46] which had itself suffered many indignities at the hands of Asian overlords. A book of rituals from the Late Period, the House of Life, with its fourfold function of library, scriptorium, school for the priests, and sanctuary,[47] reflects this attitude:

> It shall be very, very concealed.
> No one shall know it, no one see it
> Except the disk of the sun, that looks into its secret.

> Those officiating . . . shall enter in silence, their bodies covered
> So as to be protected against sudden death
> The Asiatic must not enter, he must see nothing.[48]

In Egyptian temples from the Late Period, an 'enclave' culture had emerged in order to defend itself within a wall of ritual purity, taboos, and secrecy. These boundaries provide a context for the fantastic, but probably not inaccurate statements, made by Herodotus about the purity commandments observed by the Egyptians in their contact with the Greeks and probably with all foreigners (Hdt. 2.41):

> This is the reason why no native of Egypt, whether man or woman, will give a Greek a kiss, or use the knife of a Greek, or his spit, or his cauldron, or taste the flesh of an ox, known to be pure, if it has been cut with a Greek knife.

Though categories of distinction and self-segregation had a long history in Egypt, their traditional function had been to divide sacred from profane, not indigenous from alien.[49] In the Late Period, the concept of 'profane' underwent a change. The sacred objects and rites were protected not so much from the impure and the uninitiated but from the foreigner. Foreigners symbolized the ultimate in impurity and also stood for the threat posed by Seth, the sacrilegious will to destruction, desecration, and plunder. Late Period cult texts also occasionally articulate the rule forbidding foreigners an entry to the sanctuary and attendance at the secret rites. The status of Herodotus as a Greek, and therefore as 'foreign', prevented him from being accepted in the Egyptian priestly circles. In this respect, one single and remarkable exception can be found.

Memphis and the temple of Ptah

Memphis and the Temple of Ptah are frequently mentioned in Book II. The several gates of the temple are thoroughly described. Herodotus reports quite accurately that the western gateway of the temple was built by Rhampsinitos (Ramses II) as well as the two *colossi* that stood in front of this gateway. The eastern pylon, now lost, is described as such (Hdt. 2.136):

> The eastern gateway was built by Asykhis – which in size and beauty far surpasses the other three. All the four gateways have figures graven on them, and a vast amount of architectural ornament, but the gateway of Asykhis is by far the most richly adorned.

The northern gateway of the Temple of Hephaestus (Ptah) is said to have been built by Moeris (Amenemhat III). Six statues stood in front of the temple, "two of which, representing Sesostris and his wife, are thirty cubits in height, while the remaining four, which represent his sons, are twenty cubits". The southern gate of the temple was indeed built by Psammetikhos I after he had reunified Egypt, as Herodotus mentions, which seems likely in view of the political role of the temple as the centre of the Two Lands. Next Psammetikhos built the "court for Apis, in which Apis is kept whenever he makes his appearance in Egypt. This court is opposite the gateway of Psammetikhos and is surrounded with a colonnade and adorned with a multitude of figures. Instead of pillars, the colonnade rests upon colossal statues, twelve cubits in height" (2.153).

This is an interesting piece of information since it reveals architectonic features of the temple that have completely disappeared and, thanks to this account, we have been made confident in our reconstruction.

To the southwest of the Temple of Ptah lay the Levantine quarter, mainly with a Syro-Persian population. The Phoenicians formed a long-established group in Memphis. Herodotus mentions that "Phoenicians from the city of Tyre dwell all round this precinct, and the whole place is known by the name of 'the camp of the Tyrians'. Within the enclosure stands a temple, which is called that of Aphrodite the Stranger" (2.112). This temple is surely the temple of the goddess Astarte, which was associated with Hathor, the goddess of love, who also received cult observance in this area. North of the temple of Ptah was the Carian quarter – the *Hellenion* – forming a well-established settlement of Greeks. It originated, as we have already mentioned, when Greek soldiers were moved from their camps in the Delta to the city of Memphis (Hdt. 2.154):

> The Ionians and Carians occupied for many years the places assigned them by Psammetikhos, which lay near the sea, a little below the city of Boubastis, on the Pelusiac mouth of the Nile. King Amasis long afterwards removed the Greeks hence, and settled them at Memphis to guard him against the native Egyptians.

This settlement grew up next to the Palace of Apries. It was probably to this palace that the story of the stolen treasure of the Pharaoh Rhampsinitos refers (2.121). One should not forget that the quarter continued to serve under Persian occupation as the seat of the imperial administration, and it was probably there that the treasury was kept.[50]

Contrasting with this vivid account of the city, the necropolis of Sakara is hardly mentioned at all. Furthermore, not even the burial ground of the Apis bulls, the famous Sarapeion, is mentioned, which differs from the detailed description provided by Herodotus of the sanctuary where they lived. This lacuna suggests that at this stage the necropolis was still a 'forbidden' territory, especially for foreigners. Even more striking is the absence of any reference to the burial ground of the Hellenomemphites in Abusir. The only structure of the necropolis mentioned is the temple of Isis at Memphis, "a vast structure, well worth seeing", which was dedicated to the Mother-of-Apis cows. The temple was built on the edge of the eastern escarpment along with the entrances to various catacombs, and it was easily visible from the valley,[51] which might explain why they are mentioned by Herodotus.

Besides the description of the city and its sites, Herodotus often transmits knowledge provided by the priests of Ptah. However, unlike other contexts,

Memphite sources show a significant consistency with the core of their theological framework. Book II starts right with one of the most interesting of them on how the Pharaoh Psammetikhos I used children's speech to find out which was the oldest civilization (2.1). This story assumes more relevance in light of its theological framework, the temple of Ptah. This myth in fact formulates creation itself as an act of speech by that very primeval deity.[52] In this theological vision, speech is uttered according to what is conceived in the heart. Since all creatures are conceived after the same divine model, it is nothing but natural to expect that, if not contaminated by vicarious learning, children will eventually utter the speech imprinted in their own hearts by the creator god himself. The concern given to the first word uttered by the children is thus consistent with the Memphite myth of creation, and we can trust Herodotus when he states that "these were the real facts I learnt at Memphis from the priests of Hephaestus" (2.3). From the Egyptological point of view, this excerpt clearly shows that at Memphis, the local priests introduced Herodotus to central aspects of their wisdom. Herodotus continues by saying "I got much other information also from conversation with these priests while I was at Memphis" (2.3). Most of this material deals with the history of Egypt about which they seem to be Herodotus' only reliable source. Explicit reference is made to Egyptian written sources translated directly by Memphite priests who then read them to Herodotus (Hdt. 2.100):

> They read to me from a papyrus the names of three hundred and thirty monarchs, who (they said) were his successors upon the throne. In this number of generations there were eighteen Ethiopian kings, and one queen who was a native; all the rest were kings and Egyptians.

These lists effectively existed in temple repositories, and, later on, they would be used by Manetho in his historiographical work. Some of them have even survived to our days, such as the Royal List of the Chamber of the Ancestors and the Royal List of the temple of Seti I in Abydos.[53] These monumental lists were based on historical documentation written on papyri, such as the Ramesside *Turin Canon*, the only document of its kind known so far.[54] Therefore, it was a papyrus like the *Turin Canon* – handed down in hieratic or demotic – that was translated to Herodotus by a Memphite priest. The ability of these priests to translate his source material directly into Greek is a situation that in itself deserves more active consideration.

With access to these sources, Herodotus garnered information usually omitted in the monumental Royal Lists inscribed on temple walls, for example the reign of a queen who ruled as pharaoh (Hatshepsut). The wealth of material provided by these lists probably precluded Herodotus from an exhaustive account. It is, nevertheless, interesting to point out aspects of his account that are consistent with the Egyptian historical sources.

Min or Menes is described as the first king of the Two Lands and the founder of Memphis. Herodotus says that Menes dammed the Nile south of the future site of the city, diverting it so that he could build on the reclaimed land (2.99).[55] Not surprisingly, during the First Persian Occupation, the most prominent of the pharaohs was Sesostris, about whom there is given a rich account of military conquests in Asia and Ethiopia, public works such as the irrigation system, administrative reforms, and building activity in temples. All these aspects are consistent with the Egyptian historical records with the exception of the treason of his brother. Senuseret III's exploits gathered renown over time and substantially contributed to the character of 'Sesostris' (becoming a kind of composite heroic ruler) as described by Herodotus.[56] Sesostris eventually became the quintessence of the Egyptian monarch and fully embodied the dream of military resistance towards foreign occupation.

The three builders of the Giza pyramids are correctly reported as belonging to the same dynasty, but their reigns are incorrectly dated. The description of Kheops in particular echoes the events of the Amarna period, and it is possible that some confusion has been created with Akhenaten, who indeed "closed the temples, and forbade the Egyptians to offer sacrifice" (2.124). Rulers of most of the major periods are mentioned: the Archaic Period (Min), the Old Kingdom (Nitokris, Kheops, Khephren, Mykerinos), the Middle Kingdom (Sesostris, Moeris), the New Kingdom (Rhampsinitos), the Libyan Period (Asykhis), the Ethiopian Period (Sabakos, Sethos), the Saite Period (Psammetikhos to Amasis).

Although clearly insufficient and filled with inconsistencies,[57] the inquiry carried out by Herodotus in Memphis provided him with the bulk of his historical knowledge regarding the memory of Egypt before the contacts with the Greeks. He did not have the linguistic tools or the time to cope with the enormous documental corpus. But the idea to use these lists to reconstruct the lineages of the Egyptian pharaohs would prove to be decisive in Manetho's work.

Conclusion

The country that Herodotus visited had been unified under Psammetikhos I, after nearly 500 years of political division. From the political standpoint, Egypt was unified and was highly receptive towards Greek settlers, who then lived in the country for several generations. Subsequently, the Persians maintained the Egyptian administrative system, with the addition of a satrap at the top of the administration. Although tension might have arisen in some areas, Persian occupation did not disturb the economic and cultural revival that took place during the Late Period. In this scenario, Herodotus had the perfect conditions both in terms of security and travel facilities to undertake his journey.

It is clear that Herodotus travelled all over Egypt. Greek communities in Egypt allowed him to travel and to have privileged access to historical sites. In the cities of the Delta he managed to visit the main temples, and he even participated in public festivals. Herodotus is well acquainted with the priestly mode of life. He lays great stress on their obligation to maintain a high level of ritual purity: they shaved their bodies every other day, had to be circumcised, wore only linen garments and sandals of papyrus, and washed twice a day and twice a night.[58]

With exception of the Osirian mysteries, about which, however, he does not reveal any important knowledge, the few religious references that he captured from the autochthonous sources are misleading to say the least. In the south, his reception was even worse, and he probably could not visit any important site, not even in order to view it from the exterior. Herodotus' Greek affiliation and, perhaps more importantly, his inability to speak the Egyptian language surely raised serious obstacles in the most important Egyptian temples. Egyptians considered everyone a foreigner who did not speak Egyptian (2.18, 158.5). Moreover, culture was the key factor in defining ethnicity. Eating habits that did not conform to good Egyptian practice were considered disgraceful (2.36.2). It is evident that Herodotus found the Egyptian attitude to foreigners a mixture of cultural superiority and distaste, which was reinforced by religious taboos.[59] However, despite his cold reception from the Egyptian priests, Herodotus seems to hide his discomfiture as much as possible, weaving an elaborate narrative that suggests the opposite, perhaps looking to impress his Greek audience and to validate the status of his writings.[60]

The unsoundness of information drawn from Herodotus thus gives us an important testimony about Egyptian 'xenophobia', so intensely experienced under Assyrian and Persian domination. During the Late Period, Egyptian temples became aware of their role in the preservation of the local tradition and, after the Persian invasion, they were the focus of Egyptian identity. Self-segregation was the cultural response towards foreign occupation and, in this scenario, we can understand why Herodotus would not have been welcomed. Herodotus' writings have to be examined in the light of the Egyptian reaction towards foreign occupation, and the distorted information that we find in these accounts actually provides an important and unique historical testimony concerning the Egyptian mindset during this period. On the basis of the picture that we have today regarding the priestly culture of the Late Period, it is hard to imagine that Egyptian priests would openly speak with foreigners about matters at the core of their knowledge and belief system.

Only in Memphis, where a multicultural community was gaining shape, was Herodotus able to have direct access to a mass of priestly knowledge. This Memphite connection was absolutely crucial to Herodotus. At that time, Memphis had gained an unprecedented political and religious status. During the Twenty-Fifth Dynasty, Kushite kings had launched a vast programme of cultural renewal of Egypt, and Memphis regained its status as the religious capital of the Two Lands. With the reunification of Egypt under the power of Psammetikhos I, this role gained further political significance. The exceptional status of Memphis was expressed in theological terms by reaffirming the temple of Ptah as the centre of creation, the holiest place of the Two Lands. Since the mercenaries (Greeks, Jews, and Phoenicians) played a significant role in the military unification of the country, when they moved to Memphis during the reign of Ahmose (Amasis: 570–526 BC), not only did they contribute to reshape the cultural climate of the capital of Egypt, but they also became invested in the cosmic role they played. The impact of these ideological representations on the Greek community is detected in the Greek word used to name Egypt, *Aiguptos*, which derives from the Egyptian name of the Temple of Ptah, Hutkaptah, i.e., the 'The House of the Ka of Ptah'. In other words, the Temple of Ptah in Memphis was seen by the Greeks as the seat of Egypt's quintessential identity.

The writings of Herodotus thus reflect these circumstances. Although Naukratis certainly played the role of the gateway of Egypt, Memphis was the place to go in order to gain access to the core of Egypt's wisdom and self-knowledge.

Book II reveals that Memphite priests conveyed important knowledge and provided priceless information based on their own historical records. It is also possible that these priests were able to speak Greek themselves. Since Herodotus does not reveal any knowledge of the cult, ritual, or even the sanctuaries of the temple, his contact with the priests could only have taken place in the priestly community of the House of Life, which was the academy of the temple, with scholars involved not only in the administration and management of temple properties, but also in the study and preservation of the local tradition. The writings of Herodotus are thus revealing about the contact established between autochthonous temples and foreign travellers during the Persian occupation. In the Delta, some of the temples were open to foreigners, such as the Temple of Neith in Sais, but, as far as we know, their priests hardly conveyed any important knowledge of their own traditions. The situation in Upper Egypt was even worse, and, particularly in Thebes, the priests were not receptive to foreigners.[61]

Only in Memphis, Herodotus found the openness to carry out his historical inquiry. This is explained by the multicultural status of the city. Greek settlers had lived there long enough to engage themselves in the intellectual tradition of the House of Life of the Temple of Ptah. The burial ground of the Hellenomemphites, in Abusir, has given us the earliest extant Greek book, a private fourth-century copy on papyrus of a poem by Timotheus of Miletus,[62] which shows the cultural status of this community. It is, therefore, possible that the members of this community got involved with the local intellectual elite, in the context of the House of Life, where the priests were learned both in Egyptian and Greek tradition, as Herodotus clearly shows. The importance of the Memphite House of Life also echoes in the Demotic tradition, and tales such as *Setne I* (written in *Cairo Papyrus #30646*) make clear allusion to the role played by the House of Life in the education of youngsters.[63] Documents such as the *Book of Thoth*, the *Papyrus Salt #825*, and the *Book of the Fayum*, although dating from the Graeco-Roman Period, show the vigour and richness of the Demotic tradition that flourished in the Egyptian Houses of Life.[64] In Memphis, the House of Life was the only one that, by the time of Herodotus' journey, gathered Egyptian and Greek sages. This unexpected interaction probably triggered the cultural phenomenon that would shape Graeco-Roman Egypt: the Hellenization of the Egyptian tradition.[65] The writings of Herodotus are thus crucial to document the beginning of the cultural trend that would become prevalent in Greco-Roman Egypt and, in this perspective, Herodotus offers an unrivalled historical document.

Notes

1 Néret 2002.
2 Araújo 2013: 171–95.
3 Monumental Royal Lists can be found in the cenotaph temple of Seti I in Abydos and in the Chamber of the Ancestors in Karnak. The Palermo Stone (containing royal

annals of the Old Kingdom), dating from the Fifth Dynasty, also provided an historical account of the main events of each reign. The *Canon of Turin* was written in hieratic during the Nineteenth Dynasty. See Araújo 2013: 173–4.

4   See Canhão 2013: 292.

5   Lloyd 2002: 419.

6   Herodotus relied on observation to describe the monuments: pyramids at Giza: 2.125.6; Thebes: 2.143.3; the Labyrinth: 148; Lake Moeris: 150.2; Sais: 170.2).

7   Remarks on geology and geography reveal a thorough observation of the country, with its fauna and flora (2.5.1, 8.3, 10.1, 12.1, 29.1).

8   See the description of the phoenix (2.73.1) and the skeletons of the flying snakes (2.75.1).

9   Lloyd 2002: 425.

10 Translations are adapted from Rawlinson 1942 here and elsewhere.

11 See Lloyd 1976: 237. See also Lloyd 2002: 423.

12 Herodotus' writings provide the first and earliest account of the period in any language. Lloyd 1976: 238.

13 Lloyd 1976: 231.

14 Sousa 2013: 243–7.

15 Lloyd 1976: 223.

16 Lloyd 1976: 224.

17 Lloyd 2000: 372. See also Lloyd 1983: 309–10.

18 Greek mercenaries were employed in the invasion of Nubia in 593–592 BC during the campaign of Psammetikhos II, which took them as far as the Third Cataract. On their return, while passing by Abu Simbel, a contingent of Greek soldiers recorded their passing in inscriptions on one of the *colossi* of Ramses II. See Lloyd 1976: 224.

19 Lloyd 2000: 373.

20 Lloyd 1976: 225.

21 Lloyd 1976: 225.

22 Although the city was founded by Milesians, members of other east Greek cities were also firmly established there, as well as traders from the island state of Aigina in the Saronic Gulf south of Athens. See Lloyd 1976: 224.

23 Lloyd 2000: 374.

24 Famous figures in the history of Greek culture were alleged to have visited Egypt and acquired wisdom or knowledge there, such as Homer, Lycurgus, Solon, and Pythagoras. Although the historicity of such traditions is highly questionable (Lloyd 1976: 224) some of them were certainly made available in written works. Hecataeus of Miletus is surely the most important written source for Herodotus, especially on geography and geology, zoology, Egyptian food, botany, shipping.

25 Lloyd 2000: 381.

26 The precise date of Herodotus' visit to Egypt cannot be determined, but the probabilities favour a date between 449 and 430 BC. See Lloyd 1976: 226.

27 Lloyd 1983: 321. The royal tombs stood in the courtyard preceding the hypostyle hall of the Temple of Neith and follow the temple-court burial practices found earlier at Medinet Habu and Tanis. See Wilson 2016: 86–7 and Dodson & Ikram 2008: 270–3.

28 Sousa 2007: 279–302.

29 Before the Graeco-Roman Period, there already existed many shrines dedicated to Osiris. From Abydos date the oldest known structures, such as the ritual tomb of Umm el Qaab dating from the Middle Kingdom (O'Connor 2009: 90) and the *Osireion* of the cenotaph temple of Seti I (O'Connor 2009: 50–1). In Karnak several Osirian shrines are attested, all of them built from the Third Intermediate period onwards, such as the *Osireion* of Taharka (see Sousa 2007).

30 The foundations of Khufu's causeway rose to the height of more than 40 metres. See Lehner 1997: 109.

31 Dodson & Ikram 2008: 291.
32 O'Connor 2009: 50–1. This *Osireion* is probably the prototype of the later crypts of Osiris. Note the Osireion of Taharka in the Temple of Karnak (Sousa 2007). See also Cooney 2000.
33 Sauneron 2000: 83.
34 The importance of genealogy was so strong that that Herodotus had the impression that Egypt was a caste system: "The Egyptians are divided into seven classes: priests, warriors, cowherds, swineherds, merchants, interpreters, and pilots" (2.64). See Assmann 2002: 297.
35 Andreu, Rutschowscaya, & Ziegler 1997: 114.
36 Kruchten 1989.
37 See Lloyd 1983: 303.
38 Demotic literature, such as the *Prophecy of the Lamb*, reflects these events. See Bresciani 1969: 561–2.
39 Not even a brief description of the city is provided, which might have reported interchanges revealing whether Herodotus had truly spoken with Heliopolitan priests. Probably this sort of interaction had not in fact occurred in Heliopolis.
40 Assmann 2002: 383.
41 Lloyd 1976: 226.
42 Bagnall & Rathbone 2018: 47. See Brandwood pp. 18–19.
43 See for example the story of Sethon for which see Griffith 1900: 12.
44 Clayton 1994: 48.
45 Lloyd 2000: 385.
46 Assmann 2002: 396.
47 See Wilkinson 2000: 74.
48 *Book of the Dead*, ch. 148 (P. Nu), in Assmann 2002: 394–5.
49 See Assmann (2002: 394): "Taboos were valid for the priests, not for Egyptians in general. Priests had to prepare themselves for sacred duties by strict purity and abstinence rules; analogously – within the category of secrecy – priests were subjected to arcane discipline, which was designed to preserve the sacred rites from profanation, not necessarily by foreigners but by the uninitiated."
50 See Lloyd 1983: 322–3.
51 Nicholson 2016: 27. See also Lloyd 1983: 324.
52 Sousa 2011: 97–102.
53 Araújo 2013.
54 Demichelis 2015: 257.
55 Clayton 1994: 20.
56 Callender 2000: 166.
57 The chronology is often inadequate: the pyramid builders are badly displaced (2.124.1) and their reign-lengths are incorrect (127.1, 3; 133.1, 5) as is that of Sabakos (137.2; 139.3); the order of succession is sometimes wrong (127.1; 129.1); and attempts to locate rulers in terms of years can be erroneous (13.1; 10.2; 142.2–3). However, infelicities of this kind are concentrated in the first half of the historical section, and the chronology of the account of the Saite rulers from Psammetikhos onwards is much more accurate. See Lloyd 1976: 237.
58 Lloyd 1983: 308.
59 Lloyd 1983: 316.
60 It has been pointed out that Herodotus' writings aim at correcting or developing the statements previously reported by other authors. See Thomas 2006: 67.
61 See Sousa 2013: 240–1.
62 Bagnall & Rathbone 2018: 36.
63 Griffith 1900; Lichtheim 1980: 127–37.
64 Jasnow & Zauzich 2014: 48–9.
65 Sousa 2017.

Bibliography

Andreu, G., Rutschowscaya, M.-H. & Ziegler, C. 1997. *Ancient Egypt at the Louvre*. Paris (Hachette).

Araújo, L. 2013. "Manetho and the History of Egypt." In Sousa, R., Fialho, M., Haggag, M., & Rodrigues, N., eds., *Alexandrea ad Aegyptum: The Legacy of Multiculturalism in Antiquity*. Porto & Coimbra (CITCEM, CECH), 171–95.

Assmann, J. 2002. *The Mind of Egypt: History and Meaning in the Time of the Pharaohs*. Cambridge, MA, & London (Harvard University Press).

Bagnall, R. & Rathbone, D., eds. 2018. *Egypt: From Alexander to the Copts*. Cairo (The American University in Cairo Press).

Bresciani, E. 1969. *Letteratura e Poesia dell'Antico Egitto*. Turin (Fabri Editore).

Callender, G. 2000. "The Middle Kingdom Renaissance (c. 2055–1650 BC)." In Shaw, I., ed., *The Oxford History of Ancient Egypt*. Oxford (Oxford University Press), 148–83.

Canhão, T. 2013. "A Timeless Legacy: The Calendars of Ancient Egypt." In Sousa, R., Fialho, M., Haggag, M., & Rodrigues, M., eds., *Alexandrea ad Aegyptum: The Legacy of Multiculturalism in Antiquity*. Porto & Coimbra (CITCEM, CECH), 271–82.

Clayton, P. 1994. *Chronicle of the Pharaohs: The Reign-by-Reign Record of the Rulers and Dynasties of Ancient Egypt*. London (Thames & Hudson).

Cooney, K. 2000. "The Edifice of Taharqa by the Sacred Lake: Ritual Function and the Role of the King." *Journal of the American Research Center in Egypt* 37: 15–47.

Demichelis, S. 2015. "The papyri in the Museo Egizio". *Museo Egizio*. Turin (Fondazione Museo Egizio), 254–65.

Dodson, A. & Ikram, S. 2008. *The Tomb in Ancient Egypt: Royal and Private Sepulchres from the Early Dynastic Period to the Romans*. London (Thames & Hudson).

Griffith, F. 1900. *Stories of the High Priests of Memphis: The Dethon of Herodotus and the Demotic Tales of Khamuas*, Vols. 1–2. Oxford (Clarendon Press).

Herodotus. 1942. *The Persian Wars*. Translated by G. Rawlinson. New York, NY (Modern Library/Random House).

Jasnow, R. & Zauzich, K.-T. 2014. *Conversations in the House of Life: A New Translation of the Ancient Egyptian Book of Thoth*. Wiesbaden (Harrassowitz Verlag).

Kruchten, J.-M. 1989. *Les Annales des Prêtres de Karnak (XXI–XXIII Dynasties) et Autres Textes Contemporains Relatifs à l'Initiation des Prêtres d'Amon (avec un chapitre archéologique par Thierry Zimmer)*. Orientalia Lovaniensia Analecta, 32. Louvain (Departement Oriëntalistiek).

Lehner, M. 1997. *The Complete Pyramids*. London (Thames & Hudson).

Lichtheim, M. 1980. *Ancient Egyptian Literature*, Vol. 3. Berkeley & Los Angeles, CA (University of California Press).

Lloyd, A. 1976. *Herodotus: Book II, Commentary 1–98*. Leiden (Brill).

———. 1983. "The Late Period." In Trigger, B.G., Kemp, B.J., O'Connor, D., & Lloyd, A. (eds.), *Ancient Egypt: A Social History*. Cambridge (Cambridge University Press), 279–349.

———. 2000. "The Late Period (664–332 BC)." In Shaw, I., ed., *The Oxford History of Ancient Egypt*. Oxford (Oxford University Press), 369–94.

———. 2002. "Egypt." In Bakker, E., Jong, E., & Wees, H., eds., *Brill's Companion to Herodotus*. Leiden (Brill), 415–36.

Néret, G., ed. 2002. *Description de l'Égypte*. Köln (Tashen).

Nicholson, P. 2016. "The Sacred Animal Necropolis at North Saqqara: Narrative of a Ritual Landscape." In Price, C., Forshaw, R., Chamberlain, A., & Nicholson, P., eds.,

Mummies, Magic and Medicine in Ancient Egypt: Multidisciplinary Essays for Rosalie David. Manchester (Manchester University Press), 19–31.

O'Connor, D. 2009. *Abydos: Egypt's First Pharaohs and the Cult of Osiris*. Cairo (The American University in Cairo Press).

Sauneron, S. 2000. *The Priests of Ancient Egypt²*. Ithaca, NY & London (Cornell University Press).

Sousa, R. 2007. "O edifício de Taharka no lago sagrado de Karnak: simbolismo e função ritual." In *Arte Pré-Clássica: Colóquio comemorativo dos vinte anos do Instituto Oriental da Faculdade de Letras da Universidade de Lisboa*. Lisboa (Instituto Oriental-FLUL), 279–302.

———. 2011. *O Livro das Origens: A inscrição teológica da Pedra de Chabaka*. Lisboa (Fundação Calouste Gulbenkian).

———. 2013. "Lost in Translation: The Hellenization of the Egyptian Tradition." In Sousa, R., Fialho, M., Haggag, M., & Rodrigues, M., eds., *Alexandrea ad Aegyptum: The Legacy of Multiculturalism in Antiquity*. Porto & Coimbra (CITCEM, CECH), 222–31.

———. 2017. "The Shabaka Stone and the Monumentalization of the Memphite Tradition." In Verschoor, V., Stuart, A., & Demarée, C., eds., *Imaging and Imagining the Memphite Necropolis: Liber Amicorum René van Walsem*. Leiden & Leuvein (Nederlands Instituut voor het Nabije Oosten – Peeters Publishers), 155–66.

Thomas, R. 2006. "The Intellectual Milieu of Herodotus." In Dewald, C., & Marincola, J., eds., *Cambridge Companion to Herodotus*. Cambridge (Cambridge University Press), 60–75.

Wilkinson, R. 2000. *The Complete Temples of Ancient Egypt*. London (Thames & Hudson).

Wilson, P. 2016. "A Psamtek Ushabti and a Granite Block from Sais (Sa el-Hagar)." In Price, C., Forshaw, R., Chamberlain, A., & Nicholson, P., eds., *Mummies, Magic and Medicine in Ancient Egypt: Multidisciplinary Essays for Rosalie David*. Manchester (Manchester University Press), 75–94.

10   The Greeks as seen from the east

Xerxes' European enemy

Maria de Fátima Silva

This was the vision: Xerxes saw himself crowned with a wreath of olive-tree leaves and the olive branches reach over the entire earth; but then the crown he wore would disappear.

—*Herodotus 7.19.1*

Book VII of Herodotus' *Histories* is fundamental for the establishment of the conditions under which Xerxes' military expedition against Greece began. We know that this project is not a proposal that originated with Xerxes, since it was a legacy of Darius (7.1.1–7.2.1), his father, which Xerxes now had to redefine and implement. That is why there is some relevant information on the matter that is available from the text of Herodotus before Book VII that can help us develop a more systematic appreciation of the decision to invade. Thus, the historian from Halicarnassus chooses to introduce his narrative of the campaign with a kind of prologue consisting of an analysis of the motivations, the aims, and the conditions under which the campaign eventuated, and, most particularly, a presentation of the knowledge that the Persians had, or thought they had, of their Greek enemy. Naturally our investigation of these issues sheds light primarily on Herodotean historiography – being mindful of its fundamental place in the origins of Hellenic historiography – and Herodotus' exploration of pathways by which an alien culture belonging to an Iranian people engineered in the form of Xerxes' invasion what was arguably the most momentous episode in Greek history. It is inevitable that Herodotus envision this 'clash of cultures' through a lens shaped by qualities that where distinct to the Greek *ethnos*.

For his composition of those *proemic* chapters, the author basically uses narrative models that had become a pattern in his description of various campaigns that the Persian empire waged against its successive enemies.[1] In other words, albeit in a larger dimension, given the climactic importance of the campaign against Greece, Book VII includes a kind of intratextual dialogue with the previous books in *Histories* as concerns the narrative of the main Persian campaigns in conceptual terms, such as Cyrus against the Massagetai (1.204–8), Cambyses against the Ethiopians (3.17–25.2), or Darius against the Scythians (4.1–98). This means that a discussion of the causes that trigger the expedition, a description of the nature of the enemy, or a forecast of the expected outcome has pride of place in all these episodes. In Book VII, this leading component is present at different moments. First and foremost, Herodotus establishes an *agōn* between Mardonios and Artabanos, respectively Xerxes' cousin and uncle, who have opposite opinions on the appropriateness of the campaign: while Mardonios defends it quite enthusiastically Artabanos is rather reticent concerning its timing and risks. As for the king's opinion, it wavers between the two extreme positions,[2] which serves to extend the speculation about the project's basic framework. Divine or transcendent factors intervene to settle the dispute and guarantee that the army will start its march.

There then follows a catalogue of the recruited forces and their itinerary, which, in the latter case, is quite extensive and detailed, and interspersed, at crucial moments, with new 'conversations' that provide the king with relevant information on the route to be taken, on the enemy they are fast approaching, and on how to foresee their or his reactions; this happens, first, in a dialogue between Xerxes and Artabanos who discuss the expected difficulties, globally, such as those pertaining to the terrain and its natural conditions; then, another dialogue between Xerxes and Demaratos, the Lacedaemonian, this time not based on Persian experiences or opinions but rather on a Greek exile's objective knowledge of the character of his countrymen, an interlocutor aiming to enlighten the king on the expected reaction of the enemy forces. These different episodes, corresponding to crucial moments of the narrative, symbolically signal some of the key stages of the expedition:[3] the first when they are still at Susa and when the expedition is still being planned; the second at the Hellespont, exactly when they cross the border between Asia and Europe; and, last, Demaratos' information, which had been requested in Doriskos – where the Persian king gathered, organized, and enumerated his forces – and was issued at the very last moment before the true attack on Greece, by land and by sea, was launched.

Besides establishing an internal dialogue with other passages of the *Histories*, Book VII also provides a definition of the enemy's field of reference that is consonant with its description in other contemporary sources, the most obvious case being Aeschylus' depiction in the *Persians*, despite the difference, both in basic character and in style, of the historiographical narrative and the dramatic fiction offered by the two authors. However, the version provided by the two texts is generally coincident; or, perhaps, from a more specific perspective, the dialogue of queen Atossa with the Chorus in the *Persians* (230–45), seeking to clarify her doubts as to the nature of the Greek enemy, is essentially expanded in the successive dialogues between Xerxes and his different interlocutors. Lastly, even if we decide not to identify a close, direct relationship between the two texts, we certainly must acknowledge the fact that Aeschylus and Herodotus share the same context and express a similar opinion on key events of what was then the recent history of Greece.

A background to Xerxes' campaign against Greece

> Atossa – Have they an army so well provided with men?
> Coryphaeus – Such an army as has inflicted great harm upon the Medes.
>
> Aeschylus *Persians* 235–6

Atossa, queen of Persia, wife to Darius and Xerxes' mother, who in Aeschylus' *Persians* requests some information on the Greek enemy, is the same person who, in Herodotus 3.134.1–5, takes the initiative of encouraging her husband, Darius, to wage war against Hellas; first and foremost, she advances arguments pertaining to home politics – instigating the king to honour his ancestors' tradition as conquerors, thereby ensuring the respect of his subjects[4] – while also considering the nature and characteristics of the target to be conquered (3.134.5: "from what I hear"); and, although her next argument is clearly a woman's argument – "I wish to have female servants from Lakonia, from Argos, from Attica, and from Corinth"[5] – it becomes quite obvious that the regions mentioned by the queen correspond to points of reference in the Greek map, principally known for the prominence of their peoples, especially from the cultural perspective.

With time and the different military and political experiences undergone by Persia, other more significant motives are added to these incipient reasons expressed by Atossa, the one who is a triggering element of the project in Herodotus. First, as a preamble to an Asian attack on European territory, the Persian and Greek interests had a confrontation at Sardis, during the Ionian rebellion against the Persian power, organized openly by Aristagoras of Miletos and ostensibly by Histiaios, which had the active intervention of Athens and Eretria.[6] Darius found a new pretext for his campaign in that political gambit; and he did it, very ably, though not directly highlighting the Ionians, the true promoters of the rebellion, but, in a symbolic gesture, focussing on a project of revenge against the Athenians (5.105.1–2): "He took his bow, pointed an arrow upwards towards the sky and, shooting it into the air, exclaimed: 'Zeus, let me take revenge on the Athenians!'."[7] And he committed himself to that exact purpose. That was how Mardonios (6.43.4), and Datis and Artaphernes after him, became commanders of the military forces that were to attack the two enemy cities of Athens and Eretria (6.94.2, 119.1). But the designs of the Persian king went further than that; his intention was not just vengeance; he was also seeking to expand his empire by annexing a larger territory, which corresponded to the entire Greek nation (6.44–5). Ambition was also a decisive factor in Darius' projects.

However, the outcome did not match the king's expectations. It is true that Eretria did not put up any significant resistance; its temples were burnt down, in revenge for the sanctuaries that had been destroyed before in Sardis, and its people were made slaves (6.101.3). Athens, on the contrary, put up a very successful resistance at Marathon (6.112.1–2), which became, according to Herodotus, a sort of rehearsal for resistance against the future attacks that Xerxes was planning. The different outcome in the confrontation between the Persian and Greek forces was first and foremost determined by the unawareness and the surprise natural to an invader *vis-à-vis* the strategy of their unknown enemy:

> As soon as the order to advance was issued, the Athenians charged the barbarians. . . . The Persians, however, seeing the Greeks running towards them, prepared to receive them, believing that they had gone mad, and a fatal madness it must be, because rumour had it that they were few in number and came on at a run without the support of either their troopers or their archers.

This short description includes strategic factors and criteria of analysis that serve as a preamble to other equivalent situations that will follow during Xerxes' campaign. First, the Greeks taking advantage of the invader's surprise at their unconventional actions was destined to happen again. Used to acting in a specific manner on the battlefield, the Persians were unable to understand their enemy's reactions, which they mostly disregarded as an act of mere senselessness. They were first astounded at the small number of men attacking and at the disproportion between the enemy forces and their own deployment; then they were shocked at what seemed to them to be an absence of obedience to command in the Athenians' seemingly anarchical run, with no apparent coordination between the infantry, the cavalry, and the archers. From the attackers' perspective, however, the aim was exactly to catch their enemies unawares (as Herodotus explains, "They were in fact – as far as we know – the first Hellenes to use the tactic of charging the enemy at a run" [6.112.3]), to which was added their valiant determination when the traditional fear usually produced by the mere name of 'Medes' gave way to the experience of a direct confrontation. However, the Persians did not learn their lesson of prudence and respect for their opponents at Marathon, having rather added another grievance to avenge their increasingly visible enemies, the Greeks (7.1.1).

Therefore, the symmetry set by Herodotus between the process that led Darius to attack and the one that encouraged Xerxes to take up his father's project is quite obvious. With Xerxes initially not too interested in waging warfare against the Hellenes (7.5.1), now it is Mardonios' voice – like that of Atossa had been with Darius – that provides the arguments. The first of those arguments were, as in the previous dialogue between the royal couple, reasons of internal politics (7.5.2–3, 7.8α.2, β1–2, γ1–2, 9.1–2, 11.2); the fame afforded by the expedition would bring the king not only prestige and more wealth but it would also grant him protection against any attack against his empire; furthermore, his defeats at Sardis and then at Marathon would be adequately avenged through this new campaign. These are arguments that the king himself repeats before an assembly of his leading men, which he summons to announce his plans publicly, though speaking before some who, like Artabanos, are opposed to his project. However, Mardonios had yet another private motive – which did not include gaining beautiful Greek women slaves, but rather rested on obtaining the distinction of governing Greece as satrap (7.6.1).

There is, however, a certain lack of definition as regards the concrete target of the Persian invaders, which gradually grows with time and the setbacks suffered: from Athens as the initial central target, the Persian ambition extends to the whole of Greece and, in a crescendo, to the whole of Europe (7.8.γ1, "if we subdue this people and their neighbours – the inhabitants of the land of Pelops the Phrygian – the boundaries of the Persian territory will be as large as the celestial domain of Zeus").[8] In its ambitious greatness, Xerxes' project has to overcome the obstacle interposed by the Athenians and the Lacedaemonians (7.8γ3): "From what I have heard, this is the truth: not one city, not one people will remain in this world who dare take up arms against us when those I have mentioned to you have been annihilated." In short, as Xerxes recognizes (7.11.3), "either one takes action or one must endure the attack, and either every land under the Greeks comes under Persian dominion, or vice-versa",[9] according to his belief that the world can only be owned by one of two, symmetrically equivalent, masters, Persia or Greece. With this praise Herodotus capitalizes on the national pride of his audience.

Sources of information on the Greek enemy

The whole international relations network that resulted from the successive conflicts between the eastern empire and Greece, both in Asia and in Europe, provided the Persians with a number of signs and messages on the nature and the attitude of the enemy they now planned to attack once again. With no objective planning tools – such as maps, for example – the only thing they could do was to draw up gradually an itinerary on the basis of different types of information. Both Mardonios, who had led a first attack against the European territory, and Artabanos, who had accompanied Darius' expedition against the Scythians, had well-defined ideas about the Greek enemy, although, of course, they differed as a correlative of their contradictory aims of advancing or of hampering Xerxes' plans.

However, there are repeated references in *Histories* to Greek exiles who were welcomed at the Persian court.[10] One of these men was Demokedes, a physician from Kroton, who became a paradigm of technical skills when he treated the king and the queen who were suffering from serious diseases (3.129, 133), which eventually earned him the opportunity to flee back to Greece. At a time when espionage was encouraged by the war situation, and the Persians were aware of how insufficient their knowledge was, and, therefore, how it would be prudent to try and expand it, Darius had already entrusted the Greek physician, following Atossa's suggestion, with the leadership of a reconnaissance mission in the field (3.134.6). However, this mission proved unsuccessful exactly because the Krotoniate run away to his home city (3.137.4). As Herodotus concludes (3.138.4), "these were the first Persians arriving in Greece from Asia, and they came as spies, for the reason explained above".[11]

Darius ultimately failed to obtain any benefit from the collaboration of Demokedes, the Greek physician who found the golden exile granted by Persia unacceptable.

Nonetheless, something similar occurred with Demaratos, the Lacedaemonian, a deposed Spartan king and a collaborationist who provides Xerxes with invaluable information on what to expect from the Greek military resistance. However, out of mere ignorance, according to Herodotus, Xerxes laughs at what he considers to be the disproportionate resistance predicted by the Spartan, since the Greeks were so very inferior in numbers. This means that the availability of advice from first-hand knowledge does not necessarily result in true judgment since the Persian king, blinded by the application of his own cultural criteria, is unable to understand the warnings he is given (7.103.2): "well then, if you praise them so highly, although they are of the same size as you and the Greeks I know, you should beware lest this talk of yours becomes empty bragging".

Using spies in a war situation can also serve the ends of a parallel diplomacy, aimed at influencing the enemy's decisions and changing the course of events.

That is why Xerxes behaves with interested benevolence towards Greek spies who are captured in his territory (7.146–147.1). Instead of ratifying his generals' decision to execute these prisoners, the king showed them his military camp and allowed them to estimate his infantry and cavalry units before releasing them. They thus became messengers about his formidable potential, in the hope that the message they would convey to their own people would discourage his enemies from confronting him, leading them to voluntary surrender.

It is certain that the Greeks from Ionia, despite all the differences between themselves and their continental countrymen, could provide the king with some interesting elements that would add to his knowledge of the enemy. But the opinion that the Persians gradually built of the Ionians, the Aeolians, and the east Dorians tended to portray them as politically weak and not exceedingly skilled in warfare. This is exactly the portrait conveyed by Mardonios, hoping to gain the adhesion of his audience in the Persian assembly where the decision to start the campaign or not is to be taken (7.9α1): "we know their combat strategy, we know that their resources are weak. We have dominion over their sons, those who inhabit our land, the so-called Ionians, Aeolians and Dorians". The opinion voiced contaminates the ethno-valuative profile of the European Hellenes, which, in comparison, is also described by Aeschylus' Atossa (*Pers.* 178) as the "Ionian land".

And lastly, Xerxes was in possession of a paradigmatic image of a certain Hellenic mind frame, provided by his Greek allies, which he was unable to read and interpret. A particularly significant case is that of Artemisia, queen of Halicarnassos, who joined the Persian cause for their campaign against Greece. This female figure, an exception among the male warriors, seems like a compilation of the defining traits of the 'Greek spirit'. Her qualities and motivations are clearly Hellenic (7.99.1): "endowed with courage and a virile spirit, she went on the expedition when she absolutely did not have to do it"; she was thus driven by courage and determination, and, most of all, by freedom. Her weapons for that combat also contrasted with those of her allies. First, as regards quantity of forces, her contribution was somewhat modest: a mere five ships, although the superior quality of her vessels was acknowledged by all (7.99.2–3). She was also different from the rest for her intelligence, which made her the most sensible of all the king's counsellors (7.99.2–3), showing how much the Greek character could take precedence over a certain absence of sharpness that was quite noticeable among the Persian leaders in Herodotus' telling.

Even though they had acquired all this information, the Persian kings were, nonetheless, unable to form an accurate image of the enemy they wished to confront, too convinced as they were of their advantage to be able to grasp the meaning of the different signs that they had been given.

How the Persians viewed their Greek enemy

There is no doubt that the Ionian Greek influence was responsible for the consolidation of that first image that had been gradually forming in the Persian mind for many decades and that tended to include the yet unknown peoples associated with the continental metropolis.[12] Since the submission of Ionia to Croesus of Lydia (1.6.2, 26), and then the conquest by Cyrus the Great (1.141.1–3), a proximity developed between the Asian Greeks and the lords of Susa. Although it had started with submission, the acceptance of Persian rule was then questioned by the Ionian revolt, just before the expeditions against Greece of Darius and later Xerxes. The rebellion was started by the leaders of Miletos, and assisted by their cooperation with Athens and Eritrea. This means that, when the time came for Xerxes to plan his campaign and engage his allies, he was faced with a problem of loyalty concerning his Ionian subjects.

Artabanos' advice seemed all the more prudent, for, seeing that the king's trust in the Ionians' attitudes, which had so far in fact been rather ambiguous, was risky, he urged him to exclude them from his expeditionary forces (7.51.2–3). His argument included an enumeration of the dubious relationship between the Greeks from both sides of the Aegean Sea (7.51.2):

> while, if they should follow us, they either would have to be very dishonest to be able to see their own *mētropolis* enslaved,[13] or very honest, if they seek to secure its freedom. If they prove to be very dishonest, they will be of no use to us; but if they prove very honest, they can cause serious damage to your army.[14]

Xerxes seeks to invalidate his counsellor's advice and persists in placing his trust in the Ionians, despite their ambiguous position. In order to do it, the king mentions a number of recent episodes (7.52.1–2), such as the withdrawal of Darius' expeditionary force against the Scythians – facilitated by Histiaios of Miletus, who was responsible for the continued functioning of the bridge that enabled the troops to cross the Danube and then eventually return to Asia – or the natural interests of those who had their families and properties on Persian soil. As usual, Artabanos' voice is unable to find an echo in the sovereign's perceptions.

On the other hand, the kings of Persia tended to entertain strong feelings of contempt for their enemies, no doubt based on their lack of knowledge as well as on ethnic prejudice.[15] Some intuitive gestures that multiply as the narrative unfolds serve to illustrate those deep-seated feelings. Darius, for example, wishing to show his gratitude towards Demokedes, the Greek physician who had healed him when everybody else had failed to, offers him two pairs of gold shackles (3.130.4) and is surprised at the recipient's reaction of displeasure; Darius, again as a sign of gratitude towards a Persian who had rendered him good services,[16] stated that (4.143.1) "he would rather have men like Megabyzos in a number equivalent to the seeds inside a pomegranate than to having dominion over Greece". When he regarded the Greeks as enemies, mere victory was not enough; his project always included the plan to make the defeated enemy his slaves, who must come before him in fetters (6.94.2).

In line with the symbolic practice to which the Persian king always resorted when preparing a military expedition,[17] Darius repeatedly sent for tribute of earth and water from different Greek cities as a test to see whether they would accept or resist his authority (5.17.2; 5.18.1; 5.73.2; 6.48.1–2). The same gesture of war diplomacy was repeated by Xerxes (7.32, 131–2), not as a mere *pro forma* gesture but because he believed that, given the magnitude of his campaign, even the usually uncompliant Greeks might this time adopt a different attitude as a result of their panic. The responses he obtained, i.e., whether or not those signs of submission were sent to him, gradually helped the king compose the mental portrait of the Hellenes' reaction to the Persian invasion (7.138.2), and raised different expectations, with some cities believing they were safe because they had sent the king their tokens of earth and water, and others thinking that they had become preferential targets because they had refused to comply with the king's request. Some refusals, however, were quite extreme, helping the invaders define the main foci of resistance. Disrespectful of the rules of immunity that protected messengers, the Athenians and the Lacedaemonians (6.48–49, 7.133.1) had thrown Darius' men into the *barathron* (a place of execution) and into a pit respectively, whence they were invited to "take the earth and water requested". They were thus responding to the symbolism of slavery with the symbolism of rejection and freedom. For that reason, Xerxes avoided making the same mistake for a second time, and he was able to establish a hierarchy in the conflict, having come to the conclusion that confrontation with both the Athenians and Lacedaemonians was inevitable.

Besides this objective element – the Greek cities' response to the Persian 'ultimatum' – the Achaemenid kings were overwhelmed with contradictory opinions on their European enemy, depending on their informants' differing purposes. The same Megabyzos, whose loyalty was much appreciated by Darius, had offered the king some sound advice on Histiaios of Miletos, a symbol of the Greeks of Asia Minor, describing him as "smart and ambitious" (5.23.1–2); to allow the Ionians to fortify a Thracian city would be excessively risky for the stability of Persian power in the region. In fact, that territory had all the conditions for realizing what Megabyzos outlined, even if only unconsciously, as the Greek advantages in their obstruction of Asian power: the exploitation of native wood, useful for shipbuilding, and of the silver mines that would provide them with material means for warfare, besides also the possibility of recruiting allies in a territory where the Greek and barbarian populations were very numerous. The Greeks naval skills as well as their capacity to mobilize resources were 'prophetically' implicit in Megabyzos' advice.

In the *agōn* between Mardonios and Artabanos over the timing of the expedition against Greece, the different positions of the two speakers, one in favour, the other against it, explain their different perceptions of the enemy's personality. Mardonios, who was of the opinion that the expedition should be launched, emphasizes the Hellenes' "arrogance and boorishness" (ὑπό τε ἀγνωμοσύνης καὶ σκαιότητος, 7.9β1), as shown by the wrong strategy they had used in their internal combats.[18] As for Artabanos, who was quite reticent about the possibility of success, he resorts to the similarity between this plan and the one used against the Scythians to counter Mardonios' image (7.10α3) by arguing that they are "men who are much better (ἀμείνονας) than the Scythians, men who are said to be excellent fighters (ἄριστοι) both at sea and on land", and concludes his argument by greatly praising the Athenians and the Lacedaemonians.

Xerxes' contact with Demaratos, the Lacedaemonian exile, during the expedition, completes this portrait of the enemy, although his response fails both to clarify the Xerxes' doubts and to convince him. More effectively than citing the resources or the strategies appreciated by Mardonios and Artabanos, this time the Greek informed the king about the Spartans' values. Being convinced of his advantages in terms of number and the efficiency of autocratic command, the king expresses them in the form of merely rhetorical questions (7.101.2):

[W]ould the Greeks dare to resist and raise weapons against me? In fact, it seems that even if the Greeks and all the other nations from the west were to unite against me, they would not be able to resist my attack, because there is no coordination between them.

Demaratos' answer includes a definition of the 'Greek identity' (7.102.2–3; cf. 7.104.4–5):

Greece has always been in a state of poverty, but they have brought in excellence as a result of temperance and strict laws. Thanks to that excellence, Greece has been able to defend itself from poverty and servitude. All the Greeks who live in the Dorian lands deserve my praise, although what I am going to say does not apply to all Greeks, only to the Lacedaemonians. First, it is impossible that they will accept your terms, because it would mean servitude for Greece. Besides, they would stand against you and fight you, even if all the other Greeks were to join you. As for their number, do not ask me how many they are to be able to do that, because irrespective of being a thousand in the battlefield, or less, or more than this, they will certainly put up a fight.[19]

While it defines the identity of the Hellenes, this description by Demaratos is presented as contrasting with the Persian cultural tenets. 'Poverty', which for an Asian is a derogatory word, is included in the characteristics of the Greek world and related to (σύντροφος) Greek virtues as a motivation to fight for cultural survival. Therefore, it stimulates *aretē*, which results from qualities of the mind – like moderation – in an articulation in which civic merits, starting with obedience to the law as the highest authority, are to be respected. And, lastly, these values supported their ideal comportment, which could counterbalance their numerical inferiority; on behalf of freedom, the Lacedaemonians, who, according to their countryman Demaratos, are an example of the best, will be ready to fight their enemy irrespective of the proportion of their numbers; their sense of community, the strength of a group united by the same *nomoi*, entails a different interpretation of quantity.[20]

In the face of this difference of opinions and because the criteria that have been put forward make no sense to him, Xerxes' eulogy of the enemy's virtues, delivered before his men, is meant to be nothing but words of encouragement aimed at mobilizing the eastern troops rather than enhancing the real merits of their opponents (7.53.2): "From what I have heard, we are attacking courageous men; if we shall succeed in defeating them, no other army in the whole world will stand against us."

The disproportion of the strategy: number and ideal as opposite weapons

> Atossa – And what leader will be guiding them, commanding their army?
> Coryphaeus – They are slaves or subjects to no one.
>
> Aeschylus *Persians* 241–2

Because the criterion that really impresses an eastern statesman – as Herodotus repeatedly mentions – is that of numbers, with quality only secondary, Mardonios significantly concludes his speech with the following arguments in favour of the expedition (7.9γ1):[21]

> [W]ill there be anyone, my Lord, who is capable of confronting you and fighting against you? You the leader of all the armies and ships of Asia? I do not think Greece's resources will enable them to be that daring. However, if my judgment proves to be wrong and, in an excess of optimism, they would challenge us to fight, they would learn that, in the art of war, we are the best.

Different levels of irony underlie this truly polemic statement. The order in which Mardonios highlights the superiority of the easterners – the numerical advantage of their infantry and navy – indeed corresponds to advantageous Greek qualities and to victories obtained in the most climactic moments of the expedition (first Thermopylai and Artemision and last Plataia and Mykale, all centred on the crucial moment of Salamis). On the other hand, by using the word 'optimism' Mardonios is depreciating the true Greek excellence, the political ideal that encourages Greek men to put up resistance in the face of an enemy, even if this enemy is infinitely superior in number, and an element that might counteract both the number and the fighting quality of their enemies.

With his arguments against the expedition, Artabanos indeed represents a Greek's possible defence of his position as a resistor. Using the experience of the attack against the Scythians as a term of comparison, the old counsellor subverts the criteria formerly put forward by his opponent in the debate. His first advice to Xerxes stresses the enemy's quality as an advantage that takes precedence against quantity (7.10α3; cf. 7.10β1): "but you, my king, you are going to march against men who are far better than the Scythians, men who are said to be excellent fighters both at sea and upon land". However, for the first time Artabanos associates with human excellence the issue of the 'justice' of this attack on Greece, and invokes divine intervention to preserve the balance of the universe (7.10ε). The accord between the powerful and the small depends on the gods, so that the natural asymmetry of the universe might be preserved. With his lightning, the god mostly strikes those who exalt themselves, those who stand out above the rest, inspiring panic in the small ones so that they become able to defend themselves, and this produces such outcomes as human arithmetic can neither predict nor understand.

This point of view, expounded by Artabanos during his debate with Mardonios, remains the same, despite the fact that the authoritative imposition of a dream – as fate's proxy – pushed Xerxes towards disaster, prevailing over all the arguments that he had heard (7.18.2). Before the imminence of disaster, and from the vantage point of his long experience, Artabanos can do nothing but repeat the evidence demonstrated in the past in so many Persian campaigns against enemies who were presumably weaker and more vulnerable, although in reality determined to resist, under the protection of the supreme authority of the gods. Unwavering in his position, Xerxes' uncle will have the opportunity to repeat his arguments when, before the troops gathered in the Hellespont, the king is divided between feelings of pride and safety, explained by the number of his men, and a display of his sorrow for the fragility of human life, which the passing of years must lead to extinction. Infected with the same destructive 'optimism' with which Mardonios had accused their opponent and which will prove to be the king's most injudicious imprudence, Xerxes dares to ask for Artabanos' opinion one more time (7.47.1), hoping to hear a more favourable opinion, now that the campaign is on and augurs well for them. Faced with his uncle's reservations, now stated in even more concrete terms, as the situation requires, about his power to control the situation, with Artabanos emphasizing 'the land and the sea' as two factors that could escape his grasp and would for that reason become his worst enemies, the king hastily imagines that his men are insufficient in number (7.48). This, as we shall see, demonstrates the lack of understanding persistently present in the Asian mind, epitomized by the king, in spite of all the signs conveyed by Artabanos, who reads the situation from a perspective that is more akin to the Hellenic mind frame. To the importance of quantity, the Persian mentality adds the relevance of command, which they saw as monocratic and dictatorial. This is another topic that Herodotus, like Aeschylus before him, includes in the symbolic discussions that take place in the king's presence in crucial moments of the expedition.

When Mardonios examines what could be considered Greek war diplomacy, during his debate with Artabanos in the Persian assembly, he mentions their practice in terms of condemnation. In his opinion, the way they acted in the internal conflicts, which, traditionally divided different cities, was neither adequate nor wise. With this reference, Herodotus signals Greece's traditional tendency for fragmentation, perhaps aiming to juxtapose further contemporary cohesion efforts that, in the case of their resistance to the Persians, had been an important contribution towards their victory (7.9β1–2).[22] Mardonios' first criticism is directed to the Greeks seeming preference for wide, open battlefields, where the advantages for either side are annulled and the losses become as heavy for the winners as they are for the defeated. However, even this prediction, which is, in the opinion of the author of the argument, based on the "ignorance and stupidity" of the leaders, will fail to materialize for Xerxes, because the Greeks will indeed use the characteristics of each place as their ally in their objective of neutral-izing the numerical advantage of the invader (Thermopylai and Salamis being paradigmatic cases). Not to mention, Mardonios goes on, the inconsistency of the fact that peoples that speak the same language cannot understand each other and are unable to overcome their differences through negotiation, in an attempt to avoid resorting to armed conflict. Also, in this case a complex diplomatic game is anticipated, which the Persian attack, given its characteristics, will impose itself on Greek resistance. This means that through Mardonios' criticism Herodotus indicates that the Hellenes' attitudes are adequate for their defence, while simul-taneously showing their unpredictability as an enemy that is quick and adaptable to changing circumstances.

On the Persian side, during a conversation with Demaratos, Xerxes will insist on the rigidity and predictability of a traditional eastern view of power (7.103.4):[23]

> [I]f, like us, they were led by a single commander, they would, for fear of him, become better than they naturally are, and, although they are not many, they would march under the lash upon a numerous enemy. But if they are left at liberty, they will do neither of these things.

Besides their difference, the result of this clash of cultures generates a lack of understanding of the eastern side, which Herodotus gradually identifies as one of the major reasons for the defeat of such a great power.

Phusis as a defence weapon

If, despite all the evidence offered, both the character and the strategy of the Greek enemy remained unknown to the eastern invader, the same was true as concerns the nature of the ground, which, in spite of the Persians' image of Europe, caused them some extremely unpleasant surprises.

In his intervention in favour of the expedition against Greece, Mardonios did not fail to use Europe's vigour as an incentive (7.5.3):

> this was his argument, vengeance, and to this he would add yet another one: that Europe was a very fair region, yielding all types of trees and it was incred-ibly fertile, so much so that only the Great King was worthy of possessing it.

This argument was repeated by Xerxes himself before the council members to whom the king described his plans (7.8α2).

When the expedition reached the Hellespont, Artabanos, a most sensible man, would express, among his major concerns, his opinion about how 'land and sea' would prove to be important obstacles, for he was sure that nature itself would have a word to say regarding the campaign's boldness and excess (7.49.1–2). In Artabanos' view, as a powerful ally of the Greeks, wishing to compensate for their numerical inferiority, *phusis* 'nature' might create difficulties for the invad-ers that would be associated with the disproportionality of their forces. There would not be enough harbours of sufficient scale to protect the huge eastern navy from sea storms (7.49.2) and the land would hardly yield the necessary nourishment to feed such a big army (7.49.4–5). This time Artabanos exchanges arguments with Xerxes himself. Considering that he had not omitted the importance of natural conditions, the king offers a number of precarious solutions with the same reproachful 'optimism': the care to be taken in choosing the best season for the expedition, one to avoid tempests, and the decision to seize products of the land from places occupied by farmers rather than by nomads, as had happened in the much-invoked experience of their Scythian campaign (7.50.4). This will become a starting point for the permanent refutation of these arguments, with nature systematically winning over the excess – in terms of number as well as in terms of recklessness – of the eastern invader.

References to the insufficiency of rivers and lakes to quench the thirst of the massive armed forces often appear along the Persian army's path (7.21.1, 43.1, 108.2, 109.2, 127.2), as is the overwhelming impact of the banquets that the different populations along the line of march saw as their duty to offer the Persian army (7.118–20). The land proved incapable of feeding them, as Artabanos had foreseen. And despite the king's prudent choice of the most favourable season for their journey and all the complex means aimed at subduing nature – like the canal at Mount Athos and the bridges that enabled the army to cross the Hellespont – the truth is that, also at sea, they had to endure tempests and their catastrophic consequences. The first disaster symbolically occurred in their crossing between Asia and Europe, the very first natural barrier to be conquered (7.118–20). The sophisticated engineering works of their Phoenician and Egyptian allies collapsed, being unable to halt the fury of the elements. Of course, Xerxes read all these events as an attack against him sent by the gods and the only consequence that he was able to draw from it was a reason to celebrate and openly express how proud he was in his grandiose project. Besides punishing the sea by means of lash strokes and fetters, treating it as if it were one of his vassals, he insulted it and threatened it, challenging its power (7.35): "Xerxes, the king, will cross you, whether you want it or no."

This was the Persian king's attitude of contempt and self-righteousness when he marched, with unwavering determination, upon an enemy that he in fact did not know. He pictured his adversaries as being weak and senseless; he ignored their alliances and their allies; he dismissed all the warning signs that had reached him from different sources. At the same time, he erroneously applied evaluation criteria to the enemy that pertained to his own ethnicity – number, means, leadership – and adhered to the guiding principles of the Persian Court: preserve your inheritance and strengthen its power. He did not understand how distant this mentality was from that of the Greeks. It was this distance, and ignorance as to its importance, that brought about his unforeseeable weakness. That is why, just like Aeschylus in *Persians*, Herodotus could only foresee the worst outcome for this adventure. It is certain that both authors were echoing a general *doxa*; however, they completed it with a deeper interpretation, in philosophical terms and in a poetic form.

Notes

1 Immerwahr 1966: 68–9 lists the constitutive elements of the traditional model of a military campaign in Herodotus: "1. Plan of aggressor, 2. his preparations, 3. section of causation, 4. march of aggressor to place of action, 5. preparations of defender, 6. march of defender to place of action, 7. battle, 8. epilogue." And then he points out that "the sections preceding and following the action are always more important than the battle itself".

2 For these proemic chapters dedicated to the campaign, Baragwanath 2008: 242 also highlights Herodotus' portrait of Xerxes, "a cautious and reflective, as well as self-determining ruler". This description of Xerxes' attitude creates a space for the usual intervention of the king's advisor – with the monarch promoting discussion or requiring advice – while it also suggests his permanent ineffectiveness, caused by the autocracy of his mindset as a powerful person, or, more specifically, as the holder of power in Persia. Waters (1971: 68–9) expresses a similar opinion. For Immerwahr (1966: 177), Xerxes, more than an individual character, is "a typical Persian in an extreme form, both in magnificence and in cruelty", and also "the typical tyrant . . . motivated by passion rather than by reason".

3 This narrative sequence, which alternates between 'historical' descriptions proper and fictionalized discussions on the logic behind the events, is perhaps modelled on the structure of tragedy, which had strongly influenced Herodotus. These *agones* correspond to moments of suspension and reflection, like their tragic counterparts, a device that was much used and disseminated by Euripides.

4 Cf. Aris. *Pol.* 1313b28.

5 Cf. Ael. *HN* 11.27.

6 Athens' participation in the attack against Sardis, the ancient capital of Lydia and the central pole of Persian power in western Asia Minor (Hdt. 5.99–102), was part of the Ionian revolt, triggered by the rulers of Miletos (Histiaios and Aristagoras) with the subsequent collaboration of Athens and Eretria. With this offensive, Athens became the major enemy of the homeland Greeks standing against Persian interests, and, to some extent, it could already be identified as the main focus of resistance to Xerxes' future invasion of Greek territory. Immerwahr (1956: 266) considers that "the Ionian Revolt is thus treated in the manner of an aggressive war, with the Ionians as the aggressors". Hart 1982: 87 emphasizes the imprudence of the Athenians' decision to get involved in this revolt as Aristagoras' allies: "they embroiled themselves with Persia without gaining anything themselves, they provided Persia with a pretext for imperial expansion into Greece". In the *Histories*, this daring confrontation of the great power of the Persian empire is almost an exception, since the initiative for Persian attacks is generally taken by the Great King himself. The same happened with the Spartan invasion of Samos (3.56.2), symbolically the first Greek crossing into Asia. Mardonios (7.9.2) will underline this paradox: the Persians have conquered several peoples, who have done no injury to them; thus, they have to take vengeance on the Greeks, who started the injustice.

7 This threat is proffered by Darius after asking who the Athenians are (5.105.1). Nenci (1994: 314) considers that this lack of knowledge corresponds to a Persian-centric perspective on the part of Herodotus, which necessarily had an impact on the national pride of his Greek audience. From being an 'illustrious unknown' people the Athenians had now become the winners on the battlefield. See 1.134.2–3 on the decreasing respect of the Persians towards other peoples dictated by their distance from them.

8 Martin 1965: 38–48 speculates on the king's notion of what the world to be conquered and its boundaries could be, in line with his duty of making the boundaries of his power coincide with the totality of the known world, as imposed by tradition. As regards Xerxes' project, Greece was situated at a remote, largely unknown frontier.

9 See n. 6. This mutual threat was eventually substantiated when, in the 460s BC – ten years after the end of the Persian invasion – the Greeks planned to penetrate Asian

territory during Kimon's successful campaigns (cf. Plutarch *Cimon* 6–8), with a view to gaining new territory to colonize; however, Greece's successful annexation of the East took place only much later, in the fourth century BC, through the intervention of Alexander the Great.

10 Some Greek technicians were indeed quite useful to the Persian court. For example, Mandrokles, the Samian engineer, who was commissioned by Darius to build a bridge over the Bosporus to enable the troops involved in the Scythia campaign to cross over to Europe (4.87.4. 88.1–2, 89.1).

11 This was a factfinding expedition comprising, besides Demokedes, Persian aristocrats qualified as 'observers' (κατάσκοποι). The king's comment on the outcome of this mission and its use is quite telling (3.134.6): "only then shall I rush against them knowing exactly what to expect". To illustrate the Persians' lack of knowledge about Greece, Herodotus has Darius respond, when approached in his palace by Syloson of Samos, who came to collect a favour from the king (3.140.2): "which one among the Greeks could be the benefactor to whom I owe an obligation, since I have only recently become king, if *practically none of them has come to us*, then I can say that I owe no debts to the Greeks".

12 On Herodotus' image of the Ionians, see Evans 1991: 13–4. Immerwahr 1966: 230 mentions "their lack of independence and power" and "the disunity among themselves" as Ionian traces in Herodotus. These two characteristics contribute to their bad image, among Greeks and Persians alike, as mediated by the author of the *Histories*. So Immerwahr concludes (1966: 232): "the Ionian Revolt against Darius is therefore considered by Herodotus a slave revolt, and he has little sympathy for it". Finally, although the Persian wars gave back to the Ionians their formal independence, in reality their disunity went on, as did their dependence on foreign powers.

13 When he sought the collaboration of Athens during the uprising of the Ionians against the Persians, Aristagoras of Miletos had used exactly the same argument, i.e., the bond that existed between the *metropolis* and the colony (Herodotus 5.97), which explains why Athens had strong links with some of the Asian Greeks; this was a centuries-old process of colonization since it had started in c. 1000 BC. However, in practice the relationship did not lend itself to easy collaboration; on the one hand, the Ionians tended to accept Persian authority and relinquished their freedom in order to ensure peace for their cities (cf. Herodotus 4.142); on the other, the Athenians tended to be contemptuous of these Asian Greeks, as is abundantly described by Thucydides (e.g., 5.9.1, 6.77.1, 8.25.5).

14 Artabanos' prudent words function as true prophecies as concerns a number of events that were to take place during the expedition, although at the time of creation of the narrative they were, of course, past occurrences; cf. Hdt. 9.103.

15 That was in fact a standard attitude which Herodotus underscores when mentioning the different campaigns; cf. Cyrus, 1.153.1–2; Cambyses, 2.1.2. Martin 1965: 38 defines the Persian king's political theory concerning foreign peoples as follows: "all foreign peoples are bound to come under the rule of the king, who has virtual dominion over them, as has been promised by Ahuramazda. He has but to demand that his right be acknowledged or, if challenged, enforce it. Any legal agreement with the party concerned is out of the question". This rule explains, to a good extent, the king's behaviour regarding his conquest plans.

16 Megabyzos had been charged by Darius with the submission of the regions of the Hellespont to Persian rule. This mission led to the dominion over the northern regions of Greece up to Thessaly, paving the way for a future, more extensive, invasion.

17 Cf. the same practice in Hdt. 4.126; 5.73.2.

18 Strangely enough, since the Greek territory was quite rugged, their strategy seemed to favour plains, i.e., the few available agrarian lands for hoplite warfare. Hart 1982: 80–1 believes that war was planned to erode the adversary's supplies and that this strategy

followed the ancient tradition of preferring the infantry as an army for intervention. Hart does not hesitate to identify behind Mardonios' argument the knowledge that Herodotus himself had of the preferred type of combat in Greece. The commentator also stresses an element that makes war as understood by the Persians different from the war that motivated the Greeks; perhaps Mardonios misses this aspect when he evaluates the enemy: what drove them to frequent wars with one another was the desperate quest for a bit more land to support the population or the desire to prevent any one state from achieving a dangerous eminence among its neighbours. Wars of genuine aggrandisement were extremely rare.

19 There are parallels between this episode and the dialogue between Hydarnes, the Persian, and his guests the Lacedaemonians emissaries, Sperkheios and Boulis, on the value of freedom (7.135.1–136.1). For the eastern military officer, submission to the Great King meant advantages and benefits to be gained and he advised the Lacedaemonians to adhere, for they were a worthy people who deserved the king's recognition. But for the Greeks such advice could only come from one who had never experienced freedom, because, once it has been experienced, it becomes the greatest good that is worth fighting for. And as a sign of their belief, during the royal audience that followed, they refused to prostrate themselves before the sovereign, since in their opinion only the gods deserve that type of homage.

20 As he develops a catalogue of the Greek forces, Herodotus gradually includes some more words of praise for the Persians' enemy. The Satrai, for example, are noted among the Thracians because "they have never accepted anyone's rule" and because they are "excellent warriors" (7.111.1).

21 Evans 1991: 68 describes the personality of Mardonios in Herodotus in the following terms: "The Xerxes of Aeschylus' *Persians* was an impetuous man led on by *kakoi andres*: evil men. Mardonios in the *Histories* of Herodotus took the role of the leading *kakos aner*."

22 The importance of Athens' intervention as a solution to the usual fragmentation of the Greek world and as a means to achieve cohesion in the face of their common enemy, the Persians, is made clear in 7.145. On the arguments Herodotus uses to try and legitimize the defence of private interests as a cause of that fragmentation, see Baragwanath 2008: 203–39.

23 Xerxes shows the same conservatism that had made him choose to wage the campaign against Greece, even if not very enthusiastically at first. For him, the need to prove himself worthy of his ancestors, matching up to them, was a determining factor. On the battleground, the weight of tradition proves an inhibiting factor for the invaders, who lack the flexibility to adapt their behaviour in the face of a specific enemy, with his own specific, and hitherto unknown, characteristics.

Bibliography

Baragwanath, E. 2008. *Motivation and Narrative in Herodotus*. Oxford (Oxford University Press).

Evans, J.A.S. 1991. *Herodotus, Explorer of the Past*. Princeton, NJ (Princeton University Press).

Hart, J. 1982. *Herodotus and Greek History*. London & Canberra (Croom Helm).

Hohti, P. 1974. "Freedom of Speech in Speech Sections in the 'Histories' of Herodotus." *Arctos* 8: 19–29.

Immerwahr, H.R. 1956. "Aspects of Historical Causation in Herodotus." *Transactions of the American Philological Association* 87: 241–80.

———. 1966. *Form and Thought in Herodotus*. Cleveland, OH (American Philological Association).

Martin, V. 1965. "La politique des Achéménides: L'exploration prélude de la conquête."
    Museum Helveticum 22: 38–48.

Nenci, G. 1994. *Erodoto: le Storie: V. La rivolta dell' Ionia.* Milan (Fondazione Lorenzo
    Valla).

Schrader, C. 1994. *Heródoto: Historia Livro VII.* Madrid (Gredos).

Thomas, R. 2000. *Herodotus in Context: Ethnography, Science and the Art of Persuasion.*
    Cambridge (Cambridge University Press).

Waters, K.H. 1971. *Herodotos on Tyrants and Despots.* Wiesbaden (Franz Steiner).

11 Mirages of ethnicity and the distant north in Book IV of the *Histories*

Hyperboreans, Arimaspians, and Issedones

Renaud Gagné

When Herodotus writes over the voices of others, he tends not to erase them, but rather to channel their force and take them in, to redefine them as witnesses of his narrative. The result is something that goes beyond agonistic victory and the settlement of rivalry. A virtual encyclopaedia of possible parallel understandings emerges from the uneven juxtaposition of perspectives that sustains the *Histories*. This is a text that appropriates, condenses and reframes all earlier relevant narrative. The weaving of disparate textual and non-textual presences in that work is hardly captured by the conventional understandings of 'allusion' or 'intertext'. The Herodotean kaleidoscope merges many shades into equivalent patterns. The *Histories* create uncannily familiar landscapes of alternative viewpoints that aggregate parallel versions of reality to make them part of a superior narrative configuration. This is a process I call incorporation.[1] The appropriation of voices and visions that gives such a distinctively layered texture to the *Histories* is integral to the nature of the new knowledge that is presented there. A constant concern with the limitations of cognition characterizes that text. The confines of the knowledge it explores are mostly defined through the negotiations of authority that make up the work's polyphony. Herodotus' orchestration of other voices is operative whenever distinctive knowledge is in play. The scope of the new *epistēmē*, both its reach in time and its reach in space, is largely a matter of incorporation. How does the text frame the other relevant stories on the border of its remit? Where does it situate itself in relation to these voices? And how does it rewrite them in the process? I would like in what follows to briefly revisit one case at the furthest edges of Herodotus' *historia*, and assess the way the outer boundaries of the knowledge claimed by the *Histories* are traced through the text's open engagement with other prominent voices. I will focus on the representation of *ta makrotata* in the most distant north at the beginning of Book IV, and more specifically the role given to the mirage of Hyperborea in the text.[2] Aristeas of Proconnesus, the author of the *Arimaspeia*, and Hecataeus of Miletus, are the two major interlocutors of this dialogue at the edges of text and world.[3]

The first half of Book IV is concerned with the general outlines of the populations that live north of the Pontus.[4] The first chapters deal with the original settlement of the land. Herodotus proceeds by setting various accounts side-by-side, intervening at various points, and progressively leading the audience to a conclusion.[5] After the tales told by the Scythians themselves about their own origins (Targitaus: 4.5–7), the text moves on to describe what "the Greeks who live on the Black Sea" have to say about the question (Heracles and Skythes: 4.8–10), before turning to a more plausible *logos* of successive invasions "which is told alike by Greeks and barbarians" (4.12).[6] Herodotus says explicitly that he is inclined to believe that third tale.[7] The first two stories are genealogical mythic narratives involving supernatural figures, fantastic accounts that would have struck the audience of Herodotus as fanciful fables. They serve as a colourful foil and background to the more straightforward report defended by the historian. The third account, which bluntly restates the objective course of the narrative with which Book IV opens, involves population movements and invasions: the Scythians fled the Massagetae, displacing the Cimmerians and occupying the land that was originally theirs.[8]

That privileged third *logos* is directly juxtaposed with the tale told by Aristeas in the *Arimaspeia*, where a similar pattern of invasions from the north is placed side-by-side with the narrative of invasions favoured by Herodotus.[9] In Aristeas, the flight of the Scythians also displaces the Cimmerians, but they were themselves moving away from the Issedones, not the Massagetae, and the Issedones in turn flee the Arimaspi. The passage reminds us that Aristeas claimed to have visited the Issedones himself, and his version is identified as another *logos* that disagrees with the Scythians. This statement is followed by a long disquisition on the fantastic stories told by the peoples of Proconnesus, Cyzicus, and Metapontum about the extraordinary Apolline traveller who escaped all the normal constraints of humanity (13–16). Aristeas' poem, after all, was the single most detailed and by far the most famous description of the lands beyond the Black Sea, and it comes as no surprise to find it given such a prominent position at the beginning of Herodotus' rewriting of the deep north.[10] What is Herodotus after with this alignment of his narrative with Aristeas, and how can we understand his long excursus on the poet? Are we satisfied by repeating yet again that this is just another paratactic digression? Two alternative considerations stand out.

One is the fact that Herodotus appropriates the familiarity of a standard narrative by this juxtaposition of the two parallel versions. By following the same pattern, he shows that his favoured source is indeed aligned with another well-known tale, that the one is echoed by the other. This allows him to confirm the value of the preferred version through previous knowledge. The reader is not simply asked to accept the authority of the narrator, but invited to participate in the process of evaluation. Here, as elsewhere, the familiarity of a plausible antecedent serves as a tool in the demonstration of *historia*.

Another consideration, more important than the first, is the fact that Herodotus' representation of Aristeas as a parallel account allows him to redefine the great northern epic through the categories of the new *historia*. The *Arimaspeia* was a poem chiefly concerned with what lay further than the Scythian lands, in the realm of the Issedones, the Arimaspi, and the Hyperboreans themselves. An extended, profoundly original reconfiguration of the epic travel narrative, it saw Aristeas go beyond the maritime routes of his Odyssean and Argonautic predecessors to reach deep inland into the realm of the Issedones. If we are to accept something of Maximus of Tyre's testimony, and I see no good reason not to, Aristeas even claimed to have reached the road to Hyperborea through an aerial vision, thus making his journey one that escaped the constraints of mortal travel through land or sea.[11] An extended *Dichterweihe*, the *Arimaspeia* made Aristeas become a companion of Apollo on the *thaumastē hodos* to Hyperborea and back.[12] There is no room for the reality of such claims in Herodotus, and the *Histories* remade the voyage of the possessed poet into a failed *nostos* back from an incomplete journey. The fabulous aspects of the text are transferred to the stories told about Aristeas by people in Proconnesus, Cyzicus and Metapontum.[13] Stories found over more than two centuries at the opposite extremities of the Greek world, in other words, and that can be reached and assessed perfectly well by *historia*. The claims they embody, reduced to an object of enquiry about the legends believed by the peoples of different cities, and even monumentalized in the *agora* of Metapontum, are remade into *thaumata* for the pleasures of marvel and memory. They have no purchase on the reality of lands and peoples in the far north – they are themselves objects of *historia*.

What is left of the poem as a rival voice of enquiry is the endpoint of the land travel described by Aristeas: the territory of the Issedones. The poet's knowledge up to there can be assessed as the report of an *autoptēs*.[14] Everything that lays beyond the land of the Issedones is categorised as *akoē*, and must be evaluated as such.[15] *Akoē* is, emphatically, the main tool of *historia* beyond the reach of *autopsia*.[16] At the heart of the operation is the transformation of Aristeas into an interlocutor. Separated from the eschatological horizon of its poetic narrative and transformed into the report of a travel and an enquiry, the *Arimaspeia* is remade into a claim of direct knowledge about the distant lands now claimed for itself by the new *historia*. This allows for a clear contrast between the methodical, evaluative approach to enquiry championed by Herodotus and the marvellous *apista* of his predecessor on the road to the north.

Chapter 16 begins by offering an exercise in the evaluation of this *akoē*.[17] Following patterns well established at this point in the text, Herodotus contrasts hearsay with the knowledge of *idein*:

τῆς δὲ γῆς τῆς πέρι ὅδε ὁ λόγος ὅρμηται λέγεσθαι, οὐδεὶς οἶδε ἀτρεκέως ὅ τι τὸ κατύπερθέ ἐστι. οὐδενὸς γὰρ δὴ αὐτόπτεω εἰδέναι φαμένου δύναμαι πυθέσθαι· οὐδὲ γὰρ οὐδὲ Ἀριστέης, τοῦ περ ὀλίγῳ πρότερον τούτων μνήμην ἐποιεύμην, οὐδὲ οὗτος προσωτέρω Ἰσσηδόνων αὐτὸς ἐν τοῖσι ἔπεσι ποιέων ἔφησε ἀπικέσθαι, ἀλλὰ τὰ κατύπερθε ἔλεγε ἀκοῇ, φὰς Ἰσσηδόνας εἶναι τοὺς ταῦτα λέγοντας. ἀλλ᾽ ὅσον μὲν ἡμεῖς ἀτρεκέως ἐπὶ μακρότατον οἷοί τε ἐγενόμεθα ἀκοῇ ἐξικέσθαι, πᾶν εἰρήσεται.

As for the lands of which my history has begun to speak, no one exactly knows what lies northward of it; for I can learn from none who claims to know as an eyewitness. For even Aristeas, of whom I lately made mention – even he did not claim to have gone beyond the Issedones, no, not even in his poems; but he spoke of what lay northward by hearsay; saying that the Issedones had so told him. But as far as we have been able to hear an exact report of the farthest lands, all shall be set forth.

The *akoē* of Aristeas about the *makrotaton* is to be incorporated into the *akoē* of Herodotus. Everything that follows up to 4.32 is a contribution to defining what that superior *akoē* is. In the process, elements familiar from the standard narratives are taken over, complexified, rationalized, and given a more plausible shape.[18]

As in the case of the northern invasion narrative, a number of familiar patterns and figures are pulled from the Aristean tradition and woven into the text. Their transposition generates a recurrent effect of plausibility. The *abata*, the impassable mountains that mark the ultimate northern barrier are there, but they are not identified as the Rhipaean Mountains, as even Aristotle would continue to do, and they have no Griffons or special links to Boreas.[19] Although there are no Arimaspi, gold is indeed more abundant in the distant north than just about anywhere else.[20] The just Bald Men do not wage war and are not threatened by their neighbours, like the Hyperboreans of poetic tradition.[21] Fabulous stories on the other hand, reminiscent of the Aristean material, are dismissed. There are no donkeys in the Scythian north.[22] Reports about those who live beyond the mountains, the far-fetched tales about men with goat's feet and men who sleep for six months, are all denied any credibility.[23] Both positive and negative statements draw attention to the presence of the poem.

More complex is the depiction of the Issedones in 4.26, a direct location of engagement with Aristeas.[24] The utterly strange *nomoi* of the Issedones, who give equal power to women, eat the flesh of their deceased fathers together with that of the many beasts sacrificed at the time of death, and even keep their polished skulls as *agalmata* for ritual use, are not condemned or denounced. On the contrary, the Issedones are explicitly said to be *dikaioi*, like the Bald Men, and, exactly as Aristeas himself had done in his poem, Herodotus uses their difference to make a statement about cultural relativity.[25] Contact with the difference of the Issedones is a privileged location for revisiting the sovereign *nomos*.

The cannibalistic *nomoi* of the Issedones are directly compared (*kata per Hellēnes*) to Greek cult in honour of the dead, the *Genesia*.[26] It is probably no coincidence that the one custom mentioned earlier in the *Histories* (3.38 – a programmatic passage) to illustrate the notion of cultural relativity is indeed the obligation of another people for each son to eat his dead father: the main custom that returns in Herodotus' description of the Issedones in 4.26, the people through whose eyes Aristeas had himself long ago so radically experimented with cultural perspective.[27] The material of Herodotus' predecessor, here as elsewhere, is not simply discarded, but creatively reappropriated. The location of ethnographic authority, however, is never allowed to remain in doubt.

Contrary to Hecataeus, who made them Scythian, Herodotus aligns himself with Aristeas in knowing that the Issedones are not part of that *ethnos*.[28] They are a distinct people in that part of the world, one of many in the further north. The existence of the Issedones is not questioned by Herodotus, but they are themselves firmly placed in the realm of *akoē*. What he knows about them, he knows from the Scythians, just like everybody else who has mentioned them – Aristeas included.[29] A key detail is the fact that Herodotus proposes an etymology of *Arimaspoi*, which he (wrongly) derives from the Scythian words *arima* (one) and *spou* (eye).[30] 'Arimaspoi', in other words, the all-important noun that gave the *Arimaspeia* its name, is thus not an Issedonian word, and Herodotus, like everyone else who talks about them, is dependent on the Scythians for information. The implication for the audience is that Aristeas never actually reached the Issedones, contrary to what he said, but, like Herodotus, only heard about them through the Scythians, and then embellished the rest. The poet's claim to autopsy and the value of his *akoē* can thus be properly assessed through *historia*.[31] Herodotus' knowledge of Scythian etymology allows him to tear down a fundamental claim of his ethnographic rival. Reports of reports of reports, the fables about Griffons and one-eyed men are reduced to the status of distant *apista*, like the *aigipodes andres*.[32] Just as the images of the *Arimaspeia* are reinvented for the new landscape of *historia*, the old Ionian poem is itself remade into a reflection of other stories. In Book III already, in a long disquisition on the furthest *eschatiai* and the limits of *autopsia*, the poem of Aristeas is singled out as a false report and a reflection of truth.[33] The beginning of Book IV simply expands this pattern further. Aristeas is the one single autoptic rival with a claim to the *makrotata* in the *Histories*. He deserves more attention than any other author.

What recurs as a leitmotiv throughout the passage is the fact that all of the roads north lead to inaccessible, uninhabited deserts, without exception.[34] The vast area surveyed by Herodotus' discussion of the deep north offers a detailed, precise map of peoples and rivers (much more detailed and precise than anything found in the *Arimaspeia*, one suspects), and confidently asserts that "as far as the land of these Bald Men we have full knowledge (*pollē periphaneiē*) of the country and the nations on the hither side of them" (4.24).[35] Reflecting the seven peoples of the *Arimaspeia* and the seven years of the poet's voyage, the Scythians who visit the ports of the Black Sea, like Olbia, come with seven interpreters and the knowledge of seven languages, and they allow enquiry to have direct access to every single *ethnos* mentioned, beyond the distance of individual travel.[36] Herodotus' demonstration of the range of truthful (*alētheōs*) knowledge reached by his *akoē* is impressive, but it does have very clear boundaries. The phrase (*kat*)*hoson hēmeis idmen* returns at the end of 4.17, 4.18, and 4.20 to locate exactly where it is that human life ends after the territory of the Scythians.[37] Towards the north wind (*pros boreēn anemon*), beyond (*katuperthe*) the Neuri, the Cannibals and the Blackcloaks is *to erēmon*.[38] Beyond the Bald Men and the Issedones, there are only fables. "No one can speak with exact knowledge" (*oudeis atrekeōs oide phrasai*) about those lands. The fables told by the Scythians about an impassable barrage of feathers in the deep north have nothing to do with the feathered temple of Apollo, but they simply refer to the heavy snowfall of impenetrable territory.[39] The Scythians are speaking in metaphors (*eikazontes*). The reasoned deduction of the historian can make sense of what lies behind colourful tales, and it does not limit itself to reproducing them for effect. That is what can be known about *ta makrotata*.[40] And that knowledge, by refusing the broad sweep of the poetic narrative, claims a deeper reach into the wonders of truth.

It is at the end of this virtuoso demonstration of his enquiry that Herodotus finally turns to the Hyperboreans in 4.32.[41] Everything that precedes leads to this, and the clear pattern that has by now been established by the detailed examination of the *makrotata* points to the inescapable conclusion that the Hyperboreans do not exist. Worse, they do not even belong to the fables of the northern peoples, like the Arimaspi or the *aigipodes andres*:

> Ὑπερβορέων δὲ πέρι ἀνθρώπων οὔτε τι Σκύθαι λέγουσι οὐδὲν οὔτε τινὲς
> ἄλλοι τῶν ταύτῃ οἰκημένων, εἰ μὴ ἄρα Ἰσσηδόνες· ὡς δ' ἐγὼ δοκέω, οὐδ'
> οὗτοι λέγουσι οὐδέν· ἔλεγον γὰρ ἂν καὶ Σκύθαι, ὡς περὶ τῶν μουνοφθάλμων
> λέγουσι. ἀλλ' Ἡσιόδῳ μέν ἐστι περὶ Ὑπερβορέων εἰρημένα, ἔστι δὲ καὶ
> Ὁμήρῳ ἐν Ἐπιγόνοισι, εἰ δὴ τῷ ἐόντι γε Ὅμηρος ταῦτα τὰ ἔπεα ἐποίησε.

> Concerning the Hyperborean people neither the Scythians nor any other dwellers in these lands tell us anything, except perchance the Issedones. And, as I think, even they tell nothing; for were it not so, then the Scythians too would have told, even as they tell of the one-eyed men. But Hesiod speaks of Hyperboreans, and Homer too in his poem the *Epigoni*, if that be truly the work of Homer.

The ironic *ara* of *ei mē ara Issedones* is the cue to another, devastating blow against Aristeas.[42] The *historia* of Herodotus is able to establish that the Issedones themselves do not know about the Hyperboreans. They come from the fantasies of Greek poetry, the imaginary worlds of Homer and Hesiod, and that is where the *Arimaspeia* also squarely belongs.[43] The old poem simply cannot hold its own against the *Histories* in the contest of ethnographic authority.

Herodotus goes further. In addition to the fables of Greek poetry about the Hyperboreans, he reports at length on the tales of the Delians about the Hyperborean *theōria* to the island (4.33).[44] After relating the stories of the Delians, he intervenes to assert with an emphatic *oida de autos* that this custom which the Delians describe is similar (*prospheres*) to what the Thracian and Paeonian women do in their sacrifices.[45] In other words, the extensive knowledge of the historian is able to suggest a correspondence and probable point of origin for the offerings, which does not point to the further north, but more prosaically to nearby Thrace.[46] Here, as elsewhere, the investigation of *historia* is able to recalibrate and identify the information contained in fantastic tales.[47] It does not dismiss it, but reads through it. The knowledge of the historian applies equally to the practices of the Delians themselves (*kai tauta men dē tautas oida poieusas*), and the rest of the passage in 4.34–35 goes on to show that what the Delians say about the Hyperboreans is intrinsically tied to what they do in their own local rituals. The fabled poet Olen is here a Lycian, not a Hyperborean, and the names of the Hyperborean Maidens derive from his hymns, used in local cult.[48] That is to say: the reports of the Delians are no basis for the identification of an actual Hyperborean presence in the Greek world, they only tell us something about the Delians themselves. The etiological tales of the islanders have the same truth value as the etiological tales of "the Greeks who live on the Black Sea", or any other fantastic explanatory myth in the *Histories*.[49] Like the *apista* of Aristeas, the accounts of the Delians point to the location of the Hyperboreans in the imagination of the Greeks, not the ethnographic record of real knowledge about the north defined by the radical new enquiry.[50] The Hyperboreans are a projection from the centre onto the periphery, and the new *historia* is able to see through that fog.

The last prominent Hyperborean figure to be addressed is Abaris (4.36), and Herodotus dispatches him quickly: "for I do not tell the story of that Abaris, alleged to be a Hyperborean, who carried the arrow over the whole world, fasting the while".[51] Mentioning him is enough to establish that Herodotus knows about the fabulous tales that circulate about the wandering prophet, and that he pays no credence to their veracity.[52] The critical pattern established at this point is enough to support the rejection. The consequences of Herodotus' denial of the Hyperboreans are immense. It is, at the end of the day, the whole Milesian edifice of knowledge about distant humanity and the fundamental shape of the world that is involved in Herodotus' redefinition of the limits of knowledge in the deep north. The conclusion of the Hyperborean excursus ends with this supremely confident statement:

καὶ ταῦτα μὲν Ὑπερβορέων πέρι εἰρήσθω. τὸν γὰρ περὶ Ἀβάριος λόγον· τοῦ λεγομένου εἶναι Ὑπερβορέου οὐ λέγω, λέγοντα ὡς τὸν ὀϊστὸν περιέφερε κατὰ πᾶσαν γῆν οὐδὲν σιτεόμενος. εἰ δέ εἰσι ὑπερβόρεοί τινες ἄνθρωποι, εἰσὶ καὶ ὑπερνότιοι ἄλλοι. γελῶ δὲ ὁρέων γῆς περιόδους γράψαντας πολλοὺς ἤδη καὶ οὐδένα νόον ἐχόντως ἐξηγησάμενον, οἳ Ὠκεανόν τε ῥέοντα γράφουσι πέριξ τὴν γῆν, ἐοῦσαν κυκλοτερέα ὡς ἀπὸ τόρνου, καὶ τὴν Ἀσίην τῇ Εὐρώπῃ ποιεῦνται ἴσην. ἐν ὀλίγοισι γὰρ ἐγὼ δηλώσω μέγαθός τε ἑκάστης αὐτέων καὶ οἵη τίς ἐστι ἐς γραφὴν ἑκάστη.

But if there be men beyond the north wind, then there are others beyond the south. And I laugh to see how many have ere now drawn maps of the world, not one of them showing the matter reasonably [*noon echontōs*]; for they draw the world as round as if fashioned by compasses, encircled by the river of Okeanos, and Asia and Europe of a like bigness. For myself, I will in a few words show the extent of the two, and how each should be drawn.

There follows an extensive analytical discussion of the general outline of the *oikoumenē* and the main landmasses that constitute it, and the insufficiencies of the prevalent (Milesian) division of the world into exactly parallel Europe and Asia. The mirage of the Hyperboreans is tied to nothing less than the whole mirage of continental symmetry.[53] The fundamental configuration of space in which the narrative of Persian expansion is to be related is shaped by the ultimate reach of enquiry.[54]

This is the main section of the *Histories* devoted to the shape of the world and the relative forms of the continents. It does not only have a crucial importance for

Book IV, obviously, but for the *Histories* as a whole. The removal of the Hyperboreans from the north, and the ridiculing of the logic that made the furthest men of the north exact parallels to the furthest men of the south ("Hypernotians"), is the topic that leads to those wide-ranging considerations about land shapes.[55] The geographical ethnography of Hecataeus of Miletus is one of the main targets here.[56] Following directly on his incorporation of Aristeas' claim to knowledge about the deep north, Herodotus' attack on the other monument of Milesian literature on the further limits beyond the Black Sea is the prelude to nothing less than the *Histories'* laying out of the boundaries of the world on the ruins of Milesian geography. Hecataeus' anonymity places him all the more efficiently among the *logoi polloi* that he is made to represent in the passage.[57]

A different kind of adversary than the poetic fantasies of the *Arimaspeia*, what was still the state of the art in the geographical knowledge of the age, had to be confronted head-on for the paradigm shift to take place. Herodotus does this by demonstrating the superiority of his method, systematically deconstructing what had functioned as a cornerstone of earlier thought on the topic. His intervention from 4.36 is the only place in the *Histories* where we are made to see Herodotus actually laugh at the arguments of his rivals.[58] Echoing the famous *logoi geloioi* of Hecataeus' proem, he makes that laugh his own, triumphantly turns it on its head and directs it on the pretences of his august predecessor's own failed knowledge.[59] The result is that the vast expanses of the Pontic world are now *his* to claim.[60] Herodotus' investigation of *ta makrotata* in 4.5–4.36 is the foundation of all the subsequent Scythian *logos*. Once he has established the predominance of his *epistēmē*, he can proceed to illustrate the product of its enquiry, one that does more than reflect implicit knowledge structures of geographical thought.[61] Reaching far beyond the prevailing hodological model, the long investigation of northern hydrography that follows and the massive ethnography of the peoples of the deep north all depend on that earlier section for the authority of their account.[62] The deletion of the Hyperboreans is one of the epistemological showcases of the new enquiry. Far from being *polloi*, the *logoi* of the Greeks have all followed the same fantasy, from Homer and Hesiod to Olen, Aristeas and Hecataeus, and Herodotus unveils a whole new picture on the vivid memories this fantasy has left behind.[63]

Just as Persian Empire failed in the plains of Scythia, the certitudes of Greek wisdom have been wrestling with a mirage in the distant north. Herodotus transforms both failures into objects of knowledge.[64] The errors of overextension reveal boundaries that all can see. The *eskhatia* of the distant north are no longer the limits that can authorize knowledge and wisdom, as they were for Aristeas, but the ultimate frontier for the demonstration of *historia*.[65] It would be a mistake to continue reducing the beginning of Book IV to yet another symptom of the great fantomatic movement *vom Mythos zum Logos*.[66] The critical upending of the distant north by Herodotus is not the culmination of some linear progression in the development of rationality, whatever we mean by rationality. It is, however, a triumphant claim of supercession, and a window into the mechanics of reconfiguration that allows Herodotus to bring other voices into his vast reach. This goes far beyond the contemporary debates of Hippocratic ethnography and the *periodoi gēs*.[67] The old exotic visions of epic travel poetry, the mythical aetiologies of cult, and the recent symmetries of Milesian geography, are all incorporated in the new process of knowledge. The authorities that had previously defined the edges of the world are relocated squarely in the centre and recast as witnesses to something else. By controlling the furthest boundaries of ethnicity, Herodotus controls the entire world map, and the archaeology of knowledge.[68] A long line of common errors is made plain to see and given new light. The contrasts offered by the polyphony of these other voices give shape to the distinctiveness of the Herodotean enquiry, and its ability to redirect so many perspectives together in a shared direction. That polyphony is no simple ad hoc juxtaposition of wrong alternatives. Herodotus is less wayward than some modern readers in the consistency of his views. The absence of the Hyperboreans in the Croesus story of Book I is as dramatic as anything in Book IV.[69] Both are also perfectly consistent in the scale of their consequences. Here, as elsewhere, Herodotus' rewriting of the world pushes the certainties that framed a clear centre with clear edges out of the realm of knowledge, and prepares the way for a redefinition of the certainties that make the centre itself.

Notes

1 Here is not the place for another detailed study of the narrator's complex presence within the plurality of voices staged in Herodotus' text. Among the many excellent studies that have deepened the field since Lang 1984; Dewald 1987; and Marincola 1987, the following can be mentioned: Darbo-Peschanski 1985, 1987; Lateiner 1989: 76–90; de Jong 1999, 2002; Dewald 2002; Slings 2002; Brock 2003; Giangiulio 2005; Barker 2006, 2009: 144–202; Luraghi 2006; Pelling 2006a; Scardino 2007; Baragwanath 2008; Demont 2009; Grethlein 2010: 149–204, 2013: 185–223; Branscome 2013; Mansour 2014; Marzi 2015: 59–65; Zali 2015. All translations reproduce Godley's Loeb text.

2 This study derives from the material of a chapter in my forthcoming book, *Hyperborea: Fragments of Greek Cosmography*. For the narrative tropes of the voyage to the edges of the world more generally, see, e.g., Romm 1992; Bichler 2011.

3 On Herodotus' engagement with Aristeas, West's 2004 article will continue to stand out; cf. Bolton 1962: 42–4; Bernadete 1969: 104–9; for Hecataeus, see, e.g., Gardiner-Garden 1988; West 1991; Fowler 1996; Moyer 2002.

4 See still Harmatta 1941. On the ethnography of the Scythian *logos*, see still Hartog 1980: 21–219; Lévy 1981; Shaw 1982–1983: 8–21; West 1999a, 2002a; Kim 2010.

5 The figure of the Herodotean narrator as a guide through lands of speech is a rich, recurrent trope. See now Wood 2016; cf. still the classic article of Redfield 1985 and Wakker 2007; cf. Marincola 1997: 7, 219.

6 See, e.g., Aly 1921: 116; Hadas 1935; Armayor 1978; Dumézil 1978: 169–92; Pórtulas 1994; Visintin 2000; Ivantchik 1999, 2001a; Hinge 2008; Braund 2008, 2010; Barbara 2011; Lincoln 2014, 2018: 73–83. I was not able to use Bravo 2018 before this piece was written.

7 Herodotus 4.11: ἔστι δὲ καὶ ἄλλος λόγος ἔχων ὧδε, τῷ μάλιστα λεγομένῳ αὐτὸς πρόσκειμαι: "There is yet another tale to the tradition, whereof I myself do especially incline." See Braund 2011; cf. West 2000.

8 See Harmatta 1990; Ivantchik 1993a: 58–61, 1997, 2001b, 2005: 53–66; Sauter 2000; cf. Bury 1906; Heubeck 1963.

9 Herodotus 4.12–13: οὗτος δὲ ἄλλος ξυνὸς Ἑλλήνων τε καὶ Βαρβάρων λεγόμενος λόγος εἴρηται. ἔφη δὲ Ἀριστέης ὁ Καϋστροβίου ἀνὴρ Προκοννήσιος, ποιέων ἔπεα, ἀπικέσθαι ἐς Ἰσσηδόνας φοιβόλαμπτος γενόμενος, Ἰσσηδόνων δὲ ὑπεροικέειν Ἀριμασποὺς ἄνδρας μουνοφθάλμους, ὑπὲρ δὲ τούτων τοὺς χρυσοφύλακας γρῦπας, τούτων δὲ τοὺς Ὑπερβορέους κατήκοντας ἐπὶ θάλασσαν· τούτους ὧν πάντας πλὴν Ὑπερβορέων, ἀρξάντων Ἀριμασπῶν, αἰεὶ τοῖσι πλησιοχώροισι ἐπιτίθεσθαι, καὶ ὑπὸ μὲν Ἀριμασπῶν ἐξωθέεσθαι ἐκ τῆς χώρης Ἰσσηδόνας, ὑπὸ δὲ Ἰσσηδόνων Σκύθας, Κιμμερίους δὲ οἰκέοντας ἐπὶ τῇ νοτίῃ θαλάσσῃ ὑπὸ Σκυθέων πιεζομένους ἐκλείπειν τὴν χώρην. οὕτω οὐδὲ οὗτος συμφέρεται περὶ τῆς χώρης ταύτης Σκύθῃσι. "I have now related this other tale, which is told alike by Greeks and foreigners. There is also a story related in a poem by Aristeas son of Caÿstrobius, a man of Proconnesus. This Aristeas, being then possessed by Phoebus, visited the Issedones; beyond these (he said) dwell the one-eyed Arimaspians, beyond whom are the griffins that guard gold, and beyond these again the Hyperboreans, whose territory reaches to the sea. Except the Hyperboreans, all these nations (and first the Arimaspians) ever make war upon their neighbours; the Issedones were pushed from their lands by the Arimaspians, and the Scythians by the Issedones, and the Cimmerians, dwelling by the southern sea, were hard pressed by the Scythians and left their country. Thus neither does Aristeas' story agree concerning this country with the Scythian account." See Skinner 2012: 62–78.
10 The scholarship on Aristeas is abundant. Note Meuli 1935: 153–64; Dodds 1951: 135–78; Phillips 1955; Bowra 1956; Bolton 1962; Dowden 1980, 2019; Ivantchik 1993b; Canfora 1996; Alemany i Vilamajó 1999; Bremmer 2002: 27–40, 145–51; Dettori 2005; Zhmud 2016. There is a chapter on Aristeas in the forthcoming *Hyperborea: Fragments of Greek Cosmography*.
11 See Dowden 1980, 2019; West 2004: 58.
12 Robbins 1982; cf. West 2004: 53–6; Krummen 2014: 302–11.
13 Dowden 2019.
14 See still Schepens 1980.
15 Herodotus 4.25: μέχρι μὲν δὴ τούτων γινώσκεται, τὸ δὲ τῶν φαλακρῶν κατύπερθε οὐδεὶς ἀτρεκέως οἶδε φράσαι· ὄρεα γὰρ ὑψηλὰ ἀποτάμνει ἄβατα καὶ οὐδείς σφεα ὑπερβαίνει. οἱ δὲ φαλακροὶ οὗτοι λέγουσι, ἐμοὶ μὲν οὐ πιστὰ λέγοντες, οἰκέειν τὰ ὄρεα αἰγίποδας ἄνδρας, ὑπερβάντι δὲ τούτους ἀνθρώπους ἄλλους οἳ τὴν ἑξάμηνον καθεύδουσι· τοῦτο δὲ οὐκ ἐνδέκομαι ἀρχήν. ἀλλὰ τὸ μὲν πρὸς ἠῶ τῶν φαλακρῶν γινώσκεται ἀτρεκέως ὑπὸ Ἰσσηδόνων οἰκεόμενον, τὸ μέντοι κατύπερθε πρὸς βορέην ἄνεμον οὐ γινώσκεται οὔτε τῶν φαλακρῶν οὔτε τῶν Ἰσσηδόνων, εἰ μὴ ὅσα αὐτῶν τούτων λεγόντων. "So far then as these men this country is known; but, for what lies north of the Bald Men, no one can speak with exact knowledge; for mountains high and impassable bar the way, and no one crosses them. These Bald Men say (but for my part I believe them not) that the mountains are inhabited by men with goats' feet; and that beyond these again are men who sleep for six months of the twelve. This I cannot at all accept for true. But the country east of the bald heads is known for certain to be inhabited by the Issedones; howbeit, of what lies northward either of the Bald Heads of the Issedones we have no knowledge, save what comes from the report of these latter."
16 See, e.g., Herodotus 2.29: ἄλλου δὲ οὐδενὸς οὐδὲν ἐδυνάμην πυθέσθαι, ἀλλὰ τοσόνδε μὲν ἄλλο ἐπὶ μακρότατον ἐπυθόμην, μέχρι μὲν Ἐλεφαντίνης πόλιος αὐτόπτης ἐλθών, τὸ δ' ἀπὸ τούτου ἀκοῇ ἤδη ἱστορέων. "I was unable to learn anything from anyone else, but this much further I did learn by the most extensive investigation that I could make, going as far as the city of Elephantine to look myself, and beyond that by question and hearsay." Cf. Corcella 1984: 57–67; Marincola 2007; Miltsios 2016. Nenci 1953 is still worth consulting.
17 Corcella 2007: 586–7.
18 Cf. West 2004: 51–2.
19 Herodotus 4.25. On the evolution of the Rhipean Mountains in the geographic imagination, see still Kiessling 1914; cf. Dion 1976, 1977: 260–70; Radt 2007: 248. The first

attestation of this location is in Alcman fr. 89 *PMGF*, for which see Budelmann 2013 with Cuartero 1972.

20 Herodotus 4.5; 4.7; 4.10; 4.13; 4.27; 4.71; 4.104.

21 Herodotus 4.23; see Phillips 1960. For the ethnographic mirage of the just Bald Men, cf. Lovejoy & Boas 1935: 287–367; Giraudeau 1984: 125.

22 Herodotus 4.28; 4.129; cf. Pindar, *Pythian* 10.28–36.

23 See Corcella 2007: 599–600.

24 Herodotus 4.26: νόμοισι δὲ Ἰσσηδόνες τοιοισίδε λέγονται χρᾶσθαι. ἐπεὰν ἀνδρὶ ἀποθάνῃ πατήρ, οἱ προσήκοντες πάντες προσάγουσι πρόβατα καὶ ἔπειτα ταῦτα θύσαντες καὶ κατταμόντες τὰ κρέα κατατάμνουσι καὶ τὸν τοῦ δεκομένου τεθνεῶτα γονέα, ἀναμείξαντες δὲ πάντα τὰ κρέα δαῖτα προτιθέαται. τὴν δὲ κεφαλὴν αὐτοῦ ψιλώσαντες καὶ ἐκκαθήραντες καταχρυσοῦσι καὶ ἔπειτα ἅτε ἀγάλματι χρέωνται, θυσίας μεγάλας ἐπετείους ἐπιτελέοντες. παῖς δὲ πατρὶ τοῦτο ποιέει, κατά περ Ἕλληνες τὰ γενέσια. ἄλλως δὲ δίκαιοι καὶ οὗτοι λέγονται εἶναι, ἰσοκρατέες δὲ ὁμοίως αἱ γυναῖκες τοῖσι ἀνδράσι. "It is said to be the custom of the Issedones, that whenever a man's father dies, all the nearest of kin bring beasts of the flock, and having killed these kin and cut up the flesh they cut up also the dead father of their host, and set out all the flesh mingled together for a feast. As for his head, they strip it bare and cleanse and gild it, and keep it for a sacred relic, whereto they offer yearly solemn sacrifice. Every son does so by his father even as the Greeks in their festivals in honour of the dead. For the rest, these are also said to be a law-abiding people; and the women have equal power with the men." On the Issedones see, e.g., Hennig 1935; Phillips 1955; Shaw 1982–1983; Silberman 1990; cf. Phillips 1960.

25 Cf. Humphreys 1987 and Bloomer 1993. See also Cartledge 1990; Gray 1995; Pelling 1997; Bichler 2000, 2008; Dorati 2000; Thomas 2000: 102–34.

26 Jacoby 1944; Johnston 1999: 43–6.

27 See Asheri 2007: 436–7; cf. Corcella 1984: 84–91.

28 *FGrHist* I F 186–190; see Plezia 1959–1960; cf. Dorati 1999–2000.

29 For the actual recovery of the different forms of "oral traditions" behind Herodotus' text, see, e.g., the models defended by Murray 1987; Cobet 1988; Fehling 1989; Luraghi 2001b; Hornblower 2002.

30 Herodotus 4.27: γινώσκονται μὲν δὴ καὶ οὗτοι. τὸ δὲ ἀπὸ τούτων τὸ κατύπερθε Ἰσσηδόνες εἰσὶ οἱ λέγοντες τοὺς μουνοφθάλμους ἀνθρώπους καὶ τοὺς χρυσοφύλακας γρῦπας εἶναι, παρὰ δὲ τούτων Σκύθαι παραλαβόντες λέγουσι, παρὰ δὲ Σκυθέων ἡμεῖς οἱ ἄλλοι νενομίκαμεν, καὶ ὀνομάζομεν αὐτοὺς σκυθιστὶ Ἀριμασπούς· ἄριμα γὰρ ἓν καλέουσι Σκύθαι, σποῦ δὲ ὀφθαλμόν. "Of these then also we have knowledge; but for what is northward of them, it is from the Issedones that the tale comes of the one-eyed men and the griffins that guard gold; this is told by the Scythians, who have heard it from them; and we again have taken it for true from the Scythians, and call these people by the Scythian name, Arimaspians; for in the Scythian tongue *arima* is one, and *spou* is the eye." Pinault 2008 now argues for a derivation from **áram-aspa-* or **arəmaspa-* (see especially pp. 129–36); cf. Pirart 1998. See also Hinge 2005; Schmitt 2011, 2015; cf. Harrison 1998 more generally.

31 For Herodotus' writing one type of travel narrative over another, cf. Bichler 2006a.

32 See Munson 2001.

33 Herodotus 3.114–116: ἀποκλινομένης δὲ μεσαμβρίης παρήκει πρὸς δύνοντα ἥλιον ἡ Αἰθιοπίη χώρη ἐσχάτη τῶν οἰκεομένων· αὕτη δὲ χρυσόν τε φέρει πολλὸν καὶ ἐλέφαντας ἀμφιλαφέας καὶ δένδρεα παντοῖα ἄγρια καὶ ἔβενον καὶ ἄνδρας μεγίστους καὶ καλλίστους καὶ μακροβιωτάτους. αὗται μέν νυν ἔν τε τῇ Ἀσίῃ ἐσχατιαί εἰσι καὶ ἐν τῇ Λιβύῃ. Περὶ δὲ τῶν ἐν τῇ Εὐρώπῃ τῶν πρὸς ἑσπέρην ἐσχατιέων ἔχω μὲν οὐκ ἀτρεκέως λέγειν· οὔτε γὰρ ἔγωγε ἐνδέκομαι Ἠριδανόν τινα καλέεσθαι πρὸς βαρβάρων ποταμὸν ἐκδιδόντα ἐς θάλασσαν τὴν πρὸς βορέην ἄνεμον, ἀπ' ὅτεο τὸ ἤλεκτρον φοιτᾶν λόγος ἐστί, οὔτε νήσους οἶδα Κασσιτερίδας ἐούσας, ἐκ τῶν ὁ κασσίτερος ἡμῖν φοιτᾷ. τοῦτο μὲν γὰρ ὁ Ἠριδανὸς αὐτὸ κατηγορέει τὸ οὔνομα ὡς ἔστι Ἑλληνικὸν καὶ οὐ βάρβαρον, ὑπὸ

ποιητέω δέ τινος ποιηθέν· τοῦτο δὲ οὐδενὸς αὐτόπτεω γενομένου δύναμαι ἀκοῦσαι, τοῦτο μελετῶν, ὅκως θάλασσά ἐστι τὰ ἐπέκεινα τῆς Εὐρώπης. ἐξ ἐσχάτης δ' ὧν ὅ τε κασσίτερος ἡμῖν φοιτᾷ καὶ τὸ ἤλεκτρον. πρὸς δὲ ἄρκτου τῆς Εὐρώπης πολλῷ τι πλεῖστος χρυσὸς φαίνεται ἐών. Ὅκως μὲν γινόμενος, οὐκ ἔχω οὐδὲ τοῦτο ἀτρεκέως εἶπαι, λέγεται δὲ ὑπὲκ τῶν γρυπῶν ἁρπάζειν Ἀριμασποὺς ἄνδρας μουνοφθάλμους· πείθομαι δὲ οὐδὲ τοῦτο, ὅκως μουνόφθαλμοι ἄνδρες φύονται, φύσιν ἔχοντες τὴν ἄλλην ὁμοίην τοῖσι ἄλλοισι ἀνθρώποισι. Αἱ δὲ ὧν ἐσχατιαὶ οἴκασι, περικληίουσαι τὴν ἄλλην χώρην καὶ ἐντὸς ἀπέργουσαι, τὰ κάλλιστα δοκέοντα ἡμῖν εἶναι καὶ σπανιώτατα ἔχειν αὐταί. "Where south inclines westwards, the part of the world stretching farthest towards the sunset is Ethiopia; here is great plenty of gold, and abundance of elephants, and all woodland trees, and ebony; and the people are the tallest and fairest and longest-lived of all men. These then are the most distant parts of the world in Asia and Libya. But concerning the farthest western parts of Europe I cannot speak with exactness; for I do not believe that there is a river called by foreigners Eridanus issuing into the northern sea, whence our amber is said to come, nor have I any knowledge of Tin-islands, whence our tin is brought. The very name of the Eridanus bewrays itself as not a foreign but a Greek name, invented by some poet; nor for all my diligence have I been able to learn from one who has seen it that there is a sea beyond Europe. This only we know, that our tin and amber come from the most distant parts. This is also plain, that to the north of Europe there is by far more gold than elsewhere. In this matter again I cannot say with certainty how the gold is got; some will have it that one-eyed men called Arimaspians steal it from griffins. But this too I hold incredible, that there can be men in all else like other men, yet having but one eye. Suffice it that it is but reasonable that the most distant parts of the world, as they enclose and wholly surround other lands, should have those things which we deem best and rarest." See Daverio-Rocchi 1988; Nesselrath 1995, 1996.

34 See Edelmann 1970; Kolendo 1991.

35 Maximus of Tyre (10.2f and 38.3c), it is interesting to note, insists on the extensive hydrography of the lands surveyed by Aristeas on his northern soul flight.

36 Herodotus 4.24: μέχρι μέν νυν τῶν φαλακρῶν τούτων πολλὴ περιφανείη τῆς χώρης ἐστὶ καὶ τῶν ἔμπροσθε ἐθνέων· καὶ γὰρ Σκυθέων τινὲς ἀπικνέονται ἐς αὐτούς, τῶν οὐ χαλεπόν ἐστι πυθέσθαι, καὶ Ἑλλήνων τῶν ἐκ Βορυσθένεός τε ἐμπορίου καὶ τῶν ἄλλων Ποντικῶν ἐμπορίων. Σκυθέων δὲ οἳ ἂν ἔλθωσι ἐς αὐτοὺς δι' ἑπτὰ ἑρμηνέων καὶ δι' ἑπτὰ γλωσσέων διαπρήσσονται. "Now as far as the land of these Bald Men we have full knowledge of the country and the nations on the hither side of them; for some of the Scythians make their way to them, from whom it is easy to get knowledge, and and from some too of the Greeks from the Borysthenes port and the other ports of Pontus; such Scythians as visit them do their business with seven interpreters and in seven languages." See Fehling 1989: 76. Cf. Braund 2007; Geus 2014.

37 Cf. Shimron 1973.

38 Variations on *hyper* recur throughout the passage: 4.7; 4.8; 4.9; 4.13 (5); 4.17 (2); 4.21; 4.22; 4.25 (2); 4.32 (2); 4.33 (5); 4.34; 4.35 (2); 4.36 (4); 4.37; 4.71; 4.72; 4.74; 4.93; 4.103 (4).

39 Herodotus 4.31–32: περὶ δὲ τῶν πτερῶν τῶν Σκύθαι λέγουσι ἀνάπλεον εἶναι τὸν ἠέρα, καὶ τούτων εἵνεκα οὐκ οἶά τε εἶναι οὔτε ἰδεῖν τὸ πρόσω τῆς ἠπείρου οὔτε διεξιέναι, τήνδε ἔχω περὶ αὐτῶν γνώμην. τὰ κατύπερθε ταύτης τῆς χώρης αἰεὶ νίφεται, ἐλάσσονι δὲ τοῦ θέρεος ἢ τοῦ χειμῶνος, ὥσπερ καὶ οἰκός. ἤδη ὧν ὅστις ἀγχόθεν χιόνα ἀδρὴν πίπτουσαν εἶδε, οἶδε τὸ λέγω· ἔοικε γὰρ ἡ χιὼν πτεροῖσι· καὶ διὰ τὸν χειμῶνα τοῦτον ἐόντα τοιοῦτον ἀνοίκητα τὰ πρὸς βορέην ἐστὶ τῆς ἠπείρου ταύτης. τὰ ὧν πτερὰ εἰκάζοντας τὴν χιόνα τοὺς Σκύθας τε καὶ τοὺς περιοίκους δοκέω λέγειν. ταῦτα μέν νυν τὰ λέγεται μακρότατα εἴρηται. "But as touching the feathers whereof the Scythians say that the air is full, insomuch that none can see or traverse the land beyond, I hold this opinion. Northward of that country snow falls continually, though less in summer than in winter, as is to be expected. Whoever has seen snow falling thickly near him knows

of himself my meaning; for the snow is like feathers; and by reason of the winter, which is such as I have said, the parts to the north of this continent are uninhabited. I think therefore that in this tale of feathers the Scythians and their neighbours do but speak of snow in a figure. Thus then I have spoken of those parts that are said to be most distant."

40 See Romm 1989: 111; Corcella 2007: 586.
41 Corcella 2007: 604.
42 Denniston 1954 describes the "secondary usage" of ἄρα as "surprise attendant upon disillusionment."
43 Cf. Boedeker 2002; Pelling 2006b; see still Strasburger 1972 more generally.
44 See, e.g., Kowalzig 2007: 118–24.
45 Herodotus 4.33–34: καὶ ταῦτα μὲν οὕτω προπεμπόμενα ἀπικνέεσθαι λέγουσι ἐς Δῆλον. οἶδα δὲ αὐτὸς τούτοισι τοῖσι ἱροῖσι τόδε ποιεύμενον προσφερές, τὰς Θρηΐσσας καὶ τὰς Παιονίδας γυναῖκας, ἐπεὰν θύωσι τῇ Ἀρτέμιδι τῇ Βασιληίῃ, οὐκ ἄνευ πυρῶν καλάμης ἐχούσας τὰ ἱρά. καὶ ταῦτα μὲν δὴ ταύτας οἶδα ποιεύσας. "And the offerings, it is said, come by this conveyance to Delos. I can say of my own knowledge that there is a custom like these offerings, namely, that when the Thracians and Paeonian women sacrifice to the Royal Artemis, they have wheat-straw with them while they sacrifice."
46 Cf. Asheri 1990.
47 West 2002b; cf. the various case studies in Baragwanath and de Bakker 2012.
48 For Olen as a Hyperborean, see Pausanias 10.5.7–8. Chapter 1 covers the relevant Delphian and Delian records in *Hyperborea: Fragments of Greek Cosmography*.
49 See Munson 2001.
50 Cf. Riese 1875: 14–16.
51 See e.g. Dowden 2007; Zhmud 2016.
52 Drexler 1972: 62–4. This is something rather different than the famous "Herodotean silences," for which see still Mora 1981.
53 See Sieberer 1995.
54 Lachenaud 1980; Bichler 2007; Purves 2010: 118–58.
55 See 1985; Bridgman 2010: 60; cf. Casson 1920 and Romm 1989 for a very different reading. For the symmetry between Scythia and Egypt, see still Bernadete 1969: 99–132. For Hypernotians in later literature, especially Eratosthenes, see Priestley 2014: 111–18.
56 See Aujac 1987; Boedeker 2000: 107; Bertelli 2001: 80–4; Prontera 2001; Fowler 2001: 110–11.
57 Cf. Jacoby 1912, col. 2680; 2708; 2717; Magreth 1993: 83–8.
58 See Corcella 2007: 608.
59 *FGrHist* 1 F 1: Ἑκαταῖος Μιλήσιος ὧδε μυθεῖται· τάδε γράφω, ὥς μοι δοκεῖ ἀληθέα εἶναι· οἱ γὰρ Ἑλλήνων λόγοι πολλοί τε καὶ γελοῖοι, ὡς ἐμοὶ φαίνονται, εἰσίν; cf. Armayor 1987; Marzi 2015: 54–9.
60 Kartunnen 2002.
61 See Gehrke 1998, 2007. For the notion of implicit knowledge structures and common-sense geography, see the collection of essays in Geus & Thiering 2014.
62 See Gardiner-Garden 1988. For the hodological model, see still Janni 1984.
63 See Bichler 2013.
64 For the patterns of this transformation, see Thomas 2000: 168–248; Cole 2013. Cf. Daverio-Rocchi 1988.
65 Cf. Bichler 2006b.
66 See Romm 2013: 215–20. Cf. Berger 1904; Trüdinger 1918.
67 Lloyd 1979: 15–28; Triebel-Schubert 1990; López Férez 1994; Dorati 1999–2000; Thomas 2000: 28–101; Chiasson 2001.
68 Prontera 2004.
69 Cf. Bacchylides 3, with Cairns 2010: 70–1.

Bibliography

Alemany i Vilamajó, A. 1999. "Els Cants arimaspeus d'Arísteas de Proconnès i la caiguda dels Zhou occidentals." *Faventia* 21: 45–55.

Aly, W. 1921. *Volksmärchen, Sage und Novelle bei Herodot und seine Zeitgenossen.* Göttingen (Vandenhoeck & Ruprecht).

Armayor, O.K. 1978. "Did Herodotus Ever Go to the Black Sea?" *Harvard Studies in Classical Philology* 82: 45–62.

———. 1987. "Hecataeus' Humor and Irony in Herodotus' Narrative of Egypt." *Ancient World* 16: 11–18.

Asheri, D. 1990. "Herodotus on Thracian Society and History." In Nenci, G., ed., *Hérodote et les peuples non-grecs.* Geneva (Fondation Hardt), 131–63.

———. 2007. "Book III." In Murray, O., & Moreno, A., eds., *A Commentary on Herodotus Books I-IV.* Oxford (Oxford University Press), 381–542.

Aujac, G. 1987. "The Foundation of Theoretical Cartography in Archaic and Classical Greece." In Harley, J.B., & Woodward, D., eds., *The History of Cartography I: Cartography in Prehistoric, Ancient, and Medieval Europe and the Mediterranean.* Chicago, IL (University of Chicago Press), 130–60.

Baragwanath, E. 2008. *Motivation and Narrative in Herodotus.* Oxford (Oxford University Press).

Baragwanath, E. & de Bakker, M., eds., 2012. *Myth, Truth and Narrative in Herodotus.* Oxford (Oxford University Press).

Barbara, S. 2011. "Encore sur le mythe de royauté des scythes d'après le 'logos skythikos' d'Hérodote (IV, 5–7) et le problème des sources du 'scythicos logos' (sic) d'Hérodote." In Barbara, S., Mazoyer, M., & Meurant, J., eds., *Figures royales des mondes anciens.* Paris (L'Harmattan), 31–57.

Barker, E. 2006. "Paging the Oracle: Interpretation, Identity and Performance in Herodotus' 'History'." *Greece & Rome* 53: 1–28.

———. 2009. *Entering the Agon: Dissent and Authority in Homer, Historiography, and Tragedy.* Oxford (Oxford University Press).

Berger, H. 1904. *Mythische Kosmographie der Griechen.* Leipzig (Teubner).

Bernadete, S. 1969. *Herodotean Inquiries.* The Hague (Martinus Nijhoff).

Bertelli, L. 2001. "Hecataeus: From Genealogy to Historiography." In Luraghi, N., ed., *The Historian's Craft in the Age of Herodotus.* Oxford (Oxford University Press), 67–94.

Bichler, R. 2000. *Herodots Welt: Der Aufbau der Historie am Bild der fremder Länder und Völker, ihrer Zivilisation und ihrer Geschichte.* Berlin (Akademie Verlag).

———. 2006a. "An der Grenzen zur Phantastik: antike Fahrtenberichte und ihre Beglaubigungsstrategien." In Hömke, N., & Baumbach, M., eds., *Fremde Wirklichkeiten: literarische Fantastik und antike Literatur.* Heidelberg (Winter), 237–59.

———. 2006b. "Über Grenzen und ihre Relativität im Licht von Herodots Historien." In Burtscher-Bechter, B., Haider, P.W., Mertz-Baumgartner, B., & Rollinger, R., eds., *Grenzen und Entgrenzungen: Historische und kulturwissenschaftliche Überlegungen am Beispiel des Mittelmeerraums.* Saarbrücken (Kögnigshausen & Neumann), 155–70.

———. 2007. "Herodots Historien unter dem Aspekt des Raumerfassung." In Rathmann, M., ed., *Wahrnehmung und Erfassung geographischer Räume in der Antike.* Mainz (von Zabern), 67–80.

———. 2008. "L'ethnographie d'Hérodote." In Mezzadri, B., ed., *Historiens de l'Antiquité.* Paris (Payot), 49–73.

———. 2011. "Die Fahrt zu den Grenzen der Erde: von Herodot bis zur Alexander- Historiographie." *Gymnasium* 118: 315–44.

———. 2013. "Zur Veranschaulichung des geographischen Wissens in Herodots Historien." In Boschung, D., Greub, T., & Hammerstaedt, J., eds., *Geographische Kenntnisse und ihre konkreten Ausformungen*. Munich (Wilhelm Fink), 74–89.

Bloomer, W.M. 1993. "The Superlative 'Nomoi' of Herodotus' 'Histories'." *Classical Antiquity* 12: 30–50.

Boedeker, D. 2000. "Herodotus' Genres." In Depew, M., & Obbink, D., eds., *Matrices of Genre: Authors, Canons, and Society*. Cambridge, MA (Harvard University Press), 97–114.

———. 2002. "Epic Heritage and Mythical Patterns in Herodotus." In Bakker, E.J., de Jong, I.J.F., & van Wees, H., eds., *Brill's Companion to Herodotus*. Leiden (Brill), 97–116.

Bolton, J.D.P. 1962. *Aristeas of Proconnesus*. Oxford (Clarendon Press).

Bowra, M. 1956. "A Fragment of the 'Arimaspea'." *Classical Quarterly* 6: 1–10.

Branscome, D. 2013. *Textual Rivals: Self-Presentation in Herodotus' Histories*. Ann Arbor, MI (University of Michigan Press), 2013.

Braund, D. 2007. "Greater Olbia: Ethnic, Religious, Economic and Political Interactions in the Region of Olbia c. 600–100 BC." In Braund, D., & Kryzhitskii, S.D., eds., *Classical Olbia and the Scythian World*. Oxford (Oxford University Press), 35–75.

———. 2008. "Scythian Laughter: Conversations in the Norther Black Sea Region in the Fifth Century BC." In Guldager Bilde, P., & Hjarl Petersen, J., eds., *Meetings of Cultures in the Black Sea Region: Between Conflict and Coexistence*. Aarhus (Aarhus University Press), 347–67.

———. 2010. "Teutaros, the Scythian Teacher of Herakles." In Catling, R.W.V., & Marchand, F., eds., *Onomatologos: Studies in Greek Personal Names Presented to Elaine Matthews*. Oxford (Oxbow), 381–9.

———. 2011. "Heracles the Scythian: Herodotus, Herodorus and Colonial Cultures." In Papuci-Wladika, E., ed., *PONTIKA 2008: Recent Research on the Northern and Eastern Black Sea in Ancient Times*. Oxford (Oxbow), 15–19.

Bravo, B. 2018. *Erodoto sulla Scizia et il lontano Nord-Est: Contributo all'interpretazione Del cosidetto logos scitico*. Rome (Edizioni di storia e letteratura).

Bremmer, J. 2002. *The Rise and Fall of the Afterlife*. London (Routledge).

Bridgman, T.P. 2005. *Hyperboreans: Myth and History in Celtic-Hellenic Contacts*. London (Routledge).

Brock, R. 2003. "Authoritative Voice and Narrative Management in Herodotus." In Derow, P., & Parker, R., eds., *Herodotus and His World: Essays from a Conference in Memory of George Forrest*. Oxford (Oxford University Press), 3–16.

Budelmann, F. 2013. "Alcman's Nightscapes (FRS 89 and 90 PMGF)." *Harvard Studies in Classical Philology* 107: 35–53.

Bury, J.B. 1906. "The Homeric and the Historic Kimmerians," *Klio* 6: 79–88.

Cairns, D.L. 2010. *Bacchylides: Five Epinician Odes (3, 5, 9, 11, 13)*. Cambridge (Francis Cairns).

Canfora, L. 1996. *Viaggio di Aristea*. Rome (Laterza).

Cartledge, P. 1990. "Herodotus and 'the Other': A Meditation on Empire." *Échos du Monde Classique* 34: 27–40.

Casson, S. 1920. "The Hyperboreans." *Classical Review* 34: 1–3.

Chiasson, C. 2001. "Scythian Androgyny and Environmental Determinism in Herodotus and the Hippocratic περὶ ἀέρων ὑδάτων τόπων." *Syllecta Classica* 12: 33–73.

Cobet, J. 1988. "Herodot und mündliche Überlieferung." In von Ungern-Sternberg, J., ed., *Vergangenheit in mündlicher Überlieferung*. Stuttgart (De Gruyter), 226–34.

Cole, S.G. 2013. "'I Know the Number of the Sand and the Measure of the Sea': Geography and Difference in the Early Greek World." In Raaflaub, K.A., & Talbert, R.J.A., eds., *Geography and Ethnography: Perceptions of the World in Pre-Modern Societies*. Chichester, West Sussex (Wiley-Blackwell), 197–214.

Corcella, A. 1984. *Erodoto e l'analogia*. Palermo (Sellerio).

———. 2007. "Book IV." In Murray, O., & Moreno, A., eds., *A Commentary on Herodotus Books I–IV*. Oxford (Oxford University Press), 543–721.

Cuartero i Borra, F.J. 1972. "La poética de Alcman." *Cuadernos de Filología Clásica. Estudios Griegos e Indoeuropeos* 4: 367–402.

Darbo-Peschanski, C. 1985. "Les 'logoi' des autres." *Quaderni di Storia* 22: 105–28.

———. 1987. *Le discours du particulier: Essai sur l'Enquête hérodotéenne*. Paris (Seuil).

Daverio-Rocchi, G. 1988. *Frontiera e confini nella Grecia Antica*. Rome (L'Erma di Bretschneider).

de Jong, I.J.F. 1999. "Aspects narratologiques des 'Histoires' d'Hérodote." *Lalies* 19: 217–75.

———. 2002. "Narrative Unity and Units." In Bakker, E.J., de Jong, I.J.F., & van Wees, H., eds., *Brill's Companion to Herodotus*. Leiden (Brill), 245–66.

———. 2004. "Herodotus." In de Jong, I.J.F., Nünlist, R., & Bowie, A., eds., *Narrators, Narratees, and Narratives in Ancient Greek Literature*. Leiden (Brill), 101–14.

Demont, P. 2009. "Figures of Inquiry in Herodotus' 'Inquiries'." *Mnemosyne* 62: 179–205.

Denniston, J.D. 1954. *The Greek Particles*. Oxford (Oxford University Press).

Dettori, E. 2005. "Aristea di Proconneso 'sciamano' e 'corvo': une presentazione (con qualche nota)." *Quaderni di classiconorroena* 1: 9–24.

Dewald, C. 1987. "Narrative Surface and Authorial Voice in Herodotus' 'Histories'." *Arethusa* 20: 147–70.

———. 2002. "'I Didn't Give My Own Genealogy': Herodotus and the Authorial Persona." In Bakker, E.J., de Jong, I.J.F., & van Wees, H., eds., *Brill's Companion to Herodotus*. Leiden (Brill), 267–89.

Dion, R. 1976. "La notion d'Hyperboréens, ses vicissitudes au cours de l'Antiquité." *Bulletin de l'Association Guillaume Budé* 1976: 143–57.

———. 1977. *Aspects politiques de la géographie antique*. Paris (Les Belles Lettres).

Dodds, E.R. 1951. *The Greeks and the Irrational*. Berkeley, CA (University of California Press).

Dorati, M. 1999–2000. "Le testimonianze relative alla περίοδος γῆς di Ecateo." *Geographia Antica* 8–9: 120–7.

———. 2000. *Le Storie di Erodoto: etnografia e raconto*. Pisa (Istituti editoriali e poligrafici internazionali).

Dowden, K. 1980. "Deux notes sur les Scythes et les Arimaspes." *Revue des Études Grecques* 93: 486–92.

———. 2007. "Abaris (34)." *Brill's New Jacoby Online*.

———. 2019. "Aristeas (35)." *Brill's New Jacoby Online²*.

Drexler, H. 1972. *Herodot-Studien*. Hildesheim (G. Olms).

Dumézil, G. 1978. *Romans de Scythie et d'alentour*. Paris (Payot).

Edelmann, H. 1970. "Ερημίη und ἔρημος bei Herodot." *Klio* 52: 79–86.

Evans, J.A.S. 1991. *Herodotus, Explorer of the Past*. Princeton, NJ (Princeton University Press).

Fehling, D. 1989 [1971]. *Herodotus and His "Source."* Leeds (Francis Cairns).

Fowler, R. 1996. "Herodotus and His Contemporaries." *Journal of Hellenic Studies* 116: 62–87.

———. 2001. "Early Historiē and Literacy." In Luraghi, N., ed., *The Historian's Craft in the Age of Herodotus*. Oxford (Oxford University Press), 95–115.

Gardiner-Garden, J. 1988. *Herodotos' Contemporaries on Skythian Geography and Ethnography*. Bloomington, IN (Indiana University Press).

Gehrke, H.-J. 1998. "Die Geburt der Erdkunde aus dem Geiste der Geometrie: Überlegungen zur Entstehung und zur Frühgeschichte der wissenschaftlichen Geographie bei den Griechen." In Kullmann, W., Althoff, J., & Asper, M., eds., *Gattungen wissenschaftlicher Literatur in der Antike*. Tübingen (Narr), 163–92.

———. 2007. "Die Raumwahrnehmung im archaischen Griechenland." In Rathmann, M., ed., *Wahrnehmung und Erfassung geographischer Räume in der Antike*. Mainz (von Zabern), 17–30.

Geus, K. 2014. "A Day's Journey in Herodotus' 'Histories'." In Geus, K., & Thiering, M., eds., *Features of Common Sense Geography: Implicit Knowledge Structures in Ancient Geographical Texts*. Berlin (Lit), 147–56.

Geus, K. & Thiering, M., ed. 2014. *Features of Common Sense Geography: Implicit Knowledge Structures in Ancient Geographical Texts*. Berlin (Lit).

Giangiulio, M. 2005. "Tradizione storica e strategie narrative nelle 'Storie' di Erodoto: il caso del discorso di Socle corinzio." In Giangiulio, M., ed., *Erodoto e il 'modello erodoteo': formazione e trasmissione delle tradizioni storiche in Grecia*. Trento (Università degli studi di Trento), 91–122.

Giraudeau, M. 1984. *Les notions juridiques et sociales chez Hérodote: Études sur le vocabulaire*. Paris (De Boccard).

Gray, V. 1995. "Herodotus and the Rhetoric of Otherness." *American Journal of Philology* 116: 185–212.

Grethlein, J. 2010. *The Greeks and Their Past: Poetry, Oratory and History in the Fifth Century BCE*. Cambridge (Cambridge University Press).

———. 2013. *Experience and Teleology in Ancient Historiography: 'Futures Past' from Herodotus to Augustine*. Cambridge (Cambridge University Press).

Hadas, M. 1935. "Utopian Sources in Herodotus." *Classical Philology* 30: 113–21.

Harmatta, J. 1941. *Quellenstudien zu den Skythika des Herodot*. Budapest (Kir. M. Pázmány Péter Tudományegyetemi Görög Filológiai Intézet).

———. 1990. "Herodotus Historian of the Cimmerians and the Scythians." In Nenci, G., ed., *Hérodote et les peuples non-grecs*. Geneva (Fondation Hardt), 115–31.

Harrison, T. 1998. "Herodotus' Conception of Foreign Languages." *Histos* 2: 1–45.

Hartog, F. 1980. *Le miroir d'Hérodote: Essai sur la représentation de l'autre*. Paris (Gallimard).

Hennig, R. 1935. "Herodots Handelsweg zu den sibirischen Issedonen." *Klio* 28: 248–54.

Heubeck, A. 1963. "Κιμμέριοι." *Hermes* 91: 490–2.

Hinge, G. 2005. "Herodot zur skythischen Sprache: Arimaspen, Amazonen und die Entdeckung des Schwarzen Meeres." *Glotta* 81: 86–115.

———. 2008. "Dionysos and Herakles in Scythia – The Eschatological String of Herodotus' Book 4." In Guldager Bilde, P., & Hjarl Petersen, J., eds., *Meetings of Cultures in the Black Sea Region: Between Conflict and Coexistence*. Aarhus (Aarhus University Press), 369–97.

Hornblower, S. 2002. "Herodotus and His Sources of Information." In Bakker, E.J., de Jong, I.J.F., & van Wees, H., eds., *Brill's Companion to Herodotus*. Leiden (Brill), 373–86.

Humphreys, S.C. 1987. "Law, Custom and Culture in Herodotus." *Arethusa* 20: 211–20.

Ivantchik, A. 1993a. *Les Cimmériens au Proche-Orient.* Fribourg (Éditions universitaires).

———. 1993b. "La datation du poème l'Arimaspée d'Aristéas de Proconnèse." *Antiquité Classique* 62: 35–67.

———. 1997. "Das Problem der ethnischen Zugehörigkeit der Kimmerier und die kimmerische archäologische Kultur." *Prähistorische Zeitschrift* 62: 12–53.

———. 1999. "Une légende sur l'origine des Scythes et (Hdt. IV 5–7) et le problème des sources du *Scythikos logos* d'Hérodote." *Revue des Études Grecques* 112: 141–92.

———. 2001a. "La légende 'grecque' sur l'origine des Scythes (Hérodote 4. 8–10)." In Fromentin, V., & Gotteland, S., eds., *Origines gentium.* Bordeaux (Ausonius), 207–21.

———. 2001b. *Kimmerier und Skythen: Kulturhistorische und chronologische Probleme der Archäologie der osteuropäischen Steppens und Kaukasiens in vor- und früh- skythischer Zeit.* Moscow (Paleograf).

———. 2005. *Am Vorabend der Kolonisation.* Berlin (Paleograf).

Jacoby, F. 1912. "Hekataios 3." *Realencyclopädie der classischen Altertumswissenschaft* 7.2: cols. 2667–750.

———. 1944. "ΓΕΝΕΣΙΑ: A Forgotten Festival of the Dead." *Classical Quarterly* 38: 65–75.

Janni, P. 1984. *La mappa e il periplo: Cartografia antica e spazio odologico.* Rome (Bretschneider).

Johnston, S.I. 1999. *Restless Dead: Encounters Between the Living and the Dead in Ancient Greece.* Berkeley, CA (University of California Press).

Kartunnen, K. 2002. "The Ethnography of the Fringes." In Bakker, E.J., de Jong, I.J.F., & van Wees, H., eds., *Brill's Companion to Herodotus.* Leiden (Brill), 457–74.

Kiessling, E. 1914. "'Ριπαῖα ὄρη." *Realencyclopädie der classischen Altertumswissenschaft* IA: col. 846–916.

Kim, H.J. 2010. "Herodotus' Scythians Viewed from a Central Asian Perspective: Its Historicity and Significance." *Ancient West & East* 9: 115–35.

Kolendo, J. 1991. "Les 'déserts' dans les pays barbares: Représentations et réalités." *Dialogues d'histoire ancienne* 17: 35–60.

Kowalzig, B. 2007. *Singing for the Gods: Performances of Myth and Ritual in Archaic and Classical Greece.* Oxford (Oxford University Press).

Krummen, E. 2014 [1990]. *Cult, Myth, and Occasion in Pindar's Victory Odes: A Study of Isthmian 4, Pythian 5, Olympian 1, and Olympian 3.* Prenton (Francis Cairns).

Lachenaud, G. 1980. "Connaissance du monde et représentations de l'espace dans Hérodote." *Hellenika* 32: 42–60.

Lang, M. 1984. *Herodotean Narrative and Discourse.* Cambridge, MA (Harvard University Press).

Lateiner, D. 1985. "Polarità: il principio della differenza complementare." *Quaderni di Storia* 22: 79–103.

———. 1989. *The Historical Method of Herodotus.* Toronto (University of Toronto Press).

Lévy, E. 1981. "Les origines du mirage scythe." *Ktema* 6: 57–68.

Lincoln, B. 2014. "Once Again 'the Scythian' Myth of Origins (Herodotus 4.5–10)." *Nordlit* 33: 19–34.

———. 2018. *Apples and Oranges: Explorations in, on, and With Comparison.* Chicago, IL (University of Chicago Press).

Lloyd, G.E.R. 1979. *Magic, Reason, and Experience.* Cambridge (Cambridge University Press).

López Férez, J.A. 1994. "Los escritos hipocráticos y el nacimiento de la identidad europea." In Khan, H.A., ed., *The Birth of the European Identity: The Europe-Asia Contrast in Greek Thought.* Nottingham (University of Nottingham), 90–130.

Lovejoy, O. & Boas, G. 1935. *Primitivism and Related Ideas in Antiquity*. Baltimore, MD (Johns Hopkins University Press).

Luraghi, N., ed. 2001a. *The Historian's Craft in the Age of Herodotus*. Oxford (University of Oxford Press).

———. 2001b. "Local Knowledge in Herodotus' 'Histories'." In Luraghi, N., ed., *The Historian's Craft in the Age of Herodotus*. Oxford (University of Oxford Press), 138–60.

———. 2006. "Meta-historiē: Method and Genre in the Histories." In Dewald, C., & Marincola, J., eds., *The Cambridge Companion to Herodotus*. Cambridge (Cambridge University Press), 76–91.

Margreth, D. 1993. *Skythische Schamanen? die Nachrichten über Enarees-Anarieis bei Herodot und Hippokrates*. Schaffhausen (Meier).

Mansour, K. 2014. *L'Enquête d'Hérodote: Une poétique du premier prosateur grec*. Paris (L'Harmattan).

Marincola, J. 1987. "Herodotean Narrative and the Narrator's Presence." *Arethusa* 20: 121–37.

———. 1997. *Authority and Tradition in Ancient Historiography*. Cambridge (Cambridge University Press).

———. 2007. "Odysseus and the Historians." *Syllecta Classica* 18: 1–79.

Marzi, A. 2015. "'Più vero del vero'?: la funzione del falso e della simulazione nella storiografia antica." *Quaderni di Storia* 82: 49–76.

Meuli, K. 1935. "Scythica." *Hermes* 70: 122–76.

Miltsios, N. 2016. "Sight and Seeing in Herodotus." *Trends in Classics* 8: 1–16.

Mora, F. 1981. "I silenzi Herodotei." *Social Science Research* 5: 209–22.

Moyer, I.S. 2002. "Herodotus and an Egyptian Mirage: The Genealogies of the Theban Priests." *Journal of Hellenic Studies* 122: 7–90.

Munson, R.V. 2001. *Telling Wonders: Ethnographic and Political Discourse in the Work of Herodotus*. Ann Arbor, MI (University of Michigan Press).

Murray, O. 1987. "Herodotus and Oral History." In Sancisi-Weerdenburg, H., & Kuhrt, A., eds., *Achaemenid History: II: The Greek Sources*. Leiden (Brill), 93–115 = Luraghi 2001, 16–44.

Nenci, G. 1953. "Il motivo dell'autopsia nella storiografia greca." *Studi Classici e Orientali* 3: 14–46.

Nesselrath, H.-G. 1995. "Herodot und die Enden der Erde." *Museum Helveticum* 52: 20–44.

———. 1996. "Herodot und der griechische Mythos." *Poetica* 28: 275–96.

Pelling, C. 1997. "East Is East and West Is West – Or Are They? National Stereotyping in Herodotus." *Histos* 1: 51–66.

———. 2006a. "Educating Croesus: Talking and Learning in Herodotus' Lydian 'Logos'." *Classical Antiquity* 25: 141–77.

———. 2006b. "Homer and Herodotus." In Clarke, M.J., Currie, B.G.F., & Lyne, R.O.A.M., eds., *Epic Interactions: Perspectives on Homer, Virgil, and the Epic Tradition Presented to Jasper Griffin by Former Pupils*. Oxford (Oxford University Press), 75–104.

Phillips, E.D. 1955. "The Legend of Aristeas: Fact and Fancy in Early Greek Notions of East Russia, Siberia, and Inner Asia." *Artibus Asiae* 18: 161–77.

———. 1960. "The Argippaei of Herodotus." *Artibus Asiae* 23: 124–8.

Pinault, G.-J. 2008. "La langue des Scythes et le nom des Arimaspes." *Comptes rendus des séances de l'Académie des Inscriptions et Belles-Lettres* 152: 105–38.

Pirart, E. 1998. "Le nom des Arimaspes." *Boletín de la Asociación Española de Orientalistas* 34: 239–60.

Plezia, M. 1959–1960. "Hekataios über die Völker am Nordrand des skythischen Schwarzmeergebietes." *Eos* 50: 27–42.

Pórtulas, J. 1994. "Una geografia dei limiti nell'immaginario dei Greci." *ΚΟΚΑΛΟΣ* 39–40: 297–314.

Priestley, J. 2014. *Herodotus and Hellenistic Culture*. Cambridge (Cambridge University Press).

Prontera, F. 2001. "Hekataios und die Erdkarte des Herodot." In Papenfuss, D., & Strock, V.M., eds., *Gab es das griechische Wunder? Griechenland zwischen das Ende des 6. und der Mitte des 5. Jahrhunderts v.Chr*. Mainz (von Zabern), 127–35.

———. 2004. "Karte (Kartographie*)." Reallexikon für Antike und Christentum* 20: 187–229.

Purves, A. 2010. *Space and Time in Ancient Greek Narrative*. Cambridge (Cambridge University Press).

Radt, S. 2007. *Strabons Geographika, Band 6. Buch V–VIII: Kommentar*. Göttingen (Vandenhoeck & Ruprecht).

Redfield, J. 1985. "Herodotus the Tourist." *Classical Philology* 80: 97–118.

Riese, A. 1875. *Die idealisierung der Natürvolker des Nordens in der griechische und römische Litteratur*. Frankfurt (Weiss).

Robbins, E. 1982. "Heracles, the Hyperboreans, and the Hind: Pindar, 'OL'. 3." *Phoenix* 36: 295–305.

Romm, J. 1989. "Herodotus and Mythic Geography: The Case of the Hyperboreans." *Transactions of the American Philological Association* 119: 97–113.

———. 1992. *The Edges of the Earth in Ancient Thought: Geography, Exploration, and Fiction*. Princeton, NJ (Princeton University Press).

———. 2013. "Continents, Climates and Cultures: Greek Theories of Global Structure." In Raaflaub, K.A., & Talbert, R.J.A., eds., *Geography and Ethnography: Perceptions of the World in Pre-Modern Societies*. Chichester, West Sussex (Wiley-Blackwell), 215–35.

Sauter, H. 2000. *Studien zum Kimmerierproblem*. Bonn (Habelt).

Scardino, C. 2007. *Gestaltung und Funktion der Reden bei Herodot und Thukydides*. Berlin (De Gruyter).

Schepens, G. 1980. *L'autopsie dans la méthode des historiens grecs au Ve siècle avant J.-C*. Brussels (AWLSK).

Schmitt, R. 2011. "Herodot und iranische Sprachen." In Rollinger, R., Truschnegg, B., & Bichler, R., eds., *Herodot und das persische Weltreich: Herodotus and the Persian Empire*. Wiesbaden (Harassowitz Verlag), 313–41.

———. 2015. "Herodotus as Practitioner of Iranian Anthroponomastics?" *Glotta* 91: 250–63.

Shaw, B.D. 1982–1983. "Eaters of Flesh and Drinkers of Milk: The Ancient Mediterranean Ideology of the Pastoral Nomad." *Ancient Society* 13–14: 5–31.

Shimron, B. 1973. "Πρῶτος τῶν ἡμεῖς ἴδμεν." *Eranos* 71: 45–51.

Sieberer, W. 1995. *Das Bild Europas in den Historien: Studien zu Herodots Geographie und Ethnographie Europas und seine Schilderung der persischen Feldzüge*. Innsbruck (Verlag des Instituts für Sprachwissenschaft der Universität Innsbruck).

Silberman, A. 1990. "À propos des Issédons: Hérodote (IV, 21–27) et les témoignages latins correspondants." *Revue de Philologie, de Littérature et d'Histoire Anciennes* 64: 99–110.

Skinner, J.E. 2012. *The Invention of Greek Ethnography: From Homer to Herodotus*. Oxford (Oxford University Press).

Slings, S.R. 2002. "Oral Strategies in the Language of Herodotus." In Bakker, E.J., de Jong, I.J.F., & van Wees, H., eds., *Brill's Companion to Herodotus*. Leiden (Brill), 53–77.

Strasburger, H. 1972. *Homer und die Geschichtsschreibung*. Heidelberg (Winter).

Thomas, R. 1989. *Oral Tradition and Written Record at Classical Athens*. Cambridge (Cambridge University Press).

———. 2000. *Herodotus in Context: Ethnography, Science, and the Art of Persuasion*. Cambridge (Cambridge University Press).

Triebel-Schubert, C. 1990. "Anthropologie und Norm: der Skythenabschnitt in der hippokratischen Schrift 'Über die Umwelt'." *Medizin-historisches Journal* 25: 90–103.

Trüdinger, K. 1918. *Studien zur Geschichte der griechisch-römischen Ethnographie*. Basel (E. Birkhäuser).

Visintin, M. 2000. "Echidna, Skythes e l'arco di Herakles: Figure della marginalità nella versione greca delle origini degli sciti, Herodot. 4, 8–10." *Materiali e Discussioni per l'Analisi dei Testi Classici* 45: 43–81.

Wakker, G.C. 2007. "Intentions and Future Realisations in Herodotus." In Bujis, M., ed., *The Language of Literature: Linguistic Approaches to Classical Texts*. Leiden (Brill), 168–87.

West, S. 1991. "Herodotus' Portrait of Hecataeus." *Journal of Hellenic Studies* 111: 144–60.

———. 1999a. "Introducing the Scythians: Herodotus on Koumiss (4.2)." *Museum Helveticum* 56: 76–86.

———. 1999b. "Hippocrates' Scythian Sketches." *Eirene* 35: 14–32.

———. 2000. "Herodotus in the North? Reflections on a Colossal Cauldron (4.81)." *Scripta Classica Israelica* 19: 15–34.

———. 2002a. "Scythians." In Bakker, E.J., de Jong, I.J.F., & van Wees, H., eds., *Epic Heritage and Mythical Patterns in Herodotus: Matrices of Genre: Brill's Companion to Herodotus*. Leiden (Brill), 437–56.

———. 2002b. *Demythologisation in Herodotus*. Toruń (Wydawnictwo Uniwersytetu Mikołaja Kopernika).

———. 2004. "Herodotus on Aristeas." In Tuplin, C.J., ed., *Pontus and the Outside World*. Leiden (Brill), 43–68.

Wood, C. 2016. "'I am Going to Say. . . ': A Sign on the Road of Herodotus' *Logos*." *Classical Quarterly* 66: 13–31.

Zali, V. 2015. *The Shape of Herodotean Rhetoric: A Study of the Speeches in Herodotus' Histories with Special Attention to Books 5–9*. Leiden (Brill).

Zhmud, L. 2016. "Pythagoras' Northern Connections: Zalmoxis, Abaris, Aristeas." *Classical Quarterly* 66: 446–62.

12 Ethnicity in Herodotus

The story of Helen through the Egyptians' eyes

Maria do Céu Fialho

Herodotus was undoubtedly fascinated by Egypt, which is the focus of Book II, travelling along a narrative-descriptive thread that spans from the *arkhē* 'ground beginning' of the growing opposition Asia-Europe, on what is today called the 'mythical plane', and leading up to the great conflict between Hellas and Persia – a conflict that caused great turmoil in the time period and geographical space in which Herodotus lived.

Herodotus takes obvious delight in writing about the people, the customs, the lands, and the great river Nile; Herodotus understood the interaction between the Nile and its fertile valley where such a great and ancient civilization developed, encapsulating that interaction in a formula that became universal and is still taught at schools, although the memory of its authorship has often been lost (2.5.3–4):[1]

> Αἴγυπτος ἐς τὴν Ἕλληνες ναυτίλλονται ἐστὶ Αἰγυπτίοισι ἐπίκτητός τε γῆ καὶ δῶρον τοῦ ποταμοῦ.
>
> The Egypt to which the Greeks sail is new land which the Egyptians have gained as a gift from the river.

Apart from Herodotus' *opsis* 'observation', he understood that land and its complex civilization required *akoē*, that is, listening to information and narratives from priests, the true guardians of memories, as well as deploying the hermeneutics of *gnōmē* 'intellect', for the linking of sources, translation of concepts, and the appreciation of collected data.

The length of the text dedicated to Egypt has been explained as a result either of an overwhelming fascination that consumes and drives the narrator (which, in modern terms, would raise questions over the unity of the work), or of a concern to demonstrate the importance and extent of the conquest of Egypt by the great king Cambyses. There are authors who point out that the appreciation of Egyptian civilization by the historian of Halicarnassos conveys a 'Hellenization of Egypt'.[2] In fact, as Lloyd reminds us, the Minoan traces and, later, the Mycenaean presence in Egypt, as well as that of Egyptian elements in Helladic space, are ancient. It is possible to trace the influence of Egypt on the civilizations of the Mediterranean basin back to the Neolithic and Bronze Ages.[3] The relationship between the Egyptian and the Hellenic civilizations became self-evident to an observant spirit like the author of *Histories*, who, while narrating the conflict between Europe and Asia, could not but mention the defining borders of Greece. This perspective sprang not from a synchronic standpoint but constituted a searching for the roots of a past that was poorly explored by the Greeks. These roots, which seem to show civilizational coincidences or equivalences, lead to the methodological interrogation, implemented by Herodotus, about their respective priority. The issue of the 'Hellenization of Egypt' may rest for a while open, as well as another possible opposite question – the 'de-Hellenization' of Greece.[4]

Before considering the story of Helen and Proteus in Egypt, one has to consider the global writing strategy of Book II. The book begins with Cambyses' preparations to conquer Egypt (ch. 1) and immediately proceeds with a *logos* appearing to answer the question: 'what is the nature of this civilization?' In fact, chapter 2 narrates the experiment of Psammetikhos I (663–669 BC) that was undertaken in order to establish who were the oldest people on Earth.[5] Herodotus begins by pointing out that the Egyptians thought they were the oldest (Hdt. 2.2.1):

Οἱ δὲ Αἰγύπτιοι, πρὶν μὲν ἢ Ψαμμήτιχον σφέων βασιλεῦσαι, ἐνόμιζον ἑωυτοὺς πρώτους γενέσθαι πάντων ἀνθρώπων.

Before Psammetikhos' reign, the Egyptians had regarded themselves as the oldest race on earth.

This information comes from the priests of Hephaestus in Memphis. The Egyptians' awareness of having been born into a privileged civilization on account of its ancient roots, as opposed to other known cultures, was partially corrected by an experiment on spontaneous language acquisition carried out on the pharaoh's orders: two newborns were completely isolated until they uttered their first intelligible communicative sounds (2.2.3) – hence the Phrygians were the oldest people, since the word uttered by the children corresponded to the Phrygian term for 'bread'. Therefore, the Egyptians became convinced that they were the second oldest people.

I say 'partially corrected' because if the Phrygians were the first humans to acquire language, the Egyptians took determinant steps to attain civilizational supremacy, as the historian will demonstrate. It was the Egyptians who understood and calculated the division of the year into 365 days, divided into 12 months of 3- days, plus five days extra. The calculation, based on the observation of the stars, was much more accurate than the indigenous system of the Greek calendar, according to Herodotus (2.4.1).

In as much as the author is about to approach a much more delicate matter, he warns the reader that, although he obtained information from the priests who told him about Psammetikhos' experiment, he also looked for even more credible sources to compare the resulting information. These more credible sources were the inhabitants of Thebes and Heliopolis, the most knowledgeable among the Egyptians (2.3.1): οἱ Αἰγυπτίων λογιώτατοι. Herodotus thus gives credibility to his own account, which contains more than the process of the calendaric division. The Egyptians were the first to name the 12 gods, and the Greeks adopted the names. The

Egyptians were also the ones who discovered proper forms of cult activity, like the construction of temples, the erection of altars dedicated to each god, and the sculpting of their images (2.4.2). Aside from the issue of the equivalence between gods, which is not the subject of this study and has been widely discussed,[6] it is important to note the underlying perspective: the Egyptians are, if not the oldest people, one of the oldest peoples on earth. That is because very early on the Egyptians reached a civilizational level of superiority compared to neighbouring peoples, so much so that they inspired other civilizations – in this case, that of the Greeks. The panhellenic hero Heracles, for example, originates in the Egyptian Heracles (2.43), the cult of Dionysius originates in Egypt (2.49), as well as the majority of the Greek gods. The few Greek gods that the Egyptians do not recognize (the Dioskouroi, Hera, Hestia, Themis, the Graces, and the Nereids) derive from the Pelasgians and Poseidon comes from Libya (2.50). Therefore, Egyptian deities are more ancient than those of the Greeks, and they inspired the identity of the latter (cf. 2.145–6). Likewise, according to Herodotus' interpretation, the belief in the immortality of the soul and in metempsychosis, known to the Greeks (especially to those who professed Orphic-Pythagorean convictions), has its origin in Egypt (2.123).

Even in legislation the Egyptians were inspiring: in an era closer to Herodotus' period, that wise legislator, the Attic poet Solon was likely influenced by another wise ruler, the Pharaoh Amasis, whom the historian perhaps met when in Egypt. Their mutual admiration confirms Herodotus' own opinion that men great in wisdom and excellence attract each other (2.177). Amasis is regarded by Herodotus as φιλέλλην (2.178.1). His account of Amasis favouring the Greeks, at the end of Book II, conveys the idea that the Greek civilization owes a lot to the Egyptian and that a new phase of reciprocity was underway in the historical period. The link between the gods Horus and Apollo (2.144) and the oracle of Delphi represent a continuum in this relationship, from time immemorial to the present.

In fact, in the classical Greek collective *imaginaire*, one of the hallmarks of the contact and assimilation of an ancient culture was the evocation of Egyptian provenance, either through the arrival of mysterious scholars (like the Platonic Strangers) or by means of the visit of Greek scholars to Egypt (Pythagoras, Plato, according to some *Vitae*).[7]

Helen's *logos* takes a central space in Book II (112–20) and begins immediately after the story of Pheros' divine punishment, and the blindness brought on him by his *hybris* (2.111).[8] Herodotus hastily corroborates the consistency of his narrative indicating, directly or indirectly, his sources: the description of Proteus' temple, its form and location in the Phoenician quarter of the city, the proximity of another small temple dedicated to a 'foreign Aphrodite' indicate to the reader that Herodotus knows what he depicts – in all probability, he had been there.[9] His primary information came from the priests from Memphis (Hdt. 2.112.1):

Τούτου δὲ ἐκδέξασθαι τὴν βασιληίην ἔλεγον ἄνδρα Μεμφίτην, τῶι κατὰ τὴν Ἑλλήνων γλῶσσαν οὔνομα Πρωτέα εἶναι.

The priests told me that after Pheros the kingdom passed to a man from Memphis whose name in Greek is Proteus.

This phrasing implies that 'the man from Memphis' does not belong to the same dynasty as the previous rulers, as How and Wells remark.[10]

The combination of seeing, listening, questioning, and personal interpretation is resumed, after the expressive usage of συμβάλλομαι – 'I guess' (2.112.2) – in a much more vigorous formulation (Hdt. 2.113.1):

Ἔλεγον δέ μοι οἱ ἱρέες ἱστορέοντι τὰ περὶ Ἑλένην γενέσθαι ὧδε·
On the business concerning Helen, I asked the priests what they knew and this is what they told me.

As widely known, the story of Helen's presence in Egypt represents an alternative variation of the story about her successful abduction, leading to Helen and Paris' arrival in Troy.[11] It is not possible to ascertain how deep its roots go: the first explicit testimonial is Stesichorus' famous fragment (fr. 15 Page):[12] Helen did not go to Troy. Helen's *eidōlon* seems to be Euripides' later invention. According to Herodotus, however, Homer knew the version of the arrival of Helen and Paris in Egypt but did not use it because he found it unsuitable for his designs. But there are traces of it in his text: the historian turning Homeric literary critic cites *Il.* 6.289–92, where the poet alludes to the luxurious garments brought to Troy by Alexandros (Ἀλέξανδρος) and Helen, in her journey from Phoenicia. He also cites *Od.* 4. 227–30, where Helen, already in her palace, laces her wine with a drug that will make anyone who takes it forget all their grief and suffering: she will thus prepare Menelaus and Telemachus for the banquet, once the painful memories of relatives lost in the fighting at Troy have been forgotten. The drug had been given to Helen by the Egyptian Thon's wife (2.116.4) – the name is almost coincident with that of one of the characters mentioned by Herodotus: Thonis, the guardian of the Canobic branch of the Nile delta (2.114.1). Furthermore, to attest that the author of *Odyssey* knew about Menelaus' presence in Egypt, Herodotus quotes the king of Sparta in *Od.* 4.351–2.

It is quite possible that Herodotus is right and that the version of Helen's presence in Egypt is at least contemporary with the Homeric Poems. This Egyptian version is the one chosen by Euripides for his *Helen*. According to the priests questioned by Herodotus (2.118) no *eidolon* or stolen treasures went to Troy – let us say that the only *eidolon* was in the Greeks' minds: they would not believe in the Trojans' oaths that they did not have Helen nor did they understand that, no matter how beautiful Helen was, no king would ever sacrifice his city and his people on account of a prince's whim (2.120). This is also Herodotus' *gnōmē*, which works from a rationalized version of previous sources – probably Hecataeus, according to Lloyd[13] and Vandiver.[14] Harrison notes that:[15]

Love is never said explicitly to be of divine origin, but frequently, at least, has fateful consequences. Most famous, Alexandros' desire for a Greek wife . . . attracted retribution, in Herodotus' view, in the form of the complete destruction of Troy (2.120.5).

Thus, the Greeks destroyed the city and found out too late that the Trojans had spoken the truth.

This critique of Homeric sources, intended to demonstrate the reliability of the Egyptian accounts, is typical of Herodotus' writing process: he de-mythologizes history, as How and Wells stress.[16] The epic poet and his listeners knew, at least implicitly by means of mythological narratives, about the fame of Egypt's fertility and the Egyptians' expertise in medicine and natural pharmacology. The length of the cited second excerpt of the *Odyssey* seems to play the role of making the readers of *Histories* aware of that fact.

Along the same de-mythologizing lines, Homer depicts Proteus' character not as that of a marine god with a prodigious metamorphic ability, but as a prudent and fair ruler. It is possible that among Herodotus' sources for this rationalizing account, aside from Egyptian priests, was Hecataeus.[17] Nonetheless, several aspects (to be discussed in the following section) remain unaccounted for; aspects that might provide an answer for the everlasting question: what is the extent of Herodotus' influence and how reliable is his work?

Archaeology has corroborated the existence of a temple – the one that Herodotus visited – in the urban space near Memphis, inhabited by Phoenicians. There was probably another smaller temple adjacent to it dedicated to the goddess Hathor. Two plaques with the goddess' name were found – she was the Egyptian goddess of love and beauty, equivalent to the Greek goddess Aphrodite. But while the urban layout was clearly Phoenician, the Phoenicians worshipped Astarte as the goddess of love and beauty. It would, therefore, be natural to name the patroness of the temple as 'the Foreign Astarte' (cf. Waddell[18]), which in the words of the cultural translator Herodotus would correspond to 'Foreign Aphrodite'. The conclusion that it was a temple in honour of Helen is the result of Herodotus' γνώμη; Herodotus acknowledges its application with the use of the term συμβάλλομαι (2.112.2). As far as Proteus was concerned, Herodotus could not accept the Homeric version of the shape-changing divinity.[19] Apparently the historian thought himself responsible for finding a plausible correspondence: each and every comment helps to form the hypothesis that Herodotus might have learned of an Egyptian term that designated a governing position and this fact might have led him to an incorrect or overreaching translation: Proutî (accepted by De Bakker, How and Wells, Lloyd, and Waddell). Even if such a conclusion was wrong, Herodotus probably had plausible grounds for his identification.

De Jong rightly remarks, citing one of her previous works,[20] that Homer uses two names for the Trojan seducer: Paris (19 times) and Alexandros (45 times), which are not randomly used. So De Jong argues against Lloyd in stating that the first name seems to correspond to a local name, while the second is the 'international name' of Helen's lover.[21] If this perspective might be undermined by the discussion over the name in Euripides' tragedy, it is strengthened by the exclusive usage of the name 'Alexandros' by Herodotus. Not only does Herodotus link the narrative to the Homeric reference, as De Jong maintains, but he places himself as someone who posesses an outsider's perspective of the famous story, a foreign, Egyptian perspective – indeed, Homer uses 'Paris' fewer times.

This is yet another Herodotean strategy to make his *logos* trustworthy, repeating again and again that he heard the facts of the matter from local priests. Moreover, Herodotus transfers the process of *historiē* to two entities connected with the narrative: first, to an external entity (human interlocutors) in the name of the utmost reliability and, second, to an internal entity in the name of the highest plausibility. The external entity comprises the priests from Memphis (2.119.3):

Τούτων δὲ τὰ μὲν ἱστορίηισι ἔφασαν ἐπίστασθαι, τὰ δὲ παρ'ἑωυτοῖσι γενόμενα ἀτρεκέως ἐπιστάμενοι λέγειν.

My informants told me that they learnt this as a result of their enquiries, but that they were certain of the events that had happened in their own country.

After all, the Trojan war occurred away from their homeland; it had a terrible outcome, establishing a direct link of cause and effect with the magnitude of the ἔργον ἀνόσιον (2.114.2). It was committed by a Trojan, upon whom Homer's narrative expands: not only did the Trojan abduct Helen, but he also robbed Menelaus. Such a narrative outline allowed Herodotus to conclude, maybe innovatively, that therein lay an explanation for the gods' anger and punishment of Paris. Also, as Paris and Helen sailed away from Egypt there began to blow winds that dragged the foreigners back to the Egyptian shore. These unfavourable winds or absent winds (which are closely related to the story of the war itself and Helen) were possibly elements of traditions contributed by priests or other listeners to the several episodes of cyclic stories about Helen. Besides, the Egyptians, who had been navigating the area for thousands of years, knew as well as Herodotus did the pattern of winds along the coast of their homeland.

To ask questions about the foreigners, Proteus also resorts to the same processes as Herodotus.[22] This mysterious character was the object of the priests' narrative; Herodotus translated his name and established an equivalent one. He also learned that Proteus seized Helen (and the riches stolen from Menelaus) and expelled Alexandros. Herodotus brings king Proteus to life and characterizes him as a wise and prudent man, who seeks to ascertain the provenance of those he takes in and on whom he may enact justice. His exercise of justice is firm and fair; it is fit for a royal model of *xenia*, 'an educator', using De Bakker's expression. It is worth noting Herodotus' care in having the king declare, twice, that it is not his usual practice to sacrifice foreigners (μηδένα ξείνων κτείνει, 2.115.4; μὴ ξεινοκτονέειν, 2.115.6). In fact, although they were not exactly xenophiles, apparently the Egyptians did not kill foreigners, although the Greeks attributed acts of *xeinoktonia* to the mythical Bousiris. This note – which no doubt bears Herodotus's mark – probably intends to establish a contrast between the Greek Menelaus' behaviour, and that of the Egyptians who lawfully guarded his wife and riches.

At the beginning of his *logos*, Herodotus explains that the first of the temples that formed part of the setting of this story was a coastal sanctuary dedicated to Heracles; the author asserts that the temple still exists in his time and that it was tied to the custom of conferring immunity to the slaves who went there as suppliants (2.113.2). No other source contains such information, nor is there any echo of such practice by the Egyptians. In this particular excerpt, the historian does not mention the priests as his source of information. Whether he relied on Hecataeus or not we will never know.

One thing is certain: the Egyptians are credited with respecting two determinant aspects in Greek ethics and religion, namely the respect for suppliants and the hospitality and integrity towards the guest (*xenos*): following this precedent, they accommodate first Helen, then Menelaus.[23] Regarding this issue, there is, in fact, a certain 'Hellenic perspective of Egypt' at play that draws on Greece's most noble and elevated qualities. The *logos* is expertly finished by a description of the destinies of the Trojan and the Greek. The former will witness the total destruction of his home and city; the latter, whose wife and riches Proteus kindly protected as a host in *xenia* (2.119), is expected to reciprocate in gratitude, in a pact of *philia*. However, the Atreid does no such thing. The rhythm of the narrative accelarates towards the end of the story. Chapter 120 is dedicated to Alexandros; chapter 119 to Menelaus; both proceed at a breathtaking pace: after his reception, Menelaus rushes his departure, but the winds are unfavourable (again the element of 'wind' plays a vital role in the story). He then does 'a forbidden deed', πρῆγμα οὐκ ὅσιον (2.119.2). His hastiness, paralleled by the rapid rhythm of the narrative, leads him to do what Proteus, or his people, twice declared that they would never do: human sacrifice. Thus, the Greek kills two Egyptian children and leaves behind him a reputation of hatred in the minds of the people that had taken such good care of Helen and his riches.[24] Herodotus guarantees that he heard this story from the priests – the same who sought information about what they had not witnessed. It is interesting to note that there appears to have existed a 'harbour of Menelaus' in Libya.[25]

Menelaus', or his people's, punishment remains unclear, unlike that of Alexandros. Could it be that Herodotus' objective is to leave a warning, in Aeschylean fashion, about divine justice looming and ruthlessly falling upon later generations? That is Saïd's opinion,[26] who stresses the contrast between this version of Menelaus' departure from Egypt and the excerpt from the *Odyssey* (4.585–6). She states:

> This barbarous behaviour sets in motion a new process of retaliation. The narrative of the Egyptian priests ends with Menelaus 'fleeing to Libya with his ships, hated and pursued by the Egyptians' (Hdt. 2.119.3) . . . in respect to this unhappy conclusion I would suggest that the process of guilt and counter-guilt did not end with the defeat of Xerxes and the fall of Sestos but continued with the Athenian imperialist initiatives in 479 BCE, which could be seen as the first stage of new aggression against Asia.

And thus we may now return to the question about the purpose and foundation of this *logos*. Its full scope, world view, and interpretation bear, as De Jong writes, Herodotus' fingerprint. Herodotus picks up on material remnants and narratives to tell his *logos*, albeit with hard research work and *historiē*. The equivalences are far from correct, and other elements that cannot be accounted for, such as Hecataeus' findings, permeate his narrative.

His purpose, within the context of the book dedicated to Egypt, is certainly to deconstruct the dichotomy Greek–Barbarian,[27] in terms of the Egyptians. Egypt is the origin of other civilizations, like the Greek one – how then can it be barbaric, even if its language is different (albeit lending itself to equivalences)? Egypt lives in the Greek identity, which frequently betrays itself as Egyptianizing. The process of 'barbarization of the Greek' justifies and is justified by the process of 'Hellenization of the Egyptian'.[28] The land of Egypt deserves all possible attention for it holds the civilizational key that bridges the gap between Greece and Asia. With which continent does Egypt truly identify? With itself: Egypt is different – and so is the Nile and thereby the climate, ways, and customs.

Notes

1 Herodotus' translations quoted in this chapter are borrowed from Waterfield 2008.
2 The bibliography on this question is immense. As a single but expressive example, see Burkert 1972: 126.
3 Lloyd 1975: 1–9.
4 Both topics refer to a great issue: that of the problematization and questioning of the traditional Greek/Barbarian binomial, already present in Herodotus' work. Euripides, in the *Helen,* will deepen the relativity and somehow the artificiality of this binomial. Concerning the building of this binomial, see Hall 1989. On the need for tolerance and understanding towards the differences of the 'other' in Herodotus, see Soares 2005: 95–176. For an opposite perspective see Silva 2000: 3–26, 2001: 3–48. On the first testimonies of the relativity of the binomial in Aeschylus, see Fialho 2005a: 77–93. On the critical subversion of the binomial in Euripides, see Fialho 2005b: 47–70, 2006: 13–30, 2007: 165–77. Vlassopoulos 2013, demonstrates in his book the complexity and contradictions of this binomial: the conscience of identity and difference towards the other is concomitant with the diverse ways the Greeks interact with other peoples of the Eastern Mediterranean. This phenomenon played a great and decisive role for globalization in the ancient world.
5 Gera 2003: 68–92 presents a detailed description of what it is supposed to be Psammetikhos' experiment.
6 On this equivalence, see Harrison 2000: 208–22.
7 For Pythagoras, see Isoc. *Bus.* 29 = Diels-Kranz 14 A4. According to Diog. Laert. 3.6–7, Plato travelled once to Egypt in order to made contact with the prophets there. Cf. Cic. *Rep.* 1.10.16; *Fin.* 5.29.87, who mentions two journeys. However, Plato's presence in Egypt seems to be a fiction created by subsequent tradition. See, e.g., Guthrie 1975: 14–15.
8 According to Soares (2007: 82–100), Hdt. 2.112 and 2.120 (the beginning and end of Helen's episode in the *Histories*) contain the key for an understanding of the inclusion of this episode in its context: the former contains the formal justification and the latter the moral justification. This moral justification, I think, recovers, the moral lesson of Pheros' story, under a wider perspective: all men, either Egyptians or Greeks, are equally subject to the same divine laws.
9 For a discussion on this issue, see Armayor 1978: 65–73. See also Sousa pp. 209–10.
10 How & Wells 1912: 222–3, *comm. ad loc.*
11 See, e.g., Harrison 2000: 214–15. De Bakker (2012: 109) also mentions the testimonies of Homer, Stesichorus, and of fragments of the *Cypria* and of Hecataeus. In a footnote De Bakker (2012: 109, n. 6) makes a persuasive *Quellen Kritik* and presents the state of the art of the philology concerning Herodotus' relationship towards the version of Helen's presence in Egypt. In 1963 a papyrus was found (*POxy.* #2506) that contains

a note that sheds new light on Stesichorus' *Palinode*. It informs us that his Helen went to Egypt (some scholars, like Erbse 1955; Ghali-Kahil 1955; Herther 1957; also von Fritz 1967 were convinced that Stesichorus' Helen remained in Sparta). Then, most scholars arrived at the conclusion that the lyric poet was "Herodotus' ultimate source for Helen's stay in Egypt" (Dale, Kannicht, West, Heubeck among others). How to explain, then, Herodotus' silence towards Stesichorus? De Bakker answers with Grethlein (2010): "Herodotus does not engage in polemic with Stesichorus, but with Homer, whom he considers . . . a testimony worth engaging with."

12 For the *Palinode*, see Stesich. fr. 90–1 Davies and Finglass = *PMGF* 192; Pl. *Resp.* 586c; Isoc. 10.64; Conon *FGrH* 26 F 1.18; Paus. 3.19.11. Pl. *Phaed.* 243a = Stesich. fr. 91a Davies and Finglass: οὐκ ἔστ' ἔτυμος λόγος οὗτος οὐδ' ἔβας ἐν νηυσὶν εὐσέλμοις, οὐδ' ἵκεο Πέργαμα Τροίας.

13 Lloyd 1988: 47.

14 Van Diver 2012: 147, n. 14.

15 Harrison 2000: 238.

16 How & Wells 1912: 224 *comm. ad loc.*

17 Scanlon 2015: 10–12 considers rationalizations of myth by Hecataeus and by Herodotus as well, a manifestation of the typical characteristic of Ionian scientific thought. For the relationship between Hecataeus and the Egyptian priests as the information source of the Ionian, see the the classical work of Heidel (1935, repr. now 2011).

18 Waddell 1971: 220.

19 De Bakker 2012: 124–6; De Jong 2012:140–1.

20 De Jong 2012: 132–3.

21 See also Vandiver 2012: 147, n. 14.

22 De Bakker 2012: 120–1.

23 Harrison (2000: 214) points out: "This picture of a tolerant universalism must be qualified."

24 Soares (2014: 232) underlines, in the conclusions of her paper, how much the stories told by Herodotus: "demonstrate to Herodotus' audience that rules, human and divine, . . . and notions of hospitality, must be obeyed, by barbarians and Greeks alike".

25 How & Wells 1912: *comm. ad* Hdt. 2.119.3.

26 Saïd 2012: 101.

27 See also De Bakker 2012: 116–17.

28 Cartledge & Greenwood (2002: 354) speak of 'Egyptification' of Greece. For them, "Herodotus is explicit in making Greek religious practice derive from barbarian practice and underwrites this statement with a confident truth-claim . . . This 'Egyptification' of Greece . . . informs us about Herodotus' provocative positioning of himself in relation to his audience and, while it might not score many points for accuracy, suggests an independent attitude which was to become one of the defining traits of the historian." I agree with this remark on accuracy, excepting the presuposed equation 'barbarian -= Egyptian'. In an extremely well-researched synthesis, Rood (2007: 298) observes: "Far from pandering to Greek assumptions of cultural superiority, Herodotus' account of the earth's extremities encourages readers or listeners to think through and question their own preconceptions. Elswhere, too, Herodotus relativizes notions of superiority. He notes, for instance, that the Egyptians call all those who do not speak their own language 'barbarians' (2.158.5). His point is not that they use the same word as the Greeks, but that like the Greeks, they have a single word for those who do not speak their own language: Greeks are barbarians to Egyptians just as Egyptians are barbarians to Greeks." Rood also points out Herodotus' cultural relativism: "[H]e [sc. Herodotus] encourages Greeks to think about how other cultures view foreign peoples, and so how they as Greeks appear to others in much the same way that foreign peoples appear to Greeks."

Bibliography

Armayor, O.K. 1978. "Did Herodotus Ever Go to Egypt?" *Journal of the American Research Center in Egypt* 15: 59–73.

Burkert, W. 1972. *Lore and Science in Ancient Pythagoreanism*. Translated by A.L. Minar Jr. Cambridge (Cambridge University Press).

Cartledge, P. & Greenwood, E. 2002. "Herodotus as a Critic: Truth, Fiction, Polarity." In Bakker, E.J., De Jong, I.J.F., & Van Wees, H., eds., *Brill's Companion to Herodotus*. Leiden (Brill), 351–71.

Davies, M. & Finglass, P.J. 2014. *Stesichorus: The Poems*. Cambridge (Cambridge University Press).

De Bakker, M. 2012. "Herodotus'Proteus: Myth, History, Enquiry and Storytelling." In Baragwanath, E., & De Bakker, M., eds., *Myth, Truth & Narrative in Herodotus*. Oxford (Oxford University Press), 107–26.

De Jong, I. 2012. "The Helen 'Logos' and Herodotus' Fingerprint." In Baragwanath, E., & De Bakker, M., eds., *Myth, Truth & Narrative in Herodotus*. Oxford (Oxford University Press), 127–42.

Fialho, M.C. 2005a. "Representações de identidade e alteridade em Ésquilo." In Fialho, M.C., Silva, M.F., & Rocha Pereira, M.H., eds., *Crise e consolidação da ideia de Europa: Vol. I*. Coimbra (Imprensa da Universidade), 77–94.

———. 2005b. "Crise do poder e perversão da retórica no teatro de Eurípides." *Revista de História das Ideias* 26: 47–70.

———. 2006. "A 'Medeia' de Euripides e o espaço trágico de Corinto." In Suarez de la Torre, E., & Fialho, M.C., eds., *Bajo el signo de Medea/Sob o signo de Medeia*. Coimbra & Valladolid (Imprensa da Universidade – Secretariado de Publicaciones e Intercambio Editorial), 13–30.

———. 2007. "Sedução e sofrimento em 'As Troianas' de Eurípides." In Bañuls, J., *et al.*, eds., *O Mito de Helena: de Tróia à Actualidade*. Coimbra (CECH), 165–77.

Gera, D.L. 2003. *Ancient Greek Ideas About Language, Speech, and Civilization*. Oxford (Oxford University Press).

Guthrie, W.K.C. 1975. *History of Greek Philosophy: IV: Plato: The Man and His Dialogues*. Cambridge (Cambridge University Press).

Hall, E. 1989. *Inventing the Barbarian. Greek Self-Definition Through Tragedy*. Oxford. (Clarendon Press).

Harrison, T. 2000. *Divinity and History: The Religion of Herodotus*. Oxford (Oxford University Press).

Heidel, W.A. 1935. "Hecataeus and the Egyptian Priests in Herodotus, Book 2." *American Academy of Art and Sciences: Memoirs* V. 18, pt. 2 (repr. 2011).

How, W.W. & Wells, J. 1912. *A Commentary on Herodotus: Vol. I (Books I-IV) With Introduction and Appendixes*. Oxford (Oxford University Press).

Lloyd, A.B. 1975. *Herodotus: Book II: Introduction*. Leiden (Brill).

———. 1988. *Herodotus: Book II: Commentary 99–182*. Leiden (Brill).

Rood, T. 2007. "Herodotus and Foreign Lands." In Dewald, C., & Marincola, J., eds., *The Cambridge Companion to Herodotus*. Cambridge (Cambridge University Press), 290–305.

Rosén, H.B. 1987. *Herodoti Historiae: Vol. I: Libros I-IV Continens*. Leipzig (Teubner).

Saïd, S. 2012. "Herodotus and the 'Myth' of the Trojan War." In Baragwanath, E., & De Bakker, M., eds., *Myth, Truth & Narrative in Herodotus*. Oxford (Oxford University Press), 87–105.

Scanlon, T. 2015. *Greek Historiography*. Oxford (Blackwell).

Silva, M.F. 2000. "Os desafios das diferenças étnicas em Heródoto: Uma questão de inteligência e saber." *Humanitas* 52: 3–26.

———. 2001. "Os desafios das diferenças étnicas em Heródoto: Uma questão de inteligência e saber." *Humanitas* 53: 3–48.

Soares, C. 2005. "A visão do 'Outro' em Heródoto." In Fialho, M.C., Silva, M.F., & Rocha Pereira, M.H., eds., *Crise e consolidação da ideia de Europa: Vol. I*. Coimbra (Imprensa da Universidade), 95–176.

———. 2007. "Rapto e resgate de Helena nas Historias de Heródoto." In Bañuls, J., *et al.*, eds., *O Mito de Helena: de Tróia à Actualidade*. Coimbra (CECH), 81–8.

———. 2014. "Dress and Undress in Herodotus' 'Histories'." *Phoenix* 68: 222–34.

Vandiver, E. 2012. "'Strangers Are from Zeus': Homeric 'Xenia' and the Courts of Proteus and Croesus." In Baragwanath, E., & De Bakker, M., eds., *Myth, Truth & Narrative in Herodotus*. Oxford (Oxford University Press), 143–66.

Vlassopoulos, K. 2013. *Greeks and Barbarians*. Cambridge (Cambridge University Press).

Waddell, W.G., ed. 1939 (repr. 1971). *Herodotus: Book II*. London (Methuen Educational).

Waterfield, R. 2008. *Herodotus: The Histories: A New Translation*[2]. Oxford (Oxford University Press).

Part IV

Reflections of Herodotean ethnic historiography

13 Barbarians, Greekness, and wisdom

The afterlife of Croesus' debate with Solon

Delfim F. Leão

Introduction: the historicity of the meeting

The meeting between Solon and Croesus is one of the most famous and widely discussed episodes in the history of classical culture. Although these two personalities have aroused interest independently, it is indisputable that, after Herodotus had narrated the conversation between the two men, they would remain indelibly connected to that account, which, besides being the most complete, would also serve as a model for subsequent treatments of the same topic.[1] The awareness of this reality does not, of course, compel the other *testimonia* to describe the meeting in exactly the same way. Moreover, if small variants in the exposition reinforce the influence of the pattern established by Herodotus, they may, on the other hand, help to clarify better the specific objective that has led other authors to retell the famous episode. It is precisely in these differences of detail that the theme of ethnicity and the approach to the relationship of Greek *vs.* barbarian register interesting discourse modulations.

However, before proceeding to this analysis, it is appropriate to address some preliminary problems, whose understanding may have a decisive influence on the final understanding of the question. The first is to recall a well-known fact, that is, that both Solon and Croesus are two real personalities, about whom quite precise historical data are available. For the establishment of the relative chronology between these two figures, an essential aspect lies in the exact definition of the year of Solon's archonship. This is a complex and widely debated issue, the detailed analysis of which would divert us from the objectives of this study and that I have already been able to address in detail in a previous approach to Solon's political activity.[2] For this reason, only my general conclusions about the possible historicity of the meeting and the consequences that may derive from its interpretation will now be recalled.

With regard to the date of Solon's archonship, the literary tradition provides rather precise elements, with particular emphasis on the information provided by Diogenes Laertius (1.62), which is expressly based on Sosicrates, a contemporary of Apollodorus and a recognized authority in the discussion of the life and work of the Seven Sages. Sosicrates seems to have been concerned to use the best sources at his disposal, and it is probable that the calculation of the date of Solon's office was based on the official list of eponymous archons, therefore providing fairly secure information (Miller 1969: 63; Meiggs & Lewis 1989: 9–12; Alessandrì 1989: 192, n. 4). According to this source, Solon's *akmē* is to be placed in the Forty-Sixth Olympiad (= 596–592 BC) and the archonship would fall in the third year of the same Olympiad, so in 594–593 BC. Still, according to this testimony, Solon's *nomothesia* or legislative activity would implicitly have occurred during the same period of time. It has been suggested, however, that in the year of archonship the statesman enacted only emergency provisions (the *seisakhtheia* and the reform of measures and reference weights), which he would later supplement (during 592–1) with the bulk of the constitutional reform. This is, in fact, an old suggestion, already advanced by Hammond (1940), which has the advantage of being able to harmonize better the testimony of Diogenes Laertius with that of the Aristotelian *Athenian Constitution* (*Ath. Pol.* 10.1; 14.1). For the present purposes, however, it is sufficient to emphasize as very probable the dating of Solon's archonship in 594–3.

Regarding Croesus, it is generally assumed that the Lydian monarch ascended the throne about 560 BC, ruling for 14 years in succession, until Sardis fell to Cyrus in 547–546. With these first data in mind, it is now time to evoke the elements provided by the account of Herodotus (1.29–30.1):

κατεστραμμένων δὴ τούτων καὶ προσεπικτωμένου Κροίσου Λυδοῖσι, ἀπικνέονται ἐς Σάρδις ἀκμαζούσας πλούτῳ ἄλλοι τε οἱ πάντες ἐκ τῆς Ἑλλάδος σοφισταί, οἳ τοῦτον τὸν χρόνον ἐτύγχανον ἐόντες, ὡς ἕκαστος αὐτῶν ἀπικνέοιτο, καὶ δὴ καὶ Σόλων ἀνὴρ Ἀθηναῖος, ὃς Ἀθηναίοισι νόμους κελεύσασι ποιήσας ἀπεδήμησε ἔτεα δέκα, κατὰ θεωρίης πρόφασιν ἐκπλώσας, ἵνα δὴ μή τινα τῶν νόμων ἀναγκασθῇ λῦσαι τῶν ἔθετο. αὐτοὶ γὰρ οὐκ οἷοί τε ἦσαν αὐτὸ ποιῆσαι Ἀθηναῖοι· ὁρκίοισι γὰρ μεγάλοισι κατείχοντο δέκα ἔτεα χρήσεσθαι νόμοισι τοὺς ἄν σφι Σόλων θῆται. αὐτῶν δὴ ὦν τούτων καὶ τῆς θεωρίης ἐκδημήσας ὁ Σόλων εἵνεκεν ἐς Αἴγυπτον ἀπίκετο παρὰ Ἄμασιν καὶ δὴ καὶ ἐς Σάρδις παρὰ Κροῖσον.

And after these were subdued and subject to Croesus in addition to the Lydians, all the sages from Hellas who were living at that time, coming in different ways, came to Sardis, which was at the height of its prosperity; and among them came Solon the Athenian, who, after making laws for the Athenians at their request, went abroad for ten years, sailing forth to see the world, he said. This he did so as not to be compelled to repeal any of the laws he had made, since the Athenians themselves could not do that, for they were bound by solemn oaths to abide for ten years by whatever laws Solon should make. So for that reason, and to see the world, Solon went to visit Amasis in Egypt and then to Croesus in Sardis.[3]

Herodotus reports that, shortly after the *nomothesia*, Solon left Athens for a period of ten years under the pretext of visiting other lands, although his real motive resided in the desire to avoid pressure to change the code of laws that he had just established. This information is consistent with that provided by other sources

(*Ath. Pol.* 11.1; Plut. *Sol.* 25.6), although the *Athenaion Politeia* does not refer to Solon's visit to the court of Croesus.[4] If it is accepted that the archonship of Solon occurred in 594–3, and even assuming that the legislative reform might have occupied him for some further time, it would result that the meeting with Croesus would have to have taken place within the next ten years, therefore before 580, even with the widest allowances. However, by maintaining that the Lydian monarch reached the throne only in 560, that date would make impossible the historical accomplishment of his encounter with Solon as related. In fact, to ensure the historical existence of their meeting, a number of circumstances would need to be changed. Firstly, the beginning of the ten-year voyage would have to take place not after the archonship, but after the first establishment of the tyranny by Peisistratos (561/60). And even if this could provide a good reason to leave Athens – as is maintained by Diogenes (1.50), who is committed to stressing Solon's disenchantment with the political course of his city – as a consequence it would lead, however, to lowering the date of the archonship considerably. In fact, Herodotus informs his audience that Sardis was at the height of its power (ἀκμαζούσας πλούτῳ) at the time of Solon's visit, a situation that, if taken literally, would postpone the meeting to a period subsequent to the submission to Lydia of the cities of Asia Minor and to Croesus' alliance with the Greek islands. These developments certainly demanded the course of several years to be fulfilled, which is to say that the meeting with Croesus could not take place at the beginning of his reign. Given these multiple chronological difficulties, the most natural conclusion would be to accept the historical impossibility of the dialogue between Croesus and Solon.

Recently, however, Wallace (2016) has offered significant arguments that Croesus' reign began much earlier, probably before 580, thereby calling into question Herodotus' information about the duration of the reign of Croesus, which rests in multiple values of seven: "Are Herodotus' figures for Croesus in 1.86, '14 years', '14 days' and 'twice seven *paides* of the Lydians', historical or formulaic? These numbers also look densely formulaic" (Wallace 2016: 170). At the same point, he suggests that the idea of "sacrificing or sparing 'twice seven' youths is a Greek convention", thus constituting a mode of Herodotus representing the ethnicity of the 'non-Greek' and his view or representation of what is 'Greek' (following Parker 2004: 153). According to this pattern, the 14 years of Croesus' reign would be divided into two periods of seven years, whose turning point is marked by the visit of Solon: thus a period of increasing prosperity, until the visit of the Athenian statesman, is followed by a second descending period, in which the Lydian monarch suffers divine consequences for having dared to consider himself the happiest of men. If this really was the case, Wallace's proposal could be reinforced by the connection here to Delphic morality (see later in this chapter under "Solon, Croesus and the tradition of the Seven Sages in Herodotus"), making it possible to render the encounter between Croesus and Solon historically viable at an earlier date. Admitting this hypothesis, however, is not the same as demonstrating that the meeting really took place and with the exact characteristics that made Herodotus' story famous. In other words, the effecting of such a meeting may be more or less credible from a temporal angle, but its cultural impact does not necessarily stem from the greater or lesser historical accuracy that can be conceded to it; its force actually lies in the fact that it became a civilizational paradigm and, in this viewpoint, its significance even overcomes any constraint that could be imposed from a chronological reconstruction.

Solon, Croesus, and the tradition of the Seven Sages in Herodotus

Gnomic literature is a pleasant and practical way of transmitting to young people the traditional values of their culture by helping to create a mental structure that works as a paradigm capable of influencing behaviour not only in religious and moral beliefs but also in the social and political fields.[5] Although simple and popular in its formulation, admonitory literature probably had an aristocratic origin in the sense that it represented a vehicle for conveying a system of principles generally aligned with the interests and designs of the upper classes.[6] This type of literature is not unique to Greek culture and can take many forms, although it usually conforms to a common basic scheme: it portrays the situation where an older or more experienced person gives his or her advice to a more or less skilled younger interlocutor. In Greece, the image of the Seven Wise Men is particularly representative of this phenomenon, which expresses itself in a tradition that would flourish until Roman times, maintaining the capacity to incorporate new elements throughout that period, to the point where there are more than 20 personalities that could figure in different groups of seven *sophoi* (DL 1.41–42). When one examines the profile of these *sapientes*, it becomes clear that they represent an order of values filtered by the worldliness of a small part of the community: the Sages are generally Greeks, aristocrats, and men, although, within the group could also be included some special *barbaroi* (as is seen with Croesus and Anacharsis). Certain figures of a different nature – such as the former slave Aesop or the young Kleobouline – could also come into association with the *sophoi*, to the point of being present in meetings of the Seven Wise Men and even participating in their discussions, but they still were not really part of that more restricted circle of wise persons. This is so, remarkably, in Plutarch's *Septem Sapientium Convivium*, a work that can be considered a kind of cosmopolis of different types of wisdom (Leão 2008a).

Another important element derives from the fact that the majority of these sages had a historical existence, even if their stories would subsequently attract a great deal of legendary amplification, especially with regard to biographical details. Nevertheless, the historical context in which some of these figures (such as Thales, Solon, Bias, Pittakos, Periander, Kleoboulos, Kheilon, and Croesus) operated suggests that the tradition began to take shape during the Archaic period, more specifically between the seventh and the sixth centuries BC. This process cannot be understood without recognizing that during this period Greece experienced great political and social tensions, which were accompanied by the rise of charismatic leaders who would play a central role in resolving these tensions, especially as advisers and legislators, and sometimes also as rulers of autocratic governments. It is, therefore, reasonable to suppose that, at least with the most emblematic of these personalities, their visibility as philosophers, poets, rulers, or legislators would have been a determining factor for their characterization as special individuals and, therefore, as fitting candidates for the position of paradigmatic *sophoi*.[7]

Despite the historical antiquity of various figures who came to be considered Sages, it is only in Herodotus that the first literary expression of the configuration of a legend concerning the *sophoi* appears. To be sure, the historian was probably not aware of the existence of a *sylloge* of Seven Wise Men – even if the image of the counsellor is recurrent in his work, as was long ago emphasized by Lattimore (1939: 24), who puts, for example, Amasis in the gallery of tragic counsellors. In Herodotus, what stands out most are the famous meetings promoted by Croesus and the advice he received from such figures as Thales (1.74.2, 75.3–4), Bias (or Pittakos, 1.27.1–5), and Solon (1.29–32). Herodotus also refers to Kheilon (1.59.2–3), Periander (1.20; 23), and Anacharsis (4.76–7), thus providing the first literary presentation of personalities who would play an influential role as *sophoi*.

Particularly important to this tradition (and central to the ongoing analysis) are the details of the meeting between Solon and Croesus, which give shape to the typical model of presentation of the dialogue between a Greek sage and an Eastern monarch. Moreover, the importance of Croesus himself in the development of the Seven Wise Men tradition has long been emphasized (e.g., Snell 1952: 42–3). This fact can be explained, in the first place, by the notoriety that the Lydian king enjoyed among the Greeks and by the probable influence of Delphi – a more easily understandable perspective if one takes into account the impact caused in the Greek world by the magnificent offerings made by Croesus to the oracle (cf. Hdt. 1.50–1; Bacchyl. 3.15–29; see also Parke 1984). On the other hand, it is not improbable that Solon himself played a prominent role in the First Sacred War, a conflict that must have begun shortly before the archonship of the legislator. Moreover, some *testimonia* even claim that it would have been Solon who proposed that the members of the Amphictyony come to the aid of the oracle (Aesch. 3.108; Plut. *Sol.* 11). Therefore, Delphic propaganda would have every interest in linking to each other those personalities who had played a prominent role in the history of the oracle of Apollo.

On the other hand, although there is no specific allusion to the number of seven *sapientes* in Herodotus (who refers to these special visitors vaguely as *sophistai*[8]), the number seven would become the formulaic figure used to designate the *sophoi* as a group. The importance of this number in other accounts and in other cultures is well known, but it is also defensible that it could establish a direct relationship with Delphic interests. Indeed, this was precisely the date of the birth of Apollo (which fell on the seventh day of the month *Bysios*, in February/March).[9] Apart from the relative pertinence of these interpretations, it is particularly important to note now that, although the existence of a *sylloge* of Seven Wise Men is not yet clearly detectable in Herodotus, there are still some traits that may already be found in the work of the historian that will become characteristic of the conventional way of presenting the *sophoi*: the emergence of certain influential regions such as Ionia (Pittakos, Bias, and Thales), Athens (Solon) and the Peloponnese (Kheilon, Periander); and the role of Delphi as an aggregator of these figures (Busine 2002: 17–27). From that point on, the canon would begin to establish itself, although it remained open to the inclusion of new additions and developments, as the works of Plutarch and Diogenes Laertius clearly illustrate.

The meeting of Solon and Croesus: the Herodotean paradigm

Apart from these elements that may have influenced Herodotus' options, let us now reflect on how the historian imagined the celebrated meeting of the two statesmen. The account is so well known that it would appear not to require more examination. Nevertheless, it must be justifiably invoked briefly in order to make more evident certain of its differences in detail in relation to other ancient authors who will base themselves on this Herodotean model, thus illustrating the different perspectives from which his report was being rewritten. According to Herodotus then, when Solon passes through Sardis, during his *apodēmia*, Croesus receives him in the palace and, on the third and fourth days after his arrival, he instructs the servants to show the illustrious guest the riches that he possessed. Only then, and after accentuating the wisdom of the interlocutor, in the way of a *captatio benevolentiae*, does Croesus introduce the central question of the dialogue between the two men: "so now I desire to ask you who is the most fortunate man you have seen" (1.30.2: νῦν ὦν ἐπειρέσθαι μοι ἵμερος ἐπῆλθέ σε εἴ τινα ἤδη πάντων εἶδες ὀλβιώτατον). Herodotus himself gives voice to what would be the expectation of Croesus, easy predictable after the monarch has made his treasures shown to the visitor. However, the historian notes that Solon was not impressed, a detail that, in addition to highlighting the world of higher values in which a wise man moves, foretells that he will propose a redefinition of the concept of *olbos* – since in Homer, Hesiod, and poets of the Archaic period in general, the use of the terms *olbos* and *olbios* is mainly related to material wealth. In fact, the basic notion of wealth (described by Herodotus as μεγάλα τε καὶ ὄλβια) that underlies Croesus' question corresponds to the semantic field traditionally supported by Greek aristocrats, i.e., the possession of material goods. The prospect that Solon will propose a reformulation of the concept is immediately confirmed by the evocation of the person who occupies the first place on the scale of happiness, Tellos of Athens (Hdt. 1.30.4–5):

Τέλλῳ τοῦτο μὲν τῆς πόλιος εὖ ἡκούσης παῖδες ἦσαν καλοί τε κἀγαθοί, καί σφι εἶδε ἅπασι τέκνα ἐκγενόμενα καὶ πάντα παραμείναντα, τοῦτο δὲ τοῦ βίου εὖ ἥκοντι, ὡς τὰ παρ' ἡμῖν, τελευτὴ τοῦ βίου λαμπροτάτη ἐπεγένετο· γενομένης γὰρ Ἀθηναίοισι μάχης πρὸς τοὺς ἀστυγείτονας ἐν Ἐλευσῖνι βοηθήσας καὶ τροπὴν ποιήσας τῶν πολεμίων ἀπέθανε κάλλιστα, καί μιν Ἀθηναῖοι δημοσίῃ τε ἔθαψαν αὐτοῦ τῇ περ ἔπεσε καὶ ἐτίμησαν μεγάλως.

Tellos was from a prosperous city, and his children were good and noble. He saw children born to them all, and all of these survived. His life was prosperous by our standards, and his death was most glorious: when the Athenians were fighting their neighbours in Eleusis, he came to help, routed the enemy, and died very finely. The Athenians buried him at public expense on the spot where he fell and gave him much honour.

This is, therefore, the diagnosis of the *olbiotatos*: belonging to a city worthy and prosperous; to have children of whom one may be proud and know their off-spring, free from danger; to lead a moderate existence and – a decisive aspect – to have a glorious end of life,[10] as represented by the fact that Tellos perishes in defence of his motherland, thus attracting a great 'honour' (ἐτίμησαν μεγάλως), which perhaps corresponded to the institution of a hero cult in his honour.[11] It was to be expected that Croesus would be surprised in the face of a picture so far removed from usual expectations. But the king insisted, hoping to occupy at least the second place, just to suffer a similar disappointment. Solon now referred to two Argive youths, who had sufficient means of subsistence, were endowed with great physical strength, and had even been winning athletes. Thus far they fulfill the requirements regarding place of birth, moderate existence, although still short, and some noteworthy previous achievements, which easily identify them with the level of Tellos' children (καλοί τε κἀγαθοί). Therefore, the difference in relation to the first case must be found in another aspect. It is then that Herodotus tells the story of the mother who had to be carried in a wagon to the sanctuary of Hera, but as the oxen were not available on time, her sons took the place of the draft animals and took her to the temple. So far, the two young men are still playing the role of devoted and pious children, and, therefore, the novelty must be sought in the outcome of the account (Hdt. 1.31.3–5):

ταῦτα δέ σφι ποιήσασι καὶ ὀφθεῖσι ὑπὸ τῆς πανηγύριος τελευτὴ τοῦ βίου ἀρίστη ἐπεγένετο, διέδεξέ τε ἐν τούτοισι ὁ θεὸς ὡς ἄμεινον εἴη ἀνθρώπῳ τεθνάναι μᾶλλον ἢ ζώειν. Ἀργεῖοι μὲν γὰρ περιστάντες ἐμακάριζον τῶν νεηνιέων τὴν ῥώμην, αἱ δὲ Ἀργεῖαι τὴν μητέρα αὐτῶν, οἵων τέκνων ἐκύρησε. Ἡ δὲ μήτηρ περιχαρὴς ἐοῦσα τῷ τε ἔργῳ καὶ τῇ φήμῃ, στᾶσα ἀντίον τοῦ ἀγάλματος εὔχετο Κλεόβι τε καὶ Βίτωνι τοῖσιν ἑωυτῆς τέκνοισι, οἵ μιν ἐτίμησαν μεγάλως, τὴν θεὸν δοῦναι τὸ ἀνθρώπῳ τυχεῖν ἄριστόν ἐστι. μετὰ ταύτην δὲ τὴν εὐχὴν ὡς ἔθυσάν τε καὶ εὐωχήθησαν, κατακοιμηθέντες ἐν αὐτῷ τῷ ἰρῷ οἱ νεηνίαι οὐκέτι ἀνέστησαν, ἀλλ᾽ ἐν τέλεϊ τούτῳ ἔσχοντο. Ἀργεῖοι δέ σφεων εἰκόνας ποιησάμενοι ἀνέθεσαν ἐς Δελφοὺς ὡς ἀνδρῶν ἀρίστων γενομένων.

When they had done this and had been seen by the entire gathering, their lives came to an excellent end, and in their case the god made clear that for human beings it is a better thing to die than to live. The Argive men stood around the youths and congratulated them on their strength; the Argive women congratulated their mother for having borne such children. She was overjoyed at the feat and at the praise, so she stood before the image and prayed that the goddess might grant the best thing for man to her children Kleobis and Biton, who had given great honour to the goddess. After this prayer they sacrificed and feasted. The youths then lay down in the temple and went to sleep and never rose again; death held them there. The Argives made and dedicated at Delphi statues of them as being the best of men.

As happened already with Tellos, in the case of Kleobis and Biton the moment of death is also decisive, because the two brothers perished in a moment of glory. The involuntary cause of their premature death was the mother herself who asked for her children the greatest reward that might be given to humans. And so, with their death, the divinity showed that sometimes it is better to perish in a favourable time than to face an uncertain future.[12] Now the reason for placing the two young men second in the scale of happiness seems to lie in this extemporaneous death, since, in essence, their story is similar to that of Tellos, in that they also perish in a moment of recognized glory. Moreover, a little further (1.32.2), and although with the intention of demonstrating the amount of evils to which mankind is subject during human existence, Solon puts the term of the human life at 70 years. This figure immediately evokes his poem about the ages of life, structured in ten periods of seven years.[13] It also brings to mind his alleged polemic with Mimnermus, who expresses the desire for death at the age of 60 years (fr. 6 West), while Solon raises this number to 80 (fr. 20 West). In the latter case, there is a difference of ten years from the usual figure, although poets are not obliged to be always consistent.[14] However, the most relevant aspect rests on the idea that old age is as dignified as youth, a conception opposed to the pessimism characteristic of the poets of the Archaic period. For Solon, years bring together with them the comfort of intellectual progress (fr. 18 West: γηράσκω δ' αἰεὶ πολλὰ διδασκόμενος[15]), although his poetry also registers some ideas that are a little closer to the perspective pointed out in the history of Kleobis and Biton (fr. 14 West: οὐδὲ μάκαρ οὐδεὶς πέλεται βροτός, ἀλλὰ πονηροὶ/πάντες ὅσους θνητοὺς ἠέλιος καθορᾶι[16]). However, observations of this nature are not characteristic of the statesman's poetry, where a creative optimism about existence prevails above all. Therefore, the conception of happiness of the Solon-poet is closer to the example of Tellos, who originated in the same city as the legislator, and, therefore, it seems probable that the story has an Athenian origin.

Faced with this second example of *olbos*, Croesus should have already understood that the essence of the concept would not focus on material wealth, of which he could expect to be a legitimate representative. Moreover, the wealth of the Lydian monarchs was proverbial, and before Croesus, the symbol of eastern opulence was already seen in Gyges (cf. Archil. fr. 19 West). Therefore, Croesus is eager to know in what position Solon will put his *eudaimoniē* ('good fortune') – an expression that denotes a broadening of horizons and, to a certain extent, a concession on the part of the king, for whom happiness was initially concentrated only in his concept of *olbos*, mere abundance of material goods. The legislator clarifies his position in the incisive response he gives to the king (Hdt. 1.32.1–9):

ὦ Κροῖσε, ἐπιστάμενόν με τὸ θεῖον πᾶν ἐὸν φθονερόν τε καὶ ταραχῶδες ἐπειρωτᾷς ἀνθρωπηίων πρηγμάτων πέρι. ἐν γὰρ τῷ μακρῷ χρόνῳ πολλὰ μὲν ἔστι ἰδεῖν τὰ μή τις ἐθέλει, πολλὰ δὲ καὶ παθεῖν. . . . ἐμοὶ δὲ σὺ καὶ πλουτέειν

μέγα φαίνεαι καὶ βασιλεὺς πολλῶν εἶναι ἀνθρώπων· ἐκεῖνο δὲ τὸ εἴρεό με
οὔ κώ σε ἐγὼ λέγω, πρὶν τελευτήσαντα καλῶς τὸν αἰῶνα πύθωμαι. οὐ γάρ
τι ὁ μέγα πλούσιος μᾶλλον τοῦ ἐπ' ἡμέρην ἔχοντος ὀλβιώτερός ἐστι, εἰ μή
οἱ τύχη ἐπίσποιτο πάντα καλὰ ἔχοντα εὖ τελευτῆσαι τὸν βίον. . . . πρὶν δ' ἂν
τελευτήσῃ, ἐπισχεῖν μηδὲ καλέειν κω ὄλβιον, ἀλλ' εὐτυχέα. . . . πολλοῖσι γὰρ
δὴ ὑποδέξας ὄλβον ὁ θεὸς προρρίζους ἀνέτρεψε.

Croesus, you ask me about human affairs, and I know that the divine is
entirely grudging and troublesome to us. In a long span of time it is possible
to see many things that you do not want to, and to suffer them, too. . . . To me
you seem to be very rich and to be king of many people, but I cannot answer
your question before I learn that you ended your life well. The very rich man
is not more fortunate than the man who has only his daily needs, unless he
chances to end his life with all well. . . . But refrain from calling him fortunate before he dies; call him lucky. . . . For the god promises fortune to many
people and then utterly ruins them.

Solon's explanation allows us to clarify the apparent injustice of the premature
death of Kleobis and Biton. The example of Tellos had clearly shown that the
paradigm corresponds to leading a modest and healthy existence, to live long
enough to know one's offspring and, fundamentally, to have a good death, which
can instil respect and admiration in others. This idea is in accordance with Solon's
poetry (fr. 21 West) and is central to the response now given to Croesus. The two
young athletes of Argos occupy the second place because they did not have a long
life and were, therefore, deprived of the joy of having offspring. However, in view
of the instability of human affairs, it is sometimes better to perish than to risk the
loss of what was already believed to be safe, as will happen to Croesus. In this
sense, the rich cannot be said happier than the poor. In fact, later on, on the pyre
prepared by Cyrus, Croesus recalls the conversation with Solon, from which he
retained the basic principle that it is premature to consider someone happy during
his lifetime (1.86.3).

In Solon's poetry, reflections on the character and role of wealth can often be
found, in line with the usual aristocratic perspective of the Archaic period, which
considered economic prosperity an essential feature of *aretē*.[17] His freshness lies,
therefore, in admitting the disjunction of those values, while affirming the superiority of *aretē* over wealth (fr. 15 West). In his most extensive and also most complex poem (fr. 13 West), usually known as "Elegy to the Muses", Solon asks the
daughters of Zeus and Mnemosyne for happiness (ὄλβον) from the gods and for
the grace to enjoy good fame (δόξαν ἔχειν ἀγαθήν) among humans, an aspect that
has already been seen to be important both in the history of Tellos and in that of
the Argive youths. However, in the same elegy he makes it clear that, despite the
instability of material possessions, he continues to desire them also for himself,
but with an important caveat (fr. 13.7–13): wealth is legitimate when it emanates
from the divine will, which guarantees it firmness and perenniality. Conversely,
the wealth that is the fruit of insolence (ὑφ' ὕβριος) and injustice (ἀδίκοις ἔργμασι)
soon draws man to the path of perdition (ἄτηι).[18] This happens because the

unrestrained demand for wealth does not respect the due order (οὐ κατὰ κόσμον ἔρχεται) and thus attracts the retribution of justice (πάντως ὕστερον ἦλθε δίκη), which is given by Zeus – as the poet states later on (fr. 13.17–25). Applied to the case of Croesus, these principles remain operative: the monarch, not content with his power, wishes to expand it beyond the reasonable, as symbolically is indicated by the crossing of the natural frontier that is constituted by the Halys river (1.72). On the other hand, the initial wealth of Croesus, though inherited, is not entirely legitimate, in as much as Gyges usurped the throne, after assassinating Candaules (1.7). This is an important factor, as is shown by the oracle of Apollo, whom Croesus asked to justify his fate after his fall (1.91). The Pythia explained that Loxias had endeavoured to have the punishment fall upon the sons of Croesus, and not upon the monarch himself, which proves the gratitude of the god for Croesus' offerings, though Apollo could not nullify the fate from the Moirai. Still, Apollo delayed the fall of Sardis for three years. These considerations raise the complex question of the causes of Croesus' misfortune, which amounts to asking whether he was atoning for personal faults or for hereditary guilt. The answer seemingly imposed is that the Lydian monarch has incurred this fate on both accounts, eventually receiving his punishment.[19] The Solon of the poems also acknowledges that the justice of Zeus may be delayed, but will always reach its target, whether it be the offenders themselves or future generations (fr. 13.29–32 West). Therefore, when Croesus pays for the faults of his ancestor Gyges this happens in obedience to the principle that atonement befalls all the guilty, although the punishment can at times fall not directly on the perpetrators but rather on their descendants.

This closeness between the ideas of the historical Solon and that of the character recreated by Herodotus helps to clarify the reasons that led the historian to choose the figure of the statesman, whose characterization may be heir to the memory preserved of him by the aristocratic Athenian elite, "who melded garbled anecdote with reminiscence of admonitory elegy" (Figueira 2015: 27). However, authors such as Shapiro (1996) argue, on the contrary, that the aforementioned principles express simply the beliefs of Herodotus and not those of Solon. In fact, the theme of the instability of human affairs is immediately introduced in the chapters in which Herodotus states the intention to consider large and small cities in his account (1.5.4), and is taken up, for example, when he discusses the causes of the madness of Cambyses (3.33). The mutability of fortune thus calls for the suspension of judgment on one's happiness until the circumstances of a person's death illuminate the soundness or even the nobility of the existence led (3.75.3). The contingency of human life, to be subject to the variations of luck, is related to the fact that, as Solon explains to Croesus, the gods envy and are prone to upset human successes (1.32.1: τὸ θεῖον πᾶν ἐὸν φθονερόν τε καὶ ταραχῶδες). The concept of divine *phthonos* does not appear in the poetry of Solon (unless we see it implied in the desire to hold *olbos* with *sōphrosynē*), while in Herodotus it holds a great importance. The concept is central to the relationship between Amasis and Polycrates and finds one of its clearest expressions in the words of Artabanos to his nephew Xerxes, while showing him that the animals, trees, and the most imposing houses are those that attract divine lightning, "for the god loves to bring low all things of surpassing greatness" (7.10e: φιλέει γὰρ ὁ θεὸς τὰ ὑπερέχοντα πάντα κολούειν). Therefore, the *phthonos* of the gods settles upon everything that threatens to exceed its natural limit, since divinity allows the nurturing of thoughts of greatness only to itself. There is thus a direct relationship between *hybris* and *phthonos*, and the likely consequence will be the doom of the offender so as to restore the order and balance of the world.[20] This explains the terrible punishment that will fall on Croesus in successive incidents until the day when he will have to climb the pyre prepared by Cyrus. It must, therefore, be recognized that, basically, the ideas conveyed by the Solon of the *Histories* also express notions sustained by Herodotus.[21]

It is as clearly pertinent to analyze another question, fundamental for our understanding of other sources dealing with this topic, which is to inquire whether the concepts exchanged between Solon and Croesus are to be perceived only within the framework of opposing ethnicities, i.e., Greek *vs.* barbarian, or are they intended to point out the limitations of a certain axiological universe applicable as well to the Greek society. In general, the first interpretation tends to be privileged, and Herodotus seems to support this hypothesis in the way he introduces the *logos* of the Lydian monarch (Hdt. 1.6.2–3):

Οὗτος ὁ Κροῖσος βαρβάρων πρῶτος τῶν ἡμεῖς ἴδμεν τοὺς μὲν κατεστρέψατο Ἑλλήνων ἐς φόρου ἀπαγωγήν, τοὺς δὲ φίλους προσεποιήσατο. κατεστρέψατο μὲν Ἴωνάς τε καὶ Αἰολέας καὶ Δωριέας τοὺς ἐν τῇ Ἀσίῃ, φίλους δὲ προσεποιήσατο Λακεδαιμονίους. πρὸ δὲ τῆς Κροίσου ἀρχῆς πάντες Ἕλληνες ἦσαν ἐλεύθεροι.

This Croesus was the first foreigner whom we know who subjugated some Greeks and took tribute from them and won the friendship of others: the former being the Ionians, the Aeolians, and the Dorians of Asia, and the latter the Lacedaemonians. Before the reign of Croesus, all Greeks were free.

In other passages, Herodotus seems to contradict the claim that Croesus was the first to act against Hellenic liberty, by stating that Gyges (1.14.4), Ardys (1.15), and Alyattes (1.16–22) had already attacked and even dominated some Asian Greek cities. One possible way of explaining this apparent contradiction lies in the distinction to be made between raiding operations (or temporary incursions) and the definitive establishment of dominion. In effect, the campaigns carried out by the other monarchs had not resulted in an effective and lasting submission, as in the case of Croesus, whose domain is symbolized by the obligation to pay tribute (Asheri 1988: CIII–CV). Although Croesus is clearly a barbarian – as king of Lydia, he could not belong to any group of Greeks – such a classification is not explored in the encounter between Croesus and Solon. The aspect of the sovereign of Sardis that is repeatedly emphasized is his enormous wealth, which can be both positive (as in the gifts given to Delphi) and negative, by its arousing feelings of *hybris*. However, it has already been pointed out that this notion of happiness based on material possessions ends up being characteristic of the ideals shared, in general terms, also by the Greek aristocrats.[22] Therefore,

Solon's words are not so much the mirror of a Greek *vs.* barbarian opposition, but rather a generalizing critique of the more usual conception of happiness, which finds its support, as previously discussed, in the poems of the legislator himself.[23] Moreover, in describing the fall of Sardis to Cyrus, Herodotus himself clarifies, by the mouth of Croesus, the real reach of the words of Solon: οὐδέν τι μᾶλλον ἐς ἑωυτὸν λέγων ἢ οὐκ ἐς ἅπαν τὸ ἀνθρώπινον καὶ μάλιστα τοὺς παρὰ σφίσι αὐτοῖσι ὀλβίους δοκέοντας εἶναι.[24] Therefore, to analyze the conversation between Solon and Croesus simply in the light of the Greek/barbarian binary relationship is to reduce the ethical weight of an episode that has, admittedly, much larger goals. Herodotus denounces the limitations of a certain conception of happiness that is not exclusive to a barbarian, but can also extend to the Greek aristocracy itself (and particularly to the excesses typical of a tyrant) and to the human race in general.[25] For this purpose he uses two historical figures whom he recreates in order to accentuate the two aspects under debate: on the one hand, the enormous wealth of a monarch, which can lead to arrogant blindness; on the other, the thoughtful vision of a statesman and thinker who has been concerned to avoid the ways of excess, as well as the perdition that is generally associated with them. Croesus and Solon thus overcome the frontiers of their historical existence to attain the status of paradigm (Duplouy 1999: 1–9, 21–2).

The reception and reshaping of the paradigm

Any person familiar with the tradition of the Seven Sages is well aware of the fact that it is necessary to wait until Plato's *Protagoras* (342e-343b) to find the first reference to a complete list of seven *sophoi*. This detail would suffice to guarantee Plato's testimony a special place in gnomic literature, but two other aspects deserve to be underlined: the central role that Plato attributes to Solon among the various *sapientes*, and the fact that he will certainly have influenced Plutarch in the way the latter imagined the *Septem Sapientium Convivium* – and by extension also the first book of the *Lives of the Eminent Philosophers* by Diogenes Laertius. Taken together, these three elements explain why Plato is generally a mandatory presence in discussions concerning the Seven Wise Men. One possible sign that Plato would be innovating in providing the complete *sylloge* of *sophoi* in written form is suggested by the detail that he is referring to "l'intégralité des sept noms et leurs ethniques respectifs" (Busine 2002: 33–4). In fact, if Plato were not naming them for the first time in the written tradition, it would seem more natural to refer to the Sages only through the expression *hepta sophoi*, which will later become the usual designation. This argument has a certain force, but it is not self-sufficient: in fact, Diogenes Laertius (1.41–42) gives the name of more than 20 *sophoi* and, although he wrote long after Plato, he continues to use ethnic identification and even the patronymic when referring well-known personalities of this cycle. Nevertheless, it is undeniable that the earliest reference to this *syllogē* is the passage from the *Protagoras* referenced earlier, although this does not necessarily imply that Plato was creating the tradition of the Seven Sages, as has already been maintained (e.g., by Fehling 1985: 9–19). On the contrary, Herodotus already mentions all these names (with the exception of Kleoboulos and Myson), although he presents them by association with other personalities or events and not as an autonomous group (see section "Solon, Croesus and the tradition of the Seven Sages in Herodotus").

However, more than the broader question of the Seven Wise Men, it is pertinent to analyze in particular the way in which Plato – or more probably an author writing in the tradition of Platonism – deals with the relationship between Croesus and Solon and to ponder the similarities and differences with respect to Herodotus. The author expressly references those two personalities at a time when he speaks of the natural tendency that wisdom (φρόνησις) and power (δύναμις) have to associate with each other. In the following, he illustrates several examples of this type of association (Pl. *Ep.* 2.311a):

οἶον καὶ περὶ Ἱέρωνος ὅταν διαλέγωνται ἄνθρωποι καὶ Παυσανίου τοῦ Λακεδαιμονίου, χαίρουσι τὴν Σιμωνίδου συνουσίαν παραφέροντες, ἅ τε ἔπραξεν καὶ εἶπεν πρὸς αὐτούς· καὶ Περίανδρον τὸν Κορίνθιον καὶ Θαλῆν τὸν Μιλήσιον ὑμνεῖν εἰώθασιν ἅμα, καὶ Περικλέα καὶ Ἀναξαγόραν, καὶ Κροῖσον αὖ καὶ Σόλωνα ὡς σοφοὺς καὶ Κῦρον ὡς δυνάστην.

For example, when men talk about Hieron or about Pausanias the Lacedaemonian they delight to bring in their meeting with Simonides and what he did and said to them; and they are wont to harp on Periander of Corinth and Thales of Miletus, and on Pericles and Anaxagoras, and on Croesus also and Solon as wise men and Cyrus as potentate.[26]

Notwithstanding the interest that the different examples offer, the characterization of Croesus and Solon is particularly significant here. It would be possible to invoke them both as a symbol of power or else refer to the former as a potentate and the latter as wise, as in the account of Herodotus. However, the author prefers to attribute to both the role of sapient (ὡς σοφούς) and, therefore, he is not interested in referring the details of the meeting between Croesus and Solon, but rather the relationship they establish with Cyrus as a figuration of power (ὡς δυνάστην). This detail underscores the idea that the Greeks did not see the king of Lydia as a common barbarian. This coloration mirrors Herodotus where, on several occasions, Croesus had also taken on the role of Cyrus' counsellor (cf. 1.155–156; 1.207–208).

When Diodorus, for his part, addresses this same episode, the fundamental elements of the tradition concerning the Seven Wise Men had long been fixed. In fact, the author attaches great importance to the prudential feature of the life of Solon, both in speaking of the formation of the statesman and in referring to the most important aspects of his activity. Diodorus also mentions the relation between the Athenian legislator and Croesus three times, with some variations worthy of note. In the first of them (9.2.1–4), Solon appears as the only interlocutor of the Lydian king whose answer is reproduced. But the manner in which both men are presented here deserves to be remembered, at least in part (DS 9.2.1–2):

ὅτι Κροῖσος ὁ Λυδῶν βασιλεὺς μεγάλας κεκτημένος δυνάμεις καὶ πολὺν ἐκ παρασκευῆς σεσωρευκὼς ἄργυρόν τε καὶ χρυσόν, μετεπέμπετο τῶν Ἑλλήνων τοὺς σοφωτάτους, καὶ συνδιατρίβων αὐτοῖς μετὰ πολλῶν δώρων

ἐξέπεμψε καὶ αὐτὸς πρὸς ἀρετὴν ὠφελεῖτο πολλά. ποτὲ δὲ τοῦτον [*scil.*
Σόλωνα] μεταπεμψάμενος καὶ τὰς δυνάμεις καὶ τὸν πλοῦτον ἐπιδειξάμενος,
ἠρώτησεν εἴ τις ἕτερος αὐτῷ δοκεῖ μακαριώτερος εἶναι. . . . σκοπεῖν οὖν
ἔφησε δεῖν τὴν τοῦ βίου τελευτὴν καὶ τὸν διευτυχήσαντα τότε προσηκόντως
λέγειν μακάριον.

Croesus, the king of the Lydians, who was possessed of great military
forces and had purposely amassed a large amount of silver and gold, used
to call to his court the wisest men from among the Greeks, spend some time
in their company, and then send them away with many presents, he himself
having been greatly aided thereby toward a life of virtue. And on one occasion he summoned Solon, and showing him his military forces and his wealth
he asked him whether he thought there was any other man more blest than
he. . . . Consequently, he continued, we must look to the end of life, and only
of the man who has continued until then to be fortunate may we properly say
that he is blest.[27]

Diodorus begins by accentuating the sheer scale of Croesus' power and wealth,
accumulated to serve a deliberate project (ἐκ παρασκευῆς σεσωρευκώς) – a goal
that, without being clearly identified, must correspond, in some part, to the will to
impress the people whom the king summoned to his court. These illustrious visitors were the wisest among the Greeks (τῶν Ἑλλήνων τοὺς σοφωτάτους), a detail
that underlines the relevance of the interpretation of the exchange of impressions
with Solon in the light of the Greek *vs.* barbarian opposition. However, this reading, which would tend to be unfavourable to the Lydian monarch, is mitigated by
several elements. First of all, in the socializing with the *sophotatoi*, Croesus does
not properly seek adulation, but rather the possibility of perfecting knowledge
toward virtue (καὶ αὐτὸς πρὸς ἀρετὴν ὠφελεῖτο πολλά) – a circumstance that contributes to explaining why Diodorus does not register, in this passage, any negative reaction to a tyrant in the response of Solon.[28] This praiseworthy attitude of
the monarch is reinforced by the context that precedes the passage under analysis,
where Diodorus describes how Solon has sought to discipline the indolent spirit
of his fellow citizens (9.1.4). As for Croesus' question and the answer given him
by the Athenian legislator, the essential lines of Herodotus' account are clearly
recognized in Diodorus: the different conception of richness contrasting with happiness held by both men, and the need to wait for the end of life until a reliable
diagnosis can be made of the whole existence. However, Diodorus does not record
the examples provided by the Herodotean Solon (with respect to Tellos, Kleobis,
and Biton), an omission that occurs in every passage where the author evokes
this episode, perhaps because they are already well known, as is maintained by
Diogenes Laertius, in a passage that will be discussed later (1.50). Diodorus' final,
brief description of the fate of Croesus at the hands of Cyrus (9.2.3–4) accords
with the usual elements, although he registers an oscillation that will probably
derive from an unfolding of the same tradition. According to Herodotus (1.86.5–
87.2), Cyrus ordered that the flames of the pyre be extinguished, but, in face of
the impossibility of controlling the fire that followed, the invocation of Croesus

and the saving storm sent by Apollo were necessary. Diodorus begins by affirming only that the flames were extinguished by order of Cyrus (9.2.4); however, further on (9.34) he refers only to the storm, where he sees the mark of the piety of Croesus, a circumstance that leads Cyrus to make him his adviser and to count him among the wise.[29]

Notwithstanding the interest of these details, the differences documented in the more extensive passage that Diodorus dedicates to the celebrated episode turn out to be more significant. The contrasting form of presenting the monarch and his purposes is particularly emphasized (DS 9.26.1):

Ὅτι ὁ Κροῖσος μετεπέμπετο ἐκ τῆς Ἑλλάδος τοὺς ἐπὶ σοφίᾳ πρωτεύοντας, ἐπιδεικνύμενος τὸ μέγεθος τῆς εὐδαιμονίας, καὶ τοὺς ἐξυμνοῦντας τὴν εὐτυχίαν αὐτοῦ ἐτίμα μεγάλαις δωρεαῖς. Μετεπέμψατο δὲ καὶ Σόλωνα, ὁμοίως δὲ καὶ τῶν ἄλλων τῶν ἐπὶ φιλοσοφίᾳ μεγίστην δόξαν ἐχόντων, τὴν ἰδίαν εὐδαιμονίαν διὰ τῆς τούτων τῶν ἀνδρῶν μαρτυρίας ἐπισφραγίζεσθαι βουλόμενος.

Croesus used to send for the most distinguished wise men from Greece, to display to them the magnitude of his felicity, and would honour with rich gifts those who lauded his good fortune. And he also sent for Solon as well as for such others as enjoyed the greatest fame for their love of wisdom, wishing to have the witness of these men set the seal of approval upon his own felicity[30]

In the first passage analyzed, Diodorus gestured toward the vanity of Croesus with a brief and discreet note, but now this element becomes central in the characterization of the monarch. In fact, Diodorus had previously said that the king of Lydia rewarded the illustrious visitors he summoned, but he did so in exchange for the opportunity to deepen his knowledge of virtue. However, in the text now under analysis, gifts of hospitality, although equally magnificent, are intended to reward only those who flatter the wealth that the potentate possesses (τοὺς ἐξυμνοῦντας τὴν εὐτυχίαν αὐτοῦ). This Croesus no longer wants to learn anything: he only intends to 'buy' the opinion of famous messengers who can testify abroad to the greatness of his power. The monarch thus assumes the traits of the arrogant barbarian who hopes to dazzle the representatives of Hellenic civility with a display of his power. For this reason, it is not thus surprising that Croesus has repeatedly questioned several of the Sages in the hope of obtaining a flattering response. He suffers, however, the same disappointment with Anacharsis, Solon, Bias, and Pittakos. Solon's words correspond, in essence, to the basic lines already analyzed in Herodotus: because fortune is changeable, we must wait for the end of life to evaluate one's existence properly. Even so, Diodorus again opts not to mention the example of Tellos and of the two Argive young men. He accentuates (9.27.1–2), however, a significant reversal of the path described by Herodotus' Croesus. When, in the historian's account, Croesus questioned Solon about happiness, he began by accentuating the notion of material wealth (ὀλβιώτατον), then giving way to a broadening of horizons (εὐδαιμονίη), which somehow foreshadowed the future evolution of the thought of the monarch. In Diodorus, however, the contrary process takes place, a fact that accentuates Croesus' pettiness of understanding: he begins by emphasizing the notion of happiness (εὐδαιμονέστατον) but ends up confining it to an abundance of material goods (πλουσιώτατον). Contrary to Herodotus' Solon, in Diodorus, the Athenian statesman tends to reject all material wealth, since he considers it immoral, although, as I have noted already, the historical Solon did not hold such a radical perspective.[31] The Greek *vs.* barbarian binary is also emphasized when Croesus asks Pittakos about the best form of government to which the sage responds " 'that of variously-painted wood', referring to the laws" (9.27.4: τὴν τοῦ ποικίλου ξύλου, διασημαίνοντα τοὺς νόμους). As can easily be perceived, at the base of this answer lies the idea that Croesus, being a tyrant, would judge himself above the law, unlike a Greek citizen, for whom the rules of the *polis* constituted true sovereignty.

To sum up, in the first passage analyzed, Diodorus presents an image of Croesus permeated with positive connotations, where one can easily foresee his future role of counsellor. However, the author's more extensive extract shows how, along with a consolidation of elements related to the tradition of the Seven Wise Men, a tendency to ethnicize the interview between Solon and Croesus has also been accentuated within the logic of the Greek *vs.* barbarian dichotomy. As has been suggested (Santoni 1983: 134, n. 159), this different approach may be owed to Diodorus' use of distinct sources relating to the theme of the Seven Wise Men, such as Ephorus and Hermippus.

Plutarch finally has not only the greatest number of references to the episode under analysis, but also its most elaborate and complete approach after Herodotus. Some of the references occur scattered throughout the *Moralia* (58e; 69e; 155b; 857f–858a), but they have a generalizing character and, therefore, do not justify a digression, especially when compared with the treatment that the biographer has dedicated to the meeting between Solon and Croesus in his *Solon*. This account occupies two long chapters, which represent a more carefully elaborated examination, a clear indication of the interest the episode had aroused in Plutarch. In broad terms, his exposition follows the essential lines of Herodotus' version, with the amplification of some elements and summary of others, as is common practice when approaching so well known an anecdote. However, the most noteworthy aspect lies in the profound differences that occur in the presentation of Croesus. Indeed, after stressing the simplicity of Solon's tastes before the grandeur of the Lydian court, Plutarch introduces the figure of the king in these terms (Plut. *Sol.* 27.3–4):

πᾶν ὅσον ἐν λίθοις, ἐν βαφαῖς ἐσθῆτος, ἐν τέχναις χρυσοῦ περὶ κόσμον ἐκπρεπὲς ἔχειν ἢ περιττὸν ἢ ζηλωτὸν ἐδόκει περικείμενον, ὡς δὴ θέαμα σεμνότατον ὀφθείη καὶ ποικιλώτατον. ἐπεὶ δ᾽ ὁ Σόλων ἄντικρυς καταστὰς οὔτ᾽ ἔπαθεν οὐδὲν οὔτ᾽ εἶπε πρὸς τὴν ὄψιν ὧν ὁ Κροῖσος προσεδόκησεν, ἀλλὰ καὶ δῆλος ἦν τοῖς εὖ φρονοῦσι τῆς ἀπειροκαλίας καὶ μικροπρεπείας καταφρονῶν.

[Croesus] was decked out with everything in the way of precious stones, dyed raiment, and wrought gold that men deem remarkable, or extravagant, or enviable, in order that he might present a most august and gorgeous spectacle.

But when Solon, in this presence, neither showed any astonishment at what he saw, nor made any such comments upon it as Croesus had expected, but actually made it clear to all discerning eyes that he despised such vulgarity and pettiness.[32]

It is significant to note that Plutarch, unlike Herodotus, makes the appearance of Croesus deliberately delayed, accentuating the monarch's vanity with the accumulation of details connected with the description of his rich clothing, before even showing his treasures to the Athenian guest. The aim of the king is to make of himself the most dazzling of spectacles (ὡς δὴ θέαμα σεμνότατον ὀφθείη καὶ ποικιλώτατον). Croesus himself confirms this intention later, in clarifying to Cyrus the meaning of the invocation of the name of Solon. When he had invited the Athenian statesman to stay with him, he had not done so with the intention of learning, but rather with much lesser purposes: "in order that he might behold, and, when he left me, bear testimony to the happiness I then enjoyed, the loss of which I now see to be a greater evil than its possession was a good" (*Sol.* 28.4: ὡς δή μοι θεατὴς γένοιτο καὶ μάρτυς ἀπίοι τῆς εὐδαιμονίας ἐκείνης, ἣν ἀποβαλεῖν ἄρα μεῖζον ἦν κακὸν ἢ λαβεῖν ἀγαθόν). This idea is also expressed in the *Septem Sapientium Convivium* (155b), illustrated by the very affinity of the vocabulary used in both passages (e.g., γενέσθαι θεατής). The same perspective has already been found in Diodorus (9.26.1), although, as previously noted, in this author it does still coexist with the notion that Croesus, in socializing with the Wise Men of Greece, also sought to perfect himself in the path of virtue (9.2.1).

Even before Plutarch put the famous question about happiness in Croesus' mouth, Solon's attitude already demonstrated the gap in understanding that existed between himself and the tyrant. For those who were prudent (εὖ φρονοῦσι), the exuberance of the eastern monarch was nothing more than the visible expression of the limitation of Croesus' character. The narrative thus suggests, with increasing intensity, what the Athenian legislator would soon clearly explain to a visibly upset sovereign (Plut. *Sol.* 27.8–9):

> καὶ ὁ Σόλων, οὔτε κολακεύειν βουλόμενος αὐτὸν οὔτε περαιτέρω παροξύνειν, ''Ἕλλησιν' εἶπεν 'ὦ βασιλεῦ Λυδῶν, πρός τε τἆλλα μετρίως ἔχειν ἔδωκεν ὁ θεός, καὶ σοφίας τινὸς ἀθαρσοῦς ὡς ἔοικε καὶ δημοτικῆς, οὐ βασιλικῆς οὐδὲ λαμπρᾶς, ὑπὸ μετριότητος ἡμῖν μέτεστιν, ἣ τύχαις ὁρῶσα παντοδαπαῖς χρώμενον ἀεὶ τὸν βίον, οὐκ ἐᾷ τοῖς παροῦσιν ἀγαθοῖς μέγα φρονεῖν οὐδὲ θαυμάζειν ἀνδρὸς εὐτυχίαν μεταβολῆς χρόνον ἔχουσαν. ἔπεισι γὰρ ἑκάστῳ ποικίλον ἐξ ἀδήλου τὸ μέλλον. ᾧ δ' εἰς τέλος ὁ δαίμων ἔθετο τὴν εὐπραξίαν, τοῦτον εὐδαίμονα νομίζομεν.

Then Solon, who was unwilling to flatter him and did not wish to exasperate him further, said: "O king of Lydia, as the deity has given us Greeks all other blessings in moderation, so our moderation gives us a kind of wisdom which is timid, in all likelihood, and fit for common people, not one which is kingly and splendid. This wisdom, such as it is, observing that human life is ever subject to all sorts of vicissitudes, forbids us to be puffed up by the good things we have, or to admire a man's felicity while there is still time for it to change. For the future which is advancing upon everyone is varied and uncertain, but when the deity bestows prosperity on a man up to the end, that man we consider happy."

The notion of mutability of fortune and the necessity of suspending judgment on one's happiness until knowing the end of one's existence are actually in Herodotus' account, but the purpose of Solon's words is quite different. For Plutarch, it is not only a matter of enunciating a principle applicable to the whole human race. The biographer also wishes to emphasize the different capacity of perception that exists between a Greek (Ἕλλησιν) and a barbarian (ὦ βασιλεῦ Λυδῶν). He thus praises the wise consciousness of fair measure existing in a common citizen (δημοτικῆς) of a *polis*, compared with the blind exuberance of an eastern monarch (οὐ βασιλικῆς οὐδὲ λαμπρᾶς). None of the *testimonia* so far analyzed have so clearly expressed this idea. In fact, it is in this passage of Plutarch that the clearest and most unequivocal expression of the Greek *vs.* barbarian opposition is found in the context of the celebrated interview that has motivated this analysis.

This episode had multiple posterior treatments, and it was not the purpose of this study to analyze them all in detail, but to evoke only the most paradigmatic.[33] Still, it is justifiable to comment on another author, Diogenes Laertius, not only because he is one of the more extensive sources on Solon, but also because his portrayal represents a stage of the tradition in which the elements related to the Athenian legislator and the Lydian monarch were already well crystallized. This compendious quality holds for itself some interest, but the most revealing dimension lies again in the meaning to be attributed to the differences of detail present in Diogenes' approach. The first aspect worthy of reflection concerns the fact that the doxographer places the journey of Solon in the period immediately after the beginning of the tyranny of Peisistratos, thus about 560 BC. In historical terms, this is an unlikely time scheme, which would only add further problems to Herodotus' chronological arrangement. It is, however, revealing for the intentions of Diogenes (and certainly also of some of his sources), since this dating would allow framing the voluntary exile of the old legislator (and first 'democrat') within the opposition to the tyrannical regime of Peisistratos (Leão 2008b). In the same passage where he maintains this perspective (1.50), Diogenes also refers to the journey to Egypt, Cyprus, and, finally, to Sardis. The conversation with Croesus is then briefly mentioned, and in it there is strikingly no trace of the wealth of the Eastern monarch – a determinant element in the evolution of the account. To the expected inquiry about happiness, Solon responds only with reference to the names of Tellos, Kleobis, and Biton. The other details are summed up with a vague expression, clearly indicating that they were part of a well-known cultural heritage: "and went on in words too familiar to be quoted here" (καὶ τὰ θρυλούμενα).[34] Instead of these traditional elements, Diogenes chooses to provide other picturesque data that transform the model provided by Herodotus, as usually happens in the process of legendary amplification. Among them are the letters that Solon would have exchanged with such personalities as Periander (1.64),

Epimenides (1.64–66), and Peisistratos (1.66–67). These letters are surely fabricated documents, to be read in the light of the tradition of the Seven Wise Men and of the discussions on the best form of government. The missive for Croesus will certainly have the same genesis. However, it is worth recalling it here, because it betrays marks of the theme that we have been analyzing (DL 1.67):

Σόλων Κροίσῳ
Ἄγαμαί σε τῆς περὶ ἡμᾶς φιλοφροσύνης· καὶ νὴ τὴν Ἀθηνᾶν, εἰ μὴ περὶ παντός μοι ἦν οἰκεῖν ἐν δημοκρατίᾳ, ἐδεξάμην ἂν μᾶλλον τὴν δίαιταν ἔχειν ἐν τῇ παρὰ σοὶ βασιλείᾳ ἢ Ἀθήνησι, τυραννοῦντος βιαίως Πεισιστράτου. ἀλλὰ καὶ ἡδίων ἡμῖν ἡ βιοτὴ ἔνθα πᾶσι τὰ δίκαια καὶ ἴσα. ἀφίξομαι δ' οὖν παρὰ σέ, σπεύδων τοι ξένος γενέσθαι.

Solon to Croesus
I admire you for your kindness to me; and, by Athena, if I had not been anxious before all things to live in a democracy, I would rather have fixed my abode in your palace than at Athens, where Peisistratos is setting up a rule of violence. But in truth to live in a place where all have equal rights is more to my liking. However, I will come and see you, for I am eager to make your acquaintance.

In this note, there are no signs that would clearly suggest a negative characterization of Croesus. On the contrary, Solon confesses himself honoured with the attention that he had stimulated in Croesus and even shows himself to be attracted by the idea of living in Sardis.[35] The reason is that Athens is about to be dominated by a tyrannical government.[36] It is, therefore, only this suggestion that allows framing the words of Solon within the spirit of the Greek vs barbarian opposition. Were it not for the preference for a democratic regime (οἰκεῖν ἐν δημοκρατίᾳ), in which all share the same notion of justice and equality, Solon would have preferred the king's court (ἐν τῇ παρὰ σοὶ βασιλείᾳ). At the root of the argument is easily identified the notion of the supremacy of certain Greek civilizational achievements (such as the sovereignty of the law) over the autocratic regime accepted by the barbarians. However, this idea is left flat and largely unauthorized by the fact that Athens is also at the door of tyranny.[37] Consequently, the characterization of Croesus in Diogenes ends up being mainly favourable to the king of Lydia.

Conclusion

The diachronic analysis of the main testimonies related to the meeting between Solon and Croesus shows that this episode has been used differently over time. The principles laid out by Solon in the interview with the Lydian monarch in Herodotus' work provide proof that the historian was acquainted with the poems of the statesman, whose content he knew to harmonize with his own ideas. Even so, Herodotus almost ignores the legislative work, because in Solon he was especially interested in the ethical value of the *sophos*, who established a natural alliance with Delphic morality – a source of authority to which the author also accords a place of prominence in his work. Thus, in Herodotus, the episode of Croesus and Solon is intended, above all, to define an ethics of universal and not specifically Greek application. In Plutarch, on the contrary, there is the most energetic expression of the Greek *vs.* barbarian opposition, although this account also gives rise to significant moral implications. The remaining sources move between these two perspectives, which they favour variably. In fact, the correct interpretation of the famous dialogue already divided the ancients, as Plutarch's elucidation (*Sol.* 27.1) illustrates, by referring to the chronological difficulties that accompanied the historical tradition of the meeting, but which did not prevent him from paying it much attention, precisely because of the high moral interest of the episode. It is definitely the recognition of this high ethical message that invites the reader, even today, to follow both the argument of the Athenian legislator and the growing surprise of the Lydian monarch, because in them lies one of the happiest expressions of the paradigmatic value of classical culture.

Notes

1 The *testimonia* respecting this issue were collected by Martina (1968: 32–50), whose text is adopted in those passages discussed throughout this analysis. This study resumes and expands, to varying degrees, arguments approached previously in Leão 2000, 2001: 19–42, 2010, 2013. The research was developed under the project UID/ELT/00196/2013, funded by the Portuguese FCT – Foundation for Science and Technology. I wish to thank T.J. Figueira and C.I. Soares for having invited me to contribute to this volume, and for their very helpful criticism.

2 Leão 2001: 268–75. For a recent overview of the question, see Porciani 2016: 16–20.

3 English translation of Herodotus adapted from A.D. Godley, available at the Perseus Digital Library (www.perseus.tufts.edu/hopper/text?doc=Perseus:text:1999.01.0125).

4 Markianos 1974: 15, n. 62, argues that in Aristotle there are implicit allusions to the episode in *EE* (1219b) and *EN* (1100a; 1179a), but this is a remote hypothesis.

5 For an overview of gnomic literature down to the time of Plutarch, see Wehrli 1973; Rodríguez Adrados 1996: 130–7; West 1997; Leão 2011: 13–19.

6 A point already underlined by Figueira 1995: 42, especially in what respects the *Theognidea*.

7 See the pertinent observations of Wallace 2009, whose analysis focusses on three *poleis* (Mytilene, Megara, and Athens), for which there is independent evidence contemporary to the events, respectively provided by the poetry of Alcaeus, Theognis, and Solon. Still, his opinion is disputable that the *sophoi* represent a new type of chief men in the sense that they were *sophoi* and that for this reason they became charismatic leaders (see pp. 420–1).

8 Hdt. 1.29.1. The term *sophistēs* is here used in the neutral sense of 'wise'. Further on (2.49.1), Herodotus uses the same word to designate a specialist in a particular field. The fact that Herodotus maintains that the Greek sages of the time visited Croesus has sometimes been interpreted as suggesting that the idea of the synchronous existence of these personalities, constituting a group of Seven Sages, would already have been popular before Plato. See Mosshammer 1976: 172; Martin 1998: 113; Hollmann 2015: 86, n. 3.

9 In the previous section, Wallace 2016 emphasized the "densely formulaic" nature of the number seven in Herodotus, although he did not explore this specific connection to Delphic morality, which could help to strengthen his global argument.

10 As has been amply underlined, Tellos' name suggests a connection with the *telos* of his life; see, e.g., Immerwahr 1966: 156, n. 21; Chiasson 1986: 250, n. 3; Silva 1994: 26,

n. 61. Chiasson (2005: 54–5), suggests that the term *telos*, in the context of the death of the Argive youths, who will occupy the second place in the happiness scale, "is also used as a semi-technical term in describing the successive stages of human life".

11 Or, at least, the recognition of an award of *aristeia* in the battle. On the subject of the death in Herodotus, as an element promoting *timē*, see Soares 2003: 117–32. Hollmann (2015: 91, n. 18), admits the hypothesis that the involvement of the *polis* in the burial of Tellos could be an echo of the laws of Solon that sought to restrict the excess of aristocratic funerals. On the issue of funerary restrictions introduced by Solon's legislation, see Leão & Rhodes 2015: 116–21.

12 Herodotus does not clarify what the mother's reaction to the outcome of her prayer would have been. Chiasson (1983: 115–16), argues that, among the words used by the historian to describe the sense of joy, only the adjective περιχαρής (here used to describe the joy of the youths' mother) occurs with the meaning of 'exceedingly happy' or 'overjoyed', and it always indicates the imminent presence of a serious danger that will put an end to this ephemeral joy. In a subsequent study, Chiasson (2005: 49) further emphasizes that in this case as in two others (1.119.2; 4.84.2), the use of the term by Herodotus "describes parents who are themselves indirectly responsible for the imminent deaths of their children, which in their deluded joy they cannot foresee".

13 Cf. fr. 27.17–18 West. Lefkowitz (1981: 45), usually sceptical of the value of Herodotus' testimony to the historical knowledge of Solon, unreservedly accepts this echo of Solon's poetry in his depiction by Herodotus. Noussia-Fantuzzi (2010: 388–9) emphasizes that the verb τελέω is used by Homer to complete periods of time (e.g. 10.470), so the adoption of the term τελέσας by Solon may be understood as a linguistic traditional use.

14 Thus Adkins 1995: 131, who also adds the hypothesis that in fr. 27 West, Solon might have used an alien structure of *hebdomadai*, even if expressing his own ideas on the topic.

15 "I get old, always learning many things." In contrast with this statement, see Mimnermus' pessimistic view of old age, at fr. 1.5–10; 2.9–16; 3; 4; 5.5–8 West.

16 "Not a single man is happy, but rather miserable / are all the mortals who, from above, the sun beholds." Cf. also fr. 24.10 West.

17 On this, see Figueira 1995, who provides an insightful semantic analysis of archaic attitudes regarding affluence and poverty, combined with upward and downward social mobility.

18 Chiasson (1986: 257) points out that, in the poetry of Solon, the conceptual distinction is not made, as it is in the account of Herodotus (1.32.7), between *eutukhes* (a person fortunate, but vulnerable to disaster) and *olbios* (the holder of enduring happiness). However, the opposition instability/perenniality presupposed by these principles lies in reality implicit in the possible double emanation of wealth, referred to in this poem. Figueira (2015: 29–38) analyzes what he calls "the *hybris* syndrome", in Solon, Pindar, and Bacchylides, which derives from the articulation between *koros* ('glutting'), *hybris* ('arrogance'), and *atē* ('downfall'), when one is not able to deal mentally with the *olbos* ('prosperity'); in particular, Figueira notes (p. 29), "Solon attributes this syndrome to the traditional Attic elite in fr. 4.7–10 W²."

19 The analysis of Croesus' story in terms of a tragic plot has garnered much attention, stimulating parallels mainly with the Aeschylean principle of the *pathei mathos* and with the ironic blindness of the protagonist of Sophocles' *Oedipus Rex*. E.g., Stahl 1975; Silva 1994: 30–1. Pelling (2006: 154) suggests that the fact that Solon avoided clearly censoring the Lydian monarch makes it difficult to perceive the message he intends to convey, stressing that "learning is very difficult, especially when wisdom is as elusive as this".

20 Fisher (1992: 357–60) reacts against the idea of considering as *hybris* all Croesus' acts. According to Fisher, the only action that really falls within the realm of *hybris* is the king's imperialism, which leads him to cross the Halys and unjustly enslave the

Syrians (1.76). The fall of Sardis corresponds to the punishment of a hereditary fault (it was Gyges who committed the act of *hybris*) and the death of his son Atys is an excessive atonement, responding to the fault (namely, to consider himself *olbiotatos* and not to accept the advice of Solon), which inspires tragic commiseration more than the sense of justice.

21 In any case, the harsh judgment of Plutarch or Pseudo-Plutarch (*De Her. mal.* 857f-858a) seems clearly excessive, according to whom Herodotus, in projecting his religious conceptions on Solon, would have allied evil to blasphemy. On the contrary, apart from the notion of divine *phthonos*, the ideas expressed in the poems of the legislator agree globally with the literary re-creation of Herodotus.

22 For passages respecting the term *olbos*, see de Heer 1969: 12–15 (for Homer), 32–8 (for the Archaic period), 67–72 (for the Classical period). For a table of attestations regarding wealth, affluence and moral character, acquisition, acquisitiveness, and poverty in the poetry of the Archaic period, see Figueira 1995: 56–9.

23 In some of his verses (especially in fr. 23 West), Solon also strikes some notes more in the line with the traditional approach, but these few examples are not characteristic of the statesman's thought.

24 Hdt. 1.86.5: "Speaking no more of him [i.e. Croesus] than of every human being, especially those who think themselves fortunate."

25 As Porciani (2016: 24) pertinently emphasizes: "in tutto il primo *logos* delle *Storie* prevale un clima culturale segnato da forti interrelazioni fra Oriente e Occidente, in cui non c'è posto per un'etnologia sommaria o per stereotipi".

26 English translation of Plato adapted from R.G. Bury, available at the Perseus Digital Library (www.perseus.tufts.edu/hopper/text?doc=Perseus:text:1999.01.0164).

27 English translation of Diodorus by C.H. Oldfather, available at the Perseus Digital Library (www.perseus.tufts.edu/hopper/text?doc=Perseus:text:1999.01.0083).

28 As Gazzano (2016: 43, n. 61) pertinently argues, in this passage Diodorus depicts a Croesus genuinely interested in his own moral growth. Diodorus states this positive attitude so explicitly only here.

29 The topic had indeed a tradition before Herodotus, a fact that is illustrated by a red figure amphora (dating from the early fifth century) and five fragments of a Corinthian hydria, also red figure (from about 480–450 BC), which seem to represent Croesus on the pyre; cf. the version of Bacchylides (3.15–62), in the ode in honour of Hieron of Syracuse, who won the car race at the Olympic Games of 468 BC. In the version of Bacchylides, Croesus decides to sacrifice himself, along with the wife and the daughters, when the fall of the city was imminent, but, at the last moment Zeus extinguishes the flames and Apollo takes them to the Hyperboreans, thanks to the piety of the Lydian monarch. See Evans (1978–1979: 34).

30 This translation follows that of Diodorus by C.H. Oldfather, available at the Perseus Digital Library (www.perseus.tufts.edu/hopper/text?doc=Perseus:text:1999.01.0083).

31 This difference may be justified by the influence of Cynic philosophy, as underlined by Santoni 1983: 136–8.

32 English translation of Plutarch by B. Perrin, available at the Perseus Digital Library (www.perseus.tufts.edu/hopper/text?doc=Perseus:text:2008.01.0063).

33 For an overview of the multiple literary, philosophical, and iconographic variants of this Herodotean theme, see the recent volume edited by Castelnuovo 2016.

34 English translation of Diogenes Laertius by R.D. Hicks, available at the Perseus Digital Library (www.perseus.tufts.edu/hopper/text?doc=Perseus:text:1999.01.0258).

35 Theoretically, the letter under analysis had been written before the visit to the court of Croesus, and so, after meeting the monarch personally, Solon could have changed his mind. However, it must be acknowledged that this hypothesis is a simple exercise of speculation, which finds no support in the text of Diogenes.

36 Although the letter destined to Croesus is the last one to be transcribed by Diogenes, this letter should appear first, for Solon is in Athens and the tyranny of Peisistratos is not yet an accomplished fact.

37 Still, Diogenes does not emphasize much the negative character of the government of Peisistratos, perhaps because the latter also sometimes occupies the position of sage, as the same Diogenes records (1.122). In fact, this notion generally accords with the portrait of the tyranny of Peisistratos provided, for example, by the *Athenian Constitution* (*Ath. Pol.* 16.7), which compares this period to a new age of Kronos.

Bibliography

Adkins, A.W.H. 1995. *Poetic Craft in the Early Greek Elegists*. Chicago, IL (University of Chicago Press).

Alessandrì, S. 1989. "I Viaggi di Solone." *Civiltà Classica e Cristiana* 10: 191–224.

Asheri, D. 1988. *Erodoto: Le Storie: Libro I – La Lidia e la Persia*. Milano (Fondazione Lorenzo Valla).

Busine, A. 2002. *Les Sept Sages de la Grèce antique: Transmission et utilisation d'un patrimoine légendaire d'Hérodote à Plutarque*. Paris (De Boccard).

Castelnuovo, L.M., ed. 2016. *Solone e Creso: Variazioni letterarie, filosofiche e iconografiche su un tema erodoteo*. Macerata (Università di Macerata).

Chiasson, C.C. 1983. "An Ominous Word in Herodotus." *Hermes* 111: 115–18.

———. 1986. "The Herodotean Solon." *Greek, Roman and Byzantine Studies* 27: 249–62.

———. 2005. "Myth, Ritual, and Authorial Control in Herodotus' Story of Cleobis and Biton (*Hist.* 1.31)." *American Journal of Philology* 126: 41–64.

de Heer, C. 1969. *Makar, Eudaimon, Olbios, Eutyches: A Study of the Semantic Field Denoting Happiness in Ancient Greek to the End of the Fifth-Century B.C.* Amsterdam (A.M. Hakkert).

Duplouy, A. 1999. "L'Utilization de la Figure de Crésus dans l'Idéologie Aristocratique Athénienne: Solon, Alcméon, Miltiade et le Dernier Roi de Lydie." *Antiquité Classique* 68: 1–22.

Evans, J.A.S. 1978–1979. "What Happened to Croesus?" *Classical Journal* 74: 34–40.

Fehling, D. 1985. *Die Sieben Weisen und die frühgriechische Chronologie: Eine traditionsgeschichtliche Studie*. Bern (Peter Lang).

Figueira, T.J. 1995. "'Khrēmata': Acquisition and Possession in Archaic Greece." In Irani, K.D., & Silver, M., eds., *Social Justice in the Ancient World*. London (Greenwood), 41–60.

———. 2015. "Solon in Fifth-Century Lyric." *Trends in Classics* 17: 24–42.

Fisher, N.R.E. 1992. *Hybris: A Study in the Values of Honour and Shame in Ancient Greece*. Warminster (Aris and Phillips).

Gazzano, F. 2016. "μᾶλλον ὁ Φρύξ: Creso e la Sapienza Greca." In Castelnuovo, L.M., ed., *Solone e Creso: Variazioni Letterarie, Filosofiche e Iconografiche su un Tema Erodoteo*. Macerata (Edizioni Università di Macerata), 29–50.

Hammond, N.G.L. 1940. "The 'Seisachtheia' and the 'Nomothesia' of Solon." *Journal of Hellenic Studies* 60: 71–83.

Hollmann, A. 2015. "Solon in Herodotus." *Trends in Classics* 17: 85–109.

Immerwahr, H.R. 1966. *Form and Thought in Herodotus*. Cleveland, OH (American Philological Association).

Lattimore, R. 1939. "The Wise Adviser in Herodotus." *Classical Philology* 34: 24–35.

Leão, D.F. 2000. "Sólon e Creso: Fases da Evolução de um Paradigma." *Humanitas* 52: 27–52.

———. 2001. *Sólon: Ética e política*. Lisboa (Fundação Calouste Gulbenkian).

———. 2008a. "Plutarch and the Character of the 'Sapiens'." In Nikolaidis, A.G., ed., *The Unity of Plutarch's Works: 'Moralia' Themes in the 'Lives', Features of the 'Lives' in the 'Moralia'*. Berlin (De Gruyter), 480–8.

———. 2008b. "A 'Sophos' in Arms: Plutarch and the Tradition of Solon's Opposition to the Tyranny of Pisistratus." In Ferreira, J.R., Stockt, L.V., & Fialho, M.C., eds., *Philosophy in Society: Virtues and Values in Plutarch*. Coimbra & Leuven (Imprensa da Universidade de Coimbra), 129–38.

———. 2010. "The Seven Sages and Plato." In Giombini, S., & Marcacci, F., eds., *Il Quinto Secolo: Studi di Filosofia Antica in Onore di Livio Rossetti*. Passignano (Aguaplano – Officina del Libro), 403–14.

———. 2011. "A Literatura de Sentenças." In Leão, D.F., ed., *Plutarco: Obras Morais: O banquete dos Sete Sábios*. Coimbra & São Paulo (Imprensa da Universidade de Coimbra & Annablume), 13–19.

———. 2013. "O Livro I de Diógenes Laércio: a Tradição dos Sete Sábios e a Caracterização da Figura do 'Sophos'." In Leão, D.F., Cornelli, G., & Peixoto, M.C., eds., *Dos Homens e suas Ideias: Estudos sobre as Vidas de Diógenes Laércio*. Coimbra (Imprensa da Universidade de Coimbra), 1–19.

Leão, D.F. & Rhodes, P.J. 2015. *The Laws of Solon: A New Edition with Introduction, Translation and Commentary*. London (I.B.Tauris).

Lefkowitz, M.R. 1981. *The Lives of the Greek Poets*. London (Duckworth).

Markianos, S.S. 1974. "The Chronology of the Herodotean Solon." *Historia* 23: 1–20.

Martin, R.P. 1998. "The Seven Sages as Performers of Wisdom." In Dougherty, C., & Kurke, L., eds., *Cultural Poetics in Archaic Greece: Cult, Performance, Politics*. Oxford (Oxford University Press), 108–28.

Martina, A. 1968. *Solon: Testimonia veterum*. Roma (Edizioni dell'Ateneo).

Meiggs, R. & Lewis, D. 1989. *A Selection of Greek Historical Inscriptions to the End of the Fifth Century B.C.* Oxford (Oxford University Press).

Miller, M. 1969. "The Accepted Date for Solon: Precise, but Wrong?" *Arethusa* 2: 62–86.

Mosshammer, A. 1976. "The Epoch of the Seven Sages." *California Studies in Classical Antiquity* 9: 165–80.

Noussia-Fantuzzi, M. 2010. *Solon the Athenian: The Poetic Fragments*. Leiden (Brill).

Parke, H.W. 1984. "Croesus and Delphi." *Greek, Roman and Byzantine Studies* 25: 209–32.

Parker, R. 2004. "Sacrificing Twice Seven Children: Queen Amestris' Exchange with the God Under the Earth (7.114)." In Karageorghis, V., & Taifacos, I., eds., *The World of Herodotus*. Nicosia (Foundation Anastasios G. Leventis), 151–7.

Pelling, C. 2006. "Educating Croesus: Talking and Learning in Herodotus' Lydian 'Logos'." *Classical Antiquity* 25: 141–77.

Porciani, L. 2016. "Il Dialogo tra Solone e Creso nell'Opera di Erodoto: Temi e Problemi." In Castelnuovo, L.M., ed., *Solone e Creso: Variazioni Letterarie, Filosofiche e Iconografiche su un Tema Erodoteo*. Macerata (Università di Macerata), 15–28.

Rodríguez Adrados, F. 1996. "Géneros Helenísticos en el 'Banquete de los Siete Sabios' de Plutarco." In Fernández Delgado, J.A., & Pordomingo Pardo, F., eds., *Estudios sobre Plutarco: Aspectos Formales*. Salamanca (Ediciones Clásicas), 125–42.

Santoni, A. 1983. "Temi e Motivi di Interesse Socio-economico nella Leggenda dei 'Sette Sapienti'." *Annali della Scuola Normale Superiore di Pisa* 13: 91–160.

Shapiro, S.O. 1996. "Herodotus and Solon." *Classical Antiquity* 15: 348–64.

Silva, M.F. 1994. "II: Creso e Ciro: A Figura do Rei no Livro I de Heródoto." In Ferreira, J.R., & Silva, M.F., eds., *Heródoto: Histórias – Livro 1°*. Lisboa (Edições 70), 21–49.

Snell, B. 1952. *Leben und Meinungen der Sieben Weisen*. München (Heimeran).

Soares, C. 2003. *A Morte em Heródoto: Valores Universais e Particularismos Étnicos*. Lisboa (Fundação Calouste Gulbenkian).

Stahl, H.-P. 1975. "Learning Through Suffering? Croesus' Conversations in the 'History' of Herodotus." *Yale Classical Studies* 24: 1–36.

Wallace, R.W. 2009. "Charismatic Leaders." In Raaflaub, K.A., & van Wees, H., eds., *A Companion to Archaic Greece*. Malden, MA (Wiley-Blackwell), 411–26.

———. 2016. "Redating Croesus: Herodotean Chronologies, and the Dates of the Earliest Coinages." *Journal of Hellenic Studies* 136: 168–81.

Wehrli, F. 1973. "Gnome, Anekdote und Biographie." *Museum Helveticum* 30: 193–208.

West, M.L. 1997. *The East Face of Helicon: West Asiatic Elements in Greek Poetry and Myth*. Oxford (Oxford University Press).

14   Scientific discourse in Herodotus Book II and its reflection in the age of New World discovery*

Carmen Soares

Introduction

Herodotus' nine books are the literary product of an intellectual milieu in which different areas of knowledge were originated and first developed as parts of a holistic approach toward the unknown world (that of the so-called *barbaroi* 'non-Greeks' or 'Barbarians'). Geography (including climatology), ethnography, dietetics, botany, zoology (besides politics, linguistics, literature, religion, etc.) all formed part of early historiographical research (Greek *historiē*).[1]

As Achille Olivieri has pointed out (2004: 7), it was precisely in Herodotus' methodology (so embued with ethnology, anthropology and oral history) that contemporary history took inspiration. The first purpose of my analysis is to demonstrate the many ways in which Book II of Herodotus highlights many of these scientific methodologies throughout his *logos* on Egypt (see "Foundations of scientific discourse in Herodotus' Book II"). My second goal is to illustrate the tenacity of these conceptualizations in the travel literature surrounding the Portuguese exploration of Brazil (see "Herodotus through *others'* eyes: the Herodotean matrix in the historiography of sixteenth-century Portuguese settlers concerning the land and peoples of Brazil").

In this introduction to my study I shall begin by explaining our subject's relevance. This will be followed by a discussion of literary foundations and historical context in order to approach the methodological principles of this scientific discourse, which are relevant to our subject of ethnicity and identity in Herodotus. Finally, I will discuss the reception of the aforementioned narrative model in Portuguese texts from the age of discoveries. These texts provide accounts of unknown people and places – true *barbaroi*. They elucidate a confrontation with the European cultures embodied by the authors of the texts.

As all who dedicate themselves to studying Herodotus' work know, the bibliography about the historian and his work is a true *thōma megiston*! Bringing a fresh contribution to such an extensive collection of titles is certainly a challenge. Herodotus' historiography inaugurated a new holistic approach to constructing the past of peoples through narrative. To *identify* in his *Histories* the cultural matrix behind the travel narratives written on the New World by the first Portuguese settlers is one of the 'revealed wonders' (*thōmasta*) of the classical tradition of

Western thought and a path that has not yet been well trodden by other scholars.[2] That is the reason why I decided to develop some thoughts on how Herodotus can be seen *through others' eyes*. These "others" are sixteenth-century Portuguese settlers who composed works on the land and peoples of Brazil.

Let me also explain why I decided to circumscribe my range of analysis on scientific discourse – a topic displayed through all the nine books of the *Histories* – to Book II.[3] There are several rationales behind my choice. First, within the multiethnic universe of the *Histories*, Book II is the only book that is entirely dedicated to one people, a fact which demonstrates the importance of Egypt and its people for the author, as compared with the other non-Greeks he describes[4]; consequently, this book constitutes a privileged Herodotean 'intra-text' of convergence of the three main themes of my research: scientific methodology, ethnicity, and identity.

Second, in Book II, the author devotes considerable space to what is contemporarily called 'the earth and life sciences', or, to describe it in terms more coeval with Herodotus, the questions pertaining to the 'nature' (*phusis*) of the territory and the living beings (animals and plants) that inhabit it; in the interests of brevity, I shall focus primarily on the nature of the territory, discussing such passages as the frequently evoked discussions concerning the lands of the Nile that animated 'scientists' or 'men of knowledge' (words expressed in Greek by the synonymous nouns *sophoi* and *sophistai*[5]) in Herodotus' time; this approach reveals the application of a scientific discourse to the construction of (land) *identity*, a *physical* issue always with *ethnographical* implications for the historian's portraits of peoples' and individuals' customs and characters.[6]

Third, Egyptians are the people whom the author most admired intellectually, calling them "by far the *most learned* (λογιώτατοι) people" (2.77.1) and "the *wisest* of men" (2.160.1: τοὺς σοφωτάτους ἀνθρώπων Αἰγυπτίους); and this admiration is based most particularly on the Egyptians' quest for historical knowledge, which Herodotus calls "the memory of humanity" (2.77.1: μνήμην ἀνθρώπων πάντων); thus, it can be legitimately deduced that love of knowledge (i.e., science) is in Herodotus' portrait of the Egyptians a mark of *ethnic identity*.

In the other chapters of this volume, the authors have mainly focussed on analysis of the *contents* of Herodotus to reveal the importance of ethnicity and identity in the construction of the narrative web of the *Histories*. My approach to these themes in Herodotus' work is completely distinct, as the object of this contribution is to figure how the historian's *modus (de)scribendi* serves the purpose of expressing a scientific discourse, which is itself a materialization of the text's methodological and verbal identity. For example, I shall not analyze the way Herodotus expresses, in Book II, the ethnic identity of other cultures in juxtaposition to Greek identity based on the specific criteria which Rosaria V. Munson has rightly identified (2014: 341): 'blood' (in the literal and scientific sense, and in the narrative sense, of descending from a common ancestor), physical appearance, cultural traits, territorial habitation and provenance.[7] Rather, focussed on the scientific identity of Herodotus' narrative, the emphasis of my analysis is on how the historian ethnicizes interpretations by distinguishing collective *gnōmai* (attributed to *ethnoi*) from his own individual opinions.

However, Herodotus' manner of describing land and people, with his portraits of ethnicity and identity, is only fully understood if we analyse his work through the dialectic he necessarily establishes with the intellectual context that preceded his inquiries or was contemporary with it. I would argue that even my short investigation amply reveals the *raison d'être* for the fifth-century BC Greek historiographical discourse. This purpose was to aggregate a miscellany of knowledge, a basis that only through progressive specialization – marked in the following century by, for example, the zoological and botanical treaties, respectively by Aristotle and by Theophrastus among others – would progress towards autonomy and separation. In the light of subsequent concepualizations, particularly in later historiography, the Herodotean text would not be considered 'history' but, using the description by Caroline Dewald (2008: 52), "an ongoing workshop on how to think historically".

Considering the focus of my analysis, I will review the scientific background prevailing before Herodotus and in his lifetime. Not wishing to duplicate the arguments laid out by several Herodotean specialists before me,[8] I must recall that, in order to understand the presence of the language and concepts of 'scientific discourse' (as it is generally called) in Herodotus' work, one must consider the methodological affinities between our historian and coeval intellectuals in east Greece (i.e., in the late fifth century BC). The distinctive epistemological traits of that representation of reality comprise the study of the tangible, the visible, and the empirically verifiable. There is then a clear difference between these concerns and the Ionian pre-Socratic philosophers of the sixth century BC, whose thought was based on speculations on qualities like the 'invisible', or abstractions (Thomas 2006: 62). As Rosalind Thomas has highlighted (2006: 71), Herodotus' method of presenting his material reveals his close proximity to contemporary intellectual trends. This Herodotean familiarity with other scientific works should be understood not as a relationship of dependence but as one of interaction (Raaflaub 2000: 154). As I will try to show when discussing Book II, the markers of scientific identity in the discourse of Herodotus (shared with other contemporary 'scientists') consisted in critical commentary upon his sources, stressing the central importance of eyewitness accounts (*autopsia*), and highlighting the presence of the author in the text (using the first person and including explicitly personal comments).

Concerning studies on the nature of the Earth (which were to become much later the autonomous scientific branches of geography, climatology, and geology), Herodotus reveals more scientific curiosity and power of observation than all those Greek writers before Aristotle (Romm 2006: 180). As has been well documented by Thomas (2006), Herodotus shares this interest, as well as some affinities – and many differences – with some of the contemporary Ionian natural philosophers (a group he simply calls 'Ionians'), and also Hecataeus. Covering both the 'earth sciences', an area on which many sixth and fifth-century BC authors wrote, and the 'life sciences', James Romm's apt description of Herodotus as a "proto-biologist" makes good sense (2006: 181). Not before the fourth century would studies on fauna and flora – which in Herodotus' work were still in an embryonic state and still marked by interwoven scientific and mythological arguments – achieve major scientific and generic-literary status, thanks to the works of Aristotle (*Historia Animalium*) and Theophrastus (*Historia Plantarum*).

Another scientific field where similarities with Herodotus have been examined in detail is that of the medical treatises of the *Corpus Hippocraticum*. Within this vast body of works, with the earliest quite close to Herodotus, there are some analogous texts where ethnography, dietetics, and medicine are more intricately enmeshed – the *Airs, Waters, Places* is one such text which has been quite extensively studied. In the interest of brevity, and because this 'kinship' between historiographic narrative and the Hippocratic treatises has been extensively explored,[9] I shall not be discussing in this chapter the epistemological dialogue between Herodotus and the Hippocratic treatise on dietetics. Yet I shall take into consideration the presence of the Hippocratic mode of analysis in the writings of the Portuguese settlers, another subject until now relatively neglected by scholars. To conclude this summary on the relationship between Herodotus and other 'scientific' authors before him or contemporary, it must be noted that the historian's originality consisted in applying this 'scientific discourse' to the subject of past history and not only to present days (Thomas 2006: 72–3).

Finally, I turn to the use of Herodotus' *Histories* as a model for European writers to describe the 'wonders' that the New World revealed through the discoveries presented by explorers/settlers. It was precisely the fact that the Heredotean narrative looks on unknown lands and people that contributed towards its rehabilitation as an historiographical model during that period (Dewald 2008: 53; Varotti 2012: 101). There is widespread consensus among contemporary historians concerning the classical (literary) matrix of Renaissance New World accounts (Earle 2012; Rubiés 1993, 2006; Lupher 2003). The overall influence of the Greek and Latin authors that form the basis of *litterae humaniores* was paramount in its effect upon the humanist teaching practised in colleges and universities. Nevertheless, as Joan-Pau Rubiés explains (2006: 141), the impact of the classics was not confined to an intellectual milieu; it was also perceptible in the texts of what has been named 'popular humanism', i.e., those whose authors were not trained in reading the Greek and Latin original texts of the humanist canon. He defines 'popular humanism' as an intermediate reception of classical culture. In fact, he links this concept to what he calls 'urban culture' or 'court culture' acquired by those first settlers who went to the New World for economic and political reasons – to become riche(r) and (more) powerful. Probably they did not undergo a thorough humanistic education, meaning that they had had a limited access to formal schooling (especially in Latin and Greek texts). They were interested, however, in vernacular literature, including translations of classical authors. Thus, in their works we find what Rubiés has rightly called the "humanistic flair" (2006: 144).

With this analytic perspective I propose the presence of the classical models in the works of these Portuguese settlers, directly or indirectly linked to a humanist education. Yet I surely do not intend to deny the influence that the more recent travel narratives may have had on their texts. In the Portuguese case it must be kept in mind that the medieval text by Marco Polo had been translated and published in Portugal at the beginning of the sixteenth century (1502) by Valentim Fernandes, an editor known for his taste for travel literature (an indication of the genre's popularity in vernacular languages at the time).[10] It also cannot be forgotten that the years around 1650 had been crucial in terms of the publication of key works for the imperial historiography of the Hispanic renaissance, both in Spain and Portugal.[11] While not denying the potential influence of these readings for the writings of our settler-authors' texts, I will conduct an analysis that focusses on the classic models that are the literary formative matrix of all these works of humanist inspiration.[12]

My methodology draws on comparative studies, where I have limited the range of classical primary sources to one significant literary genre, historiography, with which the texts of the Portuguese settlers containing descriptions of the 'other' or the New World are juxtaposed. In contrast, contemporary categorization of natural or anthropological phenomena entails a type of scientific discourse that is totally autonomous, and, crucially, a product of the eighteenth century.[13] Therefore, it is important to clarify, however briefly, how the *modus cogitandi* of the sixteenth-century authors (with which we are concerned here) involved 'history' in the classic (and Herodotean) understanding of *historiē* ('investigation', 'research', 'inquiry'). However, given that this conception of *historiē* involves a dialogue (which existed already at its Greek origin), with medical or scientific discourse, I shall include the Hippocratic dietary discourse as referring to the study of the classical interpretations in the works of Portuguese settlers.

Even if necessarily brief, a discussion is needed on the reception of *Histories* at the time of the pertinent Portuguese authors. As observed by Adam Foley (2016: 213–4), Herodotus is absent from fifteenth-century humanists' reception of historiography; the historians from that period seldom, if ever, adopt the Greek author's model for history writing.[14] That does not mean that they did not mention, quote, or translate him (into Latin), with the Latin translation by Lorenzo Valla having become the reference work in this area.[15] However, as Foley (2016: 220) concludes, "reading Herodotus, therefore, meant reading Valla" and for that reason the Greek historian "remained yoked to the standards of Latin prose rather than those of ancient historiography". That is, the interest of the great names of Italian humanism in the release, through translation into Latin, of the monumental historiographical work composed in Greek, was surely responsible for the increase of its circulation in European intellectual circles.

Tracing the editorial course of *Histories* in Italy and France has already elicited detailed attention and studies by Achille Olivieri (2004), Stephano Pagliaroli (2006, 2007, 2012), Carlo Varotti (2012), Adam Foley (2016), and Benjamim Earley (2016). Shortly after the first complete translation into Latin, by Mattia Palmieri (c. 1450), in 1455 Lorenzo Valla published the edition that was transformed into an editorial work of reference for the Renaissance.[16] Only a century later (in 1566), Henri Estienne published another Latin edition of the *Histories* in France. The Portuguese humanists would have surely had access to the editions by Valla and Estienne, as testified by the deposit of these works in the library of the University of Coimbra.[17] Also there were translations into the vernacular, the first in Italian by Matteo Maria Boiardo (dated 1491 but published in 1533), which also circulated in Portugal.[18] The first Greek edition is not far removed from this activity: it comes in 1502 by the hand of Aldo Manuzio.

Thus, to Adam Foley (2016: 213–4), even when some fifteenth-century humanists write about unknown lands, producing ethnographic and geographic reports and using methods from Herodotean historiography (as sometimes occurs in our testimony), seldom or never have they adopted Herodotus as model. Only in the sixteenth century will humanists reveal an interest in the 'Herodotean style' of writing history, "often by way of apology for relying on eyewitness testimony and oral tradition occasioned by the expansion of Europe into East Asia and Americas" (Foley 2016: 215). According to the humanist *modus cogitandi*, Greek antiquity (and not only Latin) offers *exempla* and embodies an *auctoritas* which modern authors still respect, even if they do it in an undeclared manner (i.e., without identifying the classical literary sources by which they have been inspired). Moreover, the *Histories* of Herodotus have become more 'credible' to the eyes of sixteenth-century readers because, as observed by Anthony Grafton (2010b: 444):

> As European knowledge of Asia and the Americas grew, what had seemed tall tales in Herodotus gained a new plausibility, and offered a powerful model for writers who set out to describe the peoples that conquistadores and missionaries met in Mexico and the Andes, China and India.[19]

This study will argue that Brazil should be included as well.

In fact, it is not only the editorial disclosure of the works which testifies to the greater or lesser vitality of Herodotean historiography in a certain period. Its inclusion in school programmes of the time also shows how some ancient texts could have entered the literary culture and intellectual ideology of the authors that we are analyzing. Herodotus enjoyed recognition at the highest level of the European Renaissance because, as underlined by Neville Morley (2016: 146), Erasmus included Herodotus in his work on grammar school curriculum, the famous *De Ratio Studii* (= *On the Right Method of Instruction*), as one of the recommended Greek prose writers. Considering that our reception focusses on Portuguese works, we shall present as follows the elements that should be appreciated in the study of Greek during the sixteenth century in the religious schools' and university curricula (the university finally being installed in Coimbra from 1537 onwards, though alternating till then its location between there and Lisbon). I focus my attention only in these centres of learning, and I will not consider the interest that the study of the Greek language and authors registered upon private courses of study (in the court and some Portuguese noble houses),[20] because the biographies of our writer-settlers indicate their attendence at public or religious teaching venues.

Thanks to studies by Sebastião T. Pinho (2006) and Carlos Morais (2009) we can assess the relevance of Greek study at Coimbra and in the religious schools of the Society of Jesus, respectively. As a preparation measure for the university's transfer from Lisbon to Coimbra, King D. João III ordered a curricular reform in the Monastery of Santa Cruz in Coimbra, a pre-university religious teaching institution where the Greek language started being taught from 1535 onwards.

A sign of the appreciation for the Hellenic language and culture was the existence (between 1530 and 1557) of a printing facility in the same convent, where not only works in Portuguese and Latin, but also in Greek, were printed.[21] In 1532, the *Lexicon Graecum et Hebraicum* by Heliodoro de Paiva was published, a work that was especially meant for the support of the Greek lessons taught in Santa Cruz's schools. There is unfortunately no surviving copy (Meirinhos 2001: 322).

With the university coming to Coimbra (1537), higher education classes (then known as 'General Studies') began taking place in the city's schools belonging to the order of Santa Cruz, and they included Greek in their curriculum. Herodotus was not included among the authors used in these classes, a situation agreeing with the general position of marginality for the Greek historian among those authors covered by Adam Foley. The preference went to another literary type (not historiography), i.e., oratory (Isocrates), or moralistic and religious literature (*Dialogues* of Lucian, St. Basil, and the Gospels).[22] From 1547 onwards, D. João III provided the city of Coimbra with minor university studies, conducted in the Royal College of Arts, where the teaching of Greek remained mandatory. With the school's direction passing to the Society of Jesus (1555), Greek would remain in the curriculum, not only in teaching particular to Coimbra, but also, as will be seen momentarily, almost homogenously in all the institutions of the Society scattered throughout the world, because of its addition to the Jesuit *Ratio studiorum* (of which the definitive form dates from 1598). Apart from the programme of general studies, the canon of Greek authors studied in Jesuit schools is known, thanks to the publication in Coimbra in 1583 of a selection of Greek authors (*Aliquot Opuscula Graeca ex variis auctoribus collecta*. Off. António Maris). Herodotus was still absent from this roster (comprising Demosthenes, Theocritus, the Homeric Hymns, Lucian, Aesop, epigrams, the *Epitaph* of Bion, and the Pythagorean *carmina aurea*).[23]

In summary, in Portuguese education, there was an obvious presence of Greek studies in the training of young scholars and elites, with an equally clear 'oblivion' of Herodotus' *Histories* in such curricula. However, it is equally clear that the reading of and influence by the Greek historian was revealed in another context, that of humanist culture not tied to school manuals or programmes. Being more difficult to track, this presence of Herodotus in non-school environments frequented by literate men of the sixteenth century indicates that Portugal was not indifferent to this pan-European cultural trend. Proof rests on the several aforementioned editions of Herodotus preserved among the rare books collection at the library of the University of Coimbra.

Regarding these introductory clarifications, let us observe, as follows, how Book II of the *Histories* reveals the exploration of scientific *identity* in Herodotean historiography.

Foundations of scientific discourse in Herodotus' Book II

Let us start by looking into the contribution of Greek terminology used in the field of science. As we shall see in the following analysis, keywords and concepts such as 'knowledge', 'wisdom' and 'reasoning' (respectively related to the roots *soph-*, *epistēm-*, *log-*) are all used in the *Histories* with meanings that can be subsumed under the common name of our object of analysis, i.e., 'science'.

As happens with any exercise of 'identity definition' (i.e., saying *what one is*), the essence (i.e., *being*) of *what is* can only be grasped against (i.e., by *contrast* with) what is not. The materialization of this exercise is achieved through verbalization, i.e., through *discourse*. In fact, as we can see in the text of Book II, the language of 'scientific discourse' becomes implicit in the simultaneous exposure of a 'non-scientific discourse'. But before we look into some passages where this mirror game is enacted, it is important to mention that the presence of this characterization of science based on non-science is mostly a consequence of the fact that the *Histories* were written at a moment in history where the emergence of this new way of thinking and this new discourse was still very recent, and, therefore, still itself struggling for self-determination (i.e., *identity*).

Of course, Herodotus' aim was not to theorize scientific thought, nor did he mean to systematize the characteristics of scientific thought or of scientific discourse. However, Herodotean clarifications on this topic enable the reader to *identify* a discursive network of a scientific nature that is responsible for conferring a level of gravity on his account of Egypt. In effect, Herodotus intentionally differentiates it from other less earnest, or even implausible, narratives. But before we consider the foundations of this methodology, we should discuss the types of discourse (and, implicitly, their underlying methods) whose use the author finds objectionable (though not necessarily entirely inapplicable[24]) in 'research' (*historiē*).

Within that plural universe of 'non-scientific' approaches, one can find seemingly scientific modes of discourse alongside others of an obviously different nature. The most difficult task is to identify alleged science, as it is often presented as genuine by its authors. The way in which Herodotus mentions the Ionians' accounts on the variations of the Nile's flow (2.20–3) leads to the conclusion that their approaches do not adopt a scientific methodology but are based on a seemingly scientific approach. According to this critique, I propose that 'science' in Herodotean discourse is defined against what I would call *pseudo*-science. In fact, Herodotus names as 'false' some of those theories, a topic to which I shall return.

In the vocabulary used by the historian we find the word *sophiē*, whose literal meaning is 'knowledge' possessed by a so-called *sophos*. Possessing that knowledge 'marks the person with a seal' (Gr. *episēmenoi*), which is equivalent to saying that he is 'distinct' from the common masses. What could be seen as the pursuit of an asset, however, is presented as a fault, since in our historian's words some individuals use their knowledge – even if this knowledge is 'false', as implied by Herodotus' use of ἔψευσται (2.22.1) – as a means of social self-promotion (2.20.1): "Three different theories have been advanced by certain Greek thinkers, who were, however, motivated by a desire (βουλόμενοι) to enhance their reputation (ἐπίσημοι) as clever (σοφίην) people."[25] All three theories on the Nile flow are devoid of 'scientific qualities', or, to use the terminology of chapter 21, where the second theory is discussed, they are 'non-scientific' (ἀνεπιστήμων).

Nevertheless, the author ranks them, describing the second one as 'more non-scientific' (ἀνεπιστημονεστέρη) than the other two, as perhaps more dangerous, we would say, since the argument of 'reasonability' only serves to give it a misleading appearance of wisdom. From the author's considerations on this theory, it becomes clear that 'being reasonable' is not synonymous with 'being true'. Note here the formulation of 2.22.1: "The third theory, despite being the *most plausible* [ἐπιεικεστάτη], is also the *furthest from the truth* [μάλιστα ἔψευσται]".

In fact, in light of Herodotus' conception of inquiry, truth is not a condition *sine qua non* for reporting.[26] Later in Book VII (152.3) he will call his readers' attention to this in the context of the issue of whether the Argives Medized in the Persian Wars, by explicitly saying: "I am obliged to record the things I am told, but I am certainly not required to believe them – this remark may be taken to apply to the whole of my account." Turning back to Book II, as for the less scientific of the theories on the Nile flow, the second one (concerning the supposed existence of a river called Ocean which surrounded the Earth, and which the Nile flowed out of), Herodotus clarifies the purpose of scientific thought and of scientific discourse: they aim to 'shed light' on issues, to 'impart knowledge on', 'to reveal' (Greek root *phan-/phain-*) what had been hidden (ἀφανής) or not yet fully known, rather than to examine or to lead to an inscrutable conclusion, or, as can be read in chapter 23, to offer what is dubious and 'cannot be proven' (οὐκ ἔχει ἔλεγχον). As mentioned earlier (pp. 298–9), Herodotus the researcher is thus distancing himself from what is intangible and invisible. This position is patent in the author's argument against the Ionian theory concerning the river Ocean (2.23): "It is impossible to argue against the person who spoke about the Ocean, because *the tale* (τὸν μῦθον) is based on something which is *obscure* (ἐς ἀφανές) and that *cannot be proven* (οὐκ ἔχει ἔλεγχον)." In some passages the historian explicitly (rather than implicitly, as in the quotation earlier) states that what motivates him, i.e., his 'object of inquiry' (τὰ ἱστορημένα), is exactly the aim of 'clearly revealing' issues that are surrounded by polemics or are simply unknown. This is his explanation, for example, when he discusses Heracles, both within the Greek and the Egyptian religions (2.44.5): "These inquiries (τὰ ἱστορημένα) of mine, then, *clearly* show (δηλοῖ σαφέως) that Heracles is an ancient god." As can be read further on, in chapter 49, that process is exactly the mission of 'men of knowledge' (σοφισταί): 'to explain, to clarify', or, using Herodotus' own terminology, *ekphainein* (cf. 2.49.1: ἐξέφηναν). However, Herodotus the researcher shares with other contemporary scientists a sense of intellectual humility,[27] that is, an awareness of the limits of human knowledge, which moderates the inquiring impulse. The author explains this when reporting on his research on the dissemination of the cult of the god and hero Heracles (2.44.1): "I wanted to understand these matters as *clearly* (σαφές τι εἰδέναι) as *I could* (οἷον τε ἦν), so I also sailed to Tyre in Phoenicia, since I had heard that there was a sanctuary sacred to Heracles there." As I mentioned before, the *identity* of scientific thought and discourse can also be demarcated through a process of contrast with diametrically opposite realities. This is to say that the same subject-matter can be viewed from quite different perspectives, each generating considerations of a different nature. Concerning the

cult of Heracles in Egypt, Herodotus mentions a version told by his fellow countrymen, of whom he says that they *inattentively* (ἀνεπισκέπτως, i.e., without a rig-
ourous observation) "say many and different things" (λέγουσι δὲ πολλὰ καὶ ἄλλα:
2.45.1). The tenor of those versions (which include the attempted human sacrifice
of the Greek hero at the hands of the Egyptians) is so inconsistent with reality (the
nature and customs of the Egyptians, as far as the historian knows them) that he
does not hesitate in describing that 'story' (μῦθος) as 'simple-minded' (εὐήθης).

Probably as a consequence of his close interaction with the Egyptians, as well
as of his direct contact with local sources and informants,[28] from the beginning of
the book he dedicates to the people of Egypt, Herodotus is particularly critical of
what many of his countrymen have had to say about the Egyptians. In chapter 5
he blames the Greeks for saying "many other *nonsensical* things" (ἄλλα τε μάταια
πολλά: 2.2.5) and declares that Psammetikhos had sent the children whose first
spoken word he wanted to know to two nannies whose tongues he had cut out.

The passages in Book II I have so far surveyed show the distinction established
by Herodotus between, on the one hand, forms of scientific discourse (i.e., oriented towards building the type of knowledge he considers to be reliable), and,
on the other, non-scientific discourse. However, in order to gain a deeper understanding of his concept of 'science', one must consider its foundations. Although
I cannot say with absolute certainty that Herodotus followed a well-defined programme for structuring his historical research (which seems to me to be anachronistic, and therefore improbable[29]), the truth is that his readers likely could find in
his narrative a description of the structuring elements of the conduct and activity
of a man of science (be it in the domain of what today are called earth sciences,
life sciences, or human sciences). Let us now focus our attention on the written
evidence for the scientific tone of the historian's research methodology.

In the opening of chapter 99 of Book II, Herodotus describes the foundations
supporting the whole structure of historical knowledge as he conceives it. When
he writes "so far my account of Egypt has been dictated by my own observations [ὄψις], judgment [γνώμη], and investigation [ἱστορίη]", his observation, the
ability to formulate one's own judgment (i.e., to examine sources critically), and
his investigations are highlighted. However, because he knows that, in some circumstances, he cannot have direct access to reality – which is known only vicari-
ously, through the knowledge of others – Herodotus does not discard indirect, oral
sources (ἀκοή), although he suggests that it is advisable to supplement them by
means of other elements which the researcher has personally gathered. This is his
position, as we see here in the passage that immediately follows my last quotation
(2.99.1): "But from now on I will be relating Egyptian accounts *as I heard them*
(κατὰ τὰ ἤκουον); but to these I will add also *what I personally saw* (τῆς ἐμῆς
ὄψιος)." *Opsis, gnōmē,* and *historiē* delineate the profile of Herodotus' scientific
method and have practical bearing on his activity as a researcher.[30] The need to
observe and to have personal contact with his research targets leads him to travel.
Among the numerous examples of the 'mobility' required from the researcher,[31]
his travels to Thebes and Memphis are mentioned as early as chapter 3, in a passage where the author explains that one of the ways of validating the reliability

of a given source is by finding other sources which contain the same content but derive from different origins (2.3.1): "The information I gained there led me to travel to Thebes and to Heliopolis, to try to find out whether their accounts would agree with *the accounts* [τοῖσι λόγοισι] heard in Memphis." This methodological requirement of *opsis* must be understood as a specific scientific practice that, nonetheless, has its origins in folk wisdom, as shown by its formulation as a maxim. This dual dimension (scientific and popular) is mentioned by the author in different passages. In the narrative concerning Gyges' ascension to the throne of Lydia, triggered by Kandaules, the monarch whose desire to prove (by showing) the extraordinary beauty of his wife and queen (about whom they were talking), Herodotus writes: "it is true that people trust their ears less than their eyes" (1.8.2).

On the other hand, when writing about his investigations regarding the headwaters of the Nile and the data he provides about that region, Herodotus confirms that direct observation (autopsy) enables him to improve his narrative greatly, as opposed to what he does when he must simply report what others have told him (ἀκοή) (2.29.1):

> I could not get any other information from anyone else, but I managed *to learn quite a bit more* (ἐπὶ μακρότατον ἐπυθόμην) about other subjects because *I have seen them with my own eyes* (αὐτόπτης), in the path to Elephantine and, from there onwards, *my research* (ἱστορέων) is based on *what I have heard* (ἀκοῆι).[32]

However, in order to be able to interpret reality, as well as formulate his own opinion on it (his *gnōmē*), the researcher must possess a quality which the author cannot praise highly enough: the 'reasoning ability' (expressed in Greek through the verb λογίζεσθαι and other compounds of the *log-* root). *Being able to think* is so important that, when coupled with direct contact with the reality under analysis, it enables the researcher to interpret that same reality even in the absence of previous knowledge on his subject-matter (conveyed by *akoē*). The historian describes that *opsis-logos gnōmē* methodological tripod in the following words (2.5.1):

> My view is that they are right in saying this about the country. Even someone – a *man of intelligence* (σύνεσιν ἔχει), at any rate – who has not already *heard about* it (προακούσαντι), but just *uses his eyes* (ἰδόντι), can easily see that the Egypt to which the Greeks sail is new in land which the Egyptians have gained as a gift from the river.

Indeed, Herodotus considers direct observation a major method of research, which is further reinforced, whenever necessary, by resorting to experimentation.[33] However, it also becomes clear how, as a man of knowledge, Herodotus acknowledges that using reason is more onerous even than observing. The author explains the critical importance of that vantage point that is exclusively reserved for the ability to reason when he refutes the theory according to which the Nile's abundant flow is a consequence of the melting of snows (2.22.2): "The idea that it rises in snowy regions makes no sense at all, as anyone *capable of rational thought* (λογίζεσθαι) could realize. The first and most convincing *piece of evidence* (μαρτύριον) is that the winds which blow from these regions are warm." As Nino Luraghi (2006: 78) rightly wrote, "logical arguments . . . are the most powerful weapon of his [sc. Herodotus'] hermeneutical arsenal". One of the most common reasoning techniques was comparison. Supported by comparative reasoning, thinkers formulated their theories (*gnōmai*), which needed no other form of validation. That is to say that knowledge is grounded not only on what one sees and hears but also in the subject's ability to formulate theories based on logical arguments. An example is the way in which Herodotus acknowledges the truth of the theory according to which the Nile divides Libya into two halves, based exactly on analogy. Logical reasoning is posited here as an act of revelation, that is, of *making visible* (adj. ἐμφανής) "that which is unknown (τὰ μὴ γινωσκόμενα)". By using the verb τεκμαίρεσθαι, the author makes it clear that another methodological pillar for a researcher is rooted in his ability to construct reasoning on the basis of previously acquired knowledge, resting in the ability to make inferences (2.33.2):

> Etearkhos thought that the river crossing the city was the Nile and that demonstrates *logic* (ὁ λόγος). In fact, the Nile comes from Libya, dividing it in half; and, *as I reckon* (ὡς ἐγὼ συμβάλλομαι), while conjecturing (τεκμαιρόμενος) from *manifest* qualities (τοῖσι ἐμφανέσι) about *what is not known* (τὰ μὴ γινωσκόμενα), the Nile starts at a distance similar to the Istros.[34]

It should be stressed that Herodotus had resorted to comparative logic before in order to confirm a thesis he had previously known (2.10–11). In fact, the Egyptian priests' theory that the regions of Memphis and Elephantine represented Nile alluvium had been readily accepted by the historian as probable, since the same natural phenomenon also occurred on the Ionian and Acarnanian coasts.[35]

From the examples mentioned earlier, one should not draw the conclusion that formulating personal interpretations is necessarily always motivated by a desire to prove or refute somebody else's thesis. Autonomous reasoning is a component of scientific thought, as is shown by the pride with which Herodotus proclaims his discovery, through personal deductive logic, of the Egyptian origins of the inhabitants of Colchis, situated on the eastern margin of the Black Sea (2.104.1–2):

> For the fact is, as *I first came to realize myself* (νοήσας δὲ πρότερον αὐτός), and then *heard from others later* (ἀκούσας ἄλλων), that Colchians *are obviously* (φαίνονται) Egyptians. When the notion *occurred to me* (μοι ἐν φροντίδι ἐγένετο), I asked both the Colchians and the Egyptians about it and found that the Colchians had a better recollection of the Egyptians than the Egyptians did of them. Some Egyptians said that they thought the Colchians originated with Sesostris army, but *I myself had guessed* (αὐτὸς δὲ εἴκασα) their Egyptian origin not only because the Colchians are dark-skinned and curly haired (which does not count for much by itself, because these features are common to others too), but more importantly because Colchians, Egyptians, and

Ethiopians are the only peoples in the world who practice circumcision and have always done so.

It follows, therefore, that, in a period where history affirms itself as science, it legitimately claims the basic and timeless principles of a research methodology that is transferable to scientific thought and scientific discourse in different domains and is built upon observation, experimentation, source criticism, and logical reasoning. The conjunction of these principles enables the researcher to formulate hypotheses and theories that are clearly different from non-scientific discourse. When the topic is 'New Worlds', that is, worlds that are unknown or little known to their readers, the historian's main object of study is the difference present in their referents when compared with the 'Old (and well-known) World', which is their own. In other words, the historian's writing focusses on surprising matters and events, which is the reason why they are called θώματα 'wonders' (sing. θῶμα) in Greek and are described as μέγιστα 'grand'. Because a θῶμα discloses what had hitherto been hidden and its appreciation is guided by the quest for truth, we may conclude that the historian's act of revelation (of creating an *identity* for his verbalization of *historiē*) takes the form of scientific discourse. We should also consider that Herodotus' scientific credit as an *histōr*, as he constantly puts it, is rooted in evaluating not an individual thesis or authorities, but collective *gnomai*. In general, he subsumes under collective designations (such as Ionians) personal references (Hecataeus). In Book II the historian offers to his public several examples of a process of ethnicizing interpretations. On geographical characterization of the Delta, he distinguishes Ionians' *gnōmē* from that of the Egyptians and Greeks (2.15–17). We should not conclude that Herodotus conceives ethnic identity as a monolithic reality. As in other perspectives (like local or regional cults and dialects), there is a place for difference in the same *ethnos*. Therefore, he says that "for some, Egyptians crocodiles are sacred, for others not" (2.69.1).

Let us now see in the case of the first writings on the Portuguese discoveries in America in the sixteenth century how the Herodotean matrix of historical narrative, as based on the methodological principles described earlier, continues to live on.

Herodotus through *other's* eyes: the Herodotean matrix in the historiography of sixteenth-century Portuguese settlers concerning the land and peoples of Brazil

The next three authors and their works share with Herodotus that they describe unknown lands and peoples. All of them produce discourses about alterity, the *identity* of the 'other'. A comparative study of works written within a time span of 20 centuries attests the vitality of Herodotus' historiographic approach in authors educated according to the principles of humanism. For this study, I shall only focus on the general alignment of early modern accounts of Brazil with classical historiographical discourse and will not proceed to the analysis of the similarities of their contents. Let me start by identifying the authors and their texts:

- Pêro de Magalhães de Gândavo: *História da Província de Santa Cruz a que vulgarmente chamamos Brasil* [*The history of the Province of Santa Cruz, in what we commonly call Brazil*], 1576;[36]
- Fernão Cardim: *Do clima e terra do Brasil e de algumas cousas notáveis que se acham na terra como no mar* [*On the weather and land of Brazil and some remarkable things that can be found on land and in the sea*], 1583–1601;[37]
- Gabriel Soares de Sousa: *Notícia do Brasil* [*News from Brazil*] (1587), which includes two works: *Descrição verdadeira da costa daquele Estado que pertence à Coroa do Reino de Portugal, sítio da Baía de Todos-os-Santos* [*The true description of the coast of the state of Bahia de Todos-os-Santos, which belongs to the Portuguese Kingdom*]; *Memorial e declaração das grandezas da Baía de Todos-os-Santos, de sua fertilidade e das notáveis partes que tem* [*Memorial and declaration of the greatness of Bay of Todos-os-Santos, of its fertility and noteworthy places that it has*].[38]

In spite of their 'humanistic flair', the works of these Portuguese authors have not yet been read in this light: thus far, the classical education of their authors and/or their alignment with a humanist *modus scribendi et cogitandi* has not been taken into consideration. This oversight, I suggest, may be owed to the fact that these texts have been studied in the context of social, political, and economic history, rather than cultural or literary history.

The works of the three abovementioned colonists are alike in describing spaces and people they themselves witnessed in their travels, which allows us to ascribe them to the literary genre of 'Travel Literature'. This denomination is quite extensive, leading literary theorists to propose numerous sub-specifications, from which we can adopt one used for such productions in Portuguese. Thus, under Fernando Cristóvão's proposal, the analysed *corpus* of texts belongs to the type named 'Expansion Travel Literature'.[39] By gathering elements regarding issues concerning the administrative and territorial implantation of the settlers, as well as descriptions of the fauna, flora, and customs of the indigenous populations, along with data on the progress of evangelization of the natives, the works of our authors amalgamated the three sub-categories defined for "Expansion Travels": political expansion, scientific expansion, and expansion of faith. Still, according to Joan-Pau Rubiés (2006: 132), we need to take account fully of the impact of travel writing upon humanistic culture in order to understand how the Renaissance eventually led to the Enlightment.

Before analysing these works, it is important to consider the biographic elements which are available on these three author-settlers, particularly concerning their probable schooling and intellectual training. We must keep in mind that "the educated traveller of the sixteenth and seventeenth centuries was essentially a humanistically educated traveller" (Rubiés 2006: 168). The available biographical data on these colonial authors reveal that one of them, Pêro de Magalhães de Gândavo, was a humanist and a teacher of Latin and Portuguese in a public school in the northwestern region of Portugal, probably in Braga, his birthplace. It was there, in 1531, in the College of Arts (also known as St. Paul's College),[40] that the first institution for public studies was created. This was followed (from 1572 onwards) by a career as a scrivener ('moço de câmara'), copying books and documents at the Royal National Archive known as Torre do Tombo. Gândavo is clearly an example of a scholar with privileged access to both classical texts and to all sorts of other 'literature' (namely official and administrative documents) that are so vitally important for Portuguese history. The addition of two poems by a giant of Portuguese Renaissance literature, Luís Vaz de Camões, for the opening of his work, is again confirmation of the circle of intellectuals with whom he had contact. The period of this first history of Portuguese America in print (1576), *The history of the Province of Santa Cruz, which we commonly call Brazil*, coincides with the author's stay in Brazil,[41] where he was appointed Commissioner for the Royal Treasury of the Captaincy of the Salvador da Bahia Province. In other words, Gândavo undoubtedly enjoyed a scholarly academic training that he cultivated thanks to his many postings in the service of the crown in the fields of culture, literature, and politics.

Fernão Cardim (1548–1625) undertook studies following the humanist canon of the Jesuits' *Ratio Studiorum*, after which he achieved a remarkable career as a Jesuit. After his studies in (the colleges of) Évora and Coimbra, in 1583 he left for Brazil as secretary to the 'visiting priest', Cristóvão de Gouveia, a prestigious position that acknowledged his standing as a man of letters. His responsibility was to follow the order's top representative in his apostolic travels and visits to the colleges and villages in which the Jesuits evangelized. The record of the information collected at these locations, of the living conditions for the religious, and the missions' progress was made through letters, sent to the province priest installed in the kingdom. Of his written production I will only speak of that treatise which, by his own initiative, or, in other words, by impulse of his humanistic disposition and from his readings of other classical and/or medieval reports describing unknown worlds, he felt compelled to write, the abovementioned *On weather and land of Brazil and some remarkable things that can be found on land and in the sea*. This Jesuit's high culture would have surely contributed towards the superior position he occupied in the province's hierarchy, as testified by his subsequent positions as dean, procurator of the Jesuit province of Brazil, and province priest.[42] Finally, as Rubiés explained (2006: 140), such missionaries are "arguably the most 'educated' of those primary travel writers".

On the other hand, regarding the colonist-conqueror Gabriel Soares de Sousa, I cannot (as yet) demonstrate his humanistic training in any particular university or religious school, but I can, nevertheless, spot a 'humanist flair' in his work, because of the presence in it of some classical *topoi*. Sousa was a layman, an explorer who arrived in Brazil in 1569, who owned two sugar cane mills in the environs of Bahia and had been nominated 'governor and captain of the discovery and conquest of the St. Francis River' (by king's charter from 18.12.1590).[43]

Because of being an archetypal work for all subsequent cultural descriptions, and notwithstanding the high regard that Pliny the Elder's *Natural History* was eventually to achieve, Herodotus' *Histories* lays down, in its prologue, the foundations for the development and increasing complexity (or diversity) of this type of humanist descriptions – whether scholarly or popular – that the present texts exemplify.[44] Although very well known, I shall present once again the *Histories'* prologue as it helps us to an easier understanding of the intertextuality between the historical proposals of Herodotus and of Portuguese writers on the New (Brazilian) World.

> Here are presented the results of the *disclosure* (ἀπόδειξις) carried out by Herodotus of Halicarnassus. The purpose is to prevent the traces of human events from being erased by time, and to preserve the fame of *the great* (μεγάλα) and *admirable* (θωυμαστά) achievements produced by both Greeks and non-Greeks; among the matters covered, in particular, the case of the hostilities between Greeks and non-Greeks.

The first conclusion to draw from this prologue is that to make history is *to disclose* (Gr. ἀπόδειξις: from ἀπο-δείνυμι)[45] what was previously hidden, meaning that what is about to be revealed is *news* for the listener or the reader. Moreover, this (written) presentation is meant to preserve the memory of what is being described, underlying those aspects that are thought to be *great* (μεγάλα) and *admirable* (θωυμαστά). In his descriptions of places and peoples, Herodotus details many aspects that would from then on be seen as characteristic of this historiographical discourse. Based on relating what is great and admirable (lands and nature included), examples include the relief, hydrographic resources, distance, climate, fauna, flora, and mineral resources of the land, and the physical and cultural description of the people.

In other words, in the days of the Portuguese colonial writers under analysis, history is viewed as a discourse in which an author presents his findings on matters that not only in antiquity, but also in the renaissance and the modern era, could easily coexist in the same literary register: geography, climate, botany, zoology, diet, concepts and practices in the realm of politics, economy, society, and culture. To sum it up, from its origin and for over 20 centuries, history would remain an eminently holistic discourse.[46]

I will structure my reflections on the reception of the scientific-historiographic methodology on Herodotean template for the writings of the Portuguese settlers in two parts. In a first aspect, there will be considered what can be called the stage of 'work conception' (title, presentation to the reader/patron, structure); followed by the stage of 'work execution' (treatment of the narrated subjects).

Markers of the Herodotean scientific-historiographic discourse in the conception of Portuguese narratives on the New World of Portuguese America

All three abovementioned texts clearly exhibit in their titles one or another of the principles of classical historiographical discourse as pioneered by Herodotus' work. The earliest of them, by P.M. Gândavo, displays the keyword and concept of the genre: *The history of the Province of Santa Cruz*. Perhaps this explicit affiliation of the work in a line of so many *Histories* (classic, medieval, and modern) may be explained by the fact that Gândavo, out of the three authors-settlers, was the one who seems to have had a more thorough humanistic training. The other two authors opted for titles that refer to the genre by resorting to other foundational methodological principles, such as truth, novelty, greatness, and memory; thus in G.S. Sousa's work: "*News* from Brazil: The *true* description of the coast. . .; *Memorial* and declaration of the *greatness* of Bahia de Todos-os-Santos, of its fertility and *famous* lands"; or, in Cardim's work, the object of study (a place with conditions for human settlement) and its remarkable elements: "On the weather and land of *Brazil* and some *remarkable things* that can be found on land and in the sea."

Both Gândavo and Sousa composed presentation letters for their treatises, containing elements on the conception of these works.[47] The first insists on the identification of his text's genre as *history*, although the insistence with which, in this letter and throughout his work, he indicates that his *History* has the particularity of being a *brief* composition seems to indicate that he and his readers must have in mind a literary *exemplum* that distinguishes it from the extensive classic writings of the genre (the nine books of *Histories* by Herodotus and the 37 of the *Natural History* by Pliny). Likewise, Gândavo does not forget the classic *topos* of novelty when he says about his work "ser cousa nova" (to be a novelty). Moreover, the criterion of autopsy is a mandatory presence in any narration that is to be trustworthy; therefore, the author is careful to mention, still in his letter of presentation, that he is a direct witness of what he narrates (eu a escrever como testemunha de vista, 'me writing as eye witness'). He proceeds, in the "Prologo ao leitor" (Prologue to the reader), with another 'founding principle' of Herodotean *historiē*: the unusual/marvellous character of what he narrates (and calls "cousas dignas de grande admiração, & tam notaveis", such remarkable and admirable things). In fact, as he clarifies further ahead in chapter 1, it has been on behalf of the report's briefness that he has been limited to "as cousas mais notaveis & principaes da terra" (the land's more remarkable and principal matters: Gândavo 1576: 10). Of course, that many of the "remarkable things" of this New World, because of the strangeness they would impart to the readers, could cause disbelief; therefore, another classic historical *topos* is found in which Gândavo insists that his is the true report. It is that insistence in the defence of a discourse based on truth, and not in the stylistic tricks, which leads him to call his work "historia tam verdadeira" (such true history). As he clarifies, it has been that same criterion that has led him to confine his report on Indian tribes to what he deems well-testified, despising what he considers as lacking in truth (such as the life of inland Indians).[48] Even when the subject could have been particularly interesting for his reader (as in the case of the local gemstones), he is inhibited from providing information on what he says he has no knowledge of, i.e., their market value.[49] Fidelity to the founding principle of preserving the memory, or saving it from oblivion, is typical of historiographic discourse in all its markers. Gândavo openly declares his inheritance of classical *auctoritas*; which expressly proclaims its placement in the wake of the classical tradition, when he composes this memorial of admirable things, specifying: "dalas a perpetua memoria, como costumavam os Antigos: aos quaes nam escapava cousa algua que por extenso nam reduzissem a historia" (giving perpetual memory, as the Ancients used to do: for whom nothing escaped so that it could not be reduced to history, in his "Prologue to the reader").

No less imbued with the ancient principles (Herodotean–Hippocratic–Plinian) for the description of place and people, Gabriel Soares de Sousa shows – both in the presentation letter of his *Notícia do Brasil* to D. Cristóvão de Moura, a member of the Council of Portugal, and in chapter 1 of the second treatise included in it (the *Memorial and declaration of the greatness of Bahia de Todos os Santos*) – an identical spectrum of historical narrative fundamentals. Let us focus on two steps revealing that affiliation. In the letter he implies, firstly, the affiliation of his report, *ipsis verbis*, to the Herodotean matrix of the *megala kai thōmasta* ("as I deeply regret the little notice this reign of ours has taken of the *greatness* and *singularity* of this province [(sc. Brazil]"). Thereupon, he continues with statements that clarify the inclusion of his writing in the classical genre of holistic history, particularly attentive to the geoclimatic coordinates of locations and living beings that inhabit them: Here it is clear:

> As my intention has not been to write *history* that delighted with style and good language, I do not expect to take praise from this writing and brief relation (containing what I could achieve in *cosmography* and *description* of this State), that I offer to Your Lordship.

In chapter 1 of the *Memorial* as well, when presenting the subject of the second part of his treatise, Sousa defines his aims clearly according to the motifs of *raising awareness* (Gr. *apodexis*), the *greatness* (*megala*) and the *wonderful* (*thaumasta*) of the territory of the 'other' (to wit, the Bahia de Todos-os-Santos). According to the method established since Herodotus, this description is based on the explanation (itself implying the presentation of the *aitia*, i.e., the 'causes' why things are how they are) and on truth. At this moment of his narration, the author evokes, as we can infer, the criterion of veracity to distance himself from other fictional reports, made by those who, unlike him, would speak of what they did not see. Sousa compensates for the lack of rhetorical artifice (a style that he names the "grave style", different from his "simple style") with a speech he claims is "all based on truth".

Yet another classical pattern of allusion – Hippocratic in this case – can be seen in chapter 1 of Sousa's *Memorial*, where the author uses the Hippocratic trio of "airs, waters, and places" to emphasize "the fertility of the *land*, the healthy *air*, the wonderful *waters*, the excellent provisions" of Bahia de Todos-os-Santos.

It must be noted that strong praise for the conquered New World is a reflection of the patriotic pride of Portuguese settlers, not only for belonging to a European kingdom combining two of the greatest engineers of overseas expansion under the same crown, Portugal and Spain (under the same crown of the Philippine dynasty, between 1580–1640), but also on account of the colony's magnificent economic potential.[50]

In what follows, I will consider how the work's own structure – that is, the subjects broached in several chapters and the order in which they are presented – is linked to Greek–Latin models. We have intentionally set aside here the first treatise of the *Notícia do Brasil* by G.S. Sousa (i.e., *The true description of the coast of the state of Bahia de Todos-os-Santos*), given that here the topic of the narrative is the cosmography of the whole of Brazil and the classical subjects of the 'customs and life modes' (Gr. *diaitai*) of the people living in those places are dealt more superficially. In the second treatise (i.e., *Memorial and declaration of the greatness of Bahia de Todos-os-Santos*), the author is focussed on one single place, precisely on the geography and the people of the region where he settled – the Bahia de Todos-os-Santos – which causes the sequence of succeeding chapters to truly reveal classical models.

In accordance with Herodotean historiography, the narrative of the New World is preceded by an account of how this land, unknown to the writer's culture, came to be discovered.[51] Both Gândavo (*History*, ch. 1) and Sousa (*Memorial*, chs. 1–5), expressly describe themselves as writers of 'history' and introduce their treatises with a more or less brief account of the events regarding the discovery of this land and the political and administrative management of the settlers. Only after that 'introduction' do the Portuguese writers describe the natural environment (Gr. *phusis*) and culture (*nomoi*) of the other (the indigenous people of Brazil). Given that the classical doctrine (thriving among fifth-century Greek authors) of climatic and geographic determinism in the physical build and way of life of peoples and individuals (common to Herodotus and *Corpus Hippocraticum*) remained valid during the sixteenth century, it is no surprise that, following those models, all the author-settlers begin their descriptions with the presentation of the virtues of the place's climate and geography, before moving on to the food products and, at the same time, pharmacology of the goods that it produces (autochthonous or imported from the settlers' lands). As is well known, in Herodotean narrative there are concerns with the climate and geography. But it is mostly in the afore-mentioned Hippocratic text *Airs, Waters, Places* that the subject is developed. As I precede, I shall stress elements that, in the works of Portuguese writers, converge in a dietetic matrix of interpretation – indeed, these topics are one more piece of evidence for their 'humanistic flair'. Rebecca Earle (2012: 21), in her study dedicated to Spanish America, has already made quite clear the application of the classical scientific body of ideas, when stressing that "Since the time of Hippocrates European writers had drawn connections between the environment in which individuals lived and their characters, and during the sixteenth and seventeenth centuries the influence of climate on the human constitution was universally acknowledged." My main contribution consists in demontrating that this classical and humanist tendency is also verifiable in Portuguese writings.

Because these writers' goal was to garner public and private good will in order to invest their resources and themselves in the colony, and because the Portuguese kingdom was also under the Spanish dual crown of Philip II and his successors (which might mean a reduction of the focus of royal power on Brazil, the New World of Portuguese colonization), all the authors under analysis are unanimous in praising the health conditions of the New World. Furthermore, they do so according to the Hippocratic criteria of air, water, and healing locales, standards that the medieval hygiene treatises (implementing *regimina sanitatis*) also promulgated.[52] Since any change in environment represents an endangerment of the balance of a subject's organism (given that it is porous and suffers the consequences from everything that may enter: air, temperature, water), the environmental qualities stressed by the writer settlers constitute an assurance of health for settlers in the New World.

Concretely, Gândavo, in order to attest to the 'good airs' from the province (Bahia), indicates the directions from which the wind usually blows (contemplating those deemed best: from the north and east). The mild climate and the abundance of water (from the three source types considered in the Hippocratic interpretative grid: rain, spring, and lake) are responsible for an eternally spring-like climate. Because spring is the season least subject to climate changes, it was also the most favourable to individual health.

In the case of the Bahia de Todos-os-Santos, described by Gabriel Soares de Sousa in his *Memorial*, there are descriptions of wind directions (which vary according to the seasons), the abundance of water and air purity (generalized to the whole day, given it is always bright). The water was also always clear, i.e., not turbid. The opening chapter of *On the weather and land of Brazil*, by the Jesuit Cardim, already explains, amid other benefits, the main virtues behind the natural properties associated with the climate and land. The first of them is the cause–effect relationship between "good, delicate and healthy airs" and the health of those who breathe them, which translates into an extraordinary general longevity ("where men live until ninety, one hundred and more years, and the land is filled with elders", p. 63). There is an insistence on the advantage of a clear sky, in which the sun shines from daybreak until night (because only so, states the author, the "morning is healthy", i.e., without morning or evening twilights). In this passage the direct relation between the stars and people's well-being is made implicit; therefore, it is important for the skies to be clear, because this allows clear conditions for observation.[53] That is, the *aer* from Brazil (as air, wind, water, climate, and stars) is an assurance of a healthy life for settlers.

When the Jesuit Cardim describes the gentle climate and the green, well irrigated land of Brazil with its diverse relief, he knows those characteristics were causes for the main factor weighed by his readers: the healthy life of the people embracing the adventure, always unsure, of travel and living in a new location. And that healthy life depends, first, on a human being having high quality food and drink available, a need that Cardim assures his readers with a sentence that I shall reproduce, in as much as it shows the key role of digestion in health, one more heritage of the classic Hippocratic (and Galenic) medical-dietetic thought: "the food supplies and water are generally healthy and of easy assimilation". These supplies are the fruits from a land that need only be described in its geomorphological characterization (as Cardim does) or in terms of implantation of colonists and territorial administration (detailing data on the architecture and planning of villages and cities and the life conditions of their populations, as was also done by Gândavo and Sousa[54]).

After the three initial subject blocks (history of the settlers' implantation in the New World, description of the place's climate and geography, and the conquerors' lifestyle in the colony, in the case of Gândavo and Sousa), or right after the geoclimatic portrait of Brazil (in the case of Cardim), there are three new subject axes, concerning the three realms of nature: animal, vegetable, and mineral. Because it is from those faunal, floral, and mineral resources that man takes the necessary ingredients for his food and health, using them in the preparation of recipes and medicine, the ancient authorities, from Herodotus to Pliny, mandatorily included them in their accounts in order to offer information about these main bases of human survival.

If we compare the order in which they appear in the Roman model of Pliny the Elder (the most organized and influential text, starting from the Middle Ages) and in the texts by Portuguese settlers, we can conclude that Sousa and Cardim present a perfect example of the classical sequence (Animals–Plants–Minerals), whereas Gândavo inverts the order of the first two groups (presenting them in the sequence Plants–Animals–Minerals). This difference does not amount to so much as a deviation from the Plinian canon as an approximation of the Herodotean principle of privileging the narration of 'marvellous' aspects. Truthfully, in light of the food norms of the narrator's culture, the basic element of the European diet (again, conforming to the classical cultural pattern) was bread (particularly, for the more priviledged classes, wheat bread). Therefore, the nonexistence in local flora of the plant that produces the grain to make (wheaten) flour, alongside a substitute of it, shaped like a root – cassava – rightly provides the opening of chapter 5, which is dedicated to plants (creeping flora, bushes, and trees) that both produce food supplies and medicines.

I end these references to the formal debts of the texts from Portuguese settlers in Brazil to the classical discursive model by mentioning that Sousa, the only one of the three authors who treats in detail the introduction of European fauna into Brazil, followed the sequence for meats established in the Hippocratic treatise *Regimen* (ch. 46), namely: bovine, sheep, goat, pork, and poultry (*Memorial*, ch. 33).

Conclusion

Through my analysis centered on Book II of *Histories*, I have argued that the scientific discourse shaped by Herodotus in the service of the construction of the *identity* of Egypt (and other cultures not highlighted earlier) was a vital force in literature of the age of discovery. As I have sought to demonstrate, both in the work of the Greek author and in the works of the sixteenth-century Portuguese settler-writers, that scientific natural discourse is a *formal schema* of 'investigation' (*historiē*) of *identity* in New Worlds, whose novelty and marvellous aspects – at least for those readers who do not yet know them – fall perforce under the narrator's competence to reveal.

From a narrative-constructive perspective, the *identity* of the scientific discourse is based, as in any identity formation process, in the distinction or confrontation with the 'other' (in this case ἀνεπιστήμων 'the non-scientific'). A fundamental characteristic of the scientific discourse consists in guiding the 'investigation' (*historiē*) towards the revelation (*apodexis*) that was hidden, even if the researcher must be aware that there are limits constraining the inquisitive impulse.

For Herodotus, the essential methodologies of research are observation (*opsis*, preferably direct observation or autopsy), source-critical sense (*gnōmē*), and reasoning (*logos*). From those three instruments of knowledge production, the author ends by emphasizing the last, mostly when used by the investigator as complementary to *opsis*. In summary, we can infer that, for the historian from Halicarnassus, the formulation of theories based on reasoning ability is what truly distinguishes the man of science from those who only appear to have such knowledge. Analogic reasoning (patent in the comparison with the hypotheses of others) and deductive reasoning (created by his own logical reasoning) are two of the investigation methods Herodotus uses.

As for the exploration carried out in the second part of my study – on the influence of the classical historic–scientific matrix (mostly Herodotean and Hippocratic in origin) in the Portuguese narratives on the land and peoples of Brazil – I sought to demonstrate that that influence becomes clear at the level of genre conception and investigative methods. In fact, in this analysis, it has been possible to detect references, explicit and implicit, to respective resonances of ancient inspiration in the modern historiographic genre. That is the case with the presence of many classical *topoi* (originarily Herodotean), such as novelty, marvellous character, and truth of the matters narrated; direct observation of the described *realia*; designs for preservation of past memory; and the holistic character of the genre. A natural consequence of the confluence of several areas of knowledge in the construction of classical historical narrative (and its revitalization during the age of discoveries) is the presence of a discourse on dietetics in the narratives of Portuguese settlers. In the settlers' texts, I have also uncovered the reuse of *topoi* of Greek origin, in this case Hippocratic, such as references to the salubrity of air, water, and place; food properties; and invocations of environmental determinism in the (good) health of the individuals who dwell in certain locations.

With this inquiry into the textual markers of the principles of historic–scientific discourse, originarily established by fifth-century BC Greek authors, in the vernacular writings of Portuguese settlers, I have intended to emphasize the presence of a 'humanistic flair' in Portuguese written works on the New World of Portuguese South America.

Notes

* Research developed under the Project UID/ELT/00196/2019, funded by the Portuguese FCT – Foundation for Science and Technology.
1 On the conception and evolution of historiography from antiquity to modern era, see Grafton 2007, 2010b; Foley 2016.
2 Note that in the *Brill's Companion to the Reception of Herodotus in Antiquity and Beyond*, edited by J. Priestley and V. Zali, appearing in the series *Brill's Companions to Classical Reception*, the authors and geographical contexts taken into account are limited to French and Italian sources. See Earley 2016; Looney 2016; Foley 2016.

3 The importance of scientific discourse in Herodotus' work has already been studied in detail by Thomas 2000, 2006, and, more recently, by Luraghi 2006 and Nicolaidou-Arabatzi 2018. Against these opinions, Fehling (1989) not only argues for the fictive character of Herodotus' source-citations (which then reflect neither oral informants nor written sources but are his own "free literary creations" (p. 9)), but he completely denies to the *Histories* any scientific–historical character (note his conclusions about "Herodotus' place in the history of science" (pp. 252–3)). In my opinion, his reasoning miscarries from the very lack of contextual comprehension for which he accuses other scholars as having regarding Herodotus' commitment to truth-telling. Fehling states that Herodotus' methods of critical research "belong not so much to the realm of science as to science fiction" (p. 252). Yet this conception of 'science' is prejudiced by its immurement in modern criteria. Thus Fehling, and some others like West (1985) and Hartog (esp. 1988) interpret the 'scientific' approach as a façade to clothe an Herodotean exposition essentially based in traditional storytelling. Not only has this view been badly damaged by Pritchett (1993), it also fails to understand that, in point of fact, 'scientific' historiography was too embryonic during the formative years of Herodotus to have had sufficient cultural visibility to be exploited or manipulated in the manner that Fehling imagines. Thus, what I would propose is to approach Herodotus' discourse as an emerging new discourse, one using methodologies common in its contexto *historiē* and other emerging areas of knowledge (such as medicine and the 'earth sciences').

4 Lloyd (2002: 418) specifically argues that Book II was originally a separate piece written as an independent ethnographic inquiry, only imported into the account of the Persian Wars when it became relevant to clarify the discussion.

5 On *sophistēs* used in the sense of 'wise man', see 2.49.1.

6 The 'natural' relationship in Herodotus' world between lands' and people's *phuseis* (the current Greek doctrine of environmental determinism, a concept virtually explicitly stated at 2.35.2 and unequivocally at 2.77.3) results from the narrow bond that since Homer, at least, the Greek writers established between geographical and anthropological speculation (Lloyd 2002: 415, 433).

7 I have largely discussed elsewhere the portraits Herodotus presents in his *Histories* of the others, the so-called *barbaroi* (Soares 2003, 2005, 2009, 2014). All the ethnographic *logoi* and some emblematic episodes were analysed there under the perspective of the relevance given to the main identity markers: physical/biological traits (of peoples and lands) and cultural features (*diaitai* lifestyles with special emphasis on food and clothing habits, social and family 'laws'/*nomoi*, religion, funerary practices, war; and also language as a cultural heritage transmitted by mothers). Concretely in Book II (18.2–3), Herodotus 'justifies' the right claim of the inhabitants of the cities of Marea and Apis on the basis of the identity markers which distinguished them from the Egyptians (language, territory, and no restrictions on meat eating).

8 See Lloyd 1976; Lateiner 1986, 1989; Fowler 2006; Thomas 2000, 2006.

9 See Thomas 2000: 28–74, 86–98 and, more recently, Pelling 2018. Note that the former was concerned with geographical and ethnographic aspects of the relations of 'affinities' (not 'influences') between Herodotus work and the Hippocratic corpus and the latter on the application of "the same intellectual tool-kit to the history of events" (Pelling 2018: 201).

10 Note the travel narratives published in Portuguese translation by Valentim Fernandes de Morávia: *Livro de Marco Polo* (= Marco Polo's Book), *Livro de Nicolau Venetto* (= Nicolau Venetto's Book) and *Carta de Jerónimo de Santo Estevão* (= Jerome of Saint Stephen's Letter).

11 Francisco López de Gómara, *Historia de las Indias y Conquista de Mexico* (1552), Pedro Cieza de León, *Parte primera de la chrónica del Perú* (1553), Agustín de Zárate, *Historia del descubrimiento y conquista del Perú* (1555), Fernão Lopes de Castanheda,

História do descobrimento et conquista da Índia pelos Portugueses (1551–1561), João de Barros, *Décadas da Ásia* (1552–1563).

12 Rubiés (1993: 172) has assertively drawn attention to the confluence of classic, medieval and modern sources at the disposal of Renaissance authors of travel reports.

13 In fact, there were no rigid boundaries between scientific or didactic literature and fictional literature. It will be necessary to wait for the eighteenth century to witness a phenomenon thus far unusual: the separation between aesthetic creation and scientific compostion. Moreover, that separation is contemporaneous with the specialization of the term 'science', which only at this time becomes used for strictly objective knowledge (Cristóvão 2002: 18).

14 Varotti (2012: 99), before Foley, underlined the non-interest of humanistic writers for Herodotus, considering his reputation of being *mendax* or *fabulosus*: "la cultura umanistico-rinascimentale per lungo tempo non sembra avere fatto dello storico di Alicarnasso né un tema centrale di ricerca, né un modelo atraente ed exemplare di scrittura storiografica".

15 The translation by Valla, finished in 1455, had a wide manuscript circulation and then had its *editio princeps* in 1474. As clarified by Pagliaroli (2007: 126), the printed edition in Venice was followed, in the next year (1475), by a printed edition in Rome. From the reedition in 1494 of the *editio princeps*, subsequent numerous editions of the text by Valla are attested, works that become the origin of what can be reasonably considered a true *vulgata*, of four centuries in duration, of this Latin translation of the *Histories* made by the Italian humanist.

16 As stated by Pagliaroli (2012: 37), the translation by Valla "renderà fruibile Erodoto ad un larghissimo pubblico di lettori occidentale, fino ad un'epoca non molto lontana da noi".

17 See, e.g., *Herodoti Halicarnassei Historiographi libri novem, musarum nominibus inscripti/interprete Laurentio Valla; Item de genere vitaque Homeri libellus, jam primum ab . . . Heresbachio e graeco in latinum conversus.* Coloniae, apud Eucharium Cervicornum, 1537; *Herodoti Halicarnassei historiarum lib. IX, IX Musarum nominibus inscripti. Eiusdem narratio de vita Homeri. Cum Vallae interpret. latina historiarum Herodoti, ab Henr. Stephano recognita. . .* Editio secunda. Genevae: excudebat Henricus Stephanus, 1592; *Herodoti Halicarnassei Historia, siue, historiarum Libri IX . . . Apologia Henr. Stephani pro Herodoto.* Genevae. Excudebat Henricus Stephanus, 1570.

18 Of which the library of the University of Coimbra has the following copy: *Herodoto Alicarnaseo Historico delle guerre de Greci et Persi/tradotto di greco in lingua italiana per il Conte Mattheo Maria Boiardo, di novo ristampato, et con summa diligentia revisto et corretto.* In Venetia: per Bernardino de Bindoni, ad instantia de M. Marchio Sessa, 1539.

19 On the plausibility of Herodotus' writings in that context, see also Grafton 2010a. Although no systematic study has been published on the presence of Herodotean *topoi* of describing the other's lands and people on Portuguese literature about the New Worlds, this is an 'impression' that the scholarship briefly mentions. In fact, as Figueira rightly pointed out (1997: 397), we should look for that invisible presence of Herodotus in works from the fifteenth century.

20 On the importance of Greek authors for the noble and court milieu and on the education of the major Portuguese humanists, see Ramalho (2000: 171–93) and Pinho (2006: 297–322).

21 The editorial activity by the monks of the Monastery of Santa Cruz has already been studied (Meirinhos 2001), and it is known that the c. 30 works published between 1530 and 1563 focussed on the following subjects: spiritual training and internal organization of the congregation, and literary studies.

22 See Pinho 2006: 9–12.

23 See Morais 2009: 121.

24 Criticizing the scientific validity of a given account does not mean that it should not be recorded. That is what Herodotus sometimes, though not always, does. If, in the case of his explanation of why the Phrygians should be considered a more ancient people than the Egyptians on the basis of their language, the historian records for posterity what he deems to be a naïve version (2.15.2: a passage which he calls it an "experiment with the infants": ἐς διάπειραν τῶν παιδίων), in other cases he simply mentions the existence of unreliable accounts, which, for that reason, are not included in his work (an example of these is the explanation concerning the use of sacrificial pigs in Egypt, which, although known to the historian, he chooses not to reveal, cf. 2.47.2).

25 For quotations of passages in Book II, I base myself on Waterfield's translation (1998), although I have adapted for more literal renderings in some places.

26 On the importance of analyzing Herodotus' conception of truth in connection with fiction and polarity, see Cartledge & Greenwood 2002.

27 See *Regimen* 67 of the *Corpus Hippocraticum* for an example of intellectual humility in medical texts.

28 Luraghi (2006) studies the importance of meta-*historiē* (that is, the information provided by the author on his use of sources, especially oral sources, as well as on the research methods adopted) for a definition of the new genre of historiography. Those are the only two aspects that enable Herodotus to create distinctive boundaries between his work and other genres dealing with the past (epic, tragedy, and elegiac or encomiastic poetry). As for his mention of collective testimonies ('the Egyptians', in this case), the historian uses this strategy to grant credibility to his narrative, since, according to his readers' expectations, communities were responsible for the preservation and dissemination of their own collective memory. At the time, written texts were not acknowledged as having the same authority as collective oral testimonies and, therefore, the strong presence of *akoē* (accounts heard from a third party) in Herodotus actually serves to legitimize the historian's narrative.

29 Thus I agree with Dewald's statement (2008: 51–2): "Herodotus' reasoning is not technical and is never encapsulated into a chapter of self/conscious methodology." This does not mean that Herodotus' readers do not find and identify evidences of a methodological discourse in his writings. Book II is where this becomes more notable; see Cartledge and Greenwood 2002: 365.

30 Lloyd (2002: 419), in his analysis of Herodotus' methods in Book II, argues that the historian uses each of these scientific strategies in different contexts: autopsy (*opsis*) mainly when discussing geography, geology, botany, zoology, customs, and sites (archaeological or inhabited); 'opinion' (*gnōmē*) in matters of religion and tradition; inquiry or hearsay (for him taken as equivalents: *historiē, akoē*) in his stock-in-trade for history and traditions. More recently, Nicolaidou-Arabatzi (2018: 224–8), arguing for the preeminence of ἱστορίη and θῶμα as supports of both the unity and the scientific character of *Histories*, defends the view, based on several occurences of ἱστορίη in Book II, that the term refers both to inquiry as whole and the method in which it was conducted.

31 Thomas (2006: 61) reminds us that this peripatetic element in Herodotus, on the basis of which some scholars before her had identified the historian as a 'tourist' (Redfield 1985), is common also to other coeval intellectuals (logographers, sophists, philosophers, and doctors), with whom Herodotus has 'scientific' affinities. On Herodotus and foreign lands, see also Rood 2006.

32 In this passage I use my own, more literal, translation.

33 Experiments may be valid or not. The former type is illustrated through the episode of casting a lead line into the waters of the Nile delta area to measure its depth (2.5.1); the latter type is exemplified through doing the same sounding experiment to prove that the Nile sources are of such depth as cannot be fathomed by using the rope method (2.28.4–5). According to the historian, this experiment is not valid because there is

behind it a misinterpretation that has simply to do with the fact that the place where the line is dropped is a whirlpool area, which prevents it from reaching the bottom.

34 Here I present my own translation.

35 In the case of Asia Minor, this refers to the plains of Troy, Teuthrania, and Ephesos, and in the case of west-central Greece, it refers to Akarnania (under the effect of the Akheloos).

36 I have used the following edition: Gândavo (1576), *História da Província de Santa Cruz a que vulgarmente chamamos Brasil*. Dirigida ao muito ilustre senhor Dom Leonis Pereira, governador que foi de Malaca e das mais partes do Sul da India. Lisboa, na typographia da Academia Real das Sciencias. Foreword by Francisco Leite de Faria, Lisboa, Biblioteca Nacional, facsimile first edition, Biblioteca Nacional, Lisboa 1984.

37 This text and another one on the Indians' way of life was first published in London, in 1625 by Samuel Purchas. The book was entitled *A Treatise of Brasil, Written by a Portugall Which Had Long Lived There*. The Portuguese edition that I consulted was: Cardim, Fernão (1583–1601), *Tratados da Terra e Gente do Brasil*. Text transcription, introduction and notes by Ana Maria Azevedo. Comissão Nacional para as Comemorações dos descobrimentos Portugueses. Lisboa, 1997.

38 I have utilized the following edition: Sousa, Gabriel Soares de (1587), *Notícia do Brasil*. Direction and commentary by Luís de Albuquerque. Current Portuguese transcription of Maria da Graça Pericão. Alfa, Lisboa 1989.

39 The literature theorist Cristóvão (2002: 37–52) states that, apart from this category, there exist four others: Pilgrimage Travel Writing; Commerce Travel Writing; Erudite Travel Writing (of training and service); and Imaginary Travel Writing. As advocated by Rubiés (2000: 36), the "Travel Writing" genre is a genre with many sub-genres, of which "Discoveries and Expansion Literature" is only one. On the literary genre of "Travel Writing", see Hulme-Youngs (2002); Bassnett (2002); and Rubiés (2000, particularly on the ethnographic impulse that characterized this genre).

40 On this teaching establishment (in northern Portugal), a competitor with the Jesuit teaching centres active at the time (in the central region, in Coimbra, and to the south, in Évora), along with its alignment with the European humanist teaching, see Miranda 2010.

41 Although it is unknown how long Gândavo remained in the province, we know that he had been appointed, for a period of six years, to the Finance Commissioner of the Salvador da Bahia Province Captaincy by a decree of August 29, 1576. Regarding the sparse information on his biography: the beginning of the Capistrano de Abreu's "Introdução" to the author's work (Gândavo 2008); Fonseca 2013: 236–7; Amorim 2015b.

42 On his life and work, see Leite 1949: 132–7. He served as dean in two colleges: in Bahia initially for three years (1590–1593), and later for another 15 years (1607 to 1625), and in the College of São Sebastião do Rio de Janeiro, between 1596 and 1598. He was in Rome for three years (1598–1601) as Procurator of the Province of Brazil. On his journey back to Brazil he was captured by English corsairs and kept in a London prison between December 1601 and March 1603. Back in Brazil he assumed the role of Provincial of the Company of Jesus (1604–1609). On this subject, see Azevedo 1997: 11–15; Amorim 2015a.

43 On the biographical data for this settler, see Varnhagem 1938: 13–14; Couto 2015.

44 Note that differently from Olivieri (2004); Pagliaroli (2006); Varotti (2012) and more recently Earley (2016) and Foley (2016), I do not approach the reception of the *Histories* as a work translated from the Greek, first into Latin and then into several modern languages. Nor do I explore how historians, since antiquity (starting with Thucydides, who was in some part responsible for the idea that historiography is made of facts, not fables, and has its focus on contemporary political events) and until the sixteenth century (more exactly until the publishing by Henri Estienne's *Apologia Pro Herodoto*, in 1566), centered the debate on the issue of truth or fiction in the Halicarnassian historian's account. My perspective is different. It focusses on how Herodotus' model of writing history inspired Portuguese works on the New World of Brazil.

45 On the Herodotian conception of *apodexis*, see the detailed analysis of Bakker (2002). He argues against other scholars' understanding of the notion ('publication', 'public performance', 'proof/display'), preferring 'achievement' or 'accomplishment'. *Apodexis* has a complex meaning in Herodotus' work; it is only rightly understandable in relation with other core concepts of the proem, like *historiē*. Thus, Bakker states (p. 28): "*apodexis* is not only *accomplishment* of great deeds, but also *recording,* which can not fail to become a great accomplishment itself, a *mega ergon,* in the process".

46 This methodological approach had to wait for the twentieth century to be recovered, through the French historiography of the *Annales* School, on which see Burke 1990.

47 Note that the letter by Gândavo was published with his work (in 1576), while the one by Sousa was first published by Varnhagen in the twentieth century (1938: 13–14).

48 See ch. 12: "por me parecer que seria temeridade & falta de consideraçam escrever em historia tam verdadeira, cousas em que por ventura podia aver falsas informações, pola pouca noticia que ainda temos da mais gentilidade que habita pela terra dentro" (for deeming to be temerity and lack of consideration to write such a true story, in which there might be false information, for the few notice that we still have more of the courtesy that dwells in the land) (Gândavo 1576: 45).

49 See ch. 12: "Do preço dellas nam rrato aqui, porque ao presente o nam pude saber" (their price I shall not tell because to this time I could not know it) (Gândavo 1576: 45).

50 The regularity of the laudatory tone of these reports on the Portuguese America has led literature theorists to creating, for the texts written on sixteenth to eighteenth-century Brazil, the subcategory of "boasting Writing" (Cristóvão 2009).

51 Compare how Herodotus Book I starts by bringing the rivalry between Greeks and non-Greeks back to the the the first Phoenician expeditions throughout the Mediterranean.

52 The regimens of health were heirs to classical traditions, mostly through the *Canon of Medicine* from the Arabic physician Avicena, one of the most widely read books in medieval universities throughout the fourteenth century. On the regimens of health, see Nicoud 2007 and Sotres 1998: esp. 296–300 ("Hygiene in Works of Arabic Origin") and 302–4 ("The Principles of Medieval Hygiene. The Environment").

53 A case stressed by the author is the influence of the moon, being, as he himself says, "mui prejudicial à saúde, e corrompe muito as coisas" (very harmful to health and [it] corrupts many things). Thus, a place with a clear sky was essential to see in what stage the moon stood in order to avoid the illness caused by its influence.

54 See chs. 3 and 4 of Gandavo's *História da Província de Santa Cruz* [*The History of the Province of Santa Cruz*] and, from Sousa's *Memorial,* chs. 7–32 (in which he writes on "the greatness of the Bahia de Todos-os-Santos and all its power") and chs. 33–196 (where he presents its fertility).

Bibliography

Amorim, M.A. 2015a. "Cardim, Fernão." In Domingues, F.C., ed., *Dicionário da Expansão Portuguesa,* Vol. I. Lisboa (Círculo de Leitores), 219–21.

———. 2015b. "Gândavo, Pêro Magalhães de." In Domingues, F.C., ed., *Dicionário da Expansão Portuguesa,* Vol. I. Lisboa (Círculo de Leitores), 428–30.

Azevedo, A.M. 1997. *Fernão Cardim, Tratados da Terra e Gente do Brasil.* Lisboa (Comissão Nacional para as Comemorações dos Descobrimentos Portugueses).

Bakker, E.J. 2002. "The Making of History: Herodotus' 'histories apodexis'." In Bakker, E.J., Jong, I.J.F. de, & Wees, H. van, eds., *Brill's Companion to Herodotus.* Leiden (Brill), 3–32.

Bassnett, S. 2002. "Travel Writing and Gender." In Hulme, P., & Youngs, T., eds., *The Cambridge Companion to Travel Writing.* Cambridge (Cambridge University Press), 225–41.

Burke, P. 1990. *The French Historical Revolution: The Annales School 1929–1989*. Cambridge (Polity Press).

Cardim, Fernão (1583–1601). *Tratados da Terra e Gente do Brasil*. Text transcription, introduction and notes by Ana Maria Azevedo. Lisboa (Comissão Nacional para as Comemorações dos Descobrimentos Portugueses), 1997.

Cartledge, P. & Greenwood, E. 2002. "Herodotus as Critical: Truth, Fiction, Polarity." In Bakker, E.J., Jong, I.J.F. de, & Wees, H. van, eds., *Brill's Companion to Herodotus*. Leiden (Brill), 351–71.

Couto, J. 2015. "Sousa, Gabriel Soares de." In Domingues, F.C., ed., *Dicionário da Expansão Portuguesa*, Vol. II. Lisboa (Círculo de Leitores), 963–5.

Cristóvão, F., ed. 2002. *Condicionantes culturais da literatura de viagens: estudos e bibliografias*. Coimbra & Lisboa (Centro de Literaturas de Expressão Portuguesa da Universidade de Lisboa, Almedina Editora).

————. 2009. "Marcas da Literatura de Viagens nos textos ufanistas brasileiros." In Cristóvão, F., ed., *Literatura de Viagens: Da Tradicional à Nova e à Novíssima*. Coimbra & Lisboa (Almedina Editora, Centro de Literaturas de Expressão Portuguesa da Universidade de Lisboa, Marcas e Temas), 19–35.

Dewald, C. 2008. "Introduction." In *Herodotus: The Histories*[2]. Translated by R. Waterfield, With an Introduction and Notes by C. Dewald. Oxford (Oxford University Press), 13–92.

Earle, R. 2012. *The Body of the Conquistador: Food, Race and the Colonial Experience in Spanish America, 1492–1700*. Cambridge (Cambridge University Press).

Earley, B. 2016. "Herodotus in Renaissance France." In Priestley, J., & Zali, V., eds., *Brill's Companion to the Reception of Herodotus in Antiquity and Beyond*. Leiden (Brill), 120–42.

Fehling, D. 1989. *Herodotus and His "Sources": Citation, Invention and Narrative Art*. Translated by J.G. Howie. Leeds (Francis Cairns Publications).

Figueira, D. 1997. "Fantasies of Faith." In Falcão, A.M., ed., *Literatura de viagem: Narrativa, história, mito*. Lisboa (Edições Cosmos), 387–98.

Foley, A. 2016. "Valla's Herodotean Labours: Towards a New View of Herodotus in Italian Renaissance." In Priestley, J., & Zali, V., eds., *Brill's Companion to the Reception of Herodotus in Antiquity and Beyond*. Leiden (Brill), 213–31.

Fonseca, J.A. 2013. "Os três 'Peros' que interessam à história do Brasil." In Alexandre Sousa Pinto, *et al.*, eds., *Brasil e Portugal: unindo as duas margens do Atlântico*. Lisboa (Academia Portuguesa da História), 224–72.

Fowler, R.F. 2006. "Herodotus and His Prose Predecessors." In Dewald, C., & Marincola, J., eds., *The Cambridge Companion to Herodotus*. Cambridge (Cambridge University Press), Cambridge Collections Online, 29–45.

Gândavo, P.M. 1576. *História da Província de Santa Cruz a que vulgarmente chamamos Brasil: Dirigida ao muito ilustre senhor Dom Leonis Pereira, governador que foi de Malaca e das mais partes do Sul da India*. Lisboa, na typographia da Academia Real das Sciencias. Foreword by Francisco Leite de Faria. Lisboa (Biblioteca Nacional, facsimile first edition, Biblioteca Nacional, Lisbon 1984).

————. 2008. *Tratado da Terra do Brasil: História da província Santa Cruz, a que vulgarmente chamamos Brasil*. Brasília (Senado Federal, Conselho Editorial).

Grafton, A. 2007. *What Was History? The Art of History in Early Modern Europe*. Cambridge (Cambridge University Press).

————. 2010a. "Herodotus." In Grafton, A., Most, G.W., & Settis, S., eds., *The Classical Tradition*. Cambridge, MA (Harvard University Press), 434–5.

————. 2010b. "Historiography." In Grafton, A., Most, G.W., & Settis, S., eds., *The Classical Tradition*. Cambridge, MA (Harvard University Press), 441–8.

Herodotus. 1998. *The Histories*². Translated by R. Waterfield, With an Introduction and Notes by C. Dewald. Oxford (Oxford University Press, reissued 2008).

Hulme, P. & Youngs, T. 2002. "Introduction." In Hulme, P., & Youngs, T., eds., *The Cambridge Companion to Travel Writing*. Cambridge (Cambridge University Press), 1–14.

Lateiner, D. 1986. "The Empirical Element in the Methods of Early Greek Medical Writers and Herodotus: A Shared Epistemological Response." *Antichthon* 20: 1–20.

————. 1989. *The Historical Method of Herodotus*. Toronto & London (University of Toronto Press).

Leite, S. 1949. *História da Companhia de Jesus no Brasil VIII: Escritores: de A a M* (*suplemento bibliográfico – I*). Rio de Janeiro (Instituto Nacional do Livro).

Lloyd, A.B. 1976. *Herodotus: Book II, Commentary 1–98*. Leiden (Brill).

————. 2002. "Egypt." In Bakker, E.J., Jong, I.J.F. de, & Wees, H. van, eds., *Brill's Companion to Herodotus*. Leiden (Brill), 415–35.

Looney, D. 2016. "Herodotus and Narrative Art in Renaissance Ferrara: The Translation of Matteo Maria Boiardo." In Priestley, J., & Zali, V., eds., *Brill's Companion to the Reception of Herodotus in Antiquity and Beyond*. Leiden (Brill), 232–53.

Lupher, D.A. 2003. *Romans in a New World: Classical Models in the Sixteenth-Century Spanish America*. Ann Arbor, MI (University of Michigan Press).

Luraghi, N. 2006. "Meta-'historie': Method and Genre in the 'Histories'." In Dewald, C., & Marincola, J., eds., *The Cambridge Companion to Herodotus*. Cambridge (Cambridge University Press), 76–91.

McInerney, J., ed. 2014. *A Companion to Ethnicity in the Ancient Mediterranean*. Chichester, West Sussex (Wiley-Blackwell).

Meirinhos, J.F. 2001. "A tipografia de Santa Cruz 1530–1563: The Typography of Santa Cruz 1530–1563." In Frias, A.F., Costa, J., & Meirinhos, J.F., eds., *Santa Cruz de Coimbra. A cultura portuguesa aberta à Europa na Idade Média: The Portuguese Culture Opened to Europe in the Middle Ages*. Porto (Biblioteca Municipal do Porto), 319–27.

Miranda, M. 2010. "O Humanismo no Colégio de São Paulo (séc. XVI) e a tradição humanística europeia." *Humanitas* 62: 243–63.

Morais, C. 2009. "As artes de gramática 'ex Clenardo' para o ensino do grego em Portugal." In Várzeas, M., & Pereira, B.F., eds., *Estudos em homenagem a Ana Paula Quintela*. Porto (Universidade do Porto-Faculdade de Letras), 117–34.

Morley, N. 2016. "The Anti-Thucydides: Herodotus and the Development of Modern Historiography." In Priestley, J., & Zali, V., eds., *Brill's Companion to the Reception of Herodotus in Antiquity and Beyond*. Leiden (Brill), 143–66.

Munson, R.V. 2014. "Herodotus and Ethnicity." In McInerney 2014, 341–55.

Nicolaidou-Arabatzi, S. 2018. "ἱστορέειν and θωμάζειν: scientific terms and signs of unity in Herodotus' 'Histories'." in Bowie, E., ed., *Herodotus – Narrator, Scientist, Historian*. Berlin (De Gruyter), 223–41.

Nicoud, M. 2007. *Les régimes de santé au Moyen Âge. Naissance et diffusion d'une écriture médicale (XIIIᵉ–XVᵉ siècle)*. Rome (École Française de Rome).

Olivieri, A. 2004. *Erodoto nel Rinascimento: l'umano e la storia*. Roma (L'Erma di Bretschneider).

Pagliaroli, S. 2006. *L'Erodoto del Valla*. Messina (Centro Interdepartimentale di Studi Umanistici).

————. 2007. "L'Erodoto del Valla." In Santoro, M., ed., *Valla e Napoli: il dibattito philologico in Età Umanista: Atti del convegno internazionale Ravello, Villa Rufolo, 22–23 settembre 2005*. Pisa-Roma (Istituti Editoriali e Poligrafici Internazionali), 113–28.

————. 2012. "Il 'proemio' di Mattia Palmieri alla traduzione latina delle 'Storie' di Erodoto." In Gambino Longo, S., ed., *Hérodote à la Renaissance*. Turnhout (Brepols Publishers).

Pelling, Ch. 2018. "Causes in Competition: Herodotus and Hippocratic." In Bowie, E., ed., *Herodotus – Narrator, Scientist, Historian*. Berlin & Boston (De Gruyter), 199–222.

Pinho, S.T. 2006. *Humanismo em Portugal: estudos*, Vol. 2. Lisboa (Imprensa Nacional-Casa da Moeda).

Pritchett, W.K. 1993. *The Liar School of Herodotos*. Amsterdam (Gieben Publishers).

Raaflaub, K.A. 2000. "Philosophy, Science, Politics: Herodotus and the Intellectual Trends of His Time." In Bakker, E.J., Jong, I.J.F. de, & Wees, H. van, eds., *Brill's Companion to Herodotus*. Leiden (Brill), 149–86.

Ramalho, A.C. 2000. *Para a história do Humanismo em Portugal*, Vol. III. Lisboa (Imprensa Nacional-Casa da Moeda).

Redfield, J. 1985. "Herodotus the Tourist." *Classical Philology* 80: 97–118.

Romm, J. 2006. "Herodotus and the Natural World." In Dewald, C., & Marincola, J., eds., *The Cambridge Companion to Herodotus*. Cambridge (Cambridge University Press), 178–91.

Rood, T. 2006. "Herodotus and Foreign Lands." In Dewald, C., & Marincola, J., eds., *The Cambridge Companion to Herodotus*. Cambridge (Cambridge University Press), 290–305.

Rubiés, J.-P. 1993. "New Worlds and Renaissance Ethnology." *History and Anthropology* 6: 157–97.

————. 2000. "Travel Writing as a Genre: Facts, Fiction, and Inventions of Scientific Discourse in Early Modern Europe." *Journeys* 1.1–2: 5–35.

————. 2002. "Travel Writing and Ethnography." In Hulme, P., & Youngs, T., eds., *The Cambridge Companion to Travel Writing*. Cambridge (Cambridge University Press), 242–60.

————. 2006. "Travel Writing and Humanistic Culture: A Blunted Impact." *Journal of Early Modern History* 10. 1–2: 131–68.

Soares, C. 2003. "A língua, um instrumento de diálogo cultural em Heródoto." *Biblos* n.s. 1: 13–22.

————. 2005. "A visão do 'outro' em Heródoto." In Fialho, M.C., Silva, M.F., & Rocha Pereira, M.H. da, eds., *Génese e consolidação da ideia de Europa: Vol. I: de Homero ao fim da Época Clássica*. Coimbra (Imprensa da Universidade de Coimbra), 95–176.

————. 2009. "Os Gregos e a sexualidade dos 'Outros': o testemunho de Heródoto." In Ramos, J.A., Fialho, M.C., & Rodrigues, N.S., eds., *A Sexualidade no Mundo Antigo*. Porto (Centro de História), 327–40.

————. 2014. "**Alimentação** e guerra nas 'Histórias' de Heródoto." *Humanitas* 66: 125–50.

Sotres, P.G. 1998. "The Regimens of Health." In Grmek, M.D., ed., *Histoire de la pensée médical en Occident: 1- Antiquité et Moyen Âge*. Paris (Éditions du Seuil), 291–318.

Thomas, R. 2000. *Herodotus in Context: Ethnography, Science and the Art of Persuasion*. Oxford (Oxford University Press).

————. 2006. "The Intellectual Milieu of Herodotus." In Dewald, C., & Marincola, J., eds., *The Cambridge Companion to Herodotus*. Cambridge (Cambridge University Press), 60–75.

Varnhagem, F.A. 1938. *Gabriel Soares de Sousa, Tratado descritivo do Brasil em 1587*. Companhia Editora Nacional, Biblioteca Pedagógica Brasileira, série 5ª, Brasiliana, Vol. 117, São Paulo, Rio de Janeiro, Recife, & Porto Alegre, 3rd ed.

Varotti, C. 2012. "Erodoto nella storiografia fra Quattrocento e primo Cinquecento." In Gambino Longo, S., ed., *Hérodote à la Renaissance*. Turnhout (Brepols Publishers), 99–125.

West, S. 1985. "Herodotus' Epigraphical Interests." *Classical Quarterly* 79: 278–305.

Index Locorum

References found exclusively in endnotes appear in *italics*.

General Index

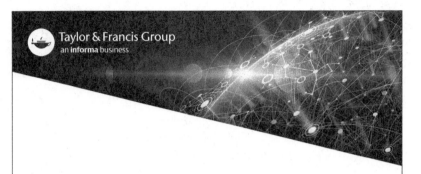